C000264158

STREET ATLAS
Oxfordshire

Abingdon, Banbury, Bicester, Didcot, Henley, Oxford, Witney

www.philips-maps.co.uk
First published in 1992 by Philip's
a division of Octopus Publishing Group Ltd
www.octopusbooks.co.uk
Endeavour House
189 Shaftesbury Avenue
London WC2H 8JY
An Hachette UK Company
www.hachette.co.uk

Fourth edition 2009
Second impression 2013
OXFDA

ISBN 978-1-84907-278-6 (spiral)

© Philip's 2009

 **Ordnance Survey®**

This product includes mapping data licensed
from Ordnance Survey® with the permission
of the Controller of Her Majesty's Stationery
Office. © Crown copyright 2009. All rights
reserved. Licence number 100011710.

Speed camera data provided by
PocketGPSWorld.com Ltd

Post Office is a trade mark of Post Office Ltd in
the UK and other countries.

Printed in China

Contents

II	Mobile speed cameras
III	**Key to map symbols**
IV	**Key to map pages**
VI	**Route planning**
VIII	Major administrative and Postcode boundaries

1	**Street maps** at 3½ inches to 1 mile
261	**Street map of Oxford city centre** at 7 inches to 1 mile

262	**Index** of towns, villages, streets, hospitals, industrial estates, railway stations, schools, shopping centres, universities and places of interest

Digital data

The exceptionally high-quality mapping found in this atlas is available as digital data in TIFF format, which is easily convertible to other bitmapped (raster) image formats.

The index is also available in digital form as a standard database table. It contains all the details found in the printed index together with the National Grid reference for the map square in which each entry is named.

For further information and to discuss your requirements, please contact
philips@mapsinternational.co.uk

Mobile safety cameras

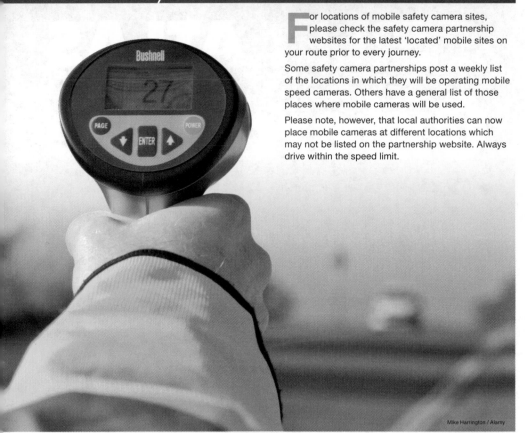

For locations of mobile safety camera sites, please check the safety camera partnership websites for the latest 'located' mobile sites on your route prior to every journey.

Some safety camera partnerships post a weekly list of the locations in which they will be operating mobile speed cameras. Others have a general list of those places where mobile cameras will be used.

Please note, however, that local authorities can now place mobile cameras at different locations which may not be listed on the partnership website. Always drive within the speed limit.

Mike Harrington / Alamy

Useful websites

Oxfordshire County Council
www.oxfordshire.gov.uk/cms/content/safety-cameras

Thames Valley Police
www.thamesvalley.police.uk/rdsafe/rdsafe-roadpol/rdsafe-roadpol-speedenforcement

Safer Roads (Berkshire)
www.saferroads.org

Gloucestershire Road Safety
www.roadsafety-gloucestershire.org.uk

Warwickshire safety cameras
www.warwickshire.gov.uk/safetycameras

Northamptonshire safety cameras
www.northamptonshire.gov.uk/en/councilservices/Transport/roads/Pages/SafetyCameraSites.aspx

Further information
www.dvla.gov.uk
www.thinkroadsafety.gov.uk
www.dft.gov.uk
www.road-safe.org

Key to map symbols

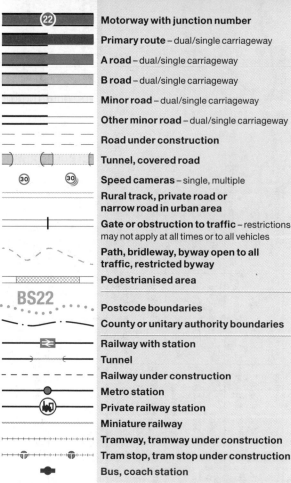

	Motorway with junction number
	Primary route – dual/single carriageway
	A road – dual/single carriageway
	B road – dual/single carriageway
	Minor road – dual/single carriageway
	Other minor road – dual/single carriageway
	Road under construction
	Tunnel, covered road
	Speed cameras – single, multiple
	Rural track, private road or narrow road in urban area
	Gate or obstruction to traffic – restrictions may not apply at all times or to all vehicles
	Path, bridleway, byway open to all traffic, restricted byway
	Pedestrianised area
BS22	Postcode boundaries
	County or unitary authority boundaries
	Railway with station
	Tunnel
	Railway under construction
	Metro station
	Private railway station
	Miniature railway
	Tramway, tramway under construction
	Tram stop, tram stop under construction
	Bus, coach station

◆	Ambulance station
◆	Coastguard station
◆	Fire station
◆	Police station
✚	Accident and Emergency entrance to hospital
H	Hospital
+	Place of worship
i	Information centre – open all year
P	Shopping centre, parking
P&R PO	Park and Ride, Post Office
⚑ ⨯	Camping site, caravan site
	Golf course, picnic site
Church ROMAN FORT	Non-Roman antiquity, Roman antiquity
Univ	Important buildings, schools, colleges, universities and hospitals
	Woods, built-up area
River Medway	Water name
	River, weir
	Stream
	Canal, lock, tunnel
	Water
	Tidal water

 Adjoining page indicators and overlap bands – the colour of the arrow and band indicates the scale of the adjoining or overlapping page (see scales below)

The dark grey border on the inside edge of some pages indicates that the mapping does not continue onto the adjacent page

The small numbers around the edges of the maps identify the 1-kilometre National Grid lines

Abbreviations

Acad	Academy	Meml	Memorial
Allot Gdns	Allotments	Mon	Monument
Cemy	Cemetery	Mus	Museum
C Ctr	Civic centre	Obsy	Observatory
CH	Club house	Pal	Royal palace
Coll	College	PH	Public house
Crem	Crematorium	Recn Gd	Recreation ground
Ent	Enterprise		
Ex H	Exhibition hall	Resr	Reservoir
Ind Est	Industrial Estate	Ret Pk	Retail park
IRB Sta	Inshore rescue boat station	Sch	School
		Sh Ctr	Shopping centre
Inst	Institute	TH	Town hall / house
Ct	Law court	Trad Est	Trading estate
L Ctr	Leisure centre	Univ	University
LC	Level crossing	W Twr	Water tower
Liby	Library	Wks	Works
Mkt	Market	YH	Youth hostel

Enlarged maps only

	Railway or bus station building
	Place of interest
	Parkland

The map scale on the pages numbered in blue is 3½ inches to 1 mile
5.52 cm to 1 km • 1:18 103

0	¼ mile	½ mile	¾ mile	1 mile
0	250m 500m	750m	1km	

The map scale on the pages numbered in red is 7 inches to 1 mile
11.04 cm to 1 km • 1:9051

0	220yds	440yds	660yds	½ mile
0	125m 250m	375m	500m	

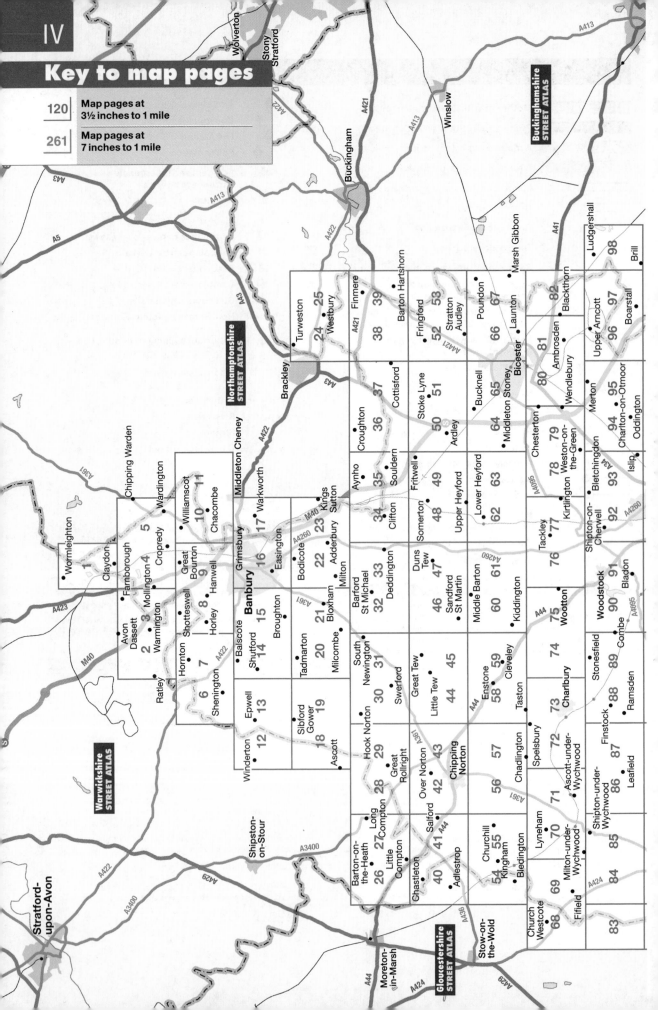

IV

Key to map pages

120 Map pages at 3½ inches to 1 mile

261 Map pages at 7 inches to 1 mile

Buckinghamshire STREET ATLAS

Northamptonshire STREET ATLAS

Warwickshire STREET ATLAS

Gloucestershire STREET ATLAS

Wolverton
Stony Stratford
Winslow
Buckingham
Ludgershall
Brill
Stratford-upon-Avon
Shipston-on-Stour
Moreton-in-Marsh
Stow-on-the-Wold
Banbury
Brackley

Turweston 24 25 Westbury
Finmere 38 39 Barton Hartshorn
Fringford 52 53 Stratton Audley
Poundon 66 67 Launton
Ambrosden 80 81
Upper Arncott 96 97 Boarstall
Blackthorn 82 98
Marsh Gibbon
Middleton Stoney Bicester
Wendlebury 94 95 Oddington
Merton Charlton-on-Otmoor
Chipping Warden
Wardington
Williamscot 10 11 Chacombe
Cropredy 5
Middleton Cheney
Warkworth 17
Kings Sutton 23
Adderbury 22
Milton
Croughton 36 37 Cottisford
Stoke Lyne 50 51
Ardley 64 65 Bucknell
Chesterton 78 79 Weston-on-the-Green
Bletchington 92 93 Islip
Aynho 34 35 Souldern
Clifton
Fritwell 48 49 Upper Heyford
Somerton
Lower Heyford 62 63
Kirtlington 76 77 Tackley
Shipton-on-Cherwell
Bladon 90 91 Combe
Wormleighton 1
Claydon
Farmborough 4 Mollington
Great Bourton 9 Hanwell
Shotteswell 8 Horley
Balscote 15 Broughton
Shutford 14
Bodicote 16 Easington
Grimsbury
Barford St Michael 32 33 Deddington
Duns Tew 47
Sandford St Martin 46
Middle Barton 60 61 Kiddington
Wootton 74 75
Woodstock 88 89
Avon Dassett 2 3 Warmington
Hornton 7 Shenington
Epwell 13
Tadmarton 20 Milcombe 21
South Newington 30 31 Swerford
Great Tew 44 45 Little Tew
Enstone 58 59 Cleveley
Taston
Charlbury 72 73
Stonesfield 86 87 Finstock
Ramsden
Winderton 12 Sibford Gower 18 19 Ascott
Hook Norton 28 29
Great Rollright 42 43 Over Norton
Chipping Norton 56 57
Chadlington
Spelsbury
Ascott-under-Wychwood 70 71
Shipton-under-Wychwood 84 85 Leafield
Barton-on-the-Heath 26 27 Long Compton
Little Compton
Chastleton 40 41 Salford
Adlestrop
Churchill 54 55 Kingham
Bledington
Lyneham
Milton-under-Wychwood 68 69 Fifield
Church Westcote 83

Aylesbury
A4010
A4129
Princes Risborough
Haddenham
A418
A4129

Chinnor 168 169
Bledlow Ridge 189
Beacon's Bottom
Kingston Blount 188
Stokenchurch 187
Henley-on-Thames 254 255
Wargrave
Twyford
A4155
A4130
A4
Sonning
A329
A327
A33
A3290
A329

Towersey 148 149
Henton
Thame 130
Sydenham 167
Aston Rowant 166
Lewknor 186
Watlington 207
Fawley 226
Lower Assendon 244
Middle Assendon 243
Shepherd's Green
Sonning Common 252 253
Tokers Green 259
Caversham
Reading

Long Crendon 128 129
Shabbington
Tiddington 146 147
Great Haseley 164 165
Stoke Talmage
Brightwell Baldwin 184 185
Ewelme 205
Greenfield 206
Crowmarsh Gifford
Nettlebed 224 225
Stoke Row 242
A4130
Whitchurch Hill 251
Shiplake 254
Pangbourne 256 257
Whitchurch Hill
A4074
A340

Horton-cum-Studley 112
Worminghall 126 127
Holton
Wheatley 144 145
Cuddesdon
Little Milton 162 163
Stadhampton
Berinsfield 182 183
Dorchester
Long Wittenham 202 203
Warborough
Benson 204
Brightwell-cum-Sotwell
Wallingford 220 221
Cholsey
South Stoke 238 239
Moulsford
Goring 248 249
Aldworth 247
A329
M4

Stanton St John 124 125
Headington
Cowley 142 143
Garsington
Horspath
A4142
A420
M40
A40

Marston 122 123
Oxford 261
Botley 140 141
North Hinksey
Kennington
A4144
A34

Noke 110 111
Beckley
Kidlington 108 109
Yarnton
Wolvercote
Cumnor 138 139
Northmoor
A40

Freeland 106 107
Cassington
Eynsham 120 121
Sutton
Stanton Harcourt

Sandford-on-Thames 160 161
Radley
Abingdon 180 181
Culham
Sutton Courtenay 200 201
Didcot
Drayton 178 179
Milton 198 199
Steventon
Milton Hill
Harwell 216 217
East Hendred
Chilton 234 235
Blewbury 236 237
Upton 218 219
Aston Upthorpe
Aston Tirrold

Wootton 158 159
Appleton
Marcham 176 177
Garford
East Hanney 196 197
Grove
Denchworth
Wantage 214 215
Ardington
Letcombe Regis
West Hanney

North Leigh 104 105
Crawley
Witney 118 119
South Leigh
Ducklington 136 137
Standlake
Cote

Curbridge 116 117
Brize Norton
Minster Lovell 102 103
Shilton 114 115
Alvescot
Carterton
Black Bourton 134 135
Aston
Bampton
Langford 132 133
Filkins

Clanfield 152 153
Littleworth
Faringdon 172 173
Charney Bassett 174 175
Hinton Waldrist 154 155
Buckland
Stanford in the Vale 194 195
Great Coxwell 192 193
Longcot
Baulking
Uffington 210 211
Woolstone
Childrey 212 213
Sparsholt
Letcombe Bassett 230 231
West Ilsley
Ashbury 228 229
A4185
A338
A417
A420

Lechlade-on-Thames 150 151
Buscot 170 171
Kelmscott
A417
Highworth 190 191
Watchfield
Shrivenham 208 209
Bourton
Bishopstone 227
Baydon 245
A419
A346
A361
Swindon

North Leigh 99 100 101
Taynton
Burford
Westwell 113
Great Barrington
Eastleach Martin
Southrop 131

246

Scale
0 5 10 15 km
0 5 10 miles

Wiltshire & Swindon STREET ATLAS
Berkshire STREET ATLAS

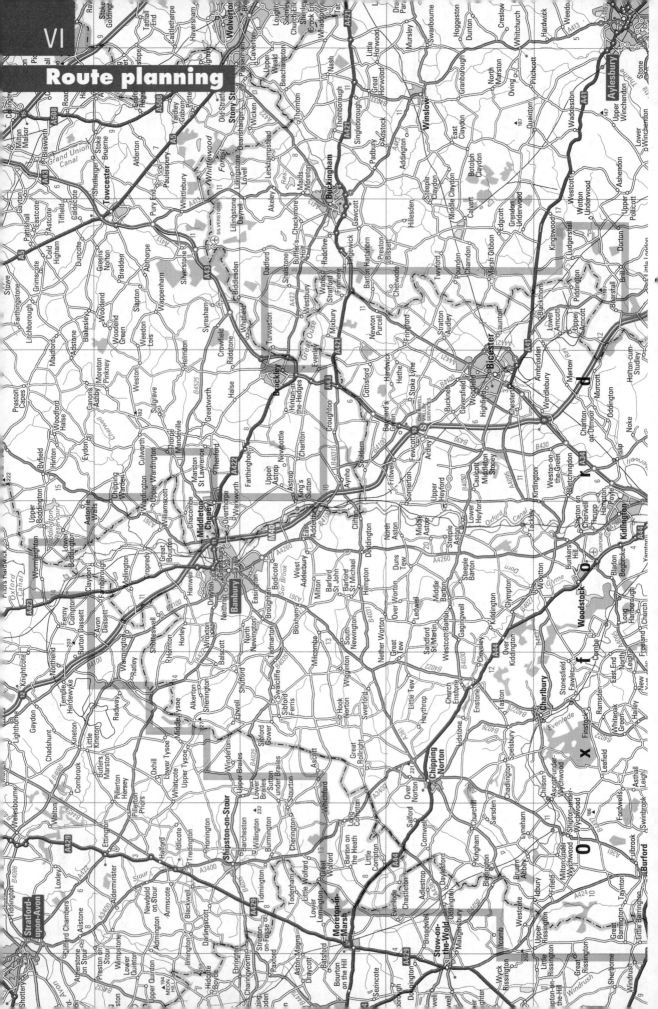

County and unitary authority boundaries
District boundaries
Postcode boundaries
Area covered by this atlas

Scale

0   5   10   15 km
0   5   10 miles

Warwickshire

Mollington
OX17

Northamptonshire

OX16
Banbury

OX15
Bloxham

Hook Norton

CV36

Westbury

NN13

GL56
Adlestrop

Chipping Norton

Aynho

Fringford
OX27

Gloucestershire

OX7

West Oxfordshire

OX25
Cherwell
Upper Heyford

OX26
Bicester

Charlbury

Tackley

OX20

Woodstock

OX25
Ambrosden

Ludgershall

GL54

Stonesfield

OX5
Kidlington

HP18

Buckinghamshire

Burford

OX29

Witney
OX28

Eynsham

OX3

OX33

Shabbington

HP17

OX18

Carterton

Oxford
OX2
Oxford

Wheatley

Thame

GL7
Bampton

Oxfordshire

OX1   OX4

Garsington

OX9

HP27

Chinnor

SP
Lechlade-on-Thames

SU

SP
SU

OX44

OX39

OX13
Marcham

Abingdon

Stadhampton

Watlington

HP14
Stokenchurch

Faringdon

SN7

OX14

Dorchester

OX49

Highworth

Vale of White Horse

South Oxfordshire

OX10

SN6
Shrivenham

Uffington

Wantage

Harwell

Didcot

Wallingford

Nettlebed
RG9

OX12
Chilton

OX11

Swindon
Bishopstone

RG17

RG20

Goring

Woodcote

Henley-on-Thames

SN4

RG8

Sonning Common
RG4

RG10

SN8

Reading

Wiltshire

West Berkshire

Reading

Wokingham

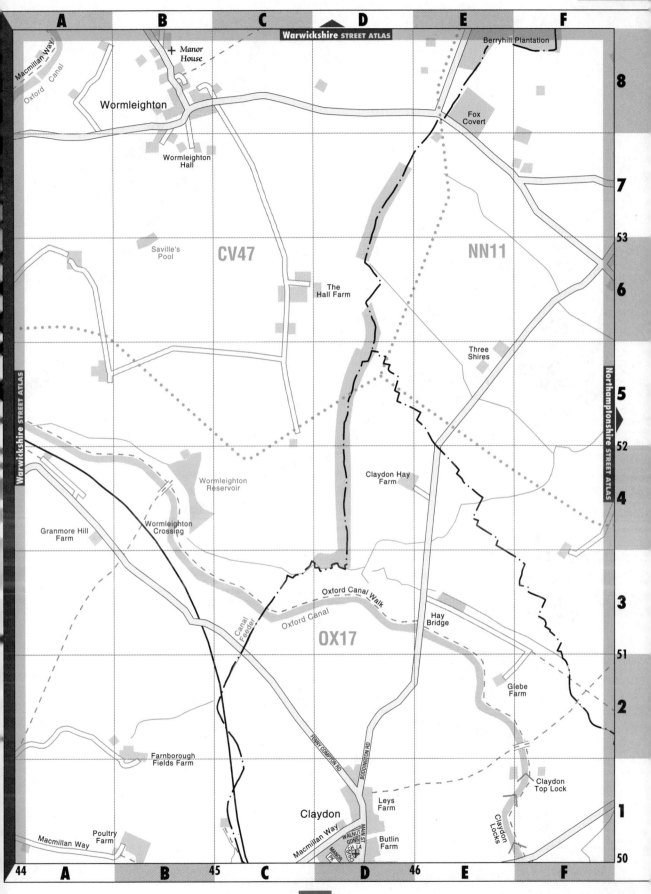

Macmillan Way

Oxford Canal

Manor House

Wormleighton

Wormleighton Hall

Saville's Pool

CV47

The Hall Farm

Berryhill Plantation

Fox Covert

NN11

Three Shires

Wormleighton Reservoir

Wormleighton Crossing

Granmore Hill Farm

Claydon Hay Farm

Canal Feeder

Oxford Canal Walk

Oxford Canal

OX17

Hay Bridge

Glebe Farm

Farnborough Fields Farm

Fenny Compton Rd

Boddington Rd

Claydon Top Lock

Claydon Locks

Claydon

Macmillan Way

Poultry Farm

Macmillan Way

Leys Farm

Butlin Farm

MANOR PK

WALNUT GDNS

CH LA

4

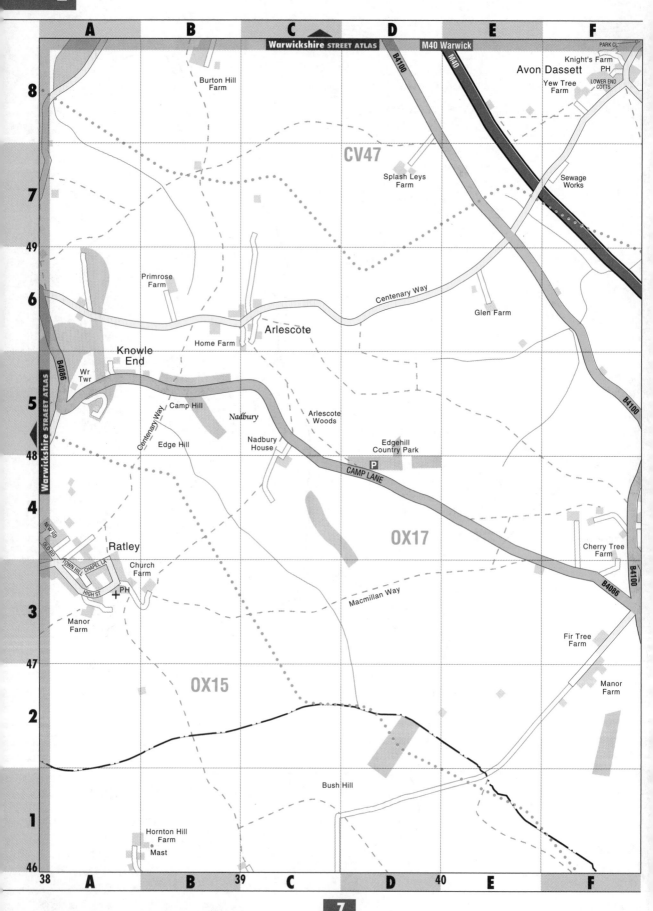

Warwickshire STREET ATLAS
M40 Warwick

CV47

Avon Dassett

Knight's Farm
PH

PARK CL

Yew Tree
Farm

LOWER END
COTTS

Burton Hill
Farm

Splash Leys
Farm

Sewage
Works

Primrose
Farm

Centenary Way

Glen Farm

Arlescote

Home Farm

Knowle
End

Wr
Twr

B4086

Camp Hill

Nadbury

Arlescote
Woods

Centenary Way

Edge Hill

Nadbury
House

Edgehill
Country Park

P

CAMP LANE

OX17

B4100

Cherry Tree
Farm

B4086

NEW RD

OLD RD

TOWN HILL

CHAPEL LA

Ratley

Church
Farm

HIGH ST

PH

Macmillan Way

Fir Tree
Farm

Manor
Farm

OX15

Manor
Farm

Bush Hill

Hornton Hill
Farm

Mast

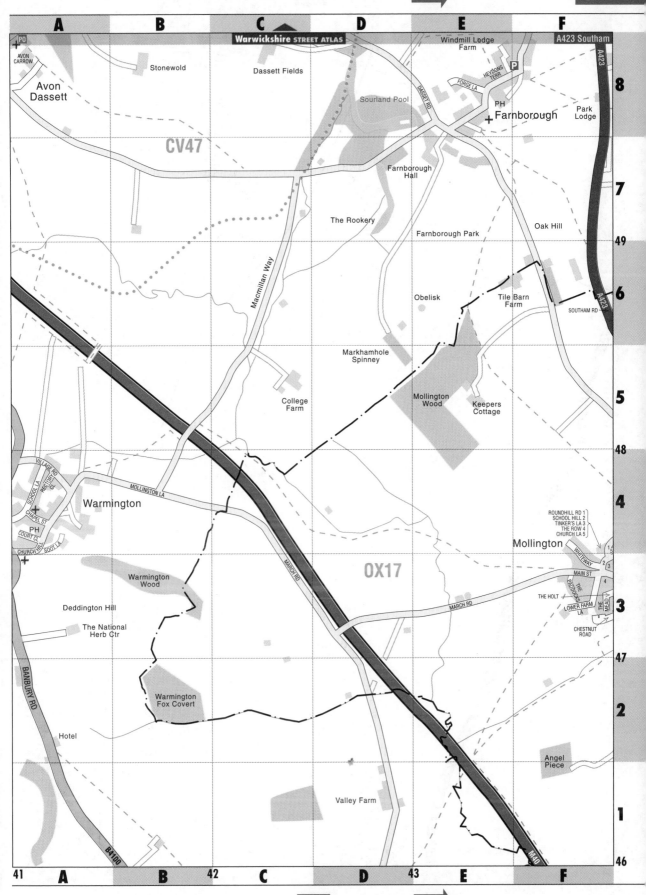

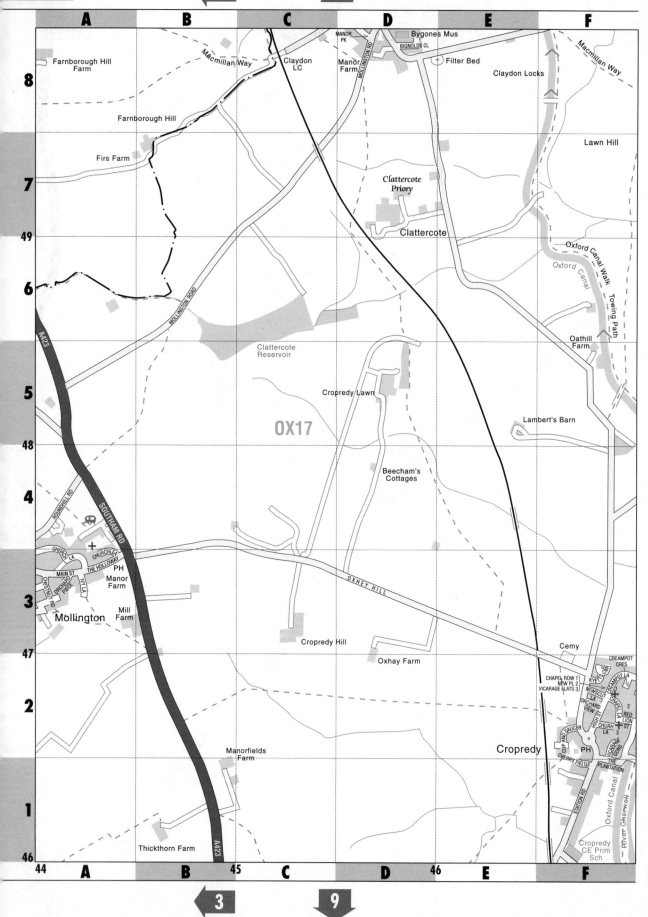

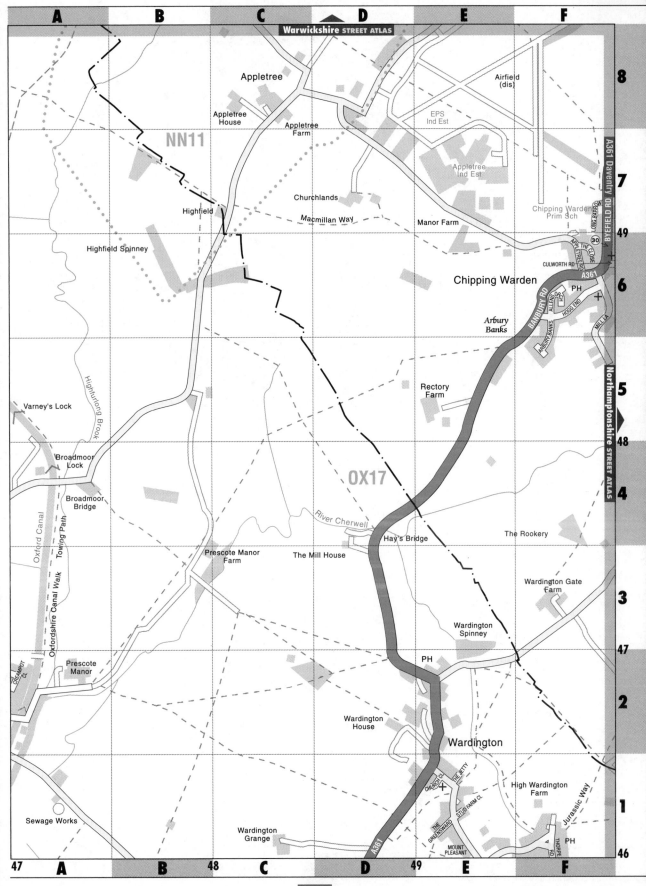

A   B   C   D   E   F

8

Appletree

Appletree
House

NN11

Appletree
Farm

Airfield
(dis)

EPS
Ind Est

Appletree
Ind Est

7

Churchlands

Highfield

Macmillan Way

Manor Farm

Chipping Warden
Prim Sch

A361 Daventry Rd

LONG BARROW

AYFIELD RD

THE CLOSE

APPLETREE RD

CULWORTH RD

A361

30

49

Highfield Spinney

Chipping Warden

6

Arbury
Banks

BANBURY RD

ALLEN'S ORCH

ARBURY BANKS

HORSE END

PH

MILL LA

Varney's Lock

Rectory
Farm

5

Northamptonshire STREET ATLAS

48

Broadmoor
Lock

OX17

Broadmoor
Bridge

River Cherwell

Hay's Bridge

The Rookery

4

Oxford Canal

Towing Path

Oxfordshire Canal Walk

Prescote Manor
Farm

The Mill House

Wardington Gate
Farm

3

47

Wardington
Spinney

Prescote Manor

PH

CREAMPOT CL

Wardington
House

2

Wardington

High Wardington
Farm

Jurassic Way

Sewage Works

CHURCH CL

THE JETTY

THE GREENSWARD

STUD FARM CL

PH

THORPE RD

1

Wardington
Grange

A361

MOUNT
PLEASANT

46

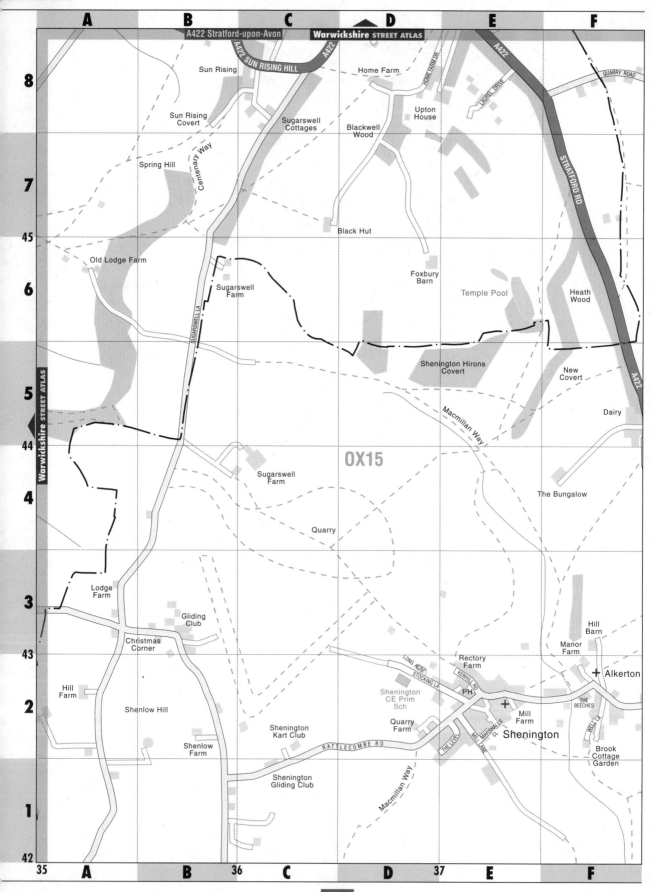

A422 SUN RISING HILL
A422
A422

Sun Rising
Home Farm
HOME FARM DR
Upton House
LAUREL DRIVE
QUARRY ROAD

Sun Rising Covert
Sugarswell Cottages
Blackwell Wood

Centenary Way
Spring Hill

STRATFORD RD

Old Lodge Farm
Black Hut
Foxbury Barn
Temple Pool
Heath Wood

Sugarswell LA

Sugarswell Farm
Shenington Hirons Covert
New Covert

A422

Warwickshire STREET ATLAS

Macmillan Way
Dairy

OX15

Sugarswell Farm
The Bungalow

Quarry

Lodge Farm

Hill Barn

Gliding Club
Manor Farm

Christmas Corner
LONG ACRE
STOCKING LA
Rectory Farm
KENHILL RD
Alkerton

Hill Farm

Shenlow Hill
Shenington CE Prim Sch
PH
THE BEECHES

MARSHALLS CL
Mill Farm
WELL LA

Shenington Kart Club
Quarry Farm
Shenington
Brook Cottage Garden

Shenlow Farm
RATTLECOMBE RD
THE LEVEL
MILL LANE

Shenington Gliding Club
Macmillan Way

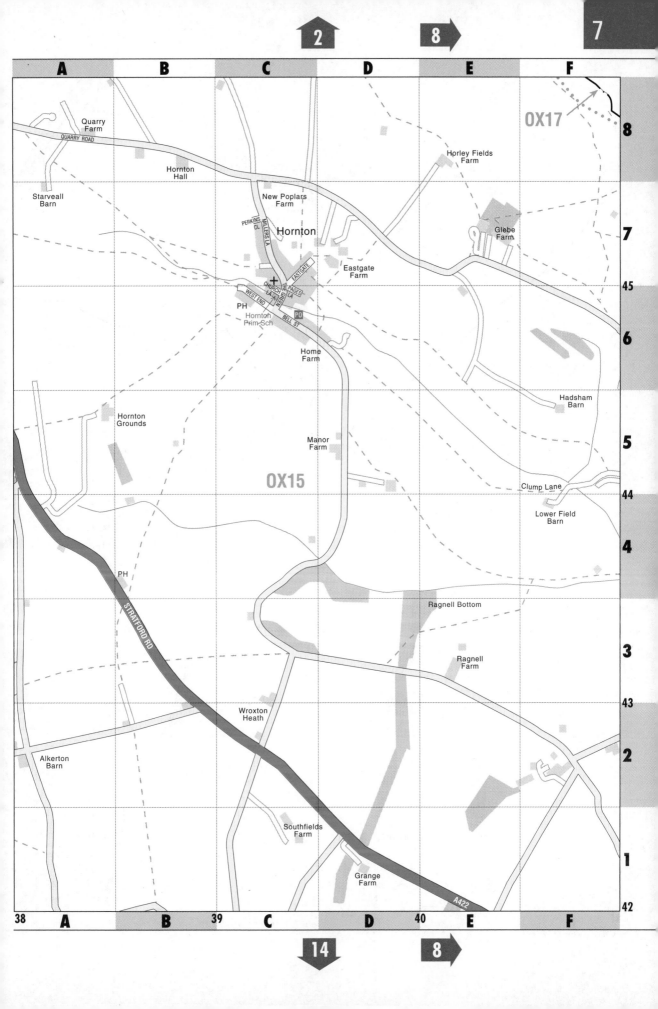

A   B   C   D   E   F

OX17

8

Quarry
Farm

QUARRY ROAD

Hornton
Hall

7

Starveall
Barn

New Poplars
Farm

PERKINS CL

MILLERS LA

Hornton

Horley Fields
Farm

Glebe
Farm

EASTGATE

THE PAGES

Eastgate
Farm

45

CHURCH LA

THE GREEN

7

WEST END

PH

BELL ST

PO

Hornton
Prim Sch

6

Home
Farm

Hadsham
Barn

Hornton
Grounds

Manor
Farm

5

OX15

Clump Lane

44

Lower Field
Barn

4

PH

Ragnell Bottom

STRATFORD RD

Ragnell
Farm

3

43

Wroxton
Heath

Alkerton
Barn

2

Southfields
Farm

1

Grange
Farm

A422

42

38   A   B   39   C   D   40   E   F

7 3

A B C D E F

8

Slated Barn

B4100

Laurel Farm

MOLLINGTON RD
BACKHOUSE LA
SNIPE LA
MIDDLE LA
CHAPEL LA
BURY CT LA
BACK HILL
PO
YEW
CORONATION LA
CHURCH LA

Bury Court Farm

Slade Barn

Shotteswell

7

45

Airstrip

OX17

6

Sor Brook

Hadsham House
Manor Farm

Water Tower

5

Horley House

Clump Lane

44

Hanwell

LITTLE LA
MANOR ORCH
PH
LANE CL
GULLIVER'S CL

SPRINGFIELD
MAIN ST
HANWELL CT
ROSE COTT
PARK CL
PH
CHURCH LA

4

Bramshill Barn

Horley

THE OLD COUNCIL HOS

THE COUNCIL HOS

SACKVILLE CT

Hanwell Castle

OX15

WARWICK RD

Park Farm

GULLICOTE LA

3

43

2

Drayton Lodge

HEREFORD WAY 1
GUERNSEY WAY 2
JERSEY DR 3
SUSSEX DR 4

Cemy

RIBSTONE PK

HORLEY PATH RD

CH

WINSTON D
ELLISON DR

WING CHELSEA CL

PITTWAYS
MELROSE CL
CL
ROW
FIRTREE CL
RYE CL

Lord's Spinney

1

HA
WICK PK
BARCOMBE
3

SAGE CL
2

QUEEN'S CRES

OX16

B4100

HORSHAM
SUSSEX DR
HIGHLANDS
CHEVIOT WAY
ROMNEY RD

42

41 A 42 B C 42 D 43 E F

A422

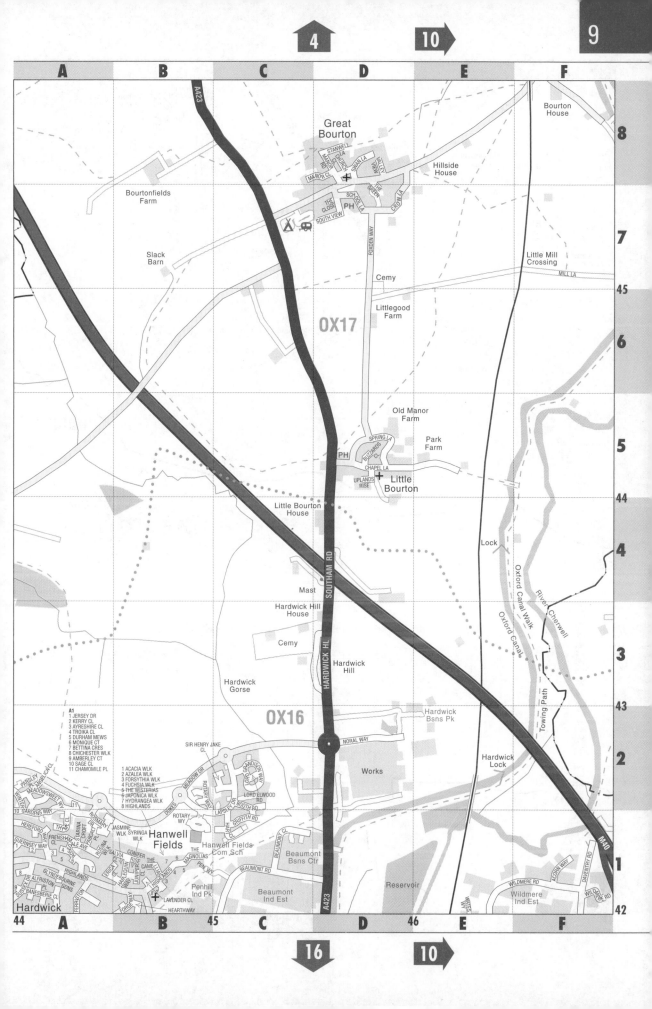

A B C D E F

8

7

45

6

5

44

4

3

43

2

1

42

Lower
Lodge

*Williamscot
House*

Weir

Oxford Canal

Oxford Canal Wlk

Peewit
Farm

River Cherwell

Williamscot Hill
Farm

Redlunch
Barn

OX17

OX16

A361

M40

Williamscot

Village
Spinney

Bell Land

Marsh Barn
Farm

The
Priory

BANBURY RD

Seale's
Farm

Huscote
Farm

A361

WARDINGTON RD

Dawkins's
Barn

Coton Farm

Works

CHURCH LA

SILVER ST N

SILVER ST S

WESLEY
RC

PH

BANBURY RD

THE SWAN

Chacombe
House

Jurassic Way

Mount
Pleasant

Barn
Farm

Bennetts
Farm

Trent
Farm

Upper
Wardington

Jurassic Way

Bridge Lake
Fisheries

Chacombe

Chacombe CE
Prim Sch

BEAN FURLONG

POPLARS RD

BENNETT CL

THORPE RD

THORNHILL

MIDDLETON RD

Castle Farm

Yew Tree
Cottage

BANBURY LA

CHENEY GDNS

KINGS
STILE

THE TYTHINGS

CHACOMBE RD

STANWELL LEA 1
STANWELL DR 2

MICHAELMAS CL

Windmill
Farm

CHENEY
CT

GLOVERS
LA

CHURCH LA

RECTORY
LA

HIGH ST

B4525

CHELMSCOTE
ROW

THE COUNCIL
HOUSES

THORPE RD

CH

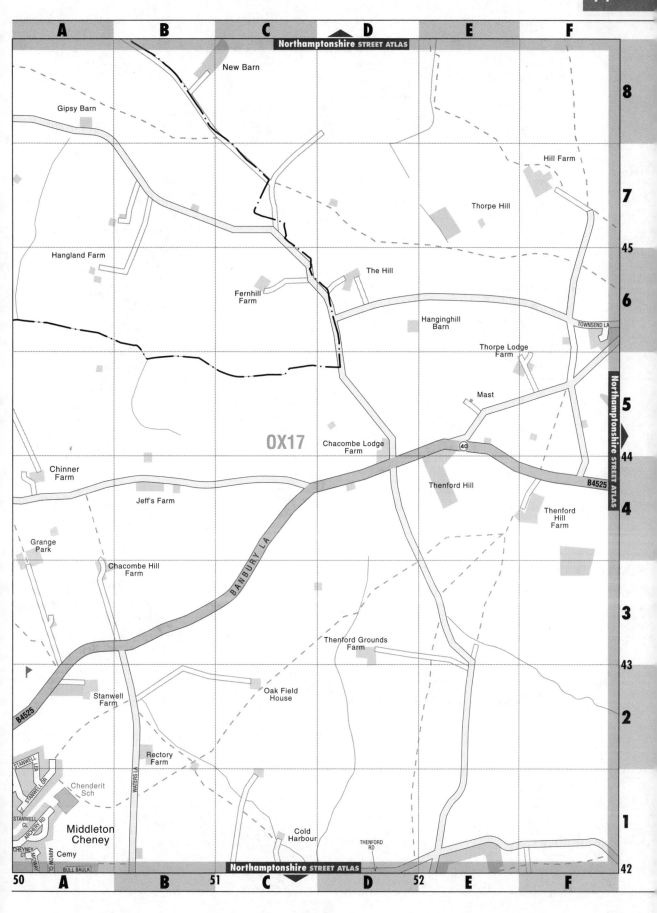

New Barn

Gipsy Barn

Hill Farm

Thorpe Hill

Hangland Farm

The Hill

Fernhill
Farm

Hanginghill
Barn

Thorpe Lodge
Farm

TOWNSEND LA

Mast

OX17

Chacombe Lodge
Farm

40

Thenford Hill

B4525

Chinner
Farm

Jeff's Farm

Thenford
Hill
Farm

Grange
Park

Chacombe Hill
Farm

BANBURY LA

Thenford Grounds
Farm

B4525

Stanwell
Farm

Oak Field
House

Rectory
Farm

WATERS LA

Chenderit
Sch

STANWELL LEA

STANWELL DR

STANWELL
CL

ARCHERY RD

Middleton
Cheney

CHEYNEY
CT

Cemy

ARROW CL

MIDWAY

Cold
Harbour

THENFORD
RD

BULL BAULK

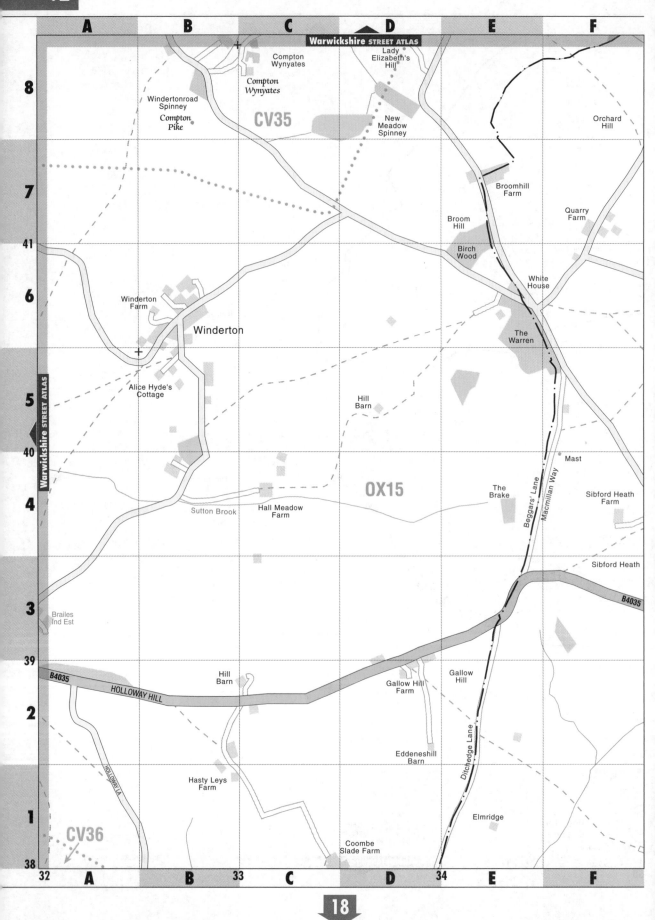

A B C D E F

8

CV35

Compton Wynyates

Compton Wynyates

Lady Elizabeth's Hill

Windertonroad Spinney

Compton Pike

New Meadow Spinney

Orchard Hill

7

Broomhill Farm

41

Broom Hill

Quarry Farm

6

Winderton Farm

Birch Wood

White House

Winderton

The Warren

Alice Hyde's Cottage

5

Hill Barn

40

Mast

The Brake

Beggars' Lane

Macmillan Way

Sibford Heath Farm

4

OX15

Sutton Brook

Hall Meadow Farm

Sibford Heath

3

Brailes Ind Est

B4035

39

Hill Barn

Gallow Hill Farm

Gallow Hill

B4035

HOLLOWAY HILL

Ditchedge Lane

2

Eddeneshill Barn

HOLLOWAY LA

Hasty Leys Farm

1

Elmridge

CV36

Coombe Slade Farm

38

32 A B 33 C D 34 E F

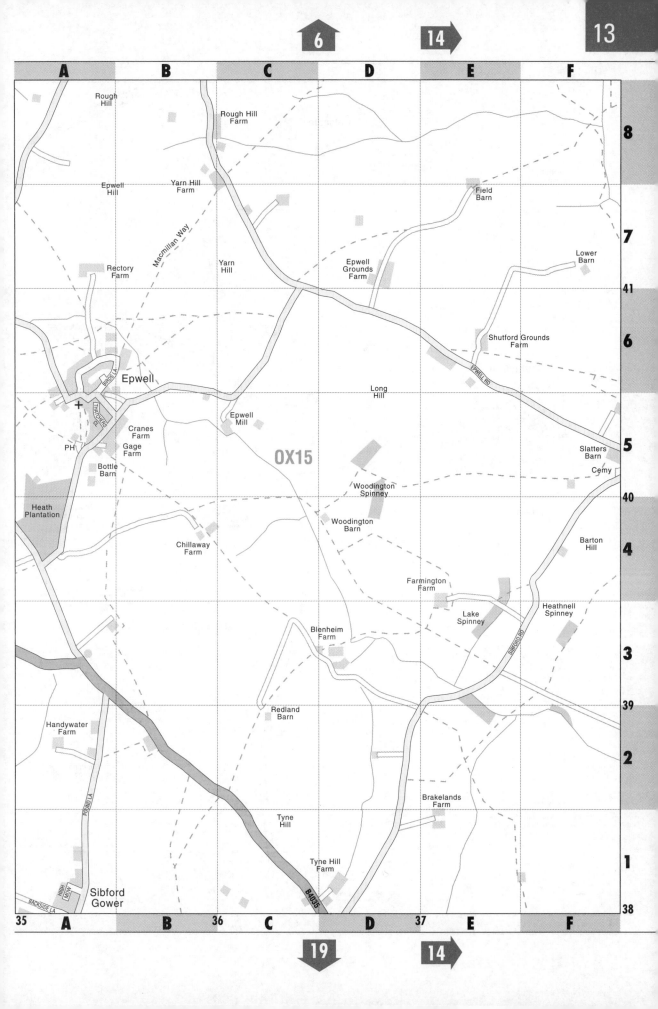

A B C D E F

8

7

41

6

5

40

4

3

39

2

1

38

Rough Hill

Rough Hill Farm

Epwell Hill

Yarn Hill Farm

Field Barn

Lower Barn

Macmillan Way

Yarn Hill

Rectory Farm

Epwell Grounds Farm

Shutford Grounds Farm

EPWELL RD

Epwell

Long Hill

Slatters Barn

Epwell Mill

OX15

Cemy

Cranes Farm

Gage Farm

PH

Woodington Spinney

Bottle Barn

Woodington Barn

Barton Hill

Heath Plantation

Chillaway Farm

Farmington Farm

Heathnell Spinney

Lake Spinney

SIBFORD RD

Blenheim Farm

Handywater Farm

Redland Barn

Brakelands Farm

POUND LA

Tyne Hill

Tyne Hill Farm

B4035

HIGH MDW

BACKSIDE LA

Sibford Gower

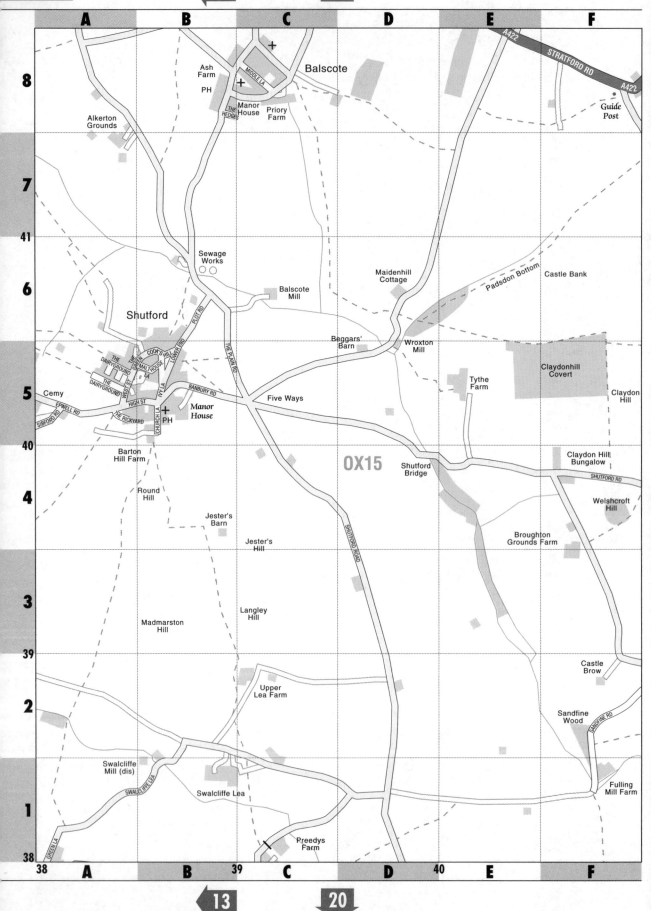

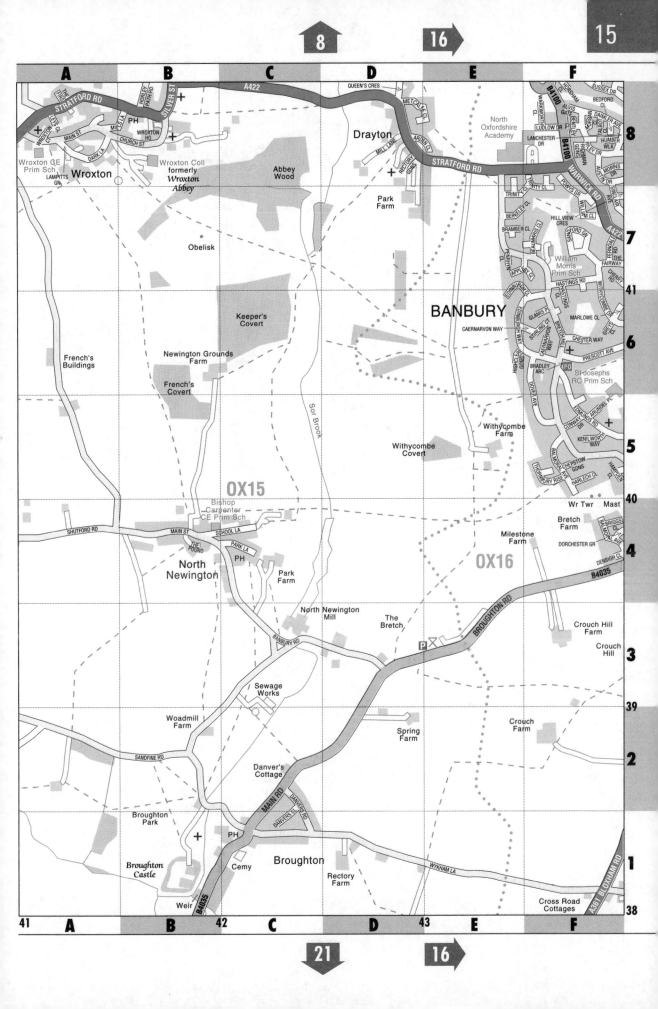

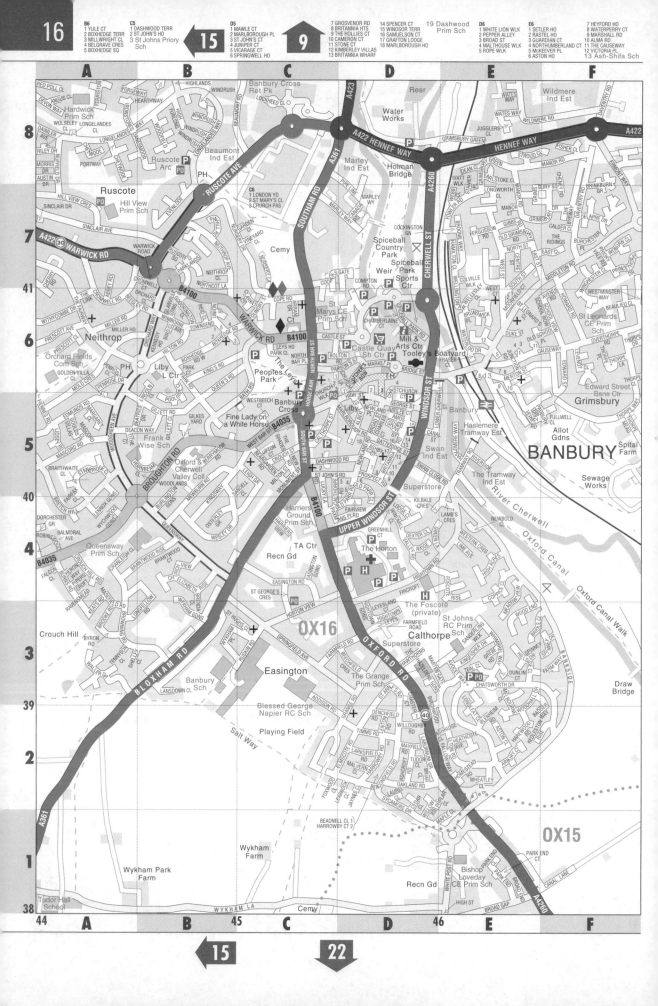

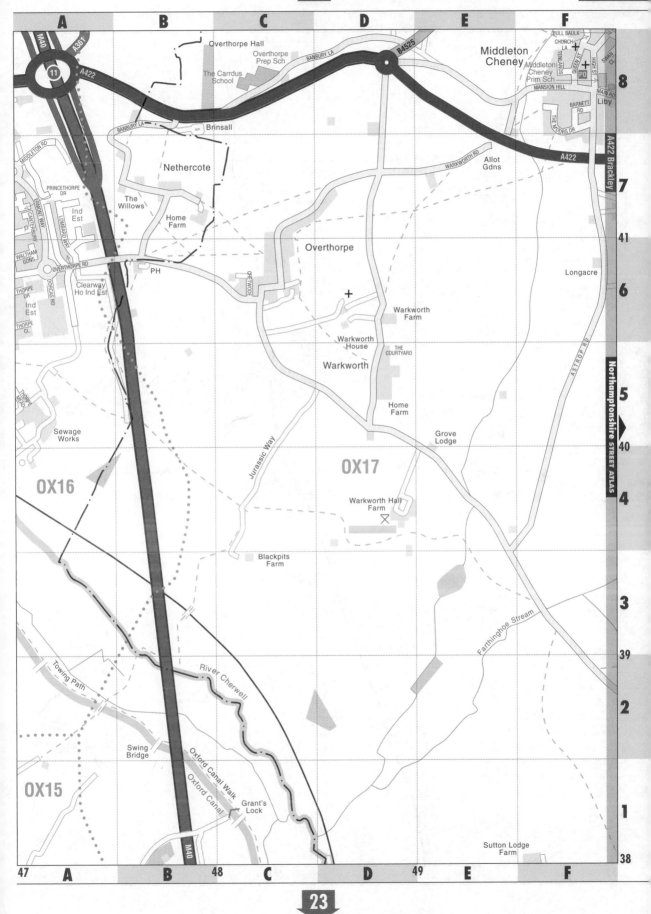

12

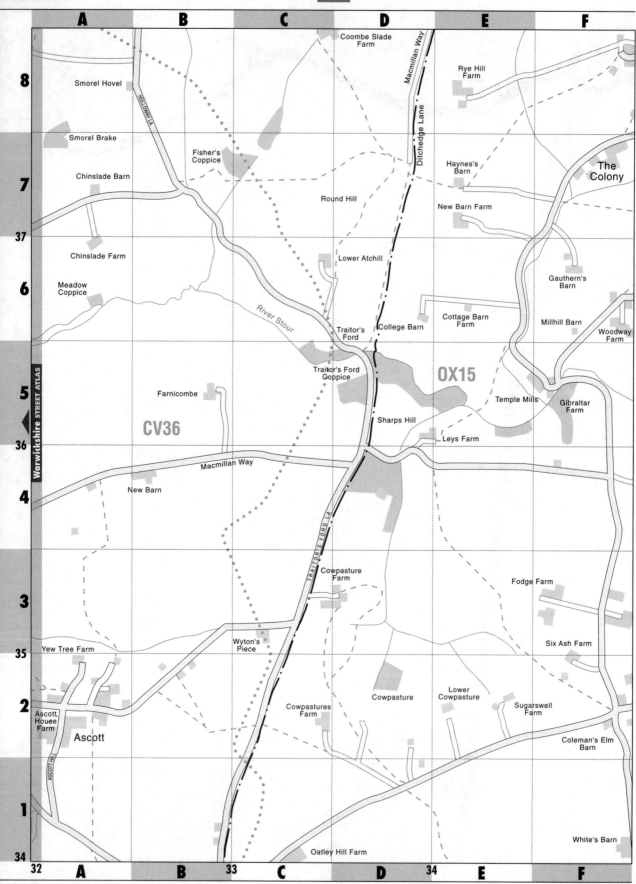

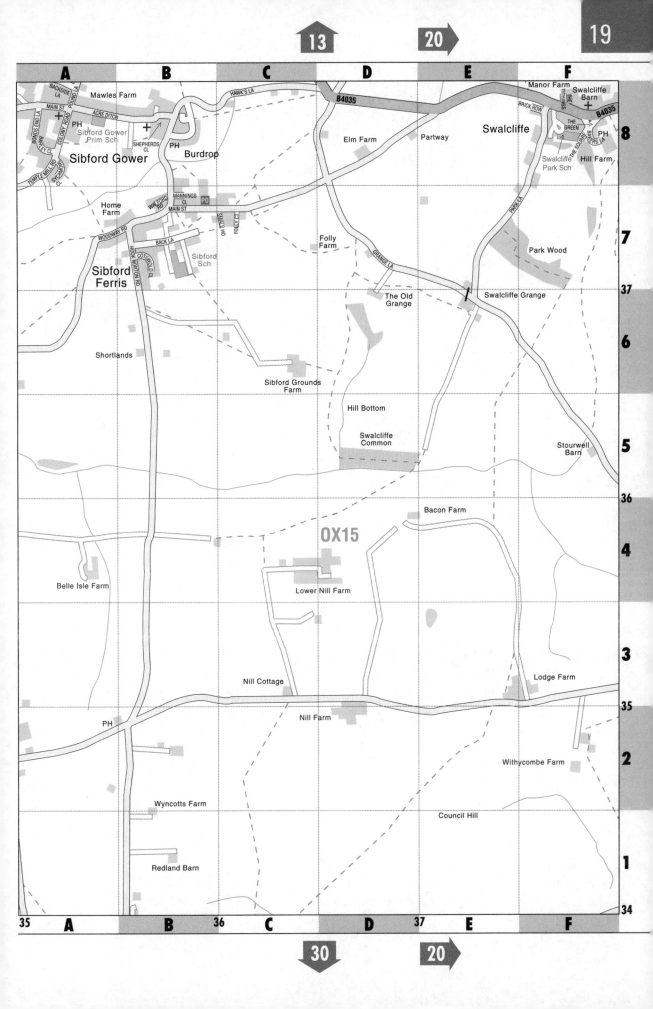

A   B   C   D   E   F

B4035
SWALCLIFFE RD
MAIN ST
GREEN LA
USHERCOMBE VIEW
OLD GLEBE
BAKERS LA
PH
Home Farm
Brick Farm

8

Tadmarton
CHURCH FURLONG
Austins Farm

Austins Farm

M A I N R D
BROOKFIELD RISE
SHUTFORD RD
Five Acres Farm

7

Ushercombe Barn
Ushercoombe Copse
DRIFT ACRE
High Meadow Farm
Lower Tadmarton
B4035
Lower Tadmarton Farm

37

6

5

36
Ushercombe Farm
Tadmarton Heath
OX15

4
CH
Rye Hill

Highways Farm

3
Wigginton Heath
CH
Fern Hill

35
Ryehill Barn

Cedar Bungalow
2
THE OLD COUNCIL HOS
PH
HEATH CL
THE GREEN

Resr
Lessor Farm

1
The Waterfowl Sanctuary & Children's Farm

34
Brickfield Farm

38   A   B   39   C   D   40   E   F

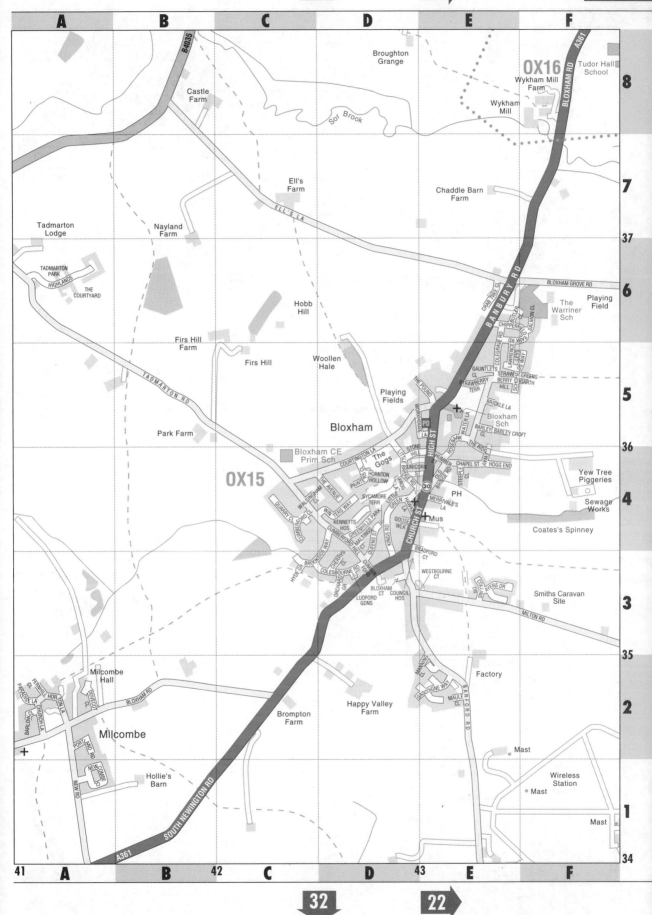

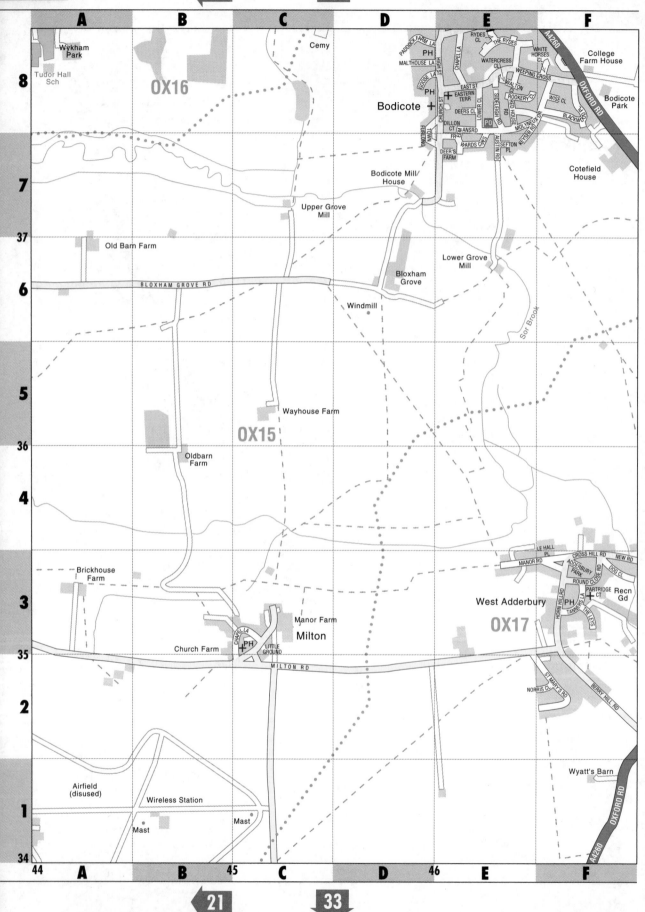

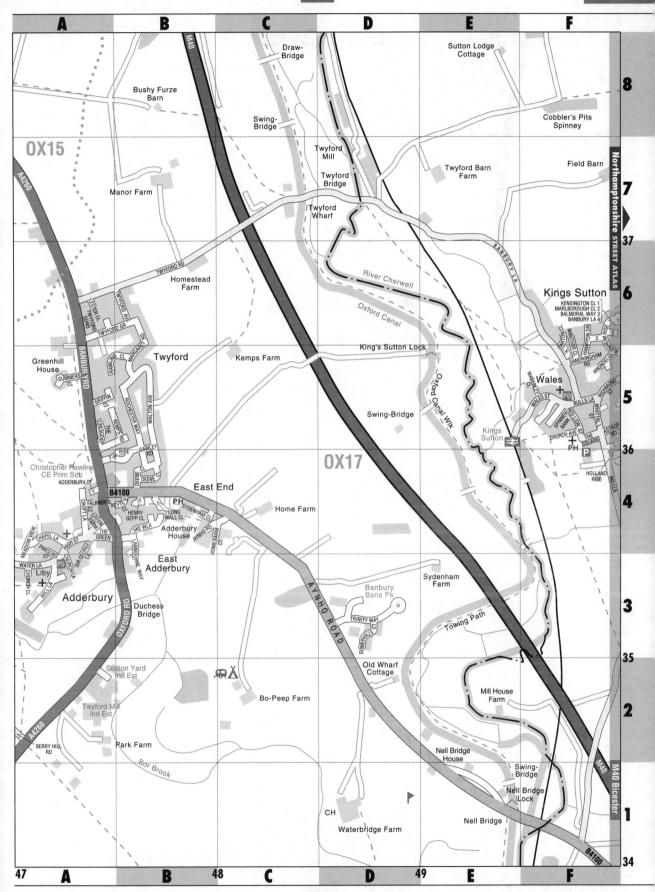

OX15

A4260

M40

Draw-Bridge

Bushy Furze Barn

Swing-Bridge

Sutton Lodge Cottage

Cobbler's Pits Spinney

Twyford Mill

Twyford Barn Farm

Field Barn

Manor Farm

Twyford Bridge

8

7

37

BANBURY LA

Twyford Wharf

River Cherwell

Kings Sutton

6

KENSINGTON CL 1
MARLBOROUGH CL 2
BALMORAL WAY 3
BANBURY LA 4

Twyford Rd

Homestead Farm

Oxford Canal

LESTER CL
TWYFORD CLMS
TWYFORD AVE
MARGARET DR

King's Sutton Lock

WINDSOR CL
SANDRINGHAM
ARUNDEL CL
HAMPTON RISE
BLENHEIM CL

Greenhill House

SUMMERS CL

RAWLINS CL
THE GRIFFIN
THE CRESCENT
KEMPS RD
ROCHESTER WAY
WALTON AVE
CAWLEY RD

Twyford

Kemps Farm

Oxford Canal Wlk

Wales

WAVERLEY CL
WALES ST
SPINNEY BANK
BULLS LA
REDLION ST
RICHMOND ST
WHITTAL

PO

5

BANBURY YRD

THE RISE

Swing-Bridge

Kings Sutton

CHURCH AVE
THE SQUARE
PH
ASTROP RD

36

Christopher Rawlins CE Prim Sch

DEENE CL
DEENE
ADDERBURY CT

B4100

East End

Home Farm

HOLLAND RISE
MILL A

FALKNER'S CL
CROFT LA
THE GREEN
KEYTES
HENRY GEPP CL
LAKE WLK
LONG WALL CL
SYDENHAM CL
HOME FARM RD
LAMBOURNE WAY

PH

4

MEADOW VIEW
CHAPEL LA
HIGH ST
PARSONS ST
CHURCH LA
ST GEORGES LA
WATER LA
CHURCH CL
MILL LA

Adderbury House

Sydenham Farm

East Adderbury

Liby

PO

Adderbury

OXFORD RD

Duchess Bridge

AYNHO ROAD

Banbury Bsns Pk

TRINITY WAY
SOMERVILLE

Sydenham Farm

Towing Path

3

35

Station Yard Ind Est

Old Wharf Cottage

Mill House Farm

A4260

Twyford Mill Ind Est

Bo-Peep Farm

2

BERRY HILL RD

Park Farm

Sor Brook

Nell Bridge House

Swing-Bridge

M40

M40 Bicester

Nell Bridge Lock

1

CH

Waterbridge Farm

Nell Bridge

B4100

34

OX17

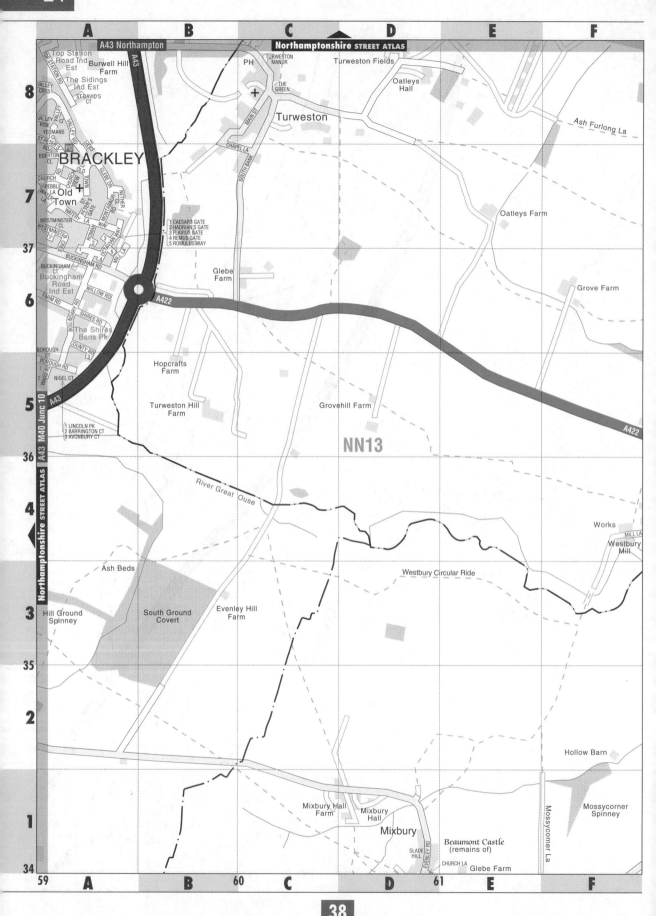

A43 Northampton

Top Station
Road Ind
Est
Burwell Hill
Farm
The Sidings
Ind Est
VALLEY
CRES
ST DAVID'S
CT
VALLEY RD

8

Turweston
Fields

TURWESTON
MANOR

THE
GREEN

PH

Oatleys
Hall

Ash Furlong La

YEOMANS
CL
VALLEY
RISE
ST PETER'S CL
EGERTON
CL
BRACKLEY
PO

Turweston

MAIN ST

CHAPEL LA

CHURCH
VIEW
Old
Town
PEBBLE
LA
CHURCH RD
OLD TOWN
WATERY LA
GLEBE DR
NETHER
ST PETER'S
WAY
ROMAN WAY
MONTABAN
PEBBLE LA

7

SOUTH BANK

Oatleys Farm

1 CAESARS GATE
2 HADRIAN'S GATE
3 FLAVIUS GATE
4 REMUS GATE
5 ROMULUS WAY

37

WESTMINSTER
WESTMINSTER CRES
BUCKINGHAM RD
BUCKINGHAM
CT
Buckingham
Road
Ind Est
WILLOW RD
OCTAVIAN WAY
VIA DEVANA
NICLA LA

Glebe
Farm

Grove Farm

6

A422

FARM RD
BOUNDARY RD
SHIRES RD
The Shires
Bsns Pk
COUNTY RD
BOROUGH
CT
BOROUGH RD
WARD RD
NIGEL CT

Hopcrafts
Farm

5

A43 M40 Junc 10
A43

1 LINCOLN PK
2 BARRINGTON CT
3 AVONBURY CT

Turweston Hill
Farm

Grovehill Farm

A422

NN13

36

River Great Ouse

4

Northamptonshire STREET ATLAS

Works

MILL LA
Westbury
Mill

Ash Beds

Westbury Circular Ride

3

Hill Ground
Spinney

South Ground
Covert

Evenley Hill
Farm

35

2

Hollow Barn

1

Mixbury Hall
Farm

Mixbury
Hall

Mixbury

Mossycorner La

Mossycorner
Spinney

SLADE
HILL
EVENLEY RD

Beaumont Castle
(remains of)

CHURCH LA
Glebe Farm

34

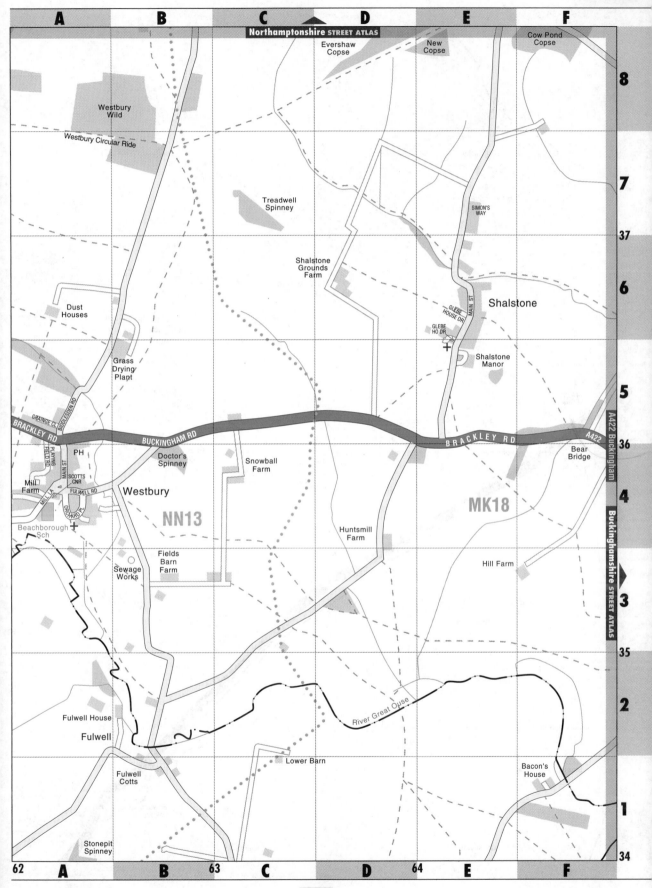

Evershaw Copse

New Copse

Cow Pond Copse

Westbury Wild

Westbury Circular Ride

Treadwell Spinney

SIMON'S WAY

Shalstone Grounds Farm

MAIN ST

Shalstone

Dust Houses

GLEBE HOUSE DR

GLEBE HO DR

Grass Drying Plant

Shalstone Manor

BRACKLEY RD

BRIDLESDEN RD

GRAINGE CL

BUCKINGHAM RD

BRACKLEY RD

A422

A422 Buckingham

Bear Bridge

PH

Doctor's Spinney

Snowball Farm

PLAYING FIELD RD

MILL LA

MILL LA

SCOTTS CNR

FULWELL RD

ORCHARD PL

Mill Farm

Westbury

NN13

MK18

Beachborough Sch

Huntsmill Farm

Hill Farm

Sewage Works

Fields Barn Farm

Buckinghamshire STREET ATLAS

Fulwell House

Fulwell

River Great Ouse

Bacon's House

Lower Barn

Fulwell Cotts

Stonepit Spinney

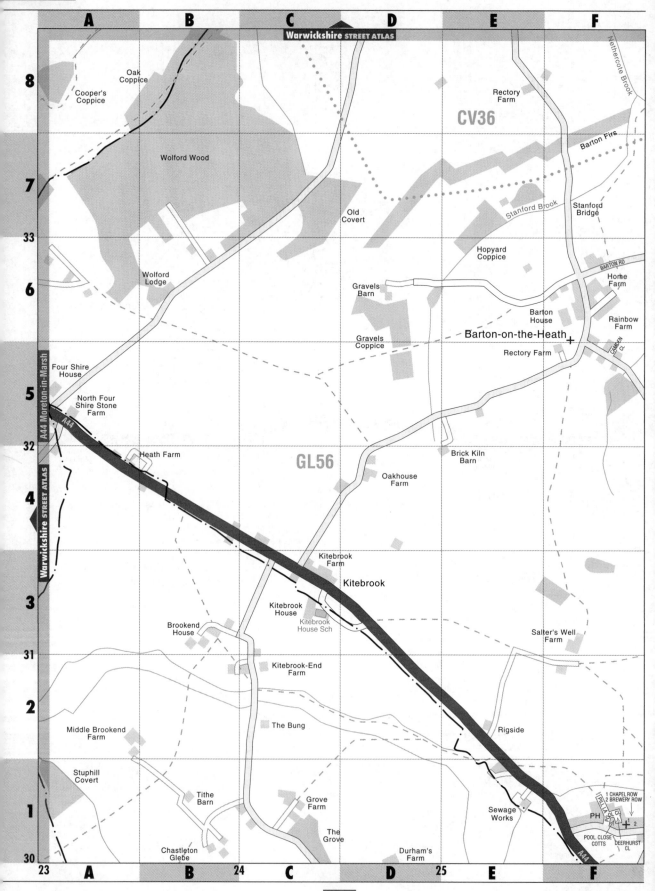

CV36

Oak
Coppice

Cooper's
Coppice

Wolford Wood

Rectory
Farm

Nethercote Brook

Barton Firs

Old
Covert

Stanford Brook

Stanford
Bridge

Hopyard
Coppice

BARTON RD

Wolford
Lodge

Gravels
Barn

Home
Farm

Barton
House

Four Shire
House

Gravels
Coppice

Barton-on-the-Heath

Rainbow
Farm

CAMDEN CL

Rectory Farm

North Four
Shire Stone
Farm

Heath Farm

GL56

Oakhouse
Farm

Brick Kiln
Barn

A44 Moreton-in-Marsh

Warwickshire STREET ATLAS

A44

Kitebrook
Farm

Kitebrook

Salter's Well
Farm

Kitebrook
House

Kitebrook
House Sch

Brookend
House

Kitebrook-End
Farm

Middle Brookend
Farm

The Bung

Rigside

Stuphill
Covert

Tithe
Barn

Grove
Farm

Sewage
Works

1 CHAPEL ROW
2 BREWERY ROW

PILLAR CL
POOL CL

PH

Pool Close
Cotts

DEERHURST
CL

Chastleton
Glebe

The
Grove

Durham's
Farm

A44

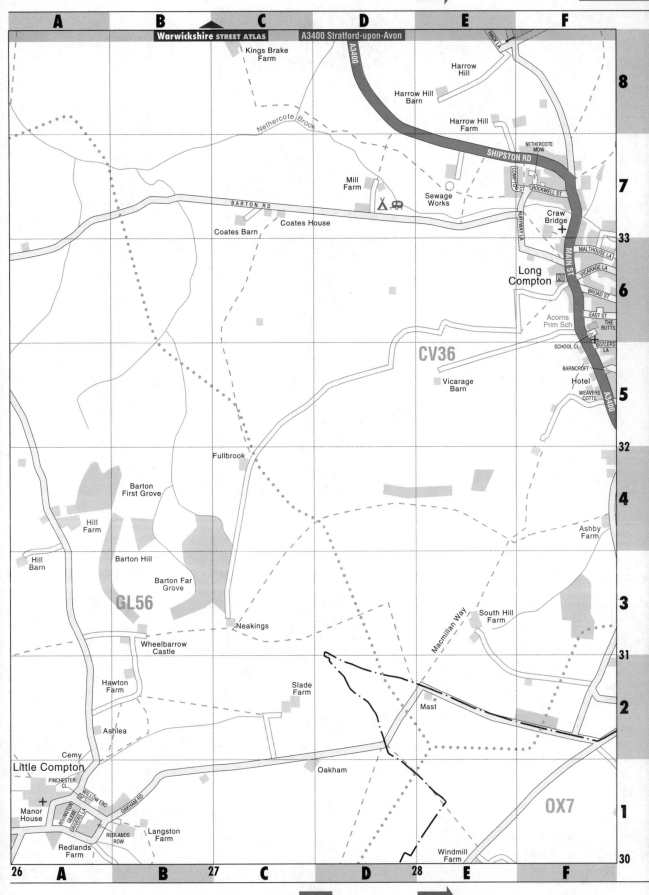

Warwickshire STREET ATLAS

A3400 Stratford-upon-Avon

Kings Brake Farm

Harrow Hill

Harrow Hill Barn

HACK LA

Harrow Hill Farm

Nethercote Brook

SHIPSTON RD

NETHERCOTE MDW

COMPTON CT

CROCKWELL ST

BARTON RD

Mill Farm

Sewage Works

Coates House

BURWAY LA

Craw Bridge

Coates Barn

MALTHOUSE LA

MAIN ST

VICARAGE LA

Long Compton

PO

BROAD ST

EAST ST

THE BUTTS

CV36

Acorns Prim Sch

SCHOOL CL

BUTLERS LA

Vicarage Barn

BARNCROFT

Hotel

WEAVERS COTTS

A3400

Fullbrook

Barton First Grove

Ashby Farm

Hill Farm

Barton Hill

Hill Barn

Barton Far Grove

GL56

Macmillan Way

South Hill Farm

Neakings

Wheelbarrow Castle

Hawton Farm

Slade Farm

Mast

Ashlea

Cemy

Oakham

OX7

Little Compton

PINCHESTER CL

WILLOW END

OAKHAM RD

Manor House

RIVINGTON GLEBE

DRIVERS LA

REDLANDS ROW

Langston Farm

Redlands Farm

Windmill Farm

8 7 33 6 5 32 4 3 31 2 1 30

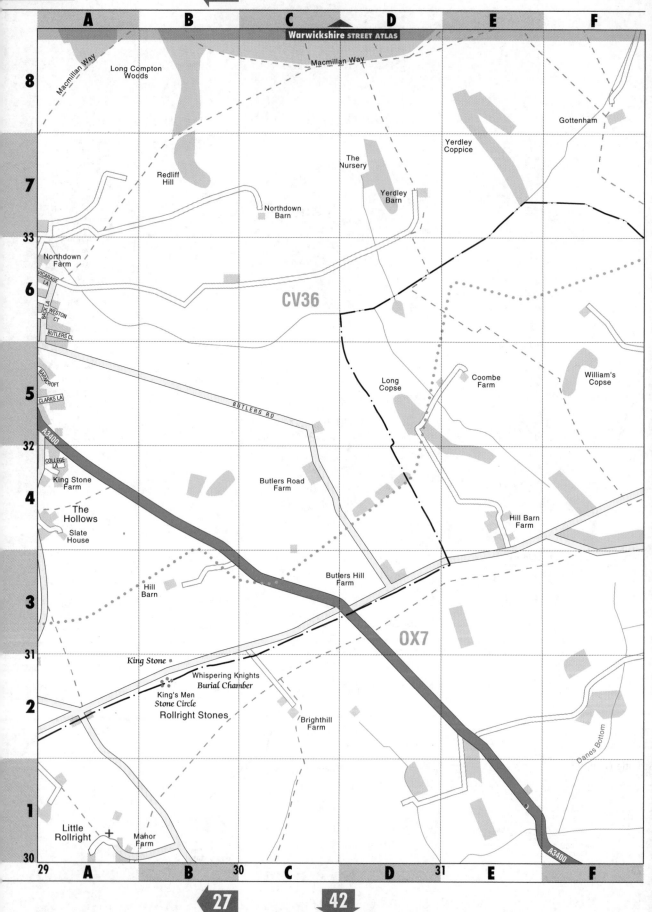

Warwickshire STREET ATLAS

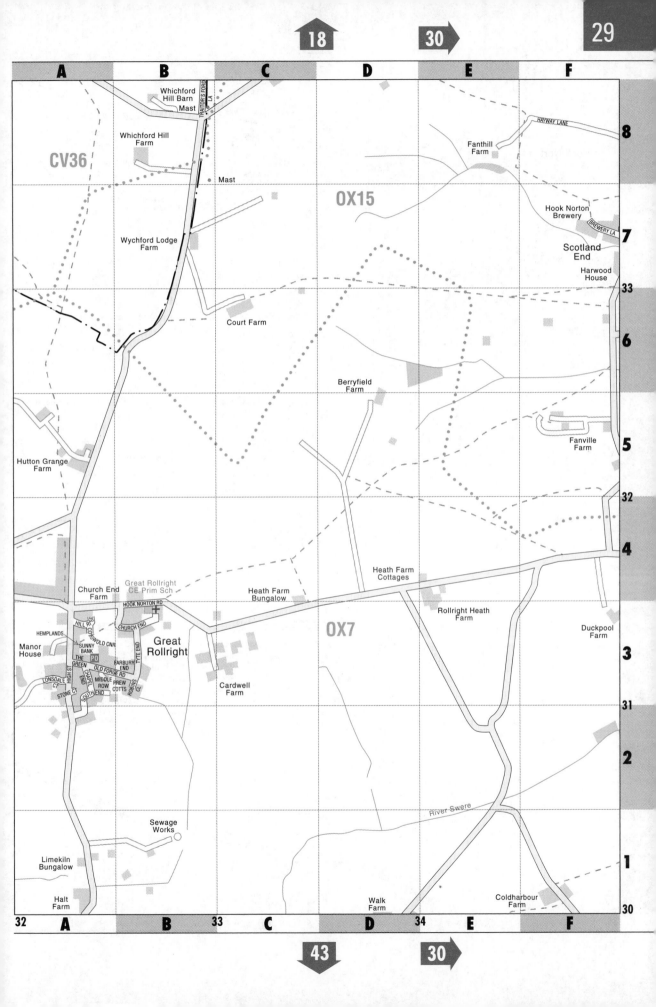

A   B   C   D   E   F

8

Round Hill

HAYWAY LA

Hook Norton

Redlands Farm

Hook Norton CE Prim Sch

Crushill Farm

Wks

Railway Farm

BRYMBO COTTS

Butter Hill

ORCHARD RD

THE GLEBE

HOLLYBUSH RD

SIBFORD RD

WHITTONS CL

RECTORY RD

BOURNE LA

East End

STATION RD

Ironstone Hollow

AUSTIN'S WAY

EAST END

Sewage Works

Manor Farm

7

ROUND CLOSE RD

CLAY BANK

BREWERY LA

OLD SCHO

THE BOURNE

CHIPPING NORTON RD

SCOTLAND END

BROOMSIDE

NETTING ST

THE SHEARINGS

WATERY LA

OSNEY CL

QUEEN ST

HIGH ST

ODILY CL

MOBBS CL

HEATH CT

DOWN END

CHAPEL ST

LA 1 ST

THE GREEN

TITE LA

WELL BANK

PARK HILL

Cemy

Wks

OX15

Down End

+ Liby

PH

Scotland End

BELT HILL

BRIDGE HILL

PARK RD

BRICK HILL

ROPE WAY

PARK CL

BEAN CRE RD

BURY GROV

SOUTHROP RD

NORTHERP V

Park Farm

33

Grounds Farm

Cradle Farm

6

CROFT'S LA

Gilden Farm

Southrop

Cradle House Farm

SWERFORD RD

Highwood Farm

5

South Hill

Cradle Barn

32

4

South Hill Farm

Archell Farm

Swerford Park

3

Swerford Park Farm

OX7

Church End +

Between Towns

East End

Ash Hill Farm

CHAPEL HILL

River Swere

ST MARY'S LA

Swerford

31

Grange Farm

2

Coltscombe

A361

BANBURY RD

1

Pomfret Castle

30

Hayes's Barn

Spring Farm

A361

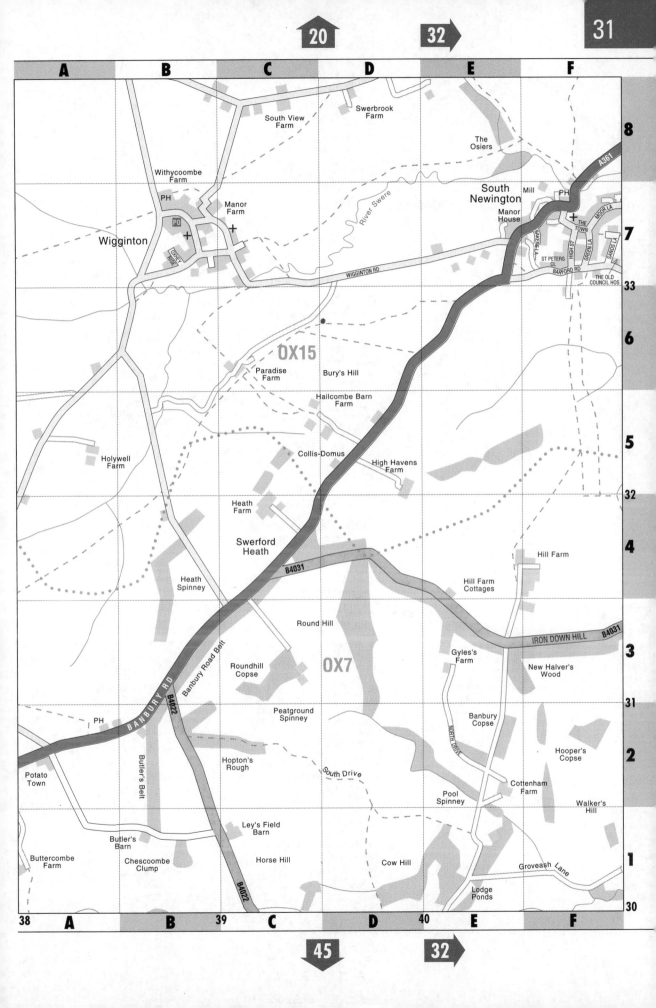

A B C D E F

8

The Bauk

A361

MOOR LA

River Swere

Barford St John

BARFORD RD

BLOXHAM RD

MEAD RD

7

Mead Farm

Manor Farm

33

BARFORD RD

Rignell Farm

Rignell Hall

The Manor House

PH

LOWER ST

6

SOUTH NEWINGTON RD

CHURCH ST

Barford St Michael

SUMMER LEY

HORN HILL

Buttermilk Farm

Barford Lodge

BROAD CL

TOWNSEND

Brasenose College Farm

5

OX15

Spring Hill Farm

THE COUNCIL HOS

HEMPTON ROAD

32

NETHERWORTON RD

4

STEEPNESS HILL

B4031

Irondown Farm

Iron Down

IRON DOWN HILL

B4031

3

Upper Grove Ash Farm

Irondown Spinney

Norton Grounds Farm

Ilbury Farm

31

Lower Grove Ash Farm

2

Raven Hill

Hawk Hill

OX7

1

Nether Worton

The Boltons

Manor Farm

Ford

Nether Worton House

FLIGHT HILL

30

41 A 42 B C 43 D E F

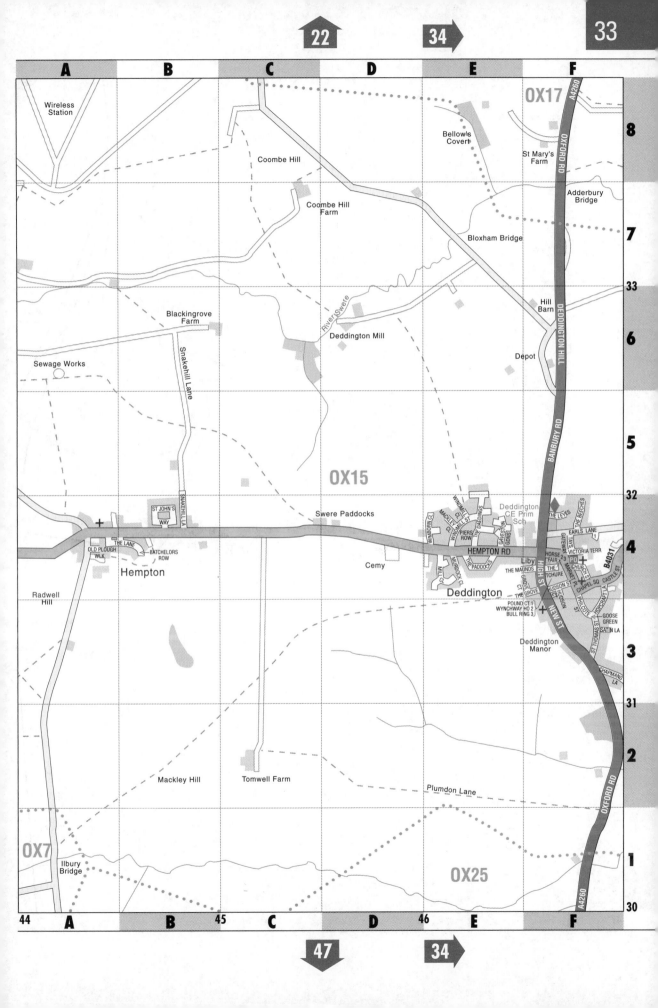

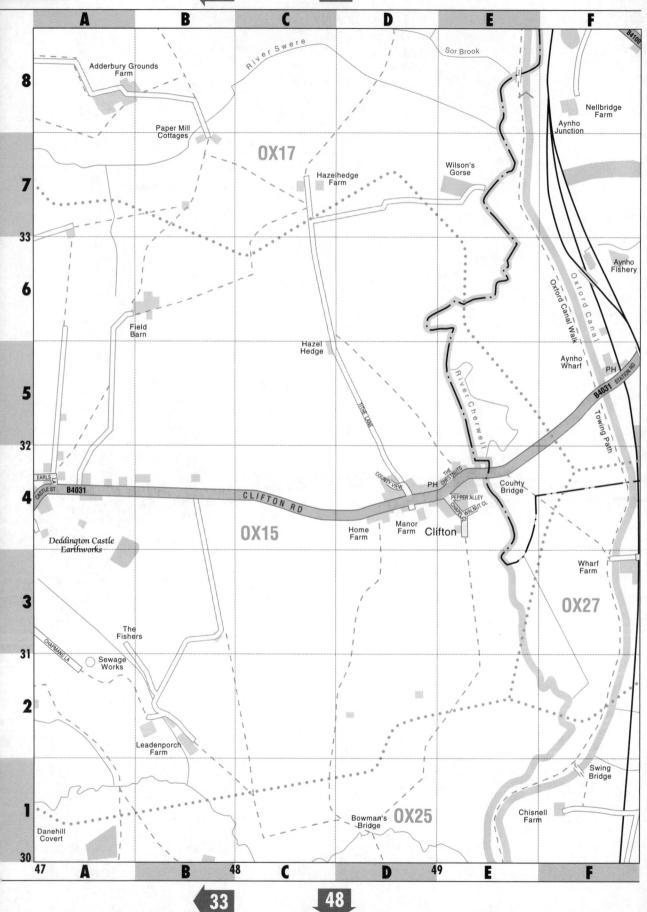

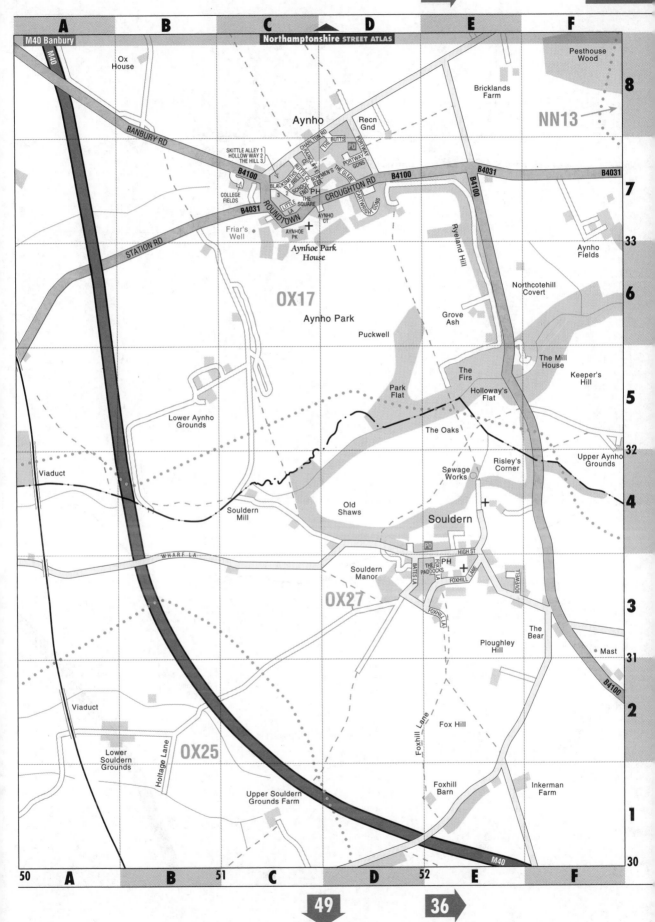

Northamptonshire STREET ATLAS

A B C D E F

M40 Banbury

M40

Ox House

Pesthouse Wood

BANBURY RD

Bricklands Farm

8

Aynho

NN13

Recn Gnd

CHARLTON RD

THE BUTTS

PO

PORTWAY

SKITTLE ALLEY 1
HOLLOW WAY 2
THE HILL 3

CHURCH LA

B4100

BUTTS LA

THE HILL

PORTWAY GDNS

B4031

B4031

B4031

7

BLACKSMITHS

SCHOOL END

THE GLEBE

B4100

COLLEGE FIELDS

3

2

LITTLE LA

PH

CROUGHTON RD

B4031

THE SQUARE

CARTWRIGHT GDNS

B4100

AYNHO CT

Friar's Well

AYNHOE PK

Ryeland Hill

Aynho Fields

33

Aynhoe Park House

OX17

Northcotehill Covert

6

Aynho Park

Grove Ash

Puckwell

The Mill House

Keeper's Hill

The Firs

5

Park Flat

Holloway's Flat

Lower Aynho Grounds

The Oaks

32

Sewage Works

Risley's Corner

Upper Aynho Grounds

Viaduct

Souldern Mill

Old Shaws

4

Souldern

WHARF LA

PO

High St

Souldern Manor

BATES LA

THE PADDOCKS

FOX LA

PH

Foxhill Lane

BOVEWELL

OX27

FOXHILL LA

FOXHILL

3

The Bear

OX25

Viaduct

Holtage Lane

Ploughley Hill

Mast

31

B4100

Foxhill Lane

Fox Hill

2

Lower Souldern Grounds

Foxhill Barn

Inkerman Farm

Upper Souldern Grounds Farm

1

M40

30

50 A B 51 C D 52 E F

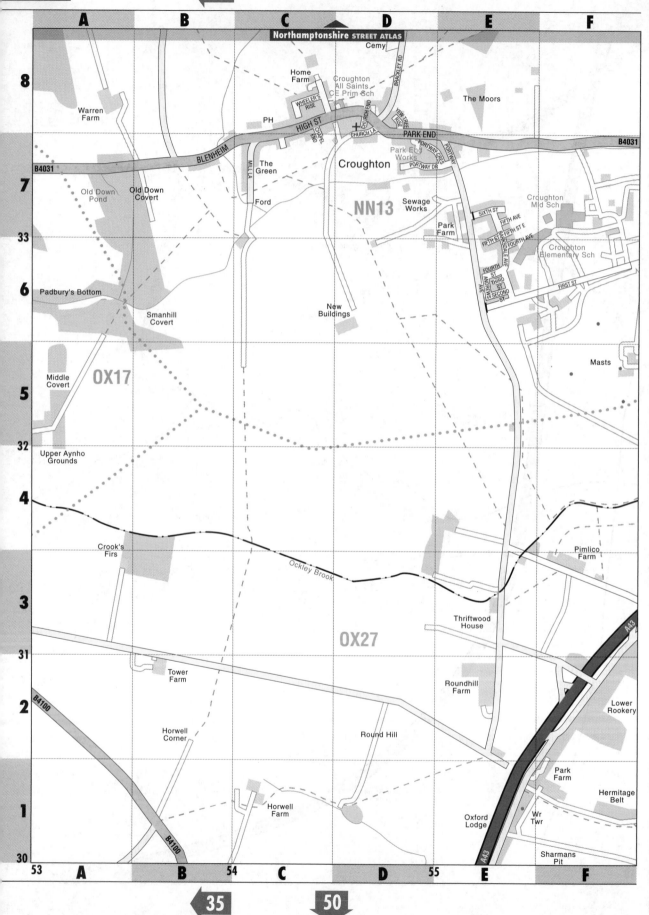

Northamptonshire STREET ATLAS

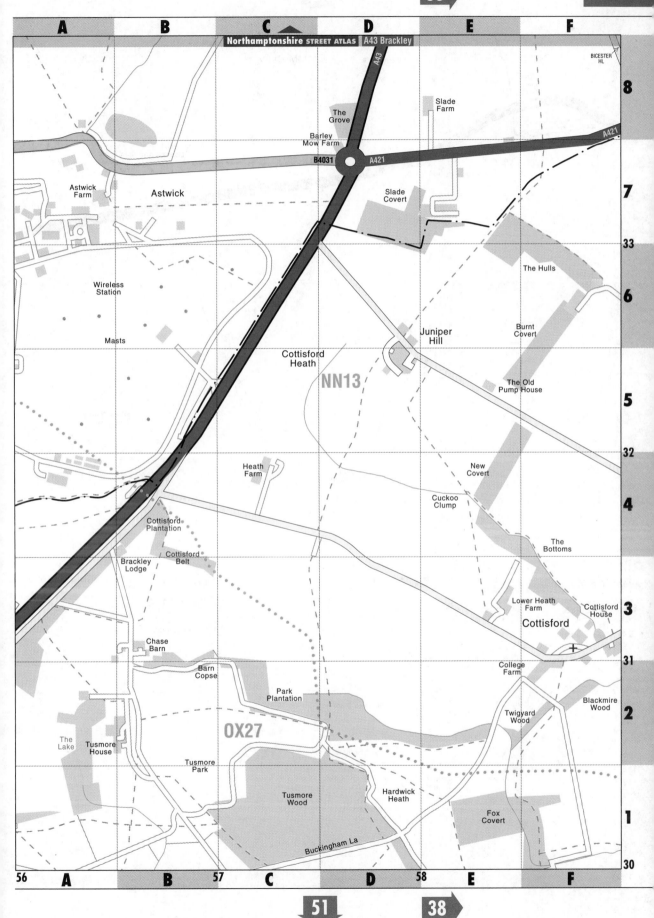

BICESTER HL

A43

A421

8

The Grove

Slade Farm

Barley Mow Farm

B4031   A421

7

Astwick Farm

Astwick

Slade Covert

33

The Hulls

Wireless Station

6

Burnt Covert

Juniper Hill

Masts

Cottisford Heath

The Old Pump House

5

NN13

32

Heath Farm

New Covert

4

Cuckoo Clump

The Bottoms

Cottisford Plantation

Brackley Lodge

Cottisford Belt

Lower Heath Farm

Cottisford House

3

Cottisford

Chase Barn

College Farm

31

Barn Copse

Blackmire Wood

Park Plantation

Twigyard Wood

2

OX27

The Lake

Tusmore House

Tusmore Park

Hardwick Heath

Tusmore Wood

Fox Covert

1

Buckingham La

30

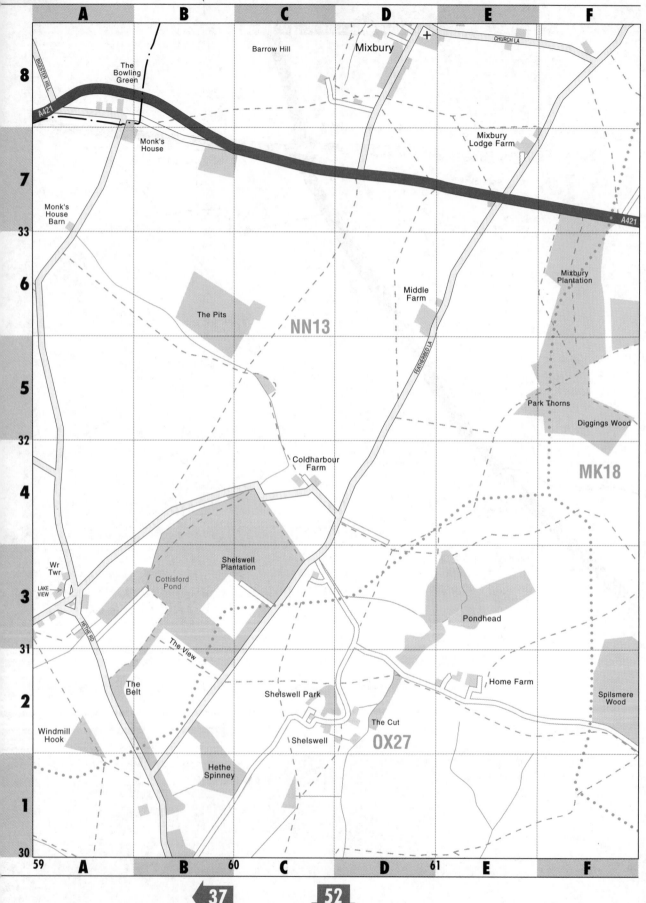

A B C D E F

8

7

33

6

5

32

4

3

31

2

1

30

59 A B 60 C D 61 E F

Mixbury

CHURCH LA

Barrow Hill

The Bowling Green

BICESTER HILL

A421

Monk's House

Monk's House Barn

Mixbury Lodge Farm

Mixbury Plantation

A421

The Pits

NN13

Middle Farm

FEATHERBED LA

Park Thorns

Diggings Wood

MK18

Coldharbour Farm

Shelswell Plantation

Cottisford Pond

Wr Twr

LAKE VIEW

HETHE RD

The View

The Belt

Windmill Hook

Shelswell Park

Hethe Spinney

Shelswell

The Cut

OX27

Pondhead

Home Farm

Spilsmere Wood

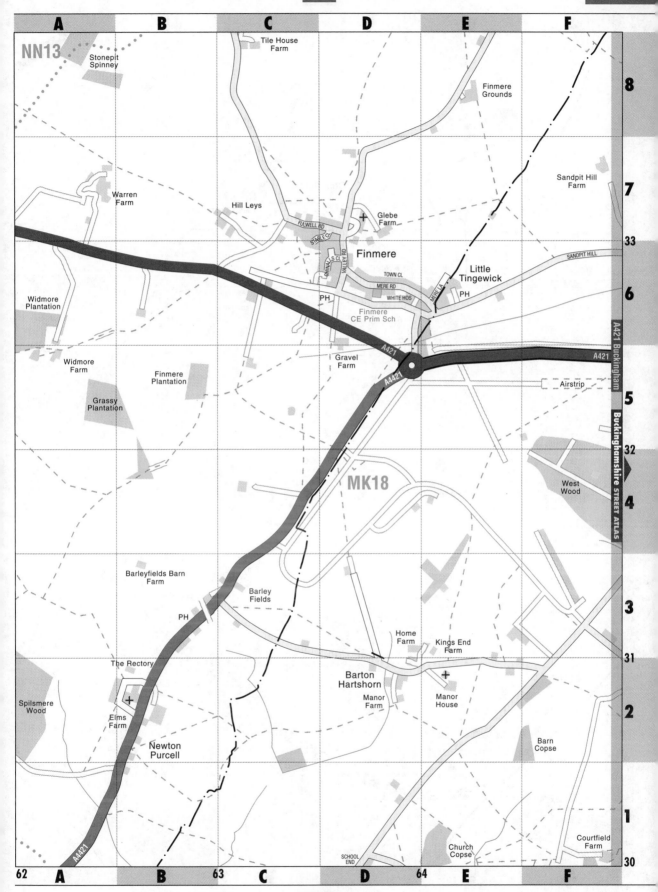

NN13

Stonepit Spinney

Tile House Farm

Finmere Grounds

8

Warren Farm

Hill Leys

Sandpit Hill Farm

7

Glebe Farm

FULWELL RD

ST MARY CE

33

Widmore Plantation

Finmere

SANDPIT HILL

Little Tingewick

VALLEY RD

LONHALL S CL

MERE LA

PH

TOWN CL

MERE RD

WHITE HOS

PH

6

PH

Finmere CE Prim Sch

A421

A421 Buckingham

Widmore Farm

Finmere Plantation

Gravel Farm

A4421

Airstrip

5

Grassy Plantation

32

West Wood

Buckinghamshire STREET ATLAS

MK18

4

Barleyfields Barn Farm

Barley Fields

3

PH

Home Farm

Kings End Farm

31

The Rectory

Barton Hartshorn

Manor Farm

Manor House

Spilsmere Wood

Elms Farm

2

Barn Copse

Newton Purcell

1

Church Copse

Courtfield Farm

A4421

SCHOOL END

30

A C D E F

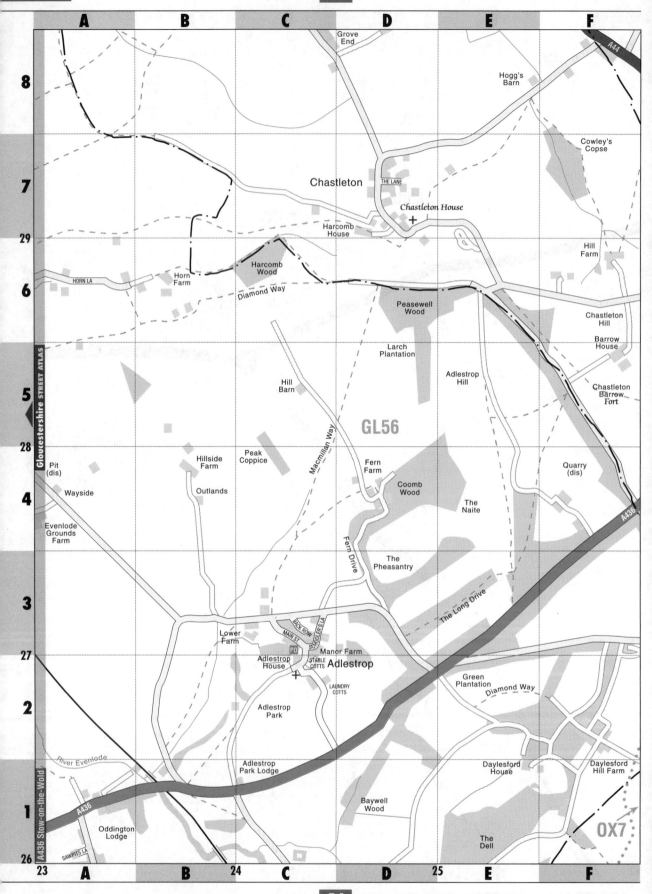

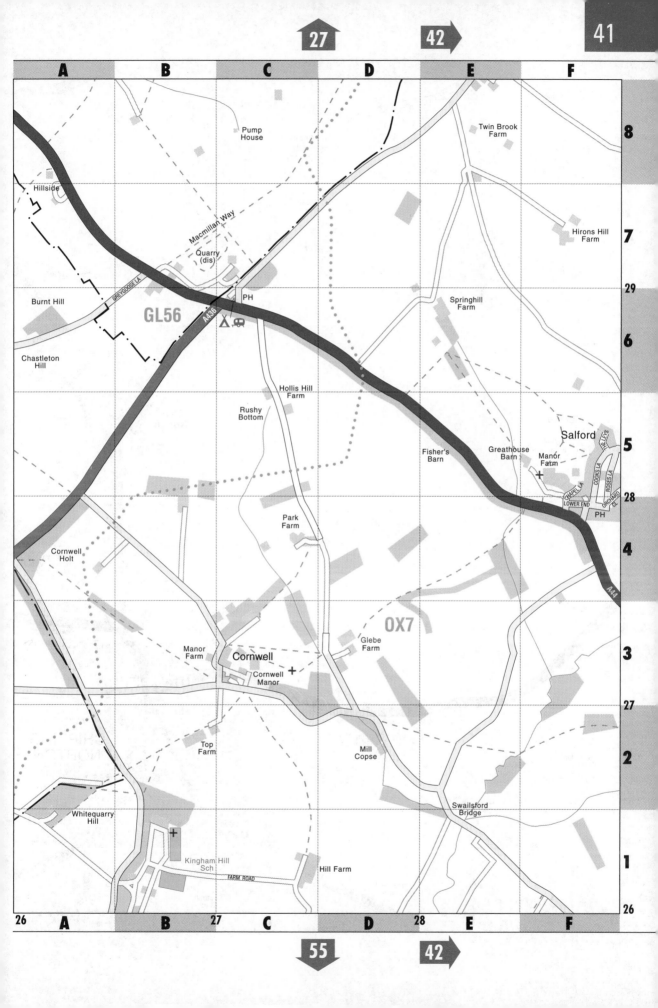

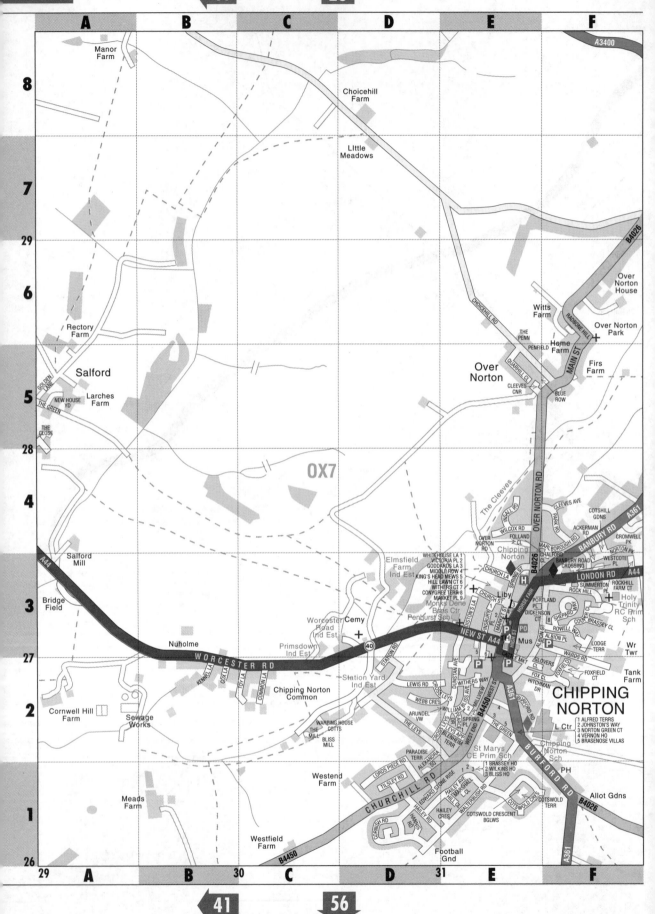

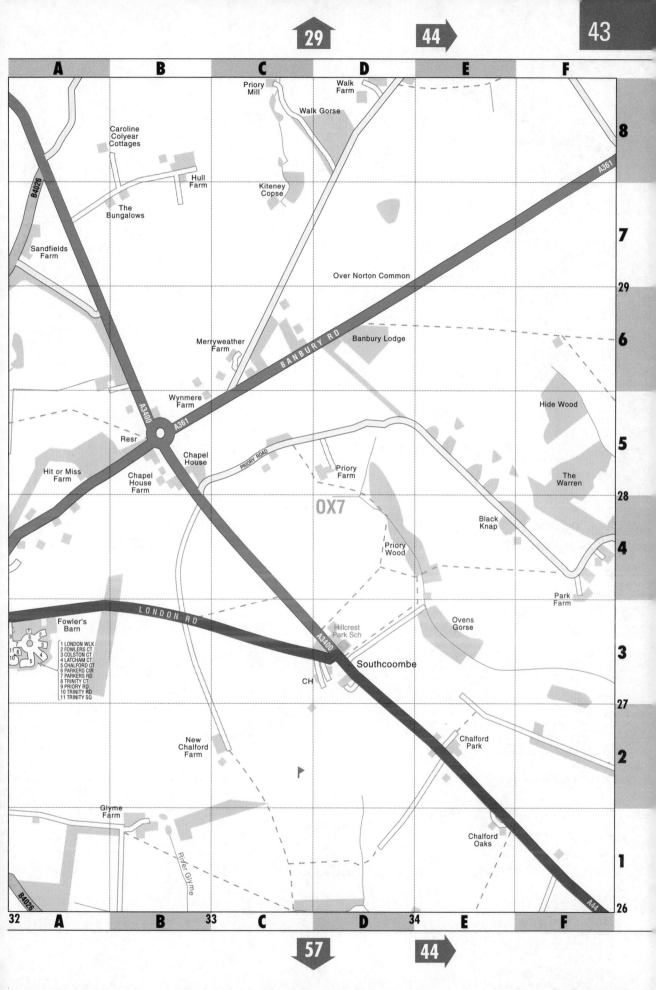

A   B   C   D   E   F

A361

BANBURY RD

Cherwell Barn

The Meetings

8

7

Showell Bungalow

Showell Farm

Showell Copse

29

River Dorn

6

Magpie Farm

Dunthrop

Chivelcorner Plantation

Chivel Farm

GREEN LA

5

OX7

28

Little Tew Grounds Farm

Heythrop

4

Wheatfield Copse

Deerpen Wood

Iron's Copse

3

Foxberry Wood

West Wood

27

Harris's Bottom

Heythrop Park

Fattingfield Copse

2

CH

Heythrop Park

Broadstone Hill

Kite Grove

1

The Wilderness

26

35   A   B   36   C   D   37   E   F

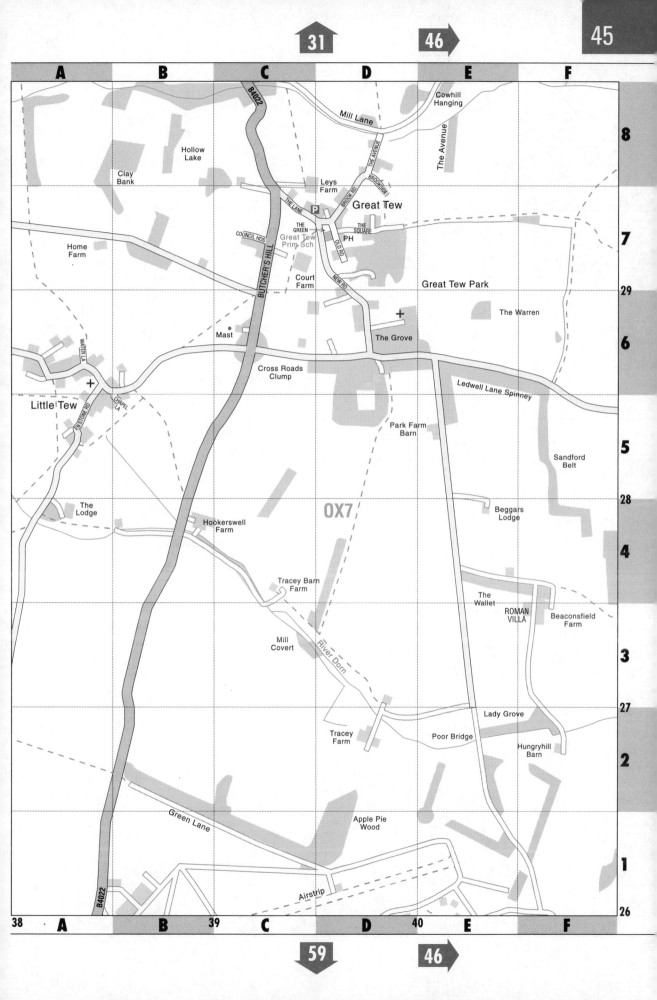

A B C D E F

B4022

Cowhill Hanging

Mill Lane

The Avenue

Hollow Lake

Clay Bank

THE AVENUE

BROOK RD

BROOKSIDE

Leys Farm

Great Tew

THE LANE

P

THE GREEN

COUNCIL HOS

Great Tew Prim Sch

THE SQUARE

PH

Home Farm

BUTCHER'S HILL

OLD RD

NEW RD

Great Tew Park

Court Farm

The Warren

Mast

WATER LA

CHAPEL LA

Little Tew

ENSTONE RD

The Grove

Cross Roads Clump

Ledwell Lane Spinney

Park Farm Barn

Sandford Belt

The Lodge

OX7

Beggars Lodge

Hookerswell Farm

Tracey Barn Farm

The Wallet

ROMAN VILLA

Beaconsfield Farm

Mill Covert

River Dorn

Lady Grove

Tracey Farm

Poor Bridge

Hungryhill Barn

Green Lane

Apple Pie Wood

B4022

Airstrip

45
32

A B C D E F

8

New House Farm

7

Flighthill Farm

Over Worton

Flighthill Cottage

Worton House

Rest Hill Farm

Hobbshole Farm

FLIGHT HILL

Grange Farm

29

Rest Hill Home

6

Lark Rise

The Bungalow

Brae

Hangman's Hill

Cockley Brook

Heath Farm

Ledwell

5

Close Farm

28

OX7

Worton Wood

WORTON ROAD

4

Conygree Wood

LEDWELL ROAD

Parkend Cottages

Heath Cottage Farm

3

Cricket Ground

High Ley

27

POUND BANK

Park Farm

Down Hill Farm

2

Sandford Park

LEDWELL RD

Sandford St Martin

Brandon Farm

River Dorn

Mill

MILL LA

Manor House

MANOR RD

Manor Farm

SANDFORD ST MARTIN RD

Manor House

ORCHARD WAY

HILLSIDE RD

WORTON RD

HOLLIERS CRES

1

THE TWIST

BALLARD CL PD

26

41 A 42 B C 42 D 43 E F

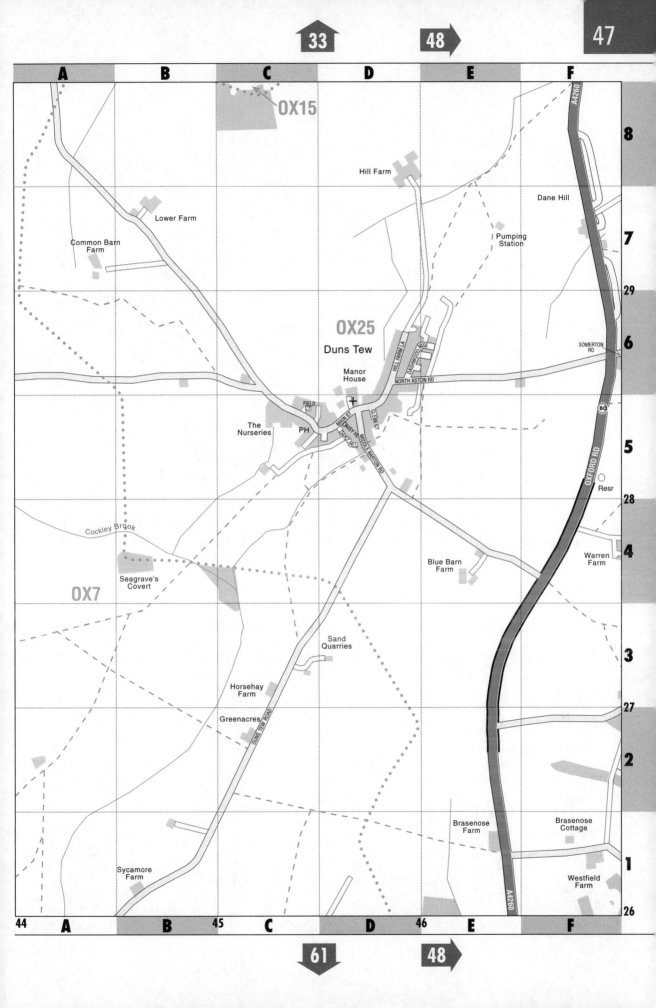

A **B** **C** **D** **E** **F**

OX15

8

Hill Farm

Dane Hill

Lower Farm

7

Common Barn
Farm

Pumping
Station

29

OX25

Duns Tew

6

SOMERTON
RD

Manor
House

NORTH ASTON RD

60

FIELD
CT

The
Nurseries

PH

MAIN ST

DAISY H

GLEBE CT

MIDDLE BARTON RD

OXFORD RD

Resr

5

28

Cockley Brook

4

Blue Barn
Farm

Warren
Farm

OX7

Seagrave's
Covert

Sand
Quarries

3

Horsehay
Farm

27

Greenacres

DUNS TEW ROAD

2

Brasenose
Farm

Brasenose
Cottage

Sycamore
Farm

1

Westfield
Farm

26

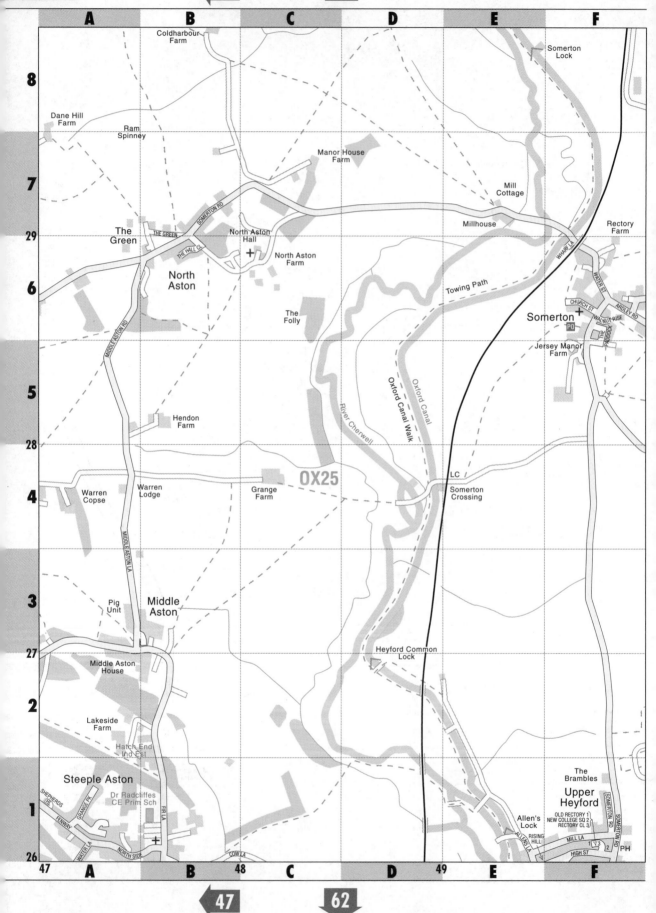

A B C D E F

8

Coldharbour
Farm

Somerton
Lock

Dane Hill
Farm

Ram
Spinney

Manor House
Farm

7

Mill
Cottage

SOMERTON RD

29

The
Green

THE GREEN

North Aston
Hall

Millhouse

Rectory
Farm

THE HALL CL

North Aston
Farm

WHARF LA

6

North
Aston

Towing Path

Somerton

CHURCH ST

WATER ST

ARDLEY RD

PO

The Folly

WALNUT RISE

NEW COL

Jersey Manor
Farm

5

MIDDLE ASTON RD

River Cherwell

Oxford Canal Walk

Oxford Canal

Hendon
Farm

28

OX25

LC

Warren
Copse

Warren
Lodge

Grange
Farm

Somerton
Crossing

4

MIDDLE ASTON LA

3

Pig
Unit

Middle
Aston

27

Heyford Common
Lock

Middle Aston
House

2

Lakeside
Farm

The
Brambles

Hatch End
Ind Est

Upper
Heyford

Steeple Aston

OLD RECTORY 1

1

SHEPHERDS

GRANGE PK

Dr Radcliffes
CE Prim Sch

FIR LA

Allen's
Lock

NEW COLLEGE SQ 2
RECTORY CL 3

FENWAY

RISING
HILL

SOMERTON RD

26

WATER LA

NORTH SIDE

COW LA

ALLEN'S LA

MILL LA

HIGH ST

PH

47 A B 48 C D 49 E F

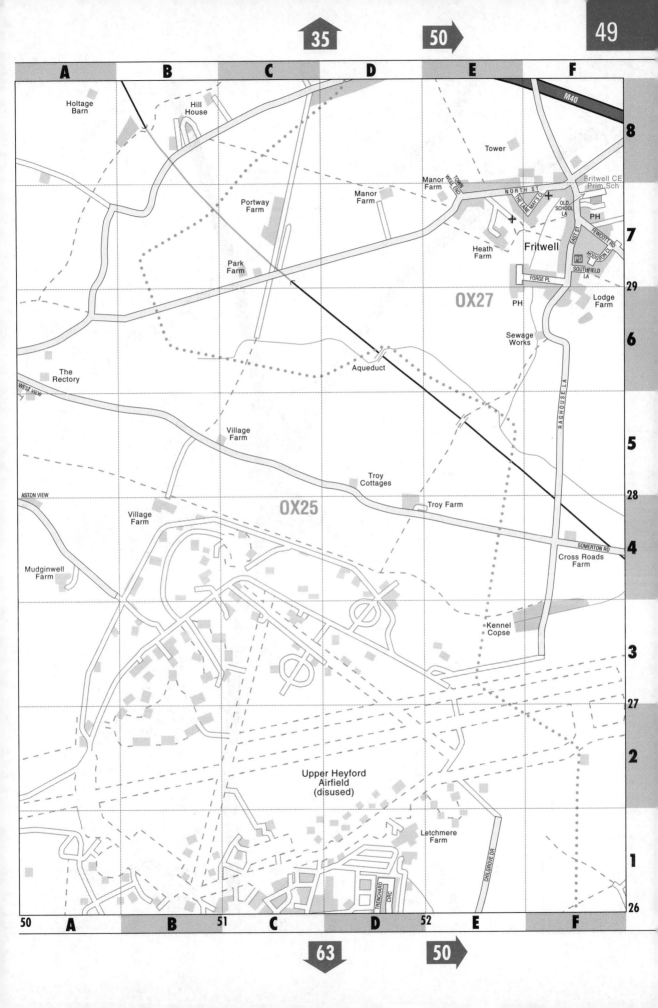

A   B   C   D   E   F

8

Holtage
Barn

Hill
House

Tower

M40

Manor
Farm

Fritwell CE
Prim Sch

NORTH ST

TOWN WELL END

THE FAIRE MAY'S CL

OLD SCHOOL LA

PH

Manor
Farm

Portway
Farm

EAST ST

FEWCOTT RD

7

Heath
Farm

Fritwell

Park
Farm

PO

HODGSON CL

SOUTHFIELD
LA

29

FORGE PL

OX27

PH

Lodge
Farm

6

Sewage
Works

The
Rectory

WEST VIEW

Aqueduct

RAGHOUSE LA

Village
Farm

5

Troy
Cottages

ASTON VIEW

28

OX25

Troy Farm

Village
Farm

Mudginwell
Farm

SOMERTON RD

Cross Roads
Farm

4

Kennel
Copse

3

27

2

Upper Heyford
Airfield
(disused)

Letchmere
Farm

CHILGROVE DR

TRENCHARD CIRC

1

26

49 36

A B C D E F

8
M40
B4100
Horwell
Green Farm
Baynards Green Farm
A43
Park Farm Belt

Baynard's Green

7
Baynard House

29

6
Lone Barn

5
OX27
Sycamore Grove
Cherwell Valley Services
A43
10

Fewcott
Manor Farm
Fewcott Farm
Sewage Works
P
B4100
Nature Trail
Stoke Wood

28
FRITWELL RD
PH
PLOUGHLEY CL
WATER LA
B430
Woodbine Cottage

4
PADDOCK RD
ORCHARD RD
KEY'S CL
RUSSET RD
ARDLEY RD
SOMERTON RD
CASTLE FIELDS
THE CROSSWAYS
FEWCOTT GREEN
Ardley

Ardley Wood
Manor Farm
PH
ST MARY'S WLK
STATION RD
CHURCH RD

Kilby's Barn

3

27
Kilby's Copse

2
Nevilles Farm
ARDLEY RD

1
Ashgrove Farm
Digging Copse
Woodlands Farm

26
B430
Ardley Fields Farm
M40

53 A B 54 C D 55 E F

49 64

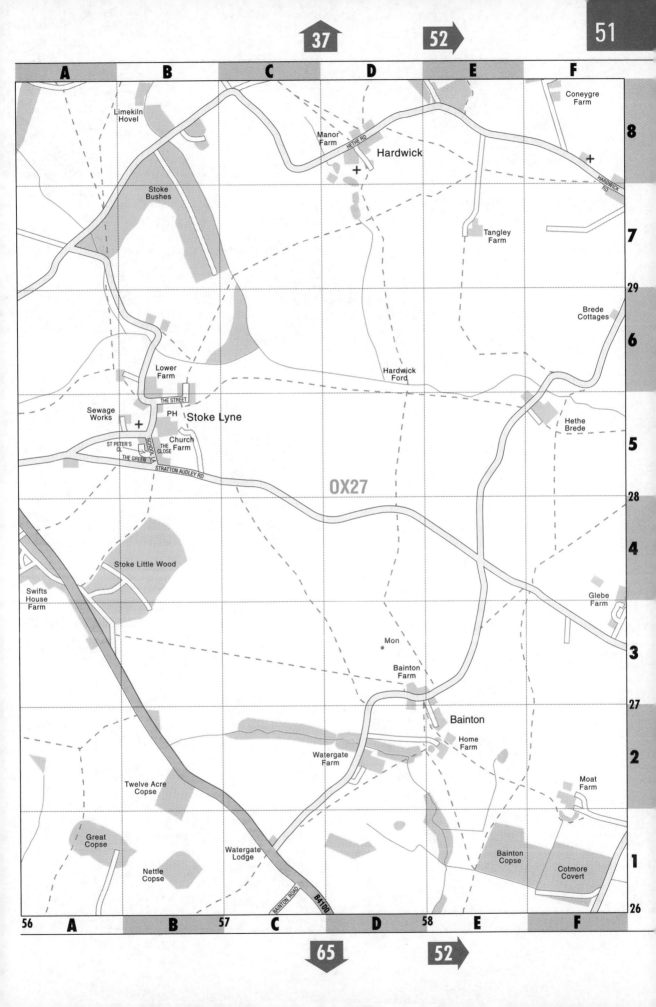

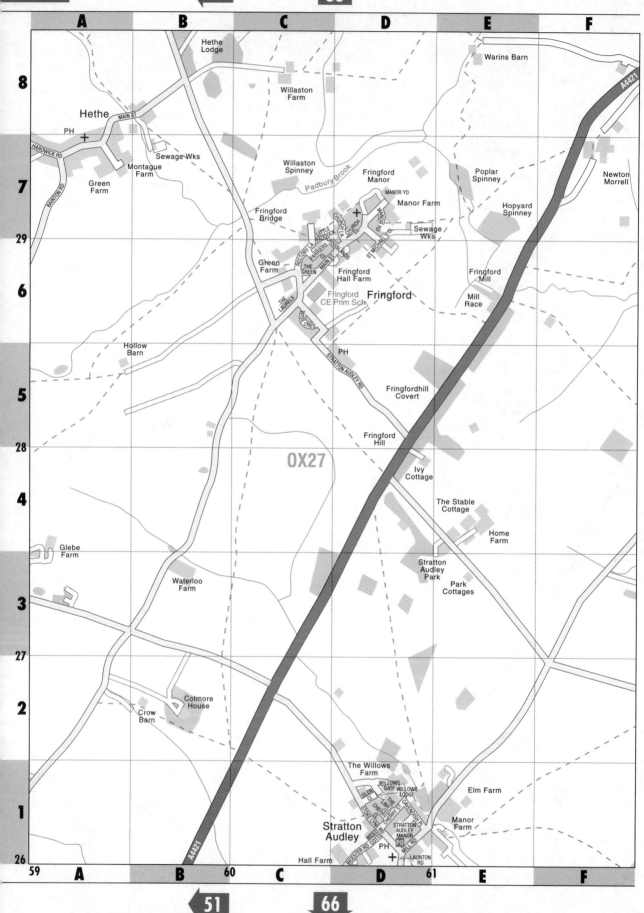

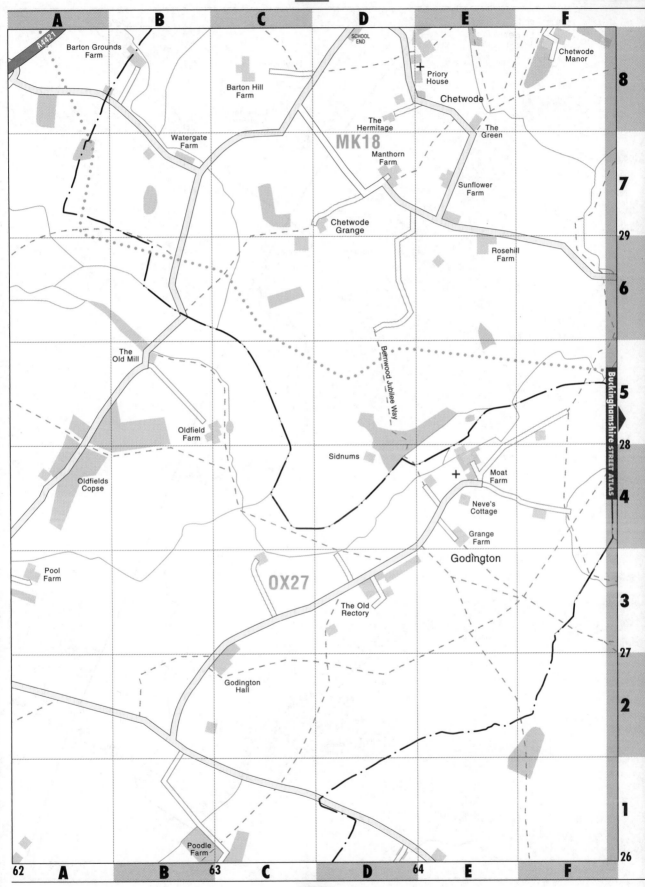

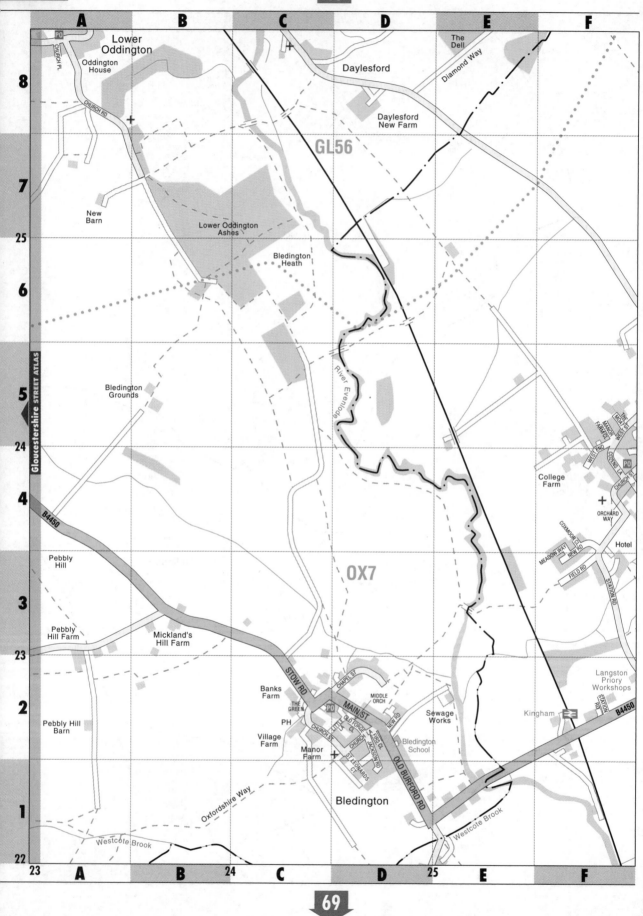

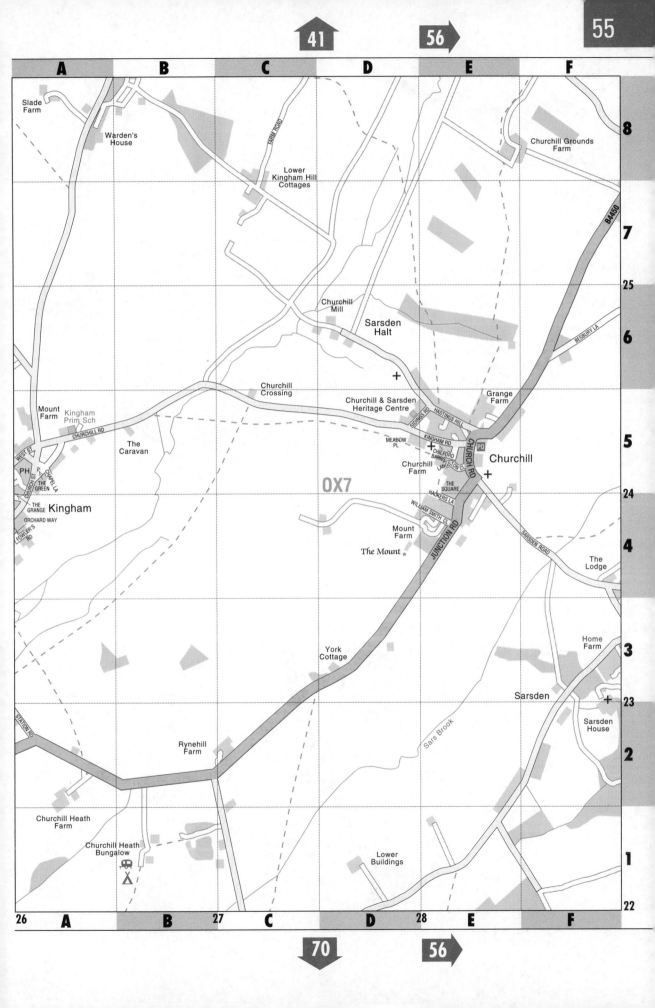

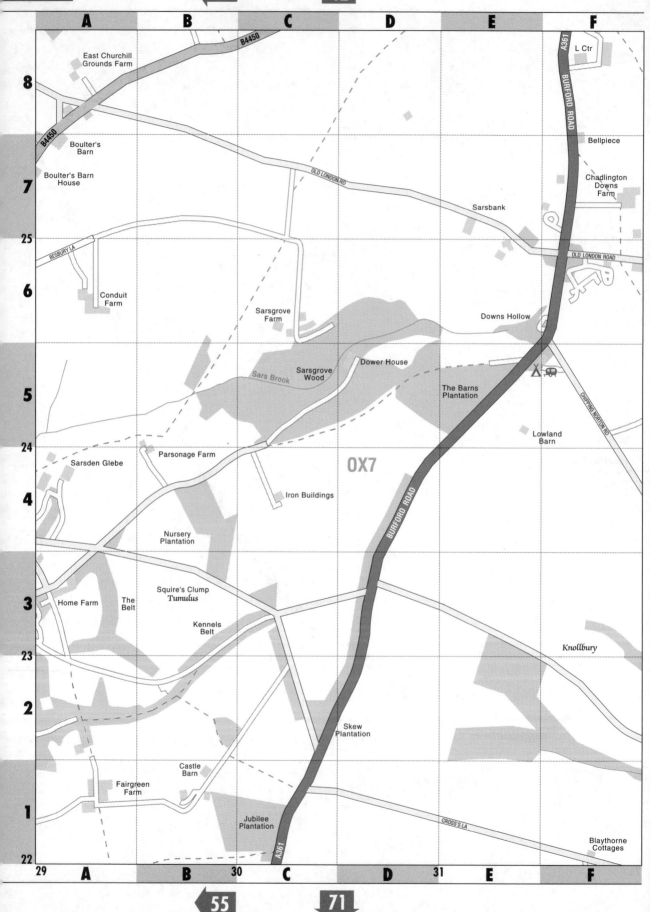

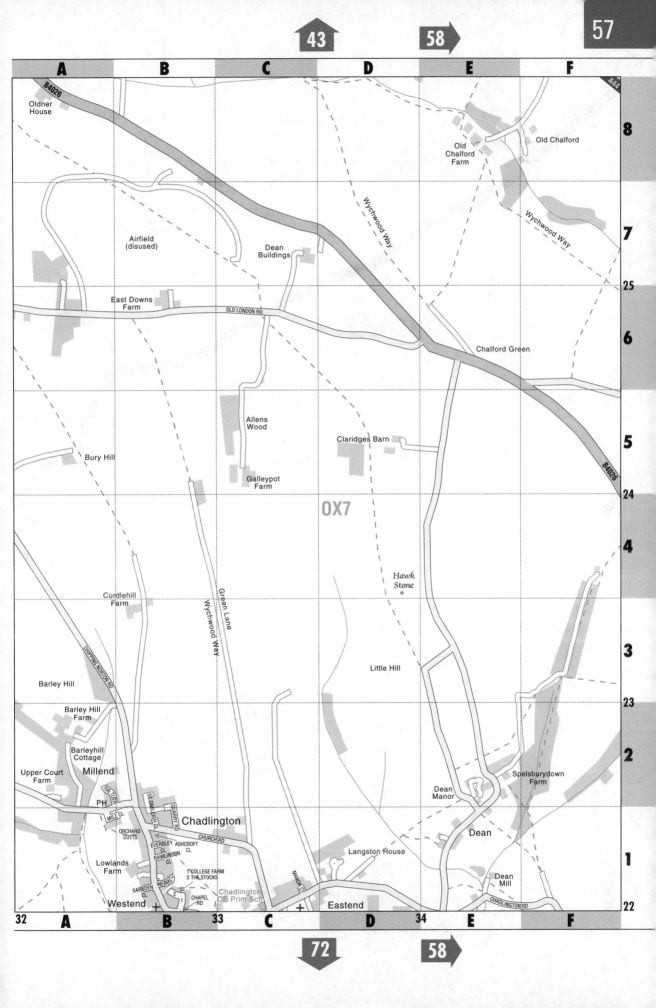

A B C D E F

8
7
25
6
5
24
4
3
23
2
1
22

B4026
A44
Oldner House
Old Chalford Farm
Old Chalford
Wychwood Way
Wychwood Way
Airfield (disused)
Dean Buildings
East Downs Farm
OLD LONDON RD
Chalford Green
Allens Wood
Claridges Barn
Bury Hill
Galleypot Farm
OX7
B4026
Hawk Stone
Curdlehill Farm
Wychwood Way
Green Lane
Little Hill
Barley Hill
CHIPPING NORTON RD
Barley Hill Farm
Barleyhill Cottage
Millend
Upper Court Farm
THE TUER
PH
MILL CL
ST ONEBRIDGE CL
QUARRY RD
Chadlington
ORCHARD COTTS
EVERSLEY CL
ASHCROFT CL
CHURCH RD
RAWLINSON CL
WEBBS
Lowlands Farm
SARSDEN CL
CHAPEL RD
Chadlington CE Prim Sch
1 COLLEGE FARM
2 THE STOCKS
MANOR CT
Langston House
Spelsburydown Farm
Dean Manor
Dean
Dean Mill
Westend
Eastend
CHADLINGTON RD

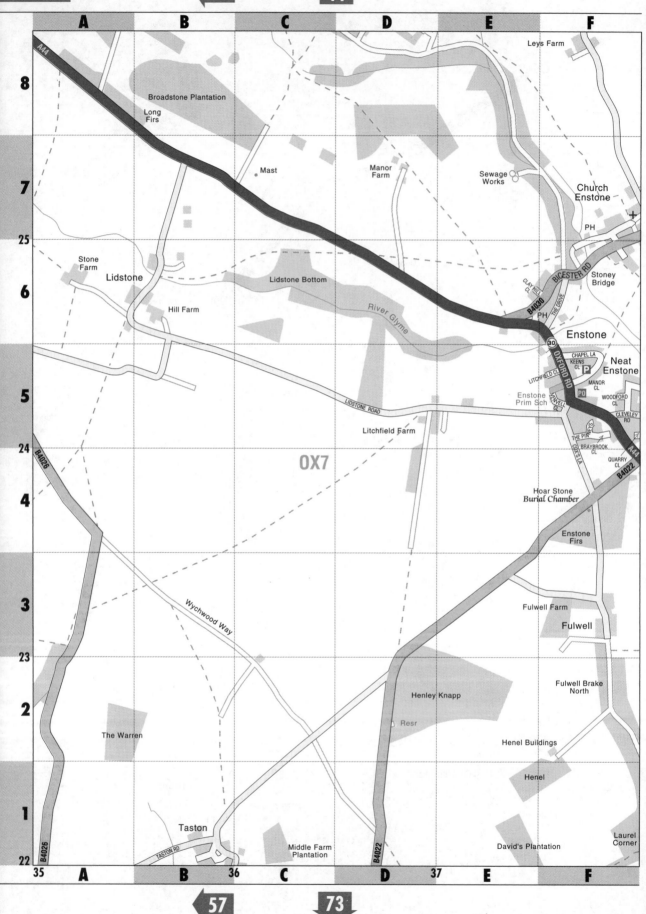

A   B   C   D   E   F

8

Long Firs

Broadstone Plantation

7

Mast

Manor Farm

Sewage Works

Leys Farm

Church Enstone

PH

25

Stone Farm

Lidstone

Hill Farm

Lidstone Bottom

River Glyme

CLAY HILL CL

B4030

PH

THE DRIVE

BICESTER RD

Stoney Bridge

6

Enstone

30

CHAPEL LA

KEENS CL

P

OXFORD RD

Neat Enstone

MANOR CL

PO

WOODFORD CL

5

Lidstone Road

LITCHFIELD CL

Enstone Prim Sch

FENWELL CL

CLEVELEY RD

Litchfield Farm

THE PINE

COX'S LA

BRAYBROOK CL

24

B4026

OX7

QUARRY CL

B4022

A44

4

Hoar Stone
Burial Chamber

Enstone Firs

3

Wychwood Way

Fulwell Farm

Fulwell

23

Fulwell Brake North

2

The Warren

Henley Knapp

Resr

Henel Buildings

Henel

1

Taston

B4022

David's Plantation

Laurel Corner

22

TASTON RD

Middle Farm Plantation

B4026

35   A   B   36   C   D   37   E   F

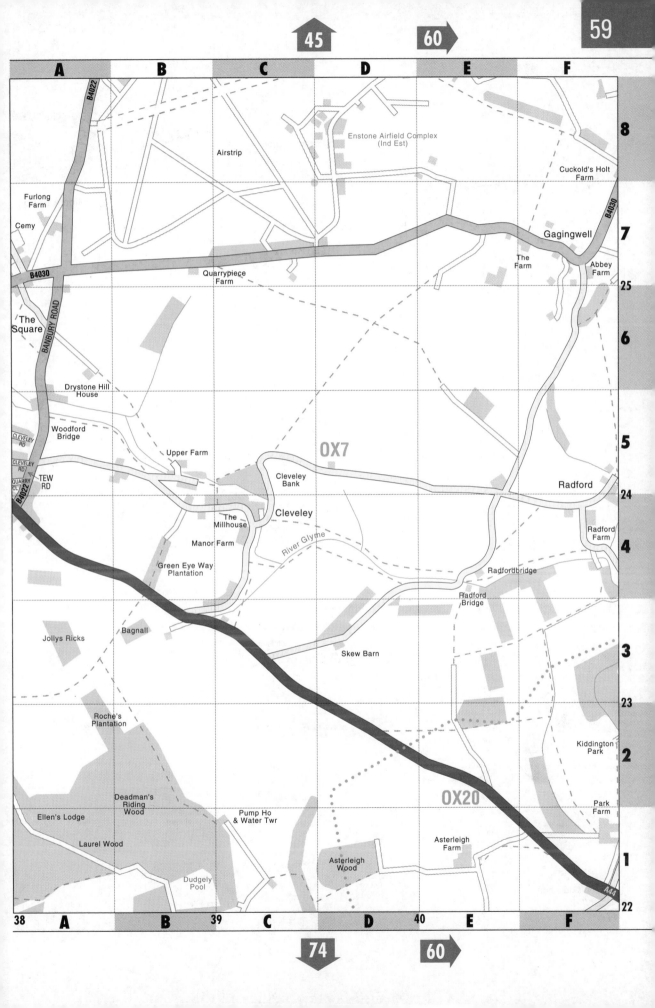

A B C D E F

8

Enstone Airfield Complex
(Ind Est)

Airstrip

Cuckold's Holt
Farm

Furlong
Farm

Cemy

7

Gagingwell

The
Farm

B4030

Abbey
Farm

Quarrypiece
Farm

25

The
Square

6

BANBURY ROAD

Drystone Hill
House

5

Woodford
Bridge

OX7

Upper Farm

Cleveley
Bank

Radford

CLEVELEY RD

CLEVELEY RD

TEW
RD

24

QUARRY CL

B4022

The
Millhouse

Cleveley

Radford
Farm

Manor Farm

River Glyme

4

Green Eye Way
Plantation

Radfordbridge

Radford
Bridge

Jollys Ricks

Bagnall

Skew Barn

3

Roche's
Plantation

23

Kiddington
Park

2

Deadman's
Riding Wood

Pump Ho
& Water Twr

OX20

Park
Farm

Ellen's Lodge

Asterleigh
Farm

Laurel Wood

Asterleigh
Wood

1

Dudgely
Pool

A44

22

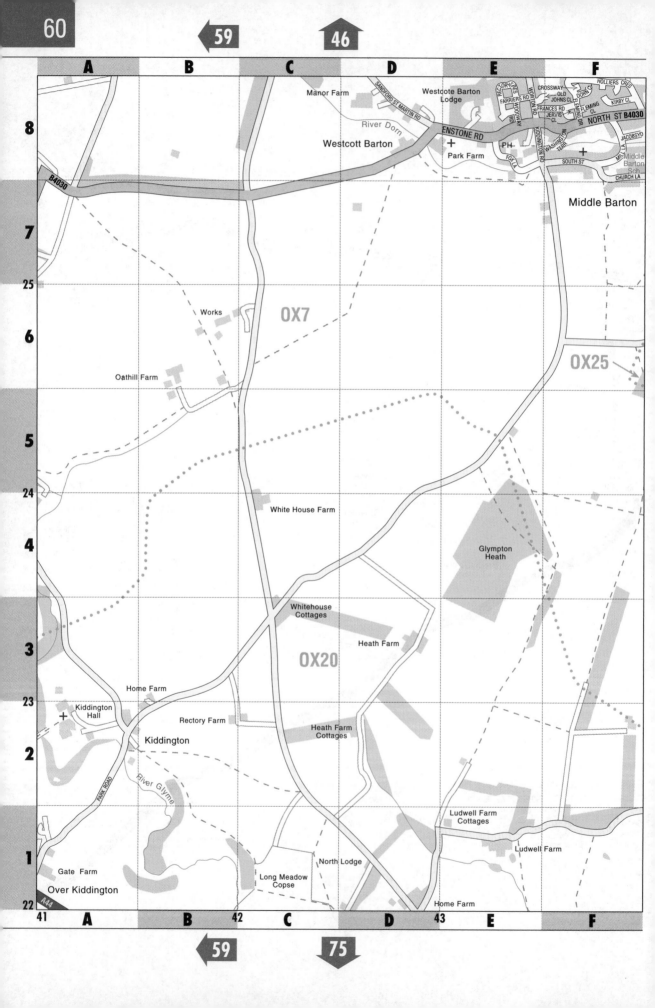

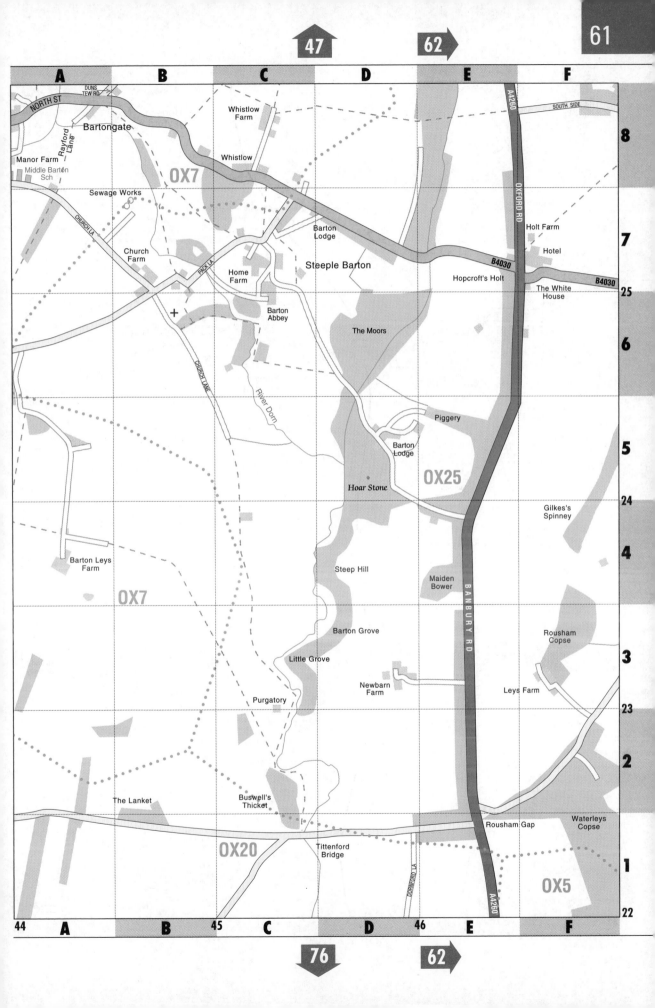

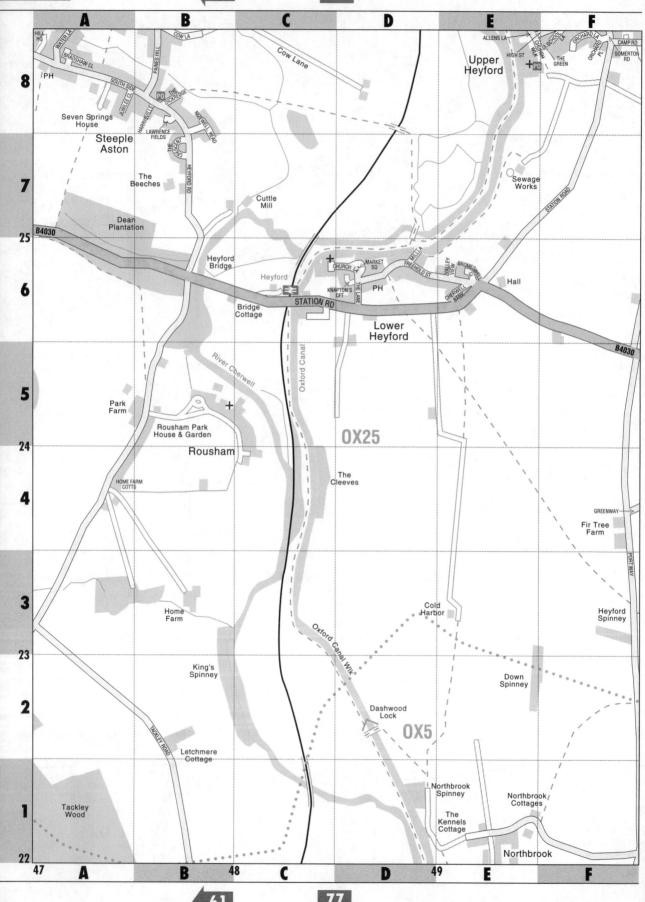

A **B** **C** **D** **E** **F**

HILL HO

WATER LA

BRADSHAW CL

PH

SOUTH SIDE

JUBILEE CT

HARRIS VILLE

PAINES HILL

COW LA

Cow Lane

PO

THE DICKREDGE

ALLENS LA

HIGH ST

SCHOOL LA

ORCHARD LA

CAMP RD

CHURCH WLK

ORCHARD PL

SOMERTON RD

Upper Heyford

THE GREEN

PO

8

Seven Springs House

Steeple Aston

LAWRENCE FIELDS

THE CRESCENT

HEYFORD RD

NIZEWELL ROAD

7

The Beeches

Cuttle Mill

Sewage Works

STATION ROAD

Dean Plantation

25 B4030

Heyford Bridge

Heyford

CHURCH

MARKET SQ

MILL LA

FREEHOLD ST

VALLEY VIEW

BROMES MRE

Hall

6

Bridge Cottage

STATION RD

KNAPTON'S CFT

THE LANE

PH

CHERWELL BANK

Lower Heyford

B4030

River Cherwell

Oxford Canal

5

Park Farm

Rousham Park House & Garden

Rousham

OX25

24

HOME FARM COTTS

The Cleeves

GREENWAY

4

Fir Tree Farm

PORT WAY

Home Farm

3

Cold Harbor

Heyford Spinney

Oxford Canal Wlk

23

King's Spinney

Down Spinney

2

Dashwood Lock

OX5

TACKLEY ROAD

Letchmere Cottage

Northbrook Spinney

Northbrook Cottages

1

Tackley Wood

The Kennels Cottage

22

Northbrook

47 **A** **B** **48** **C** **D** **49** **E** **F**

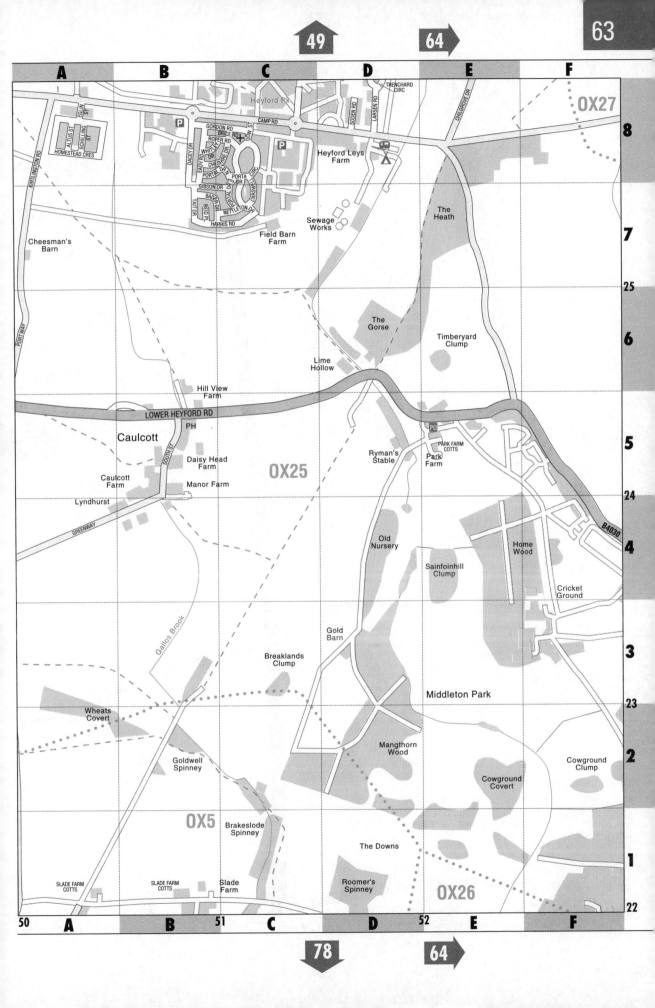

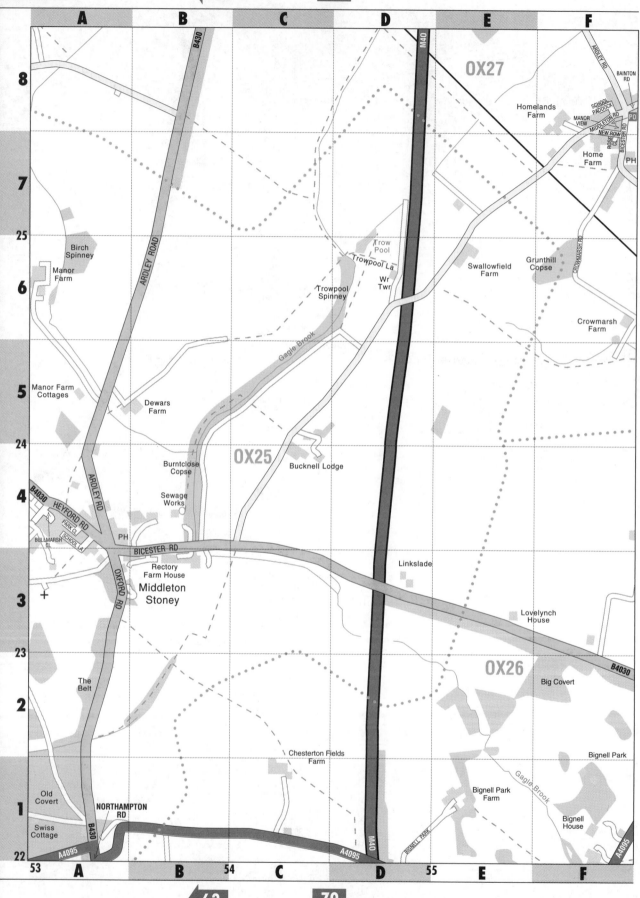

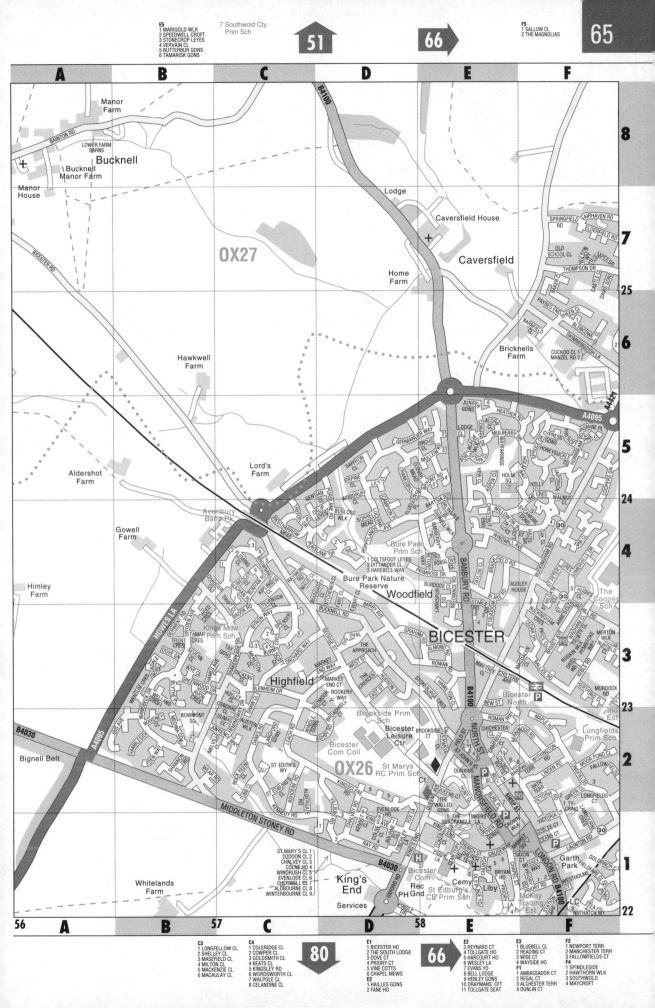

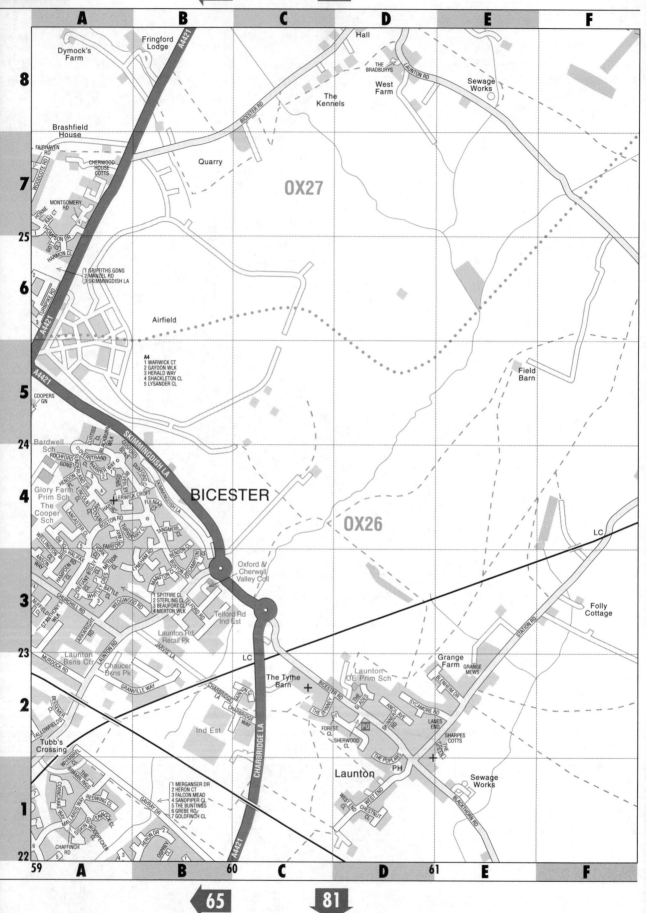

A B C D E F

8

Dymock's Farm

Fringford Lodge

Hall

The Bradburys

West Farm

Sewage Works

Brashfield House

The Kennels

FAIRHAVEN RD

CHERWOOD HOUSE COTTS

Quarry

OX27

7

HORNE RAU CT

MONTGOMERY RD

THOMPSON DR

HARMON CL

25

1 GRIFFITHS GDNS
2 MANZEL RD
3 SKIMMINGDISH LA

6

TURNPIKE RD

Airfield

A4
1 WARWICK CT
2 GAYDON WLK
3 HERALD WAY
4 SHACKLETON CL
5 LYSANDER CL

Field Barn

5

A4421

COOPERS GN

24

Bardwell Sch

ROCHFORD GDNS

CURTIS CL

BLACKBURN WLK

SUNDERLAND

OVERSTRAND

OXFORD GDNS

PUXFORD

BEVERLEY

SKIMMINGDISH LA

4

Glory Farm Prim Sch

The Cooper Sch

HENDON CL

LINCOLN

HART RV

LERWICK CROFT

FULMAR CT

BICESTER

OX26

LC

LANCASTER

BOSTON RD

AVM

TURBERRY CL

TANGMERE CL

WELLINGTON

HALIFAX

YORK

FAIRFORD

METEOR

BENSON RD

ESCAMPTON

3

NUFFIELD

HAMPDEN CL

CHURCHILL RD

BATTLE

WEDGWOOD RD

MANSTON

BOSTON CL

1 SPITFIRE CL
2 STERLING CL
3 BEAUFORT CL
4 MERTON WLK

RUFFORD RD

Oxford & Cherwell Valley Coll

Telford Rd Ind Est

Folly Cottage

ANSON WAY

ST ANN

ARKWRIGHT

DEANE BISLEY

WHITLEY

Launton Rd Retail Pk

JARVIS LA

Launton Rd

STATION RD

23

MURDOCK RD

Launton Bsns Ctr

Chaucer Bsns Pk

GRANVILLE WAY

LAUNTON RD

LC

The Tythe Barn

Grange Farm

GRANGE MEWS

Launton CE Prim Sch

BLENHEIM DR

2

BESSEMER CL

FALLOWFIELDS

CHARBRIDGE LA

CHARBRIDGE WAY

BARN CL

Ind Est

THE SPINNEY

BICESTER RD

THE GLADES

ANCIL AVE

SYCAMORE RD

SKIMMER RD

LANES END

SHARPES COTTS

Tubb's Crossing

FOREST CL

SHERWOOD CL

PO

THE POPLARS

PH

1

WHIMBREL CL

THE BRAMBLINGS

REDWING CL

CORNCRAKE WAY

MALLARDS WAY

DUNNOCK CL

SISKIN

WOODPECKER CL

GAVRAY DR

HERON DR

OSPREY CL

1 MERGANSER DR
2 HERON CT
3 FALCON MEAD
4 SANDPIPER CL
5 THE BUNTINGS
6 GREBE RD
7 GOLDFINCH CL

Launton

WEST END CL

WEST END

CHESTNUT CL

THE GREEN

BLACKTHORN RD

Sewage Works

22

CHAFFINCH RD

A4421

59 A B 60 C D 61 E F

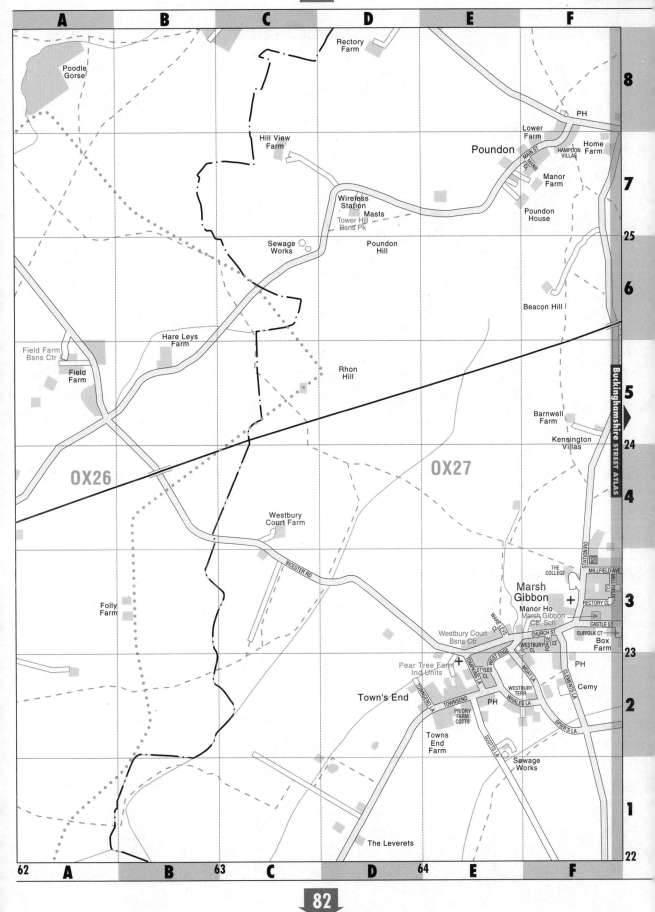

A **B** **C** **D** **E** **F**

8

Poodle
Gorse

Rectory
Farm

PH

Lower
Farm

Poundon

HAMPDON
VILLAS

Home
Farm

7

Manor
Farm

Hill View
Farm

Wireless
Station

Masts

Poundon
House

25

Tower Hill
Bsns Pk

Poundon
Hill

Sewage
Works

Beacon Hill

6

Hare Leys
Farm

Field Farm
Bsns Ctr

Rhon
Hill

Barnwell
Farm

5

Field
Farm

Kensington
Villas

24

OX26

OX27

4

Westbury
Court Farm

STATION RD

MILLFIELD AVE

THE
COLLEGE

Millfield
CL

PO

Folly
Farm

BICESTER RD

**Marsh
Gibbon**

3

Manor Ho

Marsh Gibbon
CE Sch

RECTORY CL

CASTLE ST

WARE LEYS CL

CHURCH ST

SUFFOLK CT

Box
Farm

Westbury Court
Bsns Ctr

WEST EDGE

WESTBURY
CL

FORGE CL

23

Pear Tree Farm
Ind Units

TIMPKINS LA

STYLES
CL

MOAT LA

CLEMENTS LA

PH

Cemy

WESTBURY
TERR

WHALES LA

Town's End

TOWNSEND LA

TOWNSEND

PH

2

PRIORY
FARM
COTTS

SPIER'S LA

Towns
End
Farm

SCOTTS LA

Sewage
Works

1

The Leverets

22

62   **A**   **B**   63   **C**   **D**   64   **E**   **F**

Buckinghamshire STREET ATLAS

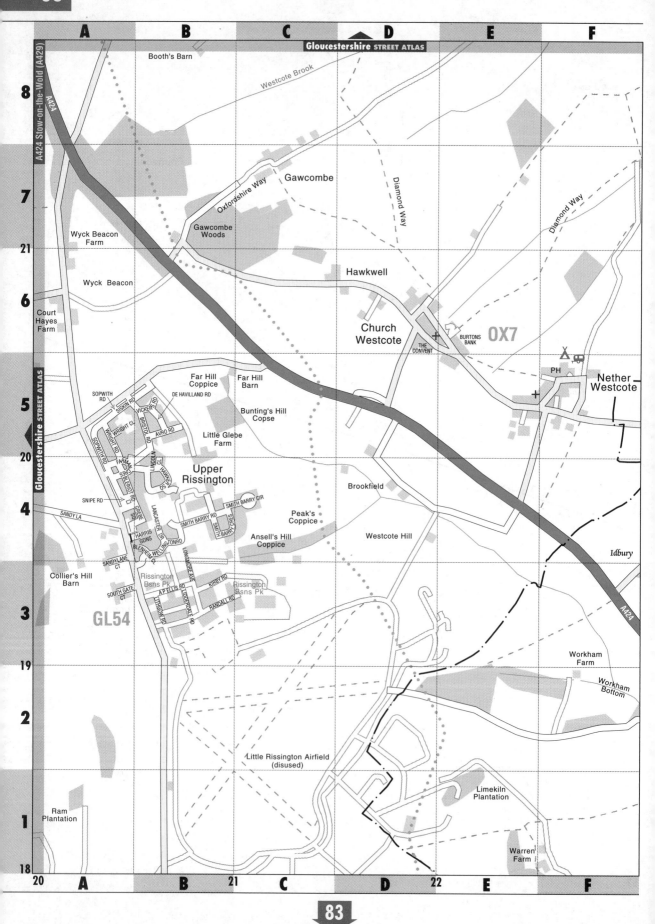

Gloucestershire STREET ATLAS

A B C D E F

Booth's Barn

Westcote Brook

Gawcombe

8

Oxfordshire Way

7

Diamond Way

Diamond Way

Gawcombe
Woods

21

Wyck Beacon
Farm

Hawkwell

6

Wyck Beacon

Church
Westcote

OX7

BURTONS
BANK

Court
Hayes
Farm

THE
CONVENT

PH

Nether
Westcote

Far Hill
Coppice

Far Hill
Barn

SOPWITH
RD

DE HAVILLAND RD

5

SISKIN RD

VICKER RD

BRISTOL RD

AVRO RD

Bunting's Hill
Copse

WRIGHT CL

WRIGHT RD

Little Glebe
Farm

SOPWITH RD

20

FARMAN

HAWKER CL

Upper
Rissington

SNIPE RD

BLERIOT RD

CRES

Brookfield

4

SANDY LA

HARRIS GDNS

LANCASTER DR

SMITH BARRY RD

SMITH BARRY CIR

Peak's
Coppice

GREER

BLENHEIM CL

WELLINGTON RD

LONGMORE AVE

SMITH
BARRY

Westcote Hill

Idbury

SANDYLANE
CT

Ansell's Hill
Coppice

Collier's Hill
Barn

SOUTH GATE
CT

Rissington
Bsns Pk

KIRBY RD

Rissington
Bsns Pk

Workham
Farm

3

GL54

AP ELLIS RD

LIDDEROLE RD

RANDALL RD

LITHGOW RD

Workham
Bottom

19

A424

2

Little Rissington Airfield
(disused)

Limekiln
Plantation

1

Ram
Plantation

Warren
Farm

18

20 A 21 B C 22 D E F

A424 Stow-on-the-Wold (A429)

Gloucestershire street atlas

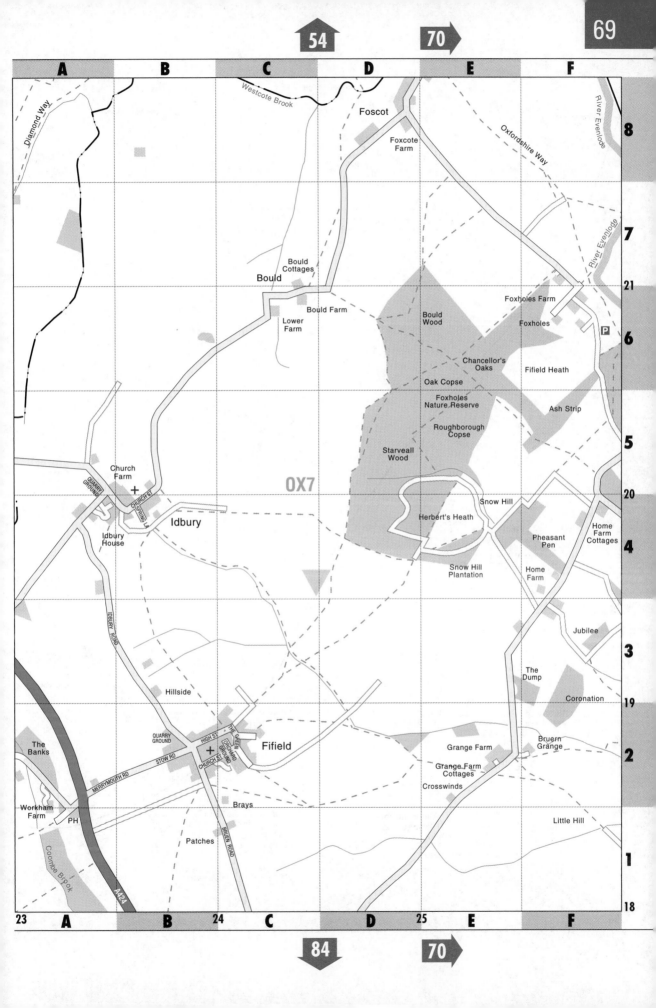

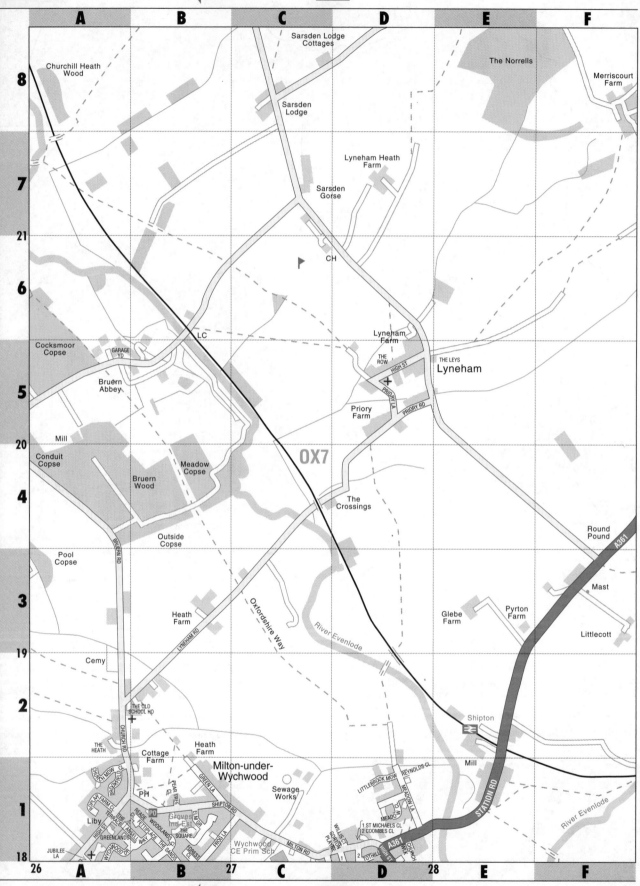

A B C D E F

8 Churchill Heath Wood

Sarsden Lodge Cottages

The Norrells

Merriscourt Farm

Sarsden Lodge

7 Lyneham Heath Farm

Sarsden Gorse

21 CH

6 Lyneham Farm

LC

Cocksmoor Copse

GARAGE YD

THE ROW
HIGH ST

Lyneham

THE LEYS

5 Bruern Abbey

PRIORY LA
PRIORY RD

Priory Farm

Mill

20 OX7

Conduit Copse

Meadow Copse

Bruern Wood

4 The Crossings

Round Pound

A361

Outside Copse

3 Pool Copse

Mast

Littlecott

Heath Farm

LYNEHAM RD

Oxfordshire Way

River Evenlode

Glebe Farm

Pyrton Farm

BRUERN RD

19 Cemy

2 THE OLD SCHOOL HO

Shipton

Mill

CHURCH RD

THE HEATH

Cottage Farm

Heath Farm

Milton-under-Wychwood

STATION RD

LITTLEBROOK MDW
REYNOLDS CL
MEADOW LN

1 CHURCH MDW
COOKSFIELD

PH

PEAR TREE CL

GREEN LA

SHIPTON RD

ELM GR

THE SQUARE

Sewage Works

MILTON RD

Mill

River Evenlode

A361

CHURCH WK

POPLAR FARM CL
HIGH ST
TERRACE
REAGE CL
TANSELL WAY
FROG LA
FOREST CL
THE SANDS

PO

Groves Ind Est

WILLIS CT
SOPWITH PLAINE

1 ST MICHAELS CL
2 COOMBES CL

MEADOW LN

Liby

GREENLANDS

WYCHWOOD DR

JUBILEE LA

Wychwood CE Prim Sch

HIGH ST
TOTHILL

18
26 A B 27 C D 28 E F

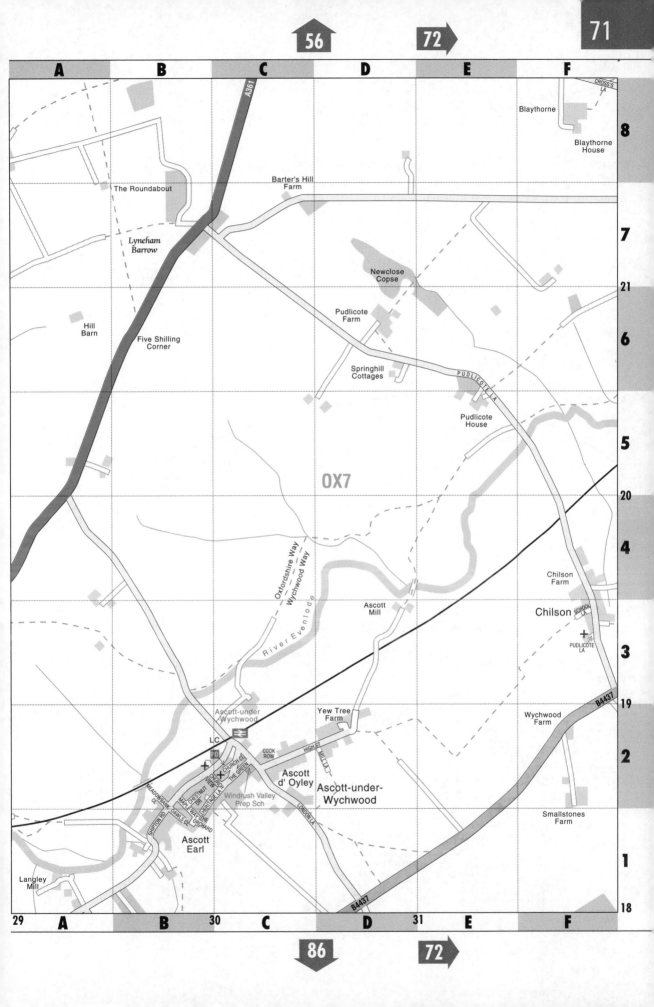

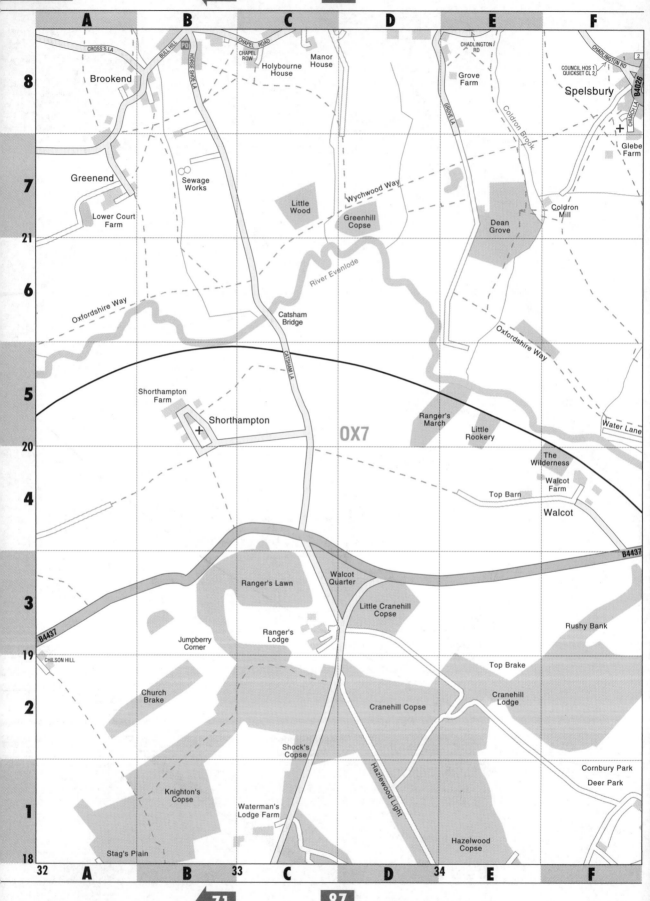

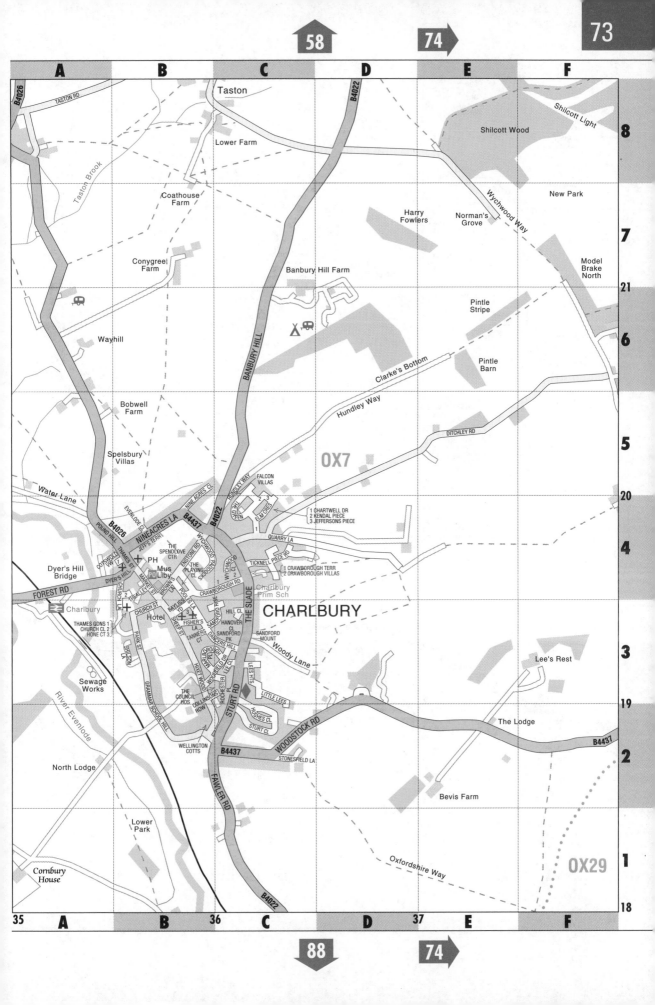

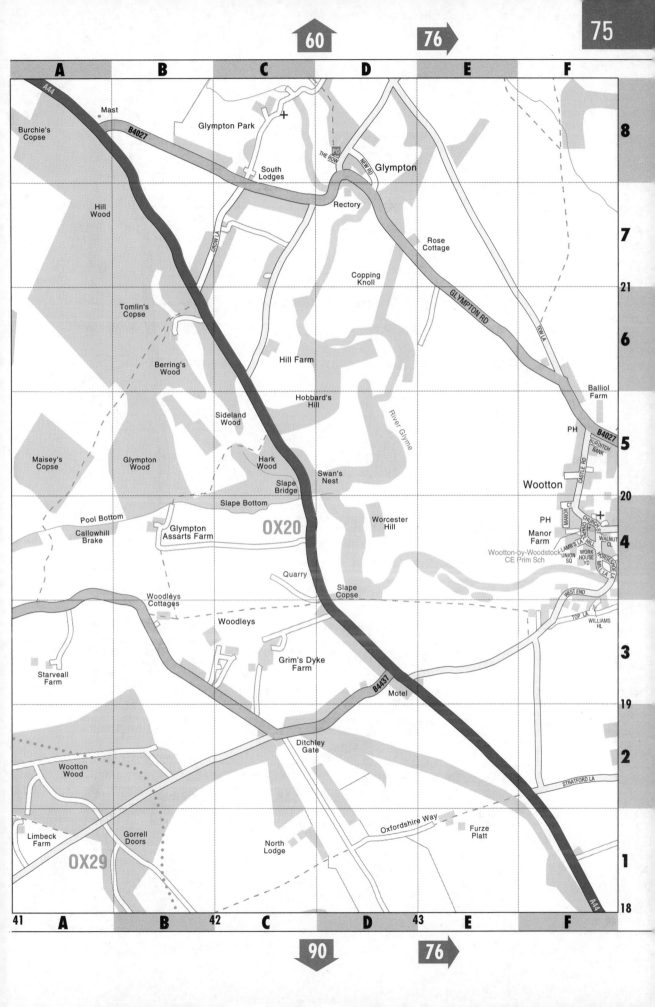

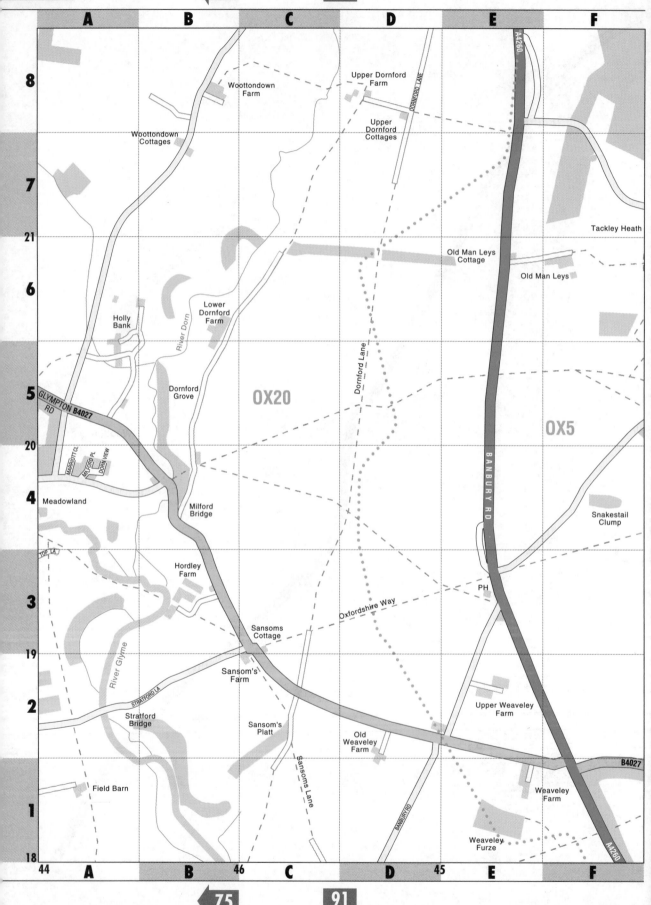

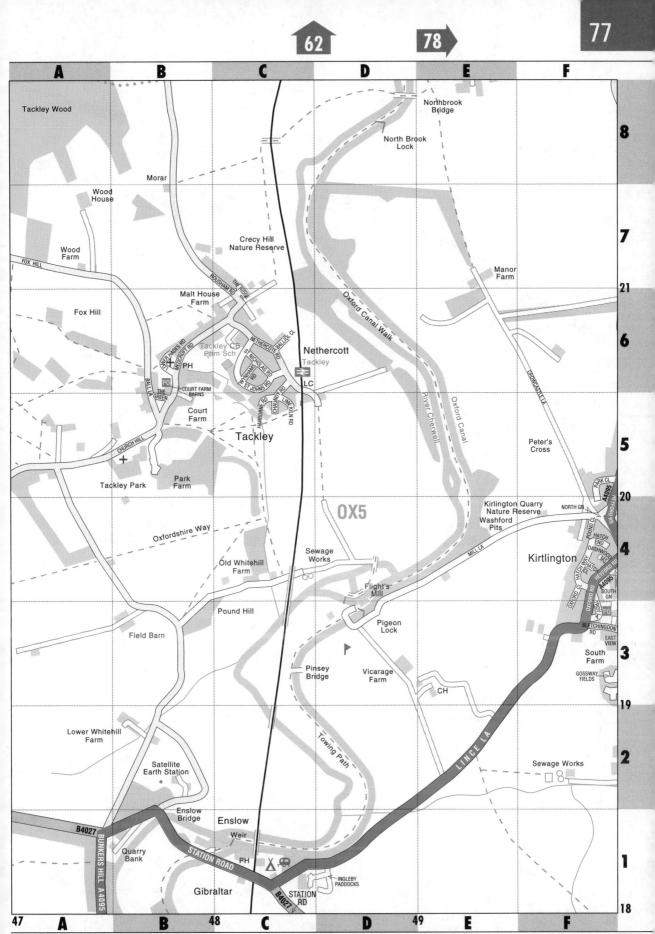

62
78

A B C D E F

8

7

21

6

Tackley Wood

Morar

Wood
House

Wood
Farm

FOX HILL

Fox Hill

Crecy Hill
Nature Reserve

ROUSHAM RD

THE RIDGE

Malt House
Farm

NETHER HAYES RD

MEDCROFT RD

ST NICHOLAS RD

NETHERCOTE RD

BALLIOL CL

Tackley CE
Prim Sch

TWYNHAMS RD

ST JOHNS RD

Nethercott
Tackley

LC

PH

PO

THE GREEN

BALL LA

COURT FARM
BARNS

HARBORNE RD

CHAUND RD

LIME KILN RD

Court
Farm

Tackley

CHURCH HILL

Tackley Park

Park
Farm

Oxfordshire Way

Old Whitehill
Farm

Pound Hill

Field Barn

Lower Whitehill
Farm

Satellite
Earth Station

Oxford Canal Walk

River Cherwell

Oxford Canal

North Brook
Lock

Northbrook
Bridge

Manor
Farm

GRIMSCOTE LA

Peter's
Cross

OX5

Sewage
Works

Flight's
Mill

Pigeon
Lock

Vicarage
Farm

CH

Pinsey
Bridge

Towing Path

MILL LA

Kirlington Quarry
Nature Reserve
Washford
Pits

NORTH GN

PARK CL

HETFORD RD

A4095

Kirtlington

HATCH
END

DASHWOOD
MWS

HATCH WAY

HATCH

OXFORD RD

POUND CL

OXFORD CL

A4095

OXFORD RD

ROY L

PO

SOUTH
GN

BLETCHINGDON
RD

EAST
VIEW

South
Farm

GOSSWAY
FIELDS

LINCE LA

Sewage Works

20

4

3

19

2

B4027

BUNKERS HILL A4095

Quarry
Bank

Enslow
Bridge

Enslow

Weir

PH

STATION ROAD

Gibraltar

B4027

STATION
RD

INGLEBY
PADDOCKS

1

18

92
78

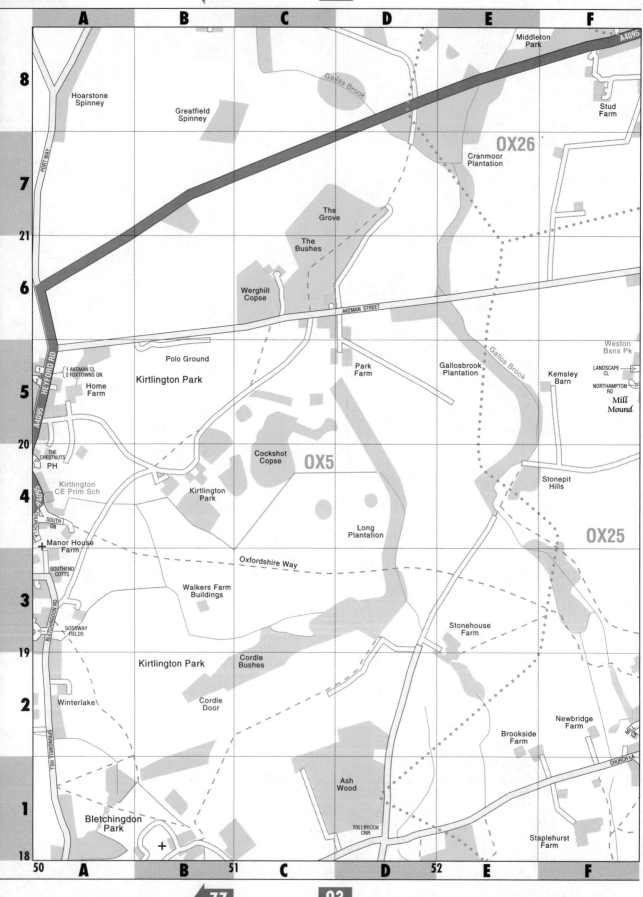

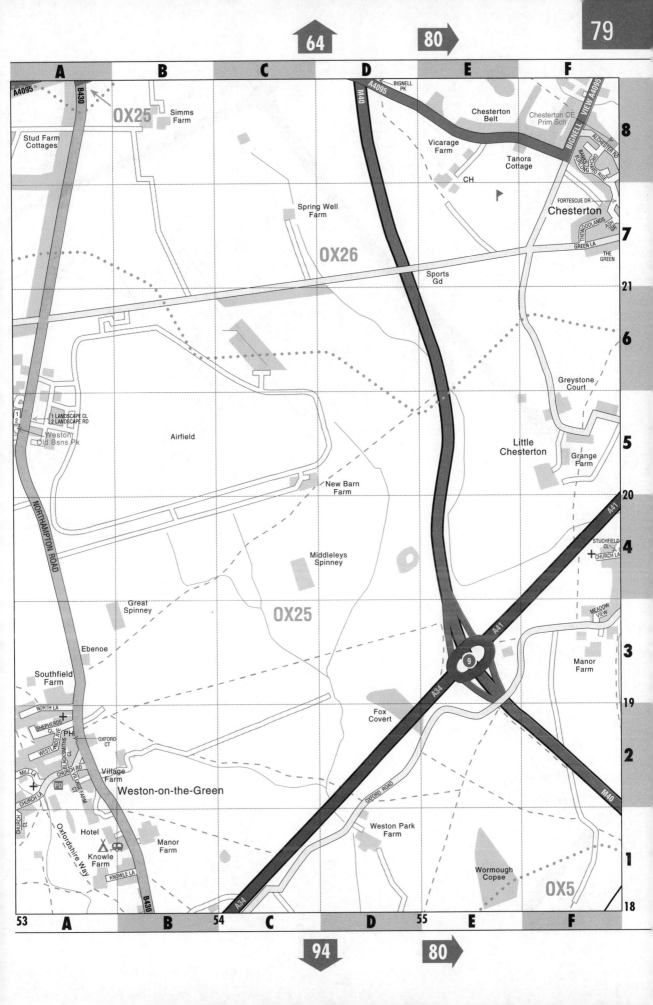

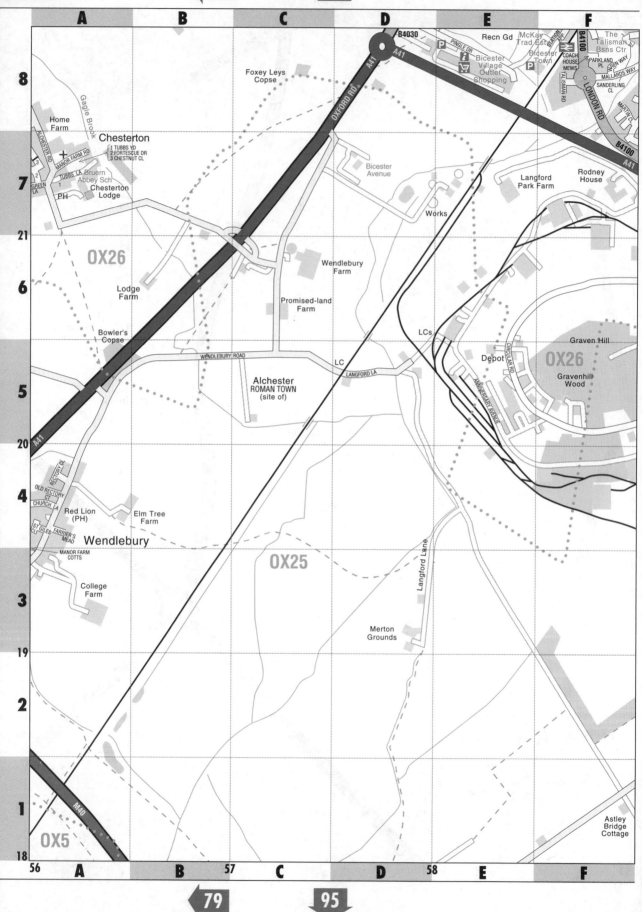

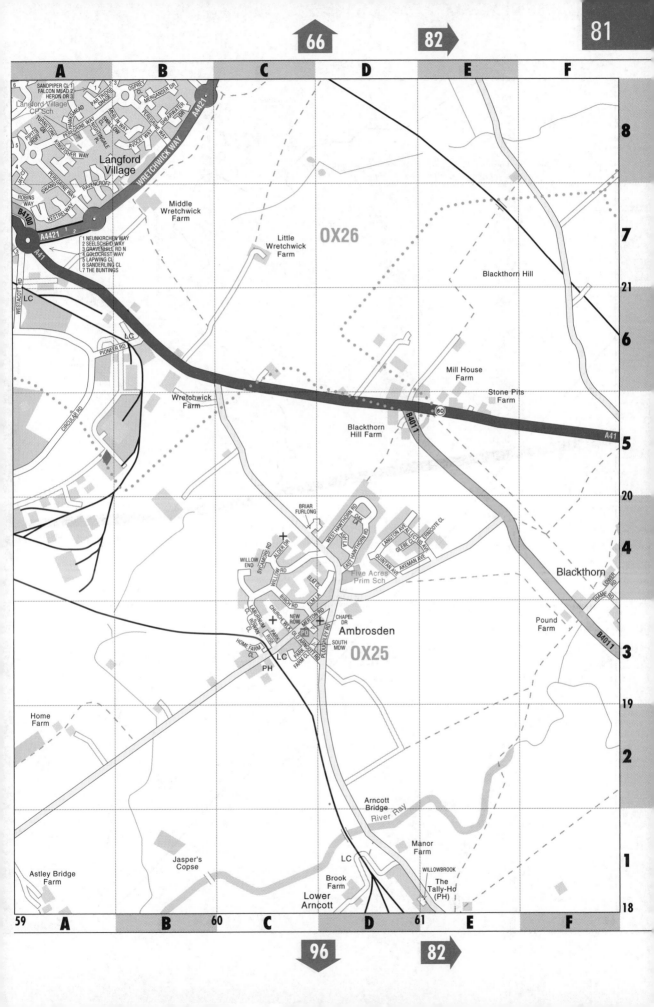

A B C D E F

SCOTTS LANE

OX26 →

Marsh-Field
Farm

Yew Elm
Farm

8

Furze
Ground

7

OX27

Bernwood Jubilee Way

Essex
Farm

21

Oakapple
Farm

6

Grange
Farm

A41 50

Heath
Bridge

5

Weir
Farm

WEIR LA

River Ray

20

Westbury
Farm

A41 Aylesbury

LOWER RD

4

Leaches
Farm

Blackthorn

ELM TREE
FARM

STATION RD

ELM TREE
CL

Lower
Cow Leys
Farm

HP18

BLACKTHORN
CL

EAST VIEW

SWAN
CL

Shaw's
Farm

Piddington
Cow Leys

3

CHAPEL
CL

THAME RD

OX25

Middle
Cow Leys
Farm

B4011

19

Blackthorn
Bridge

Bridge
Farm

Upper
Cow Leys
Farm

2

New
Farm

Treadwell's
Barn

1

HP18

18

B4011

Buckinghamshire STREET ATLAS

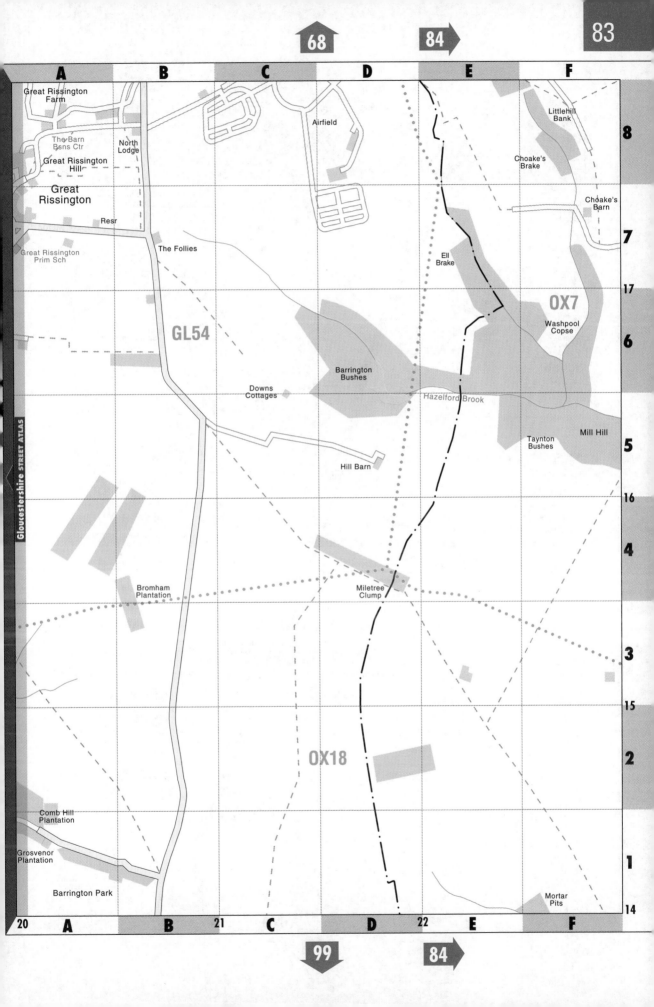

A B C D E F

Great Rissington Farm

The Barn Bsns Ctr

North Lodge

Great Rissington Hill

Great Rissington

Resr

Great Rissington Prim Sch

The Follies

Airfield

Littlehill Bank

Choake's Brake

Choake's Barn

8

7

17

GL54

Ell Brake

OX7

Washpool Copse

6

Barrington Bushes

Downs Cottages

Hazelford Brook

Taynton Bushes

Mill Hill

5

Hill Barn

16

4

Bromham Plantation

Miletree Clump

3

15

OX18

2

Comb Hill Plantation

Grosvenor Plantation

1

Barrington Park

Mortar Pits

14

Gloucestershire STREET ATLAS

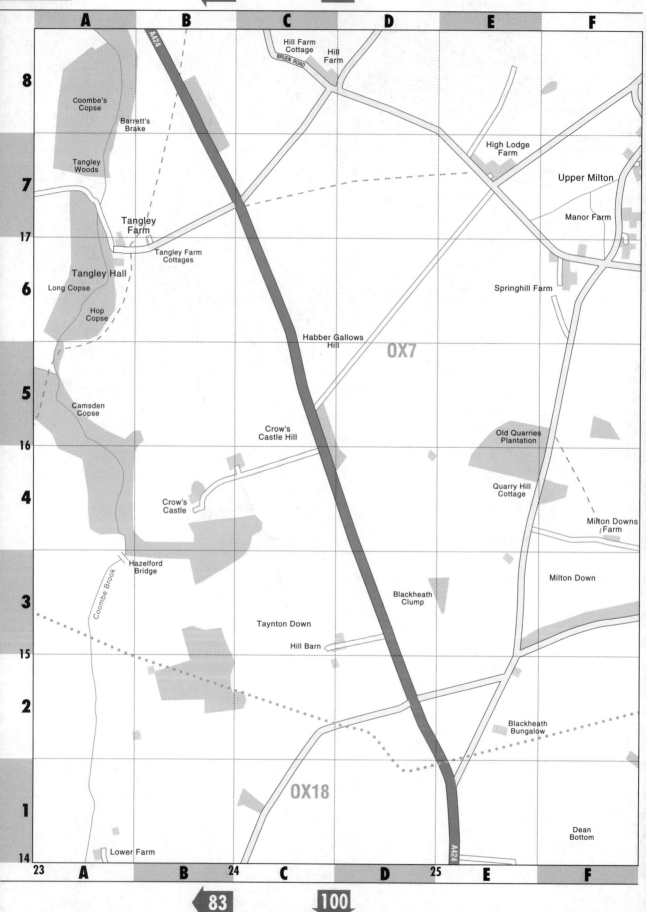

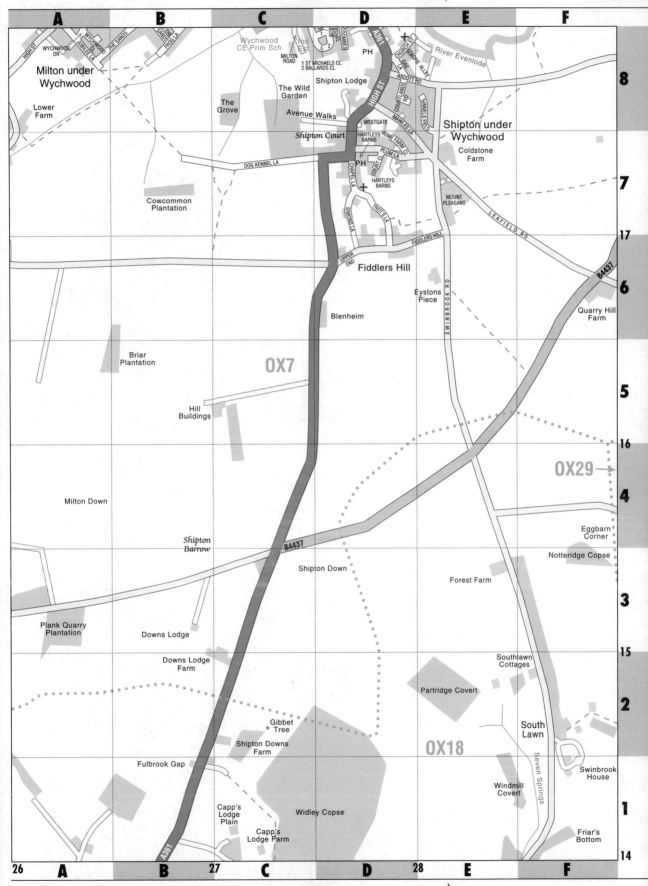

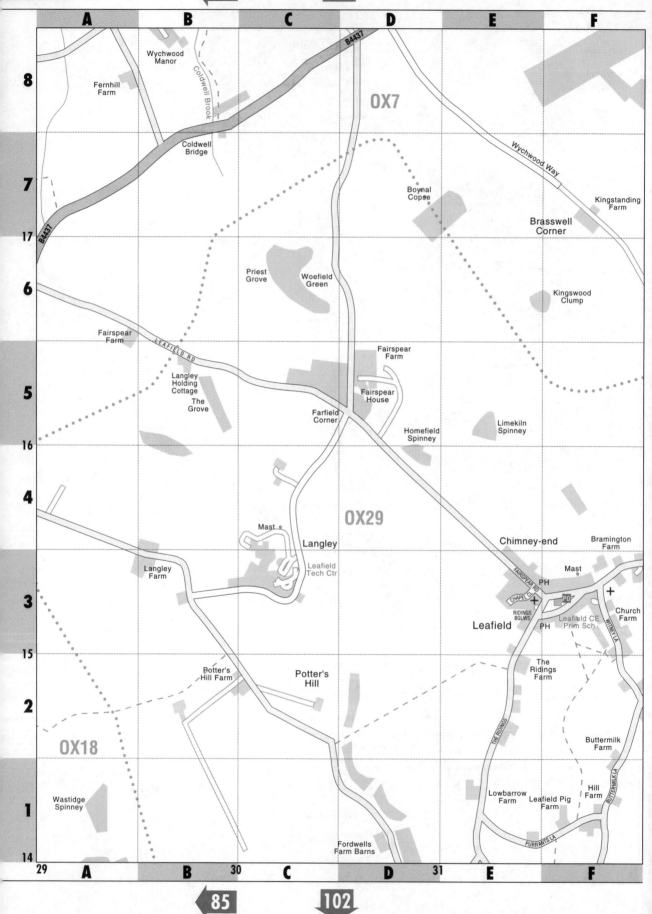

A B C D E F

8

Fernhill Farm

Wychwood Manor

Coldwell Brook

Coldwell Bridge

OX7

7

B4437

17

Woodell Way

Boynal Copse

Brasswell Corner

Kingstanding Farm

6

Priest Grove

Woefield Green

Kingswood Clump

Fairspear Farm

LEAFIELD RD

Langley Holding Cottage

The Grove

Fairspear Farm

Fairspear House

5

Farfield Corner

Homefield Spinney

Limekiln Spinney

16

4

Mast

Langley

OX29

Leafield Tech Ctr

Chimney-end

Bramington Farm

Mast

Langley Farm

FAIRSPEAR RD

PH

CHAPEL CL

PO

Church Farm

WITNEY LA

3

RIDINGS BGLWS

Leafield CE Prim Sch

Leafield

PH

15

Potter's Hill Farm

Potter's Hill

The Ridings Farm

THE RIDINGS

2

OX18

Buttermilk Farm

BUTTERMILK LA

Wastidge Spinney

Lowbarrow Farm

Leafield Pig Farm

Hill Farm

1

Fordwells Farm Barns

PURRANTS LA

14

29 A B 30 C D 31 E F

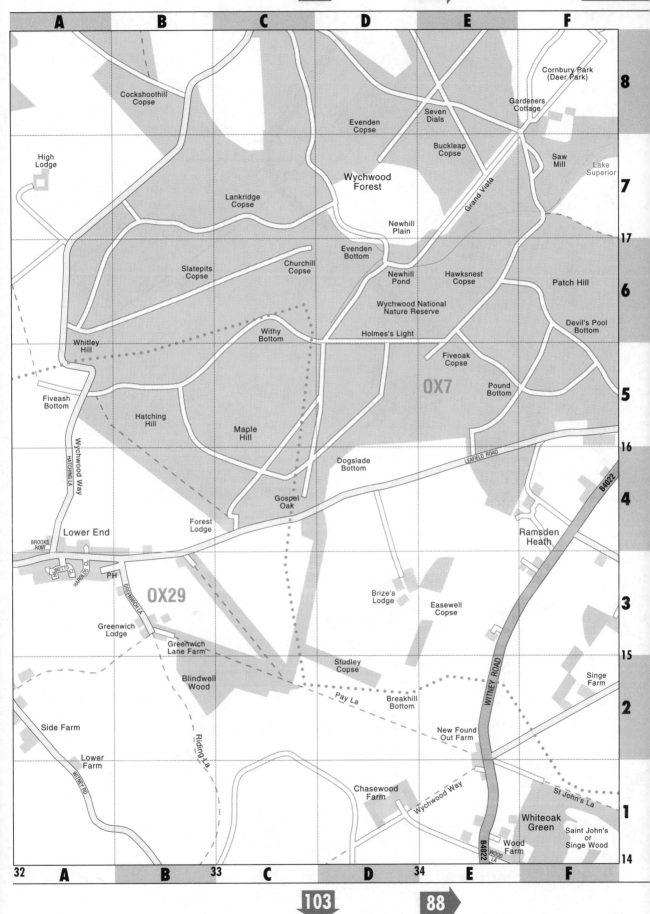

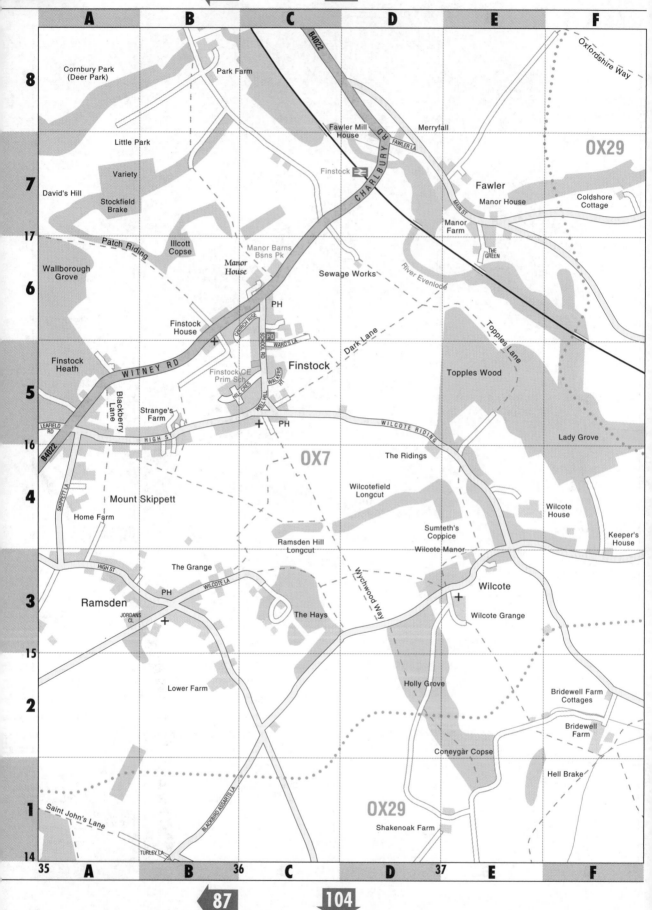

87
73

A B C D E F

8 Cornbury Park
(Deer Park)
Park Farm

Little Park

B4022

Fawler Mill
House

Merryfall

OX29

7 David's Hill
Variety

Stockfield
Brake

Finstock

Fawler

Manor House

Coldshore
Cottage

FAWLER LA

CHARLBURY RD

MAIN ST

Manor
Farm

THE GREEN

17 Patch Riding
Illcott
Copse

Wallborough
Grove

Manor Barns
Bsns Pk

Manor
House

Sewage Works

River Evenlode

6 Finstock
House

PH

CHURCH RISE

SCHOOL RD

PO

WARD'S LA

Dark Lane

Topples Lane

Finstock Heath

WITNEY RD

Finstock CE
Prim Sch

HILL CRES

WALKERS RT

WELL HILL

Finstock

Topples Wood

5 Blackberry
Lane

Strange's
Farm

HIGH ST

PH

Wilcote Riding

Lady Grove

LEAFIELD RD

B4022

16

SKIPPETT LA

OX7

The Ridings

4 Mount Skippett

Home Farm

Wilcotefield
Longcut

Wilcote
House

Keeper's
House

Ramsden Hill
Longcut

Sumteth's
Coppice

Wilcote Manor

HIGH ST

The Grange

WILCOTE LA

Wychwood Way

Wilcote

3 Ramsden

PH

JORDANS CL

The Hays

Wilcote Grange

15

Lower Farm

Holly Grove

Bridewell Farm
Cottages

2

Bridewell
Farm

BLACKBIRD ASSARTS LA

Coneygar Copse

Hell Brake

1 Saint John's Lane

OX29

Shakenoak Farm

14 TURLEY LA

35 A B 36 C D 37 E F

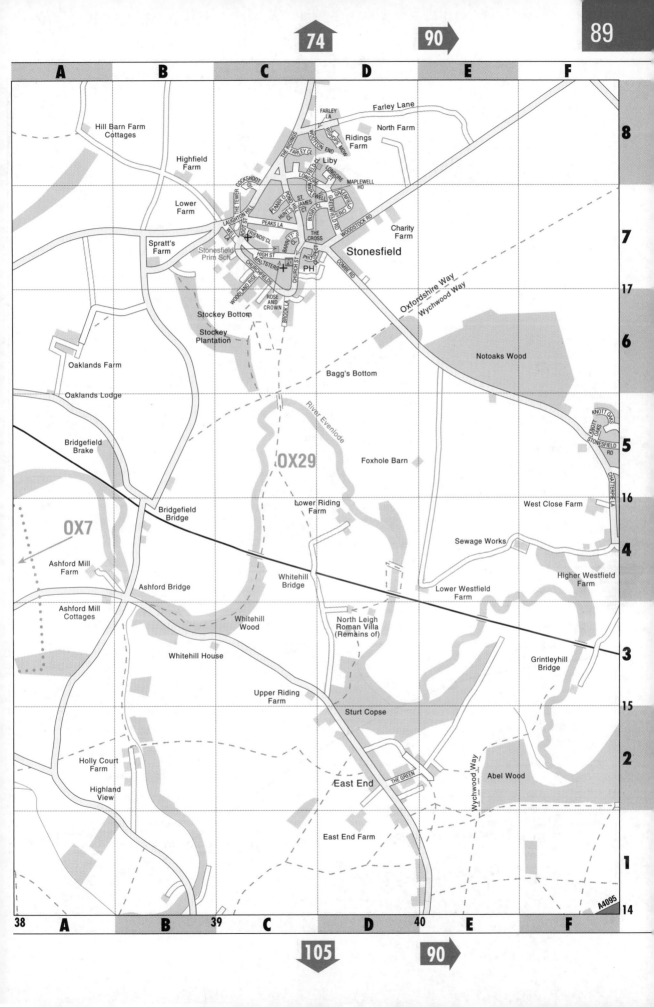

A B C D E F

8

Hill Barn Farm Cottages

Highfield Farm

FARLEY LA
Farley Lane

BISHOPS MDW

Ridings Farm

North Farm

Lower Farm

THE RIDINGS
THE FARLEY CL
WOOTTON END

Liby

COCKSHOOT CL

LONGORE
LONGORE
MAPLEWELL

MAPLEWELL HO

THE TOWER

FLYNOR'S DOWN
HUNT'S END
ST JAMES
BUSBY CL

GREENFIELD
GREENFIELD RD
G.CRES

THE TOWER

PEAKS LA

LAUGHTON LA
BOOT ST
HILL
WELL

HIGH ST
FRIENDS'CL

BARRETT'S END

WOODSTOCK RD

Charity Farm

Spratt's Farm

Stonesfield Prim Sch

MALTSTERS

CHURCHFIELDS

PO

PH

THE CROSS

PROSS

COMBE RD

Stonesfield

17

WOODLAND RISE

ROSE AND CROWN

BROOK LA

CHURCH ST

Oxfordshire Way
Wychwood Way

Stockey Bottom

Stockey Plantation

6

Oaklands Farm

Bagg's Bottom

Notoaks Wood

Oaklands Lodge

River Evenlode

KNOTT OAKS
KNOTT OAKS
STONESFIELD RD

5

Bridgefield Brake

OX29

Foxhole Barn

West Close Farm

CHATTERPIE LA

16

OX7

Bridgefield Bridge

Lower Riding Farm

Sewage Works

Higher Westfield Farm

4

Ashford Mill Farm

Ashford Bridge

Whitehill Bridge

Lower Westfield Farm

Grintleyhill Bridge

3

Ashford Mill Cottages

Whitehill Wood

North Leigh Roman Villa (Remains of)

Whitehill House

Upper Riding Farm

15

Sturt Copse

Holly Court Farm

East End

THE GREEN

Wychwood Way

Abel Wood

2

Highland View

East End Farm

1

A4095

14

← 89
↑ 75

A · B · C · D · E · F

8 · 7 · 17 · 6 · 5 · 16 · 4 · 3 · 15 · 2 · 1 · 14

Littleworth Farm

The Big Clump

Oxfordshire Way
Wychwood Way

Stonefield Steps

Mapleton Pond

Great Park

Akeman Street Farm

Park Farm

OX20

Column of Victory

Fourteen Acre Clump

Queen Pool

Square Firs

Long Firs

SQUARE FIRS

KNOTT OAKS

STONESFIELD RD

CHATTERPIE LA

Combe

Foxhole Farm

PARK RD

Manor Farm

New Park

Blenheim Park

Fair Rosamund's Well

Grand Bridge

The Lake

ORCHARD CL

PH

COMBE GATE

CHURCH WLK

WEST END

Combe CE Prim Sch

MARLBOROUGH TERR

ROBIN HILL

AKEMAN ST

Combe Lodge

High Park

Resr

Peagle Wood

Wedgehook Wood

Boltons Farm

BOLTONS LA

EAST END

High Lodge

OX29

Combe Cliff

Combe

Dog Kennel Hill

Combe Mill

River Evenlode

Millwood Farm Barns

MILLWOOD END

Millwood Farm

BOLSOVER CL

BROOK WAY

BAKER'S CT

PH

SWAN LA

Long Hanborough

Myrtle Farm

PARK LA

Long House

Long Hanborough Bridge

Hanborough Bsns Pk

LODGE DR

BANKSIDE DR

A4095

EVENLODE DR

ASH WOOD RD

MYRTLE CL

WASTIE'S ORCH

PH

MAIN RD

Mast

Oxford Bus Mus

FENLOCK CT

LOWER RD

MILLWOOD VALE

WITNEY RD

NEW RD

CHURCHILL WAY

GLYME WAY

CHURCH RD

PO

EELY CL

Motel

Hanborough

A4095

PLATTERS CT

HURDESWELL

BECKETTS CL

ROOSEVELT RD

Hanborough Manor CE Sch

41 · 42 · 43

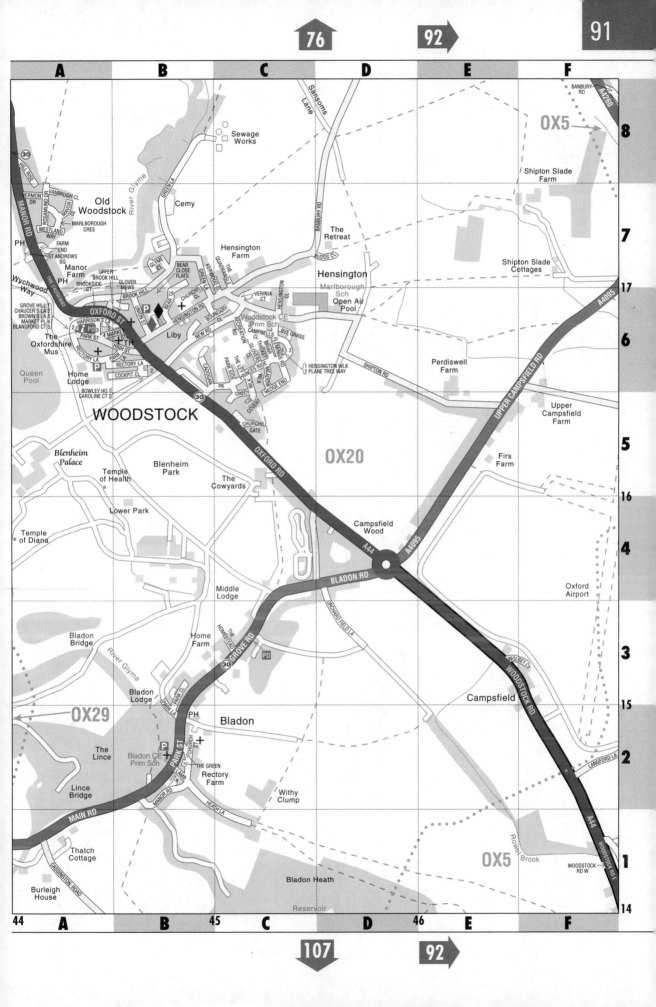

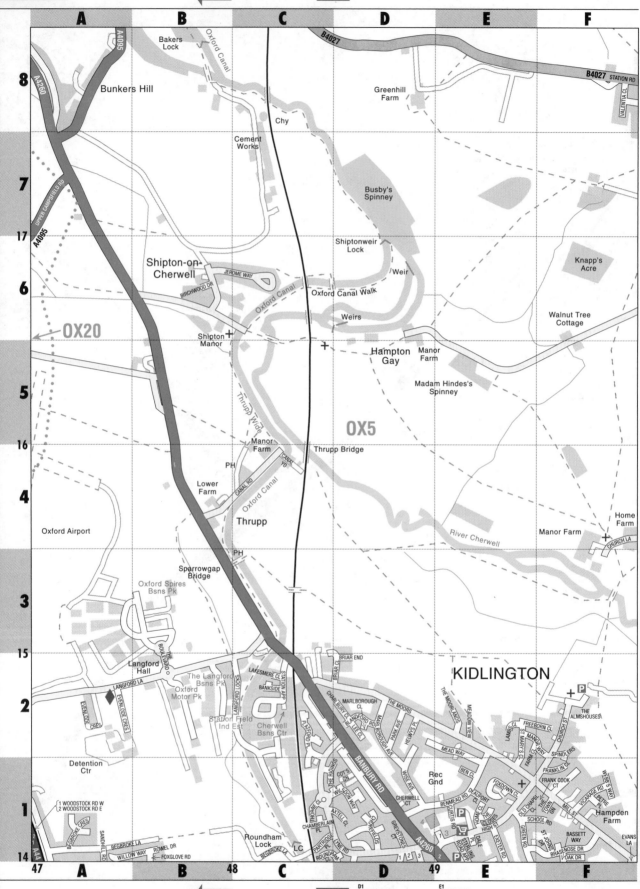

A B C D E F

8 Bunkers Hill

Bakers Lock

Oxford Canal

A4095

A4260

B4027

B4027 STATION RD

Greenhill Farm

VALENTIA CL

Chy

Cement Works

7 Busby's Spinney

UPPER CAMPSFIELD RD

17 A4095

Shiptonweir Lock

Knapp's Acre

6 Shipton-on-Cherwell

JEROME WAY

BIRCHWOOD DR

Oxford Canal

Oxford Canal Walk

Weir

Walnut Tree Cottage

OX20

Weirs

Shipton Manor

Hampton Gay

Manor Farm

Thrupp Wide

Madam Hindes's Spinney

5 Manor Farm

OX5

16 Manor Farm

Thrupp Bridge

PH

CANAL RD

CANAL YD

Lower Farm

Oxford Canal

4 Thrupp

River Cherwell

Manor Farm

Home Farm

CHURCH LA

Oxford Airport

PH

Sparrowgap Bridge

3 Oxford Spires Bsns Pk

KIDLINGTON

P

THE BOULEVARD

LANGFORD LOCKS

STATION APP

BRIAR END

THE ALMSHOUSES

15 Langford Hall

LANGFORD LA

The Langford Bsns Pk

Oxford Motor Pk

LAKESMERE CL

BANKSIDE

BRIAR CL

CHAR BURY CL

MARLBOROUGH CL

THE MOORS

PARK AVE

HELWYS PL

THE MOORLANDS

MEADOW VIEW

FREEBORN CL

ST MARY'S CL

LAMBE CL

MANOR WAY

SPINDLERS

CHURCH LA

2 EVENLODE CRES

EVENLODE CRES

Station Field Ind Est

Cherwell Bsns Ctr

LANGFORD CL

MARLBOROUGH AVE

WISE AVE

MEAD WAY

BEN CL

BEAUFORT CT

FRANKLIN CK

FRANK COOK CT

WEBBS WAY

VICARAGE RD

EXETRE

Detention Ctr

1 WOODSTOCK RD W
2 WOODSTOCK RD E

BANBURY RD

THE RODINGS

WILSON WAY

CHERWELL CT

Rec Gnd

FOXDOWN CL

BENMEAD RD

CURTIS RD

OLD CHAPEL CL

THE CLOSES

DALE CL

ST JOHNS CL

STEEL APP

GREEN RD

SCHOOL RD

Hampden Farm

1 BEGBROKE CRES

SANDHILL RD

COT'S GN

THORPE CLO

AXTELL CL

CHAMBERLAIN PL

PARTRIDGE

LYNE RD

SCOFIELDS

BRETSTONES CL

A4260

EXETER RD

BRASENOSE DR

OAK DR

BASSETT WAY

EVANS LA

A44

BEGBROKE LA

WILLOW WAY

ROWEL DR

FOXGLOVE RD

Roundham Lock

BEGBROKE LA

LC

Roundham

P

ST JOHNS APP

14 47 A 48 B C 48 D 49 E F

D1
1 THE ROOKERY
2 HEYFORD MEAD
3 CROWN RD
4 North Kidlington Prim Sch

E1
1 WATTS WAY
2 OXFORD RD
3 The Kidlington Ctr

A B C D E F

8

7

17

6

5

16

4

3

15

2

1

14

Bletchingdon Park

SPRINGWELL CL

Park Farm

TOLLBROOK CNR

Church End

Walker's Copse

Black Leys

SANDS CL

STATION RD

PH

CAUSEWAY

WESTON RD

BLENHEIM TERR

NEW RD

Bletchingdon Parochial CE Prim Sch

Grove Farm

B4027

ST GILES

DOGHILL

ISLIP RD

Bletchingdon

PINCHGATE LANE

College Farm

ANNES EV CL

LENTHAL

OXFORD RD

THE ROW

Manor Farm

Home Farm

Dolly's Barn

Diamond Farm

PH

Heathfield House

Heathfield Farm

OX25

A34

Heathfield Village

Frogsnest Farm

The Lodge

Heathfield Cottages

ISLIP RD

OX5

Brick Kiln Farm

Model Farm

Home Farm

BLETCHINGDON RD

Hampton Poyle

Hampton Gorse

Chipping Farm

CHURCH LA

PH

Field Barn Farm

OXFORD RD

River Cherwell

A34

BICESTER RD

Weir

Weir

MILL END

WATERMEAD

WOODLANDS

BLETCHINGDON RD

CONYGER CL

Islip

P

Manor Farm

Islip

Oxfordshire Way

KIDLINGTON RD

MILL LANE

CHURCH CL

Dr Southe CE Prim Sch

PO

B4027

HILLTOP GDNS

HIGH ST

MIDDLE WAY

THE WALK

NORTH ST

MIDDLE ST

CHURCH SQ

CHURCH LA

KING'S HEAD LA

LOWER ST

THE RISE

50 51 52

A B C D E F

8

PH
B430 NORTHAMPTON RD
A34
OXFORD RD
Weston Wood

7
OX25
LC
Holts Farm
MARSHMOOR RD

17
Gallos Brook
Family Farm
Oddington Wood

6
Rowles Farm
Oddington Grange

5
Barndon Farm
New House Farm

16
Oxfordshire Way
LC

4
OX5
RAY VIEW
HIGH ST

Brookfurlong Farm
Hillcroft Farm

3
Otter House

COLLEGE FRONT ST

15
Oddington
Rectory Farm
+

2
New River Ray

Logg Farm

1
River Ray

14
OX3

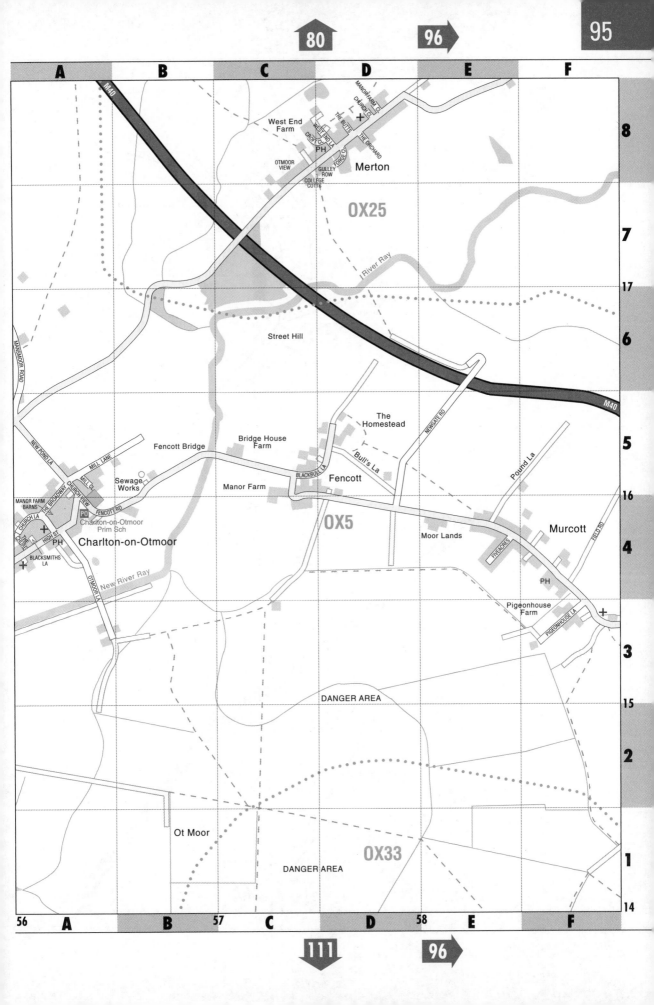

A B C D E F

M40

8

West End Farm

MANOR FARM CL
CHURCH CL
THE BUTTS
WEST END LA
CROFT CL
FORGE CL
THE ORCHARD
PH
OTMOOR VIEW
GULLEY ROW
COLLEGE COTTS

Merton

OX25

7

I River Ray

17

Street Hill

6

The Homestead

NEWGATE RD

M40

Bridge House Farm

Fencott Bridge

BLACKBULL LA

Bull's La

5

Pound La

New Pond La

MILL LANE

MILL CL

Sewage Works

Manor Farm

Fencott

Murcott

16

MANOR FARM BARNS

CHURCH VIEW

FENCOTT RD

PO

Charlton-on-Otmoor Prim Sch

OX5

Moor Lands

FIELD RD

FIVEACRES

4

CHURCH LA

THE BROADWAY

HIGH ST

THE CROSS

PH

Charlton-on-Otmoor

PH

BLACKSMITHS LA

Pigeonhouse Farm

PIGEONHOUSE LA

OTMOOR LA

New River Ray

3

DANGER AREA

15

2

Ot Moor

DANGER AREA

OX33

1

14

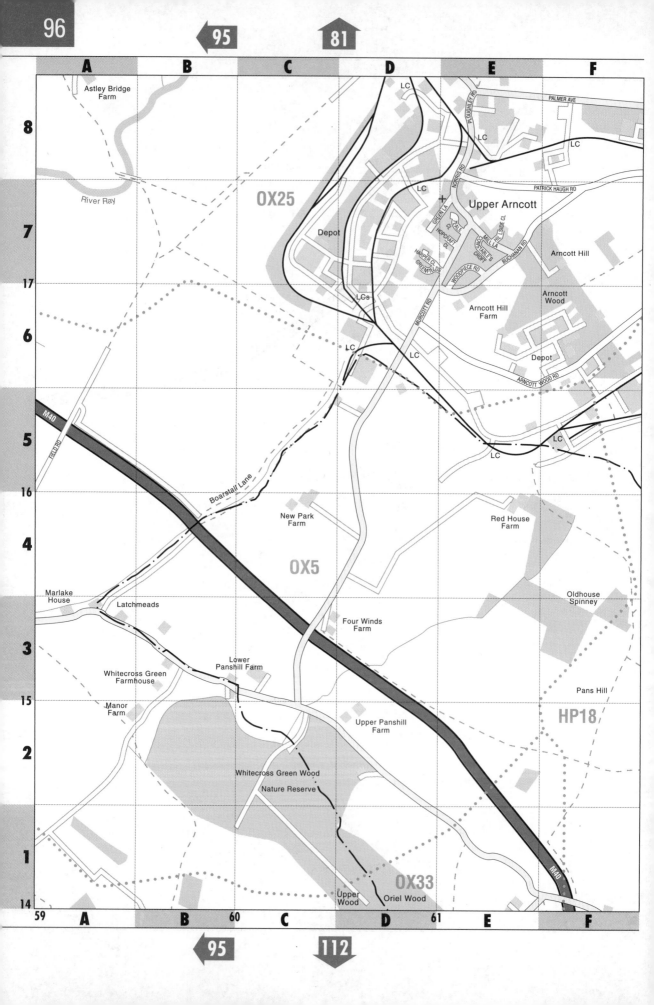

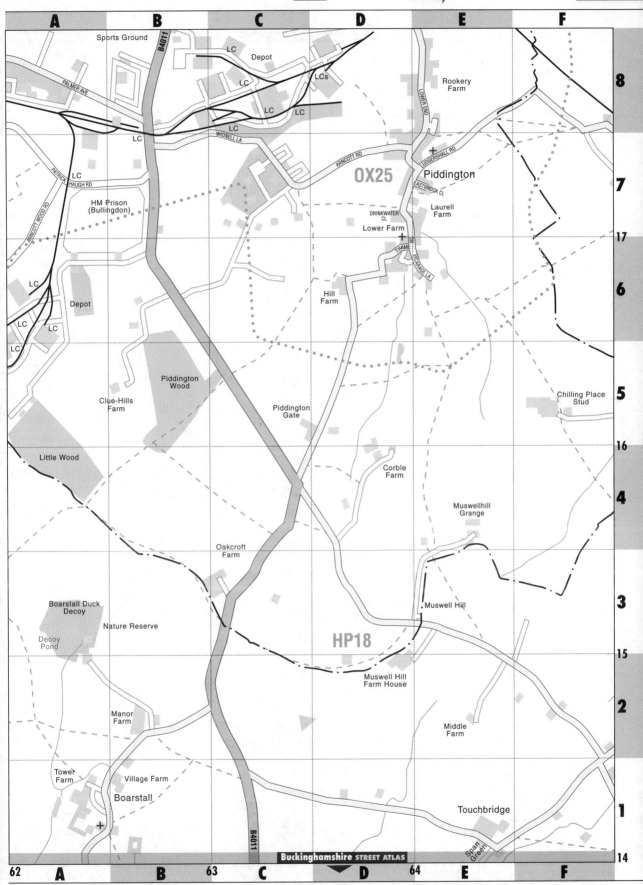

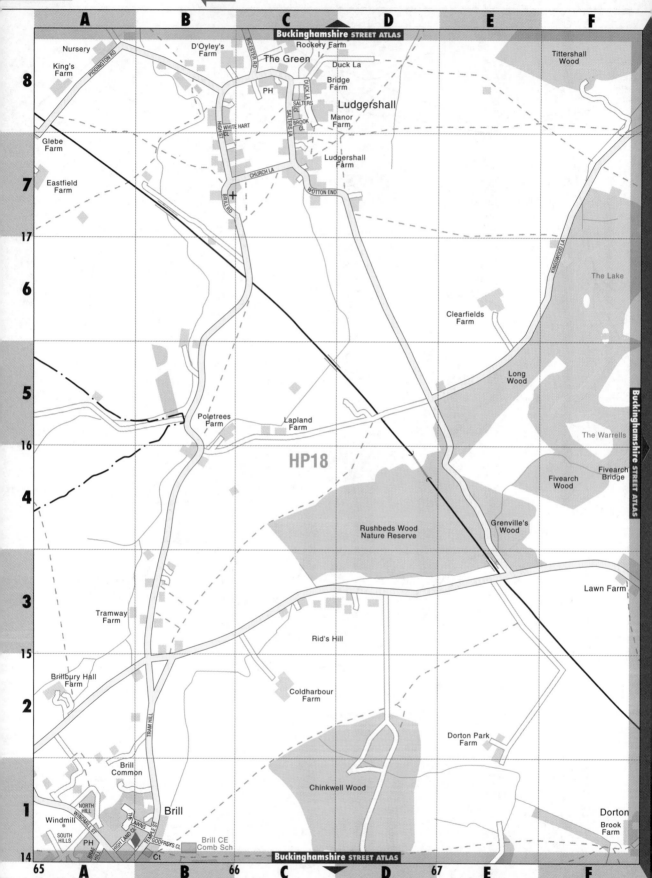

Buckinghamshire STREET ATLAS

Nursery

King's Farm

D'Oyley's Farm

Rookery Farm

The Green

PIDDINGTON RD

BICESTER RD

Duck La

Bridge Farm

Tittershall Wood

8

PH

DUCK LA

SALTERS CL

Ludgershall

Glebe Farm

WHITE HART

HIGH ST

SALTERS LA

BROOK CL

Manor Farm

7

Eastfield Farm

CHURCH LA

Ludgershall Farm

17

BRILL RD

WOTTON END

KINGSWOOD LA

The Lake

6

Clearfields Farm

5

Poletrees Farm

Lapland Farm

Long Wood

The Warrells

16

HP18

Fivearch Bridge

4

Fivearch Wood

Rushbeds Wood Nature Reserve

Grenville's Wood

3

Tramway Farm

Rid's Hill

Lawn Farm

15

Brillbury Hall Farm

Coldharbour Farm

2

Dorton Park Farm

Brill Common

Chinkwell Wood

1

Windmill

NORTH HILL

WINDMILL ST

THE LAWNS

TRAM HILL

TEMPLE ST

HIGH LAND CL

GODFREYS CL

Brill

Dorton

Brook Farm

SOUTH HILLS

PH

BRAE HILL

Ct

Brill CE Comb Sch

14

65

66

67

Buckinghamshire STREET ATLAS

A   B   C   D   E   F

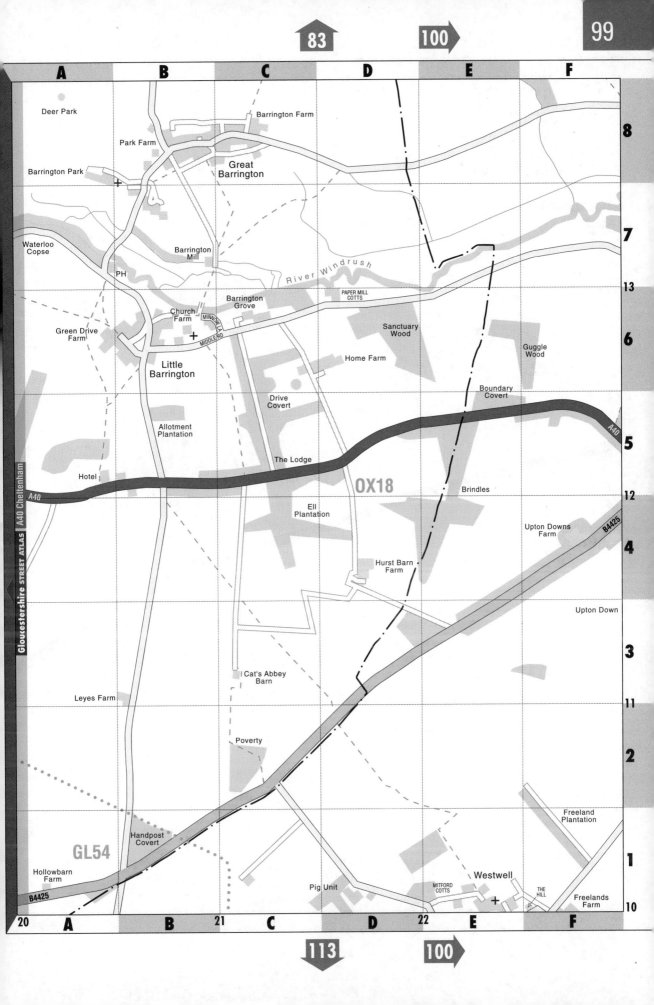

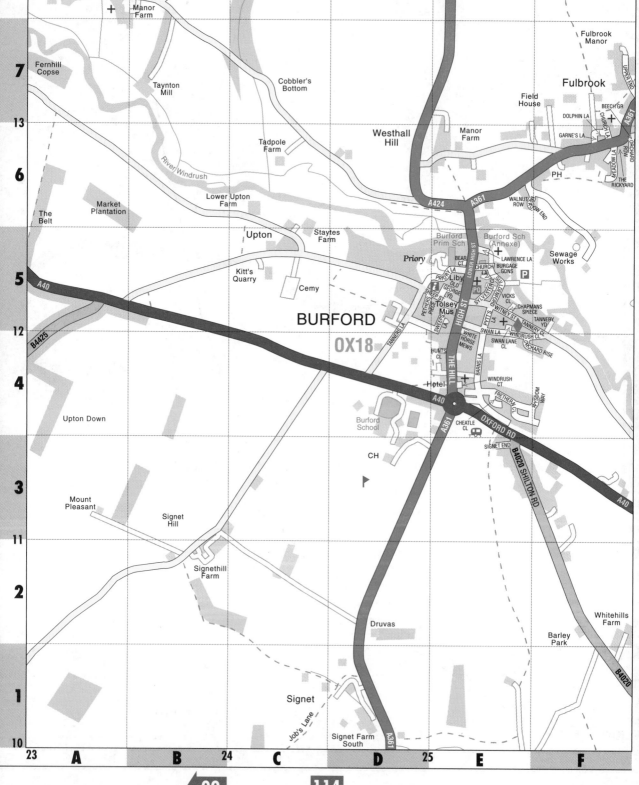

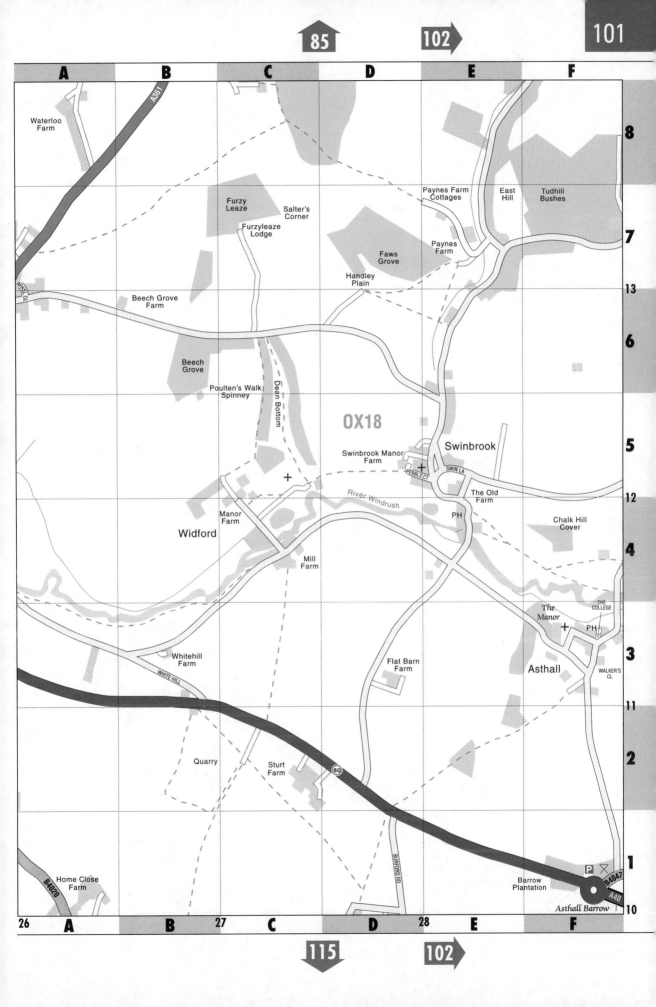

A   B   C   D   E   F

8

Waterloo
Farm

A361

Furzy
Leaze

Salter's
Corner

Paynes Farm
Cottages

East
Hill

Tudhill
Bushes

7

Furzyleaze
Lodge

AXEL CL

Faws
Grove

Paynes
Farm

13

Beech Grove
Farm

Handley
Plain

6

Beech
Grove

Poulten's Walk
Spinney

Dean Bottom

OX18

Swinbrook

5

Swinbrook Manor
Farm

PEBBLE CT

SWIN LA

The Old
Farm

12

Manor
Farm

River Windrush

PH

Chalk Hill
Cover

4

Widford

Mill
Farm

The
Manor

THE
COLLEGE

PH

3

Whitehill
Farm

WHITE HILL

Flat Barn
Farm

Asthall

WALKER'S
CL

11

2

Quarry

Sturt
Farm

60

B4020

Home Close
Farm

BURFORD RD

Barrow
Plantation

P

B4047

A40

1

Asthall Barrow

10

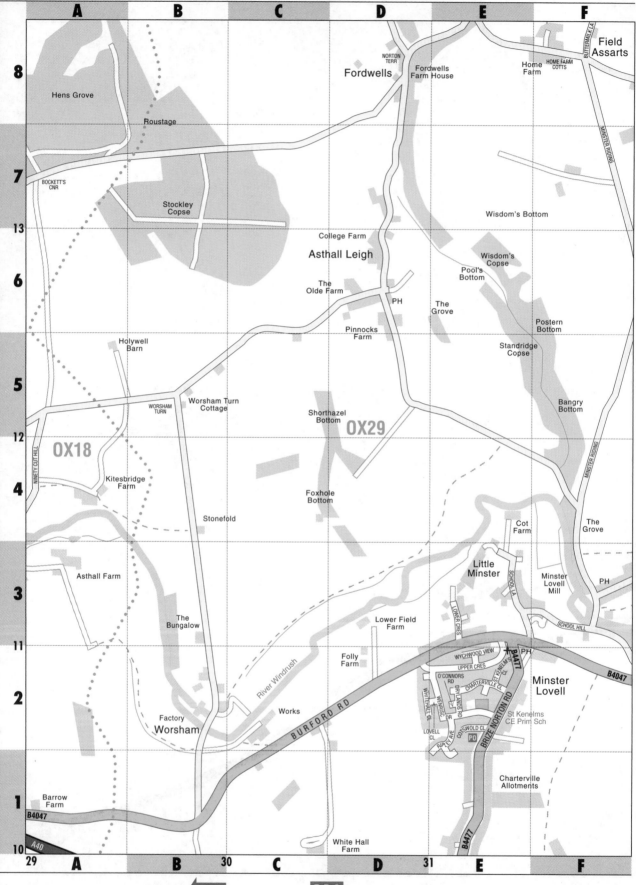

Field Assarts

Fordwells

NORTON TERR

Fordwells Farm House

Home Farm

HOME FARM COTTS

Hens Grove

Roustage

BOCKETT'S CNR

Stockley Copse

Wisdom's Bottom

College Farm

Asthall Leigh

Wisdom's Copse

Pool's Bottom

The Olde Farm

PH

The Grove

Postern Bottom

Pinnocks Farm

Standridge Copse

Holywell Barn

Worsham Turn Cottage

WORSHAM TURN

Worsham Turn

Shorthazel Bottom

OX29

Bangry Bottom

NINETY CUT HILL

OX18

Kitesbridge Farm

Stonefold

Foxhole Bottom

Cot Farm

The Grove

Asthall Farm

Little Minster

Minster Lovell Mill

PH

The Bungalow

Lower Field Farm

SCHOOL LA

LOWER CRES

SCHOOL HILL

River Windrush

Folly Farm

WYCHWOOD VIEW

B4477

PH

UPPER CRES

Minster Lovell

Works

BURFORD RD

O'CONNORS RD

CHARTERVILLE CL

ST KENELMS CL

B4047

Factory

Worsham

WHITEHALL CL

WEIRS CL

DRYLANDS RD

BRIZE NORTON RD

COTSWOLD CL

St Kenelms CE Prim Sch

LOVELL CL

RIPLEY AVE

PO

Charterville Allotments

Barrow Farm

B4047

B4477

White Hall Farm

A40

29   30   31

MINSTER RIDING

BUTTERMILK LA

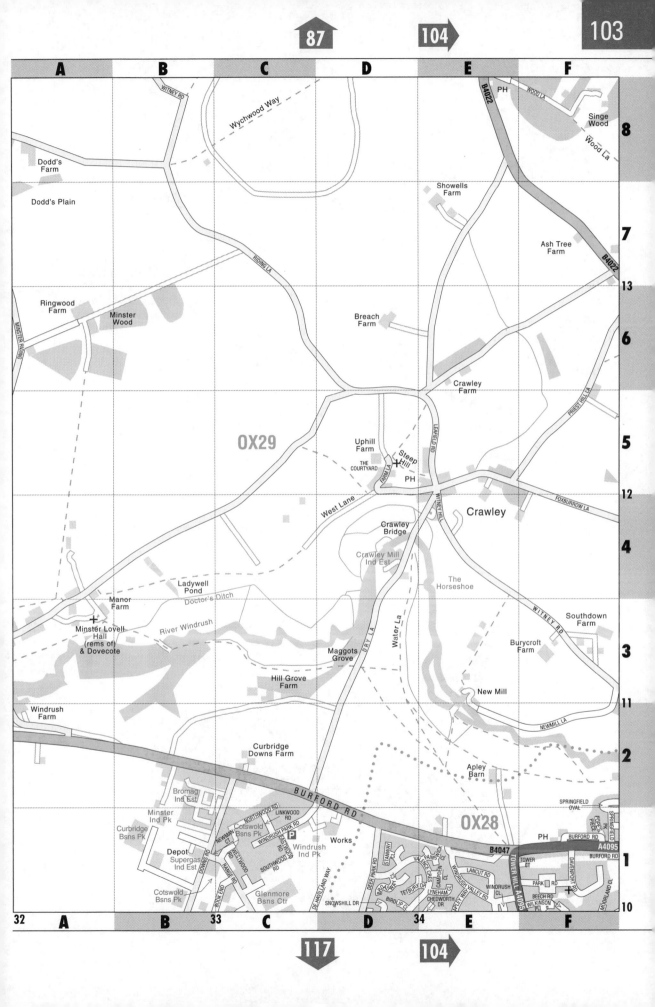

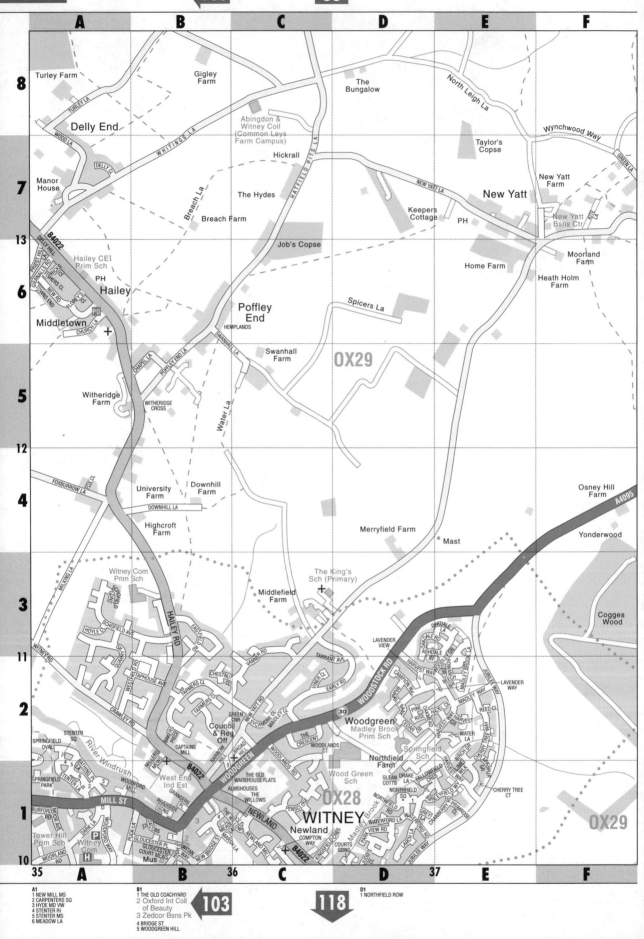

A1
1 NEW MILL MS
2 CARPENTERS SQ
3 HYDE MD VW
4 STENTER RI
5 STENTER MS
6 MEADOW LA

B1
1 THE OLD COACHYARD
2 Oxford Int Coll of Beauty
3 Zedcor Bsns Pk
4 BRIDGE ST
5 WOODGREEN HILL

D1
1 NORTHFIELD ROW

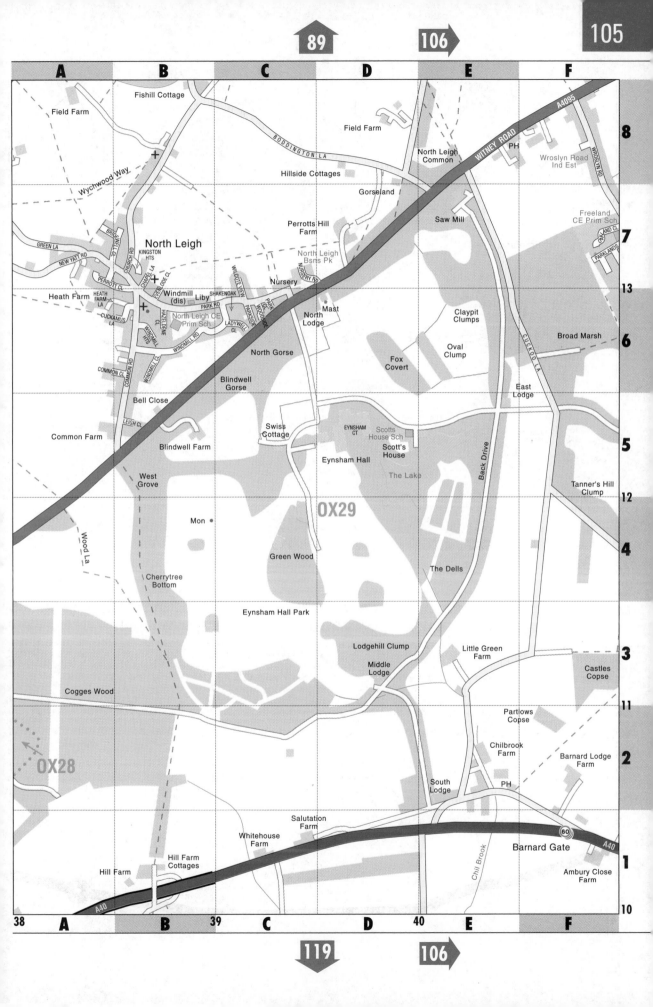

105
90

A B C D E F

8
7
13
6
5
12
4
3
11
2
1
10

LOWER RD
HURDSWELL
GLYME WAY
CHURCHILL WAY
MARLBOROUGH CRES
ROOSEVELT DR
PINSLEY RD
QUEEN ELEANOR CT

Allot Gdns

Cook's Corner Farm

Pinsley Wood

Mill Farm

OAKLAND CL
Freeland CE Prim Sch
PARKLANDS

Cemy

CHURCH RD

Freeland

WILSON RD
HURST LA
MASH LA
WOODLANDS
THE BLOWINGS
ASH LA
CHURCH LA
OXLEASE
MARSH LA
BUSBY CL
WALKERS
BLENHEIM LA
WEBSTERS CL
PH

Little Blenheim

Sewage Works

MANSELL CL

Church Hanborough
PH

College Farm

Whitehouse Farm

PIGEON HOUSE LA

Dreydon House

Goose Eye Farm

Freeland House
THE GREEN

Elm Farm

The Thrift

Lady Grove

OX29

New Barn Farm

River Evenlode

CUCKOO LA

Vincents Wood

Bowles Farm

CUCKOO LA

City Farm

Eynsham Mill

MILL LANE

Acre Hill Farm

New Wintles Farm

Mast

A40

Evenlode Farm

Acre Hill House

A40

HANBOROUGH RD

Chil Brook

41 42 43

A B C D E F

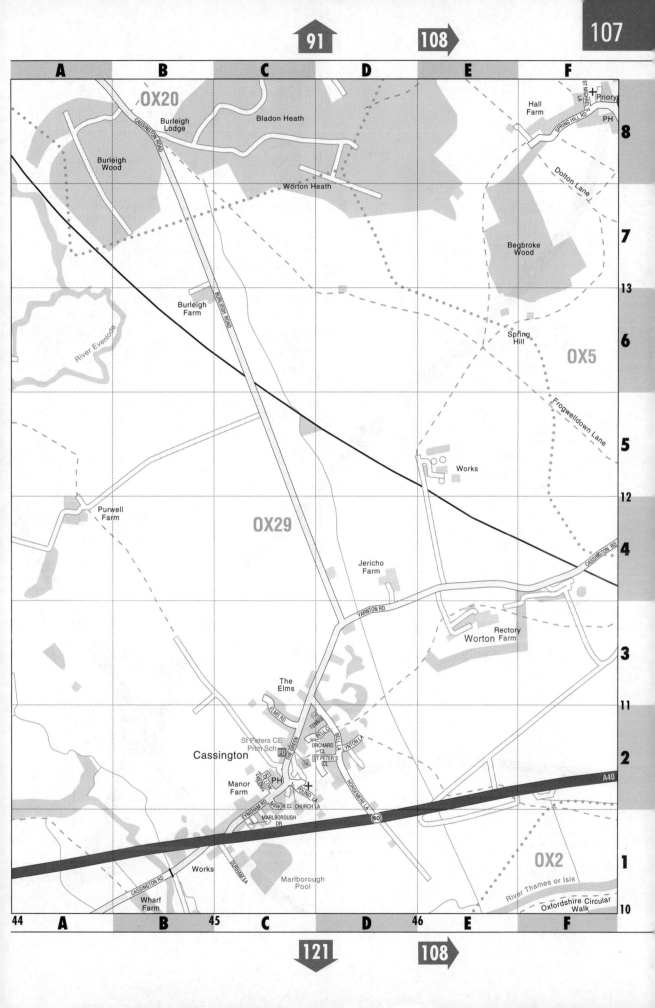

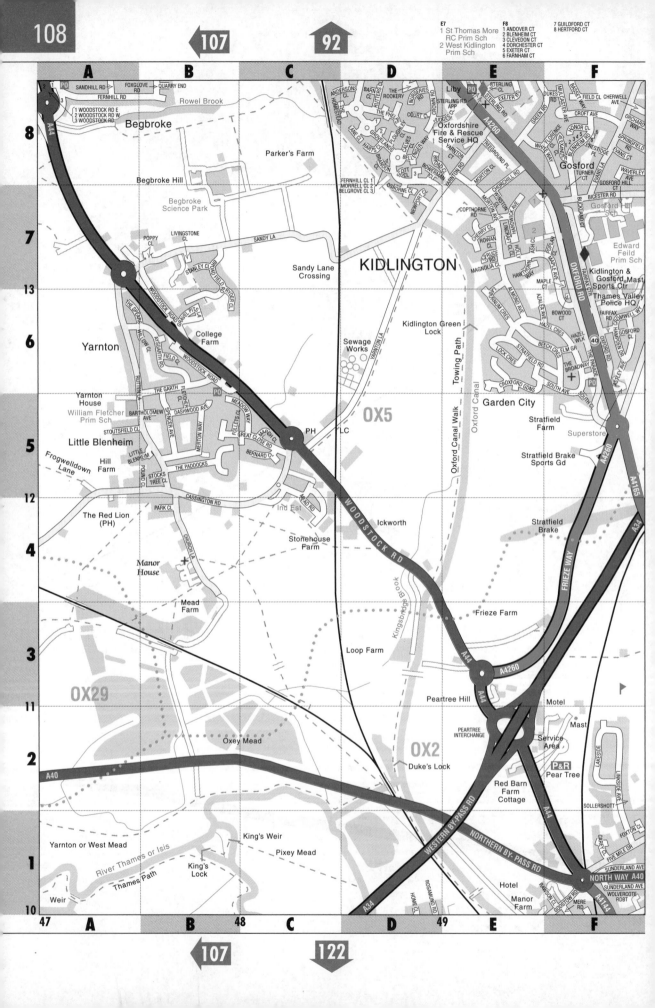

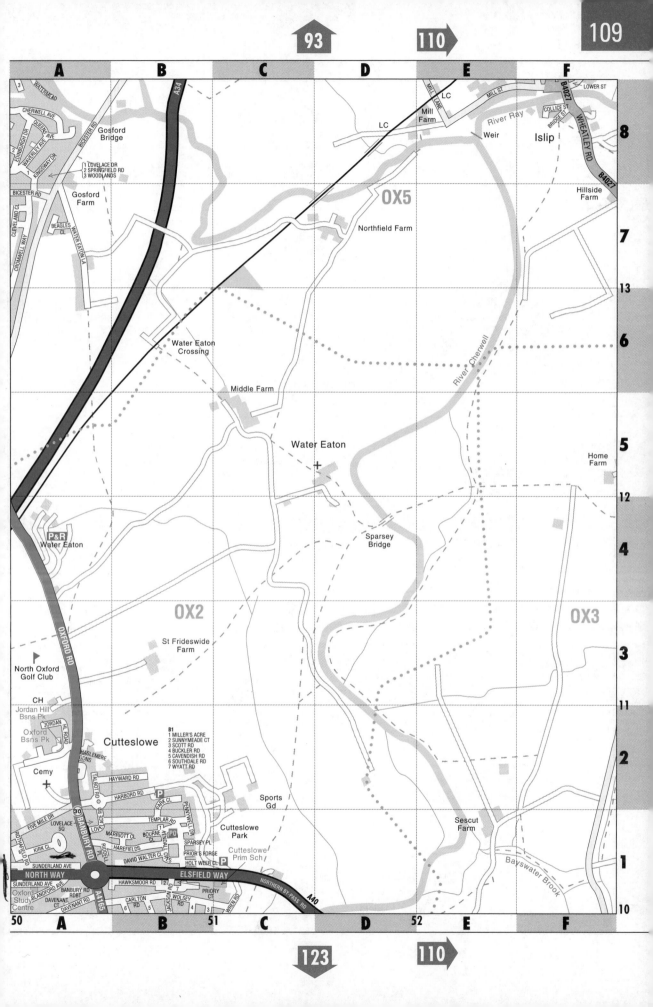

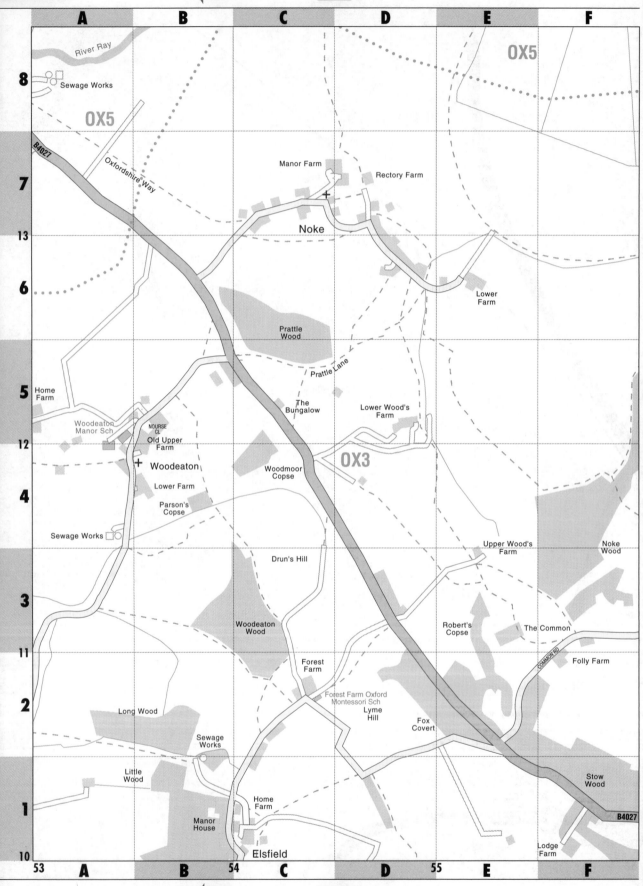

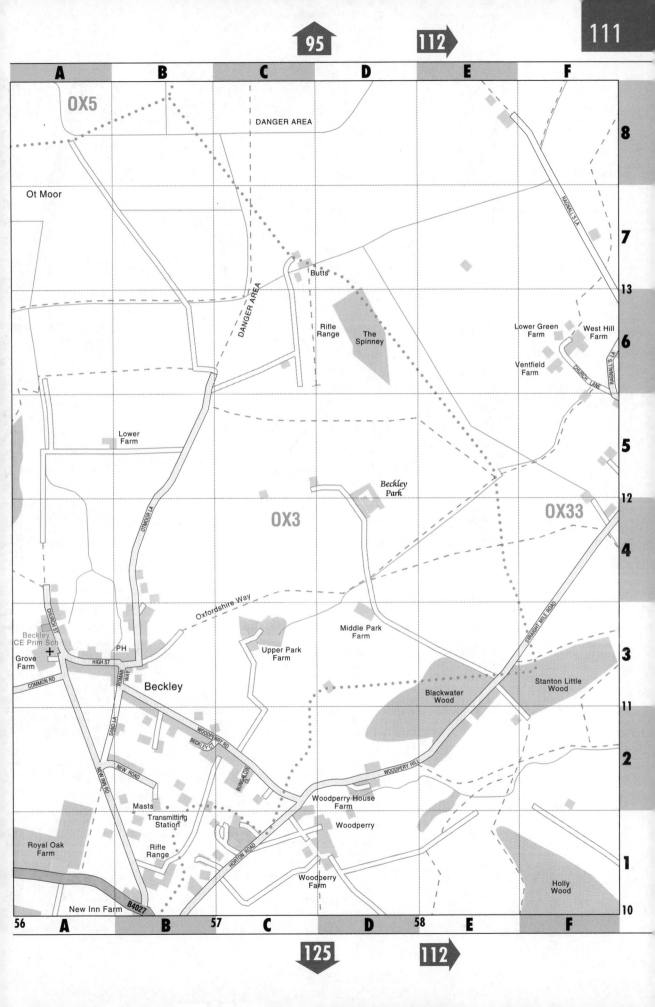

OX5

Ot Moor

DANGER AREA

DANGER AREA

Butts

Rifle
Range

The
Spinney

Lower Green
Farm

West Hill
Farm

Ventfield
Farm

CHURCH LANE

RAGNALL'S LA

Lower
Farm

Beckley
Park

OX3

OX33

Oxfordshire Way

Middle Park
Farm

STRAIGHT MILE ROAD

Beckley
CE Prim Sch

PH

Grove
Farm

HIGH ST

COMMON RD

ROMAN WAY

Beckley

Upper Park
Farm

Stanton Little
Wood

Blackwater
Wood

SAND LA

WOODPERRY RD

BECKLEY CT

NEW INN RD

NEW ROAD

BUNGALOW CL

Masts

Transmitting
Station

Woodperry House
Farm

WOODPERRY HILL

Royal Oak
Farm

Rifle
Range

HORTON ROAD

Woodperry

Holly
Wood

New Inn Farm

B4027

Woodperry
Farm

56   A   B   57   C   D   58   E   F

A   B   C   D   E   F

8

7

13

6

5

12

4

3

11

2

1

10

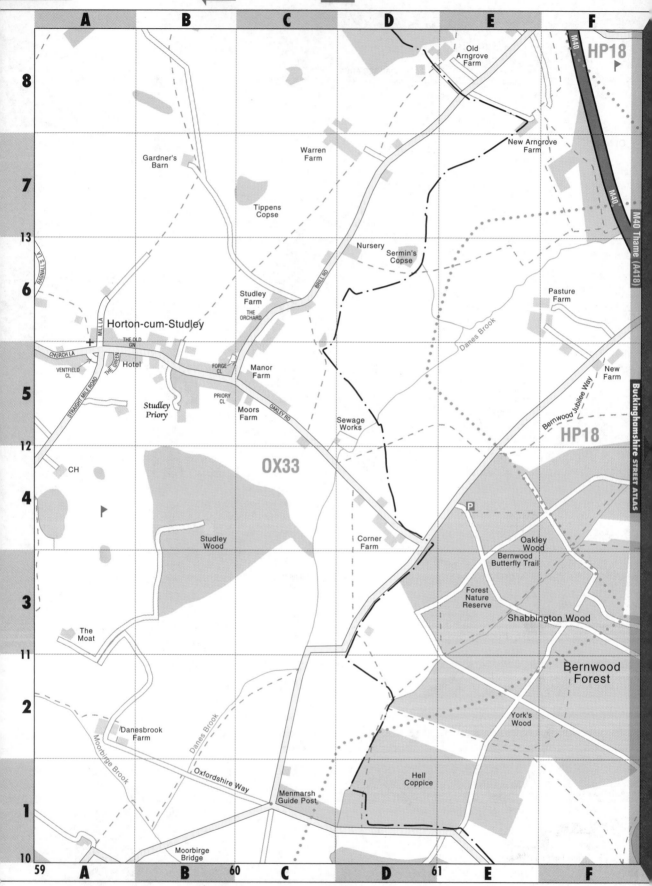

A **B** **C** **D** **E** **F**

Old Arngrove Farm

HP18

New Arngrove Farm

8

Gardner's Barn

Warren Farm

7

Tippens Copse

Nursery

13

Sermin's Copse

Pasture Farm

Studley Farm

THE ORCHARD

6

BRILL RD

Horton-cum-Studley

Danes Brook

New Farm

THE OLD GN

Hotel

Manor Farm

Bernwood Jubilee Way

CHURCH LA

VENTFIELD CL

THE GREEN

FORGE CL

HP18

STRAIGHT MILE ROAD

5

RAGNALL'S LA

MILL LA

Studley Priory

PRIORY CL

Moors Farm

OAKLEY RD

Sewage Works

12

CH

OX33

4

P

Oakley Wood

Studley Wood

Corner Farm

Bernwood Butterfly Trail

Forest Nature Reserve

Shabbington Wood

3

The Moat

Bernwood Forest

11

York's Wood

2

Danesbrook Farm

Danes Brook

Moorbirge Brook

Oxfordshire Way

Hell Coppice

Menmarsh Guide Post

1

Moorbirge Bridge

10

M40

M40 Thame (A418)

Buckinghamshire STREET ATLAS

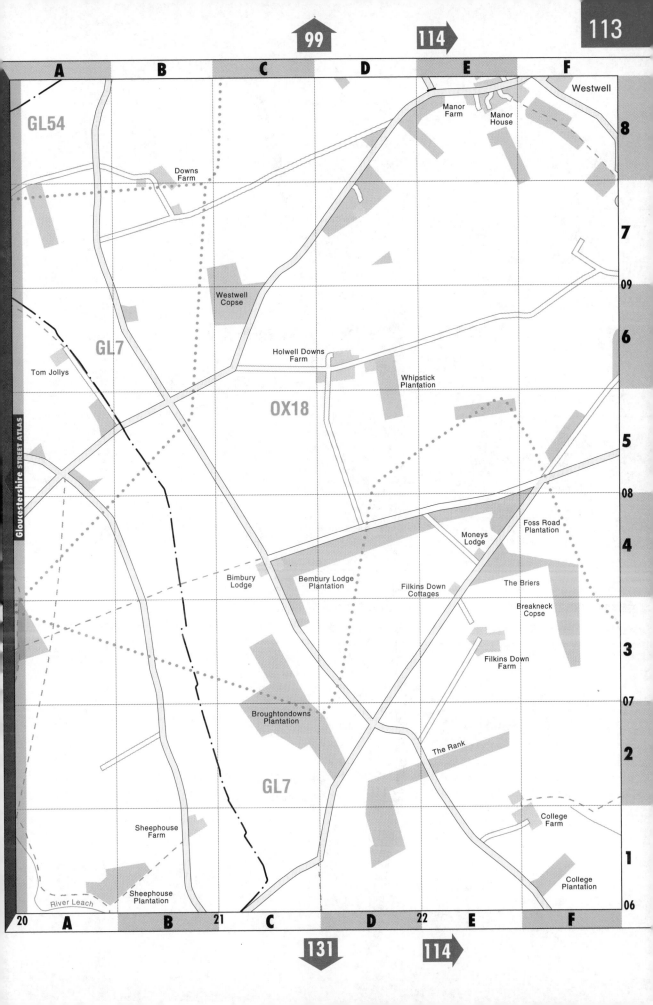

A B C D E F

Westwell

GL54

Manor
Farm
Manor
House

8

Downs
Farm

7

09

Westwell
Copse

GL7

6

Holwell Downs
Farm

Tom Jollys

Whipstick
Plantation

OX18

5

08

Foss Road
Plantation

Moneys
Lodge

4

Bimbury
Lodge

Bembury Lodge
Plantation

Filkins Down
Cottages

The Briers

Breakneck
Copse

3

07

Broughtondowns
Plantation

Filkins Down
Farm

The Rank

2

GL7

College
Farm

Sheephouse
Farm

1

Sheephouse
Plantation

College
Plantation

06

River Leach

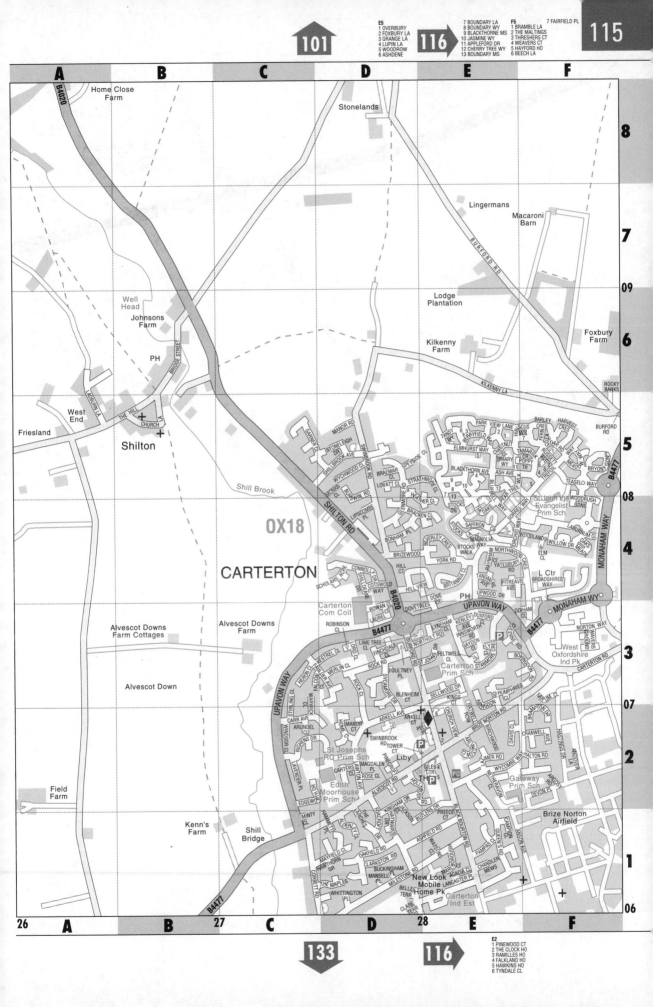

A B C D E F

8

7

09

6

5

08

4

3

07

2

1

06

A40

BRIZE NORTON RD B4477

B4477

Bushey Ground

OX29

Bushey Ground Farm

Nurseries

Grove Farm

Grove Farm Cottages

B4477

BRIZE NORTON ROAD

Rabbit's Piece Copse

CASWELL LA

BURFORD RD

Grange Farm

Astrop Cottages

WITNEY RD

Astrop Farm

Wilbro Farm

Abingdon Lane

Round Copse

B4477

MONAHAM WY

BURFORD RD

PH

MINSTER RD

ELM GR

GARSTON CT

CHAPEL HILL

Manor Farm

OX18

Brize Norton

MANOR RD

DAUBIGNY MEAD

SQUIRES CL

MOAT CL

PH

THE FOSSE WAY

CHIC

OTER PL

SOUTH MERE

CHESTNUT CL

STATION RD

HONEYHAM CL

Brize Norton Prim Sch

P

CARTERTON RD

Ten Acre Copse

Huck's Copse

Norton Ditch

Upper Haddon Farm

Sewage Works

Highmoor Brook

The Copse

Brize Norton Airfield

The Plantation

Lew Gorse

Viscount Ind Est

29

30

31

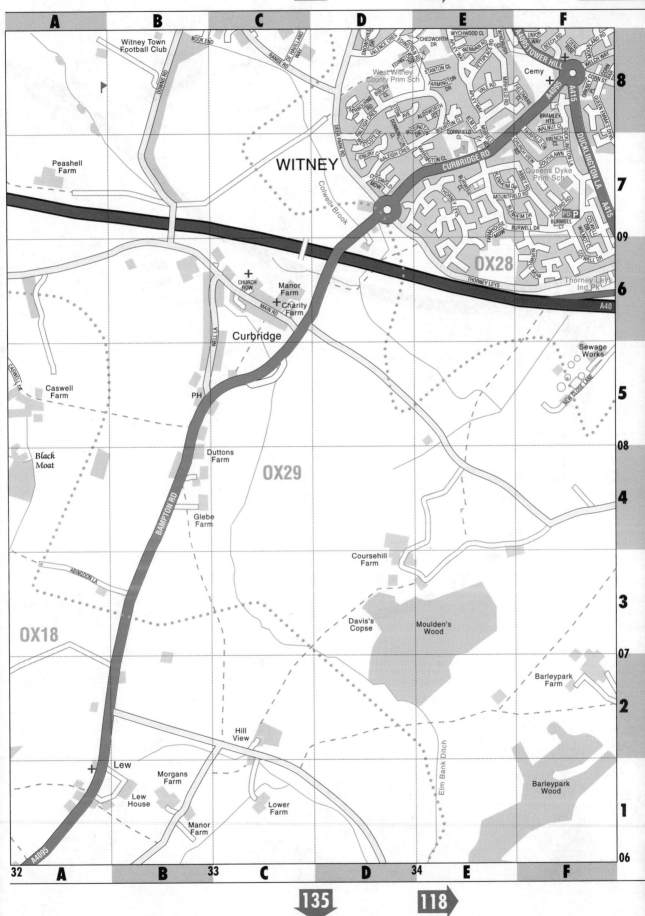

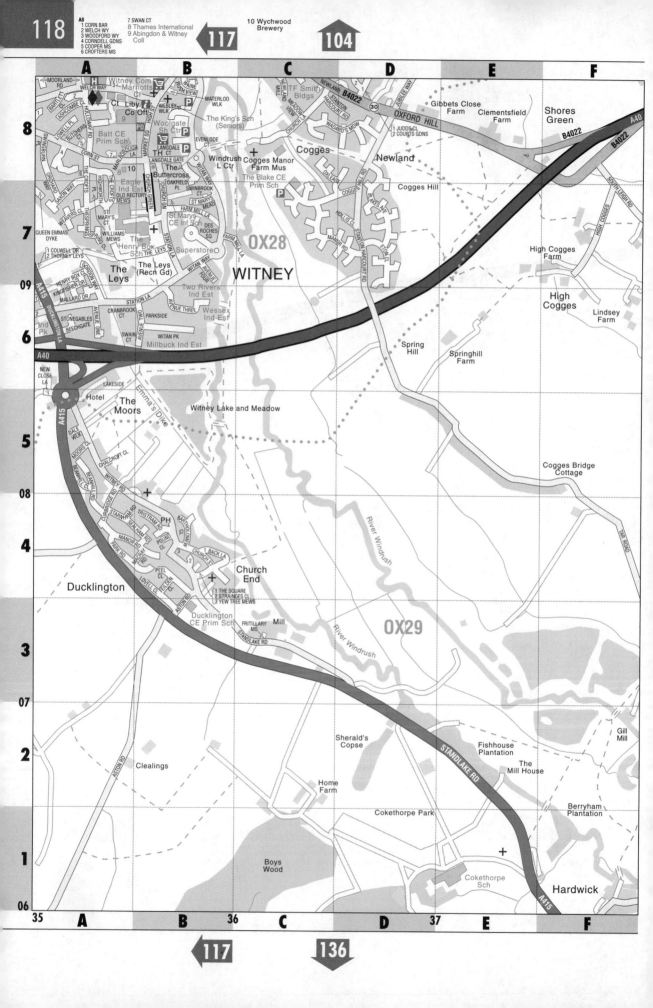

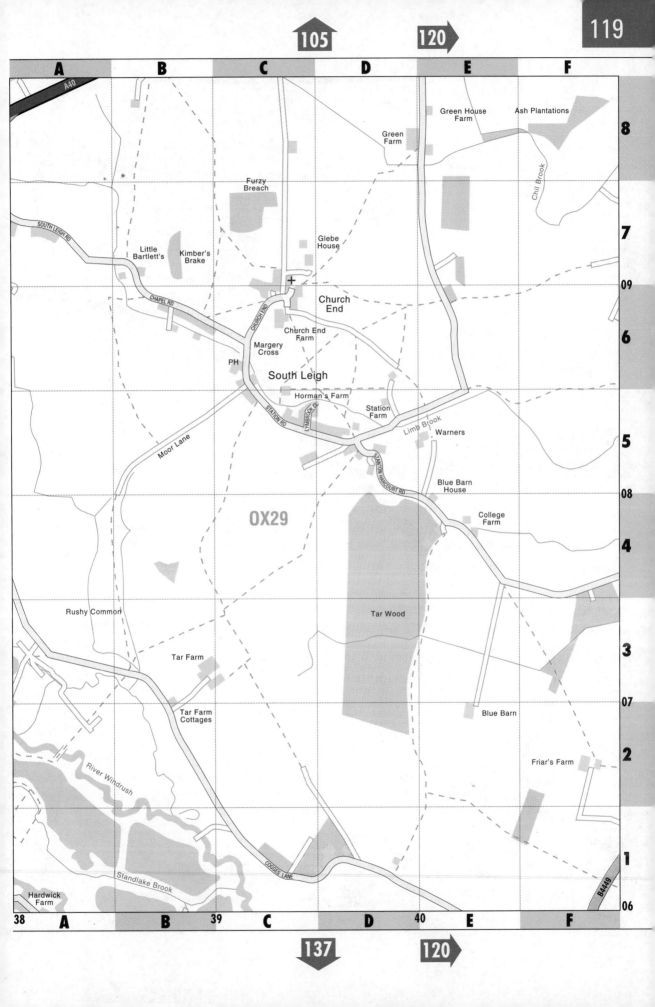

A   B   C   D   E   F

A40

8

Green House Farm
Ash Plantations
Green Farm
Chil Brook

Furzy Breach

7

SOUTH LEIGH RD

Little Bartlett's
Kimber's Brake
Glebe House

CHAPEL RD

09

Church End

6

CHURCH END
Church End Farm
Margery Cross

PH

South Leigh

Horman's Farm
STATION RD
LYMBROOK CL
Station Farm
Limb Brook
Warners

5

Moor Lane

STANTON HARCOURT RD
Blue Barn House

08

OX29

College Farm

4

Rushy Common

Tar Wood

3

Tar Farm

07

Tar Farm Cottages

Blue Barn

2

River Windrush

Friar's Farm

1

COGGES LANE

Standlake Brook

Hardwick Farm

B4449

06

38   A   B   39   C   D   40   E   F

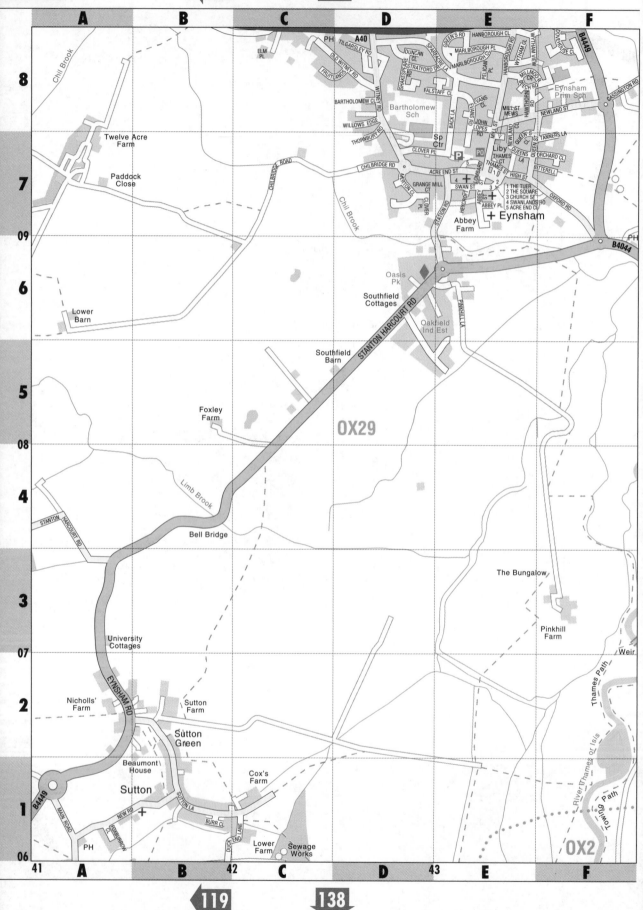

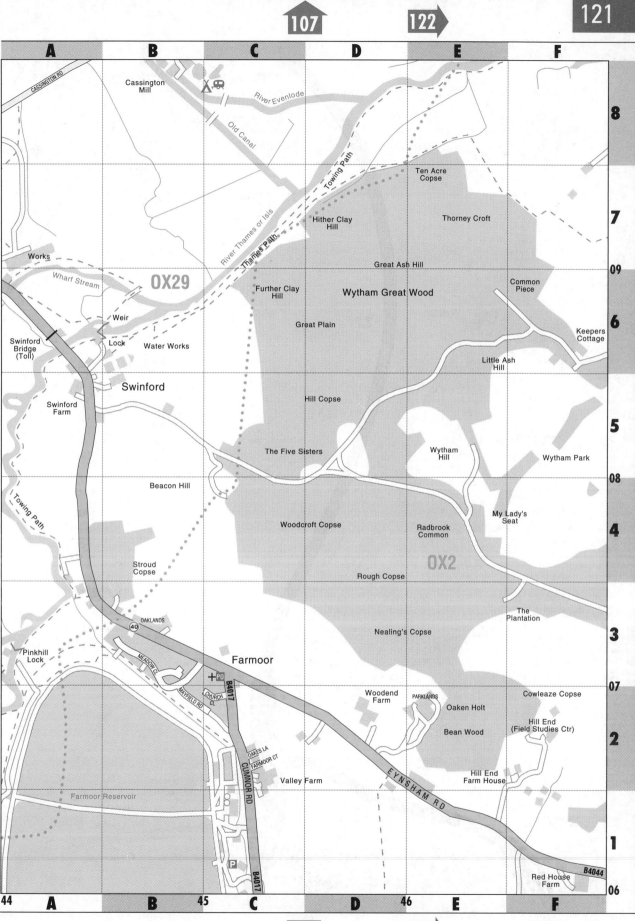

CASSINGTON RD

Cassington
Mill

River Evenlode

Old Canal

Towing Path

Ten Acre
Copse

Thorney Croft

Hither Clay
Hill

Works

OX29

Great Ash Hill

Wharf Stream

River Thames or Isis

Thames Path

Further Clay
Hill

Wytham Great Wood

Common
Piece

Weir

Great Plain

Keepers
Cottage

Swinford
Bridge
(Toll)

Lock

Water Works

Little Ash
Hill

Swinford

Hill Copse

Swinford
Farm

Wytham
Hill

Wytham Park

The Five Sisters

Beacon Hill

Woodcroft Copse

My Lady's
Seat

Towing
Path

Stroud
Copse

Radbrook
Common

OX2

Rough Copse

The
Plantation

Pinkhill
Lock

OAKLANDS
40

Nealing's Copse

Cowleaze Copse

MEADOW CL

Farmoor

Woodend
Farm

PARKLANDS

Oaken Holt

Hill End
(Field Studies Ctr)

PO

MAYFIELD RD

CHURCH
CL

B4017

Bean Wood

OAKES LA

FARMOOR CT

Hill End
Farm House

CUNNOR RD

Valley Farm

EYNSHAM RD

Farmoor Reservoir

P

B4017

Red House
Farm

B4044

44

45

46

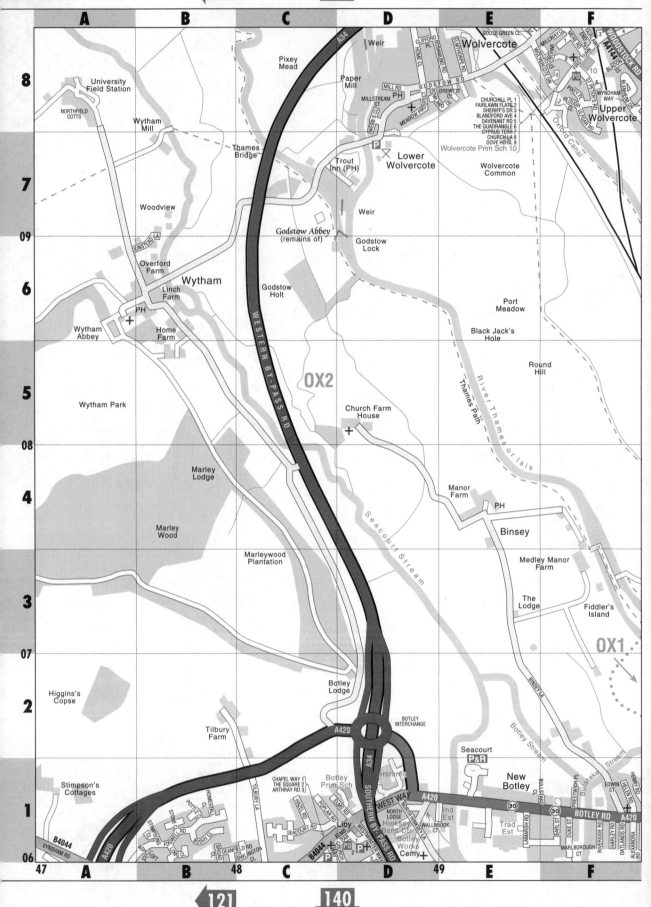

A **B** **C** **D** **E** **F**

8

University
Field Station

Weir

Pixey Mead

Paper Mill

Wolvercote

Goose Green Cl

Woodstock Rd

A44

Northfield Cotts

MILL RD

MEADOW PROSPECT

CHURCHILL PL 1
FAIRLAWN FLATS 2
SHERIFFS DR 3
BLANDFORD AVE 4
DAVENANT RD 5
THE QUADRANGLE 6
CYPRUS TERR 7
CHURCH LA 8
DOVE HO CL 9
Wolvercote Prim Sch 10

PO

PLOUGH

Upper Wolvercote

WYNDHAM WAY

Wytham Mill

Thames Bridge

7

Woodview

Dunstead La

Trout Inn (PH)

P

Lower Wolvercote

Wolvercote Common

Oxford Canal

09

Godstow Abbey
(remains of)

Godstow Lock

Overford Farm

Wytham

6

Linch Farm

Godstow Holt

Weir

PH

Home Farm

Port Meadow

Wytham Abbey

Black Jack's Hole

WESTERN BY-PASS RD

5

Wytham Park

OX2

Round Hill

Thames Path

River Thames or Isis

Church Farm House

08

Marley Lodge

Manor Farm

4

PH

Binsey

Marley Wood

Seacourt Stream

Medley Manor Farm

3

Marleywood Plantation

The Lodge

Fiddler's Island

OX1

07

Botley Lodge

BINSEY LA

2

Higgins's Copse

A420

Botley Interchange

A34

Botley Stream

Tilbury Farm

Seacourt P&R

Bulstake Stream

New Botley

SOUTHERN BY-PASS RD

Stimpson's Cottages

CHAPEL WAY 1
THE SQUARE 2
ARTHRAY RD 3

Botley Prim Sch

Superstores

WEST WAY

A420

30

30

BOTLEY RD

A420

1

B4044

A420

EYNSHAM RD

TILBURY LA

HAZEL RD

Liby

North Lodge

Hinksey Bsns Ctr
Botley Works
Cemy

Ind Est

Trad Est

MARLBOROUGH CT

RIVERSIDE RD

HARLEY RD

OATLANDS RD

ALEXANDRA

06

B4044

P

P

A **B** **C** **D** **E** **F**

47 48 49

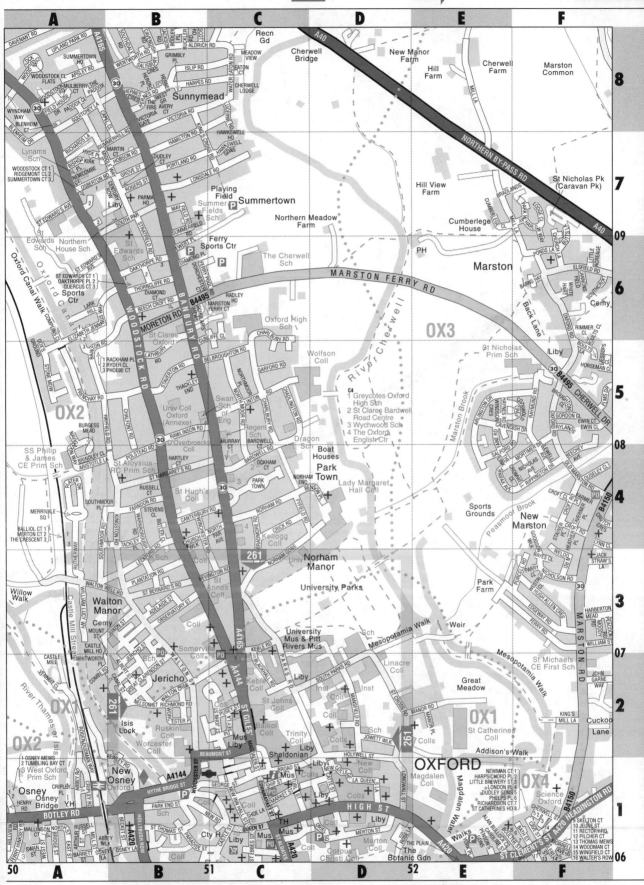

For full street detail of the highlighted area see page 261.

141 124

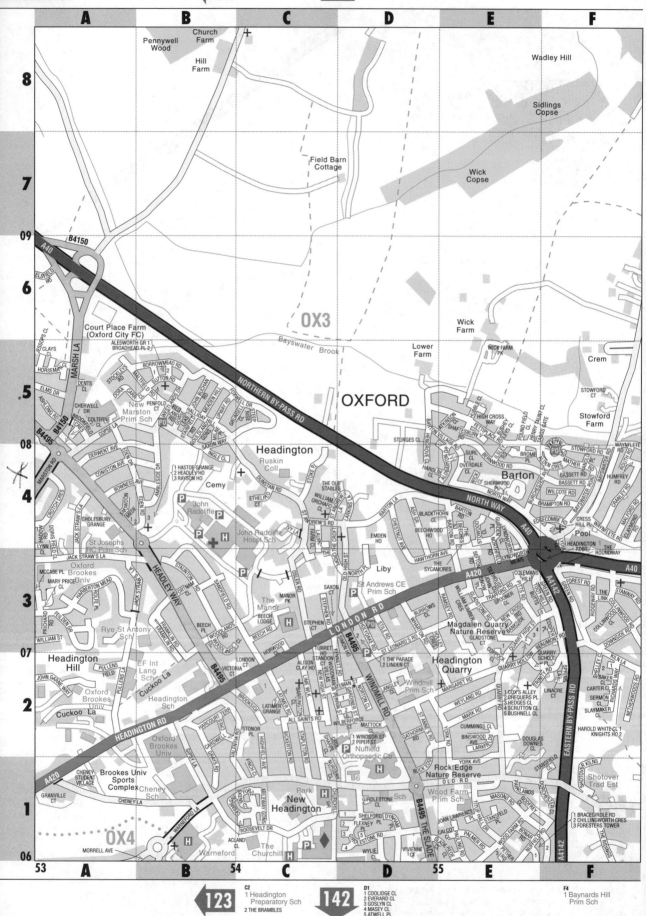

A   B   C   D   E   F

8

7

09

6

OX3

.5

OXFORD

08

Headington

B4495

08

4

1 HASTOE GRANGE
2 HEADLEY HO
3 RAYSON HO

Cemy

Ruskin Coll

Barton

John Radcliffe

John Radcliffe Hospl Sch

3

07

Headington
Hill

LONDON RD

Headington
Quarry

Magdalen Quarry
Nature Reserve

1 COX'S ALLEY
2 CHEQUERS PL
3 HEDGES CL
4 SCRUTTON CL
5 BUSHNELL CL

2

Oxford
Brookes
Univ

Cuckoo La

Headington
Sch

WINDMILL RD

1 THE PARADE
2 LINDEN CT

HEADINGTON RD

Oxford
Brookes
Univ

Nuffield
Orthopaedic Ctr

Rock Edge
Nature Reserve

Shotover
Trad Est

1 Cuckoo La

Brookes Univ
Sports
Complex

New
Headington

THE SLADE

1 BRACEGIRDLE RD
2 CHILLINGWORTH CRES
3 FORESTERS TOWER

1

OX4

The
Churchill

06

53   A   B   54   C   D   55   E   F

C2
1 Headington
Preparatory Sch
2 THE BRAMBLES

D1
1 COOLIDGE CL
2 EVERARD CL
3 GOSLYN CL
4 MASEY PL
5 ATWELL PL
6 Oxfordshire
Hospl Sch

F4
1 Baynards Hill
Prim Sch

125
112

A **B** **C** **D** **E** **F**

8

Moorbirge Brook

Wood Farm

Clearsale Hursthill

HP18

Waterperry Common

SMITHS LA

7

Bernwood Forest

Commonleys Farm

09

Waterperry Wood

6

Polecat End

Drunkard's Corner

Park Farm

Park Farm House

Oxfordshire Way

Parson's Farm

5

Polecat End Hollows

Marsh Copse

Ledall Cottage

08

Holton Wood

OX33

M40

4

Buryhook Barn

3

B4027

Keeper's Cottage

Warren Farm

Pond Farm

WHEATLEY RD

Warren Wood

Old Park Farm

Cottage Copse

Holton Brook

07

Lyehill Quarries (dis)

BURYHOOK CNR

2

A40

B4027

Warwick Close Farm

Wheatley Park Sch

The Rectory

Holton Place

Recn Gd

Holton

1

Wheatley

The Park Sports Ctr

BARNS CL

Church Farm

Garden Copse

06

WESTFIELD RD

PARK HILL

WESTFIELD RD

LONDON RD

A40

Brookes Univ (Wheatley Campus)

COLLEGE CL

M40

59 **A** **B** **60** **C** **D** **61** **E** **F**

125
144

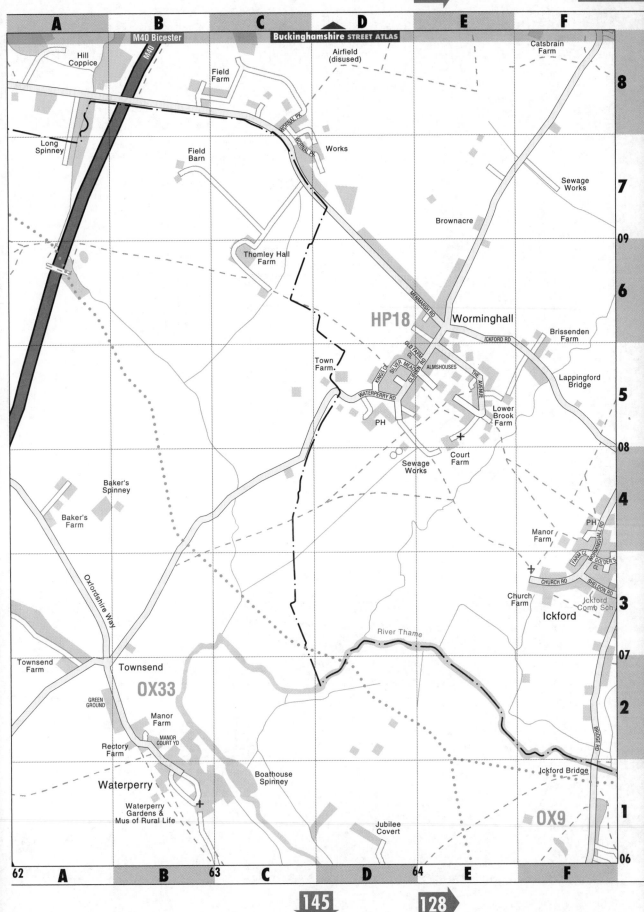

A B C D E F

Buckinghamshire STREET ATLAS

Hill Coppice

Field Farm

Catsbrain Farm

8

Long Spinney

Field Barn

Wornal Pk

Works

Sewage Works

7

Brownacre

09

Thomley Hall Farm

6

Menmarsh Rd

HP18

Worminghall

Ickford Rd

Brissenden Farm

Old Park Rd

Kings Cl

Silver Meadow

Cushens

Almshouses

The Avenue

Lappingford Bridge

Town Farm

Waterperry Rd

5

PH

Lower Brook Farm

08

Sewage Works

Court Farm

4

Baker's Spinney

Manor Farm

PH

Worminghall Rd

Golders Cl

Baker's Farm

Farm Cl

Church Rd

Sheldon Rd

Oxfordshire Way

Church Farm

Ickford Comb Sch

Ickford

3

River Thame

07

Townsend Farm

Townsend

2

OX33

Green Ground

Manor Farm

Manor Court Yd

Bridge Rd

Rectory Farm

Ickford Bridge

Waterperry

Boathouse Spinney

OX9

1

Waterperry Gardens & Mus of Rural Life

Jubilee Covert

06

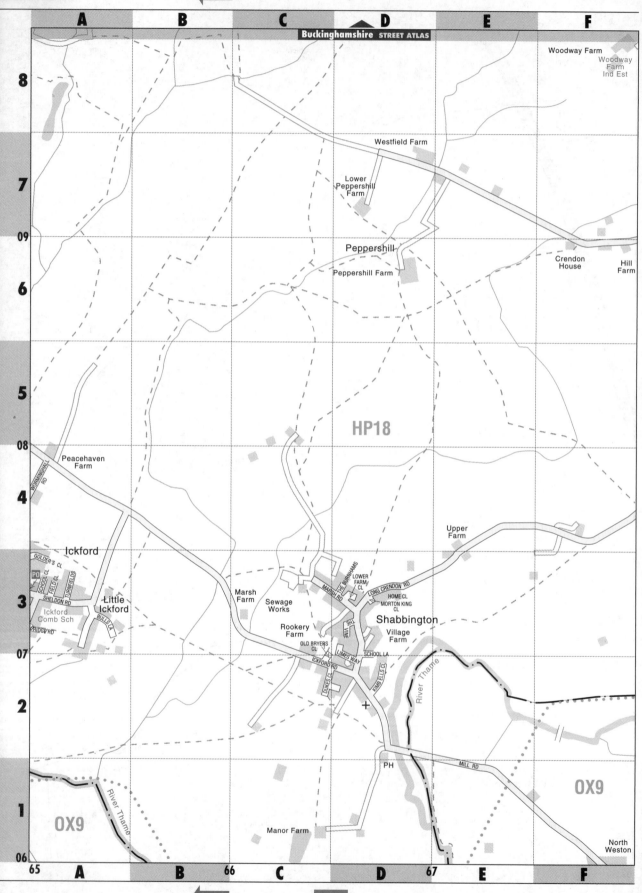

Buckinghamshire STREET ATLAS

Woodway Farm
Woodway Farm Ind Est

Westfield Farm

Lower Peppershill Farm

Peppershill

Crendon House

Hill Farm

Peppershill Farm

HP18

Peacehaven Farm

WORMINGHALL RD

Upper Farm

Ickford

GOLDER'S CL
SCHOOL CL
PO
FIELD CL
TURNFIELDS
SHELDON RD
Little Ickford
Ickford Comb Sch
BULLS LA
BRIDGE RD

Marsh Farm

Sewage Works

Rookery Farm

OLD BRYERS CL

ICKFORD RD

DUKES CL

LIMES WAY

MARSH RD

THE BURNHAMS

LOWER FARM CL

THE VINE

SCHOOL LA

KIME ELLS CL

LONG CRENDON RD

HOME CL

MORTON KING CL

Shabbington

Village Farm

River Thame

PH

MILL RD

OX9

OX9

River Thame

Manor Farm

North Weston

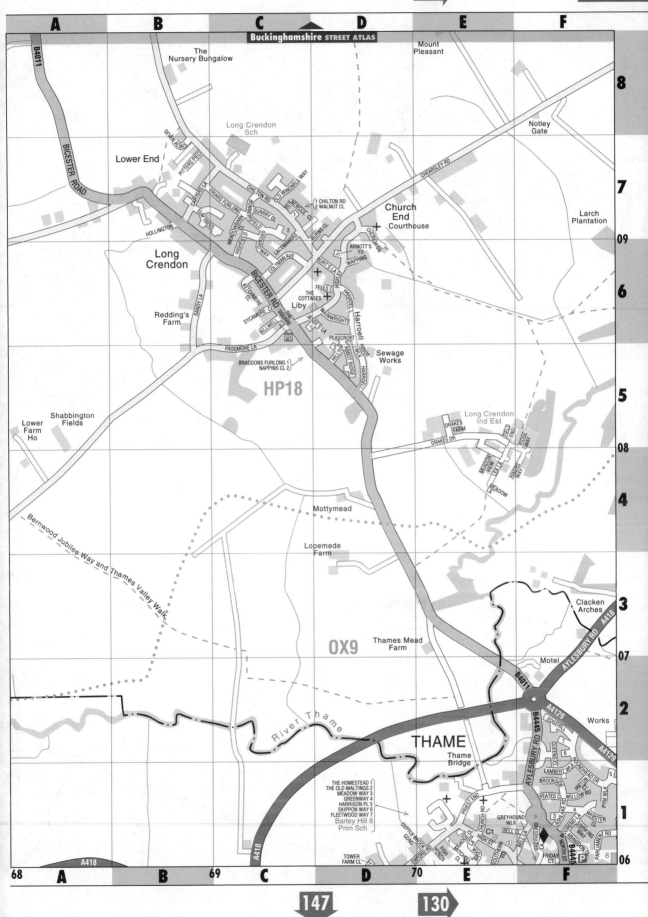

Buckinghamshire STREET ATLAS

A B C D E F

8

7

09

6

5

08

4

3

07

2

1

06

Mount Pleasant

Notley Gate

The Nursery Bungalow

Cheafsley Rd

Larch Plantation

Long Crendon Sch

Lower End

Church End
Courthouse

1 CHILTON RD
2 WALNUT CL

Long Crendon

Redding's Farm

Arnott's YD
WAPPING

FELLS CL

THE COTTAGES
Liby

PEASCROFT

Sewage Works

HP18

BRADDONS FURLONG 1
NAPPINS CL 2

Frogmore La

Lower Farm Ho

Shabbington Fields

Long Crendon Ind Est

DRAKES DR

FIELD END

RIDGE WAY

MEADOW VIEW

LEA LA

HIKERS WAY

MEADOW LA

Mottymead

Bernwood Jubilee Way and Thames Valley Walk

Lopemede Farm

OX9

Thames Mead Farm

Clacken Arches

Motel

Works

River Thame

THAME
Thame Bridge

AYLESBURY RD

A4129

B4011

EDGEHILL

QUEENS CL

ROUNDHEAD RD

BROOKSIDE

LAMBERT WY

IRETON CT

WILLOW RD

YEATES CL

PYM WLK

WEBSTER CL

MOORHEN

SIMMONS CL

ABINGDON CL

PARLIAMENT RD

THE HOMESTEAD 1
THE OLD MALTINGS 2
MEADOW WAY 3
GREENWAY 4
HARRISON PL 5
SKIPPON WAY 6
FLEETWOOD WAY 7
Barley Hill 8
Prim Sch

Greyhound WLK

BELL CL

Ct

HIGH ST

CUTTLE BROOK GDNS

FISH PONDS

MITCHELL CL

SOUTHERN RD

OXFORD RD

PRIEST END

CHURCH RD

NORTH ST

FRIDAY CT

TOWER FARM CL

A418

A418

B4011

68 A B 69 C D 70 E F

B4011
Bicester Road
CARTER LA
PITTERS PIECE
FRIARS FURLONG
ELM TREES
HOLLINGTON
SANDY LA
KETCHMORE CL
SYCAMORE CL
BILLWELL
MEADOWBANK
HIGHFIELD
GIFFARD WAY
LACEMAKERS
COLTMAN AVE
CHILTON RD
QUARRY CL
OLD WINDMILL WAY
BONNERSFIELD
CANEWODE CL
BURNS CL
BURT'S LA
HIGH ST
CHURCH RD
HARROELL
BURT'S LA
WAINWRIGHTS
JESSE'S LA
HILL
ABBOT RIDGE
HARROELL
Harroell
FROGMORE LA
THE SQUARE
PO
P

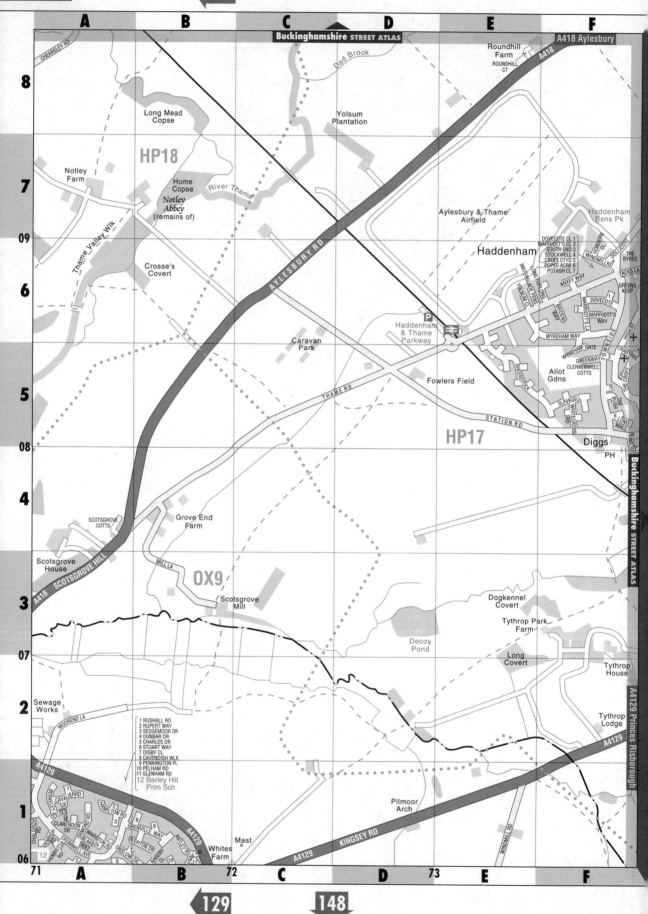

A   B   C   D   E   F

Buckinghamshire STREET ATLAS

8

CHEARSLEY RD

Long Mead
Copse

Yolsum
Plantation

Roundhill
Farm
ROUNDHILL
CT

A418

A418 Aylesbury

HP18

7

Notley
Farm

Home
Copse

*Notley
Abbey*
(remains of)

River Thame

Aylesbury & Thame
Airfield

Haddenham
Bsns Pk

09

Thame Valley Wlk

AYLESBURY RD

Haddenham

DOVECOTE CL 1
MARRIOTT'S CL 2
SOUTH END 3
STOCKWELL 4
CROFT CTYD 5
POPES ACRE 6
POTASH CL 7

6

Crosse's
Covert

WATERSIDE FERNS

LONG FURLONG

ANXEY WAY

MARRIOTT'S LA

DOVECOTE

2

MARRIOTT'S WAY

THE
BYRES

TACKS LA

GREENS
KEEP

Caravan
Park

Haddenham
& Thame
Parkway
P

WYKEHAM WAY

WYKEHAM GATE
GREENWAY
CLERKENWELL
COTTS

5

THAME RD

Fowlers Field

Allot
Gdns

SLAVEHILL

THE
BUSH

STATION RD

Diggs

SHERBOROCK

WHITECROSS
RD

LONG
WALL

HP17

PH

08

4

Scotsgrove
COTTS

Grove End
Farm

3

Scotsgrove
House

A418 SCOTSGROVE HILL

MILL LA

OX9

Scotsgrove
Mill

Dogkennel
Covert

Tythrop Park
Farm

07

Decoy
Pond

Long
Covert

Tythrop
House

2

Sewage
Works

MOOREND LA

1 RUSHALL RD
2 RUPERT WAY
3 SEDGEMOOR DR
4 DUNBAR DR
5 CHARLES DR
6 STUART WAY
7 DIGBY CL
8 CAVENDISH WLK
9 PENNINGTON PL
10 PELHAM RD
11 GLENHAM RD
12 Barley Hill
    Prim Sch

A4129

Tythrop
Lodge

A4129 Princes Risborough

A4129

Pilmoor
Arch

1

CHALGROVE RD

BERKELEY RD

CAVALIER RD

HAMILTON RD

GRENVILLE WAY

OVERTON DR

ASTLEY RD

Mast

Whites
Farm

KINGSEY RD

A4129

06

71   A   B   72   C   D   73   E   F

Buckinghamshire STREET ATLAS

113
132

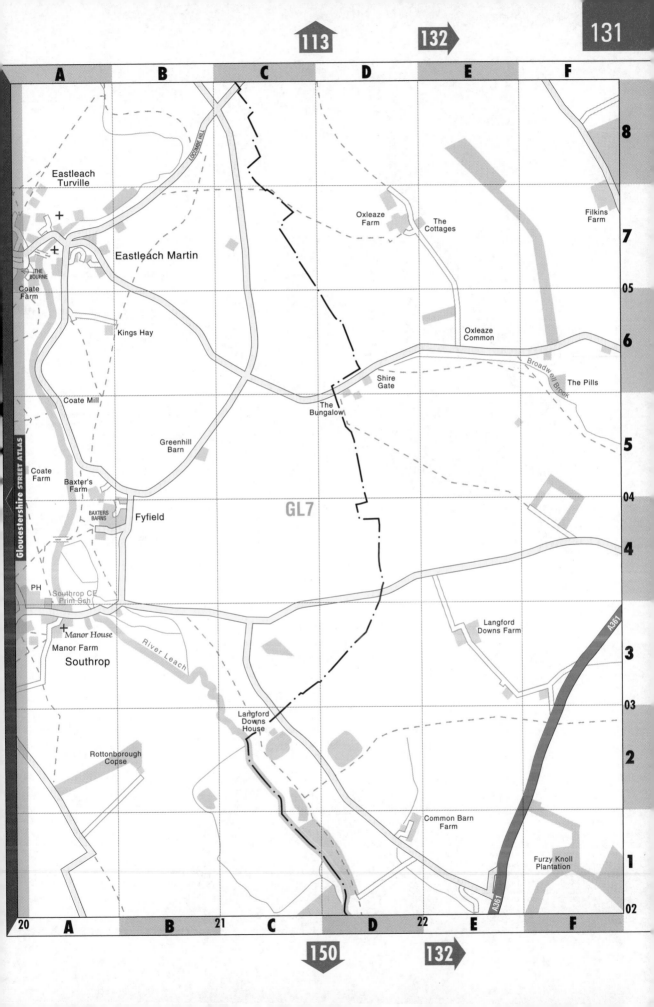

A B C D E F

8
7
05
6
5
04
4
3
03
2
1
02

Eastleach
Turville

Eastleach Martin

THE
BOURNE

Coate
Farm

Kings Hay

Coate Mill

Greenhill
Barn

Coate
Farm

Baxter's
Farm

BAXTERS
BARNS

Fyfield

PH

Southrop CE
Prim Sch

Manor House

Manor Farm

Southrop

River Leach

Rottonborough
Copse

Langford
Downs
House

The Bungalow

Shire
Gate

The Bungalow

GL7

Oxleaze
Farm

The Cottages

Oxleaze
Common

Broadwell Brook

Shire
Gate

Filkins
Farm

The Pills

Langford
Downs Farm

Common Barn
Farm

Furzy Knoll
Plantation

A361

Gloucestershire STREET ATLAS

LOCOMBE HILL

20 A B 21 C D 22 E F

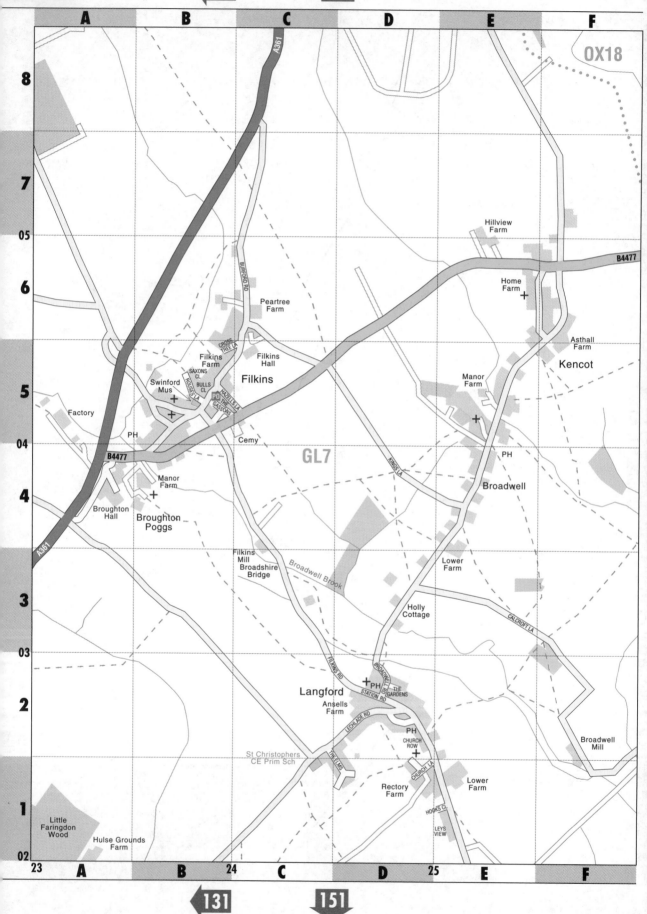

OX18

B4477

Hillview Farm

Home Farm

Asthall Farm

Kencot

Peartree Farm

BURFORD RD

Filkins Hall

Filkins Farm

Filkins

Swinford Mus

SAXONS CL

BULLS CL

ROUSES LA

PO

THE GASSONS

HAZELLS LA

Manor Farm

Factory

PH

Cemy

GL7

Broadwell

PH

KINGS LA

B4477

Manor Farm

Broughton Hall

Broughton Poggs

Filkins Mill

Broadshire Bridge

Broadwell Brook

Lower Farm

CALCROFT LA

A361

Holly Cottage

FILKINS RD

BROADWELL RD

THE GARDENS

Langford

Ansells Farm

STATION RD

PH

LECHLADE RD

PH

CHURCH ROW

Broadwell Mill

St Christophers CE Prim Sch

THE ELMS

CHURCH LA

Lower Farm

Little Faringdon Wood

Hulse Grounds Farm

Rectory Farm

HOOKS CL

LEYS VIEW

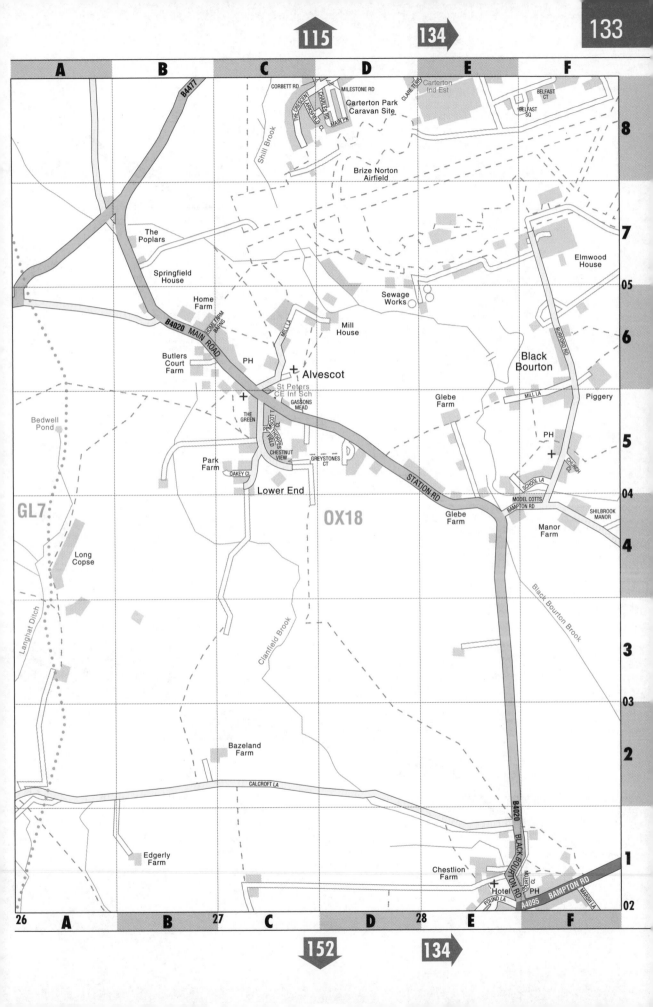

A B C D E F

8
7
05
6
5
04
4
3
03
2
1
02

CORBETT RD
THE CRESCENT
HARESFIELD
CHARLES RD
MAIN PK
MILESTONE RD
CLARE TERR
Carterton
Ind Est
Carterton Park
Caravan Site
BELFAST
CT
BELFAST
SQ
Shill Brook
Brize Norton
Airfield
The Poplars
Springfield
House
Home
Farm
HOME FARM BARNS
MILL LA
Mill
House
Sewage
Works
B4020 MAIN ROAD
Butlers
Court
Farm
PH
✛ Alvescot
St Peters
CE Inf Sch
GASSONS
MEAD
THE GREEN
ALVESCOT CL
THORPES FIELD
CHESTNUT
VIEW
GREYSTONES
CT
Park
Farm
OAKEY CL
Lower End
P
Glebe
Farm
STATION RD
Glebe
Farm
Black
Bourton
Elmwood
House
BURFORD RD
MILL LA
Piggery
PH
✛
CHURCH
CL
SCHOOL LA
MODEL COTTS
BAMPTON RD
SHILBROOK
MANOR
Manor
Farm
Bedwell
Pond
GL7
OX18
Long
Copse
Langhat Ditch
Clanfield Brook
Black Bourton Brook
Bazeland
Farm
CALCROFT LA
B4020
Edgerly
Farm
Chestlion
Farm
BLACK BOURTON RD
NORTH CL
PH
ROUND LA
Hotel
✛
A4095
BAMPTON RD
MARSH LA

26 A B 27 C D 28 E F 02

A B C D E F

8

7

05

6

5

04

4

3

03

2

1

02

Brize Norton Airfield

Lower Haddon Farm

STATION RD

Viscount Ind Est

Ven Bridge

Piggery

Lew Heath House

A4095

Deanery Farm

Hobbs Buildings

Garson's Copse

Mill Farm

The Plantation

OX18

Highmoor Brook

The Windmill

Bampton

Bampton CE Prim Sch

Field Cottage

Shill Brook

Cemy

MANOR VIEW

COLWELL

COLVILE

PEMBROKE PL

NEW RD

GREEN CL

GREEN RD

POLLARD

FOX CL

SOUTHBY

LANDELLS

GLEBELANDS

CHURCH VIEW

WINDSOR COTTS 1
VICTORIA COTTS 2
BELL LA 3
LAVENDER SQ 4

THE LANES

BUSSEY RD

LAVENDER

QUEEN ST

THE PIECES

POCOCK

MERCURY CT

CALAIS

CHENE

Liby

BROAD ST

CHEAPSIDE

DARTHURST EST

Ham Court

BOURTON COTTS

CHURCH ST

T H

SHREWSBURY

ROSEMARY LA

P

HIGH ST

ASTON RD

PH

B4449

MERCURY CL

PO

MARKET SQ

MOONRAKER LA

PH

ALBION PL

CLANFIELD RD

BRIDGE ST

CHEVY LA

The Grange

BUCKLAND RD

Shill Brook

COWLEAZE CNR

Weald Manor

BARN END

MILL GREEN CL

MILL ST

ST MARY'S CT

PRIMROSE LA

Weald Manor Farm

Backhouse Farm

THE PADDOCKS

Weald Farm

Weald

Masts

A4095

Black Bourton Brook

Glebe Farm

Masts

29 A B 30 C D 31 E F

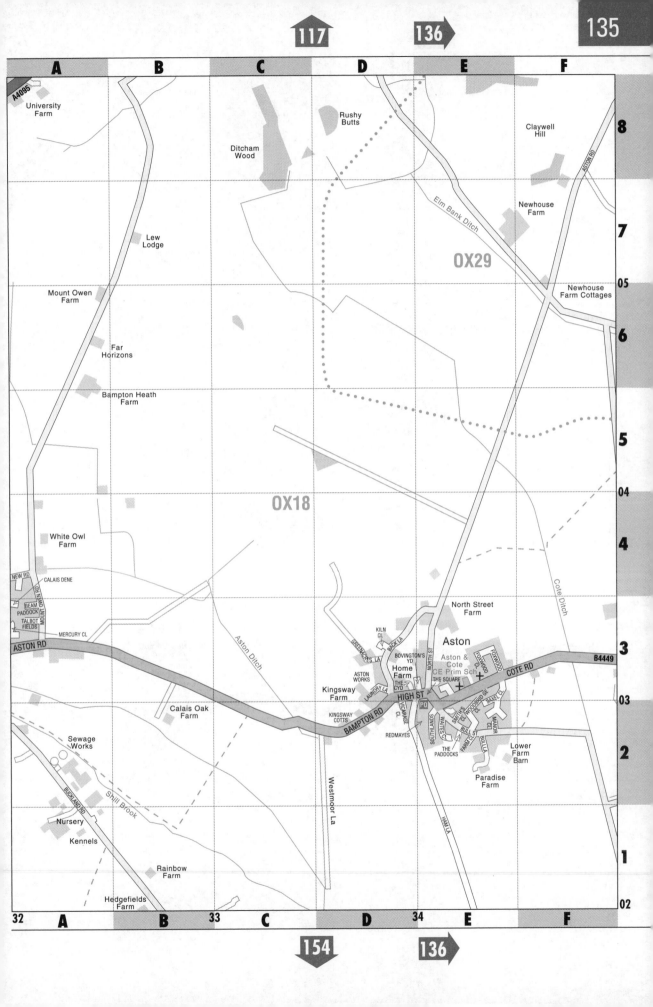

A B C D E F

8

A4095

University
Farm

Rushy
Butts

Claywell
Hill

Ditcham
Wood

Elm Bank Ditch

Newhouse
Farm

OX29

7

Lew
Lodge

ASTON RD

05

Mount Owen
Farm

Newhouse
Farm Cottages

6

Far
Horizons

Bampton Heath
Farm

5

OX18

04

4

White Owl
Farm

Cote Ditch

North Street
Farm

NEW RD

CALAIS DENE

BEAM
PADDOCK
TALBOT
FIELDS

MERCURY CL

KILN
CL

GREENACRES LA

BACK LA

Aston

North St

FOXWOOD

FOXWOOD CL

Aston &
Cote
CE Prim Sch

3

ASTON RD

Aston Ditch

BOVINGTON'S
YD

THE
CYD

Home
Farm

Kingsway
Farm

ASTON
WORKS

LAUNDRY LA

THE SQUARE

COTE RD

B4449

03

Calais Oak
Farm

KINGSWAY
COTTS

HIGH ST

PO

VICARAGE
CL

SOUTHLANDS

WAITES

SMITH'S
CL

WOODBRD CL

BULL ST

PARRY CL

MANOR CL

SAXEL CL

BULLA

BAMPTON RD

REDMAYES

Sewage
Works

THE
PADDOCKS

Lower
Farm
Barn

2

BUCKLAND RD

Shill Brook

Westmoor La

HAM LA

Paradise
Farm

Nursery

Kennels

1

Rainbow
Farm

02

Hedgefields
Farm

A B C D E F

8

Boys Wood

Long Train

Cokethorpe Park

Home Wood

A415

B4449
FAIRFIELD

Hardwick

STANDLAKE RD

A415

7

Claywell Farm

Rickless Hill

Breach Farm
Cottage

05

Manor Farm

Westfield
Farm

Hawthorn
Farm

6

Yelford

College
Farm

CALAIS LA

OX29

5

04

4

Brighthampton Cut

Cote Lodge
Farm

3

New Shifford
Farm

B4449

Green
Acres

New Shifford
Cottages

ASTON RD

03

B4449

Cote

OX18

South Farm

2

Chicken
Hatchery

New
Cottages

1

Cote
Bungalow

Cote House

Cote House
Farm

02

Shifford

35 A B 36 C D 37 E F

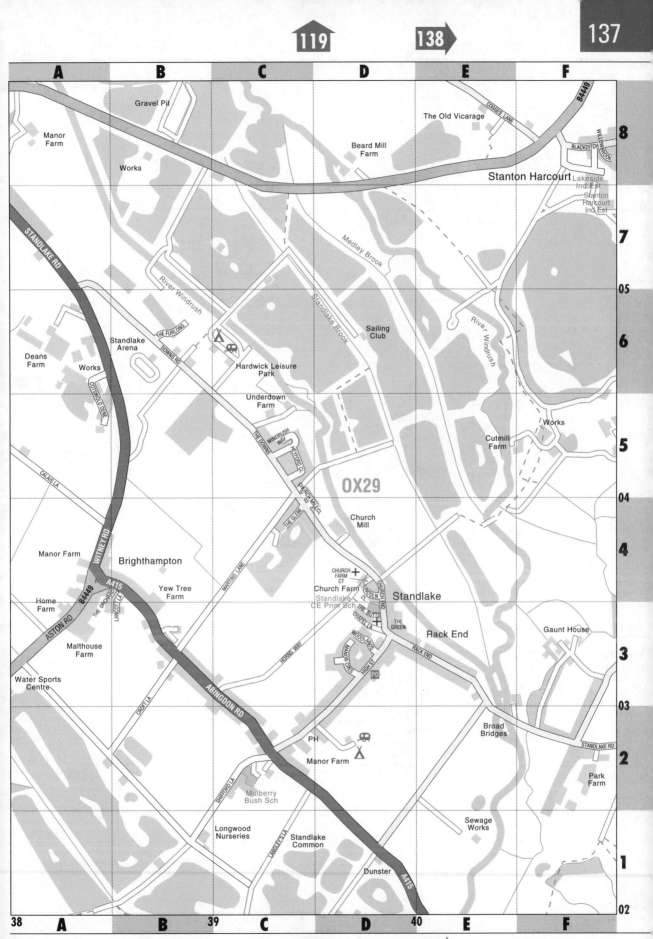

119
138

A B C D E F

8

Manor
Farm

Gravel Pit

Works

The Old Vicarage

COGGES LANE

B4449

Beard Mill
Farm

WILLOWBROOK

BLACKDITCH

Stanton Harcourt

Lakeside
Ind Est

Stanton
Harcourt
Ind Est

7

STANDLAKE RD

Medley Brook

River Windrush

Standlake Brook

05

6

THE FURLONG

DOWNS RD

Standlake
Arena

Hardwick Leisure
Park

Sailing
Club

River Windrush

Deans
Farm

Works

COTSWOLD DENE

Underdown
Farm

WINDRUSH WAY

THE DOWNS

PEYFORD CL

Works

Cutmill
Farm

5

OX29

CHURCH MILL CL

THE GLEBE

Church
Mill

04

CALAIS LA

Church
Farm

04

4

Manor Farm

WITNEY RD

Brighthampton

MARTINS LANE

CHURCH FARM CT

LINCOLN CL

CHURCH END

Standlake

Gaunt House

B4449

A415

ASTON RD

THE ORCHARD

LANCOTT LA

Yew Tree
Farm

Standlake
CE Prim Sch

Church Farm

THE BUTTS

CHAPEL LA

THE GREEN

Rack End

RACK END

Home
Farm

Malthouse
Farm

WOODLANDS

MANOR CRES

HIGH ST

PO

3

Water Sports
Centre

CROFT LA

ABINGDON RD

HORNS WAY

Broad
Bridges

STANDLAKE RD

03

PH

Manor Farm

Park
Farm

2

SHIFFORD LA

LANGLEYS LA

Mulberry
Bush Sch

Sewage
Works

Longwood
Nurseries

Standlake
Common

A415

Dunster

1

02

38 A B 39 C D 40 E F

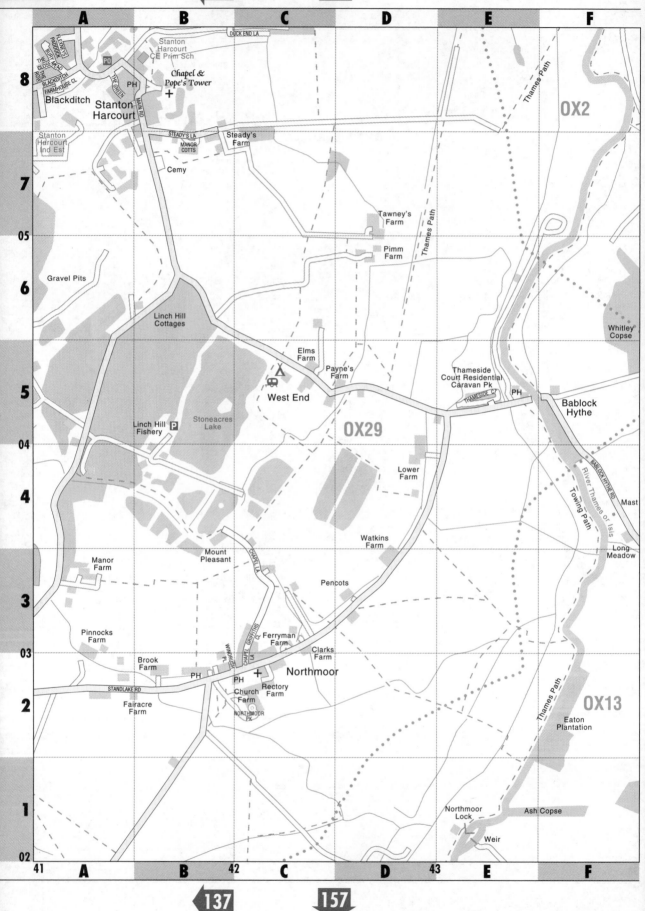

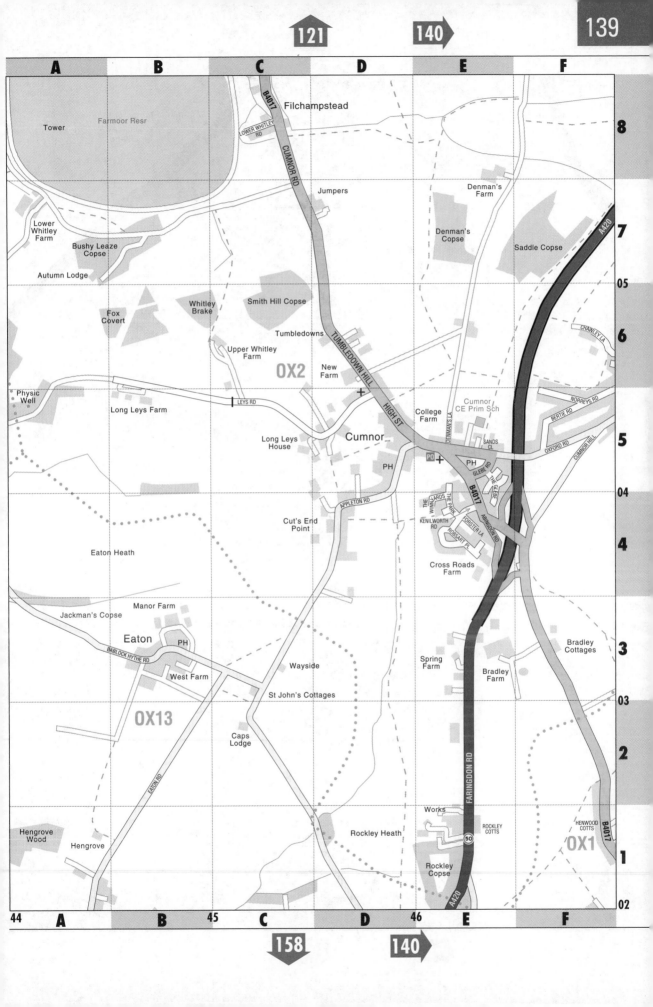

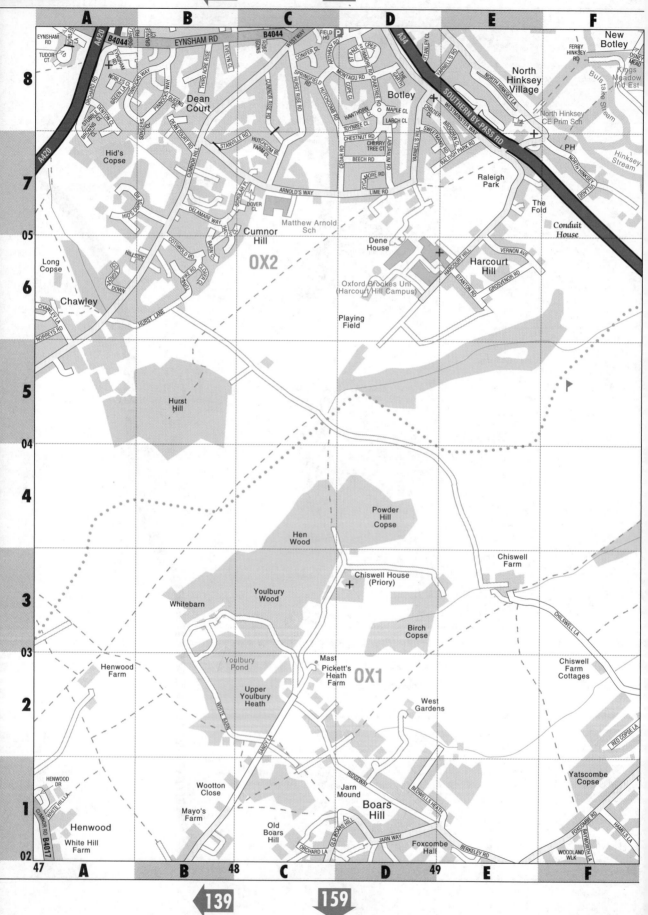

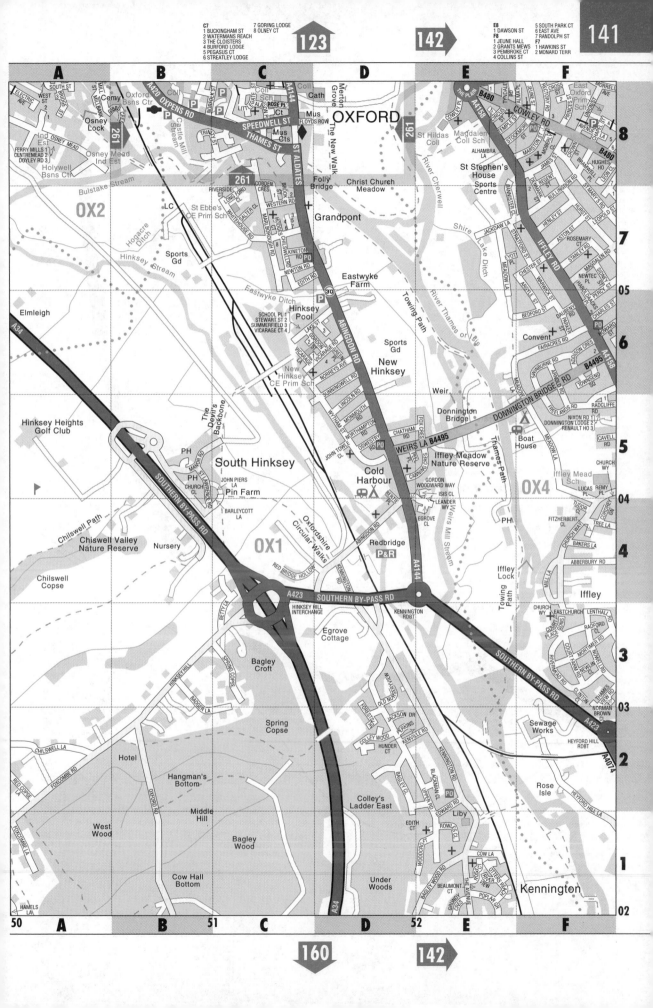

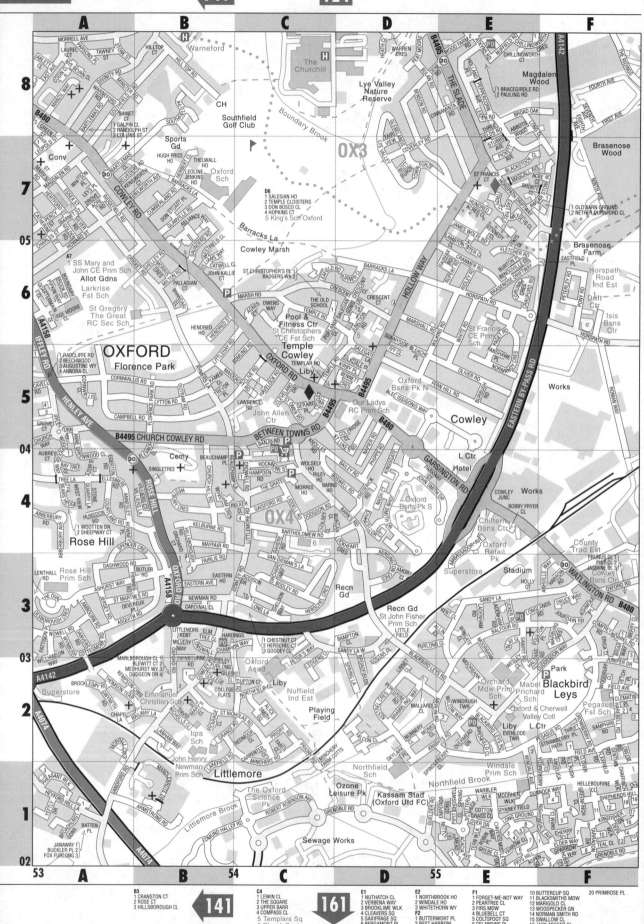

B3
1 CRANSTON CT
2 ROSE CT
3 HILLSBOROUGH CL

C4
1 LEWIN CL
2 THE SQUARE
3 UPPER BARR
4 COMPASS CL
5 SAXIFRAGE SQ
6 Church Cowley
St James Prim Sch
7 POUND WAY

E1
1 NUTHATCH CL
2 VERBENA WAY
3 BROOKLIME WLK
4 CLEAVERS SQ
5 BERGAMONT PL
6 FOXGLOVE CL
7 CRANESBILL WAY

D2
1 NORTHBROOK HO
2 WINDALE HO
3 WHITETHORN WY

F2
1 BUTTERWORT PL
2 REST HARROW
3 PERIWINKLE PL
4 STARWORT PATH
5 TIMOTHY WAY

F1
1 FORGET-ME-NOT WAY
2 PEARTREE CL
3 FIRS MDW
4 BLUEBELL CT
5 COLTSFOOT SQ
6 CELANDINE PL
7 SAGE WLK
8 POCHARD PL
9 CORIANDER WAY

10 BUTTERCUP SQ
11 BLACKSMITHS MDW
12 MARIGOLD CL
13 WOODPECKER GN
14 NORMAN SMITH RD
15 SWALLOW CL
16 JACK ARGENT CL
17 MOLE PL
18 CAMPION CL
19 SWIFT CL

20 PRIMROSE PL

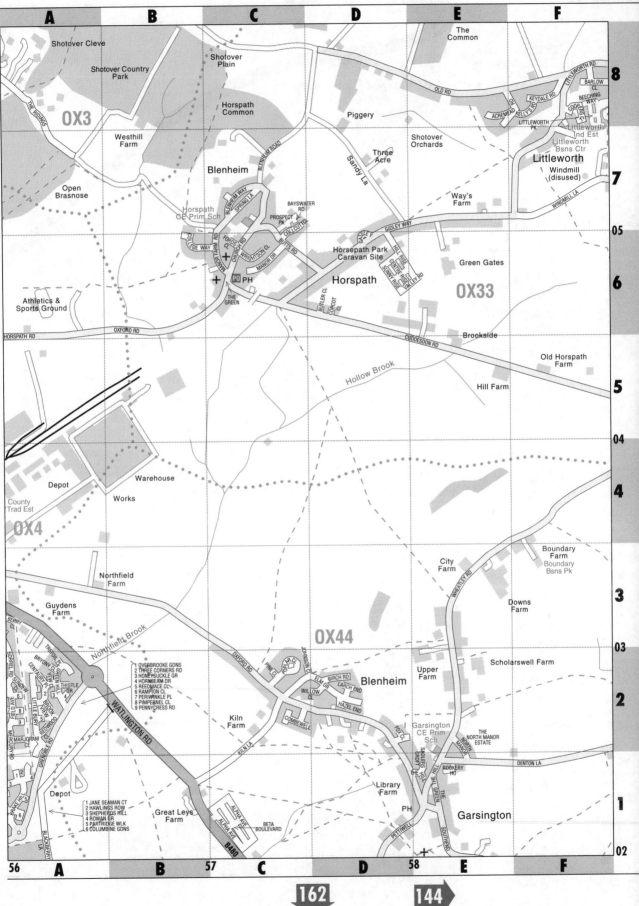

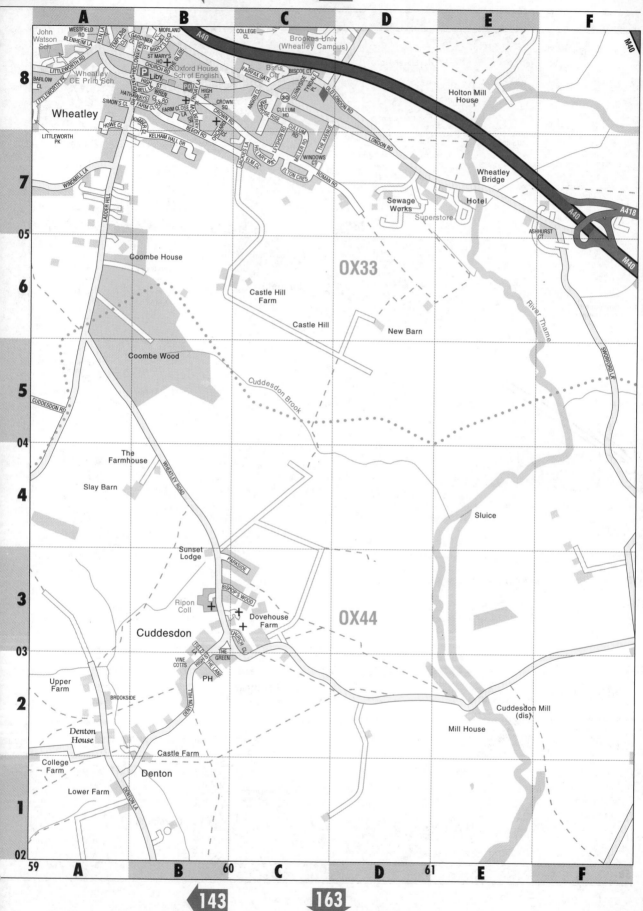

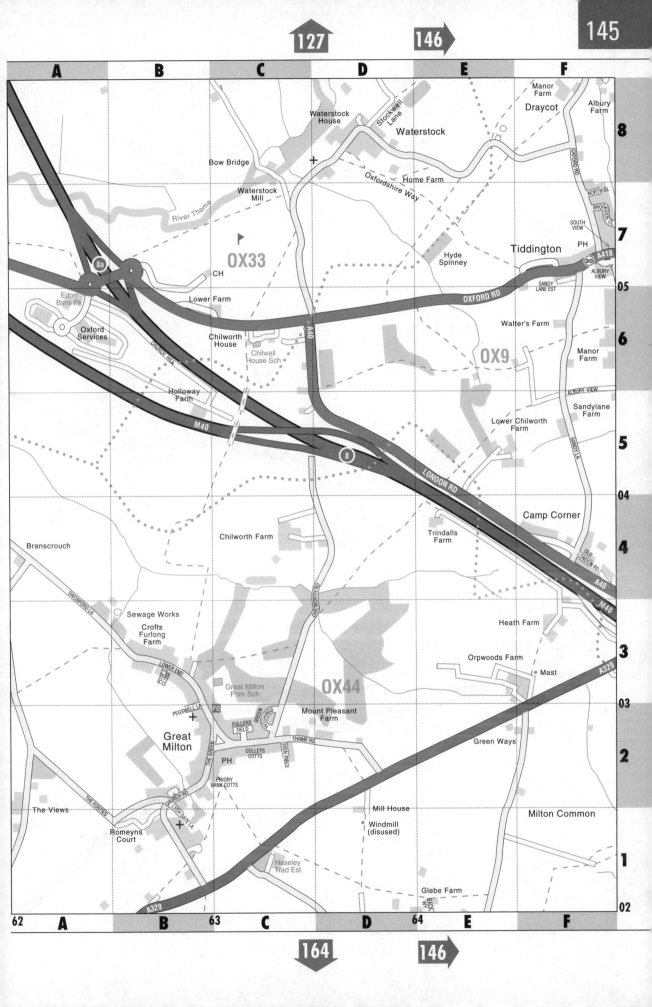

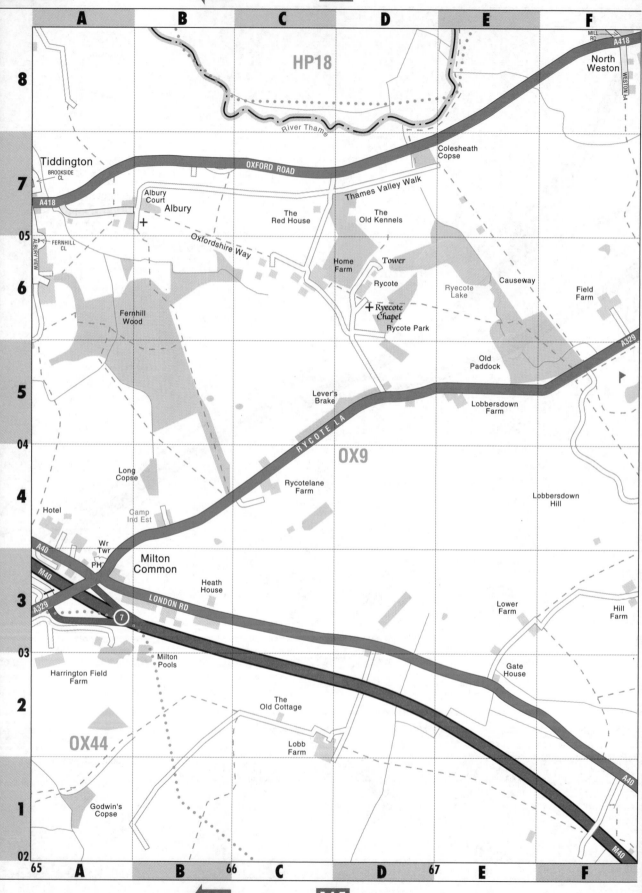

145
128

HP18

North Weston

MILL RD
A418

WESTON LA

Coleshealth Copse

OXFORD ROAD

Tiddington

BROOKSIDE CL

A418

Albury Court
Albury

Thames Valley Walk

The Red House

The Old Kennels

Oxfordshire Way

FERNHILL CL

ALBURY VIEW

Tower

Home Farm

Rycote

Rycote Chapel

Rycote Park

Ryecote Lake

Causeway

Field Farm

A329

Fernhill Wood

Old Paddock

Lever's Brake

Lobbersdown Farm

RYCOTE LA

OX9

Long Copse

Rycotelane Farm

Lobbersdown Hill

Hotel

Camp Ind Est

A40

Wr Twr

M40

PH

Milton Common

Heath House

LONDON RD

A329

7

Milton Pools

Harrington Field Farm

The Old Cottage

Lower Farm

Hill Farm

Gate House

OX44

Lobb Farm

A40

Godwin's Copse

M40

145
165

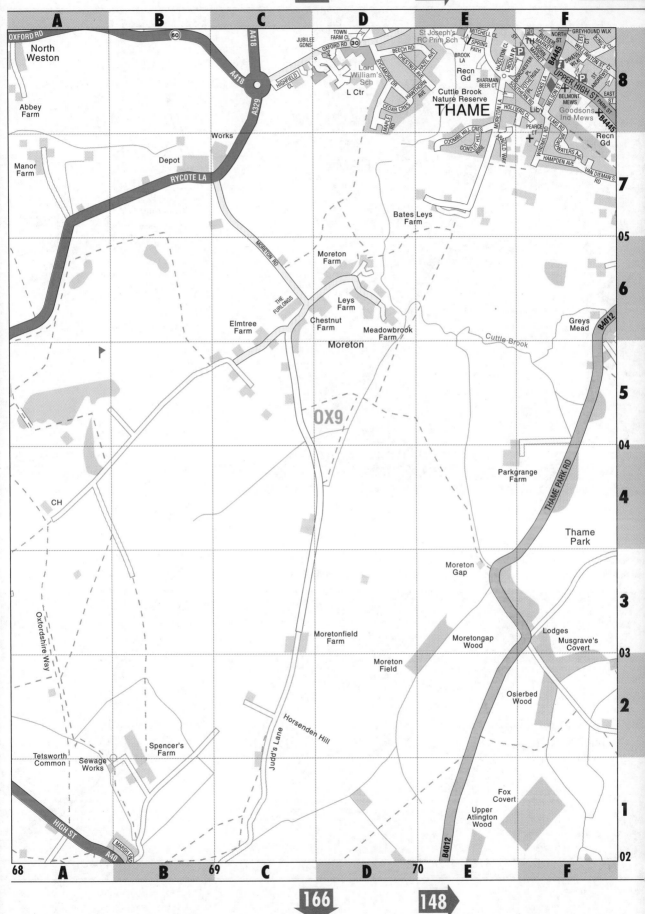

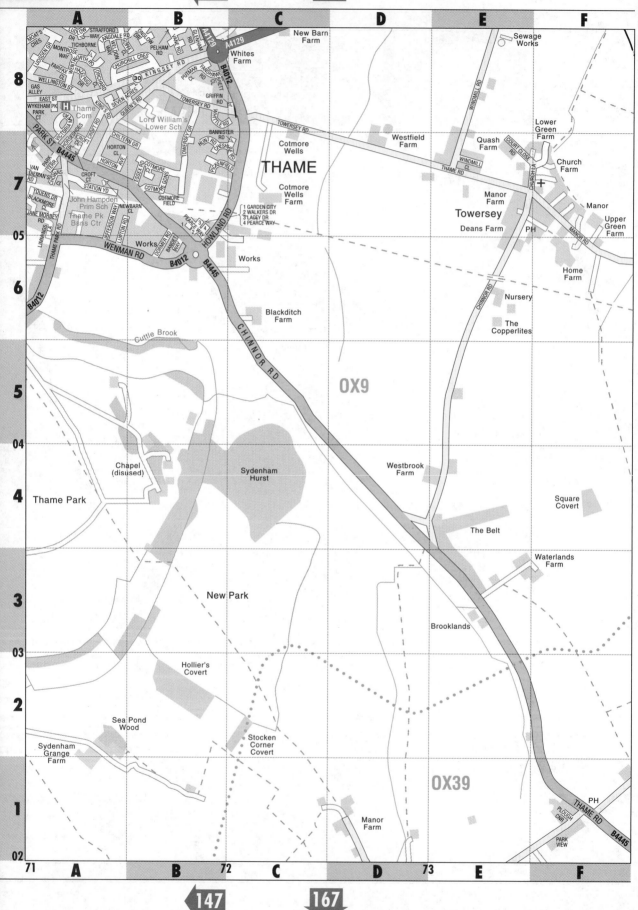

THAME

Cotmore Wells

Cotmore Wells Farm

1 GARDEN CITY
2 WALKERS DR
3 LAGEY DR
4 PEARCE WAY

New Barn Farm

Whites Farm

Westfield Farm

Sewage Works

Lower Green Farm

Church Farm

Manor

Quash Farm

Towersey

Deans Farm

PH

Upper Green Farm

Home Farm

Nursery

The Copperlites

Blackditch Farm

Guttle Brook

OX9

Chapel (disused)

Sydenham Hurst

Thame Park

Westbrook Farm

Square Covert

The Belt

Waterlands Farm

New Park

Brooklands

Hollier's Covert

Sea Pond Wood

Stocken Corner Covert

Sydenham Grange Farm

Manor Farm

OX39

Thame Rd PH
PLOUGH CNR

PARK VIEW

B4445

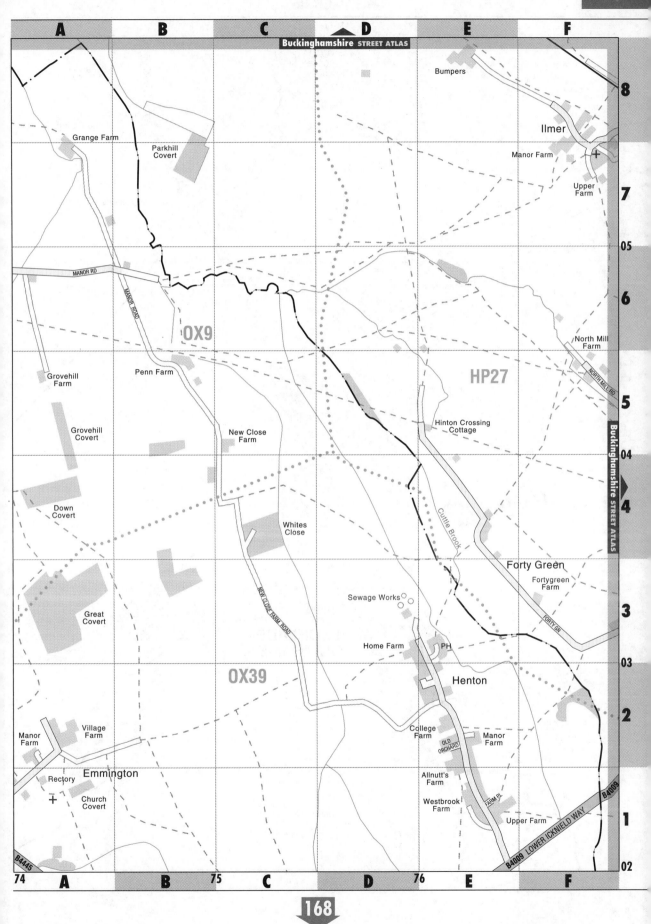

Bumpers

Ilmer

Manor Farm

Upper Farm

Grange Farm

Parkhill Covert

MANOR RD

MANOR ROAD

OX9

North Mill Farm

NORTH MILL RD

Penn Farm

HP27

Grovehill Farm

Grovehill Covert

New Close Farm

Hinton Crossing Cottage

Down Covert

Whites Close

Cuttle Brook

Forty Green

Fortygreen Farm

Great Covert

NEW CLOSE FARM ROAD

Sewage Works

FORTY GN

OX39

Home Farm

PH

Henton

Manor Farm

Village Farm

College Farm

OLD ORCHARD

Manor Farm

Rectory

Emmington

Church Covert

Allnutt's Farm

FARM PL

Westbrook Farm

Upper Farm

B4009

B4009 LOWER ICKNIELD WAY

B4445

74 75 76

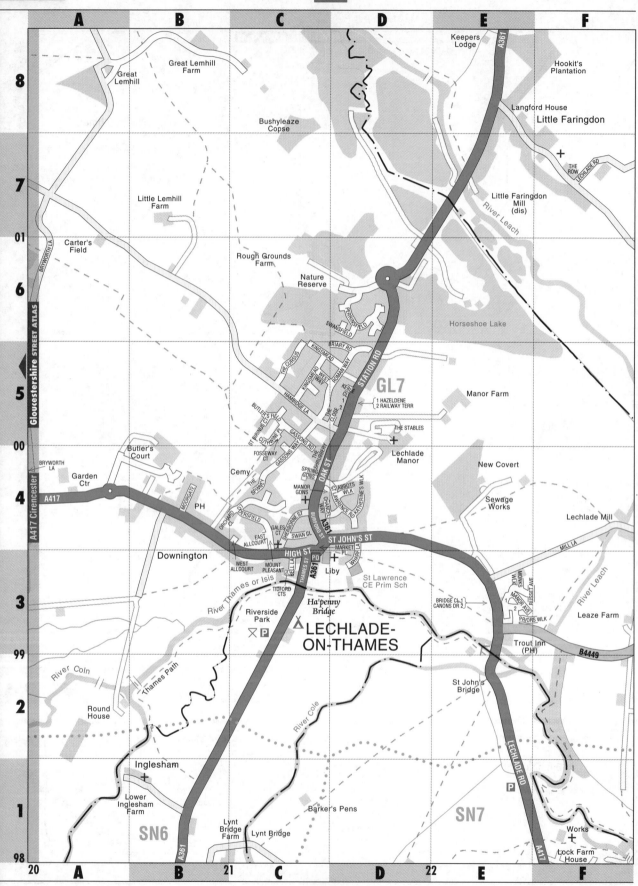

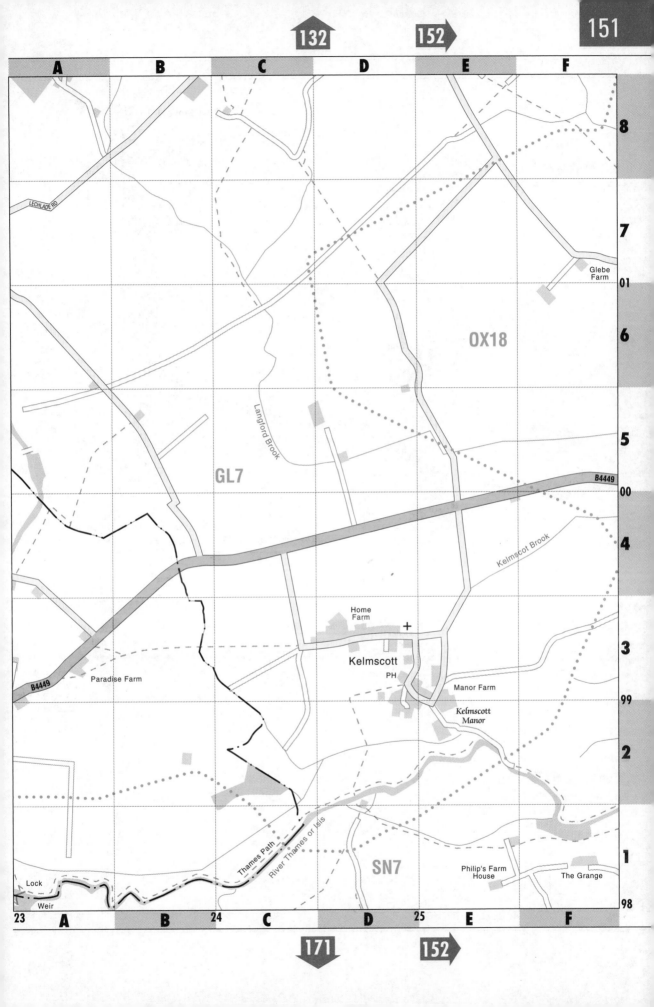

132
152

A   B   C   D   E   F

8

7

01

6

Glebe
Farm

OX18

5

Langford Brook

GL7

B4449

00

4

Kelmscot Brook

Home
Farm

+

Kelmscott

3

PH

Paradise Farm

B4449

Manor Farm

99

Kelmscott
Manor

2

Thames Path

River Thames or Isis

SN7

1

Philip's Farm
House

The Grange

Lock

Weir

98

23   A   B   24   C   D   25   E   F

171
152

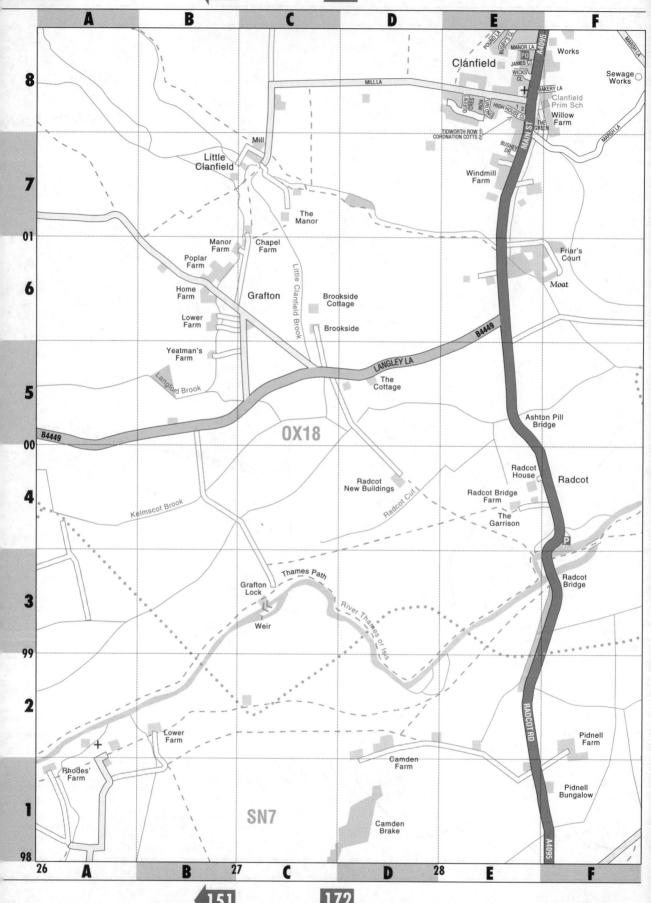

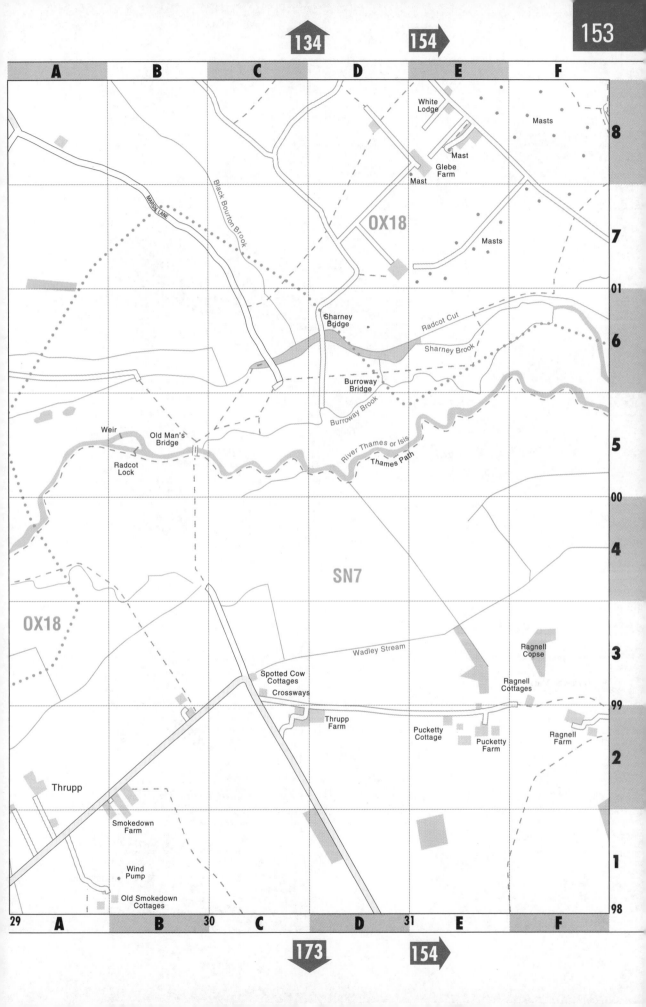

OX18

White
Lodge

Masts

Mast
Glebe
Farm
Mast

Masts

MARSH LANE

Black Bourton Brook

Sharney
Bridge

Radcot Cut

Sharney Brook

Burroway
Bridge

Burroway Brook

River Thames or Isis

Weir

Old Man's
Bridge

Thames Path

Radcot
Lock

SN7

OX18

Wadley Stream

Ragnell
Copse

Spotted Cow
Cottages

Crossways

Ragnell
Cottages

Thrupp
Farm

Pucketty
Cottage

Pucketty
Farm

Ragnell
Farm

Thrupp

Smokedown
Farm

Wind
Pump

Old Smokedown
Cottages

153
135

A **B** **C** **D** **E** **F**

8

Meadow
Arch Bridge

Meadow Farm
Cottages

Shill Brook

HAM LA

Meadow Brook

BUCKLAND RD

OX18

7

Meadow
Farm

Great Brook

01

Hoskins
Barn

Isle of Wight
Bridge

6

Tadpole
Bridge

Thames Path

PH

Tadpole

5

Rushey
Lock

River Thames or Isis

Weir

00

4

Buckland
Marsh

Buckland Marsh
Farm

SN7

3

Carswell Marsh

Gore Farm

99

2

Vicar's
Copse

Marriage
Hill

The
Lakes

Weir

Deer Park

Manor
House

Sewage
Works

CARSWELL LA

Middle
Brake

Rivey
Brake

Buckland
House

Buckland

1

Rivey
Copse

Arch
Plantation

BUCKLAND RD

ORCHARD RD

98

ST GEORGE'S RD

32   **A**   **B**   33   **C**   **D**   34   **E**   **F**

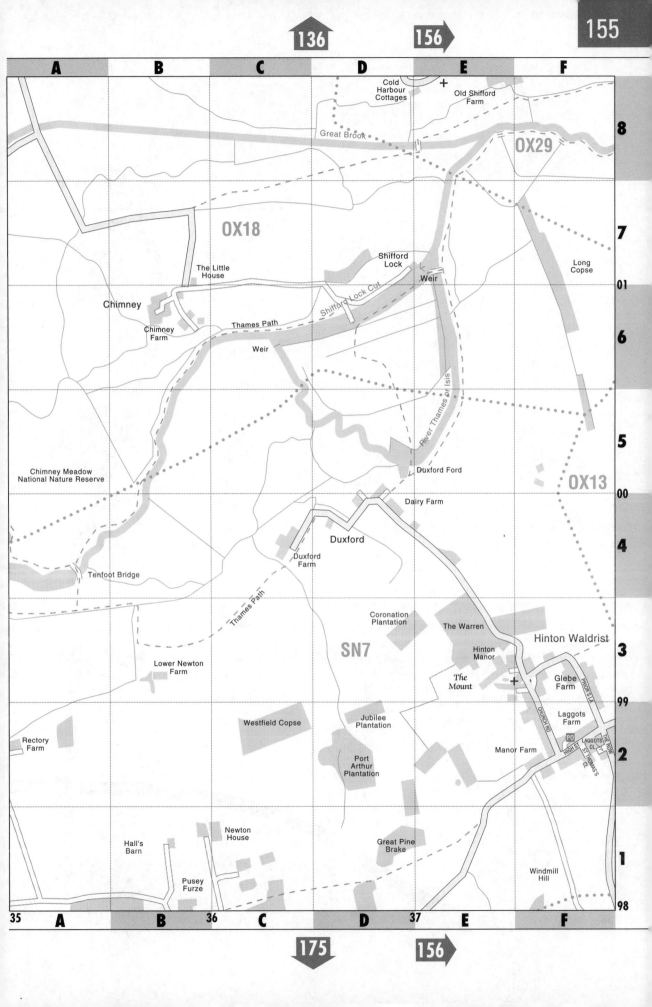

A B C D E F

Cold
Harbour
Cottages

Old Shifford
Farm

Great Brook

OX29

8

OX18

7

The Little
House

Shifford
Lock

Long
Copse

01

Chimney

Weir

Shifford Lock Cut

Chimney
Farm

Thames Path

6

Weir

River Thames or Isis

Duxford Ford

5

Chimney Meadow
National Nature Reserve

Dairy Farm

OX13

00

Duxford

4

Duxford
Farm

Tenfoot Bridge

Thames Path

Coronation
Plantation

The Warren

Hinton Waldrist

SN7

Hinton
Manor

3

Lower Newton
Farm

The
Mount

Glebe
Farm

PRIOR'S LA

99

Westfield Copse

Jubilee
Plantation

Laggots
Farm

Rectory
Farm

PO

LAGGOTS
CL

THE ROW

Manor Farm

HIGH ST

ST THOMAS'S
CL

2

Port
Arthur
Plantation

CHURCH RD

Hall's
Barn

Newton
House

Great Pine
Brake

1

Pusey
Furze

Windmill
Hill

98

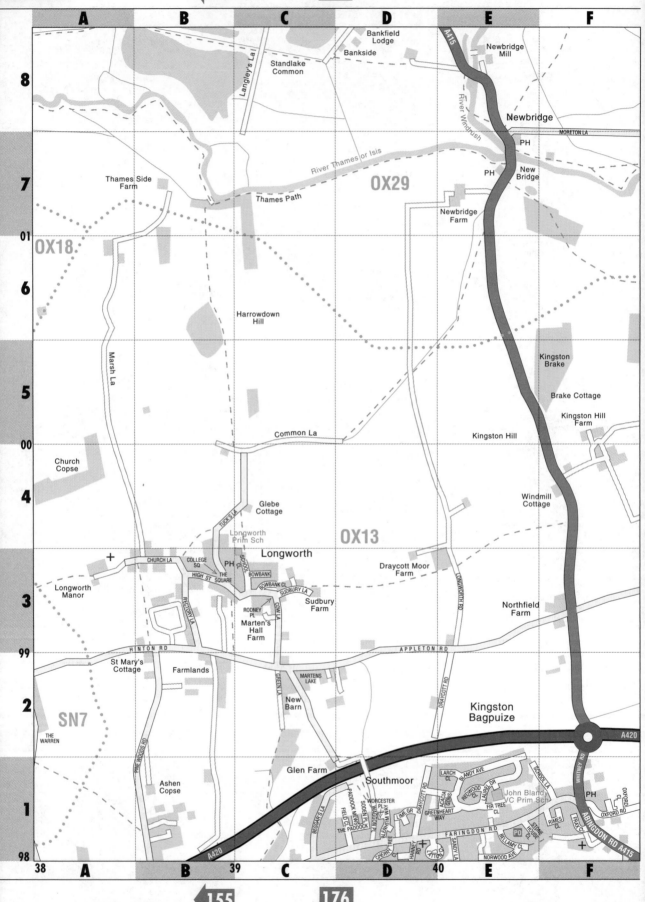

A B C D E F

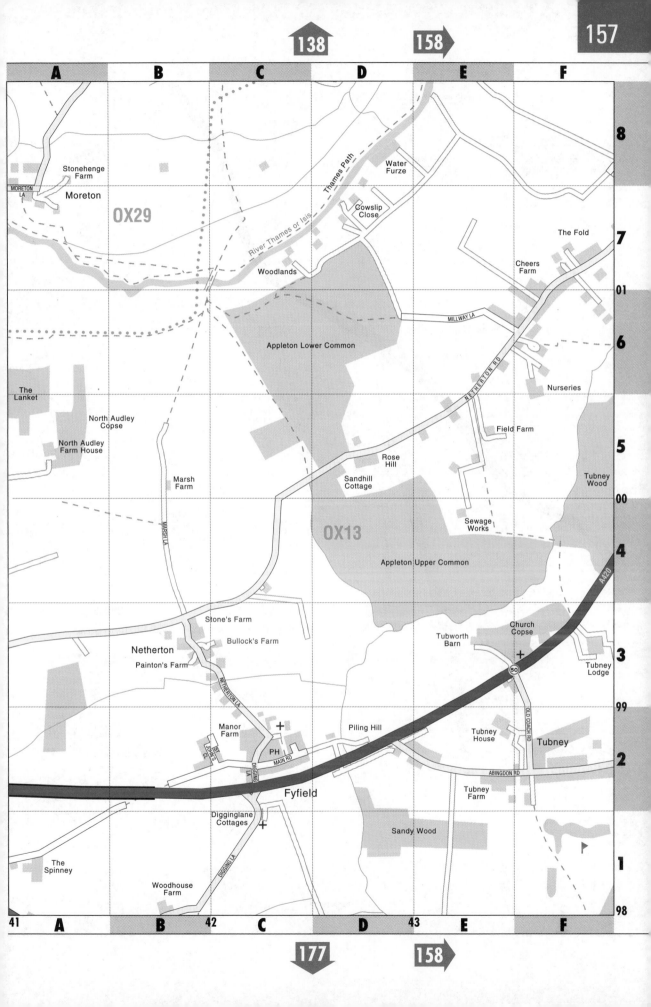

Stonehenge Farm

MORETON LA

Moreton

OX29

Thames Path

Water Furze

River Thames or Isis

Cowslip Close

The Fold

Woodlands

Cheers Farm

MILLWAY LA

Nurseries

Appleton Lower Common

The Lanket

NETHERTON RD

North Audley Copse

Field Farm

North Audley Farm House

Rose Hill

Tubney Wood

Marsh Farm

Sandhill Cottage

MARSH LA

OX13

Sewage Works

Appleton Upper Common

A420

Stone's Farm

Church Copse

Tubworth Barn

Bullock's Farm

Netherton

50

Tubney Lodge

Painton's Farm

NETHERTON LA

Manor Farm

Piling Hill

Tubney House

Tubney

OLD COACH RD

ST JOHN'S CL

PH

DIGGING LA

MAIN RD

ABINGDON RD

Fyfield

Tubney Farm

Digginglane Cottages

Sandy Wood

The Spinney

DIGGING LA

Woodhouse Farm

157
139

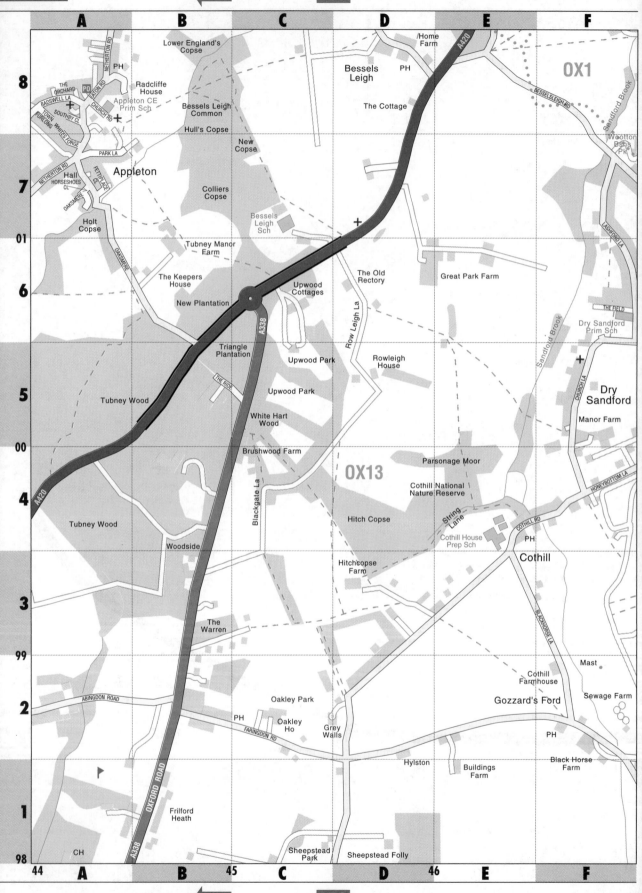

157
178

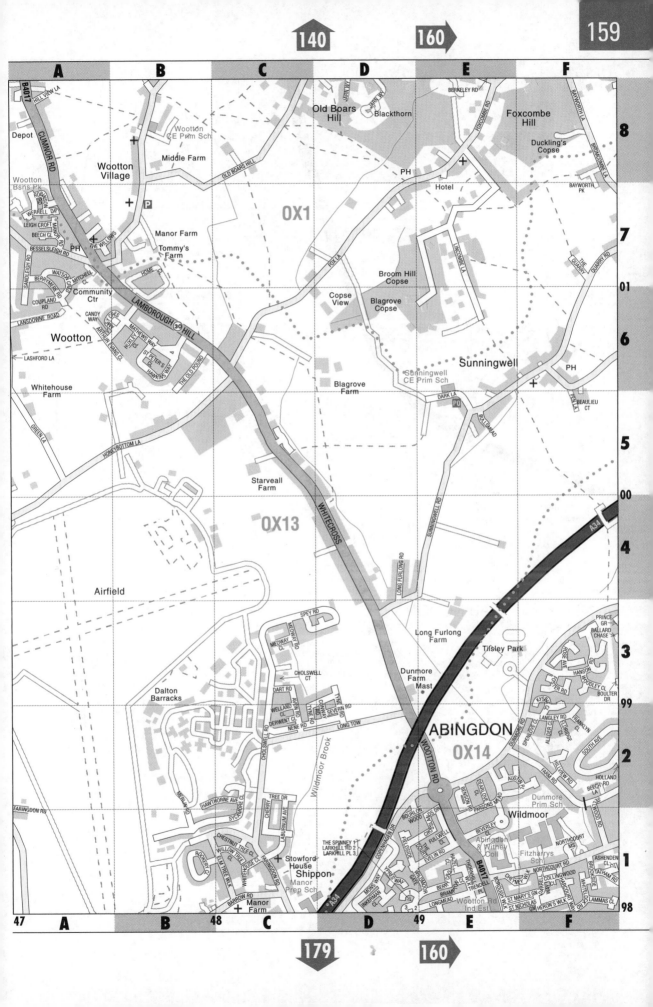

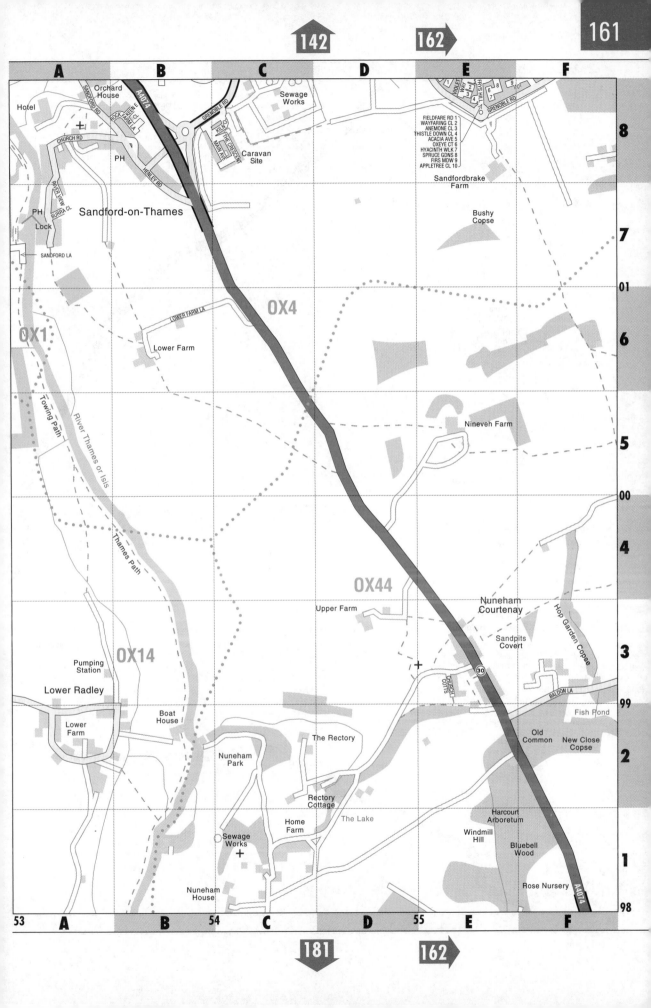

A   B   C   D   E   F

Hotel
Orchard House
SANDFORD RD
ROCA CL
KEM E
FARM LA
A4074
GRENOBLE RD
KILN CL
THE CRESCENT
MAIN AV
Sewage Works
FIELDFARE RD 1
WAYFARING CL 2
ANEMONE CL 3
THISTLE DOWN CL 4
ACACIA AVE 5
OXEYE CT 6
HYACINTH WLK 7
SPRUCE GDNS 8
FIRS MDW 9
APPLETREE CL 10
VIOLET WAY
FRY'S HILL
GRENOBLE RD

8

CHURCH RD
PH
HENLEY RD
Caravan Site
Sandfordbrake Farm

Sandford-on-Thames
Bushy Copse

PH
RIVER VIEW CL
BURRA CL
Lock
SANDFORD LA

7

OX4
01

LOWER FARM LA
OX1
6

Lower Farm
Nineveh Farm

Towing Path
5

River Thames or Isis
00

Thames Path
4

OX44
OX14
Upper Farm
Nuneham Courtenay
Hop Garden Copse

Pumping Station
Sandpits Covert
3

Lower Radley
✛
CHURCH COTTS
30
BALDON LA
99

Lower Farm
Boat House
The Rectory
Old Common
New Close Copse
Fish Pond
2

Nuneham Park
Rectory Cottage
Harcourt Arboretum

Home Farm
The Lake
Windmill Hill
Bluebell Wood
1

Sewage Works
✛
Nuneham House
Rose Nursery
A4074
98

53   A   B   54   C   D   55   E   F

161
143

161
182

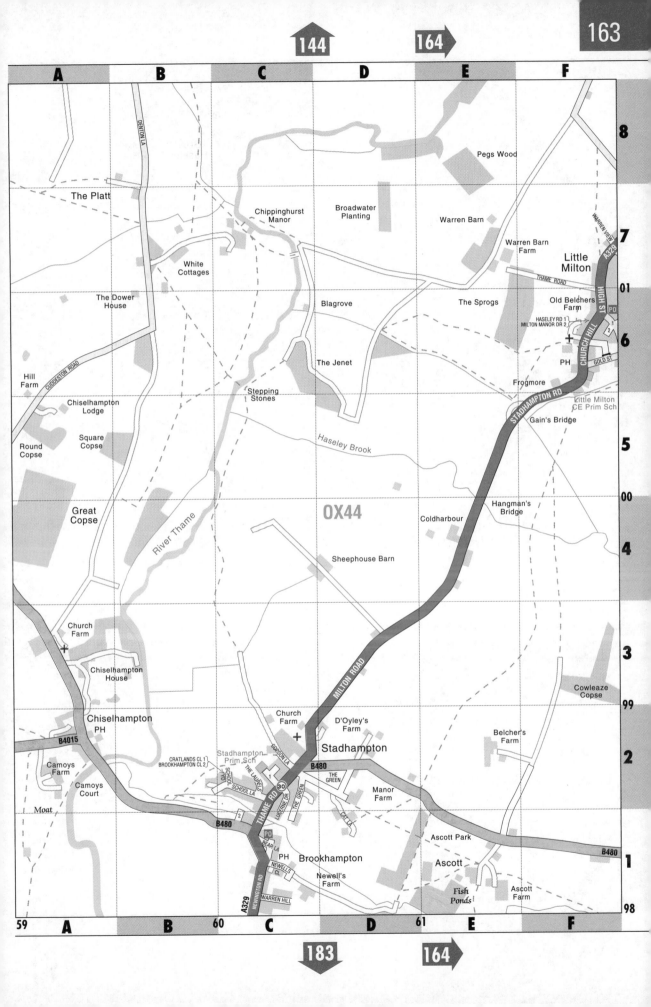

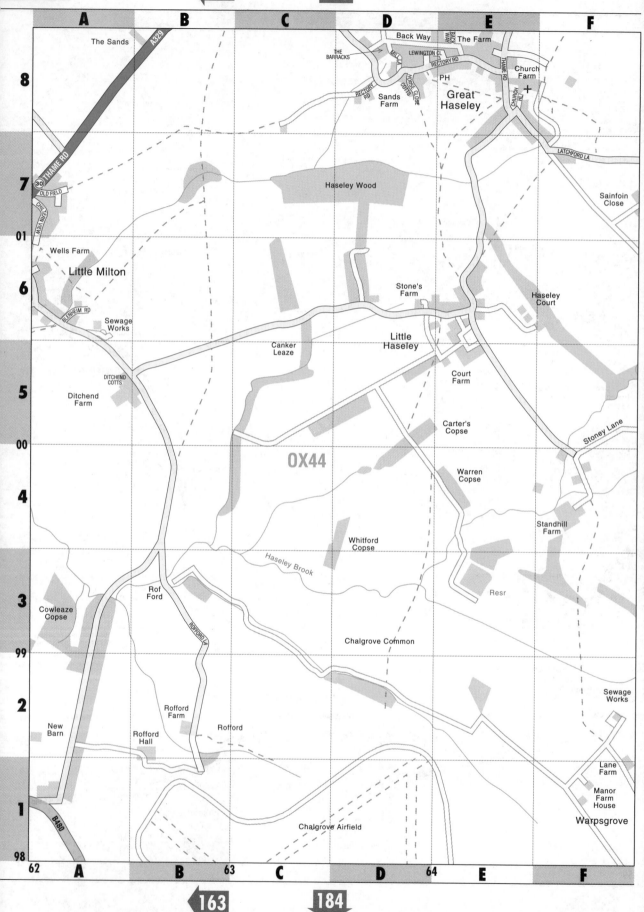

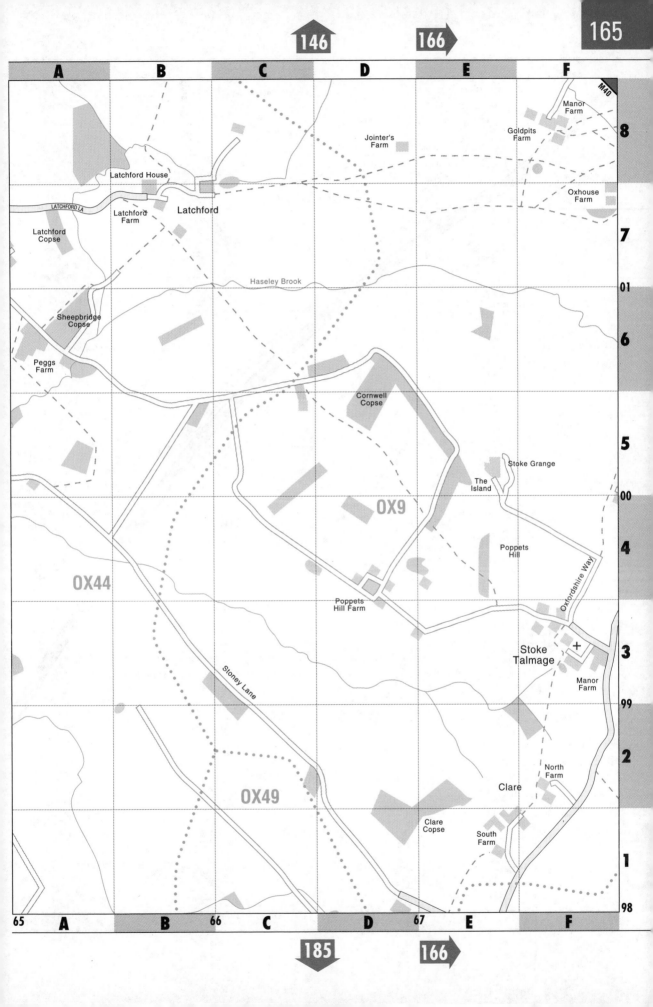

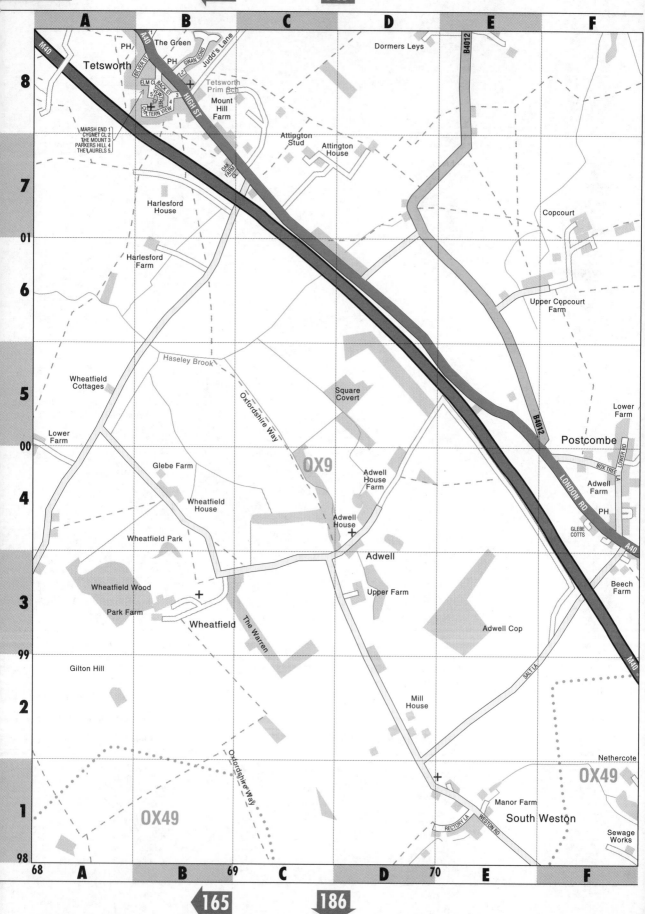

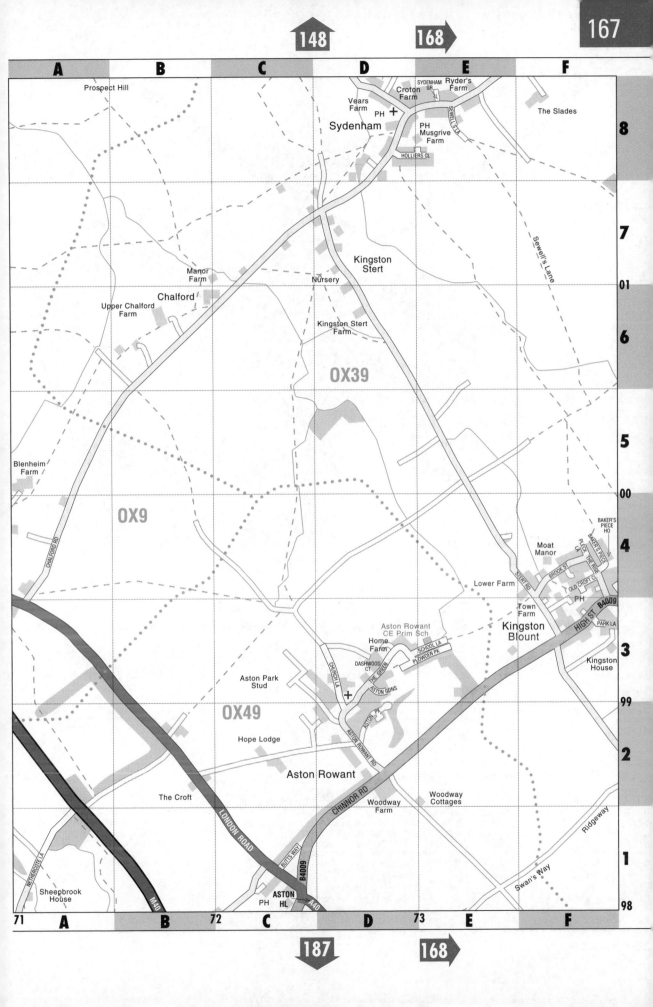

148
168

A B C D E F

8 7 01 6 5 00 4 3 99 2 1 98

Prospect Hill

Vears Farm
PH
Sydenham
Croton Farm
SYDENHAM GR
Ryder's Farm
The Slades
PH
Musgrive Farm
HOLLIERS CL
SEWELL'S LA

Kingston Stert

Manor Farm
Nursery
Chalford
Upper Chalford Farm
Kingston Stert Farm

OX39

Sewell's Lane

Blenheim Farm

OX9

CHALFORD RD

BAKER'S PIECE HO
Moat Manor
PLECK THE RISE
BAKER'S PIECE LA
BROOK ST
OLD CROFT CL
STERT RD
Lower Farm
Town Farm
PH
Kingston Blount
HIGH ST
B4009
PARK LA
Kingston House

Aston Rowant CE Prim Sch
Home Farm
SCHOOL LA
PLOWDEN PK
DASHWOOD CT
THE GREEN
ASTON GDNS
CHURCH LA
Aston Park Stud

OX49

Hope Lodge
ASTON PK
ASTON ROWANT RD

Aston Rowant
Woodway Farm
Woodway Cottages
The Croft
CHINNOR RD
Ridgeway

NETHERCOTE LA
LONDON ROAD
BUTTS WAY
B4009
M40
Swan's Way
Sheepbrook House
ASTON HL
PH
A40

71 A B 72 C D 73 E F

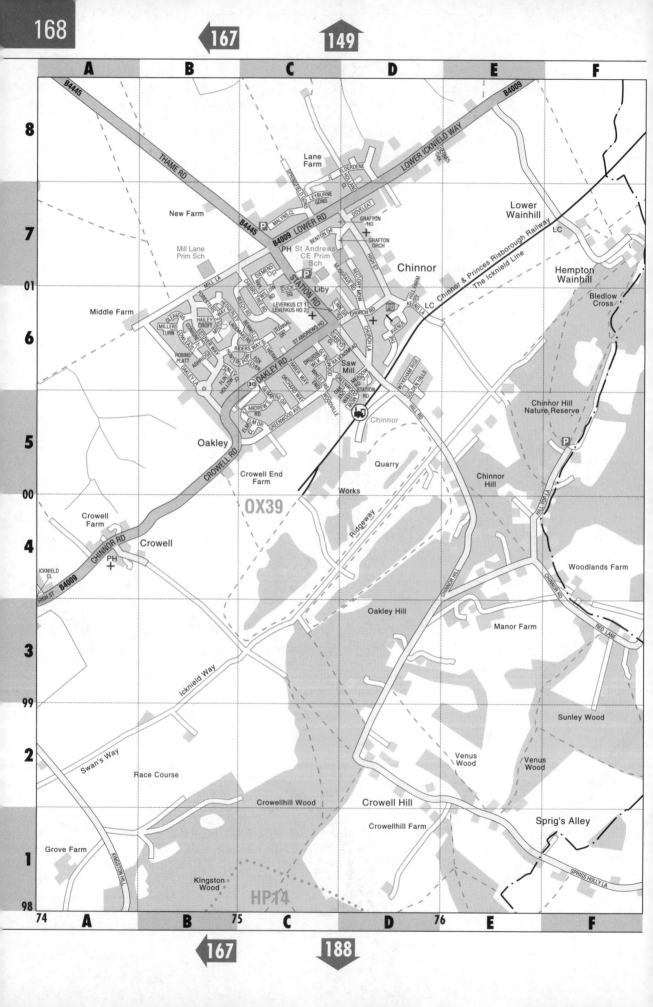

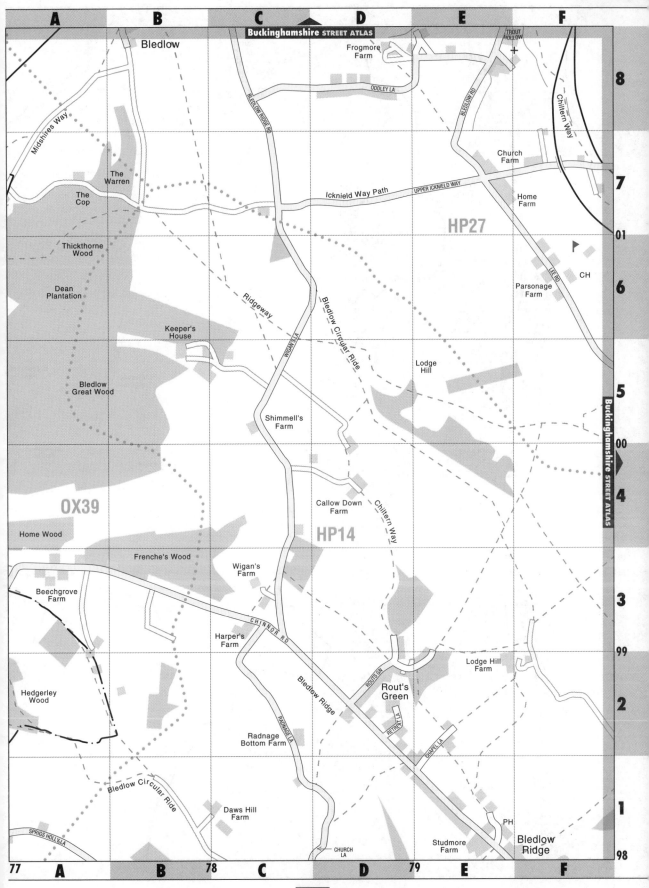

Bledlow

Frogmore
Farm

TROUT
HOLLOW

Oddley La

Bledlow Ridge Rd

Bledlow Rd

Chiltern Way

Midshires Way

Church
Farm

8

The Warren

Icknield Way Path   UPPER ICKNIELD WAY

Home
Farm

7

The
Cop

HP27

01

Thickthorne
Wood

Lee Rd

CH

6

Dean
Plantation

Ridgeway

Bledlow Circular Ride

Parsonage
Farm

Keeper's
House

Wigan's La

Lodge
Hill

5

Bledlow
Great Wood

Shimmell's
Farm

00

OX39

Callow Down
Farm

Chiltern Way

4

Home Wood

HP14

Frenche's Wood

Wigan's
Farm

Beechgrove
Farm

CHINNOR RD

3

Harper's
Farm

Lodge Hill
Farm

99

Hedgerley
Wood

Bledlow Ridge

Routs Gn

Rout's
Green

Radnage La

Retreat La

Chapel La

2

Radnage
Bottom Farm

Bledlow Circular Ride

Daws Hill
Farm

PH

1

SPRIGS HOLLY LA

CHURCH
LA

Studmore
Farm

Bledlow
Ridge

98

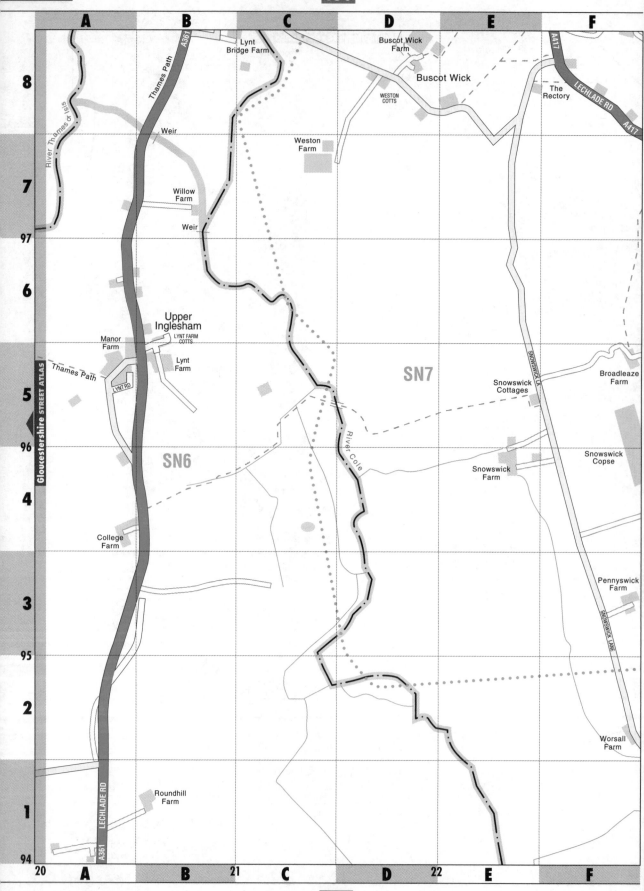

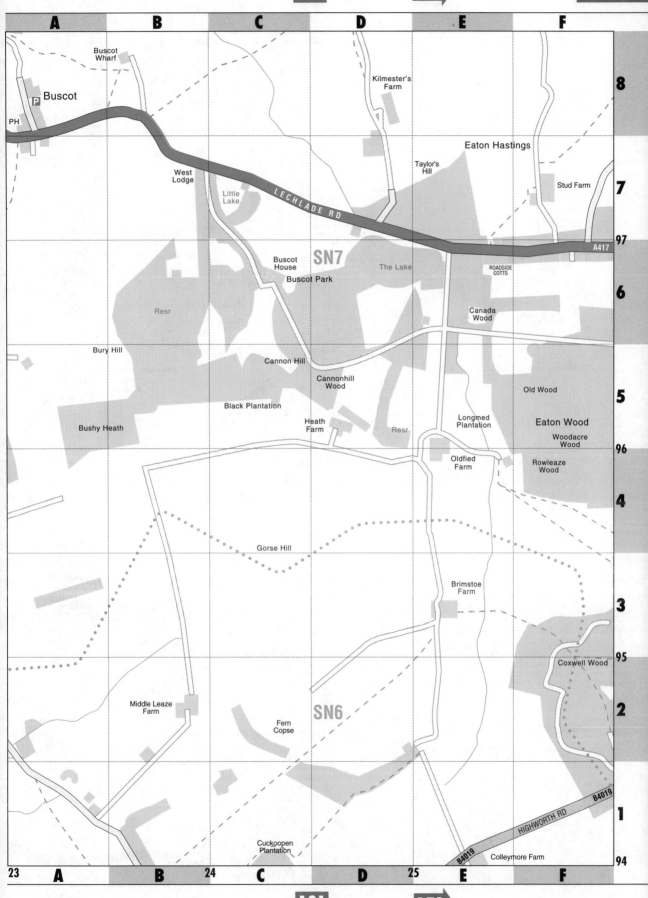

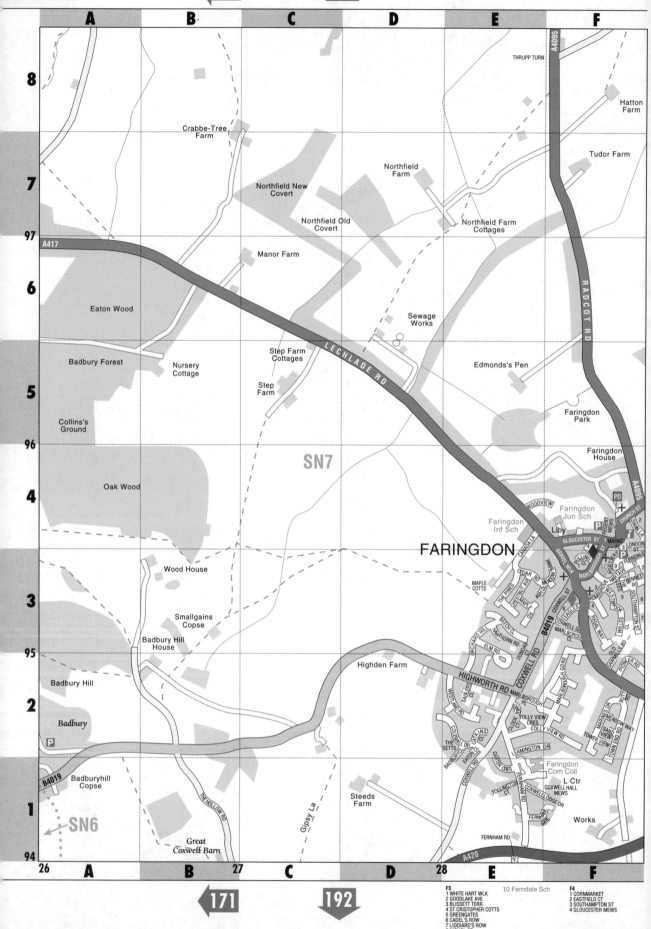

A B C D E F

8

7

97 A417

6

5

96

SN7

4

FARINGDON

3

95

2

1

SN6

94

26 A B 27 C D 28 E F

Crabbe-Tree Farm

Northfield New Covert

Northfield Old Covert

Northfield Farm

Thrupp Turn

A4095

Hatton Farm

Tudor Farm

Northfield Farm Cottages

Manor Farm

RADCOT RD

Eaton Wood

LECHLADE RD

Sewage Works

Edmonds's Pen

Faringdon Park

Badbury Forest

Nursery Cottage

Step Farm Cottages

Step Farm

Faringdon House

Collins's Ground

Oak Wood

A4095

Woodview

Faringdon Jun Sch

PO

Church St

SN7

Faringdon Inf Sch

Liby

Gloucester St

P

Regent Mews

Market

London

Wood House

Maple Cotts

Cedar Rd

Chestnut Ave

Canada La

Gravel Wlk

Marlborough Rd

Portland

P

Bennett

Southampton St

Smallgains Copse

The Pines

Beech Cl

Hawthorn Cl

Coxwell Gdns

Coxwell Rd

B4019

Eagles

Marlborough Cl

Westbrook

Regal Way

Old

Pidnell Rd

Badbury Hill House

Orchard Hill

Elm Rd

HIGHWORTH RD

COXWELL RD

Marlborough Pl

Marlborough Gdns

95

Highden Farm

Badbury Hill

Westland Rd

Sadlers Cl

Coxwell Rd

Eaton Cl

Folly View Cres

Clock

Folly View Rd

Leamington Dr

Tower View

Martins Dr

Meadow Way

Sand View

Town End Rd

Badbury

P

The Setts

Badbury Dr

Catlins Cl

Carter Cres

Tollington Ct

Ferngrove

Faringdon Com Coll

L Ctr

Coxwell Hall Mews

Coxwell Lodge Dr

Butts

B4019

Badburyhill Copse

THE HOLLOW RD

Gipsy La

Steeds Farm

Fernham Gate

Fernham Rd

Works

SN6

Great Coxwell Barn

Fernham Rd

A420

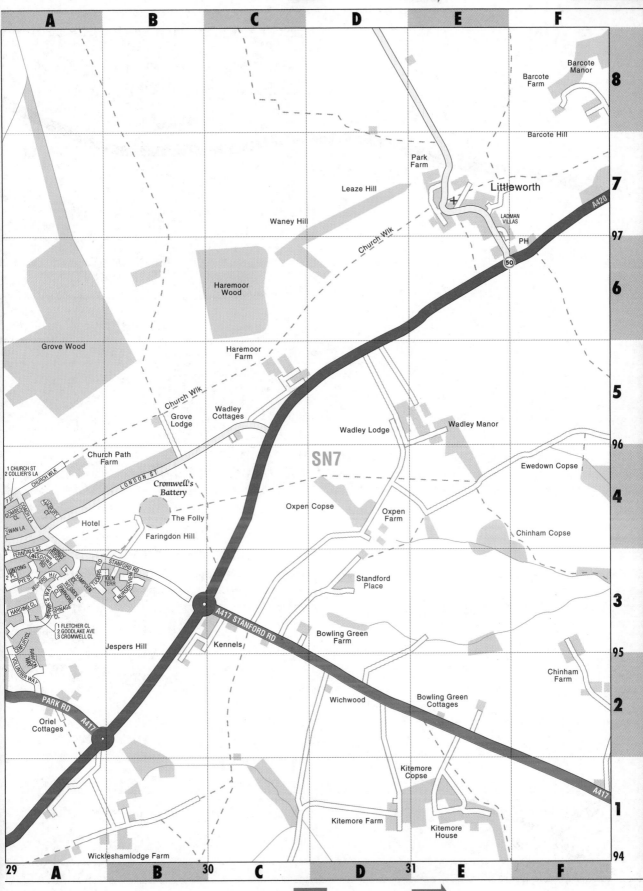

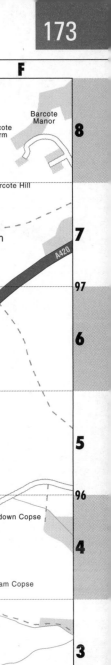

A   B   C   D   E   F

8

Barcote Manor

Barcote Farm

Barcote Hill

Park Farm

Leaze Hill

Littleworth

7   A420

Waney Hill

Church Wlk

LADMAN VILLAS

PH

97

50

6

Haremoor Wood

Grove Wood

Haremoor Farm

5

Church Wlk

Grove Lodge

Wadley Cottages

Wadley Lodge

Wadley Manor

96

Church Path Farm

SN7

Ewedown Copse

1 CHURCH ST
2 COLLIER'S LA

Church Wlk

LONDON ST

Cromwell's Battery

Oxpen Copse

Oxpen Farm

Chinham Copse

4

COOMBE LA
COACH LA

SAVORY CL

Hotel

The Folly

Faringdon Hill

SWAN LA

FERNDALE ST

WINDY
RIDGE

LANSDOWN RD

Standford Place

3

JESPERS HILL

STANFORD RD

TUCKERS RD

KILN TERR

NURSERY VIEW

A417 STANFORD RD

Bowling Green Farm

PYE ST
UNTONS PL

HAMPTON

MESSRS CL

BERNER'S WAY

SPINAGE CL

1 FLETCHER CL
2 GOODLAKE AVE
3 CROMWELL CL

Jespers Hill

Kennels

95

HARDING CL

CENTURY CL

Chinham Farm

RADNOR WAY

VOLUNTEER WAY

PARK RD

Wichwood

Bowling Green Cottages

2

Oriel Cottages

A417

Kitemore Copse

Kitemore Farm

Kitemore House

A417

1

Wickleshamlodge Farm

94

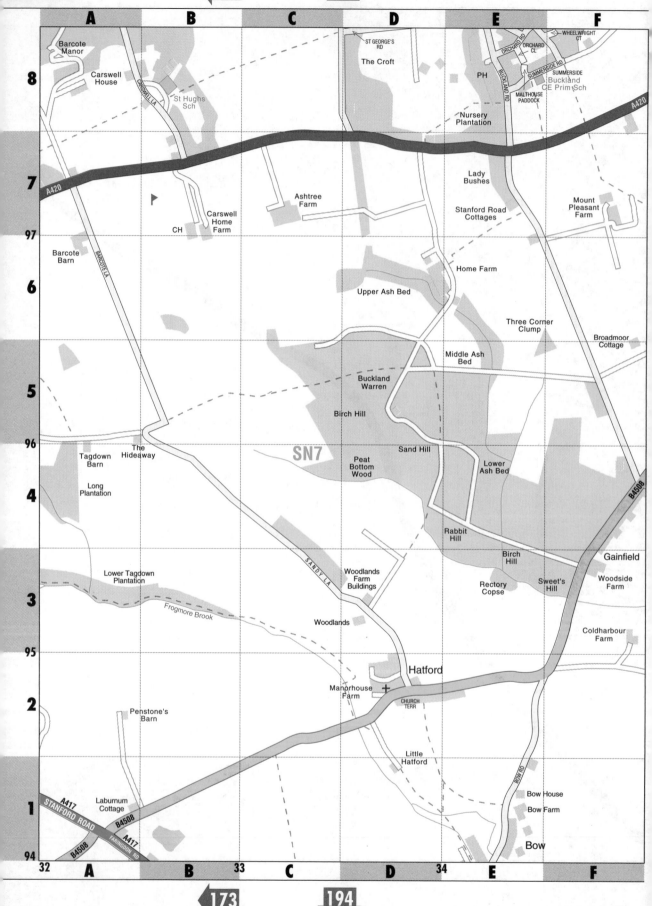

Barcote
Manor

Carswell
House

St Hughs
Sch

CARSWELL LA

CH

Carswell
Home
Farm

Ashtree
Farm

Barcote
Barn

BARCOTE LA

A420

A420

St George's
Rd

The Croft

PH

ORCHARD RD
ORCHARD
CL

WHEELWRIGHT
CT

SUMMERSIDE RD
SUMMERSIDE

BUCKLAND RD

MALTHOUSE
PADDOCK

Buckland
CE Prim Sch

Nursery
Plantation

A420

Lady
Bushes

Stanford Road
Cottages

Mount
Pleasant
Farm

Home Farm

Upper Ash Bed

Three Corner
Clump

Broadmoor
Cottage

Middle Ash
Bed

Buckland
Warren

Birch Hill

SN7

Sand Hill

Lower
Ash Bed

B4508

Tagdown
Barn

The
Hideaway

Peat
Bottom
Wood

Long
Plantation

Rabbit
Hill

Birch
Hill

Gainfield

SANDY LA

Woodlands
Farm
Buildings

Rectory
Copse

Sweet's
Hill

Woodside
Farm

Lower Tagdown
Plantation

Frogmore Brook

Woodlands

Coldharbour
Farm

Hatford

Manorhouse
Farm

CHURCH
TERR

Penstone's
Barn

Little
Hatford

BOW RD

Bow House

Bow Farm

Bow

A417

STANFORD ROAD

B4508

A417
FARINGDON RD

Laburnum
Cottage

B4508

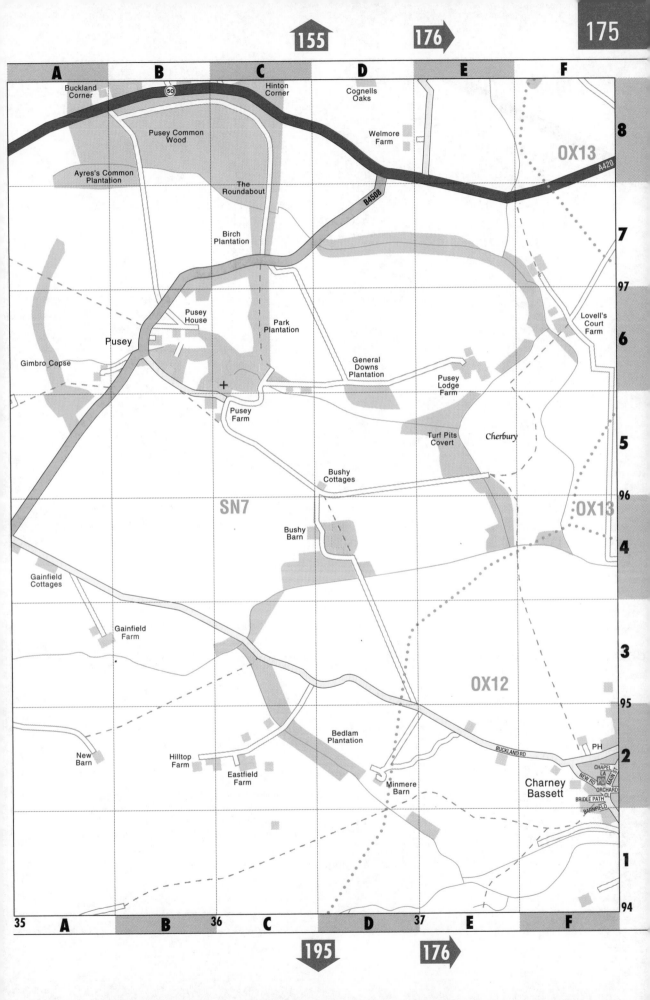

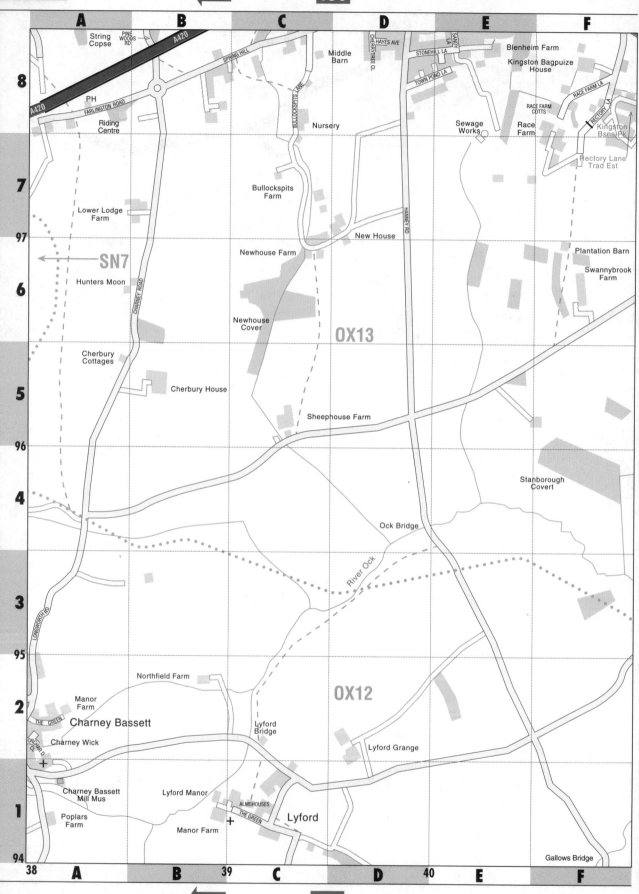

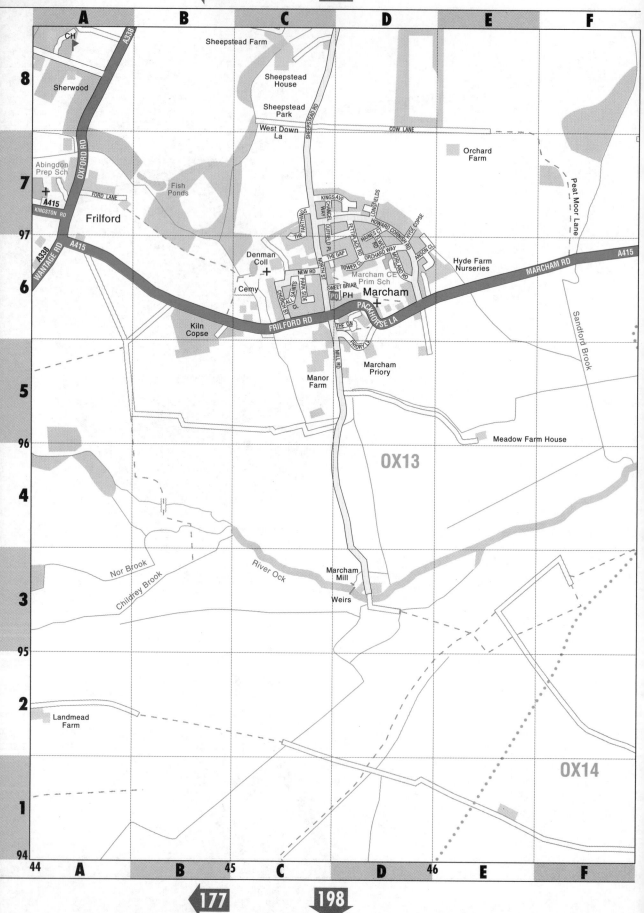

A B C D E F

8

CH
Sherwood

Sheepstead Farm

Sheepstead House

Sheepstead Park

West Down La

COW LANE

Orchard Farm

Abingdon Prep Sch

7

A415

KINGSTON RD

OXFORD RD

FORD LANE

Frilford

Fish Ponds

SHEEPSTEAD RD

KINGS AVE

CHANCEL WAY

LONGFIELDS

HOWARD CORNISH RD

HYDE COPSE

Peat Moor Lane

97

A338

WANTAGE RD

A415

THE CROSS

WHITTY WAY

DUFFIELD PL

HAINES CT

FETTIPLACE RD

ELWES RD

ORCHARD WAY

ANSON CL

6

Denman Coll

NEW RD

NORTH ST

TOWER CL

THE GAP

MORLAND RD

Marcham CE Prim Sch

Hyde Farm Nurseries

A415

MARCHAM RD

Cemy

PARK SIDE

SAINTS CL

CHURCH ST

SWEET BRIAR

PO PH

Marcham

MARCHAM RD

Kiln Copse

FRILFORD RD

THE GN

PACKHORSE LA

PRIORY LA

Manor Farm

MILL RD

Marcham Priory

Sandford Brook

5

96

Meadow Farm House

OX13

4

Nor Brook

Childrey Brook

River Ock

Marcham Mill

Weirs

3

95

2

Landmead Farm

OX14

1

94

44 A B 45 C D 46 E F

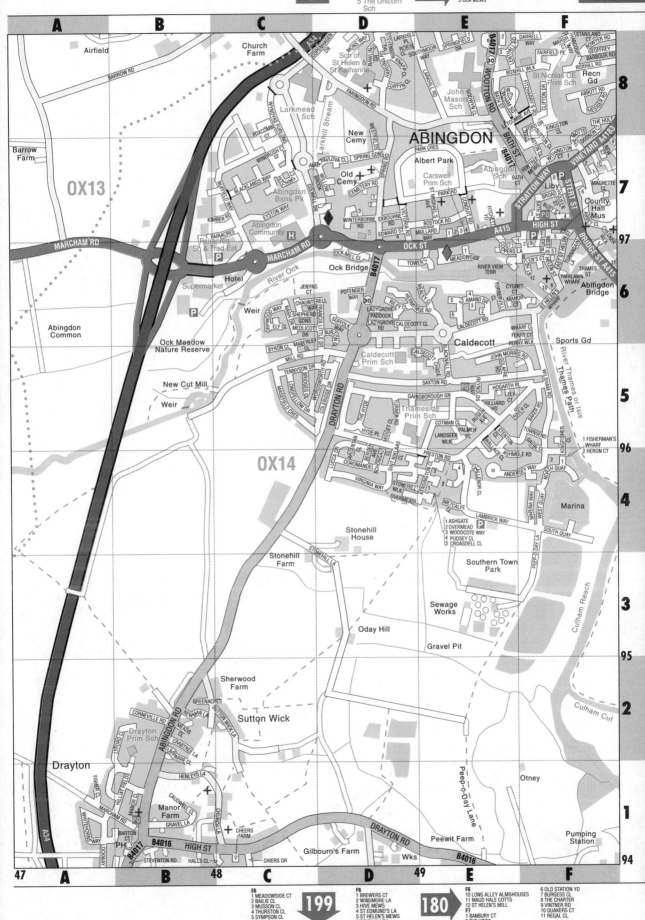

159

D7
1 BUCKLES CL
2 SPRING TERR
3 BUCKLAND MEWS
4 JUNIPER CT
5 The Unicorn Sch

180

E7
1 MAYOTT'S RD
2 CARSWELL CT
3 CROWN MEWS
4 TOMKIN'S ALMSHOUSES
5 OCK MEWS

E8
1 THORNHILL WLK
2 BOROUGH WLK
3 FINMORE CL

179

E6
1 MEADOWSIDE CT
2 BAILIE CL
3 MUSSON CL
4 THURSTON CL
5 SYMPSON CL
6 GODFREY CL
7 DRAYMANS WLK

199

F6
1 BREWERS CT
2 WINSMORE LA
3 HIVE MEWS
4 ST EDMUND'S LA
5 ST HELEN'S MEWS
6 BRICK ALLEY
7 MILL PADDOCK
8 GEORGE MORLAND HO
9 NEAVE MEWS

180

F6
10 LONG ALLEY ALMSHOUSES
11 MAUD HALE COTTS
12 ST HELEN'S MILL
F7
1 BANBURY CT
2 THE VINES
3 THE SQUARE
4 MARKET PL
5 LOMBARD ST

6 OLD STATION YD
7 BURGESS CL
8 THE CHARTER
9 VINTNER RD
10 QUAKERS CT
11 REGAL CL

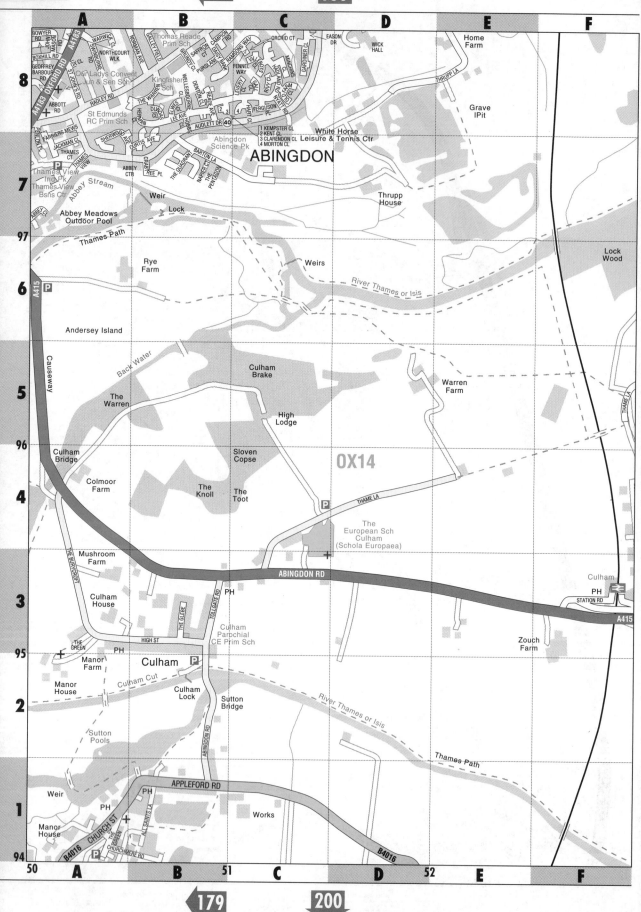

A **B** **C** **D** **E** **F**

BOWYER RD
MASON
WARWICK
SWINBURNE
NORTHCOURT WLK
Thomas Reade Prim Sch
GALLEY FIELD
SAFFRON
DAISY BANK
CAMPION RD
RAMSONS WAY
ORCHID CT
GARDINER CL
EASON DR
WICK HALL
Home Farm

BOXHILL RD
GEOFFREY BARBOUR RD
OX CL
ST JOHN'S RD
A4183 OXFORD RD
Our Ladys Convent Jun & Sen Sch
NORMAN AVE
BRUNEL CL
PURSLANE
FENNEL WAY
LEVERT
Kingfisher Sch
THRUPP LA

8

ABBOTT RD
A4183
RADLEY RD
WELLESBOURNE
DENTON CL
READE AVE
FERGUSON PL
Grave Pit

FARRIERS MEWS
FALCON CT
JACKMAN CL
St Edmunds RC Prim Sch
THE WARREN
SHERWOOD AVE
HERMAN
DUNBAR
ELMES RD
HOBBS
LEE AVE
AUDLETT DR 40
1 KEMPSTER CL
2 KENT CL
3 CLARENDON CL
4 MORTON CL
White Horse
Leisure & Tennis Ctr

THAMES CT
THAMES VIEW
CURTIS AVE
ABBEY CTR
CRABTREE PL
THE QUADRANT
BARTON LA
NAPIER CL
THE PENTAGON
Abingdon Science Pk
ABINGDON

7

Thames View Ind Pk
Thames View Bsns Ctr
Abbey Meadows Outdoor Pool
Abbey Stream
Weir
Lock
Thrupp House

ABBEY CL

97

Thames Path

Rye Farm
Weirs
River Thames or Isis
Lock Wood

6

A415
P
Andersey Island

Causeway
Back Water
Culham Brake
Warren Farm

5

The Warren
High Lodge

96

Culham Bridge
Sloven Copse
OX14

4

Colmoor Farm
The Knoll
The Toot
P
THAME LA
The European Sch Culham (Schola Europaea)

THE BURYCROFT
Mushroom Farm
ABINGDON RD
Culham
PH
STATION RD
A415

3

Culham House
TOLLGATE RD
PH
TOLL GATE RD
THE GLEBE
Culham Parochial CE Prim Sch
Zouch Farm

THE GREEN
HIGH ST
PH

95

Manor Farm
P
Culham
Culham Cut
Culham Lock
Sutton Bridge
River Thames or Isis

2

Manor House
Sutton Pools
ABINGDON RD

Thames Path

Weir
APPLEFORD RD

1

PH
PH
Works

Manor House
CHURCH ST
ALL SAINTS LA
THE GREEN
B4016

94

B4016
P
CHURCHMERE RD
B4016

50 **A** **B** **51** **C** **D** **52** **E** **F**

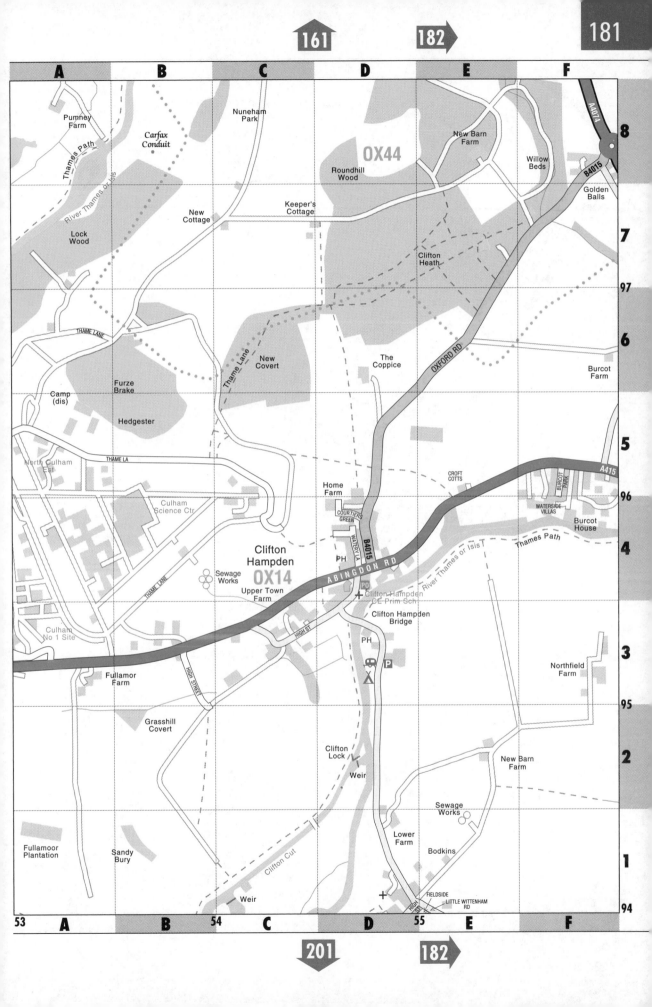

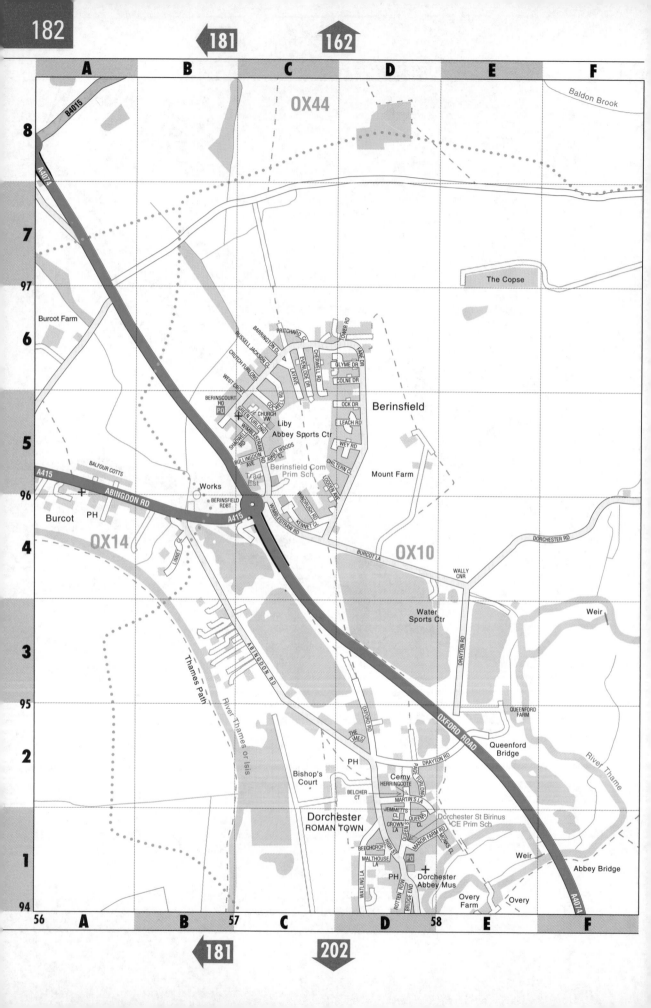

181
162

OX44

Baldon Brook

B4015

A4074

The Copse

97

Burcot Farm

RUSSELL JACKSON CL
BARRINGTON CL
PRITCHARD CL
TOWER RD
FANE DR
CRUTCH FURLONG
EVENLODE DR
CHERWELL RD
GLYME DR
COLNE DR
WEST CROFT
LATANE
BERINSCOURT HO PO
GREEN FURLONG
CHURCH
OCK DR
Berinsfield
LEACH RD
Liby
Abbey Sports Ctr
WIMBLESTRAW RD
SHACWELL RD
BULLINGDON AVE
WEY RD
ABBEY CL
ABBEY WOODS
CHILTERN CL
A415
BALFOUR COTTS
Works
Trad Est
Berinsfield Com Prim Sch
LODER AVE
Mount Farm
A415
ABINGDON RD
BERINSFIELD RDBT
96
WINDRUSH RD
Burcot
PH
WIMBLESTRAW RD
KENNET CL
A415
LINNET CL
OX14
BURCOT LA
OX10
DORCHESTER RD
WALLY CNR
Weir
Water Sports Ctr
ABINGDON RD
DRAYTON RD
Thames Path
River Thames or Isis
95
QUEENFORD FARM
THE JAMES
OXFORD RD
Queenford Bridge
OXFORD ROAD
River Thame
PH
DRAYTON RD
Bishop's Court
PAGE FURLONG
Cemy
HERRINGCOTE
BELCHER CT
MARTIN'S LA
JEMMETTS CL
QUEENS
Dorchester St Birinus CE Prim Sch
CROWN LA
QUEENS CL
Dorchester
ROMAN TOWN
MANOR FARM RD
NORRIS CL
BEECHCROFT
HIGH ST
QUEEN ST
Weir
MALTHOUSE LA
PO
WATLING LA
PH
Dorchester Abbey Mus
Abbey Bridge
ROTTEN ROW
BRIDGE END
Overy Farm
Overy
A4074

56   57   58

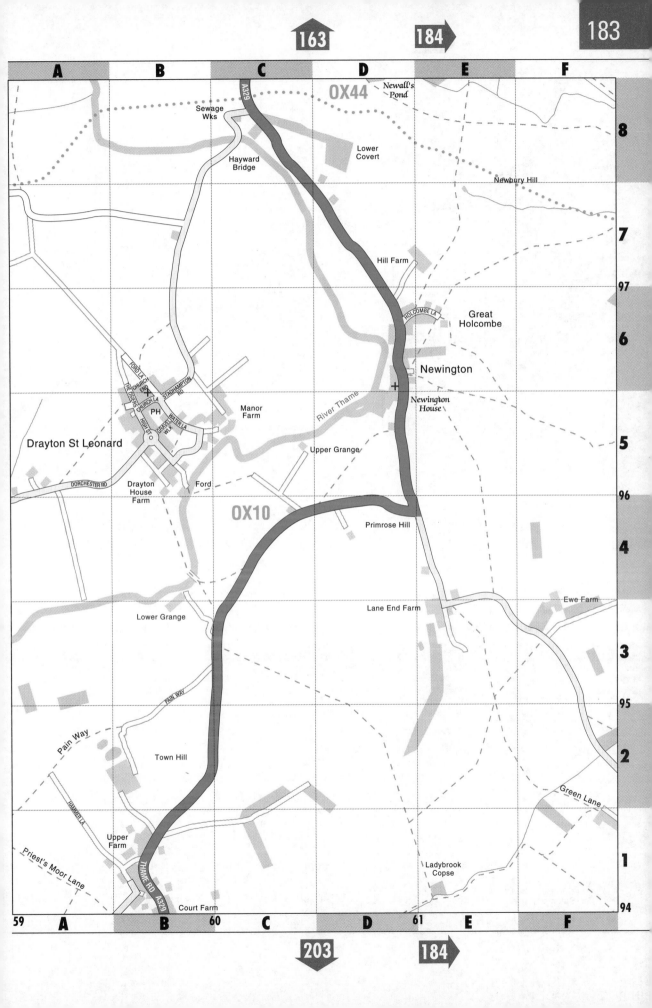

← 183
164

A B C D E F

8

Newbury
Hill

Chalgrove
Airfield

Hitchcox
Poultry
Farm

7

Fox
Covert

Monument
Ind Pk

Chalgrove
Field

MARKET LA
BOWER END
BROOKSIDE EST
CINNAMON CL
POPLAR FARM RD

PH
HIGH ST
BAKERY CT

Hampden's
Monument

97

Little Holcombe
Covert

Manor
Farm

Mill
House
THE RICKYARD

FLEMMING AVE
ADEANE RD
QUARTERMAIN RD
ORCHARD CL
BRINKINFIELD RD
PADDOCK CL
GARAGE LA

LUTON RD
FRENCH LAURENCE WAY
SIXPENNY LA

6

Langley Field
Farm

Langley
Hall

OX44

Chalgrove
Com Prim Sch

SWINSTEAD CT
LANGLEY RD
THE GREEN
HAMONDS
HAMPDEN
COPPICE LA
CHAPEL LA
MITCHELL CL
HECTON RD
FAIRFAX RD
BEVERLEY CL
ARGOSY CL
FARM CL
MONUMENT RD
CHILTERN CL

MILL LA
CHINALL CL
DICKENSHURST CL

RUPERT RD
RUPERT CL
+ ST MARY'S
CHURCH LA
WILLOW MEAD
FRANKLIN CL
CROMWELL CL

Chalgrove

Church
Farm

BERRICK RD

B480

5

Chalgrove
Farm

96

Hares Leap

Southfield
Barn

CADWELL LA

4

Hollandstide
House

Cadwell
Covert

Cadwell
Farm

3

OX10

OX49

Whitehouse
Farm

95

Lonesome
Farm

2

Manor
Farm

Rumbolds La

Berrick
Prior

Green La

Hollandtide Bottom

1

PH
Ivyhouse
Farm +

Rumbolds
Farm

94

Berrick
Salome

62 A B 63 C D 64 E F

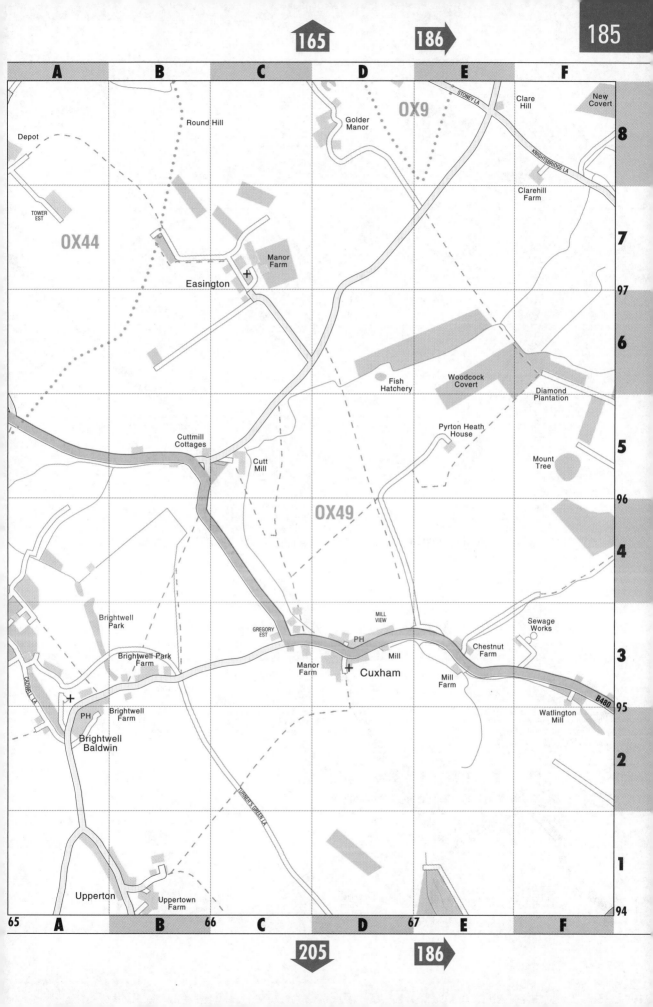

185
166

A B C D E F

8

Stokefield Farm

WESTON RD

OX9

Moor Court

Brookside Covert

7

Knightsbridge Farm

Model Farm

B4009

97

Field Farm House

6

WATLINGTON RD

Oxfordshire Way

Shirburn Farm

5

New Farm

Home Farm

PH

Shirburn Castle

KNIGHTSBRIDGE LA

96

Cemy

HALL CL

OX49

CASTLE RD

BLENHEIM RD

MAFEKING ROW

Pyrton

CHURCH LA

Shirburn

Lower Farm

4

Pyrton Manor

3

Pyrton Field Farm

Middle Way Plantation

Ridgeway

95

B480

Icknield Com Coll

Watlington Prim Sch

Eastfield Farm

Oxfordshire Way

Beechwood

Caravan Park

WILLOW CL
ASH CL
PYRTON LA
FORDENS CL

LOVE LA

STATION ROAD

Swan's Way

Watlington Ind Est

CUXHAM RD

PROSPECT PL

MEADOWS END

NEW RD

CHURCH ST

PAULS WAY

SAUNDERS

ORCHARD WLK

CHAPEL ST

SHIRBURN ST

SHIRBURN RD

2

SHELDONS PIECE 1
BEECH CL 2
SYCAMORE CL 3

WINDMILL PIECE

HURDLERS GN

BROOKS ACRE

GORWELL

HIGH ST

Liby

PO

Watlington

BRITWELL RD

THE GOGGS

BARNACRE

ALCHESTER

BROOK ST

B4009

GORWELL

CHESTNUT CL

COUCHING ST

WATCOMBE RD

P

PH

HILL RD

1

White House Farm

FARMHOUSE MEWS 1
DAVENPORT PL 2
OLD SCHOOL PL 3
INGHAM LA 4
QUARRINGTON PL 5

ILLES PL

Watcombe Manor Ind Est

HOME RD

SPRING LA

STENOR CM

CHILTERN GDNS

SPRINGFIELD CL

PARSLOW HO

B480

Chiltern Farm

Watlington Chalk Pit Nature Reserve

Pyrton Hill House

B4009

Watcombe Manor

94

68 A B 69 C D 70 E F

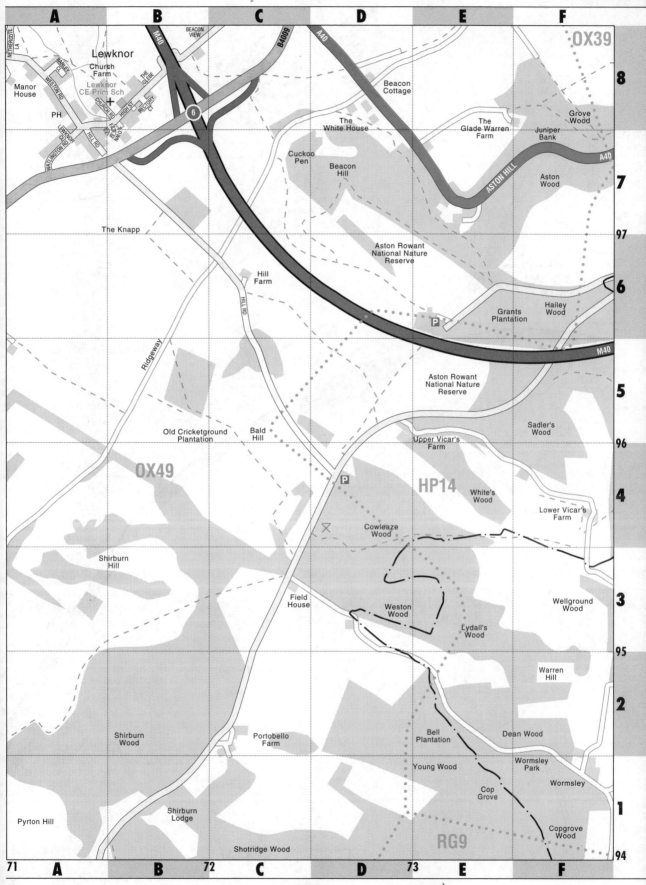

167
188
207
188

OX39

OX49

HP14

RG9

Lewknor

Manor House

Church Farm

Lewknor CE Prim Sch

PH

NETHEROTE LA

BARLEY CL

WESTON RD

HIGH ST

THE GLEBE

CHURCH RD

RECTORY CT

HILL RD

WATLINGTON RD

B4009

M40

A40

Beacon View

BEACON VIEW

The White House

Beacon Cottage

Beacon Hill

Cuckoo Pen

The Glade Warren Farm

Grove Wood

Juniper Bank

ASTON HILL

Aston Wood

The Knapp

Aston Rowant National Nature Reserve

Hill Farm

HILL RD

Ridgeway

Grants Plantation

Hailey Wood

M40

Aston Rowant National Nature Reserve

Sadler's Wood

Old Cricketground Plantation

Bald Hill

Upper Vicar's Farm

White's Wood

Lower Vicar's Farm

Shirburn Hill

Cowleaze Wood

Weston Wood

Lydall's Wood

Wellground Wood

Field House

Warren Hill

Shirburn Wood

Portobello Farm

Bell Plantation

Dean Wood

Young Wood

Wormsley Park

Wormsley

Cop Grove

Copgrove Wood

Pyrton Hill

Shirburn Lodge

Shotridge Wood

187
168

187

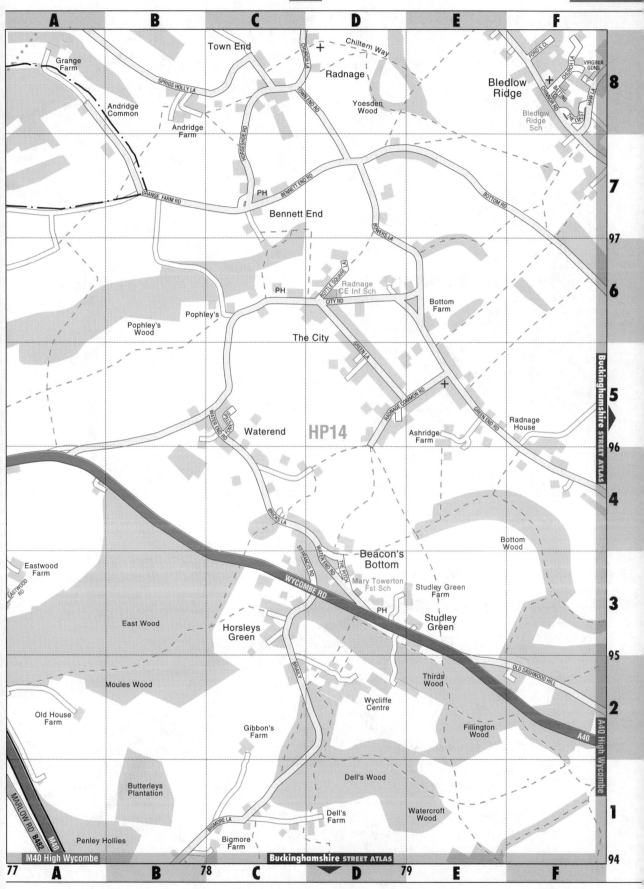

Buckinghamshire STREET ATLAS

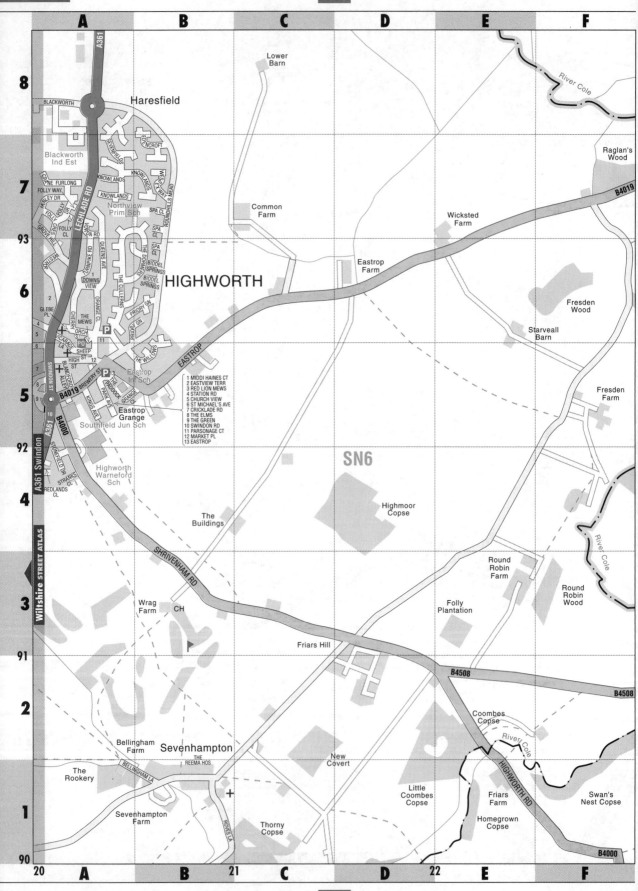

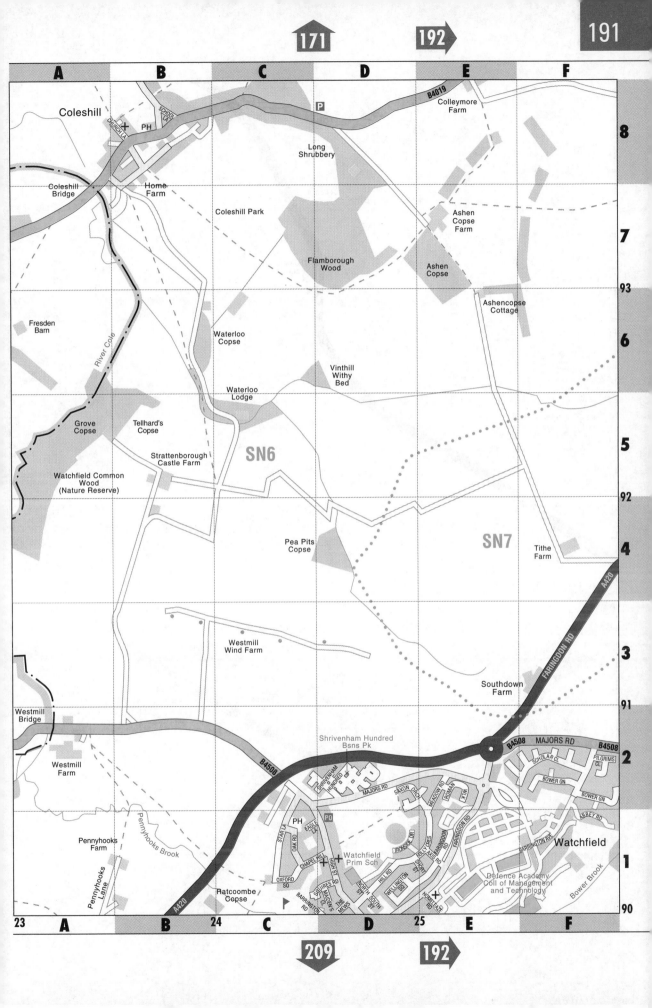

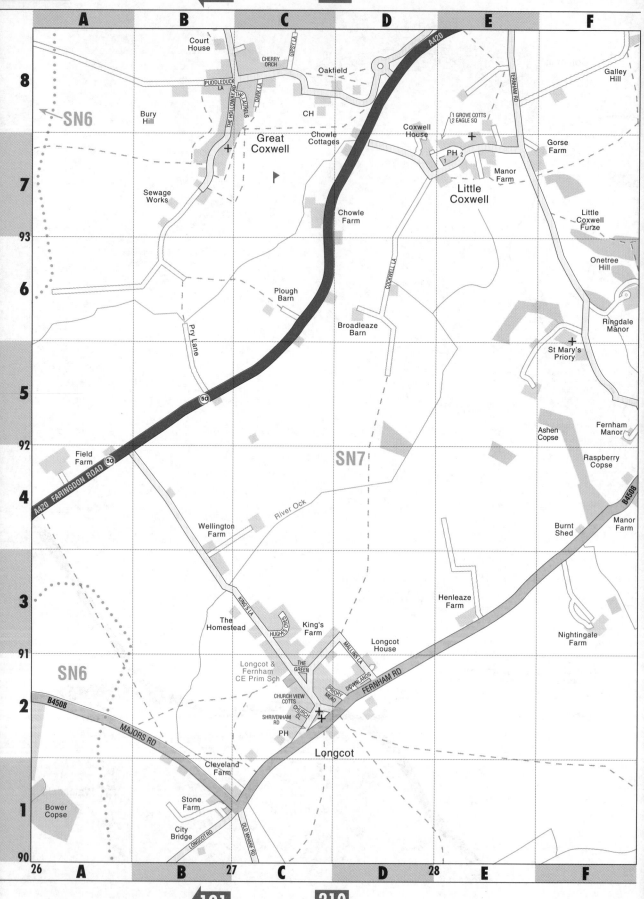

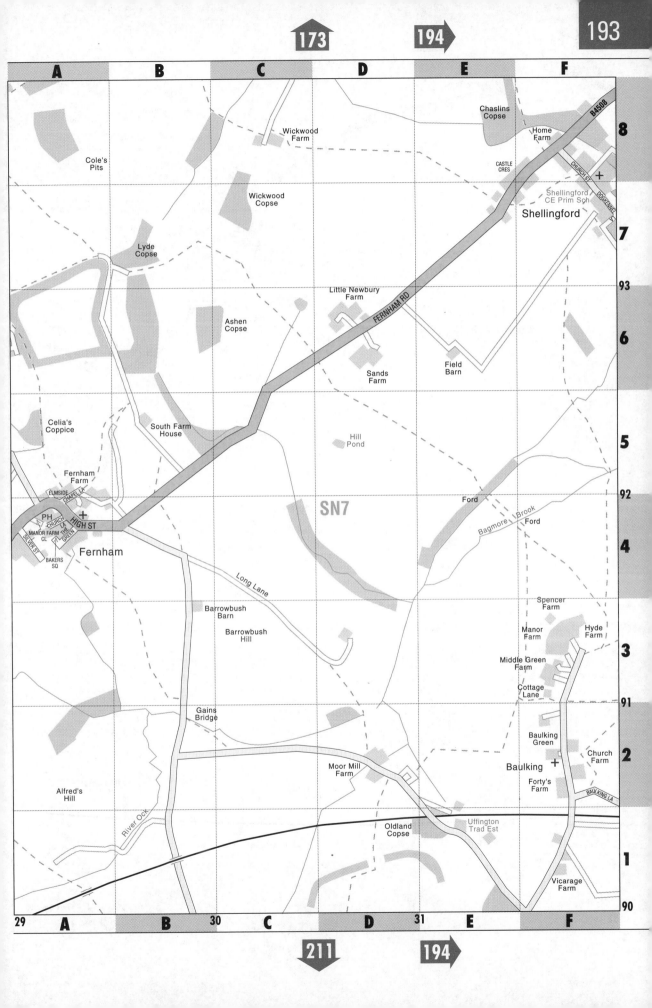

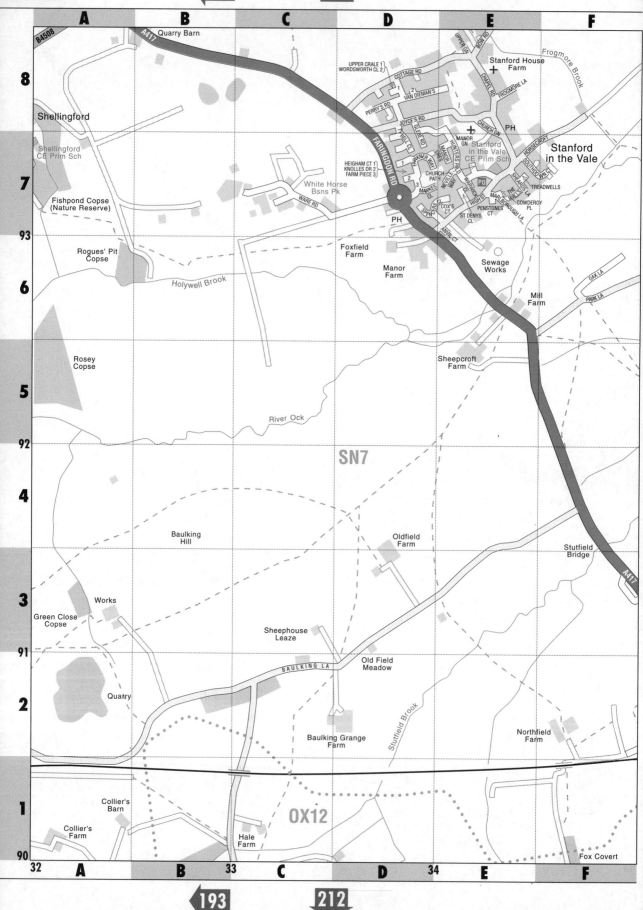

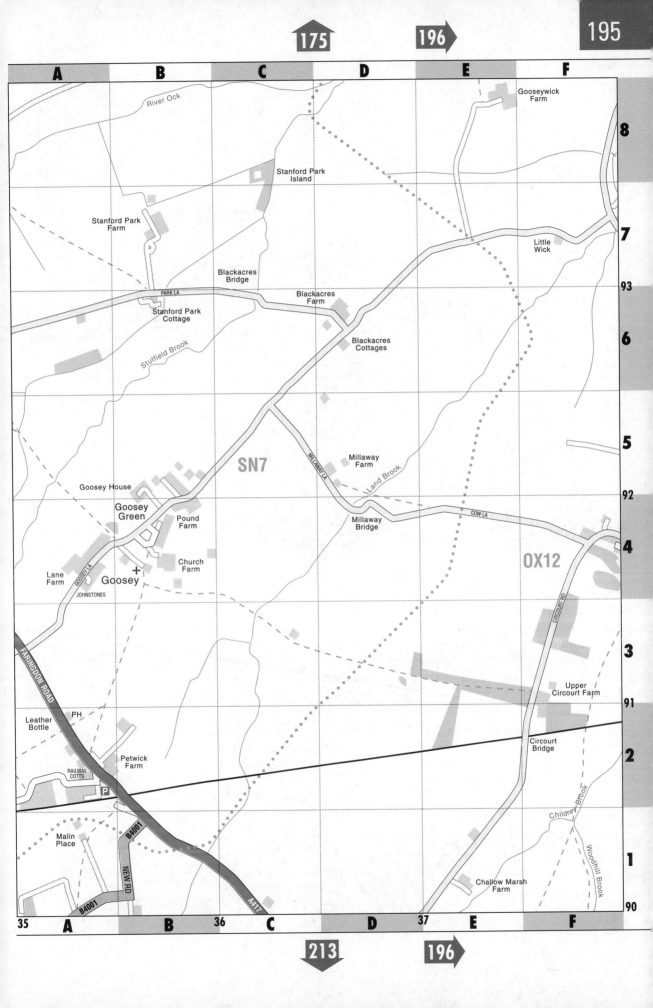

195
176

A B C D E F

8

Land Brook

Hedges
Farm

7

Northmead La

Flapp's
Barn

Bailey's Mead
Copse

Botney
Meadows
Farm

RECTORY
FARM CL

93

Grange
Farm

The Meads

Main St

Lydbrook
Farm

Church St

Monks Cl

North

Winter La

The Croft

PH

The Green

School Rd

West
Hanney

6

Hyde
Farm

Pike's Barn

Childrey Brook

Hyde Rd

Manor
Farm

Cow La

5

South Denchworth
Farm

Home
Farm
Mews

Kimbers Cl

92

Circourt
Rd

Brook La

Denchworth

Brooklane
Bridge

Rose
Terr

OX12

Hill Barn

Sewage
Works

Cow La

Bradfield Grove
Farm

4

P

3

Hanney
Bridge

Grove Wick
Farm

Works

A338

91

Denchworth Road
Bridge

Denchworth Rd

Cemy

Monk's
Farm

Townsend

Grove
CE Sch

North Dr

Tulwick La

2

The Maples

Churchward Cl

Kestrel

Shepherds Cl

Westbrook

Denchworth Rd

Wick
Green

Oxford La

Fulmar Pl 1
Hawksworth Cl 2

The
Kestrels

Peregr

Cygnet Way

Noble's Cl

Farmstead

Gdn

Church
View

St John's
Ct

Godfreys

Howard Ave

Shannon Cl

Mayfield Ave

Station Rd

1

Little Woodhill

Woodhill La

New Lands Dr

Swan Cl

Teal

Mallard Way

Mandarin Pl

Breer Dr

Sycamore Wlk

Evenlode Cl

Hardwell

Wayland Rd

School La

Old Mill Cl

Millbrook
Prim Sch

Millbrook
Sq

Easterfield

Vicarage Cl

St John's Rd

Glebe Gdns

Valeave

Caldwell La

Hunslow

Meadow Cl

Linden Cres

Minns Rd

Grove

Gipsy
Lane

CARLTON CL 1
HUNTERS CL 2
GROVELANDS CTR 3
BROADMARSH CL 4
FAIRFIELD CL 5

Savile Way

Blenheim
Gdns

Kenne Cl

Woodgate Cl

Colne

Windrush

Tree Cl

Letcombe

Bosley's Orch

Bell Cl

Harlington Ave

A338

90

38 A 39 B C 40 D E F

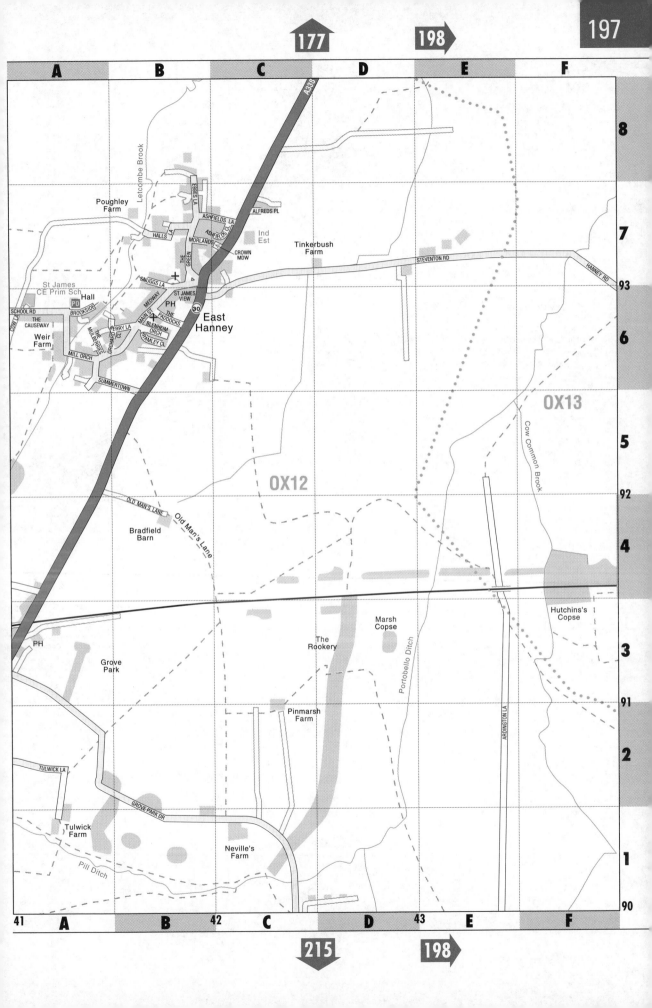

A B C D E F

8
7
93
6
5
92
4
3
91
2
1
90

OX13

OX12

Letcombe Brook

Poughley
Farm

ASHFIELDS LA
ALFREDS PL
ASHFIELDS CL
HALLS LA
MORLANDS
THE GREEN
EBBES LA
A338
CROWN
MDW
Ind
Est

Tinkerbush
Farm

STEVENTON RD

HANNEY RD

St James
CE Prim Sch
Hall
PO
SCHOOL RD
CROFT CL
BROOKSIDE
THE
CAUSEWAY
Weir
Farm
THE MULBERRIES
MILL ORCH
ORCHARD CL
PERRY LA
SNUGGS LA
MEDWAY
MAIN ST
THE PADDOCKS
BLENHEIM
ORCH
BRAMLEY CL
PH
St JAMES
VIEW
30
East
Hanney
SUMMERTOWN

Cow Common Brook

OLD MAN'S LANE
Old Man's Lane

Bradfield
Barn

PH
Grove
Park

Marsh
Copse

The
Rookery

Portobello Ditch

Hutchins's
Copse

ARDINGTON LA

Pinmarsh
Farm

TULWICK LA

GROVE PARK DR

Tulwick
Farm

Neville's
Farm

Pill Ditch

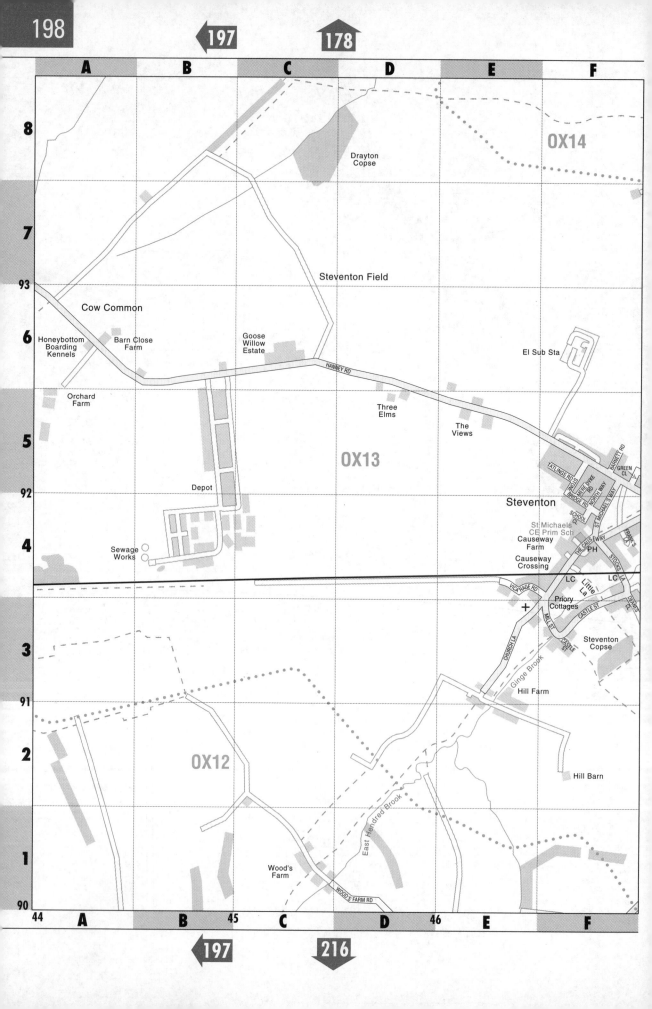

8

OX14

Drayton
Copse

7

Steventon Field

93

Cow Common

6

Honeybottom
Boarding
Kennels

Barn Close
Farm

Goose
Willow
Estate

HANNEY RD

El Sub Sta

Orchard
Farm

Three
Elms

The
Views

5

OX13

TATLINGS RD
BRIDGE RD
MERE DYKE RD
NORTH WAY
ST MICHAEL'S WAY
BARNETT RD
GREEN
CL

92

Depot

SCHOOL
CL

Steventon

St Michaels
CE Prim Sch

FRANK'S

4

Sewage
Works

Causeway
Farm

THE CAUSEWAY
PH

STOCKS LA

Causeway
Crossing

LC

LC

Little
La

VICARAGE RD

Priory
Cottages

DEANE'S
CL

3

Steventon
Copse

CHURCH LA

CASTLE ST

MILL ST

CASTLE
S'LE

Ginge Brook

91

Hill Farm

2

OX12

Hill Barn

East Hendred Brook

1

Wood's
Farm

90

WOOD'S FARM RD

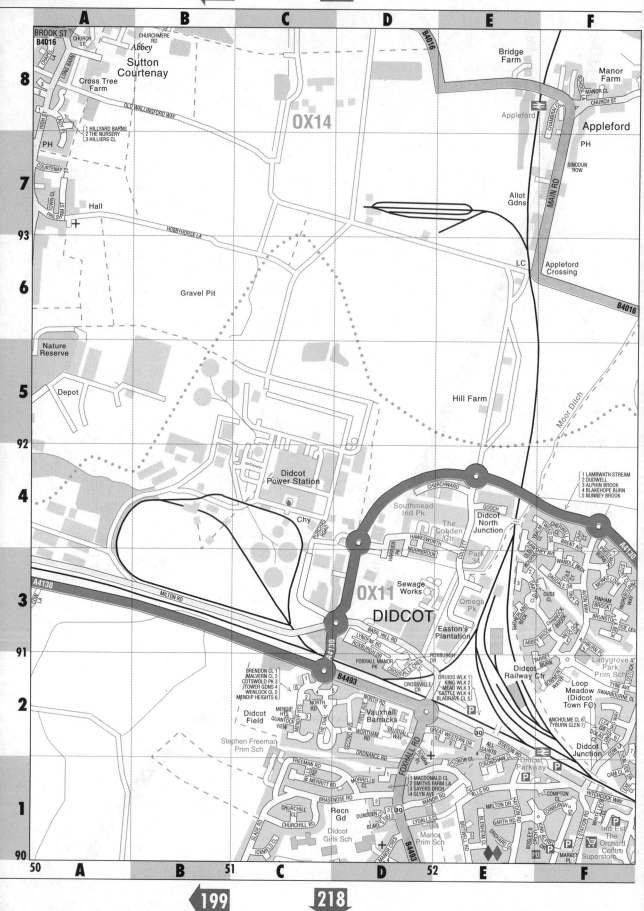

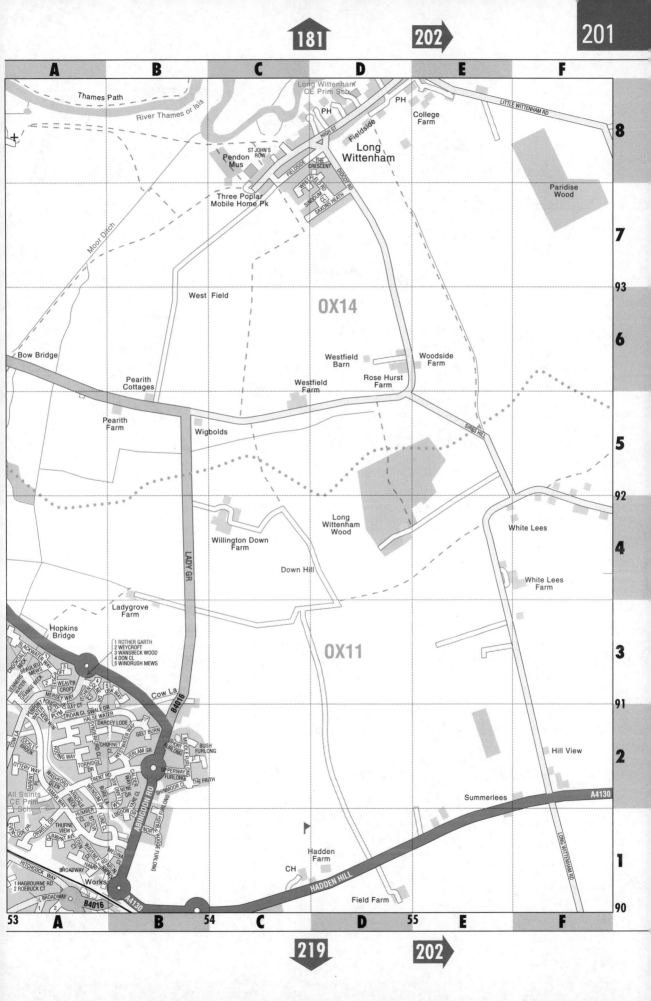

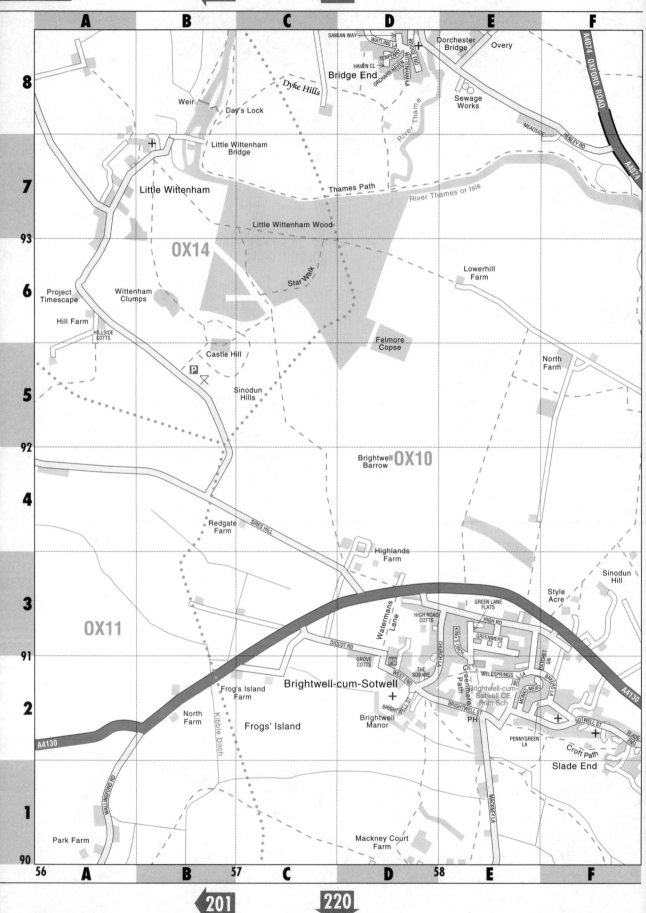

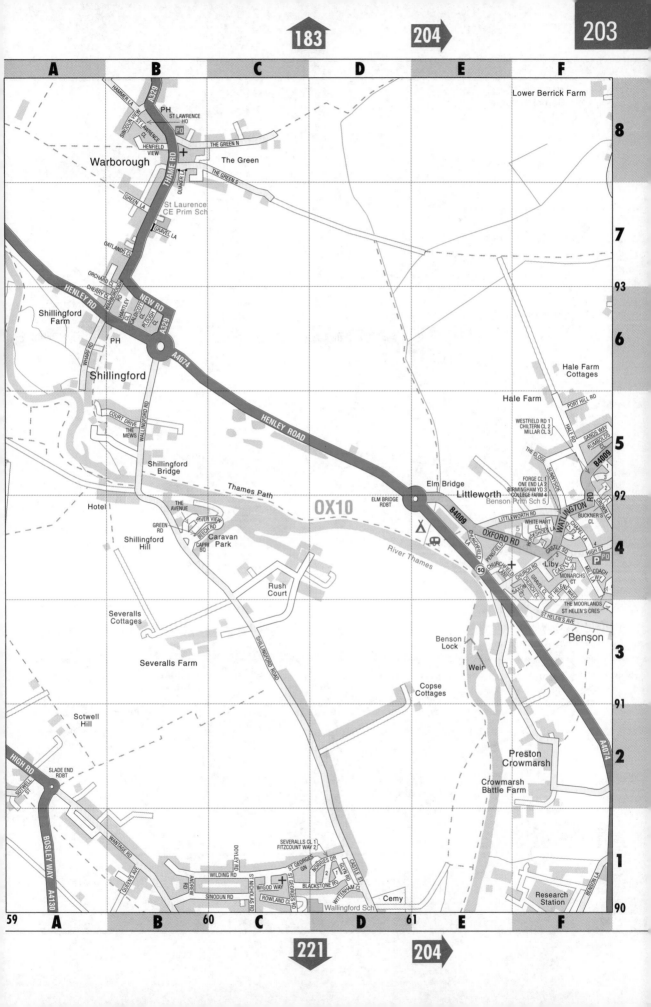

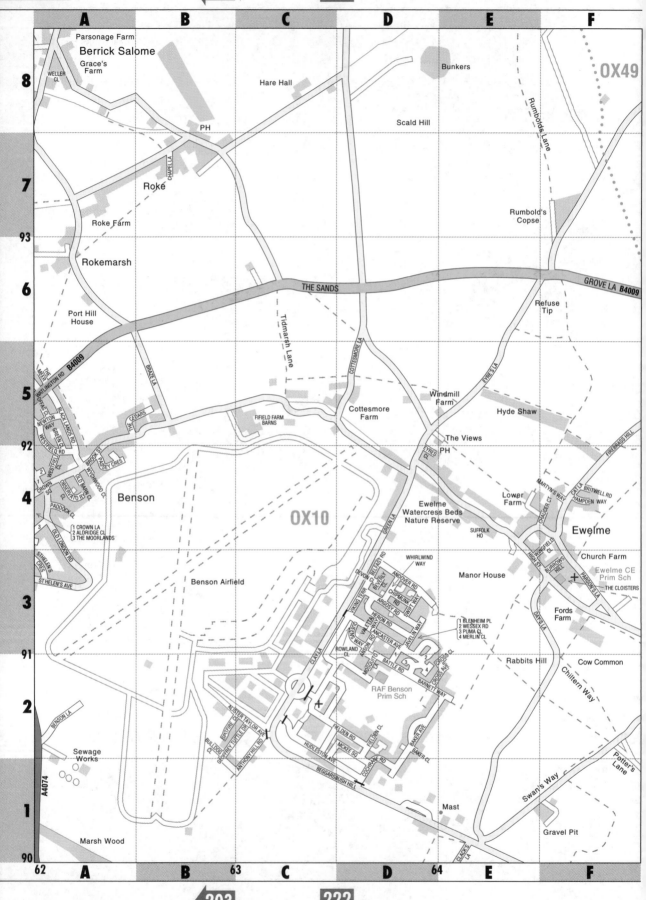

OX49

Parsonage Farm

Berrick Salome

Grace's Farm

WELLER CL

Hare Hall

Bunkers

Scald Hill

Rumbolds Lane

PH

CHAPEL LA

Roke

Rumbold's Copse

Roke Farm

93

Rokemarsh

THE SANDS

GROVE LA B4009

6

Port Hill House

Refuse Tip

Tidmarsh Lane

COTTESMORE LA

EYRE'S LA

B4009

THE MEER
WATLINGTON RD

Windmill Farm

Hyde Shaw

BRAZE LA

FIREBRASS HILL

5

THE CEDARS

Fifield Farm Barns

Cottesmore Farm

SHOPFIELD
NEWTON WAY

BLACK LANDS RD
GREEN LA

Westfield Rd

BROOK ST
PASSEY CRES
WYCHWOOD CL

The Views

EYRES CL

PH

92

RESERVOIR CL
OLD BARN CL

MARTYN'S WAY

CA LA
BRITWELL RD
HAMPDEN WAY

CROWN SQ

PADDOCK CL

Benson

Ewelme Watercress Beds Nature Reserve

Lower Farm

CHAUCER CL

Ewelme

4

1 CROWN LA
2 ALDRIDGE CL
3 THE MOORLANDS

OX10

SUFFOLK HO

HIGH ST
WINGFIELD CL
BURROWS HILL

Church Farm

OLD LONDON RD

STAPLES CRES

GREEN LA

Manor House

Ewelme CE Prim Sch

THE CLOISTERS

ST HELEN'S AVE

Benson Airfield

WHIRLWIND WAY

PARSON'S LA

Fords Farm

DAYS LA

3

ANDOVER RD
BEVERLEY
CHIPMUNK RD
ARGOSY RD

VIKING TERR
DEVON
BELFAST RD
SWIFT WAY

1 BLENHEIM PL
2 WESSEX RD
3 PUMA CL
4 MERLIN CL

VALETTA
HERON RD
LANCASTER AVE
JAVELIN WAY

CLAY LA
MOSQUITO RD
ANSON RD
STIRLING WAY

ROWLAND CL

BATTLE RD

CROSS CL
CROSS AVE

Rabbits Hill

Cow Common

91

BARNETT WAY

Chiltern Way

2

ALISTER TAYLOR AVE

SPITFIRE
GEOFFREY TUTTLE DR

RAF Benson Prim Sch

BAKER AVE
BAKER CL

BULLDOG CL

ANTHONY HILL RD

FIELDEN RD
MCKEE SQ

FIELDER CL

Swan's Way

Potter's Lane

BENSON LA

HUDLESTON AVE

COCHRANE RD

Sewage Works

BEGGARSBUSH HILL

Mast

Gravel Pit

A4074

1

Marsh Wood

CLACK'S LA

90

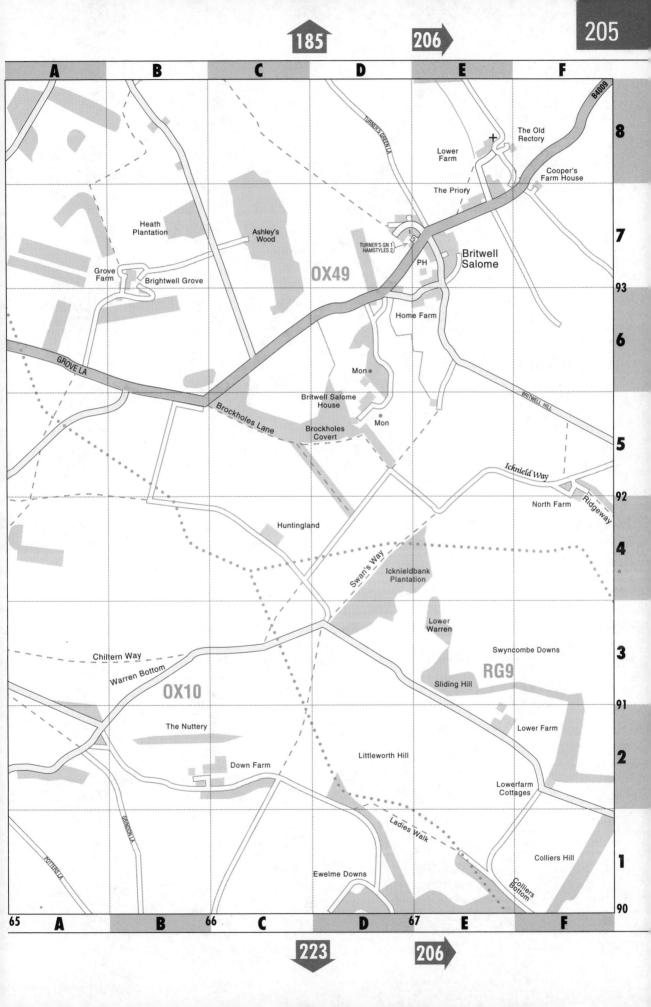

205
186

A   B   C   D   E   F

8

Springfield Farm

White Mark Farm

White Mark

HILL RD

Cobditch Hill

Watlington Hill

P

7

B480

HOWE RD

Icknield House

Piggery

Swan's Way

Ridgeway

Lys Farm House

93

Lower Dean

Lower Deans Wood

6

OX49

Dumbe Dore

Watlington Park

Dame Alice Farm

5

The Howe

Howe Combe

Greenfield Copse

92

Howe Farm

Britwell Hill

HOWE HILL

4

Britwell Hill Farm

Ridgeway

BRITWELL HILL

Howe Wood

Dean Wood

Woods Farm

Westernend Shaw

Mast

3

Ploughmans

Greenfield Manor

Lower Greenfield Farm

Coates Farm

91

COATES LANE

B481

B480

2

Coates Copse

PATEMORE LA

Grove Farm

RG9

RED LA

Wr Twr

CHURCH LA

White Hill

The Rectory

Cookley Green

1

Colliers Hill

RECTORY HILL

LADIES WLK

Church Wood

Reading La

Cookley Farm

B481

Van Diemans

Swyncombe House

90

68   A   B   69   C   D   70   E   F

205
224

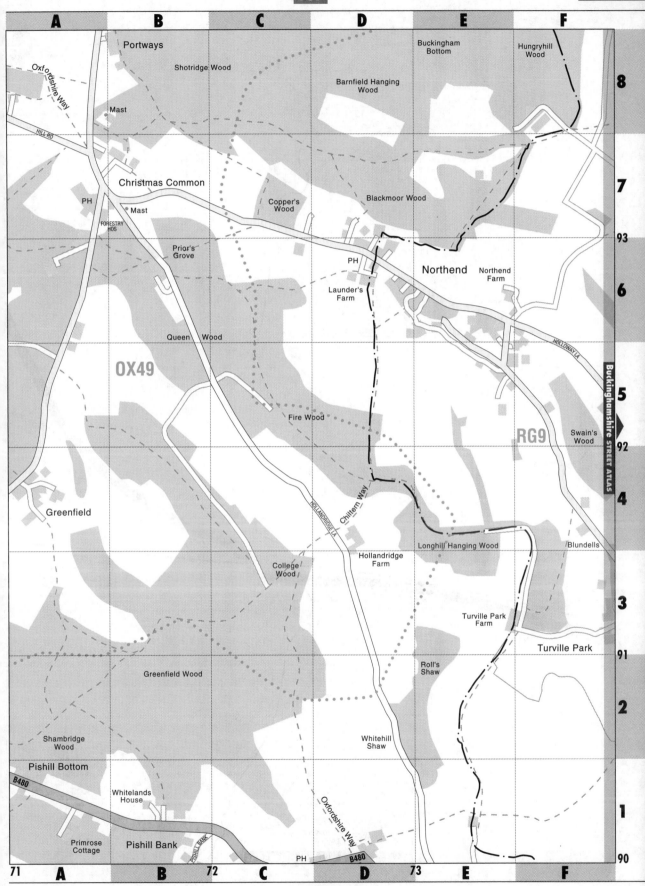

A B C D E F

Portways

Shotridge Wood

Buckingham
Bottom

Hungryhill
Wood

Oxfordshire Way

Barnfield Hanging
Wood

8

Mast

HILL RD

7

Christmas Common

PH

Copper's
Wood

Blackmoor Wood

93

Mast

FORESTRY
HOS

Prior's
Grove

PH

Northend

Northend
Farm

6

Launder's
Farm

Queen Wood

OX49

HOLLOWAY LA

Fire Wood

5

RG9

Swain's
Wood

92

Greenfield

HOLLANDRIDGE LA

Chiltern Way

4

Longhill Hanging Wood

Blundells

College
Wood

Hollandridge
Farm

Turville Park
Farm

3

Turville Park

91

Greenfield Wood

Roll's
Shaw

2

Shambridge
Wood

Whitehill
Shaw

Pishill Bottom

B480

Whitelands
House

Oxfordshire Way

1

Primrose
Cottage

Pishill Bank

PISHILL BANK

PH

B480

90

71 A B 72 C D 73 E F

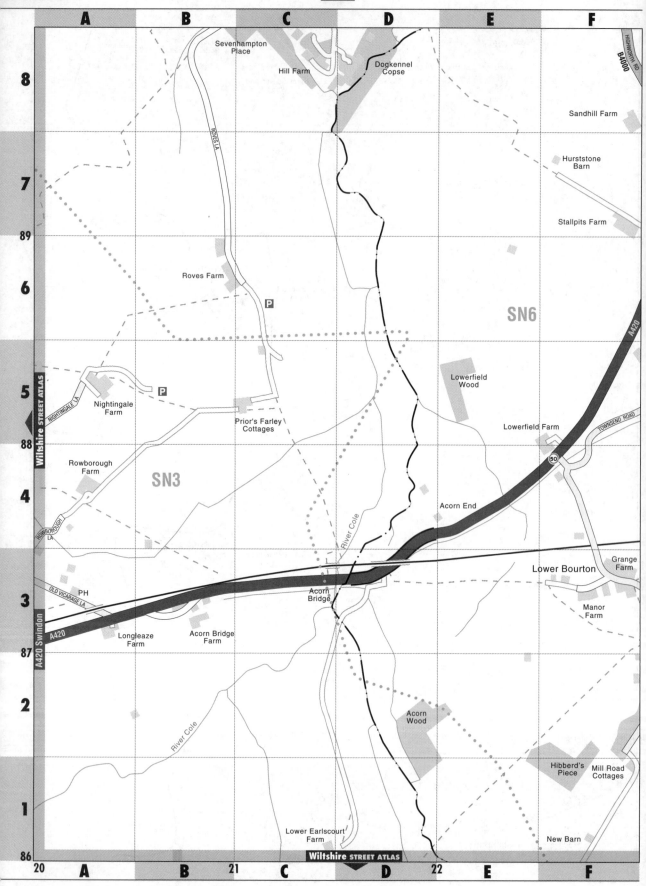

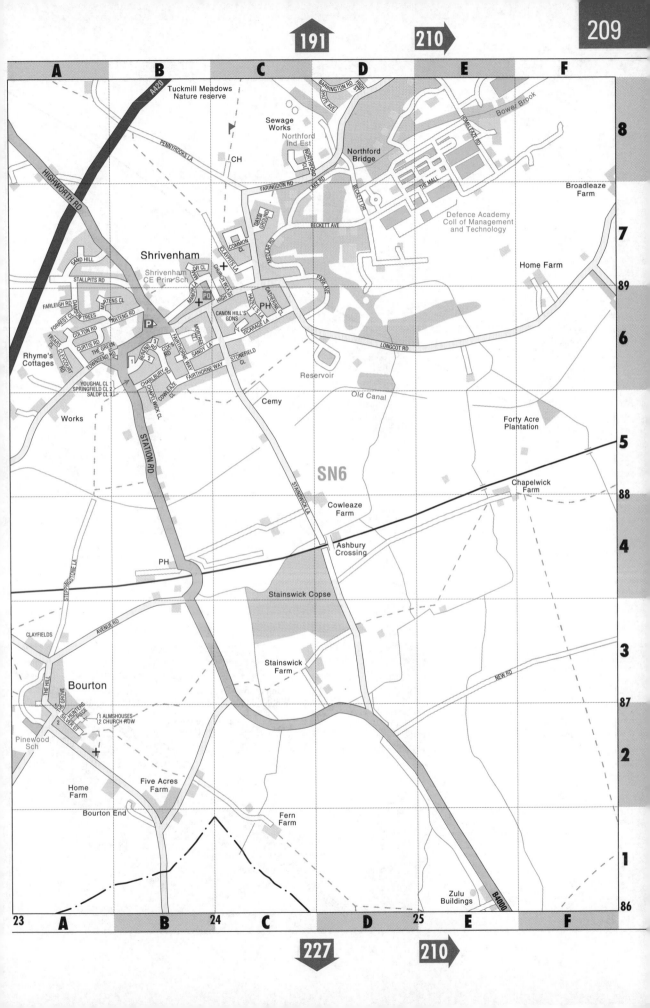

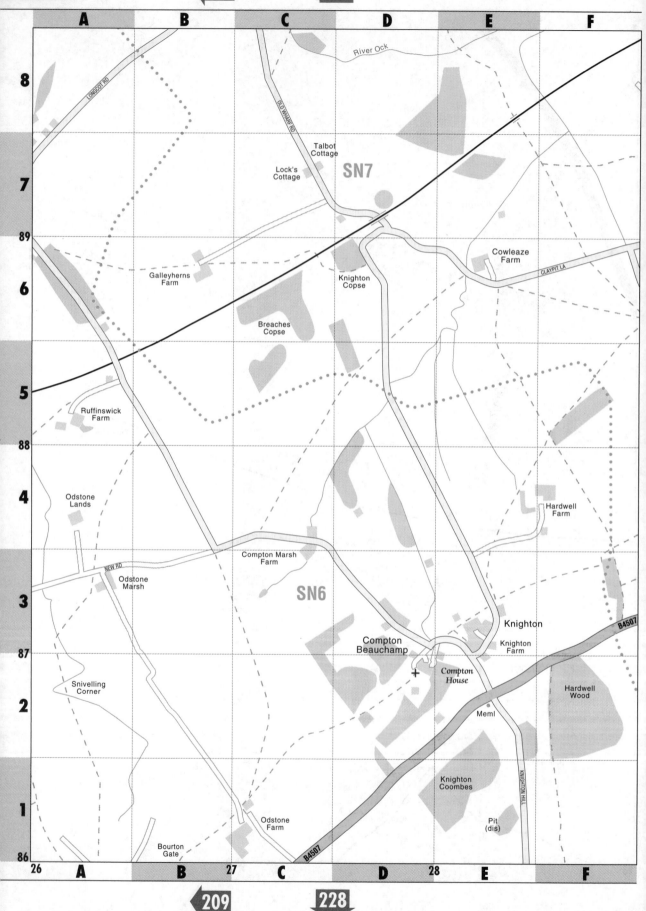

A B C D E F

8

7

89

6

5

88

4

3

87

2

1

86

River Ock

SN7

Talbot Cottage

Lock's Cottage

Cowleaze Farm

CLAYPIT LA

LONGCOT RD

OLD WHARF RD

Galleyherns Farm

Knighton Copse

Breaches Copse

Ruffinswick Farm

Odstone Lands

NEW RD

Odstone Marsh

Compton Marsh Farm

SN6

Hardwell Farm

Knighton

B4507

Snivelling Corner

Compton Beauchamp

Compton House

Knighton Farm

Hardwell Wood

Meml

KNIGHTON HILL

Knighton Coombes

Pit (dis)

Bourton Gate

Odstone Farm

B4507

26 A B 27 C D 28 E F

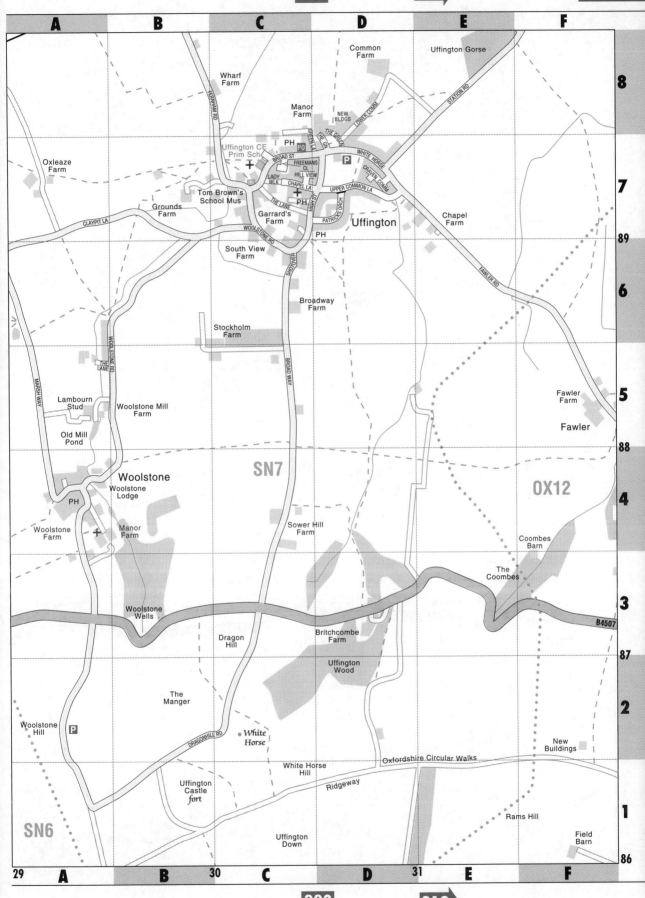

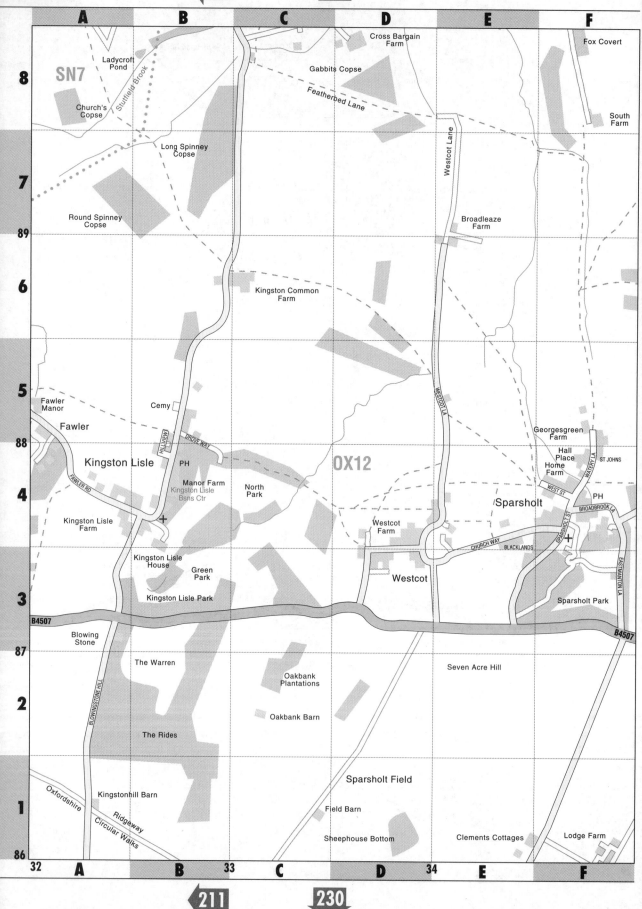

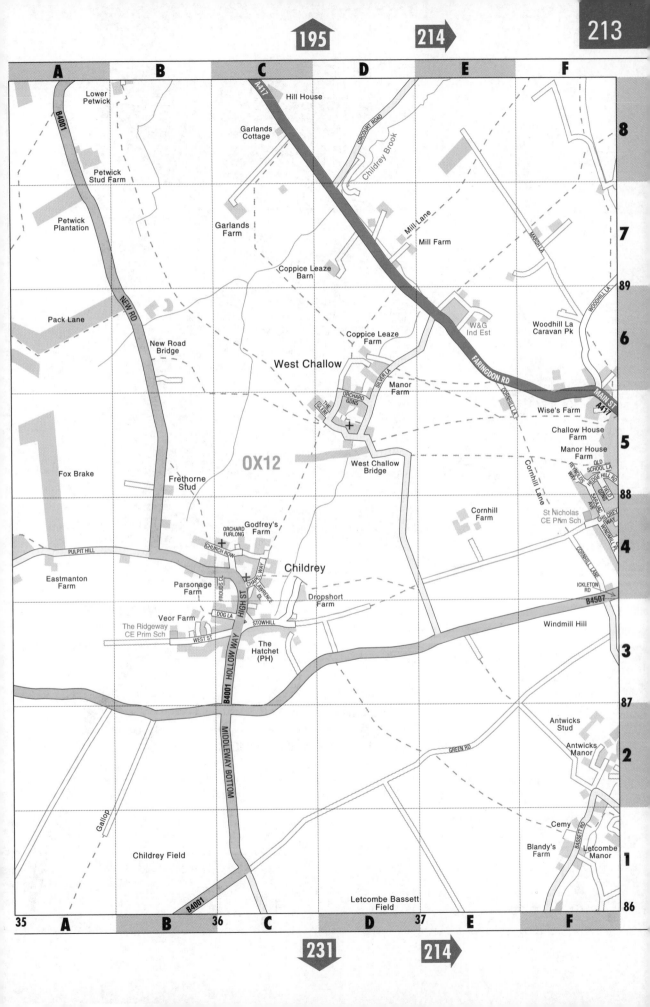

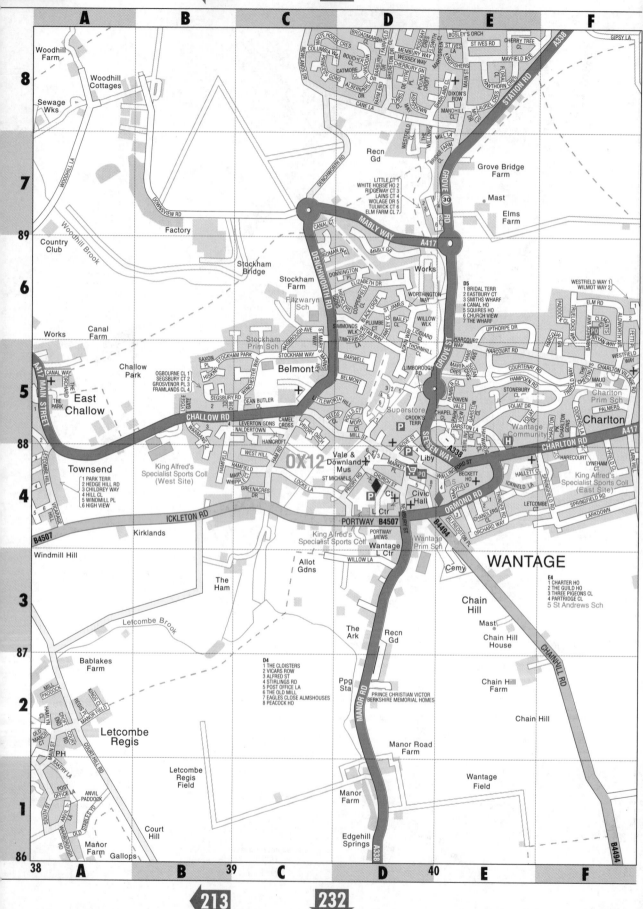

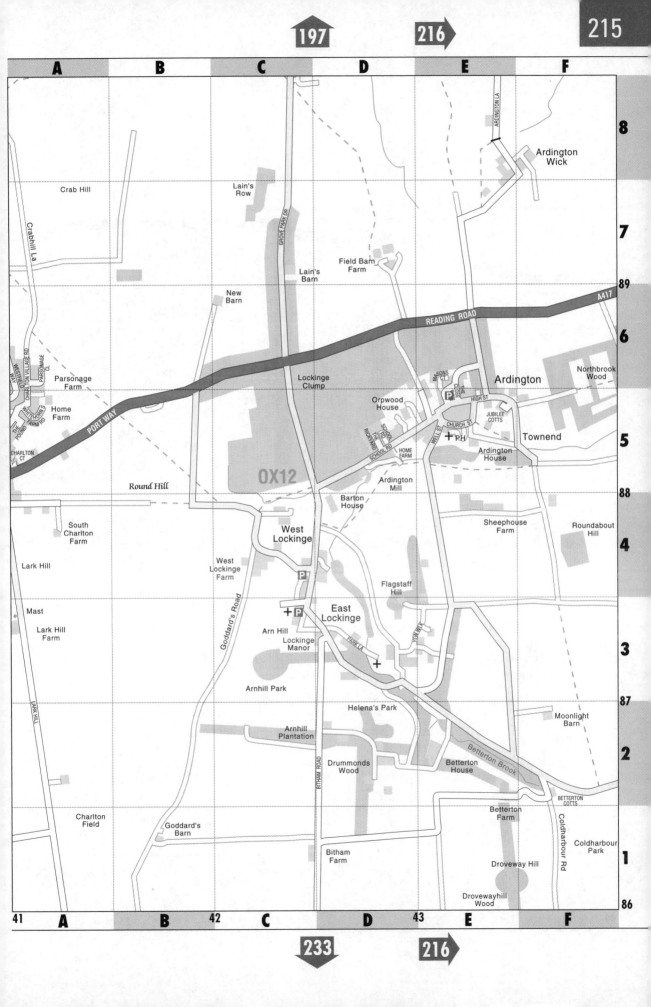

A B C D E F

8

Crab Hill

Lain's Row

Ardington Wick

7

GROVE PARK DR

Lain's Barn

Field Barn Farm

89

A417

Crabhill La

New Barn

Lain's Clump

Lockinge Clump

READING ROAD

6

Northbrook Wood

CHARLTON VILLAGE RD

Parsonage Farm

PARSONAGE CL

Lockinge Clump

MASONS

THE CLOSE

Ardington

P

HIGH ST

WESTFIELD WAY

THE POUND

WHITECROSS

Home Farm

PORT WAY

Orpwood House

SCHOOL RD

THE RICKYARD

SCHOOL RD

HOME FARM

WELL ST

CHURCH ST

JUBILEE COTTS

Townend

CHARLTON FARM RD

CHARLTON CT

PH

5

Ardington House

Round Hill

OX12

Ardington Mill

88

South Charlton Farm

Barton House

Sheephouse Farm

Roundabout Hill

4

Lark Hill

West Lockinge Farm

West Lockinge

P

LARK HILL

Mast

Lark Hill Farm

GODDARD'S ROAD

P

East Lockinge

Flagstaff Hill

Arn Hill

Lockinge Manor

PARK LA

YEW WK

3

Arnhill Park

Helena's Park

87

Moonlight Barn

Arnhill Plantation

Betterton Brook

2

BITHAM ROAD

Drummonds Wood

Betterton House

Betterton COTTS

Goddard's Barn

Charlton Field

Bitham Farm

Betterton Farm

Coldharbour Rd

Coldharbour Park

1

Droveway Hill

Drovewayhill Wood

86

41 A B 42 C D 43 E F

215
198

A417
Quab Hill
Quab Hill Farm
Greensands
East Hendred Brook
Ludbridge Mill (disused)
New Barn
Lud Bridge
50
A417
PH
READING RD
Sheephouse Barn
WOOD'S FARM RD
ALLIN'S LA
SMITH'S RUCKYARD
HOME FARM CL
COULINGS CL
ORCHARD CL
WHITE RD
East Hendred
A417
FEATHERBED LA
THE GREENWAY
BANKSIDE
MILL LA
MILL LA
ORCHARD LA
CHAPEL SQ
Champs Chapel Mus
OX11
Recreation Ground
The Mill
The Hendreds CE Prim Sch
West Hendred
THE MILLHAM
FORDY LA
CAT ST
HIGH ST
PH
PO
Hall
GINGE RD
MANOR LA
THE SPINNEY
CHURCH ST
Hendred House
ST MARY'S RD
Lydebank Plantation
The Moors
MOUNT PLEASANT COTTS
HORN LA
St Amand RC Prim Sch
Red Barn
THE LYNCH
Hill Farm
Cow Road
GINGE ROAD
Goldbury Hill
Park Hill
NEWBURY RD
GOLDBURY COTTS
OX12
Park Hill Row
Icknield
Pump House
Aldfield Common
Shadwell's Row
Black Mills Row
Parsonage Barn
Lower Farm
STILEWAY ROAD
West Ginge
Ellaway's Barn
TWENTIETH ST
Ginge House
East Ginge
Upper Farm
Ginge Manor
Deer Park
OX11
RUTHERFORD AVE
White Way
Downs Cottage
Meashill Plantation

Lockinge Brook
Ginge Brook

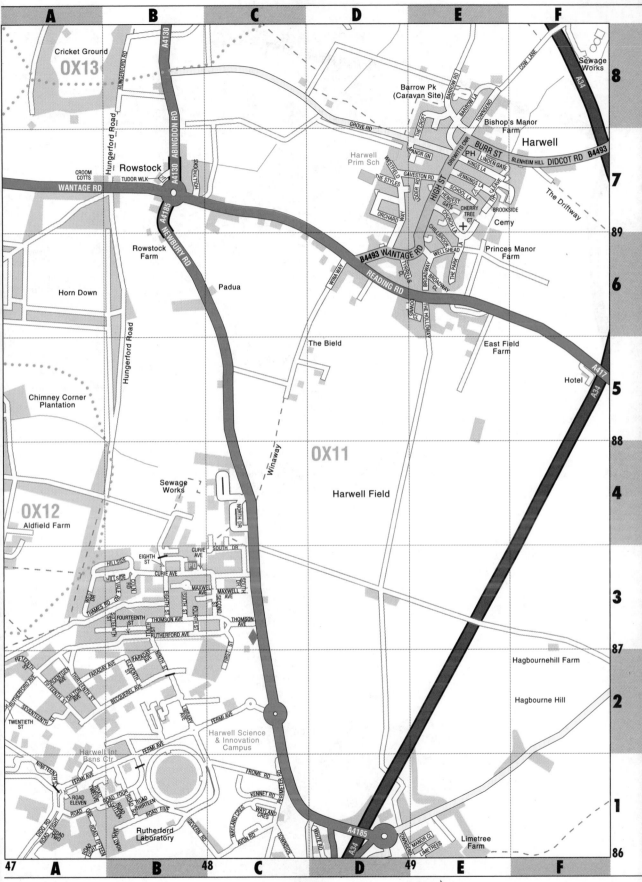

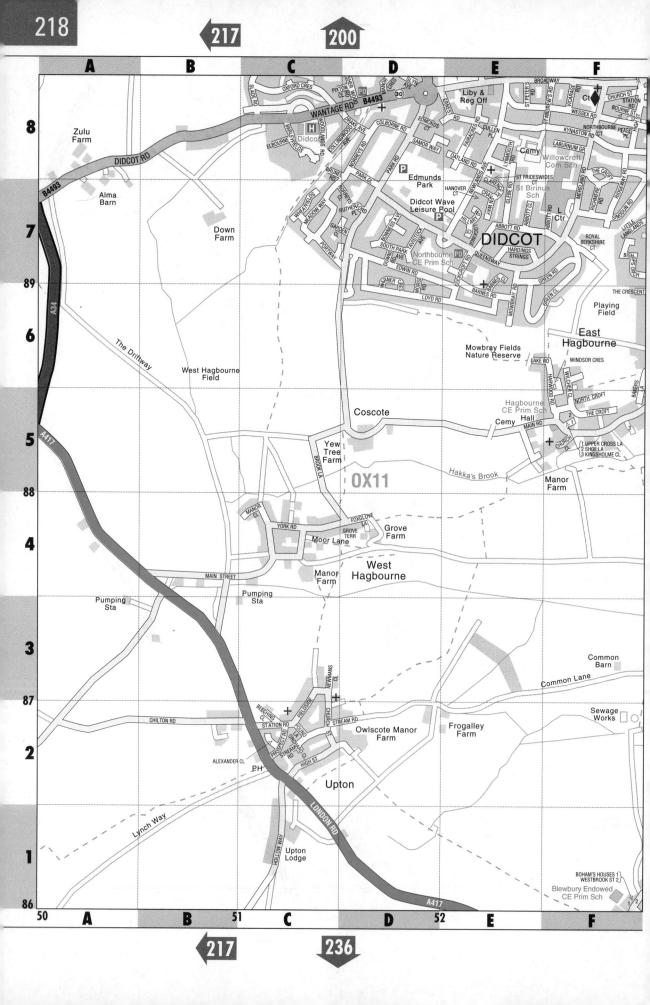

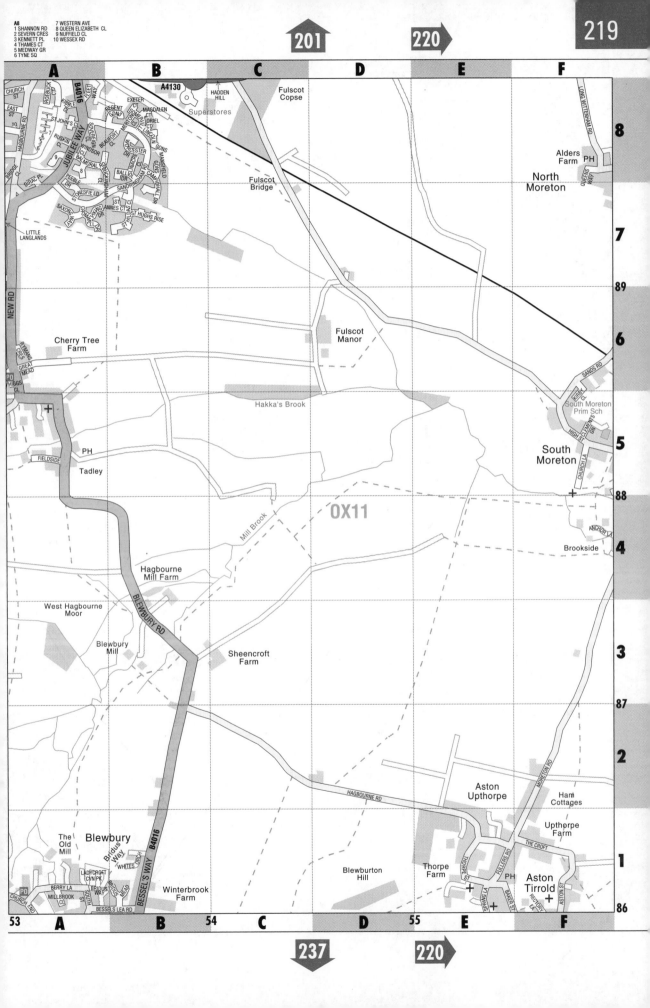

A8
1 SHANNON RD
2 SEVERN CRES
3 KENNETT PL
4 THAMES CT
5 MEDWAY GR
6 TYNE SQ
7 WESTERN AVE
8 QUEEN ELIZABETH CL
9 NUFFIELD CL
10 WESSEX RD

201
220

A4130
HADDEN HILL
Superstores
Fulscot Copse
Fulscot Bridge

8

Alders Farm PH

North Moreton

CHURCH ST
EAST ST
ROEBUCK CTP
JUBILEE WAY
B4016
JUBILEE WAY
HAGBOURNE RD
ST JOHN'S
RUSKIN CL
WINDSOR CL
BALMORAL RD
PEEBLE DR
NESFIE LD
DIRAC PL
SAXONS WAY
VIKING DR
ANNES CT
ST HUGHS RISE
CROMWELL DR
EXETER
REGENT GDNP
SOVEREIGN
MAGDALEN CT
LINCOLN CT
ORIEL
GONS
BEAUFORT CL
WORCESTER DR
LANCESTER GDNS
MANSFIELD
BRACKNALL DR
SANDRINGHAM DR
CAMPBELL DR

7

LITTLE LANGLANDS

NEW RD

Cherry Tree Farm

BYRONS CRES
GREAT MEAD
HIGGS CL
PO

89

6

Fulscot Manor

SANDS RD
KIRBY CL
South Moreton Prim Sch
HIGH ST
ST ANDREWS GDN

Hakka's Brook

PH
FIELDSIDE
Tadley

5

South Moreton

88

OX11

Mill Brook

Brookside
ANCHOR LA

4

Hagbourne Mill Farm

West Hagbourne Moor

BLEWBURY RD

Blewbury Mill

Sheencroft Farm

3

87

2

Aston Upthorpe

MORETON RD
Ham Cottages

Upthorpe Farm
THE CROFT

HAGBOURNE RD

The Old Mill
Blewbury
Bridus Way
LADYCROFT CVN PK
WHITES
NEAD
B4016
BESSEL'S WAY

Blewburton Hill

Thorpe Farm
THORPE ST
FULLERS RD
PH
SPRING LA
BAKER ST
ASTON ST
RECTORY LA

Aston Tirrold

1

PO
CHURCH END
MILLBROOK CL
BERRY LA
SOUTH BRIDUS WAY
BESSELS LEA RD

Winterbrook Farm

86

53
A
54
B
C
55
D
E
F

237
220

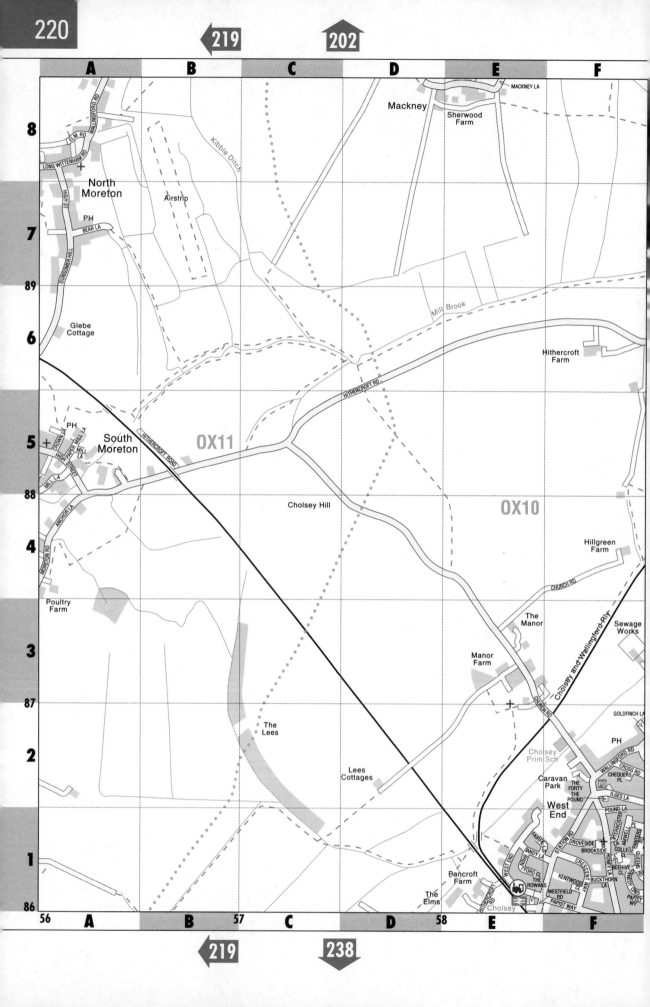

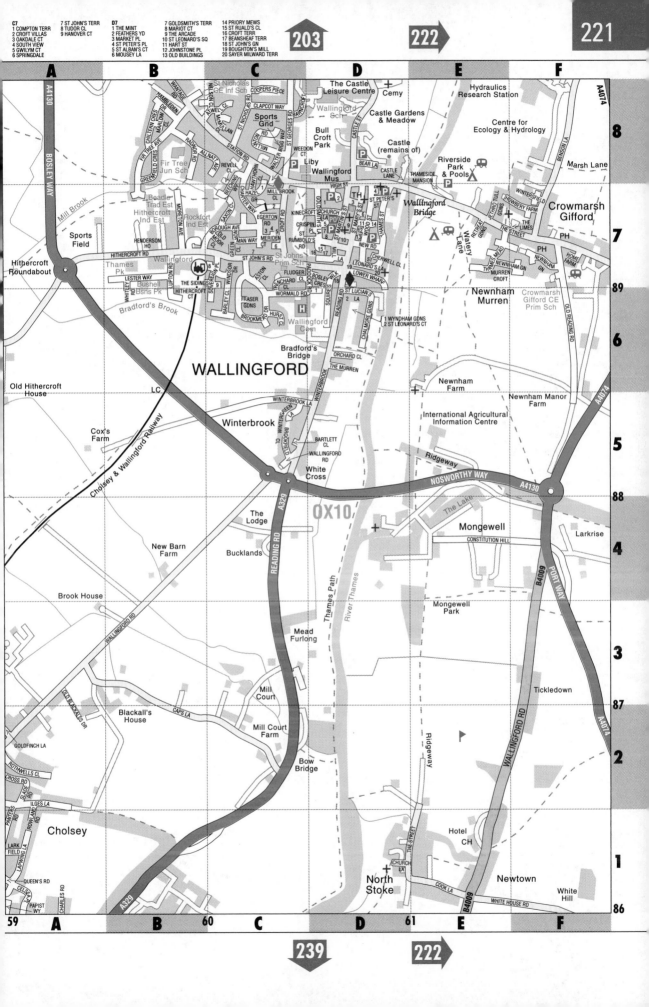

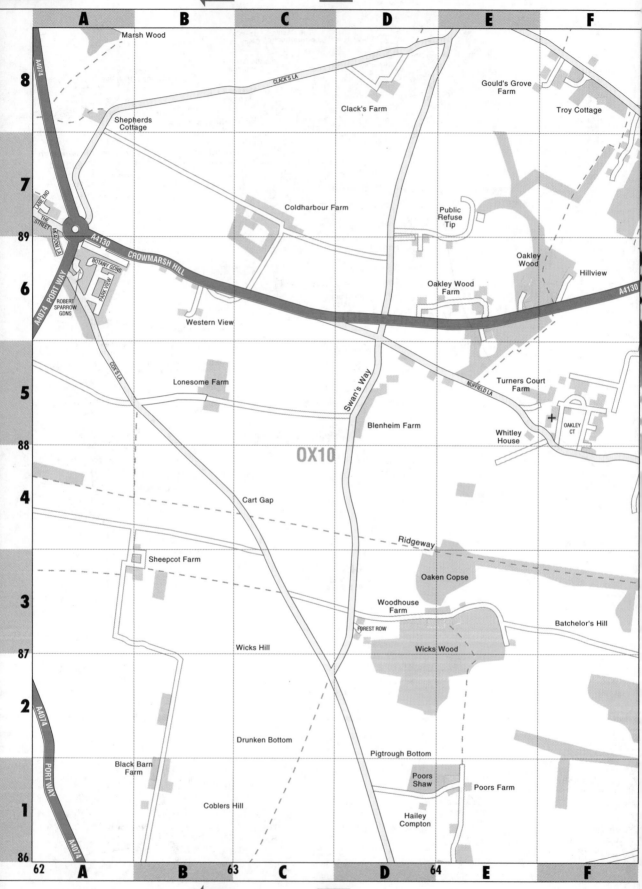

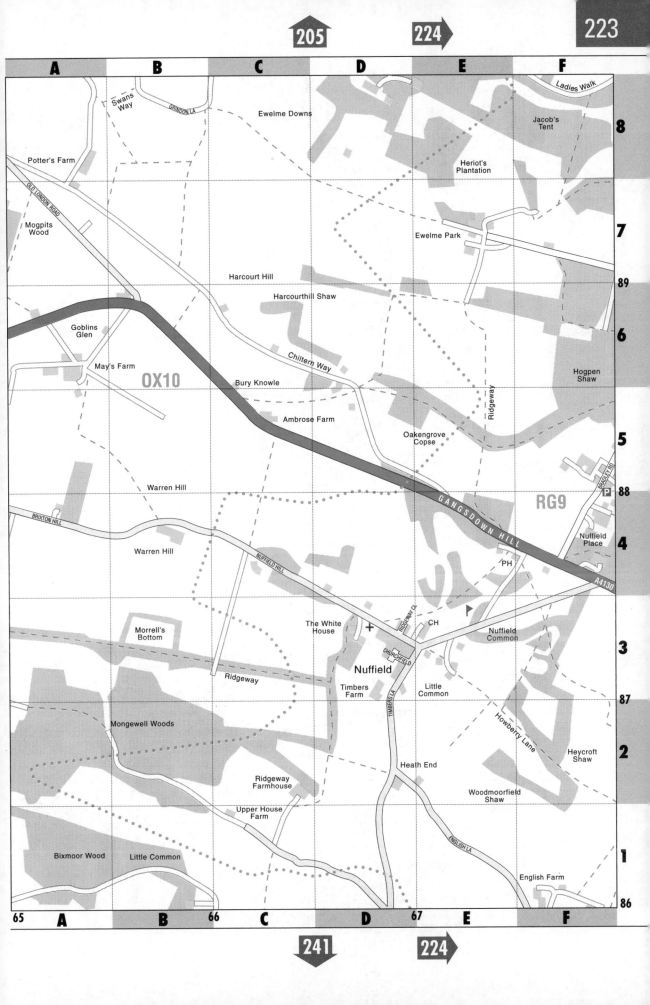

A B C D E F

8

7

89

6

5

88

4

3

87

2

1

86

Ladies Walk

Ewelme Downs

Jacob's Tent

Heriot's Plantation

Potter's Farm

Swans Way

GRINDON LA

Ewelme Park

Mogpits Wood

OLD LONDON ROAD

Harcourt Hill

Harcourthill Shaw

Goblins Glen

May's Farm

OX10

Chiltern Way

Bury Knowle

Hogpen Shaw

Ambrose Farm

Ridgeway

Oakengrove Copse

Warren Hill

BRIXTON HILL

GANGSDOWN HILL

RG9

Warren Hill

NUFFIELD HILL

Bradley RD

Nuffield Place

A4130

Morrell's Bottom

The White House

RIDGEWAY CL

CH

PH

Nuffield Common

Ridgeway

CHURCHFIELD

Nuffield

Timbers Farm

Little Common

Mongewell Woods

TIMBERS LA

Howberry Lane

Heycroft Shaw

Ridgeway Farmhouse

Heath End

Woodmoorfield Shaw

Upper House Farm

ENGLISH LA

Bixmoor Wood

Little Common

English Farm

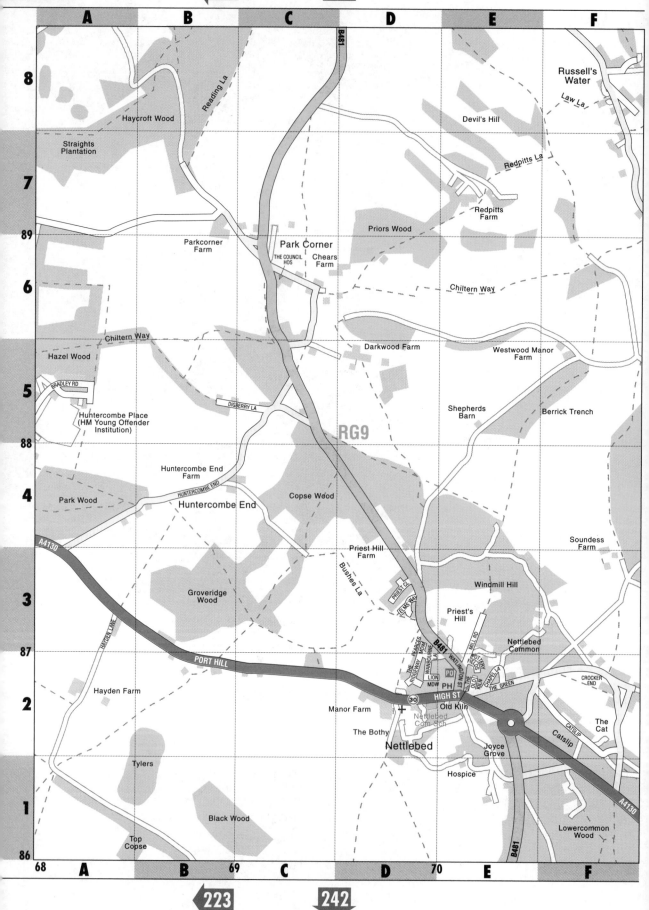

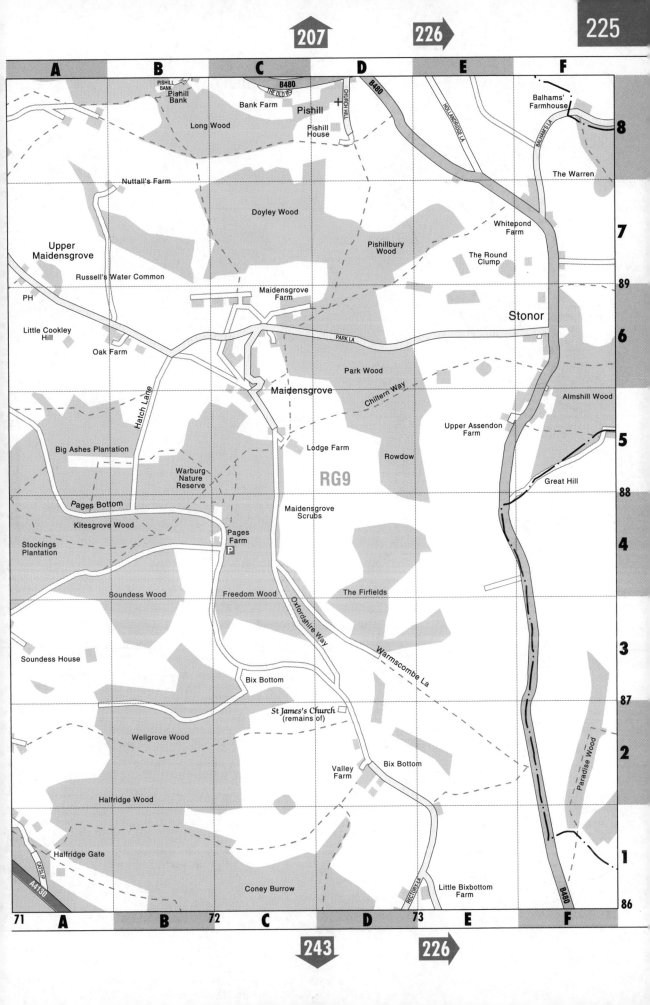

Buckinghamshire STREET ATLAS

Buckinghamshire STREET ATLAS

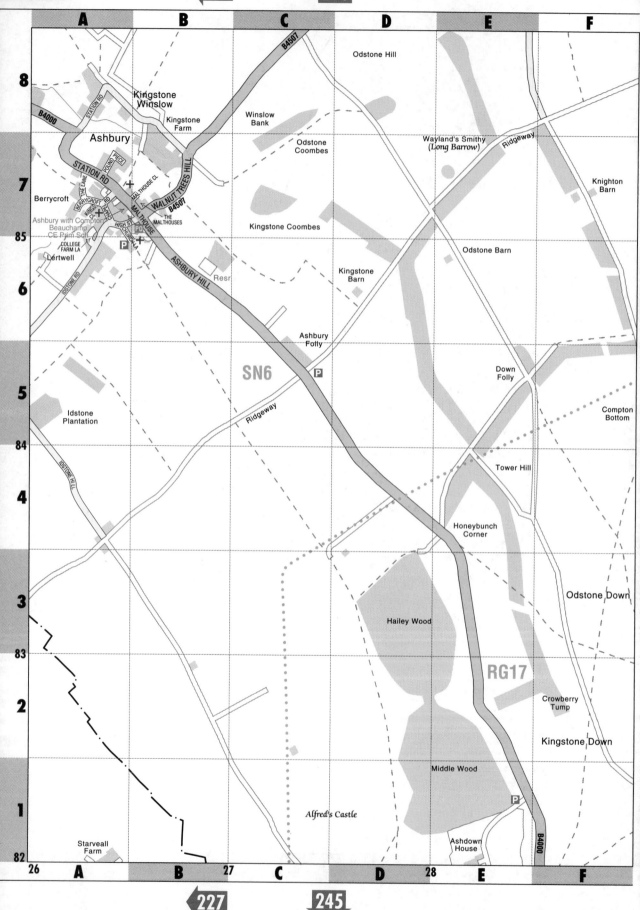

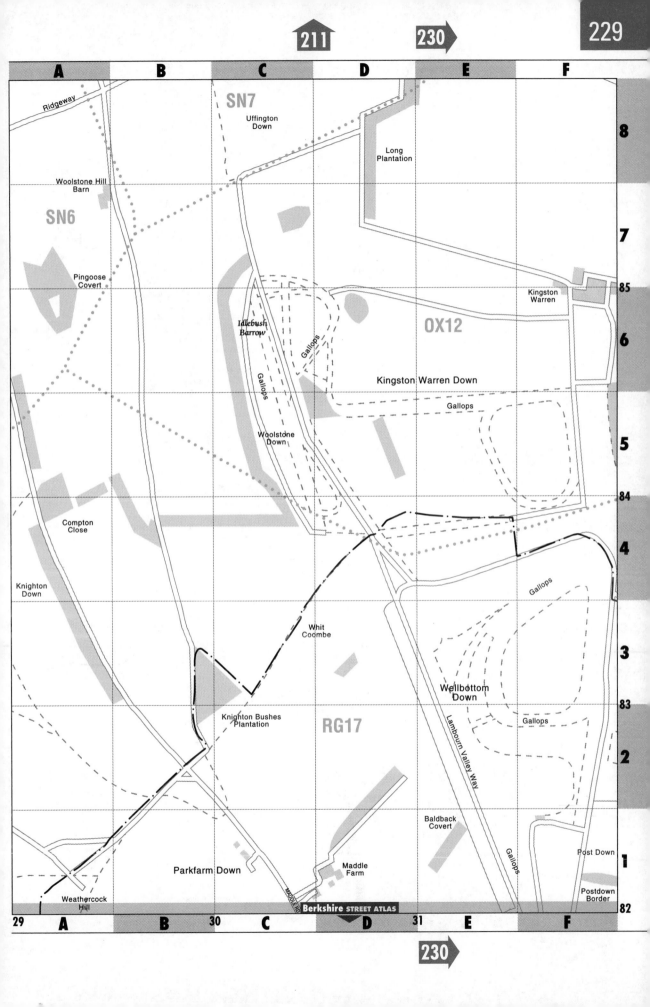

A B C D E F

8

7

85

6

5

84

4

3

83

2

1

82

SN7
Uffington Down
Long Plantation

Woolstone Hill Barn

SN6

Pingoose Covert

Kingston Warren

OX12

Idlebush Barrow

Gallops

Gallops

Kingston Warren Down

Gallops

Woolstone Down

Gallops

Compton Close

Knighton Down

Whit Coombe

Gallops

Wellbottom Down

Gallops

Knighton Bushes Plantation

RG17

Lambourn Valley Way

Baldback Covert

Gallops

Post Down

Parkfarm Down

Maddle Farm

Postdown Border

Weathercock Hill

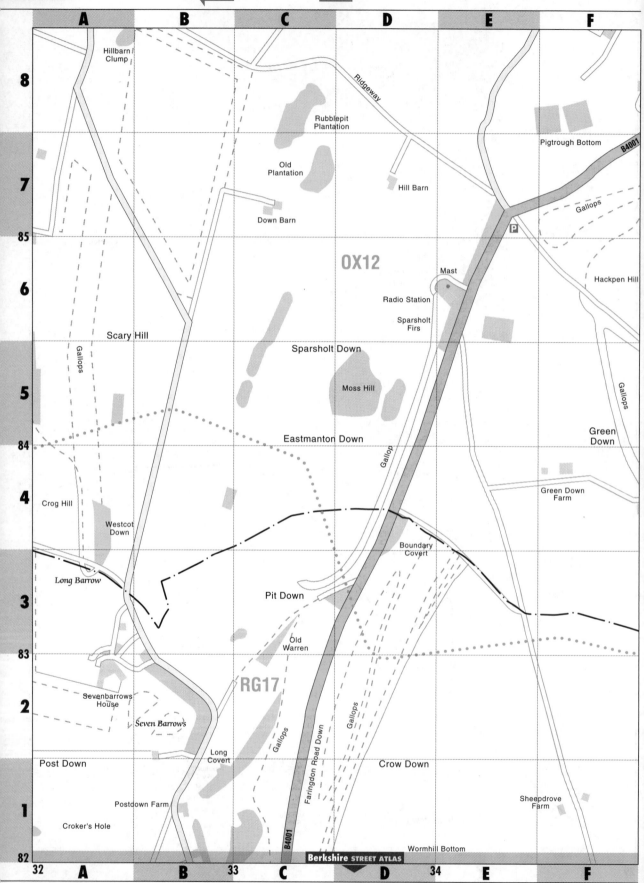

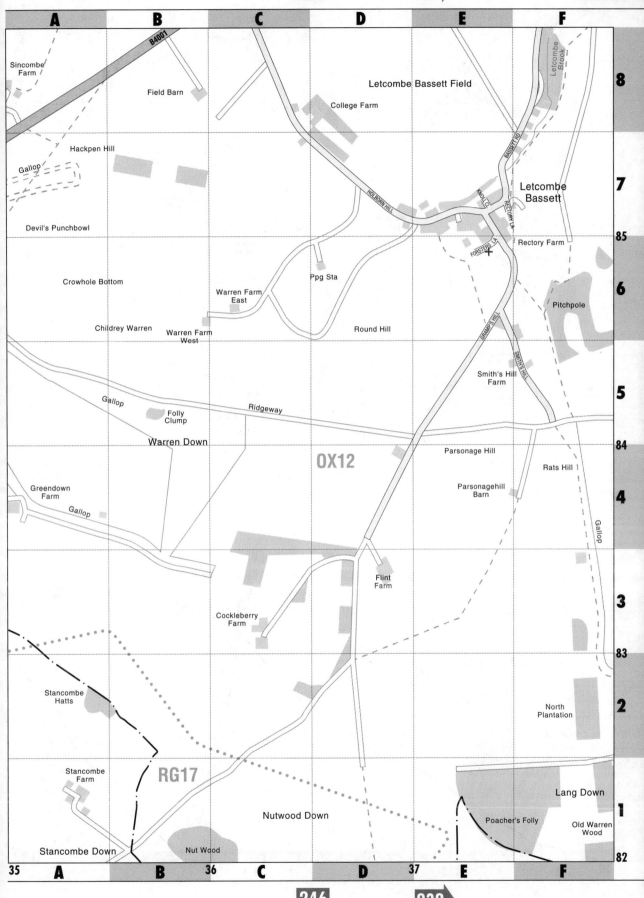

A B C D E F

8

7

85

6

5

84

4

3

83

2

1

82

Sincombe Farm

B4001

Field Barn

Letcombe Bassett Field

College Farm

Letcombe Brook

Hackpen Hill

Bassett Rd

Gallop

Letcombe Bassett

Devil's Punchbowl

Holborn Hill

Knoll Cp

Rectory La

Rectory Farm

Crowhole Bottom

Ppg Sta

Forsters La

Pitchpole

Warren Farm East

Childrey Warren

Warren Farm West

Round Hill

Gramp's Hill

Smith's Hill Farm

Smith's Hill

Gallop

Folly Clump

Ridgeway

Warren Down

OX12

Parsonage Hill

Rats Hill

Greendown Farm

Gallop

Parsonagehill Barn

Gallop

Flint Farm

Cockleberry Farm

North Plantation

Stancombe Hatts

RG17

Stancombe Farm

Lang Down

Nutwood Down

Poacher's Folly

Old Warren Wood

Stancombe Down

Nut Wood

35 A B 36 C D 37 E F 82

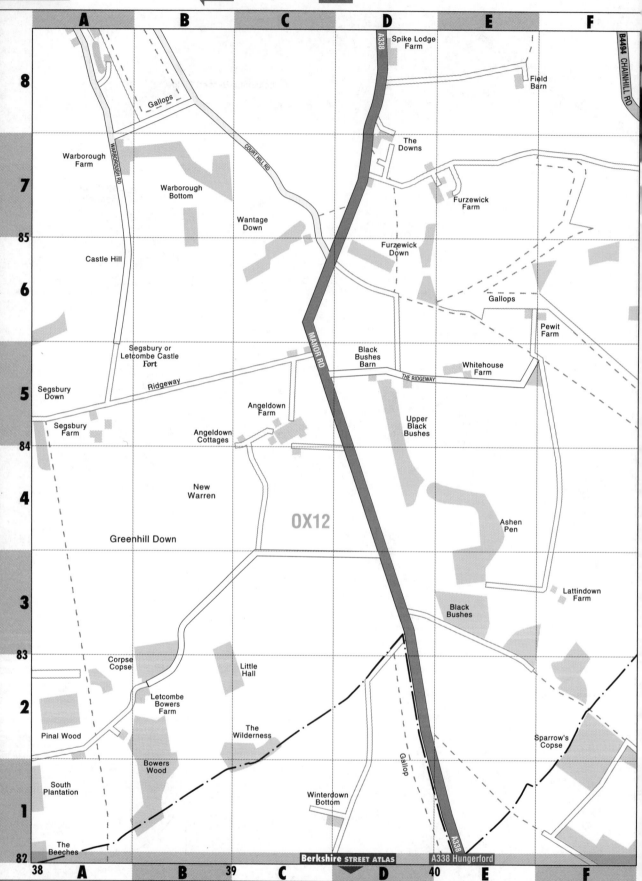

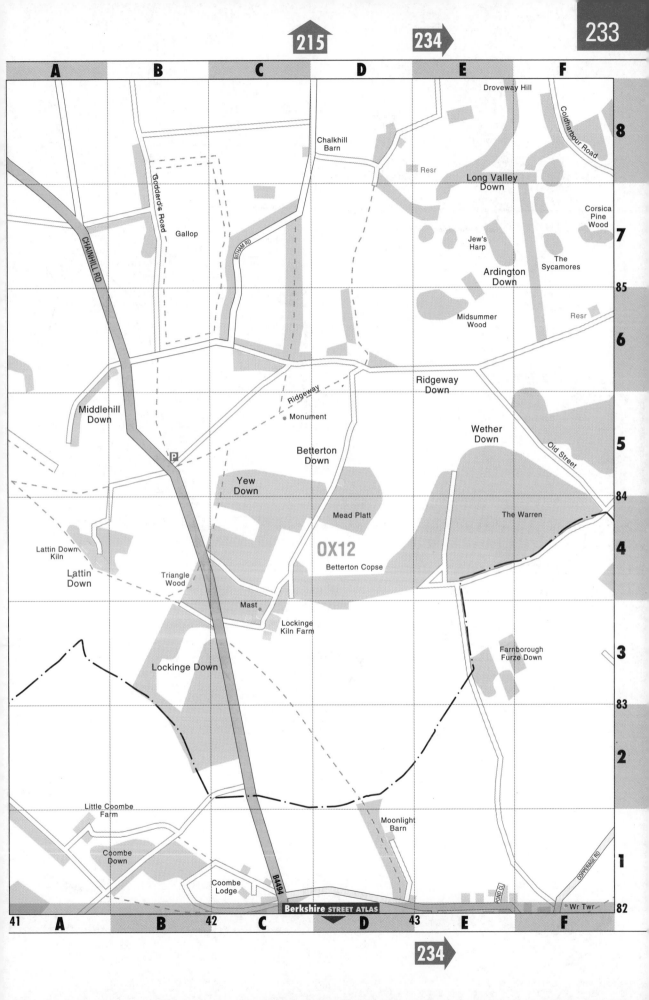

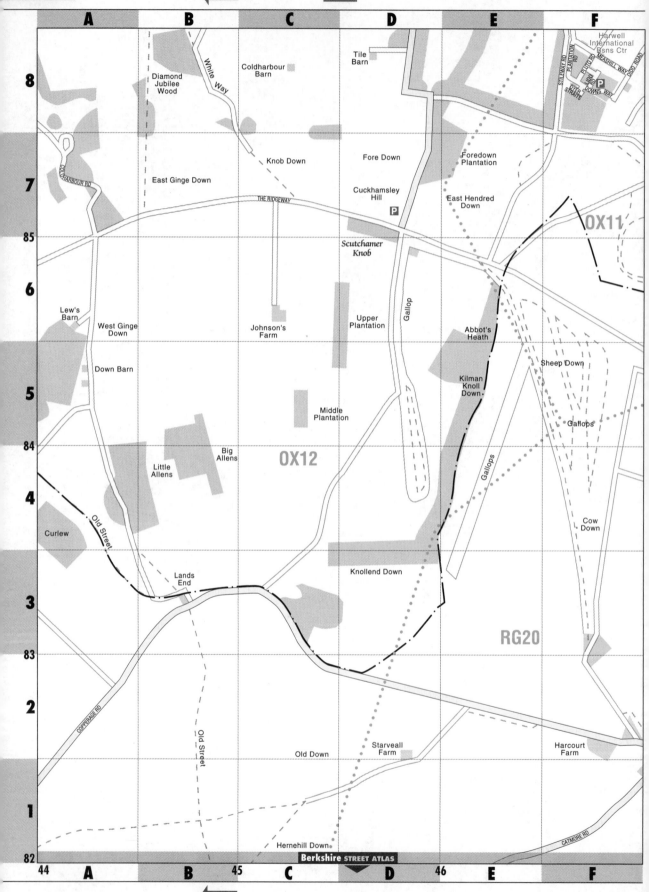

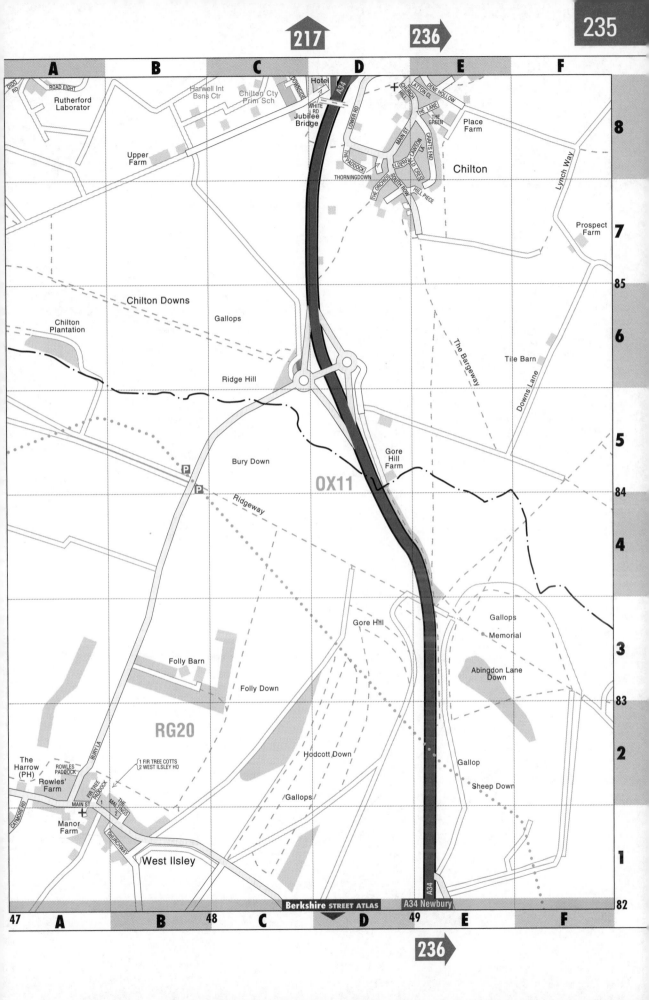

A B C D E F

DIDO RD
ROAD EIGHT
Rutherford
Laborator

Harwell Int
Bsns Ctr

Chilton Cty
Prim Sch

DOWNSIDE

Hotel

WHITE RD
Jubilee
Bridge

A34

LOWER RD

CHURCH HILL

LATTON CL

DENE HOLLOW

THE LANE

THE GREEN

Place
Farm

8

Upper
Farm

THE PADDOCK

THORNINGDOWN

THE ORCHIDS

MAIN ST

ELDERS
LAWSON LA

CRAFTS END

OLD CRES

SOUTH ROW

HILL PIECE

Chilton

Prospect
Farm

7

Chilton Downs

Gallops

Lynch Way

85

Chilton
Plantation

Ridge Hill

The Bargeway

Tile Barn

Downs Lane

6

Bury Down

OX11

Gore Hill
Farm

5

P

P

Ridgeway

84

4

Folly Barn

Folly Down

Gore Hill

Gallops
Memorial

Abingdon Lane
Down

3

RG20

1 FIR TREE COTTS
2 WEST ILSLEY HO

83

Hodcott Down

Gallop

Sheep Down

2

The
Harrow
(PH)

ROWLES
PADDOCK

BURY LA

FIR TREE
PADDOCK

Rowles'
Farm

CATMORE RD

MAIN ST

THE MALTINGS
1
2

Gallops

Gallops

Manor
Farm

CHURCHWAY

West Ilsley

1

82

47 A 48 B C 49 D E F

A **B** **C** **D** **E** **F**

HOLLOW WAY

WESTBROOK ST
WESTBROOK GN
NOTTINGHAM RD
Waterly La

A417
LONDON RD

A417

PH

8

New
Buildings

7

Alden
Farm

85

Churn
Knob

6

The
Kennels

Churn Knob

Tile
Barn

BOHAM'S RD

Saltbox

Rose
Cottage

Churn Hill

5

OX11

Upper Chance
Farm

84

Gallops

Old
Butts

4

Churn
Farm

The
Firs

Gallops

3

Gallops

Several Down

Gallops

Gallops

83

Ridgeway

Gallops

2

Compton
Downs

Gallops

Lower Chance
Farm

Blewbury
Down

Ridgeway

Gallops

1

Gallops

CHURN RD

Ridgeway

82

50 **A** **B** 51 **C** **D** 52 **E** **F**

219
238

A **B** **C** **D** **E** **F**

CHURCH
END
WATT'S
LA
GRAHAM CL
SOUTH ST
CHURCH RD
DIBLEYS
EASTFIELD
BESSEL'S WAY
CHAPEL LA
RUMSEY'S
ROBINSON CL
B4016

Blewbury

LONDON RD

1 FORTY CROSS
2 TREBLE HOUSE TERR
3 NOTTINGHAM FEE

BLEWBURY HILL

Hunt's
Grave

Golf Driving
Range

Blewbury
Barn

Copse Style
Farm

RECTORY LA

THE
CLOSE
DOWNS
VIEW

BAKER ST

ASTON ST

SPRING LA

**Aston
Tirrold**

CHALK HILL

8

WOODWAY RD

Downside
Farm

Baldon Hill

Lid's Down

Gallops

A417

Carrimers
Farm

7

85

WHITE SHOOT

Riddle Hill

Chalk Hill Bottom

6

Sheepcot
Farm

OX11

Hill
Barn

Hogtrough
Bottom

5

84

Woodway

Gallops

Upper Hill
Barn

The
Plantation

4

Langdon
Hill

Big Bull
Hill

Oven Bottom

Gallop

3

Gallops

Aston Upthorpe
Downs

83

The Fair Mile

2

Gallops

Fuller's Firs

Lowbury
Hill

RG8

Dean's Bottom

1

Ridgeway

82

53 **A** 54 **B** **C** 55 **D** **E** **F**

247
238

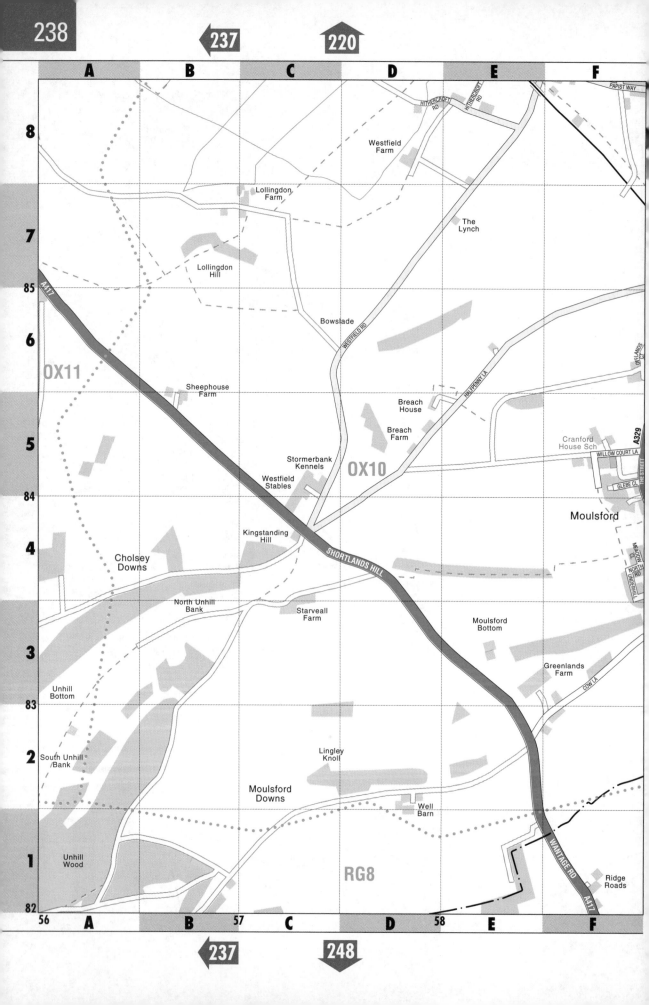

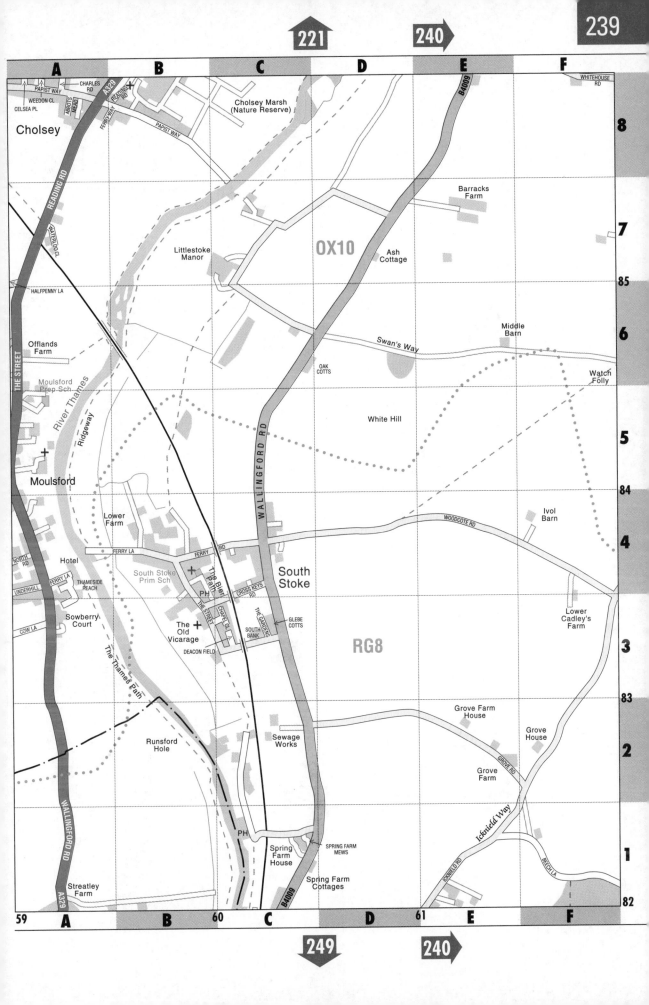

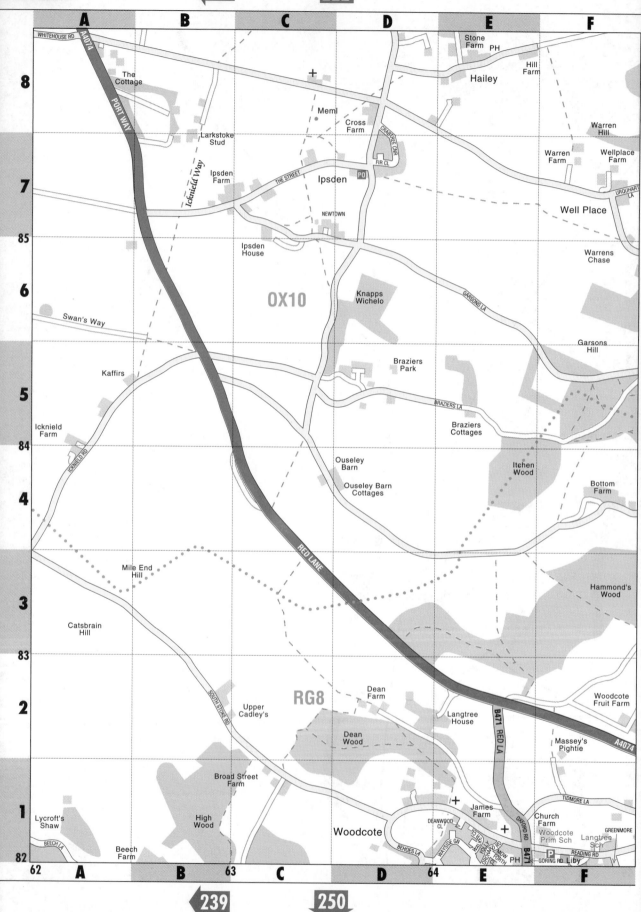

A | B | C | D | E | F

8

WHITEHOUSE RD

PORT WAY

A4074

The Cottage

Stone Farm
PH
Hill Farm
Hailey

Larkstoke Stud

Icknield Way

Meml
Cross Farm

Warren Hill

Ipsden Farm

THE STREET

Ipsden

CRABTREE CHH

FIR CL
PO

Warren Farm
Wellplace Farm

7

Well Place

URQUHART LA

NEWTOWN

85

Ipsden House

Warrens Chase

OX10

6

Knapps Wichelo

GARSONS LA

Swan's Way

Garsons Hill

Braziers Park

BRAZIERS LA

5

Kaffirs

Braziers Cottages

Icknield Farm

ICKNIELD RD

84

Ouseley Barn

Itchen Wood

Bottom Farm

Ouseley Barn Cottages

4

Mile End Hill

RED LANE

Hammond's Wood

3

Catsbrain Hill

83

Dean Farm

Woodcote Fruit Farm

RG8

2

SOUTH STOKE RD

Upper Cadley's

Langtree House

B471 RED LA

Massey's Pightie

A4074

Dean Wood

Broad Street Farm

TIDMORE LA

1

Lycroft's Shaw

High Wood

James Farm

Church Farm

DEANWOOD CL

Woodcote Prim Sch

GREENMORE

Langtree Sch

BEECH LA

Woodcote

BEHOES LA

WAYSIDE GN

ORCHARD RD

OXFORD RD

PH

READING RD

Beech Farm

MDW
ZORTH

B471

P

GORING RD
Liby

82

62 | A | B | 63 | C | D | 64 | E | F

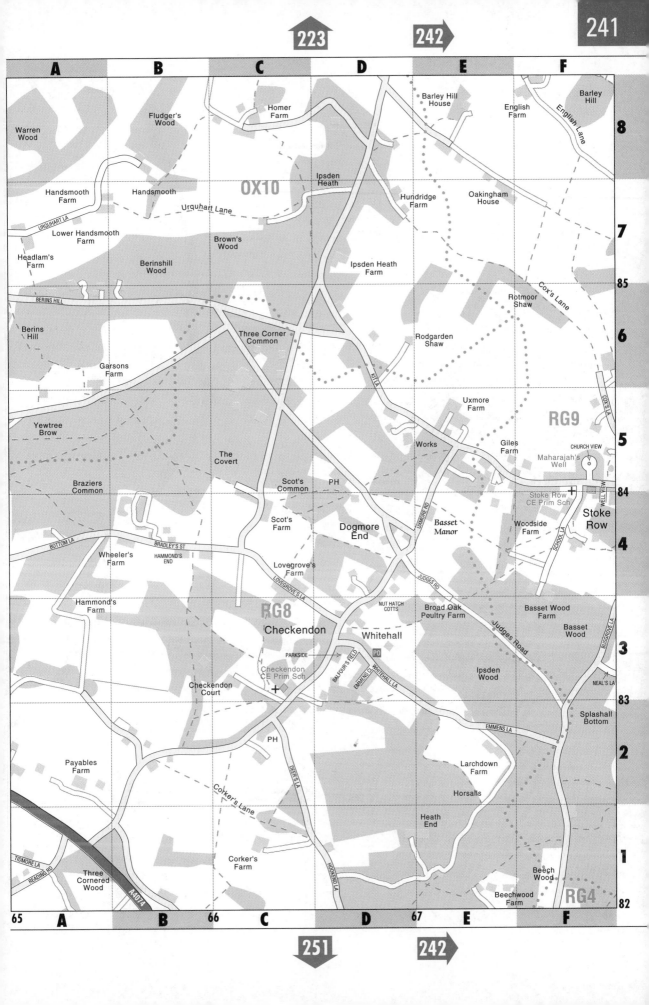

← 241
224

A B C D E F

8
Kate's Copse
Howberrywood Farm
Devil's Hill
Deadman's Lane
Swan Wood
Oxlands Bottom
Highmoor Trench
Upper Shaw

English Lane
Hall Farm
Highmoor Common Wood
Merrimoles

7
Oakingham Bottom
Nott Wood
Highmoor

Newnham Hill
B481

85
Newnhamhill Farm
Lower Highmoor

6
Strokerow Farm
Bush Wood
Little Farm
Highmoor Farm
PH
Holly Grove

NEWNHAMHILL BOTTOM

Stoke Row
Church Farm
CHERRY TREE CL
THE GLEBE
HOLLY CL
Highmoor Cross
Scotland

5
NOTTWOOD LA
NEWLANDS
Witheridge Hill
PH
Stonehouse Farm
ROCKY LA

84
ISHREE COTTS
PH
BENARES
GR
PO
ALMA GN
Van Alloys Bsns Pk
Bear Wood
RG9
Padnell's Wood
Orchard Copse

4
BUSHMORE LA
Busgrove Wood
STOKE ROW ROAD
Clayhill Wood
Satwell

Stag Hall
Greyhone Wood
Satwell House Farm
Oveys Wood
PH

3
Burnt Platt
Greyhone Plantation

COLMORE LANE
Coldmoor Wood
Greatbottom Wood
Kibes
B481

83
Neal's Lane
Neal's Shaw

2
Neal's Farm
Barn Farm
Great David's
Kennels

Neal's Wood
BARON WAY
PH
Kingwood Common

ASHDOWN WAY
HAWTHORN DR
WYFOLD CT
Cheriton House
HAZEL GR
LIME AVE
Hazel Grove
COLMORE LA

1
Littlebottom Wood

82

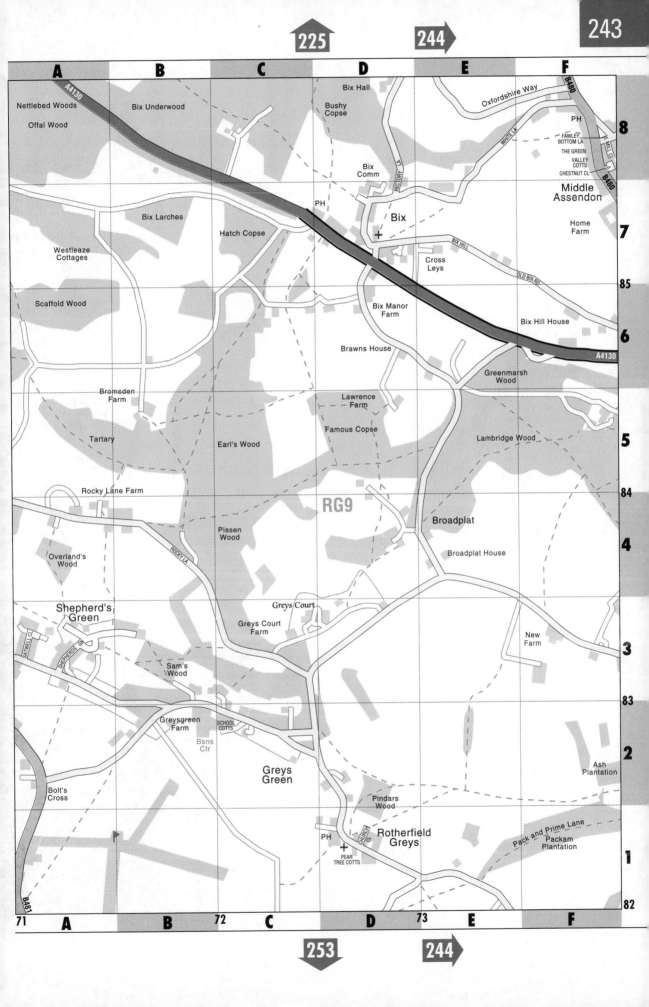

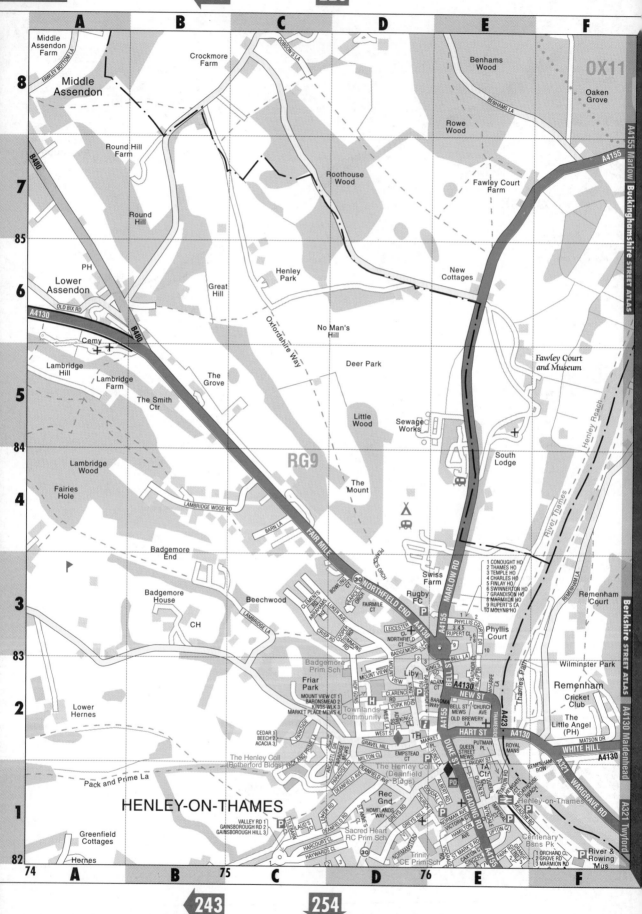

A B C D E F

8

SN6

7

81

RG17

6

5

80

SN8

4

3

79

2

1

78

26 A B 27 C D 28 E F

Starveall Farm

Swinley Down

Swinley Copse

Ashdown House

B4000

Ashdown Farm

B4000

Harley Bushes

Upper Wood

Pumping Station

Whiteshere

Russley Downs

Bishopstone Downs

Botley Bottom

Idstone Down

Dean Bottom

Botley Copse

Russley Park

THE MEWS

Bailey Hill

Gore Lane Farm

GORE LA

SN8

Bailey Hill Copse

Peaks Downs

Hazelbury Farm

Peaks Wood

Galiop

Bailey Hill Farm

THE FINCHES

THE GREEN

Baydon

RUSSLEY'S GR
AVENWAY CL

BAYDON RD

DOWNSMEAD

PO

Baydon St Nicholas CE Prim Sch
FINCHES LA

East Leaze Farm

Wiltshire STREET ATLAS

M4 Swindon
M4

M4

M4 Newbury

Wiltshire STREET ATLAS

Berkshire STREET ATLAS

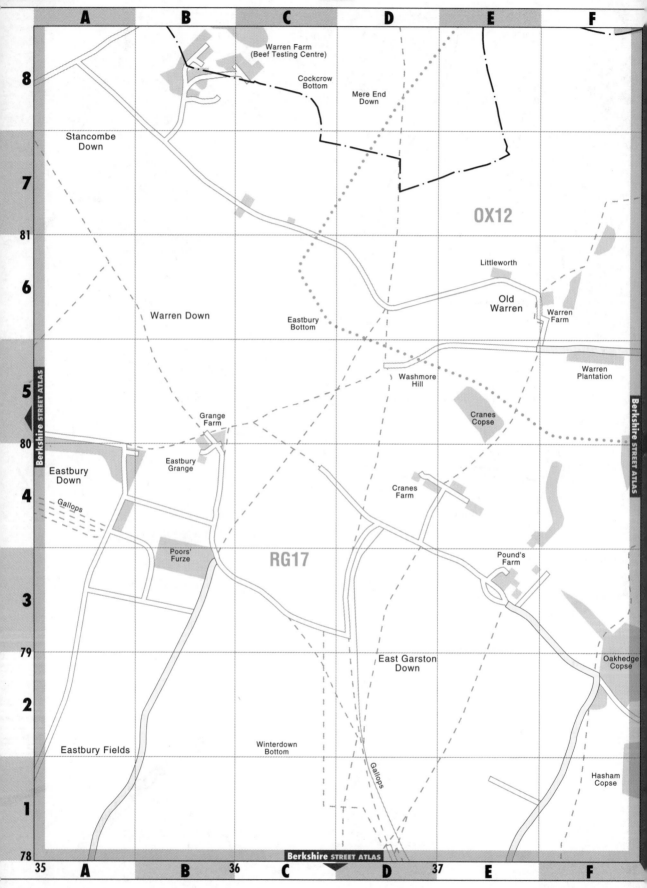

Warren Farm
(Beef Testing Centre)

Cockcrow
Bottom

Mere End
Down

Stancombe
Down

OX12

Littleworth

Old
Warren

Warren Down

Warren
Farm

Eastbury
Bottom

Warren
Plantation

Washmore
Hill

Cranes
Copse

Grange
Farm

Eastbury
Down

Eastbury
Grange

Cranes
Farm

Gallops

Poors'
Furze

RG17

Pound's
Farm

East Garston
Down

Oakhedge
Copse

Winterdown
Bottom

Eastbury Fields

Gallops

Hasham
Copse

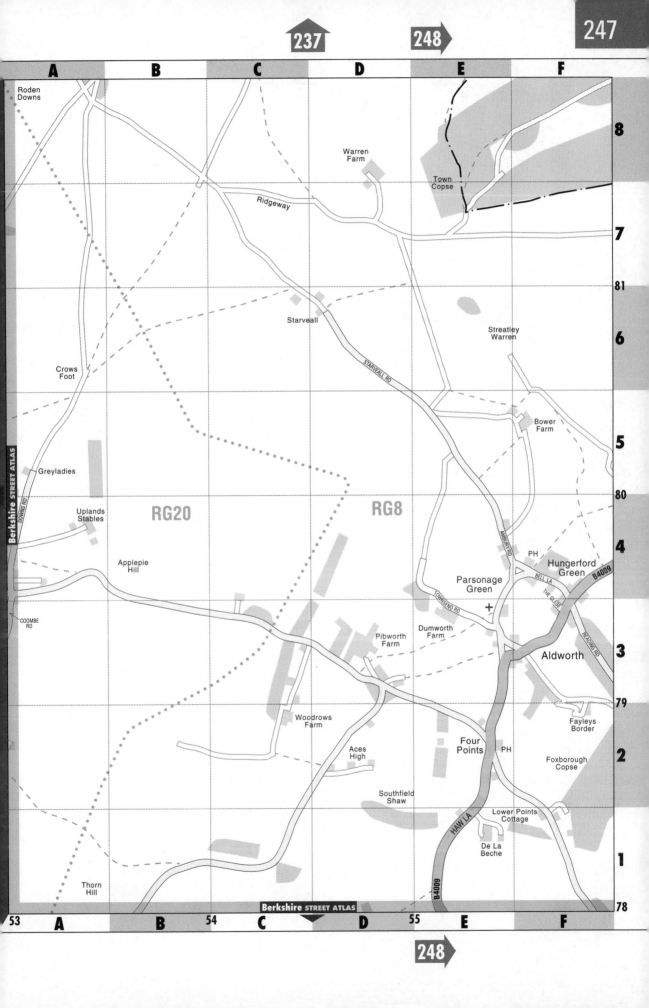

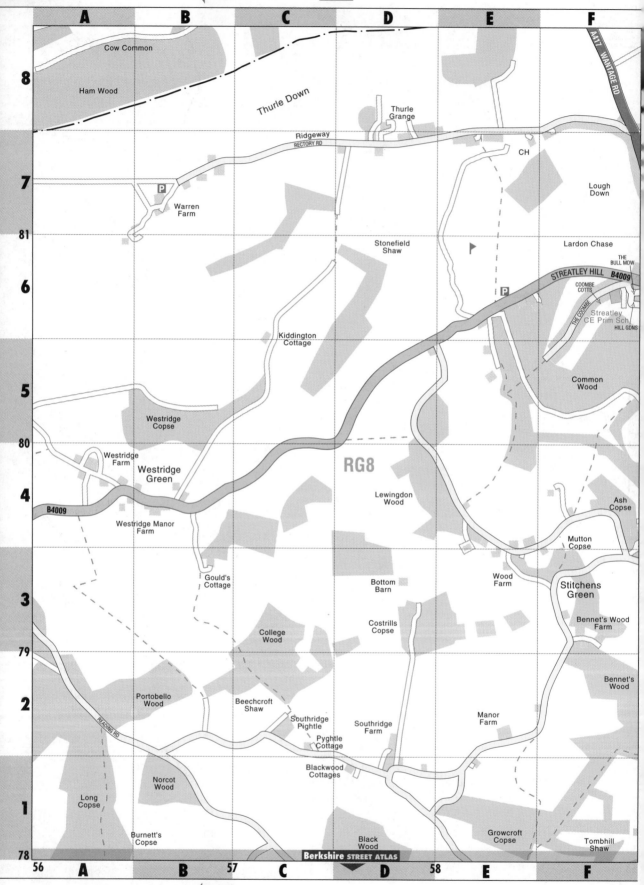

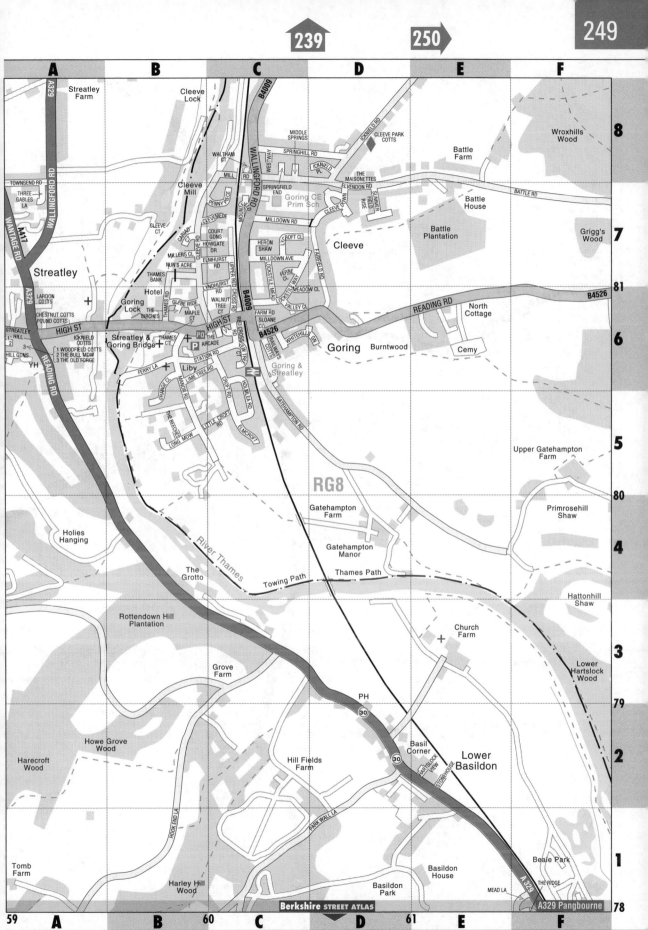

A B C D E F

8 Wroxhills Wood

Streatley Farm
Cleeve Lock
MIDDLE SPRINGS
Cleeve Park Cotts
ICKNIELD RD
Battle Farm

TOWNSEND RD
THREE GABLES LA
Cleeve Mill
WALTHAM CT
MILL RD
WESTWAY
SPRINGHILL RD
SPRINGHILL PL
ICKNIELD PL
Goring CE Prim Sch
THE MAISONETTES
ELVENDON RD
SUMMER FIELD RISE
Battle House
BATTLE RD

7 Cleeve
Grigg's Wood
CLEEVENEDE
PENNY PIECE
CARMAD CT
CLEEVE CT
CLEEVE RD
COURT GDNS
HOWGATE DR
ELMHURST RD
HERON SHAW
MILLDOWN AVE
MILLDOWN RD
CROFT CL
LYCROFT CL
FAIRFIELD RD
ELVENDON RD
CLEEVE DOWN
Battle Plantation

WALLINGFORD RD
B4009
WANTAGE RD
A417
A329

Streatley
MILLERS CL
NUN'S ACRE
THAMES BANK
THAMES RD
GLEBE RIDE
MAPLE CT
LYNDHURST RD
WALNUT TREE CT
FERNE CL
LOCKSTILE MEAD
LOCKSTILE WAY
MEADOW CL
VALLEY CL
B4009
READING RD
North Cottage
B4526

81

Goring Lock
Hotel
THE BIRCHES
FARM RD
SLOANE CL
B4526
WHITEHILLS GN
Goring
Burntwood
Cemy

6
LARDON COTTS
CHESTNUT COTTS
POUND COTTS
HIGH ST
STREATLEY HILL
HILL GDNS
YH
1 WOODFIELD COTTS
2 THE BULL MDW
3 THE OLD FORGE
ICKNIELD COTTS
Streatley & Goring Bridge
THAMES CT
PO
THE ARCADE
P
RED CROSS RD
UPPER RED CROSS RD
HIGH ST
RAILWAY COTTS

FERRY LA
ORANGE CL
STATION RD
Liby
LIME TREE RD
MANOR RD
CROFT RD
HOLMLEA RD
GATEHAMPTON RD
Goring & Streatley

THE BEECHES
LONG MDW
LITTLE CROFT RD
ELMCROFT

5 RG8
Upper Gatehampton Farm

80
Primrosehill Shaw

4
Holies Hanging
River Thames
Gatehampton Farm
Gatehampton Manor
Hattonhill Shaw

The Grotto
Towing Path
Thames Path

Rottendown Hill Plantation

3
Church Farm
Lower Hartslock Wood

79
PH
30

Grove Farm
Howe Grove Wood
Harecroft Wood
Hill Fields Farm
30
Basil Corner
HARTSLOCK VIEW
STOREHOUSE
Lower Basildon
2

HOOK END LA
PARK WALL LA
Basildon House
Basildon Park
Beale Park
THE RIDGE
1
Tomb Farm
Harley Hill Wood
MEAD LA
A329
A329 Pangbourne
78

249

240

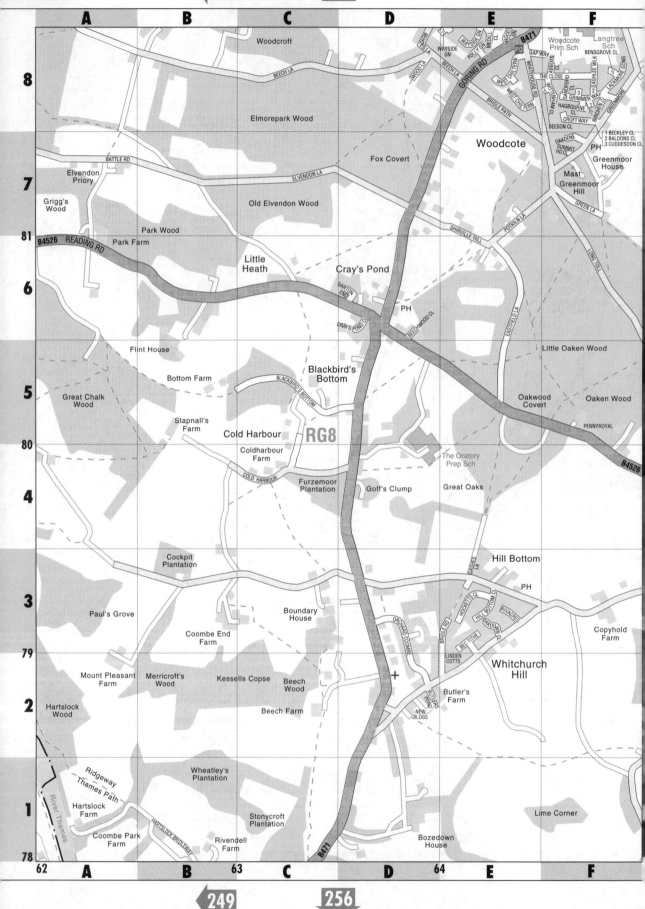

249

256

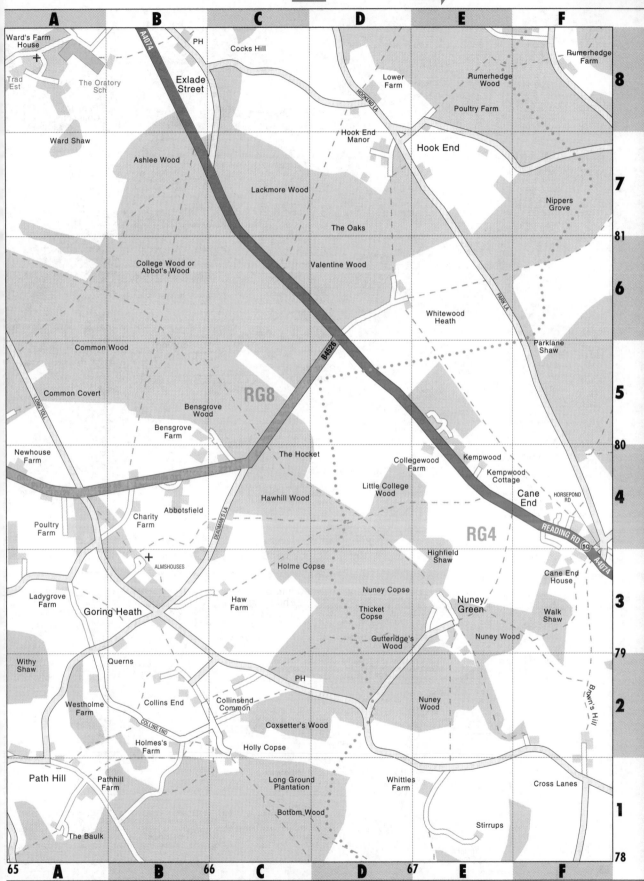

Ward's Farm House

Trad Est

The Oratory Sch

Cocks Hill

PH

Exlade Street

Lower Farm

Rumerhedge Farm

Rumerhedge Wood

8

Ward Shaw

Ashlee Wood

Hook End Manor

Poultry Farm

Hook End

7

Lackmore Wood

Nippers Grove

81

The Oaks

College Wood or Abbot's Wood

Valentine Wood

Whitewood Heath

6

Common Wood

Parklane Shaw

5

RG8

Common Covert

Bensgrove Wood

Bensgrove Farm

The Hocket

Collegewood Farm

Kempwood

80

Newhouse Farm

Little College Wood

Kempwood Cottage

Cane End

4

Poultry Farm

Charity Farm

Abbotsfield

Hawhill Wood

RG4

Highfield Shaw

HORSEPOND RD

Cane End House

READING RD

Walk Shaw

ALMSHOUSES

Holme Copse

Nuney Copse

Nuney Green

Ladygrove Farm

Goring Heath

Haw Farm

Thicket Copse

Nuney Wood

3

Withy Shaw

Querns

Gutteridge's Wood

79

Westholme Farm

Collins End

Collinsend Common

PH

Nuney Wood

2

COLLINS END

Coxsetter's Wood

Holmes's Farm

Holly Copse

Path Hill

Pathhill Farm

Long Ground Plantation

Whittles Farm

Cross Lanes

1

Bottom Wood

Stirrups

The Baulk

78

A B C D E F

8

7

81

6

80

5

4

79

2

1

78

Manor Farm Cottages

Park Farm

STEVENS LA
COLMORE LA
COVE LA
ESTER CARLING LA

COLLIERS LA

B481

Peppard Hill

Peppard Common

Peppard Hill

WYFOLD LA

RG9

CHURCH LA

Wyfold Grange

STOKE ROW RD
CHILTERN RD

SPRINGWOOD LA

PEPPARD HILL

Wyfold Wood

New Copse

CHILTERN BANK

PH

GALLOWSTREE RD

HILLCREST LA
BUTLERS YD
GRAVEL HILL
GREEN TREES
SHIPLAKE BOTTOM
BLOUNTS COURT RD
ARTORY COPSE

READES LANE

SHIPLAKE BOTTOM
GRAVEL HILL
OLD COPSE
CARLING RD
BEECH RISE
GDNS

NEWFIELD RD
SEDGEWELL RD
WOODLANDS RD

Withy Copse

Common Farm

THE HAMLET

HEARNS LA

WOODSIDE LA

Gallowstree Common

Bishopswood Farm

Sonning Common

ORCHARD AVE
APPLETREE
SMITH CL
WALNUT
HAZEL GDNS
WOOD LANE
INGLEWOOD CL
PO

COUNCIL COTTS

HORSEPOND RD

PH

ORCHARD FIELD

READE'S LA

LAMBOURNE RD
RUSSET CL
BASKERVILLE RD
WYCHWOOD CL
GREEN LA
CROMSEY WAY
ILSLEY RD
PAGES ORCH

Sonning Common Prim Sch

Liby

Bishopswood Sch

RG4

Chiltern Edge Sch

ASHFORD AV
FARM CL
GROVE RD
CHERITON CL
FONTAN PL
WESTLEIGH DR
ELM CT
SCH CL
ILEX CL
KENNYLANDS RD

Coldnorton Wood

Coldnorton Shaw

HAZELMOOR LA

Oakridge Farm

WOOD LA

CRANSLEAZE

Holly Tree Farm

KIDMORE LA

Cane End Farm

READING RD
A4074

Kidmore End CE Prim Sch

Kidmore End

Curtis Farm

PH
COOPERS PIGHTLE
Cemy

BUTLERS ORCH

Vines Farm

Stocking Shaw

Madge Gray's Wood

Highland Wood

Cross Farm

CHALKHOUSE GREEN RD

Kidmore House

Green Dean Wood

Tankers Table Farm

MILL LA

Bardolph's Wood

GREEN DEAN HILL
A4074

Hodmore Farm

SHEEPWAYS LA

TOKERS GREEN LA

Dyson's Wood

DYSONSWOOD LA
CHALKHOUSE GREEN LA
TANFERS LA
KIDMORE LA

Hodmore Farm Cottage

Tinker's Green

PH

68 A B 69 C D 70 E F

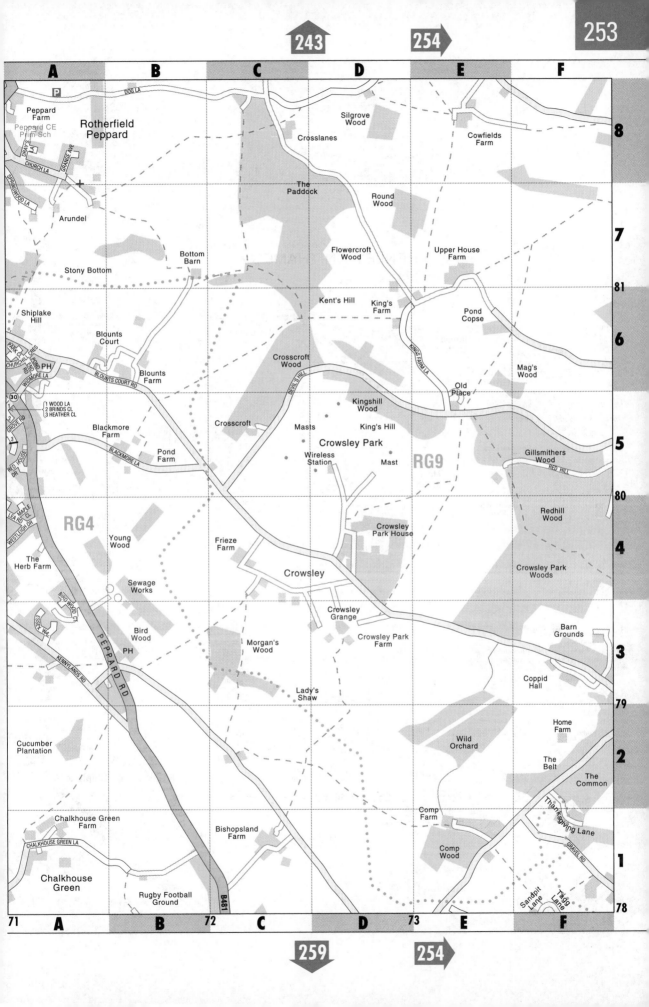

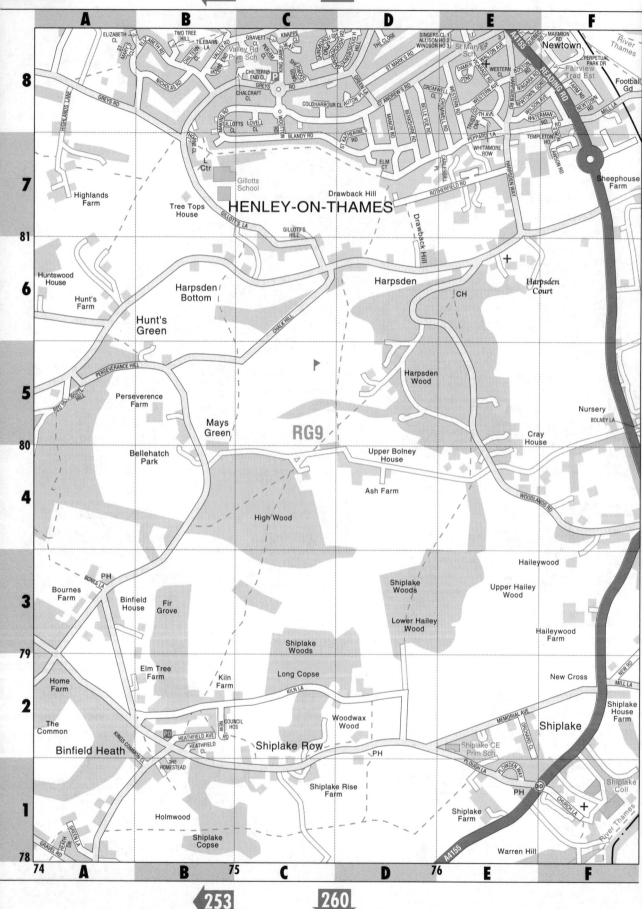

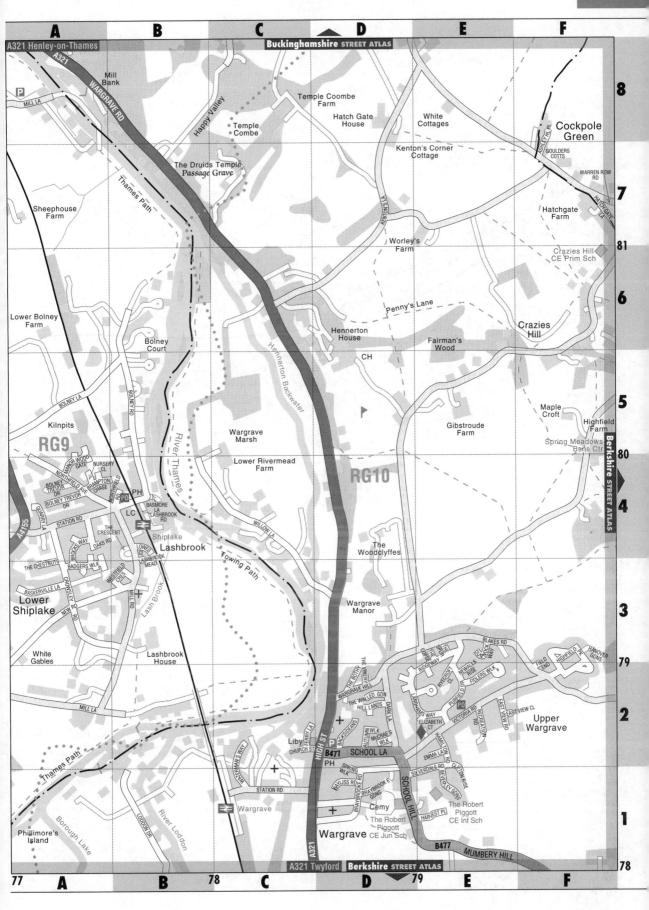

A321 Henley-on-Thames

A B C D E F

8
7
81
6
5
80
4
3
79
2
1
78

77 A 78 B C 78 D 79 E F

Berkshire STREET ATLAS

Mill Bank
WARGRAVE RD
Thames Path
Happy Valley
Temple Combe
The Druids Temple
Passage Grave
Temple Coombe Farm
Hatch Gate House
White Cottages
Kenton's Corner Cottage
Cockpole Green
GOULDERS COTTS
WARREN ROW RD
ASHLEY PL
HATCHGATE LA
Hatchgate Farm
Sheephouse Farm
Worley's Farm
Crazies Hill CE Prim Sch
Lower Bolney Farm
Penny's Lane
Hennerton House
CH
Fairman's Wood
Crazies Hill
Bolney Court
BOLNEY LA
BOLNEY RD
Kilnpits
RG9
Wargrave Marsh
Maple Croft
Highfield Farm
Spring Meadows Bsns Ctr
Gibstroude Farm
Lower Rivermead Farm
River Thames
Hennerton Backwater
RG10
MANOR WOOD GATE
NURSERY CL
BRAMPTON CHASE
NORTHFIELD AV
BOLNEY TREVOR DR
BOLNEY TREVOR DR
NORTHFIELD
PH
PO
LC
BASMORE LA
LASHBROOK RD
WILLOW LA
QUARRY LA
A4155
STATION RD
THE CRESCENT
OAKS RD
BROOKS WAY
Shiplake
Lashbrook
Towing Path
The Woodclyffes
THE CHESTNUTS
BADGERS WLK
WESTFIELD CRES
CROWSLEY RD
LOWES CL
LASHBROOK MEAD
Lash Brook
MILL RD
Lower Shiplake
BASKERVILLE LA
NEW RD
Wargrave Manor
BLAKES RD
HANOVER GDNS
White Gables
Lashbrook House
MILL LA
THE SPUR
THE COPSE
RIDGEWAY
NEWALLS RISE
DOWN WAY
FIDLERS WLK
PURFIELD DR
HIGHFIELD PK
FIELD END
Upper Wargrave
Phillimore's Island
Borough Lake
River Loddon
LODDON DR
Thames Path
WATERMAN'S WAY
STATION RD
Wargrave
FERRY LA
CHURCH ST
Liby
HIGH ST
BACKSIDEANS
WLK
McCRAE'S WLK
THE BOTHY
THE VINERY
WARGRAVE HILL
THE WALLED GDN
HILL LANDS
DARK LA
LARGHANS WAY
ELIZABETH CT
VICTORIA RD
HAMILTON RD
EMMA LA
CLIFTON RISE
EAST VIEW CL
EAST VIEW RD
RECREATION RD
P
B471
PH
SCHOOL LA
SPRING WLK
BAYLISS RD
BAYLISS RD E
BRAYBROOKE RD
BRAYBROOKE E GDNS
SCHOOL HILL
SILVERDALE RD
BEVERLEY GDNS
HARVEST PL
Cemy
The Robert Piggott CE Jun Sch
The Robert Piggott CE Inf Sch
Wargrave
B477
MUMBERY HILL

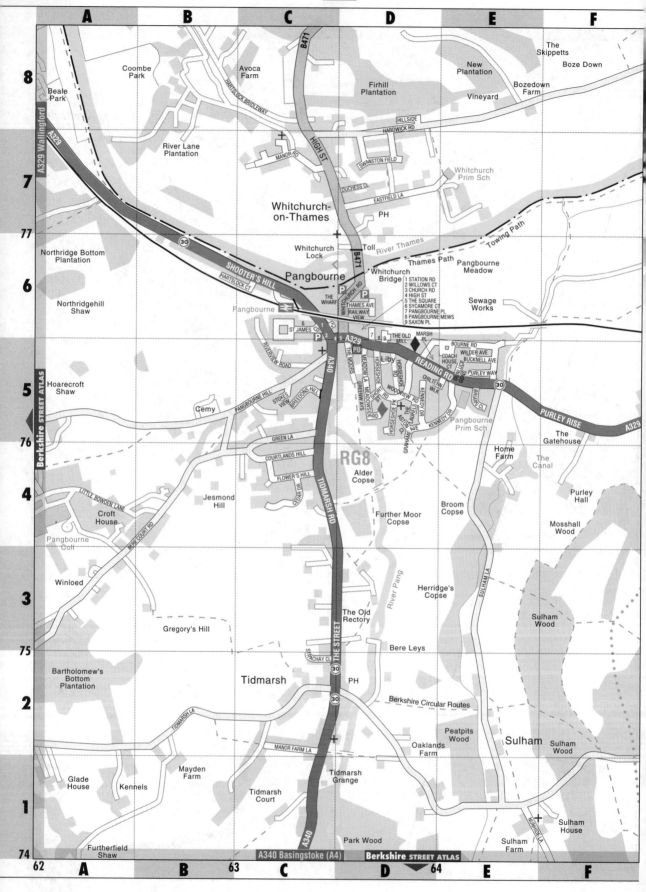

A B C D E F

8

Coombe Park

Beale Park

A329 Wallingford

Avoca Farm

Firhill Plantation

New Plantation

The Skippetts

Boze Down

HARTSLOCK BRIDLEWAY

B471

HIGH ST

Bozedown Farm

Vineyard

7

River Lane Plantation

MANOR RD

HILLSIDE

HARDWICK RD

Whitchurch Prim Sch

DUCHESS CL

SWANSTON FIELD

EASTFIELD LA

Whitchurch-on-Thames

PH

Northridge Bottom Plantation

77

A329

SHOOTER'S HILL

30

Whitchurch Lock

Toll

B471

River Thames

Towing Path

6

Northridgehill Shaw

HARTSLOCK CT

Pangbourne

Pangbourne

Whitchurch Bridge

Thames Path

Pangbourne Meadow

THE WHARF

P

P

Sewage Works

WHITCHURCH RD

THAMES AVE
RAILWAY VIEW

1 STATION RD
2 WILLOWS CT
3 CHURCH RD
4 HIGH ST
5 THE SQUARE
6 SYCAMORE CT
7 PANGBOURNE PL
8 PANGBOURNE MEWS
9 SAXON PL

ST JAMES

6
1

P
PO

7

A329

8 9

THE OLD MILL

MARSH RD

Liby

BOURNE RD

WILDER AVE

BUCKNELL AVE

COACH HOUSE CT

PURLEY WAY

5

Hoarecroft Shaw

Berkshire STREET ATLAS

RIVERVIEW ROAD

A340

THE MOORS

HORSESHOE RD

READING RD

DUNLUCE GDNS

BRIARS CL

30

Cerny

Pangbourne Hill

STOKES VIEW

BREEDONS HILL

MEADOW LA

GREEN WS

MEADOWS RD

HORSESHOE PK

WOODVIEW RD

KENNEDY DR

CHILTERN WLK

KENNEDY DR

Pangbourne Prim Sch

PURLEY RISE

A329

76

GREEN LA

HORSESHOE RD

SHORT ST

THE LAURELS

ASTON CL

GRAHAME AVE

Home Farm

The Gatehouse

The Canal

RG8

COURTLANDS HILL

Alder Copse

Broom Copse

Purley Hall

4

Little Bowden Lane

Croft House

BERE COURT RD

FLOWER'S HILL

CEDAR DR

Jesmond Hill

TIDMARSH RD

Further Moor Copse

Mosshall Wood

Pangbourne Coll

Winloed

Gregory's Hill

THE STREET

River Pang

Herridge's Copse

SULHAM LA

Sulham Wood

3

75

Bartholomew's Bottom Plantation

STRACHAY CL

30

Bere Leys

PH

2

Tidmarsh

30

Berkshire Circular Routes

Peatpits Wood

Sulham

Sulham Wood

TIDMARSH LA

MANOR FARM LA

Oaklands Farm

Glade House

Kennels

Mayden Farm

Tidmarsh Court

Tidmarsh Grange

NUNHIDE LA

Sulham House

1

A340

Furtherfield Shaw

Park Wood

Sulham Farm

74

62

A340 Basingstoke (A4)

Berkshire STREET ATLAS

63

64

A B C D E F

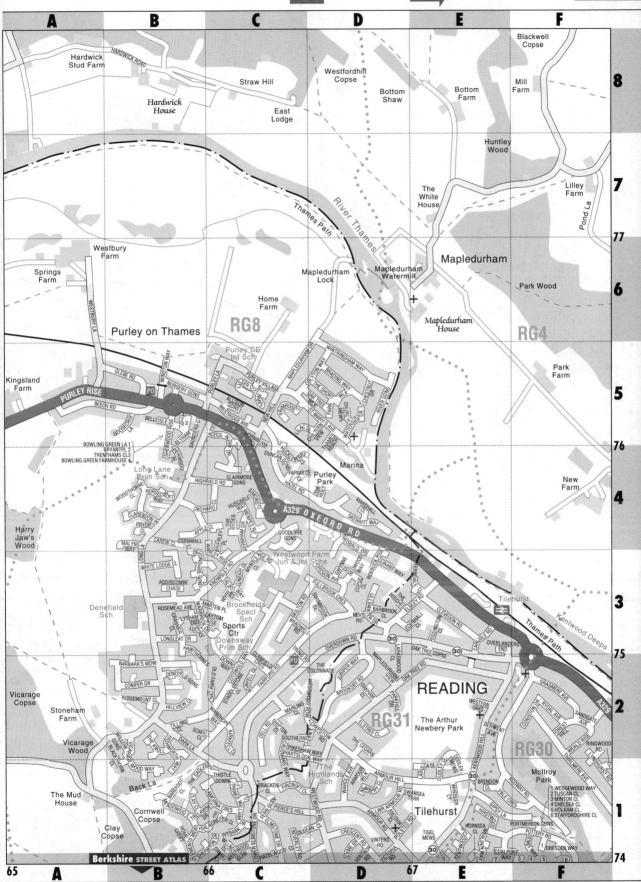

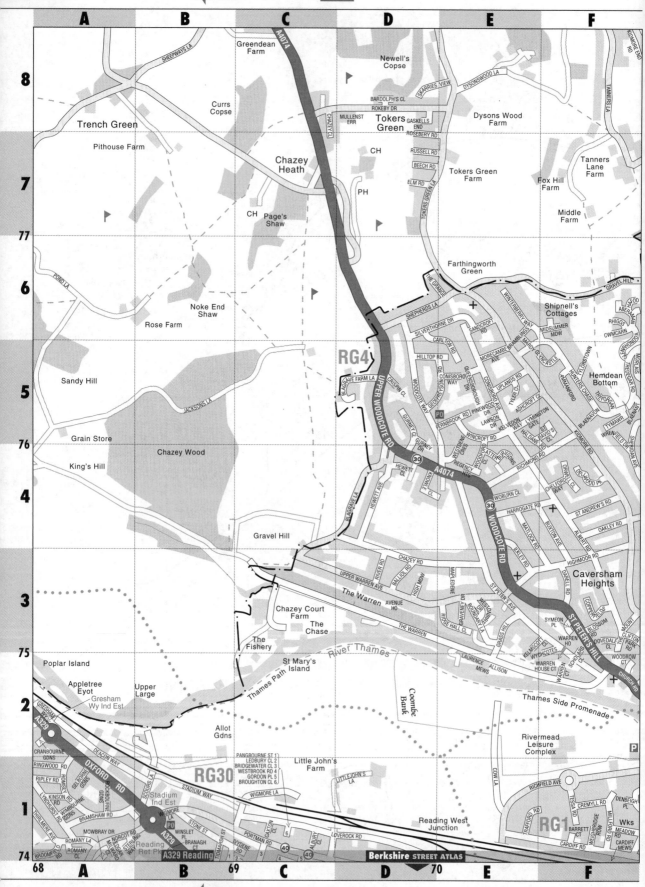

	A	B	C	D	E	F

8

Trench Green

Greendean Farm

Currs Copse

Newell's Copse

SKARRIES VIEW

DYSONSWOOD LA

Pithouse Farm

BARDOLPH'S CL
ROKEBY DR

MULLENST ERR

Dysons Wood Farm

Tokers Green

GASKELLS END

7

Chazey Heath

CH

ROSEBERY RD

RUSSELL RD

Tokers Green Farm

Fox Hill Farm

Tanners Lane Farm

CH

Page's Shaw

PH

BEECH RD

ELM RD

Middle Farm

77

Farthingworth Green

THE GRANGE

GRAVEL HILL

6

POND LA

Noke End Shaw

SHEPHERDS LA

Shipnell's Cottages

WINTERBURY WAY

MIDSUMMER MDW

Rose Farm

SILVERTHORNE DR

SANDCROFT RD

MORECAMBE

BRAMBLINGS

MARDY

GLYNCASTLE

RHIGOS

CWMCARN

RG4

CARLTON RD

HILLTOP RD

CONISBORO AVE

MORAS

Sandy Hill

JACKSONS LA

QUEENSBOROUGH DR

PINEWOOD DR

ASHCROFT CL

UPLANDS RD

HUNTERS CHASE

ANNAMFORD

Hemdean Bottom

5

UPPER WOODCOTE RD

GURNEY CL

FERNBROOK RD

WESTDENE CRES

LAWSON

KELVEDON WAY

LYMINGTON GATE

TYLER CL

PEPPARD

BLAGRAVE FARM LA

CRISPIN CL

GEOFFREY CLEY

PO

DAVID'S ST

WREN

WIMBOROUGH

76

Grain Store

Chazey Wood

HEWETT CL

WINCROFT RD

REGENCY

WOODCOTE WAY

RICHMOND RD

King's Hill

30

A4074

4

HEWETT AVE

BLAGRAVE LA

WOBURN CL

CHILFORD CL WAY

ST ANDREW'S RD

Gravel Hill

30

HARROGATE RD

BUXTON AVE

ALBERT RD

OAKLEY RD

3

CHAZEY RD

RIVER RD

HIGH VIEW

MAPLEDENE

WOODCOTE RD

HIGHMOOR RD

Caversham Heights

UPPER WARREN AVE

BALLIOL RD

The Warren

AVENUE HO

RIDGE HALL CL

SYMEON PL

BLOSSOM

CLIFTON PARK

Chazey Court Farm

The Chase

THE WARREN

GRASS HILL

WARREN HO

WYCHCOTES

WOODROW

75

The Fishery

St Mary's Island

LAURENCE MEWS

ALLISON

WARREN HOUSE CT

SCHOLARS

CHURCH RD

River Thames

Thames Path

2

Poplar Island

Appletree Eyot

Gresham Wy Ind Est

Upper Large

Thames Side Promenade

GRESHAM WAY

A329

Coombe Bank

Rivermead Leisure Complex

P

CRANBOURNE GDNS

DEACON WAY

OXFORD RD

Allot Gdns

RICHFIELD AVE

RINGWOOD RD

PANGBOURNE ST 1
LEDBURY CL 2
BRIDGEWATER CL 3
WESTBROOK RD 4
GORDON PL 5
BROUGHTON CL 6

Little John's Farm

RG1

RG30

DENBEIGH PL

1

RIPLEY RD

KINSON RD

ROMSEY

Stadium Ind Est

WIGMORE LA

LITTLEJOHN'S LA

COW LA

Reading West Junction

TRAFFORD RD

RICHFIELD AVE

TESSA RD

CREMYLL RD

MILLFORD RD

Wks

MOWBRAY DR

BRAMSHAW RD

STADIUM WAY

STONE ST

WINSLET PL

PORTMAN RD

LOVEROCK RD

BARRETT CT

CARDIFF RD

MEADOW

CARDIFF MEWS

74

ROMANY LA

BROOMFIELD

A329 Reading

Reading Ret Pk

BRANAGH CT

ALBURY CL

Berkshire STREET ATLAS

	A	B	C	D	E	F
68		69		70		

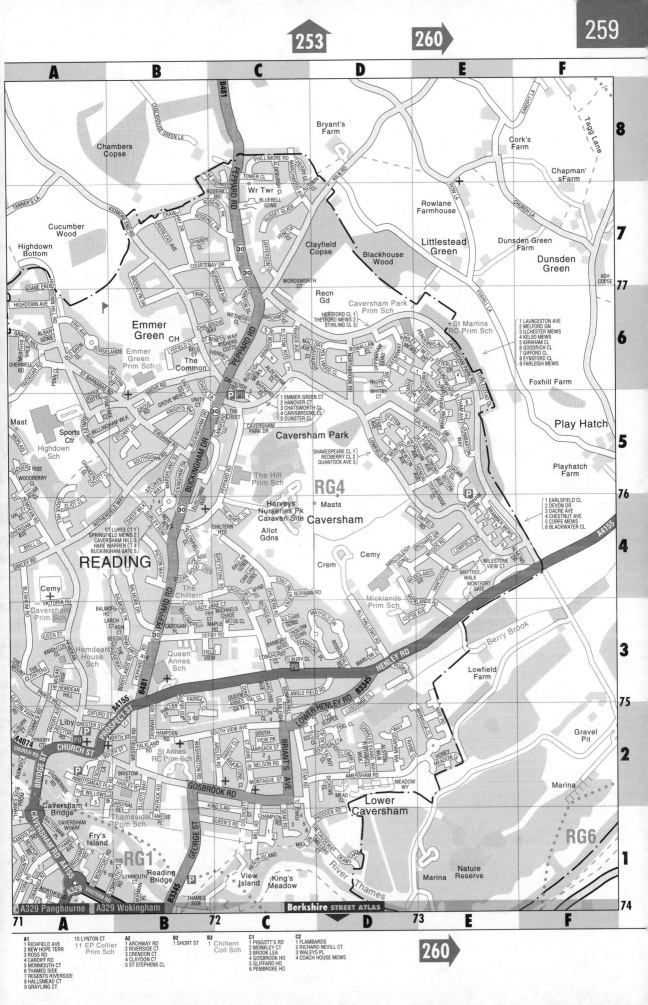

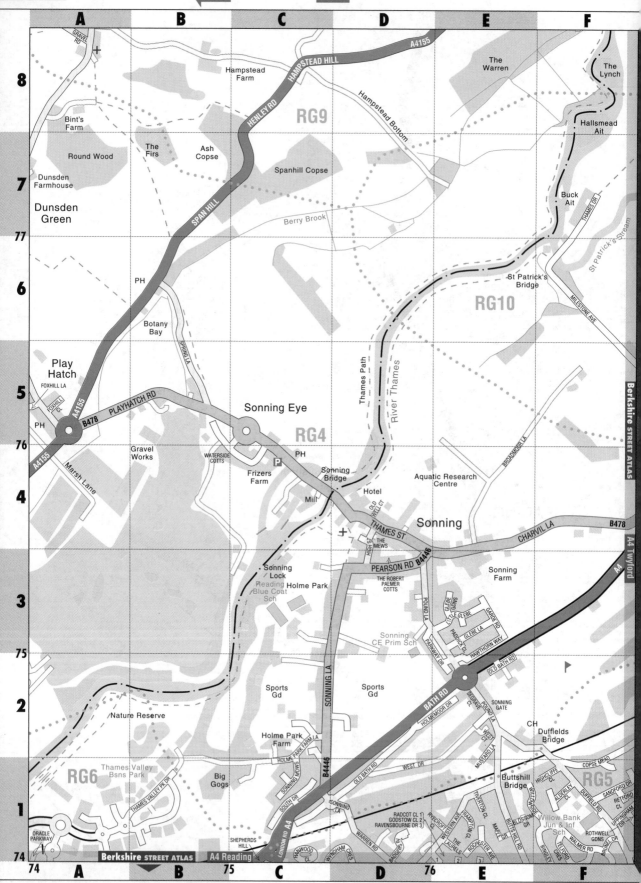

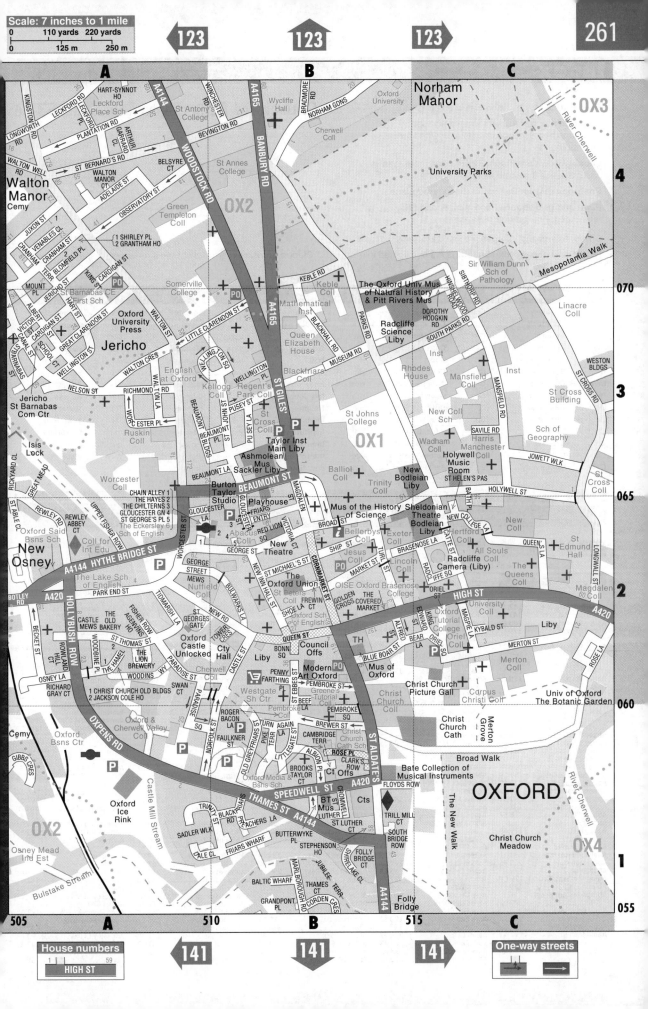

Index

Place name May be abbreviated on the map	**Church Rd** 6 **Beckenham BR2**..........**53 C6**
Location number Present when a number indicates the place's position in a crowded area of mapping	
Locality, town or village Shown when more than one place has the same name	
Postcode district District for the indexed place	
Page and grid square Page number and grid reference for the standard mapping	

Cities, towns and villages are listed in CAPITAL LETTERS

Public and commercial buildings are highlighted in magenta   **Places of interest** are highlighted in blue with a star★

Abbreviations used in the index

Acad	**Academy**	Comm	**Common**	Gd	**Ground**	L	**Leisure**	Prom	**Promenade**
App	**Approach**	Cott	**Cottage**	Gdn	**Garden**	La	**Lane**	Rd	**Road**
Arc	**Arcade**	Cres	**Crescent**	Gn	**Green**	Liby	**Library**	Recn	**Recreation**
Ave	**Avenue**	Cswy	**Causeway**	Gr	**Grove**	Mdw	**Meadow**	Ret	**Retail**
Bglw	**Bungalow**	Ct	**Court**	H	**Hall**	Meml	**Memorial**	Sh	**Shopping**
Bldg	**Building**	Ctr	**Centre**	Ho	**House**	Mkt	**Market**	Sq	**Square**
Bsns, Bus	**Business**	Ctry	**Country**	Hospl	**Hospital**	Mus	**Museum**	St	**Street**
Bvd	**Boulevard**	Cty	**County**	HQ	**Headquarters**	Orch	**Orchard**	Sta	**Station**
Cath	**Cathedral**	Dr	**Drive**	Hts	**Heights**	Pal	**Palace**	Terr	**Terrace**
Cir	**Circus**	Dro	**Drove**	Ind	**Industrial**	Par	**Parade**	TH	**Town Hall**
Cl	**Close**	Ed	**Education**	Inst	**Institute**	Pas	**Passage**	Univ	**University**
Cnr	**Corner**	Emb	**Embankment**	Int	**International**	Pk	**Park**	Wk, Wlk	**Walk**
Coll	**College**	Est	**Estate**	Intc	**Interchange**	Pl	**Place**	Wr	**Water**
Com	**Community**	Ex	**Exhibition**	Junc	**Junction**	Prec	**Precinct**	Yd	**Yard**

Index of towns, villages, streets, hospitals, industrial estates, railway stations, schools, shopping centres, universities and places of interest

262 Aba–Ann

A

Abacus Coll OX1....... **261** B2
Abberbury Ave OX4 ..... **142** A4
Abberbury Rd OX4 ..... **141** F4
Abbey Brook OX11 ..... **200** E3
Abbey Cl OX14......... **179** F7
Abbey Ctr OX14 .... **180** A7
Abbey Fishponds Nature Reserve★ OX14.........**160** C1
Abbey Mdws Outdoor Pool OX14.................**180** A7
Abbey Pl OX29 .... **120** E7
Abbey Rd
  Banbury OX16 .... **16** A7
  Oxford OX2 .... **123** A1
  Watchfield SN6 .... **191** F2
  Witney OX28 .... **117** F7
Abbey Sports Ctr OX10 .. **182** C5
Abbey St OX29......... **120** E7
Abbey Wlk OX1 .... **123** A1
Abbey Woods Cl OX10.. **182** C5
Abbot Ridge HP18 ..... **129** D5
Abbots Cl RG8........ **250** F8
Abbots Mead OX10..... **239** A8
Abbotsleigh Gdns RG4 .. **259** D4
Abbotsmead Pl RG4..... **259** A2
Abbots Wlk GL7........ **150** D4
Abbots Wood OX3 ..... **142** E8
Abbott Cl OX11 .... **218** E7
Abbott Rd
  Abingdon OX14 .... **179** F8
  Didcot OX11.......... **218** E7
Abbot Wlk HP18 ...... **129** D5
Abelwood Rd OX29..... **90** A1
ABINGDON **179** E7
Abingdon Bsns Pk OX14 . **179** C7
Abingdon Cl OX9....... **129** F1
Abingdon Com Hospl OX14.................**179** C7
Abingdon County Hall Mus★ OX14.................**179** F7
Abingdon Dr RG4 ...... **259** C6
Abingdon La OX29 ..... **117** A3
Abingdon Prep Sch OX13.................**178** A7

Abingdon Rd
  Carterton OX18......... **115** E3
  Clifton Hampden OX14 ...**181** D4
  Culham OX14.......... **180** C3
  Cumnor OX2 .... **139** E4
  Didcot OX11.......... **201** B1
  Dorchester OX10....... **182** C3
  Drayton OX14 .... **179** B2
  Kennington OX1....... **141** D4
  Kingston Bagpuize OX13 . **177** A8
  Oxford OX1 .... **141** D6
  Rowstock OX11 .... **217** B7
  Standlake OX29 .... **137** C3
  Steventon OX13....... **199** A5
  Sutton Courtenay OX14.. **180** B2
  Tubney OX13 .... **157** E2
Abingdon Sch OX14 .... **179** E7
Abingdon Science Pk OX14.................**180** B7
Abingdon Terr OX11 ... **218** C8
Abingdon & Witney Coll (Abingdon Campus) OX14.................**159** E1
Abingdon & Witney Coll (Common Leys Farm Campus) OX29 .....**104** C8
Abingdon & Witney Coll (Witney Campus) 9 OX28.................**118** A8
Ablett Cl OX4 .... **142** A8
Abrahams Rd RG9...... **244** C3
Acacia RG9 .... **244** D2
Acacia Ave OX4 .... **142** E1
Acacia Cl OX18 .... **115** E1
Acacia Gdns OX13..... **156** E1
Acacia Wlk
  Banbury OX16 .... **9** B1
  Bicester OX26 .... **65** E5
Acer Cl OX18 .... **114** D7
Ackerman Rd OX7 ..... **42** F3
Acland Cl OX3 .... **124** C1
Acorn Cl OX26 .... **65** E5
Acorns Prim Sch CV36 .. **27** F6
Acorn Way OX16........ **9** F1
Acre Cl OX3 .... **142** F7
Acre Ditch OX15 ...... **19** A8
Acre End Cl OX29 ..... **120** E7
Acre End St OX29 ..... **120** E7
Acremead Rd OX33 .... **143** F8
Adam Ct RG9.......... **244** E2
ADDERBURY **23** A3
Adderbury Ct OX17.... **23** A4
Adderbury Pk OX17 .... **22** F3

Addiscombe Chase RG31 ....**257** B3
Addison Cres OX4...... **141** F6
Addison Dr OX4 .... **142** C3
Addison Rd
  Banbury OX16 .... **16** C3
  Reading RG1 .... **259** A1
Adeane Rd OX44....... **184** C7
Adelaide St OX2 ...... **261** A4
Adkin Way OX12 ...... **214** D6
ADLESTROP **40** D2
ADWELL................ **166** D3
Adwell Sq RG9........ **244** D2
Agenvins Ho OX1 ..... **261** A2
Agnes Ct OX4 .... **142** C6
Akeman Ave OX25 ..... **81** D4
Akeman Cl OX5 .... **78** A5
Akeman St
  Combe OX29 .... **90** A6
  Kirtlington OX5 .... **78** A6
Alan Bullock Cl OX4.... **123** C1
Albany Gdns RG4 ..... **259** A6
Albermarle Dr OX12... **214** D8
Albert Rd
  Henley-on-Thames RG9... **244** E1
  Reading RG4 .... **258** F4
Albert St
  Banbury OX16 .... **16** D5
  Oxford OX2 .... **261** A3
Albion Pl
  Bampton OX18........ **134** E3
  Chipping Norton OX7... **42** F3
  Oxford OX1 .... **261** B1
Albion St OX7......... **42** E3
ALBURY................ **146** B7
Albury Cl RG30........ **258** C1
Albury View OX9...... **146** A6
Alchester Rd OX26 .... **80** A7
Alchester Terr 3 OX26.. **65** F1
Aldbarton Dr OX3..... **124** E4
Aldbourne Cl OX26.... **65** D2
Aldeburgh Cl RG4..... **259** C8
Alden Cres OX3....... **124** F4
Aldenham Cl RG4 ..... **259** C6
Alder Dr OX25 .... **81** C4
Aldergate Rd OX26.... **65** C2
Alderley Cl
  Carterton OX18........ **115** D1
  Sonning RG5 .... **260** F1
Aldrich Rd OX2 .... **123** B8
Aldridge Cl OX10...... **204** A4
Aldsworth OX28 ...... **117** E8
ALDWORTH............. **247** F3

Aldworth Ave OX12 .... **214** F6
Alec Issigonis Way OX4 . **142** D5
Alesworth Gr OX3..... **124** B5
Alexander Cl
  Abingdon OX14 .... **160** A3
  Kidlington OX5....... **108** F6
  Upton OX11.......... **218** C2
Alexandra Rd OX2..... **122** F1
Alexandra Sq OX7..... **42** D1
Alfreds Pl OX12....... **197** C7
Alfred St
  Oxford OX1 .... **261** B2
  3 Wantage OX12...... **214** D4
Alfredston Pl OX12.... **214** E4
Alfred Terraces OX7 ... **42** E2
Alfriston Pl OX16 ..... **9** A1
Alhambra La OX4 ..... **141** E8
Alice Smith Sq OX4 ... **142** C2
Alison Clay Ho OX3 ... **124** C2
Alister Taylor Ave OX10 . **204** C2
ALKERTON.............. **6** F2
Allder Cl OX14 .... **159** F2
Allectus Ave OX25 .... **81** D4
Allens La OX25........ **48** E1
Allens Orch OX17 ...... **5** F6
Alley The OX7 .... **73** B4
All Hallows Rd RG4 ... **259** D3
Allin Cl OX4 .... **142** E3
Allin's La OX12........ **216** D7
Allison Gdns RG8 ..... **257** C5
Allison Ho RG9 .... **254** E8
Allnatt Ave OX10...... **221** C8
Allnut Cl OX49 .... **186** B1
All Saints CE Prim Sch
  Didcot OX11.......... **201** A2
  Sutton Courtenay OX14 . **199** F6
All Saints Cl OX13..... **178** C6
All Saints Ct OX11..... **200** E2
All Saints La OX14 .... **180** B1
All Saints Rd OX3 .... **124** C2
All Soul's Coll OX1.... **261** C2
Alma Gn RG9 .... **242** A4
Alma Pl OX4.......... **141** F8
Alma Rd 10 OX16...... **16** E6
Almhouses OX28...... **104** C1
Almond Ave OX5...... **108** E6
Almond Dr RG4 ...... **259** F4
Almond Rd OX26...... **65** E3
Almshouses
  Bourton SN6 .... **209** A2
  Goring Heath RG8..... **251** B3
  Lyford OX12.......... **176** C1
  Worminghall HP18..... **127** E5

Almshouses The OX5..... **92** F2
Alpha Ave OX44........ **143** C1
Alphin Brook OX11..... **200** E3
Alston Wlk RG4....... **259** D2
Altus St OX25........ **63** A8
ALVESCOT.............. **133** C6
Alvescot Rd OX18..... **115** D3
Alvis Gate OX16...... **15** F8
Ambassador Ave OX4 .. **142** E4
Ambassador Ct 1 OX26.. **65** F1
Amberley Ct 9 OX16... **9** A1
Ambleside Dr OX3 .... **124** B4
AMBROSDEN **81** D3
Ambrose Rise OX33.... **144** C8
Ambury Rd RG8........ **247** E4
Amersham Rd RG4 .... **259** C5
Amey Cres OX13 ...... **159** B6
Ammanford RG4....... **258** F5
Amory Cl OX4......... **142** D3
Amos Ct OX16 .... **16** C5
Ampney Orch OX18 ... **134** F3
Amwell Pl OX10....... **220** F1
Amyce Cl OX14 .... **160** B2
Ancastle Gn RG9...... **244** D2
Ancholme Cl OX11.... **200** F2
Anchor La OX11....... **220** A4
Ancil Ave OX26 .... **66** D2
Andersey Way OX14 ... **179** F4
Anderson Cl HP14..... **188** E5
Andersons Cl OX5..... **108** D8
Andover Cl
  Bicester OX26 .... **66** A4
  Reading RG31 .... **257** D1
Andover Ct 1 OX5..... **108** F8
Andover La OX18...... **115** F2
Andover Rd OX10 ..... **204** D3
Andrew Rd OX10...... **203** B1
Andrews Ave NN13..... **36** C6
Andromeda Cl OX4.... **142** F1
Anemone Cl OX4...... **161** E8
Angelica Cl
  Hardwick OX16 .... **9** A2
  Oxford OX4 .... **142** F1
Angle Field Rd RG4 ... **259** D3
Anglesey Ct HP14..... **188** E5
Angus Cl OX16........ **16** A8
Anna Pavlova Cl OX4... **179** D7
Anne Greenwood Cl OX4 .... **142** A4
Annesley Cl OX5...... **93** A8
Anglesey Ct HP14..... **188** E5
Annesley Rd OX4 ..... **142** A4
Anniversary Ave OX25, OX26 ....**80** E5

Annora Cl OX4 142 A5
Ansell Way OX7 70 B1
Anson Ave OX18 115 E1
Anson Cl
Marcham OX13 178 D6
Wheatley OX33 144 C8
Anson Rd OX10 204 D3
Anson Way OX26 66 A3
Anthony Hill Rd OX10 204 C1
Anvil Ct SN7 194 E7
Anvil La OX12 214 A1
Anvil Paddock OX12 214 A1
Anxey Way HP17 130 F6
AP Ellis Rd GL54 68 B3
Apley Way OX28 117 E8
Appleby Cl OX16 15 E7
Apple Cl RG31 257 B4
APPLEFORD 200 F8
Appleford Dr
Abingdon OX14 160 B2
11 Carterton OX18 115 E5
Appleford Rd OX14 180 B1
APPLETON 158 A7
Appleton CE Prim Sch OX13 158 A8
Appleton Rd
Cumnor OX2 139 D4
Longworth OX13 156 D3
APPLETREE 5 C8
Appletree Cl
Sandford-on-Thames OX4 161 F8
Sonning Common RG4 252 E6
Appletree Ind Est OX17 5 E7
Appletree Rd OX17 5 F6
Approach The OX26 65 D3
Apsley Rd OX2 123 A8
Arbury Banks OX17 5 F5
Arbury Cl OX16 16 E2
Arcade The
Goring RG8 249 C6
9 Wallingford OX10 221 D7
Archery Rd OX17 11 A1
Archway Rd 1 RG4 259 A2
Arden Cl OX15 15 D8
ARDINGTON 215 E6
Ardington La OX12, OX13 197 E2
ARDINGTON WICK 215 F8
Ardler Rd RG4 259 C2
ARDLEY 50 C4
Ardley Rd
Ardley OX27 50 C4
Bucknell OX27 50 E2
Middleton Stoney OX25 64 A4
Somerton OX25 48 F6
Argentan Cl OX14 179 D4
Argosy Cl OX44 184 E6
Argosy Rd
Benson OX10 204 D3
Carterton OX18 115 F2
Argyle St OX4 141 F6
Aristotle La OX2 123 A4
Arkel Cl OX18 101 A6
Arkell Ave OX18 115 D2
Arkell Ct OX18 115 D2
Arkwright Rd OX26 66 A3
ARLESCOTE 2 C6
Arlington Cl OX18 115 E2
Arlington Dr OX3 123 E5
Armour Hill RG31 257 D1
Armour Rd RG31 257 D1
Armour Wlk RG31 257 D1
Armstrong Rd OX4 142 B1
Arncott Rd OX25 97 D7
Arncott Wood Rd OX25 96 E6
Arndale Beck OX11 201 A2
Arnold Rd OX4 141 F6
Arnold's Way OX2 140 C7
Arnold Way OX9 147 E7
Arnott's Yd HP18 129 D6
Arran Gr OX16 16 C6
Arrow Cl OX17 11 A1
Arthray Rd OX2 140 D8
Arthur Evans Cl OX13 159 A6
Arthur Garrard Cl OX2 261 A4
Arthur St OX2 123 A1
Arundel Cl
Carterton OX18 115 C2
Kings Sutton OX17 23 F5
Arundel Pl OX16 15 F5
Arundel View OX7 42 D2
Arun Mews OX11 201 A1
ASCOTT
Hook Norton 18 A2
Stadhampton 163 E1
ASCOTT D' OYLEY 71 C2
ASCOTT EARL 71 B1
Ascott Hill CV36 18 A1
Ascott Rd OX7 85 D8
ASCOTT-UNDER-WYCHWOOD 71 D2
Ascott-under-Wychwood Sta OX7 71 C2
Ash Ave OX18 115 E5
Ashburn Pl OX11 200 F3
Ashburton La OX15 30 B6
ASHBURY 228 A7
Ashbury Hill SN6 228 B6
Ashbury with Compton Beauchamp CE Prim Sch SN6 228 A7
Ashby Ct OX16 16 D5
Ashby Rd OX26 65 D2
Ash Cl
Faringdon SN7 172 E3
Kidlington OX5 108 E7
Watlington OX49 186 A2
Ashcombe Cl OX28 118 A8
Ash Copse RG4 259 F7
Ashcroft Cl
Chadlington OX7 57 B1
Oxford OX2 122 B1
Reading RG4 258 E5
Ashcroft Rd OX16 16 D2
Ash Ct RG4 259 B3
Ashdale Ave OX28 104 D3
Ashdene 6 OX18 115 E5
Ashdene Rd OX26 65 C2
Ashdown House★ RG17 245 E8
Ashdown Way RG9 242 A1
Ashenden Cl OX14 159 F1
Ashfield Rd OX18 115 E1
Ashfields Cl OX12 197 C7
Ashfields La OX12 197 C7
Ashford Ave RG4 252 E5
Ashgate OX14 179 E4
Ash Gr
Chesterton OX26 79 F7
Oxford OX3 124 D4
Ashhurst Ct OX33 144 F7
Ash La OX25 81 D4
Ashlee Wlk RG8 250 F8
Ashley Hill Pl RG10 255 F7
Ashlong Rd OX3 124 A5
Ashmead Rd OX16 8 F1
Ashmolean Mus★ OX1 261 B3
Ashmole Pl OX4 142 F3
Ashmole Rd OX14 179 E4
Ashridge OX39 168 B6
Ashridge Cl OX16 16 E2
Ashsdown Way OX12 214 D8
Ash-Shifa Sch 13 OX16 16 E6
Ashurst Way OX4 142 A3
Ashville Way OX4 142 F3
Aspen Cl OX26 65 E5
Aspen Sq OX4 142 E1
Asquith Rd OX4 142 A3
ASTHALL 101 F3
ASTHALL LEIGH 102 D6
Astley Ave OX5 108 F6
Astley Rd OX9 130 B1
ASTON 135 E3
Aston Cl
Abingdon OX14 179 F7
Banbury OX16 16 E2
Pangbourne RG8 256 D5
Wallingford OX10 221 C7
Aston & Cote CE Prim Sch OX18 135 E3
Aston Gdns OX49 167 D3
Aston Hill OX49 187 E7
Aston Ho 6 OX16 16 E6
Aston Pk OX49 167 D2
Aston Rd
Bampton OX18 134 F3
Ducklington, Church End OX29 118 B3
Ducklington OX29 118 A2
Standlake OX29 137 A3
ASTON ROWANT 167 C2
Aston Rowant CE Prim Sch OX49 167 E3
Aston Rowant National Nature Reserve★ HP14 187 E5
Aston Rowant Rd OX49 167 D2
Aston St
Aston Tirrold OX11 237 F8
Oxford OX4 141 F7
ASTON TIRROLD 237 E8
ASTON UPTHORPE 219 E2
Aston View OX25 49 A5
Aston Works OX18 135 D3
Astrop Rd
Kings Sutton OX17 23 F5
Middleton Cheney OX17 17 F6
ASTWICK 37 B7
Atkinson Cl OX3 124 E5
Atkyns Rd OX3 142 E8
Atterbury Gdns RG4 258 E4
Atwell Cl OX10 221 C8
Atwell Pl 5 OX3 124 D1
Aubrey Ct OX4 142 A4
Auburn Ct RG4 259 A2
Audlett Dr OX14 180 B8
Audley Ho OX26 65 F4
Augustine Way OX4 142 A5
Austen Wlk OX26 65 C2
Austin Dr OX16 15 F8
Austin Pl OX14 159 E2
Austin Rd OX15 22 E7
Austin's Way OX15 30 C8
Auton Pl RG9 254 D8
Autumn Cl RG4 259 C7
Autumn Wlk RG10 255 D2
Avens Way OX4 142 E1
Avenue Four OX28 118 B7
Avenue Ho RG4 258 D3
Avenue La OX4 141 F8
Avenue One OX28 118 A6
Avenue Rd
Banbury OX16 16 F6
Bourton SN6 209 A3
Avenue The
Bloxham OX15 21 D4
Chinnor OX39 168 D6
Great Tew OX7 45 D8
Kennington OX1 160 E8
Shillingford OX10 203 B4
Wheatley OX33 144 C7
Worminghall HP18 127 E5
Avenue Three OX28 118 B6
Avenue Two OX28 118 B6
Avery Ct OX2 123 B8
Avocet Way
Banbury OX16 16 E3
Bicester OX26 81 B8
Avonbury Bsns Pk OX26 65 C4
Avonbury Ct NN13 24 A5
Avon Carrow OX17 3 A8
Avon Cres OX26 65 B3
AVON DASSETT 2 F8
Avon Rd
Abingdon OX13 159 C2
Harwell OX11 217 C1
Avon Way OX11 200 F3
Avro Rd GL54 68 B5
Awgar Stone Rd OX3 142 F7
Axis Rd SN6 191 E1
Axtell Cl OX5 92 D1
Ayers Dr OX15 21 E3
Aylesbury Rd
Haddenham OX9 130 C6
Thame OX9 129 F3
Aylesbury & Thame Airfield HP17 130 E7
AYNHO 35 C8
Aynho Ct OX17 35 D7
Aynhoe Pk OX17 35 C7
Aynho Fishery★ OX17 34 F6
Aynho Rd
Adderbury OX17 23 C3
East Adderbury OX17 23 B4
Ayrshire Cl 3 OX16 9 A1
Aysgarth Rd OX5 108 B6
Azalea Ave OX5 108 E6
Azalea Wlk OX16 9 B1
Azor's Ct OX4 142 A4

B

BABLOCK HYTHE 138 F5
Bablock Hythe Rd OX13 139 B3
Back Hill OX17 8 C8
Back La
Aston OX18 135 D3
Ducklington OX29 118 B4
Eynsham OX29 120 E8
Long Compton CV36 28 A6
Sibford Ferris OX15 19 B7
Back Row GL56 40 C3
Backsideans RG10 255 D2
Backside La OX15 19 A8
Back St OX9 166 B8
Badbury Cl SN7 172 E2
Bader Dr OX25 63 B7
Badgemore La RG9 244 D3
Badgemore Prim Sch RG9 244 D2
Badger Cl OX33 125 E4
Badger La OX1 141 B3
Badgers Copse OX14 160 E2
Badgers Rise
Reading RG4 259 A5
Reading RG5 260 D1
Badgers Wlk
Lower Shiplake RG9 255 A3
Temple Cowley OX4 142 C6
Badger Way OX16 16 F3
Badswell La OX13 158 A8
Bagley Cl OX1 141 D2
Bagley Wood Rd OX1 160 D7
Bailey Cl OX12 214 D6
Bailey Rd OX4 142 D4
Bailie Cl 2 OX14 179 E6
BAINTON 51 E2
Bainton Cl OX26 66 C2
Bainton Rd
Bucknell OX27 65 A8
Hethe OX27 52 A7
Oxford OX2 123 A5
Bakehouse La OX17 8 D8
Baker Ave OX10 204 D2
Baker Cl
Benson OX10 204 D2
Bicester OX27 65 F7
Oxford OX3 124 F2
Baker Rd OX14 179 F5
Baker's Ct OX29 90 B1
Bakers La
Brightwell-cum-Sotwell OX10 202 F2
East Hagbourne OX11 218 F6
Oxford OX4 141 F4
South Newington OX15 31 F7
Swalcliffe OX15 19 F8
Tadmarton OX15 20 C8
Bakers Piece OX28 104 B2
Baker's Piece OX39 167 F4
Baker's Piece Ho OX39 167 F4
Bakers Sq SN7 193 A4
Baker St OX11 237 F8
Bakery Cl OX44 184 D7
Bakery La
Clanfield OX18 152 F8
Letcombe Regis OX12 214 A1
Baldon La OX44 161 F3
BALDON ROW 162 B5
Baldons Cl RG8 250 F8
Balfour Cotts OX14 182 A5
Balfour Rd OX4 142 E3
Balfour's Field RG8 241 D3
Balham's La RG9 225 F8
Ballard Chase OX14 160 A3
Ballard Cl OX7 46 E1
Ballards Cl OX7 85 D8
Balliol Cl OX5 77 C6
Balliol Coll OX1 261 B3
Balliol Ct OX2 123 A4
Balliol Dr OX11 219 B8
Balliol Rd
Bicester OX26 65 F3
Reading RG4 258 D3
Ball La OX5 77 B5
Balmoral Ave OX16 15 F4
Balmoral Rd OX11 219 A8
Balmoral Way OX17 23 F6
Balmore Dr RG4 259 B4
Balmore Ho RG4 259 B3
Balmore Pk RG4 259 B3
BALSCOTE 14 C8
Baltic Wharf OX1 261 B1
BAMPTON 134 F4
Bampton CE Prim Sch OX18 134 F4
Bampton Cl OX4 142 D3
Bampton Rd
Aston OX18 135 D2
Black Bourton OX18 133 E4
Clanfield OX18 133 F1
Curbridge OX18, OX29 117 B4
BANBURY 16 F5
Banbury Bsns Pk OX17 23 D3
Banbury Cross Ret Pk OX16 16 C8
Banbury Ct 1 OX14 179 F7
Banbury Gdns RG4 259 C3
Banbury Hill OX7 73 C5
Banbury La
Banbury OX17 17 D8
Kings Sutton OX17 23 F5
Middleton Cheney OX17 11 C3
Banbury Mus★ OX16 16 D6
Banbury Rd
Adderbury OX17 23 A6
Aynho OX17 35 B8
Bicester OX26 65 E4
Bloxham OX15 21 E6
Chacombe OX17 10 D4
Chipping Norton OX7 42 F4
Chipping Warden OX17 5 F6
Cutteslowe OX2 109 A1
Deddington OX15 33 F5
Enstone OX7 59 A6
Kidlington OX5 92 D1
North Newington OX15 15 C3
Over Norton OX7 43 D6
Oxford OX2 123 B6
Shipton-on-Cherwell OX5 92 B5
Shutford OX15 14 B5
Swerford OX7 30 D1
Tackley OX5 76 E4
Warmington OX17 3 A2
Woodstock OX20 91 D7
Banbury Road Crossing OX7 42 F3
Banbury Road Rdbt OX2 109 A1
Banbury Sch OX16 16 B3
Banbury Sta OX16 16 E5
Bandet Way OX9 148 B6
Banesberie Cl OX16 9 A1
Banjo Rd OX4 142 C5
Bank Cotts OX33 125 E4
Banks Furlong OX26 79 F8
Bankside
Banbury OX16 16 F3
Kidlington OX5 92 C2
Long Hanborough OX29 90 F1
Oxford OX3 124 E3
West Hendred OX12 216 B6
Bannister Cl OX4 141 E7
Bannister Rd OX9 148 C7
Barbara's Mdw RG31 257 B2
Barberry Pl OX26 65 E4
Barbrook Cl RG31 257 D3
Barbury Dr OX12 214 D8
Barclose Ave RG4 259 C3
Barcombe Cl OX16 8 F1
Barcote La SN7 174 A6
Bardolph's Cl RG4 258 D8
Bardwell Ct OX2 123 C4
Bardwell Rd OX2 123 C4
Bardwell Sch OX26 66 A4
Bardwell Terr OX26 65 F2
Barefoot Cl RG31 257 B1
Barfleur Cl OX14 160 B3
Barford Rd
Bloxham OX15 21 E2
South Newington OX15 32 A6
BARFORD ST JOHN 32 F7
BARFORD ST MICHAEL 32 E5
Bargus Cl OX13 199 A4
Barksdale Ave NN13 36 E6
Barkus Way HP14 188 F5
Barley Cl
Bloxham OX15 21 E5
Lewknor OX49 187 A8
Sibford Gower OX15 19 A8
Wallingford OX10 221 C6
Barleycott La OX1 141 C4
Barley Cres OX18 115 F5
Barley Croft OX15 21 E5
Barleyfields OX11 218 C8
Barleyfield Way OX28 104 E1
Barley Hill Prim Sch OX9 130 A1
Barlow Cl
Milcombe OX15 21 A2
Wheatley OX33 143 F8
Barnacre OX49 186 B1
Barnard Cl RG4 259 C6
BARNARD GATE 105 F1
Barnards Way OX12 214 F6
Barn Bsns Ctr The GL54 83 A8
Barn Cl
Denchworth OX12 196 A4
Kidlington OX5 108 D8
Oxford OX2 140 B6
Barncroft
Long Compton CV36 28 A5
Wallingford OX10 221 C8
Barn End OX18 134 E2
Barnes Cl OX11 218 E7
Barnes Rd OX11 218 E6
Barnet St OX4 142 A7
Barnett Rd
Middleton Cheney OX17 17 F8
Steventon OX13 198 F5
Barnett Way OX10 204 D2
Barnfield OX12 175 F1
Barnfield Cl OX27 65 F6
Barn La RG9 244 C4
Barns Cl OX33 126 B1
Barns Hay OX3 123 F6
Barns Ho OX4 142 C4
Barns La OX18 100 E4
Barn's Rd OX4 142 D4
Baroma Way RG9 244 E2
Baronshurst Dr OX44 184 D6
Baronsmead RG9 244 D2
Baron Way RG9 242 A2
Barracks La OX4 142 B7
Barracks The OX44 164 D8
Barrett Ct RG1 258 F1
Barrett's Cl OX29 89 C7
Barrett St OX2 123 A1
Barrett's Way OX14 199 F6
Barrington Ave SN6 191 F1
Barrington Cl
Berinsfield OX10 182 C6
Oxford OX3 124 C2
Witney OX28 117 E7
Barrington Ct NN13 24 A5
Barrington Rd SN6 209 D8
Barrow Hill Cl OX14 160 C2
BARROW HILLS 160 D1
Barrow La OX11 217 E8
Barrow Pk (Cvn Site) OX11 217 E8
Barrow Rd
Abingdon OX13 179 B8
Harwell OX11 217 E8
Barry Ave OX26 65 D3
Bartholomew Ave OX5 108 B5
Bartholomew Cl
Ducklington OX29 118 B4
Eynsham OX29 120 D8
Bartholomew Rd OX4 142 C4
Bartholomew Sch OX29 120 D8
Bartholomew Sports Ctr OX29 120 D7
Bartholomew Tipping Way HP14 188 F5
Bartlemas Cl OX4 142 A7
Bartlemas Rd OX4 142 A8
Bartlett Cl
Wallingford OX10 221 C5
Witney OX28 118 A8
BARTON 124 E4
Barton Cl OX17 23 F6
Barton Ct OX14 179 B1
BARTONGATE 61 A8
BARTON HARTSHORN 39 D2
Barton La
Abingdon OX14 180 B7
Oxford OX3 124 D4
BARTON-ON-THE-HEATH 26 E6
Barton Pool OX3 124 F4
Barton Rd
Long Compton CV36 27 C7
Oxford OX3 124 E4
Barton Village Rd OX3 124 E5
Bartsia Rd OX26 65 E4
Barwell OX12 214 D5
Basildon Park★ RG8 249 D1
Basil Hill Rd OX11 200 D3
Baskerville La RG9 255 A3
Baskerville Rd RG4 252 E5
Basmore La RG9 255 B4
Basset Ave OX26 65 F3
Bassett Rd
Letcombe Bassett OX12 231 F7
Oxford OX3 124 F4
Basset Way OX5 108 F8
Batchelors Row OX15 33 B4
Bate Collection of Musical Instruments★ OX1 261 B1
Bateman St OX3 124 D2
Bates La OX27 35 D3
Bath Ct OX14 179 F7
Bathing Pl La OX28 104 A1
Bath Pl OX1 261 C2
Bath Rd
Banbury OX16 16 C6
Sonning RG4 260 E2
Bath St
Abingdon OX14 179 E8
Oxford OX4 123 F1
Bath Terr OX26 65 F2
Batt CE Prim Sch OX28 118 A8
Batten Pl OX4 142 A1
Batting Cl HP14 189 F8
Battle Cl OX26 66 A3
Battle Rd
Benson OX10 204 D2
Goring RG8 249 F7
BAULKING 193 F2
Baulking La SN7 194 C2
Baxters Barns GL7 131 A4
Bayards Hill Prim Sch 1 OX3 124 F4
BAYDON 245 E1
Baydon Rd SN8 245 D1
Baydon St Nicholas CE Prim Sch SN8 245 E1
Bayliss Rd RG10 255 D1

Bayliss Yd OX7. . . . . 73 B3
BAYNARD'S GREEN 50 D7
Bayswater Farm OX3. . 125 A4
Bayswater Farm Rd OX3. 125 A4
Bayswater Rd
　Blenheim OX33. . . . . . . 143 C7
　Oxford OX3. . . . . 124 E4
　Rissinghurst OX3. . . . . . 125 A1
Bay Tree Cl OX4 . . . . . . 142 A4
BAYWORTH. 160 A7
Bayworth La OX1 . . . . . 159 F8
Bayworth Pk OX13 . . . . 159 F7
Beachborough Sch NN13 . 25 A4
BEACON'S BOTTOM 189 D3
Beaconsfield Rd OX16. . . 16 D2
Beacon View OX49. . . . . 187 B8
Beadle Trad Est OX10. . . 221 B7
Beadnell Cl OX16 . . . . . . 16 D2
Beagle Cl OX14 . . . . . . 160 C2
Beagles Cl OX5 . . . . . . 109 A7
Beale Park★ RG8. . . . . . 249 F1
Beam Paddock OX18. . . 135 A3
Beanacre Rd OX15. . . . . . 30 B6
Bean Furlong OX17. . . . . . 10 E4
Beanhill Cl OX29. . . . . . 118 A5
Beanhill Rd OX29. . . . . . 118 A5
Beansheaf Terr 17 OX10 221 D7
Bear Cl OX20 . . . . 91 B6
Bear Close Flats OX20. . . 91 B6
Bear Ct OX1 . . . . 100 E5
Beargarden Rd OX16. . . . 16 C5
Bear La
　North Moreton OX11. . . . 220 A7
　Oxford OX1. . . . . 261 C2
　Stadhampton OX44. . . . . 163 C1
　Wallingford OX10 . . . . . 221 D8
Bears Hedge OX4 . . . . . 142 A4
Beatrice Dr OX16 . . . . . . 16 A5
Beauchamp La OX4 . . . . 142 B4
Beauchamp Pl OX4 . . . . 142 B4
Beaufort Cl
　Bicester OX26 . . . . 66 A3
　Didcot OX11. . . . . 219 B8
Beaulieu Cl OX16 . . . . . . 16 F6
Beaulieu Ct OX13 . . . . . 159 F5
Beaulieu Mews OX11. . . 201 A3
Beaumaris Cl OX16. . . . . 15 F7
Beaumont Bldgs OX1. . . . 9 C1
Beaumont Bsns Ctr OX16 . 9 C1
Beaumont Cl OX16 . . . . . 9 C1
Beaumont Ct OX1. . . . . 141 E1
Beaumont Ind Est OX16 . . 9 C1
Beaumont La OX1. . . . . 261 B3
Beaumont Pl OX1. . . . . 261 B3
Beaumont Rd
　Banbury OX16 . . . . 9 C1
　Oxford OX3 . . . . 124 F3
Beaumont St OX1. . . . . 261 B3
Bec Cl OX12 . . . . 214 B5
Beckdale Cl OX26 . . . . . . 65 B3
Becket St OX1. . . . . . . 261 A2
Beckett Ave SN6. . . . . . 209 D7
Beckett Dr SN6. . . . . . . 209 D7
Beckett Ho OX12 . . . . . 214 E4
Becketts Cl OX29 . . . . . . 90 B1
BECKLEY. 111 B3
Beckley CE Prim Sch
　OX3. . . . . 111 A3
Beckley Cl RG8 . . . . . . 250 F8
Beckley Ct OX3 . . . . . . 111 B2
Becquerel Ave OX11 . . . 217 B2
Bec Tithe RG8. . . . . . . 250 E3
Bedford Cl OX16 . . . . . . 15 F8
Bedford St OX4 . . . . . . 141 F6
Bedwells Heath OX1. . . 140 D1
Beech RG9. . . . . 244 D2
Beech Cl
　Faringdon SN7. . . . . . . 172 S4
　Stokenchurch HP14 . . . . 188 F3
　Watlington OX49. . . . . . 186 A2
　Wootton OX13 . . . . 159 A7
Beech Cres OX5 . . . . . . 108 F6
Beechcroft OX10. . . . . . 182 D1
Beech Croft Rd OX2. . . . 123 B6
Beech Ct RG4. . . . . . . 259 B3
Beeches The
　Deddington OX15. . . . . . 33 F4
　Goring RG8. . . . . 249 B5
　Oxford OX3. . . . . 124 E4
　Reading RG31 . . . . 257 D3
　Shenington OX15. . . . . . .6 F2
Beechey Ave OX3 . . . . . 123 F4
Beechfield Cres OX16 . . . 16 D3
Beechgate OX28 . . . . . 118 A6
Beech Gr
　Fulbrook OX18. . . . . . . 100 F6
　Woodgreen OX28. . . . . . 104 E2
Beeching Cl OX11. . . . . 218 C2
Beeching Way
　Wallingford OX10 . . . . . 221 C7
　Wheatley OX33. . . . . . . 143 F8
Beech La
　Abingdon OX14 . . . . . . 159 F2
　6 Carterton OX18 . . . . . 115 F5
　Woodcote RG8. . . . . . . 250 C8
Beech Lodge OX3. . . . . 124 C3
Beech Pl OX3. . . . . 124 B3
Beech Rd
　Chinnor OX39. . . . . 168 C6
　Eynsham OX29. . . . . . . 120 E8
　Oxford, Botley OX2 . . . . 124 A1
　Oxford, Headington OX3 . 124 C3
　Purley on Thames RG8. . . 257 B4
　Shillingford OX10. . . . . . 203 B4
　Thame OX9. . . . . 147 D8

Beech Rd continued
　Tokers Green RG4. . . . . 258 D7
　Wheatley OX33. . . . . . . 144 B7
　Witney OX28 . . . . 117 F8
Beech Rise RG4. . . . . . 252 F6
Beechwood OX4 . . . . . . 142 A5
Beechwood Cl RG8. . . . 250 D6
Beechwood Ho OX3. . . . 124 E4
Beef La OX1 . . . . 261 B2
Beehive Cl OX10 . . . . . 220 F1
Beesley Rd OX16. . . . . . 16 A6
Beeson Cl RG8. . . . . . . 250 F8
BEGBROKE. 108 B8
Begbroke Cres OX5. . . . . 92 A1
Begbroke La
　Begbroke OX5 . . . . 92 A1
　Kidlington OX5. . . . . . . 92 C1
Begbroke Science Pk
　OX5. . . . . 108 B7
Beggarsbush Hill OX10. . 204 D1
Beggar's La OX13 . . . . . 156 C1
Behoes La RG8 . . . . . . 240 D1
Belbroughton Rd OX2. . . 123 C5
Belcher Ct OX10 . . . . . . 182 D2
Belfast Ct OX18 . . . . . . 133 F8
Belfast Rd OX10. . . . . . 204 D3
Belfast Sq OX18. . . . . . 133 F8
Belgrave Cres 4 OX16 . . 16 B6
Belgrave Cl OX5 . . . . . . 108 D8
Bellamy Cl OX13 . . . . . 156 E1
Bell Cl
　Cassington OX29. . . . . . 107 D2
　Grove OX12. . . . . 196 F1
　Thame OX9. . . . . 129 E1
Bell Ct RG4. . . . . 259 B6
Belleisle RG8 . . . . 257 B5
Bellenger Way OX5 . . . . 108 D8
Belle Terr OX18 . . . . . . 115 D1
Belle Vue Rd RG9 . . . . . 254 D8
Bellingham La SN6. . . . . 190 A1
Bellingham Wlk RG4 . . . 259 A5
Bell La
　Aldworth RG8 . . . . 247 F4
　Bampton OX18. . . . . . . 134 E3
　Bicester OX26 . . . . 65 E2
　Brightwell-cum-Sotwell
　　OX10. . . . . 202 E2
　Cassington OX29. . . . . . 107 D2
　Henley-on-Thames RG9. . 244 E3
　Lechlade-on-Thames GL7 . 150 C3
　Thame OX9. . . . . 129 F1
　Wheatley OX33. . . . . . . 144 B8
Bell Lodge 8 OX26. . . . . 65 E2
Bell's La OX15 . . . . 30 B7
Bell St
　Henley-on-Thames RG9 . . 244 E2
　Hornton OX15. . . . . .7 C6
Bell Street Mews RG9 . . 244 E2
BELMONT. 214 C5
Belmont OX12. . . . . . . 214 D5
Belmont Mews OX9 . . . 147 F8
Belsyre Ct OX1. . . . . . . 261 A4
Belvedere Rd OX4. . . . . 142 A7
Benares Gr RG9. . . . . . 242 A4
Ben Cl OX5 . . . . 92 E1
Benhams La RG9. . . . . . 226 D2
Benmead Rd OX5 . . . . . . 92 E1
Bennett Cl OX17 . . . . . . 10 E4
Bennett Cres OX4. . . . . 142 D5
BENNETT END. 189 C7
Bennett End Rd HP14 . . 189 D7
Bennett Rd SN7. . . . . . 172 F3
Benouville Cl OX4. . . . . 142 E6
Bensgrove Cl RG8. . . . . 250 F8
BENSON. 204 A4
Benson Cl OX26. . . . . . . 66 B3
Benson La
　Benson OX10. . . . . 204 A2
　Crowmarsh Gifford OX10 . 221 F8
Benson Pl OX1. . . . . . . 123 D4
Benson Prim Sch OX10. . 203 E4
Benson Rd
　Abingdon OX14 . . . . . . 159 E2
　Oxford OX3 . . . . 142 D8
Bentley Cl OX16. . . . . . . 15 F8
Benton Dr OX39. . . . . . 168 D7
Benwells OX39. . . . . . . 168 C6
Bere Court Rd RG8. . . . 256 B4
Berens Rd SN6. . . . . . . 209 B6
Bergamont Pl 6 OX4 . . . 142 E1
Bergen Ave OX14 . . . . . 179 D4
Berinscourt Ho OX10. . . 182 B5
BERINSFIELD. 182 D5
Berinsfield Com Prim Sch
　OX10. . . . . 182 C5
Berinsfield Rdbt OX10. . . 182 B4
Berins Hill OX10 . . . . . . 241 A6
Berkeley Cl OX16 . . . . . . 15 E7
Berkeley Rd
　Boars Hill OX1 . . . . 140 E1
　Thame OX9. . . . . 130 A1
Berkshire Rd RG9 . . . . . 254 D8
Bernard Cl OX5 . . . . . . 108 C5
Berner's Way SN7. . . . . 173 A3
Bernewode Cl HP18. . . . 129 C7
Bernwood Butterfly Trail★
　OX33. . . . . 112 F2
Bernwood Forest★ OX33 112 F2
Bernwood Rd
　Bicester OX26 . . . . 65 F2
　Oxford OX3 . . . . 124 E4
BERRICK PRIOR. 184 A2
Berrick Rd OX44. . . . . . 184 D5
BERRICK SALOME. 184 A1
Berry Cl OX4. . . . . 142 F3
Berrycroft SN6 . . . . . . 228 A7

Berry Croft OX14. . . . . . 159 E1
Berryfield Way OX18. . . . 115 E5
Berry Hill Rd OX17 . . . . . 22 F2
Berry La
　Blewbury OX11 . . . . . . 219 A1
　East Hanney OX12. . . . . 197 B6
Berrylands Rd RG4. . . . . 259 B3
Berrymere Rd OX13 . . . . 159 A7
Berrymoor Rd OX16. . . . . 16 B5
Bertie Pl OX1. . . . . 141 D5
Bertie Rd OX2. . . . . . . 139 F5
Besbury La OX7. . . . . . . 55 F6
Bessels Lea Rd OX11. . . . 219 A1
Bessels Leigh Rd OX13. . 158 F8
Bessels Leigh Sch OX13 158 C7
Bessel's Way OX11. . . . 237 B8
Bessemer Cl OX26 . . . . . 66 A2
Beta Bvd OX44. . . . . . . 143 C1
Betony Way OX26. . . . . . 65 E4
Betterton Cotts OX12. . . 215 F2
Bettina Cres 7 OX16 . . . . 9 A1
Betty La OX1. . . . . 141 C3
Between Towns Rd OX4 . 142 C5
Beverley Cl
　Abingdon OX14 . . . . . . 159 E1
　Chalgrove OX44. . . . . . 184 E6
Beverley Cres OX18 . . . . 115 E4
Beverley Gdns
　Bicester OX26 . . . . 66 A4
　Wargrave RG10. . . . . . . 255 E1
Beverley Rd RG31. . . . . 257 C1
Beverly Cl OX10. . . . . . 204 D3
Bevington Rd OX2 . . . . . 261 B4
Bhandari Cl OX4 . . . . . . 142 B6
Bibury Cl OX28. . . . . . . 117 D8
BICESTER. 65 E3
Bicester Ave OX25 . . . . . 80 D7
Bicester Com Coll OX26 . 65 D2
Bicester Hill NN13 . . . . . 38 A8
Bicester Ho 1 OX26 . . . . 65 E1
Bicester L Ctr OX26 . . . . 65 D2
Bicester North Sta OX26. 65 F3
Bicester Rd
　Bucknell OX27 . . . . 64 F7
　Enstone OX7 . . . . 58 F6
　Kidlington OX5. . . . . . . 108 F7
　Launton OX26 . . . . 66 C2
　Long Crendon HP18. . . . 129 C6
　Ludgershall HP18 . . . . . . 98 C8
　Marsh Gibbon OX27. . . . . 67 C3
　Middleton Stoney OX25. . . 64 B3
　Stratton Audley OX27. . . . 66 C8
Bicester Town Sta OX26. . 80 F8
Bicester Village Outlet
　Shopping OX26. . . . . . . 80 E8
Bickerton Rd OX3. . . . . 124 C2
Biddel Springs SN6. . . . 190 B6
Biddlesden Rd NN13 . . . . 25 A5
Bigmore La HP14 . . . . . 189 C1
Bignell Pk OX26. . . . . . . 64 D1
Bignell View OX26. . . . . . 79 F8
Bignolds Cl OX17 . . . . . . 4 D8
Bigwood Cvn Pk OX14. . . 160 E6
Billings Cl HP14. . . . . . 188 F5
Billwell HP18 . . . . 129 C6
BINFIELD HEATH. 254 A2
Bingley Gr RG5 . . . . . . 260 F1
Binning Cl OX11. . . . . . 199 B8
BINSEY. 122 E4
Binsey La OX2 . . . . 122 E2
Binswood Ave OX3. . . . . 124 E2
Birch Cl RG4. . . . . 252 F4
Birch Dr OX18 . . . . 114 C7
Birchen Cl RG8 . . . . . . 250 F8
Birches The RG8. . . . . . 249 B6
Birch Gr OX28 . . . . 104 C2
Birch Rd
　Ambrosden OX25. . . . . . . 81 C3
　Garsington OX44 . . . . . . 143 D2
Birchwood
　Banbury OX16 . . . . 16 D3
　Carterton OX18 . . . . . . 115 E2
Birchwood Cl RG4 . . . . . 259 C6
Birchwood Dr OX5 . . . . . 92 B6
Bird Cl OX16. . . . . 16 B6
Bird Wood Ct RG4 . . . . . 253 A3
Birdlip Cl OX28. . . . . . . 103 D1
Birds La OX15. . . . . 13 A6
Birinus Ct RG4 . . . . 259 C6
Birmingham Yd OX10 . . . 203 F4
Biscoe Ct OX33 . . . . . . 144 C8
Bishop Carpenter CE Prim
　Sch OX15. . . . . 15 B4
Bishop Kirk Pl OX2. . . . . 123 A7
Bishop Loveday CE Prim Sch
　OX15. . . . . 16 E1
Bishops Cl OX15 . . . . . . 32 E6
Bishops Mdw OX29 . . . . 89 D8
Bishops Orch OX11. . . . 218 F7
BISHOPSTONE. 227 C3
Bishopstone Prim Sch
　SN6. . . . . 227 D4
Bishop's Wood OX44 . . . 144 C3
Bishopswood Sch RG4. . 252 F5
Bisley Cl OX26. . . . . 66 A3
Bitham Rd OX12 . . . . . . 233 C7
Bitterell OX29 . . . . 120 F7
BIX 243 D7
Bix Comm RG9. . . . . . . 243 D8
Bix Hill RG9. . . . . 243 E7
Blackberry La OX4 . . . . . 162 A8
Blackbird Assarts La
　OX29. . . . . 88 B1
BLACKBIRD LEYS. 142 F2
Blackbird Leys L Ctr OX4 142 F2
Blackbird Leys Rd OX4 . . 142 D2

BLACKBIRD'S BOTTOM. . . 250 D5
Blackbird's Bottom RG8. 250 C5
BLACK BOURTON. 133 F6
Black Bourton Rd
　Carterton OX18 . . . . . . 115 E1
　Clanfield OX18. . . . . . . 133 E1
Blackbull La OX5. . . . . . . 95 C5
Black Croft OX12. . . . . . 214 D6
BLACKDITCH. 138 A8
Blackditch OX29 . . . . . . 138 A8
Blackfriars Coll OX1 . . . 261 B3
Blackfriars Rd OX1. . . . . 261 B1
Blackhall Rd OX1 . . . . . 261 B3
Blackhorse La OX13. . . . 158 F3
Blacklands OX12. . . . . . 212 E4
Blacklands Way OX14. . . 179 C2
Black Lands Rd OX10. . . 204 A5
Blackman Cl OX1 . . . . . 141 E2
Blackmore Cl OX9 . . . . . 148 A7
Blackmore La RG4 . . . . 253 B5
Blacknall Rd OX14. . . . . 179 E5
Blacksmiths Cl OX25 . . . . 79 A2
Blacksmiths Hill OX17. . . 35 C7
Blacksmiths La OX5. . . . . 95 A4
Blacksmiths Mdw 11
　OX4. . . . . 142 F1
Blackstock Cl OX3 . . . . 142 E7
Blackstone Rd OX10. . . . 203 D1
BLACKTHORN. 82 A4
Blackthorn Ave OX18. . . 115 E5
Blackthorn Cl
　Blackthorn OX25 . . . . . . 82 A3
　Oxford OX3 . . . . 124 E4
　Reading RG31 . . . . 257 B1
Blackthorne Mews 9
　OX18 . . . . 115 E5
Blackthorn Rd OX26. . . . . 66 E5
Blackwater Cl RG4 . . . . 259 E4
Blackwater Way OX11. . . 201 A3
Blackwood Pl OX15. . . . . 22 F8
Blackworth SN6. . . . . . 190 A8
Blackworth Ind Est SN6 . 190 A7
BLADON. 91 C2
Bladon CE Prim Sch OX20 91 B2
Bladon Cl OX2 . . . . 122 F8
Bladon Rd OX20 . . . . . . 91 D4
Blaenant RG4. . . . . 258 F5
Blaenavon RG4. . . . . . . 258 F5
Blagrave Cl OX11 . . . . . 200 E1
Blagrave Farm La RG4. . 258 D5
Blagrave La RG4. . . . . . 258 D4
Blake CE Prim Sch The
　OX28. . . . . 118 C8
Blakehope Burn OX11. . . 200 F3
Blake Rd OX26 . . . . 65 E4
Blakes Ave OX28 . . . . . 118 D7
Blake's Field OX11 . . . . 200 D1
Blakes Rd RG10. . . . . . 255 E3
Blake Way OX9 . . . . . . 130 A1
Blandford Alley SN6. . . . 190 A5
Blandford Ave OX2. . . . . 109 A1
Blandford Ct OX20 . . . . . 91 A6
Blandford Rd OX5. . . . . . 92 D7
Blandy Ave OX13 . . . . . 156 E1
Blandy Rd RG9. . . . . . . 254 C7
Blay Cl OX4. . . . . 142 E3
Bleache Pl OX4 . . . . . . 142 D5
BLEDINGTON. 54 D1
Bledington Sch OX7. . . . . 54 D2
BLEDLOW. 169 B8
Bledlow Rd HP27 . . . . . 169 E8
BLEDLOW RIDGE. 189 E8
Bledlow Ridge Rd HP27 . 169 C8
Bledlow Ridge Sch HP14 189 E8
Blencowe Cl OX27 . . . . . 65 F6
BLENHEIM
　Garsington. 143 D2
　Horspath 143 C7
Blenheim Cl
　Didcot OX11. . . . . 200 E1
　Upper Rissington GL54 . . 68 B4
Blenheim Ct
　Carterton OX18 . . . . . . 115 D3
　2 Kidlington OX5. . . . . . 108 F8
　Oxford OX2 . . . . 123 A8
Blenheim Dr
　Bicester OX26 . . . . 65 C3
　Launton OX26 . . . . 66 E2
　Oxford OX2 . . . . 123 A7
　Witney OX28 . . . . 117 C2
　Wolvercote OX2. . . . . . 122 F8
Blenheim Gdns OX12. . . 196 C1
Blenheim Hill OX11 . . . . 217 F2
Blenheim La
　Freeland OX29. . . . . . . 106 A6
　Wheatley OX33 . . . . . . 144 A8
Blenheim Orch OX12. . . 197 B6
Blenheim Palace★ OX20 . 91 A5
Blenheim Pl OX10. . . . . 204 D2
Blenheim Rd
　Banbury OX16 . . . . 16 E2
　Horspath OX33. . . . . . . 143 C7
　Kidlington OX5. . . . . . . 108 F8
　Little Milton OX44 . . . . . 164 A6
　Reading RG4. . . . . 259 A3
　Shirburn OX49. . . . . . . 186 A4
Blenheim Rise OX17. . . . . 23 F6
Blenheim Terr
　Bletchingdon OX5. . . . . . 93 A8
　Chipping Norton OX7. . . . 42 E2
Blenheim Way
　Horspath OX33 . . . . . . 143 C7
　Kingston Bagpuize OX13 . 156 D1
Bleriot Rd GL54. . . . . . . 68 A4
Blessed George Napier RC
　Sch OX16. . . . . 16 C3

BLETCHINGDON. 93 B8
Bletchingdon Parochial CE
　Prim Sch OX5. . . . . 93 A8
Bletchingdon Rd
　Bletchingdon OX5 . . . . . 78 A3
　Hampton Poyle OX5. . . . . 93 A4
　Islip OX5 . . . . 93 E2
BLEWBURY. 237 B8
Blewbury Endowed CE Prim
　Sch OX11. . . . . 218 F1
Blewbury Hill OX11 . . . . 237 B8
Blewbury Rd OX11 . . . . 219 B3
Blewitt Ct OX4. . . . . . . 142 B2
Blissett Terr 3 SN7. . . . . 172 F3
Bliss Ho OX7. . . . . 42 E1
Bliss Mill OX7. . . . . 42 C2
Blomfield Pl OX2. . . . . . 261 A4
Blossom Gr RG5 . . . . . . 260 E1
Blossom Rd RG4. . . . . . 258 F3
Blossoms Glade OX14 . . 160 E6
Blounts Court Rd RG4,
　RG9 . . . . 253 B6
Blowings The OX29 . . . . 106 A7
Blowingstone Hill OX12 . 212 A2
BLOXHAM. 21 D5
Bloxham CE Prim Sch
　OX15. . . . . 21 C4
Bloxham Ct OX15 . . . . . . 21 D8
Bloxham Grove Rd OX15. . 22 B6
Bloxham Rd
　Banbury OX16 . . . . 16 B3
　Barford St Michael OX15. . 32 F7
　Milcombe OX15. . . . . . . 21 B2
Bloxham Sch OX15. . . . . 21 E5
Bloxham Village Mus★
　OX15. . . . . 21 E4
Bluebell Cl 1 OX26 . . . . 65 E3
Bluebell Ct 4 OX14 . . . . 142 F1
Bluebell Gdns RG4 . . . . 259 C7
Bluebell Ride OX14 . . . . 160 E7
Bluebell Way OX18. . . . . 115 F4
Blue Boar St OX1 . . . . . 261 B2
Blue Row OX7. . . . . 42 E5
Blythe Pl OX26. . . . . 65 B3
BOARS HILL. 140 D1
BOARSTALL. 97 B1
Boarstall Duck Decoy★
　HP18. . . . . 97 A1
Boathouse Reach RG9. . 244 E1
Bobby Fryer Cl OX4 . . . . 142 E4
Bockett's Cnr OX18 . . . . 102 A7
Boddington La OX29 . . . 105 C8
Boddington Rd OX17. . . . . 1 D1
BODICOTE. 22 D8
Bodleian Liby★ OX1. . . . 261 C2
Bodleian (New Liby)★
　OX1. . . . . 261 C3
Bodley Pl OX2 . . . . 123 B8
Bodley Rd OX4. . . . . . . 142 C3
Boham's Houses OX11 . . 218 F1
Boham's Rd OX11. . . . . 236 D6
Bolney La RG9. . . . . . . 255 A5
Bolney Rd RG9. . . . . . . 255 B5
Bolney Trevor Dr RG9. . . 255 A4
Bolsover Cl OX29 . . . . . . 90 A1
Bolton Rd OX16 . . . . 16 C6
Bolton's La OX29. . . . . . . 90 C3
Bonar Rd OX3 . . . . 124 C1
Bonds End La OX15 . . . . . 19 A8
Bones La RG9. . . . . 254 A3
Bonham Pl OX18. . . . . . 115 D4
Bonnersfield HP18 . . . . 129 C7
Bonn Sq OX1 . . . . 261 B2
Book End OX29 . . . . . . 103 C1
Booth Cl OX16 . . . . 9 C2
Boreford Rd OX14. . . . . 160 B2
Boroma Way RG9 . . . . . 244 E1
Borough Ave OX10 . . . . 221 C7
Borough Ct NN13 . . . . . . 24 A5
Borough Rd NN13. . . . . . 24 A5
Borough Wlk OX14. . . . . 159 E1
Borrowmead Rd OX3. . . 124 B5
Borwood Ct OX5. . . . . . 108 F6
Bosley Cres OX10 . . . . . 221 D7
Bosley's Orch
　Didcot OX11. . . . . 200 E1
　Grove OX12. . . . . 196 E1
Bosley Way OX10 . . . . . 221 A8
Bostock Rd OX14 . . . . . 179 E7
Boston Rd
　Bicester OX26 . . . . 66 A3
　Henley-on-Thames RG9. . 254 E8
Boswell Rd OX4 . . . . . . 142 C4
Botanic Garden The (Univ of
　Oxford)★ OX1 . . . . . . 261 C2
Botany Gdns OX10 . . . . 222 A6
Bothy The RG10. . . . . . 255 D2
BOTLEY. 140 D8
Botley Intc OX2 . . . . . . 122 D2
Botley Prim Sch OX2. . . 122 D1
Botley Rd OX2. . . . . . . 122 F1
Botley Works OX2. . . . . 122 D1
Bottle Square La HP14 . . 189 D6
Bottom La RG8 . . . . . . 241 A4
Bottom Rd HP14 . . . . . 189 E7
Boucher Cl OX12. . . . . . 214 D8
Boughton's Mill 10 OX10 221 D7
BOULD. 69 C7
Boulevard The OX5 . . . . . 92 B2
Boulter Dr OX14 . . . . . . 160 A3
Boulter St OX4. . . . . . . 123 F1
Boults Cl OX3. . . . . 123 F5
Boults La OX3. . . . . 123 F5
Boundary Brook Rd OX4. 142 A6
Boundary Bsns Pk OX44. 143 F3
Boundary Cl OX20. . . . . . 91 C6

Boundary La
7 Carterton OX18 . . . . 115 E5
Reading RG4 . . . . 258 E3
Boundary Mews 13 OX18 115 E5
Boundary Rd NN13 . . . . . . 24 A6
Boundary Way 8 OX18. . 115 E5
Bourlon Wood OX14 . . . . 159 D1
Bourne Cl
Bicester OX26 . . . . 65 D1
Cutteslowe OX2 . . . . 109 B1
Bourne La OX15 . . . . 30 A8
Bourne Rd RG8 . . . . 256 E5
Bourne St OX11 . . . . 218 F8
Bourne The
Eastleach Martin GL7 . . . 131 A7
Hook Norton OX15 . . . . . . 30 A7
BOURTON 209 A3
Bourton Cl
Clanfield OX18 . . . . 133 F1
Witney OX28 . . . . 117 E8
Bourton Cotts OX18 . . . . 134 E3
Bovewell OX27 . . . . 35 E3
Bovingdon Rd OX18 . . . . 115 F3
Bovington's Yd OX18 . . . 135 D3
BOW 174 E1
Bowbank OX13 . . . . 156 C3
Bowbank Cl OX13 . . . . . . 156 C3
Bower End OX44 . . . . 184 C7
Bower Gn SN6 . . . . 191 F2
Bowerman Cl OX5 . . . . . . 108 D8
Bowers La HP14 . . . . 189 D7
Bowfell Cl RG31 . . . . 257 C2
Bowgrave Copse OX14 . . 160 C1
Bowley Ho OX20 . . . . 91 B6
Bowling Ct RG9 . . . . 244 D3
Bowling Gn HP14 . . . . . . 188 D5
Bowling Green Cl OX18 . 134 F4
Bowling Green Farmhouse
RG8 . . . . 257 B5
Bowling Green La RG8 . . 257 B5
Bowmen's Lea OX17 . . . . 35 C7
Bowmont Sq OX26 . . . . . . 65 B2
Bowmont Water OX11 . . 200 F2
Bowness Ave
Didcot OX11 . . . . 218 D7
Oxford OX3 . . . . 124 A4
Bow Rd SN7 . . . . 174 E1
Bowyer Cl OX14 . . . . 160 F2
Bowyer Rd OX14 . . . . 179 F8
Boxhedge Rd OX16 . . . . . 16 B6
Boxhedge Road W OX16 . 16 B6
Boxhedge Sq 5 OX16 . . . 16 B6
Boxhedge Terr 2 OX16 . . 16 B6
Boxhill Rd OX14 . . . . 179 E8
Boxhill Wlk OX14 . . . . . . 179 E8
Box Tree La OX9 . . . . 166 F4
Boxwell Cl OX14 . . . . 160 B2
Bracegirdle Rd OX3 . . . . 124 C1
Bracken Cl
Carterton OX18 . . . . 115 D4
Reading RG31 . . . . 257 C1
BRACKLEY 24 A7
Brackley Rd
Croughton NN13 . . . . 36 D8
Shalstone MK18 . . . . 25 E5
Westbury NN13 . . . . 25 A5
Brackstone Cl RG4 . . . . . 259 C2
Bradburys The OX27 . . . . 66 D8
Bradfield Ct OX15 . . . . . . 21 D4
Brading Way RG8 . . . . . . 257 D5
Bradlands OX3 . . . . 123 E7
Bradley Arc OX16 . . . . . . 15 F6
Bradley Rd RG9 . . . . 224 A5
Bradley's St RG8 . . . . 241 B4
Bradmore Rd OX2 . . . . . . 123 C4
Bradshaw Cl OX25 . . . . . 62 A8
Bradstock's Way OX14 . . 199 F6
BRADWELL GROVE 114 B6
Bradwell Rd RG31 . . . . . . 257 C3
Brae Hill HP18 . . . . 98 A1
Braemar Cl OX18 . . . . . . 115 D5
Brailes Ind Est OX15 . . . . 12 A3
Braithwaite Cl OX16 . . . . 16 A5
Brake Hill OX4 . . . . 143 A1
Bramber Cl OX16 . . . . 15 E7
Bramber Mews OX14 . . . 259 E4
Bramble Bank OX28 . . . . 104 D2
Bramble La 1 OX18 . . . . 115 F5
Brambles The 2 OX3 . . . 124 C2
Bramblings RG4 . . . . 258 E6
Bramblings The OX26 . . . 66 A1
Brambling Way OX4 . . . . 142 D2
Bramley Cl OX12 . . . . 197 B6
Bramley Cres RG4 . . . . . 252 E5
Bramley Hts OX28 . . . . . . 117 F8
Brampton Chase RG9 . . . 255 A4
Brampton Cl OX14 . . . . . 159 E1
Brampton Dr OX18 . . . . . 115 F2
Brampton Rd OX3 . . . . . . 124 F4
Bramshaw Rd RG30 . . . . 258 A1
Bramwell Pl OX4 . . . . 141 F8
Branagh Ct RG30 . . . . . . 258 B1
Brandon Cl OX5 . . . . 108 D8
Brantwood Ct OX16 . . . . 16 B4
Brantwood Rise OX16 . . . 16 B4
Brasenose Coll OX1 . . . . . 261 C2
Brasenose Dr OX5 . . . . . . 92 F1
Brasenose Driftway OX4. 142 E6
Brasenose La OX1 . . . . . . 261 C2
Brasenose Rd OX11 . . . . 200 D1
Brasenose Villas OX7 . . . 42 E2
Brashfield Rd OX26 . . . . . 65 E4
Brassey Cl OX7 . . . . 42 E3
Brassey Ho OX7 . . . . 42 E3
BRASSWELL CORNER 86 F7
Braybrooke Cl OX7 . . . . . 58 F5

Braybrooke Gdns RG10 . . 255 D1
Braybrooke Rd RG10 . . . . 255 D1
Braze La OX10 . . . . 204 A6
Braziers La OX10 . . . . 240 E5
Breedons Hill RG8 . . . . . . 256 C5
Brenda Cl OX16 . . . . 16 B4
Brendon Cl
Didcot OX11 . . . . 200 C2
Reading RG30 . . . . 257 C1
Brent Ave OX11 . . . . 200 F4
Brentford Cl OX10 . . . . . . 220 E1
Brereton Dr OX12 . . . . . . 196 D1
Brett Cl OX9 . . . . 148 B8
Brewer Cl OX13 . . . . 199 A4
Brewers Ct 1 OX14 . . . . . 179 F6
Brewer St OX11 . . . . 261 B1
Brewery La OX15 . . . . 29 F7
Brewery Row GL56 . . . . . 26 F1
Brewery St SN6 . . . . 190 A5
Briaily HP14 . . . . 189 C2
Briants Ave RG4 . . . . 259 C2
Briant's Ave RG4 . . . . . . 259 C2
Briar Cl
Banbury OX16 . . . . 16 D2
Kidlington OX5 . . . . 92 C2
Reading RG4 . . . . 259 A5
Briar Cl OX5 . . . . 92 C2
Briar Furlong OX25 . . . . . 81 C4
Briars Cl RG8 . . . . 256 E5
Briarswood Cl HP14 . . . . 188 E5
Briar Thicket OX20 . . . . . 91 C6
Briar Way OX4 . . . . 142 F3
Briary Rd GL7 . . . . 150 D6
Briary Way OX14 . . . . . . 115 E5
Brice Rd OX25 . . . . 63 C8
Brick Alley 6 OX14 . . . . . 179 F6
Brick Hill OX15 . . . . 30 B6
Brickle La OX15 . . . . 21 E5
Brick Row OX15 . . . . 19 F8
Bricks La HP14 . . . . 189 C4
Bridal Terr 1 OX12 . . . . . 214 D5
Bridens Way HP17 . . . . . 130 F6
Bridewell Cl OX29 . . . . . . 105 B7
Bridge Cl
Didcot OX11 . . . . 219 A8
Lechlade-on-Thames GL7 . 150 E3
BRIDGE END 202 D8
Bridge End OX10 . . . . . . 202 D8
Bridge Farm Cl OX12 . . . 214 E7
Bridge Hill OX15 . . . . 30 B7
Bridge Rd HP18 . . . . 127 F2
Bridges Cl OX14 . . . . 179 C5
Bridge St
Abingdon OX14 . . . . 179 F6
Bampton OX18 . . . . 134 E3
Banbury OX16 . . . . 16 D6
Islip OX5 . . . . 109 F8
Oxford OX2 . . . . 123 A1
Reading RG4 . . . . 259 A2
Shilton OX18 . . . . 115 B6
4 Witney OX28 . . . . 104 B1
Bridgewater Ct RG30 . . . 258 C1
Bridle Cl OX16 . . . . 16 E3
Bridle Path
Charney Bassett OX12 . . . 175 F2
Woodcote RG8 . . . . 250 E8
Bridle Rd RG8 . . . . 250 D2
Bridus Mead OX11 . . . . . 219 B1
Bridus Way OX11 . . . . . . 219 A1
Brierley Pl RG31 . . . . 257 C4
Briggs Cl OX16 . . . . 15 F4
Brigham Rd RG1 . . . . 259 A1
BRIGHTHAMPTON 137 B4
BRIGHTWELL BALDWIN . . 185 A2
BRIGHTWELL-CUM-
SOTWELL 202 C2
Brightwell-cum-Sotwell CE
Prim Sch OX10 . . . . 202 E2
Brightwell St OX10 . . . . . 202 E2
BRILL 98 B1
Brill CE Comb Sch HP18 . . 98 B1
Brill Cl RG4 . . . . 259 A4
Brill Rd
Horton-cum-Studley
OX33 . . . . 112 C6
Ludgershall HP18 . . . . . . 98 B7
Brindley Cl OX2 . . . . 123 A4
Brinds Cl RG4 . . . . 253 A5
Brinkburn Gr OX16 . . . . . 16 F8
Brinkinfield Rd OX44 . . . 184 D7
Bristol Rd
Bicester OX26 . . . . 66 A4
Upper Rissington GL54 . . 68 B5
Bristow Ct RG4 . . . . 259 B2
Britannia Cl OX18 . . . . . . 115 E4
Britannia Hts 8 OX16 . . . 16 D5
Britannia Rd OX16 . . . . . 16 D5
Britannia Wharf 13 OX16 . 16 D5
Britnell Ct HP14 . . . . 188 E5
Britwell Hill OX49 . . . . . . 206 B4
Britwell Rd
Didcot OX11 . . . . 200 E1
Ewelme OX10 . . . . 204 F4
Watlington OX49 . . . . . . 186 A1
BRITWELL SALOME 205 E7
Brixton Hill OX10 . . . . . . 223 A4
BRIZE NORTON 116 C4
Brize Norton Airfield
OX18 . . . . 116 A1
Brize Norton Prim Sch
OX18 . . . . 116 C3
Brize Norton Rd
Carterton OX18 . . . . 115 E2
Minster Lovell OX29 . . . . 102 E2
Brizewood OX18 . . . . 115 D4
Broadbrook La OX12 . . . . 212 F4

Broad Cl
Barford St Michael OX15 . . 32 E5
Kidlington OX5 . . . . 108 D3
Oxford OX2 . . . . 122 B1
Broad End OX15 . . . . 16 E1
Broad Field Rd OX5 . . . . . 108 B7
Broadfields OX4 . . . . 142 C2
Broad Gap OX15 . . . . 16 E1
Broadhead Pl OX3 . . . . . . 124 B5
Broad Hill OX28 . . . . 104 C2
Broadhurst Gdns OX4 . . . 142 A1
Broadmarsh Cl OX12 . . . 214 D8
Broad Marsh La OX29 . . . 106 A6
Broadmoor La RG5 . . . . . 260 E4
Broad Oak OX3 . . . . 142 E8
BROADPLAT 243 E4
Broadshires Way OX18 . . 115 F3
Broad St
Abingdon OX14 . . . . 179 F7
Bampton OX18 . . . . 134 E3
3 Banbury OX16 . . . . . . 16 D6
Long Compton CV36 . . . . 27 F6
Oxford OX1 . . . . 261 B2
Uffington SN7 . . . . 211 D1
Broadwaters Ave OX9 . . . 147 F7
Broadway
Didcot OX11 . . . . 218 E8
Harwell OX11 . . . . 217 E6
Broad Way SN7 . . . . 211 C5
Broadway Cl
Harwell OX11 . . . . 217 E6
Witney OX28 . . . . 103 D1
Broadway The
Charlton-on-Otmoor OX5 . 95 A4
Kidlington OX5 . . . . 108 F6
BROADWELL 132 E4
Broadwell Ct OX26 . . . . . 65 D2
Broadwell Rd GL7 . . . . . . 132 D2
Brocklesby Rd OX4 . . . . . 142 A2
Brocks Way RG9 . . . . 255 A4
Brode Cl OX14 . . . . 160 B2
Brogden Cl OX2 . . . . 140 E7
Brome Cl OX3 . . . . 124 E4
Bromeswell Cl OX25 . . . . 62 E6
Bromsgrove SN7 . . . . 172 F3
Brook Cl HP18 . . . . 98 C8
Brook Cottage Gdn★ OX15 . 6 F2
BROOKEND 72 A8
Brooke Rd OX16 . . . . 16 A3
Brookfield Cl
Milton-under-Wychwood
OX7 . . . . 70 A1
Wallingford OX10 . . . . . . 221 C5
Brookfield Cres OX3 . . . . 124 A5
Brookfield Rise OX15 . . . . 20 D7
Brookfields Specl Sch
RG31 . . . . 257 B5
BROOKHAMPTON 163 C1
Brookhampton Cl OX44 . 163 C1
Brook Hill OX20 . . . . 91 B6
Brook La
Denchworth OX12 . . . . . 196 A4
Stonesfield OX29 . . . . . . 89 C6
Thame OX9 . . . . 129 E1
West Hagbourne OX11 . . 218 C5
Brook Lea 8 RG4 . . . . . . 259 C1
Brooklime Wlk 3 OX4 . . 142 E1
Brooklyn Dr RG4 . . . . . . 259 B6
Brookmead Dr OX10 . . . . 221 C6
Brook Rd
Bicester OX26 . . . . 65 C3
Great Tew OX7 . . . . 45 D7
Brooksby Rd RG31 . . . . . 257 D2
Brookside
Abingdon OX14 . . . . 159 F1
Cholsey OX10 . . . . 220 F1
Cuddesdon OX44 . . . . . . 144 A2
East Hanney OX12 . . . . . 197 A6
Great Tew OX7 . . . . 45 D7
Harwell OX11 . . . . 217 E7
Hook Norton OX15 . . . . . 30 A7
Oxford OX3 . . . . 124 C2
Thame OX9 . . . . 129 F1
Watlington OX49 . . . . . . 186 B2
Brookside Cl OX9 . . . . . . 145 F7
Brookside Ct
Bicester OX26 . . . . 65 E2
Woodstock OX20 . . . . . . 91 A6
Brookside Est OX44 . . . . 184 C7
Brookside Way OX15 . . . . 21 C4
Brooks Row OX29 . . . . . . 87 A4
Brook St
Benson OX10 . . . . 204 A4
Kingston Blount OX39 . . . 167 F4
Oxford OX1 . . . . 141 C7
Sutton Courtenay OX14 . . 200 A8
Watlington OX49 . . . . . . 186 B1
Brooks Taylor Ct OX1 . . . 261 B1
Brook View OX4 . . . . 143 A2
Brook Way OX29 . . . . 90 A1
Broome Way OX16 . . . . . 16 E7
Broomfield Rd RG30 . . . . 258 A1
BROUGHTON 15 C1
Broughton Castle★ OX15 . 15 B1
Broughton Cl RG30 . . . . . 258 C1
BROUGHTON POGGS 132 A4
Broughton Rd OX16 . . . . 15 E3
Broughtons Cl OX3 . . . . . 123 F5
Browning Dr OX26 . . . . . 65 C4
Browning Rd OX16 . . . . . 16 A3
Browns Cl OX2 . . . . 140 A8
Brown's La
Charlbury OX7 . . . . 73 B4
Woodstock OX20 . . . . . . 91 A6
Bruen Rd OX7 . . . . 69 C1
Bruern Abbey Sch OX26 . . 80 A7

Bruern Rd OX7 . . . . 70 A3
Brumcombe La OX1,
OX13 . . . . 159 F8
Brunel Cres OX12 . . . . . . 196 D1
Brunel Dr RG5 . . . . 260 F1
Brunel Rd OX11 . . . . 218 C8
Brunstock Beck OX11 . . . 200 F3
Brunswick Pl OX16 . . . . . 16 E6
Bryan Ho OX26 . . . . 65 E1
Bryant Pl RG8 . . . . 257 B5
Bryan Way OX12 . . . . . . 214 F6
Brymbo Cotts OX15 . . . . 30 D8
Bryony Cl OX4 . . . . 143 A2
Bryony Gdns OX18 . . . . . 115 F5
Bryony Rd OX26 . . . . 65 E5
Bryworth La GL7 . . . . . . 150 A6
Buchanan Rd OX25 . . . . . 96 E7
Buchan Rd OX26 . . . . 65 C4
Buckingham Cl OX11 . . . 219 B8
Buckingham Cres OX26 . . 65 F3
Buckingham Ct NN13 . . . 24 A6
Buckingham Dr RG4 . . . . 259 B5
Buckingham Gate RG4 . . 259 B4
Buckingham Pl OX18 . . . 115 D1
Buckingham Rd
Bicester OX26 . . . . 65 F4
Brackley NN13 . . . . 24 A6
Westbury NN13 . . . . 25 B5
Buckingham Road Ind Est
NN13 . . . . 24 A6
Buckingham St 1 OX1 . . 141 C7
BUCKLAND 154 E1
Buckland CE Prim Sch
SN7 . . . . 174 E8
Buckland Ct OX5 . . . . 108 F7
BUCKLAND MARSH 154 D4
Buckland Mews 3 OX14 . 179 D7
Buckland Rd
Bampton OX18 . . . . 154 C7
Buckland SN7 . . . . 174 E8
Charney Bassett OX12 . . . 175 D2
Buckler Pl OX4 . . . . 142 A1
Buckler Rd OX2 . . . . 123 B8
Bucklers Bury Rd OX4 . . 160 B3
Buckles Cl 1 OX14 . . . . . 179 D7
BUCKNELL 65 A8
Bucknell Ave RG8 . . . . . . 256 E5
Bucknell Rd OX26 . . . . . . 65 D3
Buckner's Cl OX10 . . . . . 203 F4
Buckside RG4 . . . . 259 A2
Buckthorn La OX10 . . . . . 220 F1
Budds Cl OX20 . . . . 91 D7
Bugloss Wlk OX26 . . . . . . 65 D4
Bulan Rd OX3 . . . . 142 E8
Bull Baulk OX17 . . . . 11 A1
Bulldog Cl OX10 . . . . 204 B2
Bull Hill OX7 . . . . 72 B8
Bullingdon Ave OX10 . . . 182 C5
Bullingdon Rd OX4 . . . . . 141 F7
Bull La OX15 . . . . 135 E2
Bullmarsh Cl OX25 . . . . . 64 A4
Bull Mdw The RG8 . . . . . 248 F6
Bullockspits La OX13 . . . 176 C8
Bull Ring OX15 . . . . 33 F4
Bulls Cl GL7 . . . . 132 B5
Bulls La
Ickford HP18 . . . . 128 A3
Kings Sutton OX17 . . . . . 23 F5
Bullsmead OX13 . . . . 159 E5
Bull St OX15 . . . . 135 E2
Bulrush Rd OX4 . . . . 142 F1
Bulwarks La OX1 . . . . . . 261 B2
Bungalow Cl OX3 . . . . . . 111 C2
BUNKERS HILL 92 A8
Bunkers Hill OX5 . . . . . . 77 A1
Buntings The OX26 . . . . . 81 A8
Bunyan Rd OX26 . . . . 65 C4
Burbush Rd OX4 . . . . 142 E5
Burchester Ave OX3 . . . . 124 E4
Burchester Pl OX16 . . . . . 16 F7
BURCOT 182 A4
Burcot La OX10 . . . . 182 D4
Burcot Pk OX14 . . . . 181 F5
Burdell Ave OX3 . . . . 125 A4
Burdock Cl OX26 . . . . 65 E4
BURDROP 19 B8
Bure La OX11 . . . . 200 D5
Bure Park Nature Reserve★
OX26 . . . . 65 D4
Bure Park Prim Sch OX26 . 65 D4
Bure Pl OX11 . . . . 200 D5
BURFORD 100 D5
Burford Lodge 4 OX1 . . . 141 C7
Burford Prim Sch OX18 . . 100 D8
Burford Rd
Black Bourton OX18 . . . . 133 F6
Brize Norton OX18 . . . . . 116 A5
Carterton OX18 . . . . 115 D3
Carterton OX18 . . . . 115 E7
Chipping Norton OX7 . . . 42 E2
Filkins GL7 . . . . 132 C6
Minster Lovell OX29 . . . . 102 C2
Witney OX29 . . . . 103 D2
Burford Sch OX18 . . . . . . 100 A8
Burford Sch (Annexe)
OX18 . . . . 100 C5
Burford St GL7 . . . . 150 C4
Burgage Gdns OX18 . . . . 100 E5
Burgan Cl OX4 . . . . 142 D4
Burgess Mead OX2 . . . . . 123 A5
Burgess Cl 7 OX14 . . . . . 179 F7
Burleigh Mews RG4 . . . . 259 C6
Burleigh Rd OX20 . . . . . . 107 C6
Burlington Cres OX3 . . . . 125 A3
Burlington Gdns OX16 . . 16 B4

Bou–Cal 265

Burnham Rise RG4 . . . . . 259 C7
Burnhams The HP18 . . . . 128 D3
Burns Cl HP18 . . . . 129 D7
Burns Cres OX26 . . . . 65 C3
Burns Rd OX16 . . . . 16 A4
Burra Cl OX4 . . . . 161 A4
Burr Cl OX29 . . . . 120 B1
Burrows Cl OX3 . . . . 124 D3
Burrows Hill OX10 . . . . . 204 F3
Burr St OX11 . . . . 217 E7
Bursill Cl OX3 . . . . 125 A3
Burswin Rd OX18 . . . . . . 115 D5
Burton Cl OX14 . . . . 179 D6
Burton Pl OX4 . . . . 142 E6
Burtons Bank OX7 . . . . . 68 E6
Burton Taylor Studio★
OX1 . . . . 261 B2
Burt's La HP18 . . . . 129 D6
Burwell Cl OX28 . . . . 117 E7
Burwell Ct OX28 . . . . 117 F7
Burwell Dr OX28 . . . . 117 F7
Burwell Mdw OX28 . . . . . 117 F6
Bury Court La OX17 . . . . 8 D8
Bury Croft Rd OX15 . . . . 30 B6
Burycroft The OX14 . . . . 180 A3
Buryhook Cnr OX33 . . . . 126 C2
Bury La RG20 . . . . 235 A2
Bury Mead OX29 . . . . . . 138 A8
Bury St OX14 . . . . 179 F7
Buryway La CV36 . . . . . . 27 F7
Busby Cl
Freeland OX29 . . . . 106 A6
Stonesfield OX29 . . . . . . 89 D7
Busby's Cl OX18 . . . . 152 E8
BUSCOT 171 A8
Buscot Dr OX14 . . . . 160 B2
Buscot Pk★ SN7 . . . . 171 C6
BUSCOT WICK 170 D8
Bushell Bsns Pk OX10 . . . 221 B7
Bushey Dr OX18 . . . . 152 E7
BUSHEY GROUND 116 E8
Bushey Leys Cl OX3 . . . . 124 E5
Bushey Row OX18 . . . . . 134 F3
Bush Furlong OX11 . . . . . 201 B2
Bushnell Cl OX3 . . . . 124 F3
Bush The HP17 . . . . 130 F5
Bushy Cl OX2 . . . . 122 B1
Bushy Gd OX29 . . . . 116 F8
Butchers Cl OX28 . . . . . . 118 A8
Butcher's Hill OX7 . . . . . 45 C7
Butcher's Row OX16 . . . . 16 D6
Butler Cl
Bloxham OX15 . . . . 21 E6
Horspath OX33 . . . . 143 D6
Oxford OX2 . . . . 123 B4
Butler Ho OX4 . . . . 142 B3
Butlers Cl CV36 . . . . 28 A6
Butlers Dr OX18 . . . . 115 E2
Butler's Field GL7 . . . . . . 150 C5
Butlers La CV36 . . . . 27 F5
Butlers Orch RG4 . . . . . . 252 D3
Butlers Pond RG8 . . . . . . 250 D2
Butlers Rd CV36 . . . . 28 C5
Butler's Yd RG9 . . . . 252 F7
Butterbur Gdns RG4 . . . . 65 C5
Buttercross The★ OX28 . . 118 B8
Buttercup Sq 10 OX4 . . . 142 F1
Butterly Rd HP14 . . . . . . 188 F4
Butter Market OX9 . . . . . 147 F8
Buttermilk La OX29 . . . . . 86 F1
Butterwort Pl 1 OX4 . . . 142 F2
Butterwyke Pl OX1 . . . . . 261 B1
Butts Cl OX17 . . . . 35 C7
Butts Hill Rd RG5 . . . . . . 260 E1
Butts La OX3 . . . . 123 F7
Butts Rd
Faringdon SN7 . . . . 172 F2
Horspath OX33 . . . . 143 C6
Butts The
Aynho OX17 . . . . 35 D7
Long Compton CV36 . . . . 27 F6
Merton OX25 . . . . 95 D8
Standlake OX29 . . . . 137 D3
Butts Way OX49 . . . . 167 C1
Buxton Ave RG4 . . . . 258 F4
Buzzards Cl OX17 . . . . . . 9 D5
Byefield Rd OX17 . . . . . . 5 F7
Bygones Mus★ OX17 . . . . 4 D8
Byres The HP17 . . . . 130 F6
Byron Cl OX14 . . . . 179 C5
Byron Rd OX16 . . . . 16 A3
Byron Way OX26 . . . . 65 C3

C

Cadel's Row 6 SN7 . . . . . 172 F3
Cadogan Pk OX20 . . . . . . 91 B6
Cadogan Pl RG4 . . . . 259 B3
Cadwell La OX44, OX49 . . 184 E4
Caernarvon Way OX16 . . 15 F6
Caesars Gate NN13 . . . . . 24 A6
Calais Dene OX18 . . . . . . 134 F4
Calais La OX29 . . . . 136 E6
Calcot Cl OX3 . . . . 124 E1
Calcroft La
Clanfield OX18 . . . . 133 C2
Langford GL7 . . . . 132 E2
CALDECOTT 179 E6
Caldecott Chase OX14 . . 179 E5
Caldecott Cl OX14 . . . . . 179 D6
Caldecott Prim Sch
OX14 . . . . 179 D5

Caldecott Rd OX14 . . . . . . **179** E6
Calder Cl OX16 . . . . **16** F7
Calder Way OX11 . . . . **201** B2
Caldicott Cl OX10 . . . . **203** B6
Caleta Cl RG4 . . . . **259** D2
CALTHORPE **16** D3
Calthorpe Rd OX16 . . . . . . **16** C5
Calthorpe St OX16 . . . . . . **16** C5
Calves Cl OX5 . . . . **108** D8
Cambridge Terr OX1 . . . . . **261** B1
Cam Cl OX11 . . . . **200** F1
Camden Cl GL56 . . . . **26** F5
Camel Cross OX12 . . . . . . **214** C5
Camellias The OX16 . . . . **9** B1
Cameron Ave OX14 . . . . . . **160** C1
Cameron Ct **10** OX16 . . . . . **16** D5
Campbell Cl OX26 . . . . . . **65** E2
Campbell Rd OX4 . . . . . . **142** A5
Campbells OX20 . . . . **91** C6
CAMP CORNER **145** F4
Campden Cl OX28 . . . . . . **103** E1
Camp Ind Est OX9 . . . . . . **146** B4
Campion Cl
  Carterton OX18 . . . . **115** E1
  18 Sandford-on-Thames
  OX4 . . . . **142** F1
Campion Hall Dr OX11 . . . **219** B7
Campion Pl OX26 . . . . **65** D4
Campion Rd OX14 . . . . . . **180** B8
Campion Way OX28 . . . . . **104** D2
Camp La OX17 . . . . **2** D4
Camp Rd OX25 . . . . **63** C8
CAMPSFIELD **91** E3
Canada La SN7 . . . . **172** E4
Canada Rd OX16 . . . . **16** D7
Canal Ct OX12 . . . . **214** C7
Canal Ho **4** OX12 . . . . . . **214** D5
Canal La OX15 . . . . **16** F1
Canal Rd OX5 . . . . **92** C4
Canal St
  Banbury OX16 . . . . **16** D5
  Oxford OX2 . . . . **261** A3
Canal Way OX12 . . . . **214** A5
Canal Yd OX5 . . . . **92** C4
Candy Way OX13 . . . . **159** B6
CANE END **251** F4
Cane La OX12 . . . . **214** D8
Canning Cres OX1 . . . . . . **141** E5
Cannons Field OX3 . . . . . . **123** F6
Canon Hill's Gdns SN6 . . . **209** C6
Canons Dr GL7 . . . . **150** E3
Canterbury Cl OX16 . . . . . . **17** A7
Canterbury Rd OX2 . . . . . **123** B4
Capel Cl OX2 . . . . **123** B8
Capri Sq OX10 . . . . **203** B4
Caps La OX10 . . . . **221** B2
Captains Mill OX28 . . . . . **104** B2
Cardiff Mews RG1 . . . . . . **258** F1
Cardiff Rd RG1 . . . . **258** F1
Cardigan St
  Oxford OX2 . . . . **261** A3
  Oxford OX2 . . . . **261** A4
Cardinal Cl
  Oxford OX4 . . . . **142** B3
  Reading RG4 . . . . **259** B2
Cardwell Cres OX3 . . . . . . **124** B2
Carew Cl RG31 . . . . **257** B4
Carey Cl OX2 . . . . **108** F1
Cariad Ct OX4 . . . . **249** B7
Carisbrooke Cl RG4 . . . . . **259** C6
Carlesgill Pl RG9 . . . . **254** E7
Carling Rd RG4 . . . . **252** E6
Carlisle Rd RG31 . . . . **257** E3
Carlton Cl OX12 . . . . **196** C1
Carlton Rd
  Cutteslowe OX2 . . . . **109** B1
  Reading RG4 . . . . **258** E5
Caroline Cl OX20 . . . . **91** B6
Caroline St OX4 . . . . **123** E1
Carpenter Cl OX4 . . . . . . **142** C2
Carpenters Sq **2** OX28 . . **104** A1
Carr Ave OX18 . . . . **115** C2
Carrdus Sch The OX17 . . . **17** C8
Carse Cl OX14 . . . . **160** B3
Carswell Circ OX5 . . . . . . **63** C8
Carswell Ct **2** OX14 . . . . . **179** E7
Carswell La SN7 . . . . **154** A1
CARSWELL MARSH **154** A3
Carswell Prim Sch OX14 . . **179** E7
Carter Cl OX3 . . . . **124** F2
Carter Cres SN7 . . . . **172** E1
Carters Cl OX18 . . . . **115** D2
Carters La HP18 . . . . **129** B7
CARTERTON **115** C4
Carterton Com Coll
  OX18 . . . . **115** D3
Carterton Ind Est OX18 . . **115** F4
Carterton L Ctr OX18 . . . . **115** F4
Carterton Park Cvn Site
  OX18 . . . . **133** D8
Carterton Prim Sch
  OX18 . . . . **115** E3
Carterton Rd OX18 . . . . . . **116** B3
Cartwright Gdns OX17 . . . **35** D7
CASSINGTON **107** C2
Cassington Rd
  Bladon OX20 . . . . **107** B8
  Eynsham OX29 . . . . **121** A8
  Yarnton OX5 . . . . **108** B4
Castle Cl
  Benson OX10 . . . . **203** F4
  Bicester OX27 . . . . **65** F7
Castle Cres SN7 . . . . **193** B8
Castle Fields OX27 . . . . . . **50** B4
Castle La OX10 . . . . **221** D8

Castle L Ctr The OX10 . . . **221** D8
Castle Mews OX1 . . . . **261** A2
Castle Mill OX1 . . . . **123** A2
Castle Mill Ho OX2 . . . . . . **123** A3
Castle Quay Sh Ctr OX16 . . **16** D6
Castle Rd
  Shirburn OX49 . . . . **186** D4
  Wootton OX20 . . . . **75** F5
Castle Sq OX10 . . . . **203** F4
Castle St
  Banbury OX16 . . . . **16** C6
  Deddington OX15 . . . . . . **33** F4
  Marsh Gibbon OX27 . . . . **67** F3
  Oxford OX1 . . . . **261** B2
  Steventon OX13 . . . . **198** F3
  Wallingford OX10 . . . . . **221** D8
Castle Wlk OX11 . . . . **200** E2
Caswell La OX18 . . . . **116** F6
Catharine Cl OX14 . . . . . . **160** F3
Catherine Cl SN6 . . . . **209** C6
Catherine St OX4 . . . . . . **142** A7
Catkins Cl SN7 . . . . **172** E2
Cat La
  Ewelme OX10 . . . . **204** F4
  Stadhampton OX44 . . . . **163** D1
Catmore Cl OX12 . . . . **214** D8
Catmore Rd RG20 . . . . . . **234** F1
Catsham La OX7 . . . . **72** C5
Catslip RG9 . . . . **224** F2
Cat St OX12 . . . . **216** D6
Catte St OX1 . . . . **261** C2
Cattle Mkt OX7 . . . . **42** E3
Catwell Cl OX4 . . . . **142** B6
Caudwell Cl
  Drayton OX14 . . . . **179** B1
  Grove OX12 . . . . **196** E1
CAULCOTT **63** B6
Causeway
  Banbury OX16 . . . . **16** F6
  Bicester OX26 . . . . **65** E1
  Bletchingdon OX5 . . . . . . **93** A8
Causeway The
  11 Banbury OX16 . . . . . **16** E6
  East Hanney OX12 . . . . . **197** A6
  Reading RG4 . . . . **259** D1
  Steventon OX13 . . . . **198** F4
  Woodstock OX20 . . . . . . **91** A6
Causmans Way RG31 . . . . **257** C2
Cavalier Rd OX9 . . . . **130** A1
Cavell Rd OX4 . . . . **142** A5
Cavendish Dr OX3 . . . . . . **123** E5
Cavendish Pl OX27 . . . . . . **52** D1
Cavendish Rd
  Oxford OX2 . . . . **123** B8
  Reading RG4 . . . . **259** C6
Cavendish Wlk OX9 . . . . . **130** B1
Cave St OX4 . . . . **123** F1
Cawley Rd OX17 . . . . **23** B5
Cawsam Gdns RG4 . . . . . . **259** C4
Caxton Cl RG30 . . . . **258** C1
Caxton Ct RG9 . . . . **244** E1
Cecil Aldin Dr RG31 . . . . . **257** C4
Cecil Sharpe Cl OX3 . . . . . **124** C2
Cedar RG9 . . . . **244** D2
Cedar Cl OX16 . . . . **16** D2
Cedar Cres OX9 . . . . **147** D8
Cedar Ct OX4 . . . . **142** C5
Cedar Dr
  Bicester OX26 . . . . **65** F3
  Pangbourne RG8 . . . . . . **256** C4
  Witney OX28 . . . . **104** D2
Cedar Rd
  Carterton OX18 . . . . **115** F5
  Faringdon SN7 . . . . **172** E3
  Oxford OX2 . . . . **140** D7
Cedars The
  Benson OX10 . . . . **204** A5
  Reading RG31 . . . . **257** D2
Cedar Villa OX16 . . . . **16** B6
Cedar Wood Cres RG4 . . . **259** B4
Celandine Cl **8** OX26 . . . . **65** C4
Celandine Pl **6** OX4 . . . . **142** F1
Celsea Pl OX10 . . . . **221** A1
Cemetery Rd
  Abingdon OX14 . . . . **179** D7
  Bicester OX26 . . . . **65** E1
Centaury Pl OX4 . . . . **143** A2
Centenary Bsns Pk RG9 . . **244** F1
Centremead OX2 . . . . **141** A8
Centre Rise OX33 . . . . . . **143** D6
Centre St OX16 . . . . **16** E7
Century Cl SN7 . . . . **173** A3
Century Row OX2 . . . . . . **123** B7
CHACOMBE **10** F4
Chacombe CE Prim Sch
  OX17 . . . . **10** F4
Chacombe Rd OX17 . . . . . **10** F1
CHADLINGTON **57** B1
Chadlington CE Prim Sch
  OX7 . . . . **57** C1
Chadlington Rd
  Chadlington OX7 . . . . . . **57** F1
  Oxford OX2 . . . . **123** C6
  Spelsbury OX7 . . . . **72** F8
Chaffinch Rd OX26 . . . . . . **66** A1

Chaffinch Wlk OX4 . . . . . . **142** F1
Chain Alley OX1 . . . . **261** A2
Chainhill Rd
  Wantage OX12 . . . . **214** F2
  West Ilsley OX12 . . . . . . **233** A1
Chalcraft Cl RG9 . . . . **254** C8
Chalcroft Cl OX29 . . . . . . **118** A5
Chalfont Rd OX2 . . . . **123** B5
CHALFORD **167** B6
Chalford Cl OX7 . . . . **42** F3
Chalford Ct OX7 . . . . **43** A3
Chalford Rd OX9 . . . . **167** A4
CHALGROVE **184** E6
Chalgrove Com Prim Sch
  OX44 . . . . **184** D6
Chalgrove Rd OX9 . . . . . . **130** A1
Chalgrove Way RG4 . . . . . **259** B6
Chalk Farm Rd HP14 . . . . **188** D5
Chalk Hill
  Aston Tirrold OX11 . . . . . **237** F8
  Hunt's Green RG9 . . . . . . **254** A1
CHALKHOUSE GREEN . . . **253** A1
Chalkhouse Green La
  RG4 . . . . **253** A1
Chalkhouse Green Rd
  RG4 . . . . **252** E2
Challenor Cl OX14 . . . . . . **179** E4
Challow Rd OX12 . . . . **214** B5
Chalmore Gdns OX10 . . . . **221** D6
Chalvey Cl OX26 . . . . **65** D1
Chalvey Rd OX26 . . . . **65** D1
Chamberlaine Cl OX16 . . . . **16** D6
Chamberlain Pl OX5 . . . . . **92** C1
Chambrai Cl OX14 . . . . . . **200** F8
Chamomile Pl OX16 . . . . . . **9** A2
Champion Rd RG4 . . . . . . **259** C1
Champion Way OX4 . . . . . **142** B3
Champs Chapel Mus★
  OX12 . . . . **216** E6
Champs Cl OX14 . . . . **160** C2
Chancellor Ct OX4 . . . . . . **142** D4
Chancel Way
  Lechlade-on-Thames
  GL7 . . . . **150** C4
  Marcham OX13 . . . . **178** C7
Chandler Cl OX18 . . . . . . **134** F4
Chandler Mews OX18 . . . . **115** E1
Chandlers Cl
  Abingdon OX14 . . . . **160** C1
  Wantage OX12 . . . . **214** E4
Chandlings Manor Sch
  OX1 . . . . **160** B7
Chapel Cl
  Blackthorn OX25 . . . . . . **82** A3
  Deddington OX15 . . . . . . **34** E4
  Leafield OX29 . . . . **86** E3
  South Stoke RG8 . . . . . . **239** C3
  Wantage OX12 . . . . **214** E5
Chapel Dr OX25 . . . . **81** C3
Chapel End
  Croughton NN13 . . . . . . **36** C8
  Great Rollright OX7 . . . . . **29** A3
Chapel Hill
  Brize Norton OX18 . . . . . **116** B4
  Swerford OX7 . . . . **30** F3
  Watchfield SN6 . . . . **191** C1
  Wootton OX20 . . . . **75** F4
Chapel La
  Adderbury OX17 . . . . **23** A4
  Benson OX10 . . . . **203** F4
  Berrick Salome OX10 . . . . **204** B7
  Bledlow Ridge HP14 . . . . **169** E2
  Blewbury OX11 . . . . **237** A8
  Bodicote OX15 . . . . **22** E8
  Chalgrove OX44 . . . . . . **184** D6
  Charney Bassett OX12 . . . **175** F2
  Cropredy OX17 . . . . **4** F2
  Enstone OX7 . . . . **58** F5
  Fernham SN7 . . . . **193** A4
  Great Bourton OX17 . . . . . **9** D5
  Kingham OX7 . . . . **55** A5
  Little Tew OX7 . . . . **45** B5
  Milton OX15 . . . . **22** C3
  Nettlebed RG9 . . . . **224** E2
  North Leigh OX29 . . . . . **105** B7
  Northmoor OX29 . . . . . . **138** C2
  Oxford OX4 . . . . **142** B2
  Poffley End OX29 . . . . . **104** B5
  Ratley OX15 . . . . **2** A3
  Salford OX7 . . . . **41** F5
  Shipton-under-Wychwood
  OX7 . . . . **85** D7
  Shotteswell OX17 . . . . . . **8** C7
  Standlake OX29 . . . . . . **137** D3
  Sutton Courtenay OX14 . . **200** A8
  Turweston NN13 . . . . . . **24** B7
  Uffington SN7 . . . . **211** C7
Chapel Mews **6** OX26 . . . **65** E1
Chapel & Pope's Tower★
  OX29 . . . . **138** B8
Chapel Rd
  Ashbury SN6 . . . . **228** A7
  Brookend OX7 . . . . **72** C8
  South Leigh OX29 . . . . . **119** B6
  Stanford in the Vale SN7 . . **194** E8
Chapel Row
  Chadlington OX7 . . . . . . **72** C8
  Cropredy OX17 . . . . **4** F2
  Little Compton GL56 . . . . **26** F1
Chapel Sq
  Deddington OX15 . . . . . . **33** F4
  East Hendred OX12 . . . . **216** D6
Chapel St
  Bicester OX26 . . . . **65** E1
  Bledington OX7 . . . . **54** D2
  Bloxham OX15 . . . . **21** E4
  Hook Norton OX15 . . . . . **30** B7
  Oxford OX4 . . . . **141** F8

Chapel St continued
  Warmington OX17 . . . . **3** A4
  Watlington OX49 . . . . . . **186** B2
Chapel Way
  Childrey OX12 . . . . **213** C4
  Oxford OX2 . . . . **122** D1
Chapelwick Cl SN6 . . . . . **209** B6
Chapmans La OX15 . . . . . . **34** A3
Chapmans Piece OX18 . . . **100** E5
Charbridge La OX26 . . . . . **66** C2
Charbridge Way OX26 . . . . **66** C1
CHARLBURY **73** C3
Charlbury Cl OX5 . . . . **92** D2
Charlbury Mus★ OX7 . . . . **73** B4
Charlbury Prim Sch OX7 . . **73** C4
Charlbury Rd
  Finstock OX7 . . . . **88** D7
  Oxford OX2 . . . . **123** C5
  Shrivenham SN6 . . . . . . **209** B6
Charlbury Sta OX7 . . . . . . **73** A3
Charles Ct OX16 . . . . **16** D5
Charles Dr OX9 . . . . **130** A1
Charles Evans Way RG4 . . **259** D2
Charles Ho RG9 . . . . **244** E3
Charles Rd
  Carterton OX18 . . . . **133** D8
  Cholsey OX10 . . . . **239** A8
Charles St OX4 . . . . **141** F6
CHARLTON **214** F5
Charlton Ct OX12 . . . . **215** A5
Charlton Gdns OX12 . . . . . **214** F5
CHARLTON-ON-
  OTMOOR **95** A4
Charlton-on-Otmoor CE
  Prim Sch OX5 . . . . **95** A4
Charlton Pk OX12 . . . . . . **214** F5
Charlton Prim Sch OX12 . . **214** F5
Charlton Rd
  Aynho OX17 . . . . **35** C7
  Wantage OX12 . . . . **214** F5
Charlton Village Rd
  OX12 . . . . **214** F5
Charney Ave OX14 . . . . . . **160** C2
CHARNEY BASSETT **176** A2
Charney Bassett Mill Mus★
  OX12 . . . . **176** A1
Charney Rd OX13 . . . . . . **176** B6
Charter Ho **1** OX12 . . . . **214** E4
Charter The **8** OX12 . . . **179** F7
Charterville Cl OX29 . . . . . **102** E2
Charter Way OX10 . . . . . . **221** C7
Chartwell Dr OX7 . . . . **73** C4
Charvil La RG4 . . . . **260** F4
Chase Barn OX27 . . . . **37** B3
CHASTLETON **40** D7
Chastleton Ho★ GL56 . . . . **40** D7
Chatham Rd OX1 . . . . **141** D5
Chatsworth Cl RG4 . . . . . . **259** C6
Chatsworth Dr OX16 . . . . . **16** E3
Chatterpie La OX29 . . . . . . **89** F5
Cheatle Cl OX18 . . . . **100** E4
CHECKENDON **241** C3
Checkendon CE Prim Sch
  RG8 . . . . **241** C3
Checker Wlk OX14 . . . . . . **179** F7
Chedworth Dr OX28 . . . . . **117** E8
Cheers Farm OX14 . . . . . . **179** C1
Chelford Way RG4 . . . . . . **258** F4
Chelmscote Row OX17 . . . . **10** F8
Chelsea Cl RG30 . . . . **257** F1
Chenderit Sch OX17 . . . . . **11** A1
Cheney Cl OX17 . . . . **10** F1
Cheney Gdns OX17 . . . . . . **10** F1
Cheney La OX3 . . . . **124** A1
Cheney Rd OX16 . . . . **16** F8
Cheney Sch OX3 . . . . **124** B1
Cheney Student Village
  OX3 . . . . **124** A1
Chepstow Gdns OX16 . . . . **15** F5
Chepstow Rd RG31 . . . . . **257** D2
Chequers Cl OX33 . . . . . . **125** D7
Chequers Pl
  Cholsey OX10 . . . . **220** F2
  Oxford OX3 . . . . **124** E3
Cherbury Gn OX12 . . . . . . **214** D8
Cheriton Pl RG4 . . . . **252** F5
Cherry Cl
  Kidlington OX5 . . . . **108** E7
  Reading RG4 . . . . **259** C8
  Sandford-on-Thames OX4 . **142** F1
  Stratton Audley OX27 . . . . **52** D1
  Warborough OX10 . . . . . **203** B6
Cherry Fields OX17 . . . . **4** F1
Cherry Orch
  Great Coxwell SN7 . . . . . **192** C8
  Highworth SN6 . . . . **190** A6
Cherry Rd OX16 . . . . **16** A7
Cherrys Cl OX15 . . . . **21** D3
Cherry St OX6 . . . . **52** D1
Cherry Tree Cl
  Grove OX12 . . . . **214** E8
  Kingston Bagpuize OX13 . . **176** D8
  Stoke Row RG9 . . . . **242** A5

Cherry Tree Ct
  Harwell OX11 . . . . **217** E7
  Oxford OX2 . . . . **140** D7
  Woodgreen OX28 . . . . . . **104** E1
Cherry Tree Dr OX13 . . . . **159** C2
Cherry Tree Rd OX39 . . . . **168** C6
Cherry Tree Way
  12 Carterton OX18 . . . . **115** E5
  Witney OX28 . . . . **104** E1
Cherwell Ave OX5 . . . . . . **109** A8
Cherwell Bank OX25 . . . . . **62** E6
Cherwell Bsns Ctr OX5 . . . **92** C2
Cherwell Cl
  Abingdon OX14 . . . . **160** B1
  Bicester OX26 . . . . **65** D1
  Didcot OX11 . . . . **200** F4
  Wallingford OX10 . . . . . **221** D7
Cherwell Coll (Bradmore
  Hall) OX2 . . . . **261** B4
Cherwell Coll (Greyfriars)
  OX1 . . . . **261** B2
Cherwell Ct OX5 . . . . **92** D1
Cherwell Dr
  Headington OX3 . . . . . . **124** A5
  Marston OX3 . . . . **123** F5
Cherwell Lodge OX2 . . . . . **123** C8
Cherwell Rd
  Berinsfield OX10 . . . . . . **182** C6
  Reading RG4 . . . . **259** A6
Cherwell Sch The OX2 . . . **123** C6
Cherwell St
  Banbury OX16 . . . . **16** D7
  Oxford OX4 . . . . **123** F1
Cherwood House Cotts
  OX27 . . . . **66** A7
Cheshire Dr OX25 . . . . **63** C8
Cheshire Rd OX9 . . . . **148** B7
Chester St
  Oxford OX4 . . . . **141** F7
  Reading RG4 . . . . **259** A2
CHESTERTON **79** F7
Chesterton CE Prim Sch
  OX26 . . . . **79** F8
Chester Way OX16 . . . . . . **15** F6
Chestnut Ave
  Faringdon SN7 . . . . **172** E3
  Oxford OX3 . . . . **124** D4
  Radley OX14 . . . . **160** E4
  Reading RG4 . . . . **259** E4
  Thame OX9 . . . . **147** D8
Chestnut Cl
  Brize Norton OX18 . . . . . **116** C3
  Carterton OX18 . . . . **115** E5
  Chesterton OX26 . . . . . . **80** A7
  Launton OX26 . . . . **66** D1
  Middle Assendon RG9 . . . **243** F8
  Witney OX28 . . . . **104** B2
Chestnut Cotts RG8 . . . . . **249** A6
Chestnut Ct OX4 . . . . **142** C5
Chestnut Dr OX7 . . . . **71** B2
Chestnut End OX26 . . . . . **65** E4
Chestnut Gr RG8 . . . . **257** D5
Chestnut Pl OX49 . . . . . . **186** B1
Chestnut Rd
  Mollington OX17 . . . . **4** A3
  Oxford OX2 . . . . **140** D7
Chestnuts The
  Abingdon OX14 . . . . **160** C1
  Deddington OX15 . . . . . . **34** E4
  Kirtlington OX5 . . . . **78** A4
  Lower Shiplake RG9 . . . . **255** A3
  Wantage OX12 . . . . **214** F5
Chestnut Tree Cl OX13 . . . **159** C1
Chestnut View OX18 . . . . . **133** C5
CHETWODE **53** E8
Chetwode
  Banbury, Overthorpe
  OX17 . . . . **17** C6
  Banbury OX16 . . . . **16** A8
Chetwyn Mead OX18 . . . . **134** E4
Cheviot Way OX16 . . . . **8** F1
Cheyne La OX18 . . . . **134** E3
Cheyney Wlk OX14 . . . . . . **159** E1
Chibnall Cl OX44 . . . . **184** D6
Chichester Cl OX26 . . . . . . **65** E2
Chichester Pl OX18 . . . . . **116** C3
Chichester Wlk **8** OX16 . . . **9** A1
Chiers Dr OX14 . . . . **179** C1
Chilbridge Rd OX29 . . . . . **120** C7
CHILDREY **213** C4
Childrey Way
  Abingdon OX14 . . . . **160** B2
  East Challow OX12 . . . . . **213** F4
Chilford Barns OX7 . . . . . . **55** C5
Chilgrove Dr OX25 . . . . . . **49** E1
Chillbrook OX11 . . . . **217** C6
Chillingworth Cres OX3 . . **142** E8
Chillingworth Ct OX3 . . . . **142** E8
CHILSON **71** F3
Chilson Hill OX7 . . . . **72** A2
Chilswell La
  Boars Hill OX1 . . . . **140** F3
  Sunningwell OX1 . . . . . . **141** A2
Chilswell Rd OX1 . . . . **141** C7
Chilswell Valley Nature
  Reserve★ OX1 . . . . **141** A4
Chiltern App OX26 . . . . . . **65** E3
Chiltern Bank RG9 . . . . . . **252** E7
Chiltern Bsns Ctr OX4 . . . **142** E4
Chiltern Cl
  Benson OX10 . . . . **203** F5
  Berinsfield OX10 . . . . . . **182** D5
  Chalgrove OX44 . . . . . . **184** D6
  Henley-on-Thames RG9 . . **254** B8
Chiltern Coll Sch **1** RG4 . **259** B3
Chiltern Coll The RG4 . . . **259** B3
Chiltern Cres OX10 . . . . . **221** B8
Chiltern Ct RG4 . . . . **259** B6

Chiltern Edge Sch RG4.. 252 E4
Chiltern Gdns OX49 . . . . . 186 C1
Chiltern Gr OX9 . . . . 148 A4
Chiltern Hts RG4 . . . . 259 C4
Chiltern Rd
  Reading RG4 . . . . 259 C4
  Rotherfield Peppard RG9.. 252 E7
Chiltern Ridge HP14 . . . . . 188 C4
Chilterns End Cl RG9 . . . . 254 C8
Chilterns The OX1 . . . . . . 261 B2
Chiltern View
  Little Milton OX44 . . . . . 164 A7
  Purley on Thames RG8. . . 257 D5
  Tetsworth OX9 . . . . 166 B8
Chiltern Wlk RG8 . . . . . . 256 D5
CHILTON 235 E8
Chilton Cl OX14 . . . . 160 B1
Chilton Cty Prim Sch
  OX11. . . . . 235 C8
Chilton Rd
  Long Crendon HP18. . . . 129 C7
  Upton OX11 . . . . 218 B2
Chilwell House Sch
  OX33. . . . . 145 C6
Chilworth Rd OX44 . . . . . 145 D3
CHIMNEY 155 B6
CHIMNEY-END 86 E4
Chimney Meadow National
  Nature Reserve★ OX18 155 A5
Chinalls Cl MK18 . . . . 39 D6
Chinnock Brook OX11. . . 200 F3
CHINNOR 168 D7
Chinnor Hill OX39 . . . . . . 168 E4
Chinnor Hill Nature
  Reserve★ OX39 . . . . . . 168 F5
Chinnor & Princes
  Risborough Rly★ OX39. 168 E7
Chinnor Rd
  Aston Rowant OX9. . . . . 167 D2
  Bledlow Ridge HP14 . . . 169 C2
  Chinnor, Crowell Hill OX39. 168 F4
  Chinnor, Crowell OX39. . 168 A4
  Thame OX9 . . . . 148 C5
  Towersey OX9 . . . . 148 E6
Chinnor Sta★ OX39 . . . . . 168 D5
Chipmunk Rd OX10 . . . . . 204 D3
Chipperfield Park Rd
  OX15 . . . . 21 F6
CHIPPING NORTON 42 F2
Chipping Norton Hospl
  OX7 . . . . 42 E3
Chipping Norton L Ctr
  OX7. . . . . 42 F2
Chipping Norton Mus★
  OX7. . . . . 42 F2
Chipping Norton Rd
  Chadlington OX7 . . . . . . 57 A3
  Hook Norton OX15 . . . . 30 A2
Chipping Norton Sch OX7 42 F2
CHIPPING WARDEN. 5 E6
Chipping Warden Prim Sch
  OX17. . . . . 5 F7
CHISELHAMPTON 163 A2
Chiselhampton Hill
  OX44 . . . . 162 F5
Choicehill Rd OX7 . . . . . . 42 E6
CHOLSEY. 221 A1
Cholsey Cl OX4 . . . . 142 C4
Cholsey Prim Sch OX10 . 220 C2
Cholsey Sta OX10 . . . . . . 220 E1
Cholsey & Wallingford Rly★
  OX10. . . . . 220 E1
Cholswell Ct OX13 . . . . . 159 C3
Cholswell Rd OX13 . . . . . 159 C2
Chorefields OX5 . . . . 92 D1
Choswell Spring OX4. . . . 142 E1
Chowns Cl OX9 . . . . 148 A7
Christ Church Cath★
  OX1. . . . . 261 C1
Christ Church Cath Sch
  OX1. . . . . 261 B1
Christ Church Coll OX1. . 261 B2
Christchurch Ct OX16 . . . 16 D6
Christ Church Old Bldgs
  OX1 . . . . 261 A2
Christ Church Picture Gall★
  OX1. . . . . 261 C2
CHRISTMAS COMMON . . 207 B7
Christopher Rawlins CE Prim
  Sch OX17. . . . . 23 A4
Church Ave
  Henley-on-Thames RG9 . 244 E2
  Kings Sutton OX17. . . . . 23 F5
Church Cl
  Adderbury OX17 . . . . . . 23 A3
  Ascott-under-Wychwood
    OX7. . . . . 71 C2
  Benson OX10 . . . . 203 F4
  Black Bourton OX18 . . . 133 F5
  Charlbury OX7 . . . . 73 B3
  Cuddesdon OX44 . . . . . 144 C3
  East Hagbourne OX11. . . 218 F5
  Farmoor OX2 . . . . 121 C2
  Fringford OX27 . . . . 52 D7
  Great Bourton OX17 . . . . 9 D8
  Islip OX5 . . . . 93 F1
  Longcot SN7 . . . . 192 C2
  Merton OX25 . . . . 95 D8
  Rotherfield Greys RG9.. . 243 D1
  South Hinksey OX1 . . . . 141 B5
  Stanton St John OX33 . . 125 D7
  Wardington OX17 . . . . . . 5 E1
  Weston-on-the-Green OX25 79 A1
Church Cotts OX44 . . . . . 161 E3
Church Cowley Rd OX4.. 142 B5
Church Cowley St James
  Prim Sch ⑥ OX4. . . . . . 142 C4

CHURCH END
  Bletchington 93 B8
  Ducklington 118 C4
  Long Crendon 129 D7
  South Leigh 119 D6
  Swerford 30 E3
Church End
  Blewbury OX11 . . . . 219 A1
  Croughton NN13 . . . . . . 36 D8
  Drayton St Leonard OX10 183 B6
  Great Rollright OX7 . . . . 29 B3
  South Leigh OX29 . . . . . 119 C6
  Standlake OX29 . . . . . . 137 D3
CHURCH ENSTONE 58 F7
Church Farm Ct OX29 . . . 137 D4
Churchfield RG9 . . . . 223 D3
Churchfield La OX10 . . . . 203 E4
Churchfields OX29 . . . . . 89 C7
Church Furlong OX15 . . . 20 C8
Church Gn
  Long Crendon HP18. . . . 129 D7
  Stanford in the Vale SN7.. 194 E8
  Witney OX28 . . . . 118 B7
CHURCH
  HANBOROUGH. 106 D6
Church Hill
  Chilton OX11 . . . . 235 D8
  Forest Hill OX33 . . . . . . 125 E3
  Great Haseley OX44 . . . 164 E8
  Little Milton OX44 . . . . . 163 F6
  Stonor RG9 . . . . 225 D8
  Tackley OX5 . . . . 77 B5
  Tiddington OX33 . . . . . . 145 B6
  Warmington OX17 . . . . . 3 A4
Church Hill Rd OX4 . . . . . 142 B4
CHURCHILL. 55 E5
Churchill Cl
  Didcot OX11. . . . . 200 C1
  Woodstock OX20 . . . . . . 91 B6
Churchill Cres
  Sonning Common RG4. . . 253 A6
  Thame OX9 . . . . 148 B8
Churchill Dr OX3. . . . . . . 124 C1
Churchill Gate OX20. . . . . 91 C5
Churchill Hospl The OX3 142 C8
Churchill Pl OX2 . . . . 122 F8
Churchill Rd
  Bicester OX26 . . . . 65 F3
  Chipping Norton OX7. . . 42 D1
  Didcot OX11. . . . . 200 C1
  Kidlington OX5 . . . . 108 E8
  Langford OX7 . . . . 55 A5
Churchill & Sarsden Heritage
  Ctr★ OX7 . . . . 55 D5
Churchill Way OX29 . . . . 106 B8
Church La
  Adderbury OX17 . . . . . . 23 A3
  Ashbury SN6 . . . . 228 A7
  Aston Rowant OX9. . . . . 167 D3
  Banbury OX16 . . . . 16 D6
  Bicester OX26 . . . . 65 E1
  Bladon OX20 . . . . 91 B2
  Bledington OX7 . . . . 54 D2
  Bledlow Ridge HP14 . . . 189 F8
  Bledlow Ridge, Radnage
    HP14. . . . . 189 D8
  Brightwell-cum-Sotwell
    OX10. . . . . 202 E3
  Burford OX18 . . . . 100 E5
  Cassington OX29 . . . . . 107 C2
  Chacombe OX17 . . . . . . 10 E4
  Chalgrove OX44 . . . . . . 184 D6
  Charlbury OX7 . . . . 73 B3
  Charlton-on-Otmoor OX5. . 95 A4
  Chinnor OX39. . . . . 168 D6
  Chipping Norton OX7. . . 42 E3
  Claydon OX17 . . . . 1 D1
  Coleshill SN6. . . . . 191 B8
  Cropredy OX17 . . . . .4 F2
  Croughton NN13 . . . . . . 36 D8
  Drayton OX14 . . . . 179 C1
  Drayton St Leonard OX10 183 B6
  Dry Sandford OX13 . . . . 158 F5
  Ewelme RG9 . . . . 206 B1
  Fernham SN7. . . . . 193 A4
  Fringford OX27 . . . . 52 D7
  Fulbrook OX18 . . . . 100 F6
  Hailey OX29 . . . . 104 A6
  Hampton Poyle OX5. . . . 93 A4
  Hanwell OX17 . . . . .8 F4
  Harwell OX11 . . . . 217 E7
  Hornton OX15 . . . . 7 C6
  Horton-cum-Studley OX33 112 A5
  Islip OX5 . . . . 93 F1
  Kirtlington OX5 . . . . 78 A4
  Langford GL7 . . . . 132 D1
  Longworth OX13 . . . . . . 156 B3
  Lower Heyford OX25 . . . 62 D6
  Ludgershall HP18 . . . . . 98 C7
  Marston OX3 . . . . 123 F6
  Middle Barton OX7 . . . . 61 A7
  Middleton Cheney OX17. . 10 F1
  Milcombe OX15 . . . . . . 21 A2
  Mixbury NN13 . . . . 38 E8
  Mollington OX17 . . . . . . .4 A3
  North Stoke OX10 . . . . . 221 D1
  Pyrton OX49. . . . . 186 B4
  Reading RG4 . . . . 259 F7
  Rotherfield Peppard RG9.. 253 A8
  Shilton OX18 . . . . 115 B5
  Shiplake RG9 . . . . 254 F1
  Shotteswell OX17 . . . . . .8 D7
  Shutford OX15. . . . . 14 B5
  South Moreton OX11. . . . 219 F5
  Spelsbury OX7 . . . . 72 F2
  Steventon OX13 . . . . . . 198 E3
  Towersey OX9 . . . . 148 E7
  Wallingford OX10 . . . . . 221 D7

Church La continued
  Wendlebury OX26 . . . . . 80 A4
  Weston-on-the-Green OX25 79 A2
  Witney OX28 . . . . 118 C8
  Wolvercote OX2. . . . . . . 122 F8
  Yarnton OX5 . . . . 108 A4
Churchlea OX17 . . . . 4 A3
Church Mdw OX7 . . . . 70 A1
Churchmere Rd OX14 . . . 180 B1
Church Mews RG8 . . . . . . 257 D5
Church Mill Cl OX29. . . . . 137 C4
Church Pas ⑧ OX16. . . . . 16 C6
Church Path
  Stanford in the Vale SN7.. 194 E7
  Stokenchurch HP14 . . . . 188 D5
Church Pl GL56 . . . . 54 A8
Church Rd
  Appleton OX13 . . . . 158 A8
  Ardley OX27. . . . . 50 C3
  Benson OX10 . . . . 203 F4
  Blewbury OX11 . . . . 237 A8
  Brackley NN13 . . . . 24 A7
  Chadlington OX7 . . . . . . 57 C1
  Chinnor OX39. . . . . 168 D6
  Cholsey OX10. . . . . 220 D2
  Churchill OX7. . . . . 55 E5
  Great Milton OX44. . . . . 145 B2
  Hinton Waldrist SN7 . . . 155 F2
  Horspath OX33 . . . . 143 C6
  Ickford HP18 . . . . 127 F3
  Lewknor OX49 . . . . 187 B8
  Long Hanborough OX29.. 106 C7
  Lower Odington GL56 . . . 54 A8
  Milton-under-Wychwood
    OX7. . . . . 70 A2
  North Leigh OX29 . . . . . 105 B8
  Pangbourne RG8 . . . . . . 256 C6
  Radley OX14 . . . . 160 E3
  Reading RG4 . . . . 258 F2
  Sandford-on-Thames OX4 161 A1
  Thame OX9 . . . . 129 E1
  Weston-on-the-Green OX25 79 A1
  Wheatley OX33 . . . . 144 B8
Church Rise OX7 . . . . 88 C6
Church Row
  Bourton SN6 . . . . 209 A2
  Childrey OX12 . . . . 213 C4
  Curbridge OX29 . . . . . . 117 C6
  Hinton Parva SN4 . . . . . 227 A3
  Langford GL7 . . . . 132 C2
Church Sq OX5 . . . . 93 F1
Church St
  Appleford OX14 . . . . . . 200 F8
  Ardington OX12 . . . . . . 215 E5
  Bampton OX18 . . . . 134 E3
  Barford St Michael OX15.. 32 E6
  Beckley OX3. . . . . 111 A3
  Bicester OX26 . . . . 65 E1
  Bladon OX20 . . . . 91 B2
  Bloxham OX15 . . . . 21 D4
  Bodicote OX15 . . . . 22 E8
  Charlbury OX7 . . . . 73 B3
  Chipping Norton OX7. . . 42 E3
  Deddington OX15. . . . . . 33 F4
  Didcot OX11. . . . . 218 F8
  Ducklington OX29 . . . . . 118 B4
  East Hendred OX12. . . . . 216 D6
  Eynsham OX29 . . . . 120 E7
  Fifield OX7 . . . . 69 B2
  Henley-on-Thames RG9.. 244 D1
  Idbury OX7 . . . . 69 B4
  Kidlington OX5. . . . . . . 92 F2
  Kingham OX7 . . . . 55 A4
  Marcham OX13 . . . . 178 C6
  Marsh Gibbon OX27. . . . 67 F3
  Reading RG4 . . . . 259 A2
  Shellingford SN7 . . . . . . 193 F8
  Shipton-under-Wychwood
    OX7. . . . . 85 D8
  Somerton OX25 . . . . 48 F6
  Stokenchurch HP14 . . . . 188 D5
  Stonesfield OX8. . . . . . . 89 C7
  Sutton Courtenay OX14.. 180 A1
  Upton OX11. . . . . 218 C2
  Wantage OX12. . . . . 214 D4
  Wargrave RG10. . . . . . . 255 C2
  Watlington OX49 . . . . . . 186 B2
  West Hanney OX12 . . . . 196 E6
  Wootton OX20 . . . . 75 F4
  Wroxton OX15 . . . . 15 B8
Church Terr
  Bicester OX26 . . . . 65 E1
  Hatford SN7. . . . . 174 D2
Church View
  Ascott-under-Wychwood
    OX7. . . . . 71 C2
  Bampton OX18. . . . . . . 134 E3
  Banbury OX16 . . . . 16 B4
  Berinsfield OX10 . . . . . . 182 C5
  Brackley NN13 . . . . 24 A7
  Carterton OX18 . . . . 115 E2
  Charlton-on-Otmoor OX5.. 95 A5
  Freeland OX29. . . . . 106 A6
  Grove OX12 . . . . 196 E1
  Highworth SN6 . . . . 190 A6
  Stoke Row RG9 . . . . 241 F5
  ⑥ Wantage OX12. . . . . 214 D5
Church View Cotts SN7.. 192 C2
Church View Rd OX28 . . . 117 F7
Churchward OX11. . . . . . . 200 E4
Churchward Cl OX12 . . . . 196 D2
Churchway RG20. . . . . . . 235 B1
Church Way
  Oxford, Dean Court OX2.. 122 D1
  Oxford, Iffley OX4 . . . . . 141 F4
  Sparsholt OX12 . . . . 212 E4

CHURCH WESTCOTE 68 D6
Church Wlk
  Ambrosden OX25. . . . . . 81 C3
  Banbury OX16 . . . . 16 C5
  Bishopstone SN6 . . . . . 227 C4
  Combe OX29 . . . . 90 A4
  Faringdon SN7 . . . . 173 A4
  Oxford OX2 . . . . 123 B4
  Shipton-under-Wychwood
    OX7. . . . . 70 D1
  Shrivenham SN6 . . . . . . 209 C7
  Upper Heyford OX25 . . . 62 F8
Chure The OX5 . . . . 95 A4
Churnet Cl OX11 . . . . 201 B2
Churn Rd OX11 . . . . 236 B1
Cinnaminta Rd OX3 . . . . . 142 E8
Cinnamon Cl OX44 . . . . . 184 C2
Circourt Rd OX12 . . . . . . 195 F3
Circular Rd OX5, OX26 . . . 80 E5
Circus St OX4. . . . . 141 E8
City Rd HP14. . . . . 189 D6
CITY THE 189 D6
Clack's La OX10 . . . . 222 C8
Clairmore Gdns RG31 . . . 257 C5
CLANFIELD 152 E8
Clanfield Cres RG31 . . . . 257 C2
Clanfield Prim Sch OX18 152 E8
Clanfield Rd OX18. . . . . . 134 E2
Clapcot Way OX10 . . . . . 221 C8
CLARE 165 E2
Clarence Pl OX11 . . . . . . 218 E7
Clarence Rd RG9. . . . . . . 244 D2
Clarendon Cl OX14 . . . . . 180 B8
Clarendon Dr OX9 . . . . . . 130 A1
Clarendon Rise RG31 . . . . 257 B4
Clare Terr 115 D1
Clarkes Ct OX16 . . . . 16 C6
Clarks La CV36. . . . . 28 A5
Clark's Row OX1 . . . . 261 B1
Clarkston Rd OX18 . . . . . 115 D1
CLATTERCOTE 4 D7
Clay Bank OX15 . . . . 30 A7
Clay Cl RG31 . . . . 257 B5
CLAYDON 1 D1
Claydon Ct ④ RG4 . . . . . 259 A2
Claydon Rd OX17 . . . . . . .4 F4
Clayfields SN6 . . . . 209 A3
Clay Hill Cl OX7 . . . . 58 E6
Clay La OX10 . . . . 204 C2
Claymond Rd OX3. . . . . . 124 F4
Claypit La SN7 . . . . 211 A7
Claypits La SN6 . . . . 209 C7
Clays Cl OX3. . . . . 124 A5
Clearway House Ind Est
  . . . . 17 A6
Cleavers OX39 . . . . 168 B6
Cleavers Sq ④ OX4 . . . . . 142 E1
Cleave The OX11. . . . . . . 217 E7
CLEEVE 249 B7
Cleeve Ct RG8 . . . . 249 B7
Cleeve Down OX1. . . . . . 249 B7
Cleeve Park Cotts RG8 . . 249 D8
Cleeve Rd RG8 . . . . 249 B7
Cleeves Ave OX7 . . . . 42 F4
Cleeves Cnr OX7 . . . . 42 E5
Clematis Pl OX4 . . . . 142 F2
Clements Cl OX12 . . . . . . 214 F6
Clements Green OX11 . . . 219 F5
Clements La OX27. . . . . . 67 C2
Clements Mead RG31 . . . 257 B1
Clements Rd RG9 . . . . . . 244 C3
Clerkenwell Cotts HP17 . 130 F5
Clevedon Ct ⑧ OX5 . . . . 108 F8
Clevedon Rd RG31 . . . . . 257 E3
Cleveland Cl OX5 . . . . . . 109 A7
Cleveland Dr OX4 . . . . . . 142 C5
Clevelands OX14 . . . . 160 A1
CLEVELEY 59 C4
Cleveley Rd OX7 . . . . 58 F5
Clevemede RG8. . . . . 249 C7
Cleycourt Rd SN6 . . . . . . 209 A6
Clifden Rd HP18 . . . . 127 E5
Clifford Pl OX2 . . . . 122 D8
CLIFTON 34 E4
Clifton Dr OX14 . . . . 179 E8
CLIFTON HAMPDEN 181 C2
Clifton Hampden CE Prim
  Sch OX14. . . . . 181 D4
Clifton Hamton Rd OX44. 162 F2
Clifton Park Rd RG4. . . . . 259 A3
Clifton Rd OX15. . . . . 34 C4
Clifton Rise RG10 . . . . . . 255 E1
Clinton Cl OX4 . . . . 141 F3
Clive Rd OX4 . . . . 142 C5
Clock Ho The ② OX18. . . 115 E2
Clock Tower Ct SN7. . . . . 172 E2
Cloisters The
  Ewelme RG9 . . . . 204 F3
  ⑧ Oxford OX1. . . . . . . 141 C7
  Reading RG4 . . . . 259 A3
  ① Wantage OX12 . . . . . 214 D4
Clonmel Cl RG4 . . . . 259 D2
Closes The OX5 . . . . 92 C1
Close The
  Ardington OX12 . . . . . . 215 E5
  Aston Tirrold OX11 . . . . 237 F8
  Benson OX10. . . . . 203 F5
  Chipping Warden OX17 . . .5 F6
  Great Bourton OX17 . . . . 9 D7
  Henley-on-Thames RG9.. 254 D8
  Lechlade-on-Thames GL7 150 C5
  Salford OX7 . . . . 42 A5
  Stanton Harcourt OX29.. 138 A8
  Stoke Lyne OX27 . . . . . 51 B5
  Woodcote RG8. . . . . . . 250 F8
Clover Cl OX2. . . . . 140 B6
Clover Mead OX26 . . . . . 65 E5

Clover Pl
  Eynsham OX29. . . . . . . 120 D7
  Oxford OX4 . . . . 142 F2
Clump La OX29 . . . . 8 A5
Coach House Ct RG8 . . . . 256 E5
Coach House Mews
  Bicester OX26 . . . . 80 F8
  ④ Reading RG4. . . . . . 259 C2
Coach La SN7. . . . . 173 A4
Coach Way OX10 . . . . . . 203 F4
Coalport Way RG30 . . . . . 257 E1
Coates La
  Cookley Green OX49 . . . 206 C2
  Ewelme RG9 . . . . 206 C2
Cobden Cres OX1. . . . . . 141 C7
Cobden Ctr The OX11 . . . 200 E4
Cochrane Rd OX10 . . . . . 204 D1
Cockcroft Rd OX11. . . . . 218 E2
Cockington Gn OX16 . . . . 16 E7
Cockpit Cl OX20 . . . . 91 B6
COCKPOLE GREEN. 255 F8
Cockshoot Cl OX29. . . . . 89 C7
Cockwell La SN7 . . . . . . 192 C6
COGGES. 118 C8
Cogges Hill Rd OX28 . . . 118 D7
Cogges La OX29 . . . . 119 C1
Cogges Manor Farm Mus★
  OX28. . . . . 118 C8
Coghill OX5 . . . . 93 A8
Coker Cl OX26 . . . . 65 E1
Colborne Rd OX11 . . . . . 218 D8
COLD HARBOUR
  Oxford 141 D5
  Woodcote. 250 C5
Cold Harbour RG8 . . . . . 250 C4
Coldharbour Cl RG9. . . . 254 C8
Coldharbour Rd OX12 . . . 234 A7
Coldicutt St RG4 . . . . 259 C1
Cole Ct OX11 . . . . 200 F3
Colegrave Rd OX15. . . . . 21 E5
Colegrove Down OX2 . . . 140 A6
Colemans Hill OX3 . . . . . 124 E3
Coleridge Cl
  ① Bicester OX26 . . . . . 65 C4
  Oxford OX4 . . . . 142 D5
Coleridge Dr OX14 . . . . . 179 D5
Colerne Rd OX18. . . . . . . 115 E3
Colesbourne Rd OX15 . . . 21 D3
COLESHILL 191 A8
Coleshill Dr SN7 . . . . 172 E2
Coles La 184 C2
Collcutt St OX33 . . . . 143 C7
College Cl
  Cholsey OX10. . . . . 220 F1
  Holton OX33 . . . . 126 C1
College Cotts OX25 . . . . . 95 C8
College Farm
  Benson OX10. . . . . 203 F4
  Chadlington OX7 . . . . . . 57 B1
College Farm Cotts
  OX13 . . . . 177 D4
College Farm La SN6. . . . 228 A6
College Fields OX17. . . . . 35 C7
College Flats OX14 . . . . . 142 B2
College for Int Ed OX1 . . 261 A2
College Front St OX5. . . . 94 E2
College La
  Long Compton CV36 . . . 28 A4
  Oxford OX4 . . . . 142 B2
College Sq OX13 . . . . . . 156 B3
College The
  Marsh Gibbon OX27. . . . 67 F3
  Swinbrook OX18 . . . . . . 101 F3
College Way OX33 . . . . . 143 B6
Collets Cotts OX44 . . . . . 145 C2
Collett OX11 . . . . 200 E4
Collett Way OX12 . . . . . . 196 D1
Colley Wood OX1 . . . . . . 141 D2
Collice St OX5 . . . . 109 F4
Colliers La RG9 . . . . 252 F8
Collier's La SN7. . . . . 173 A4
Collingwood Ave OX11 . . 218 D8
Collingwood Cl OX14 . . . 159 F1
Collins Dr OX15 . . . . 21 E5
Collins End RG8 . . . . 251 B2
Collinsmith Dr OX12 . . . . 196 E1
Collinsons Row OX7. . . . . 73 B3
Collins St ④ OX4 . . . . . . 141 F8
Collinwood Cl OX3 . . . . . 124 F3
Collinwood Rd OX3 . . . . . 124 F3
Collyer Rd HP14 . . . . 188 E4
Colmore La RG9 . . . . 252 E8
Colne Cl
  Bicester OX26 . . . . 65 D1
  Grove OX12 . . . . 196 C1
Colne Dr
  Berinsfield OX10 . . . . . . 182 D6
  Didcot OX11. . . . . 201 A3
Coln Rd OX11 . . . . 217 B3
Colonnade The RG31 . . . . 257 C2
Colony Rd OX15. . . . . 19 A8
Colony The OX15 . . . . . . 18 F7
COLONY THE. 18 F7
Colston Ct OX7 . . . . 43 A3
Colterne Cl OX3 . . . . 124 A5
Coltman Ave HP18 . . . . . 129 C6
Colton Rd SN6. . . . . 209 A6
Coltsfoot Leyes OX26. . . . 65 D4
Coltsfoot Sq ⑤ OX4. . . . . 142 F1
Columbia Way OX12. . . . . 214 C8
Columbine Gdns OX4 . . . 143 A1
Colvile Cl OX18 . . . . 134 F4
Colville Wlk OX16 . . . . . . 16 E7

Colwell Dr
Abingdon OX14 . . . . .179 D7
Oxford OX3 . . . . .125 A4
Witney OX28 . . . . .117 F6
Colwell Rd OX10 . . . . .182 C5
Colyton Way RG8 . . . . . . .257 D5
COMBE 90 A5
Combe CE Prim Sch OX29 90 A4
Combe Gate OX29 . . . . .90 A4
Combe Mill★ OX29 . . . . . . .90 B3
Combe Rd
Oxford OX2 . . . . .123 A2
Stonesfield OX8 . . . . .89 D7
Combes Cl SN7 . . . . .173 A4
Combe Sta OX29 . . . . .90 B3
Combewell OX44 . . . . .143 C2
Comfrey Rd OX4 . . . . .142 F3
COMMON BEAUCHAMP . . .210 D3
Common Cl
North Leigh OX29 . . . . . . .105 B6
Shrivenham SN6 . . . . .209 C7
Common La OX7 . . . . .42 C2
Common Rd
Beckley OX3 . . . . .110 F2
North Leigh OX29 . . . . . . .105 B6
Common The HP14 . . . . . . .188 E5
Compass Cl ◢ OX4 . . . . . .142 C4
Complins Cl OX2 . . . . .123 A6
Compton Cl OX11 . . . . . . .200 F1
Compton Ct CV36 . . . . . . .27 F7
Compton Dr OX14 . . . . . . .160 B2
Compton Rd OX16 . . . . . . .16 D6
Compton Terr ◼ OX10 . . . .221 C7
Compton Way OX28 . . . . . .104 C1
Concord Ave OX16 . . . . . . .16 D6
Condor Cl RG31 . . . . .257 C3
Conduit Hill Rise OX9 . . . .147 E7
Conduit House (North
Hinksey)★ OX2 . . . . .140 F7
Conduit Rd OX14 . . . . .179 C6
Conifer Cl OX2 . . . . .140 C8
Conifer Dr
Bicester OX26 . . . . .65 E5
Reading RG31 . . . . .257 B2
Conifer Rise OX16 . . . . .9 B1
Conigre OX39 . . . . .168 B6
Conisboro Ave RG4 . . . . . .258 E5
Conisboro Way RG4 . . . . . .258 E5
Coniston Ave OX3 . . . . . . .124 A4
Coniston Dr RG30 . . . . . . .257 F2
Connaught Ho RG9 . . . . . .244 E3
Connolly Dr OX18 . . . . . . .115 D4
Constable's Croft OX25 . . .96 E7
Constitution Hill OX10 . . . .221 E4
Convent The OX7 . . . . .68 D6
Conway Dr OX16 . . . . .15 F5
Conway Rd OX13 . . . . .159 D2
Conyger Cl OX5 . . . . .93 E1
Conygree Terr OX7 . . . . . . .42 F3
Cook La OX10 . . . . .221 E1
COOKLEY GREEN 206 D1
Cook Row OX7 . . . . .71 C2
Cook's Hill OX15 . . . . .14 B5
Cooks La OX7 . . . . .41 F5
Coolidge Cl ◼ OX3 . . . . . .124 D1
Coombe Cotts RG8 . . . . . .248 F6
Coombe Hill Cres OX9. . . .147 E8
Coombe Rd RG20 . . . . . . .247 A3
Coombes Cl OX7 . . . . .85 D8
Coombe The RG8 . . . . .248 F6
Cooper Cl OX7. . . . . .42 F3
Cooper Mews ◣ OX28 . . . .118 A8
Cooper Pl OX3 . . . . .124 F3
Cooper Rd RG9 . . . . .244 D3
Cooper Sch The OX26 . . . . .65 F4
Coopers Cl OX33 . . . . .143 D6
Cooper's Court Rd HP14 . . .188 D5
Coopers Gate OX16 . . . . . .16 C7
Coopers Gn OX26 . . . . .65 F5
Coopers La
Abingdon OX14 . . . . .179 E6
Wantage OX12 . . . . .214 F5
Coopers Piece OX10 . . . . . .221 C8
Coopers Pightle RG4 . . . . .252 B3
Copcot Cl OX33 . . . . .143 D6
Cope Cl OX2 . . . . .140 D8
Copenhagen Dr OX14 . . . . .159 D1
Cope Rd OX16 . . . . .16 C6
Copperage Rd
Chilton OX11 . . . . .234 A2
West Ilsley OX12 . . . . .233 F1
Copperfield Cl OX12 . . . . . .214 D6
Copperfields RG4 . . . . . . .258 F3
Coppice Cl OX16 . . . . .16 E4
Coppice The HP14 . . . . . . .188 E5
Coppock Cl OX3 . . . . .124 E2
Copse Ave RG4 . . . . .259 E3
Copse Cl RG31 . . . . .257 D3
Copse La OX3 . . . . .124 A5
Copse Mead RG5 . . . . .260 F1
Copse The
Abingdon OX14 . . . . .160 C1
Wargrave RG10 . . . . .255 D5
Copson La OX44 . . . . .163 C2
Copthorne Rd OX5 . . . . . . .108 E7
Corbett Rd OX18 . . . . .115 C1
Cordrey Dr OX4 . . . . .141 F4
Corfe Mews RG4 . . . . .259 C4
Coriander Way �791 OX4 . .142 F1
Corn Avill Cl OX14 . . . . . . .160 C2
Corn Bar ◼ OX28 . . . . . . .117 F8
Corncrake Way OX26. . . . . .66 A1
Corndell Gdns ◢ OX28 . . . .118 A8
Corneville Rd OX14 . . . . . .179 B2
Cornfield Cl OX28 . . . . . . .117 E7

Cornhill La OX12 . . . . .213 E5
Cornish Rd OX7 . . . . .42 D1
Cornmarket
◼ Faringdon SN7 . . . . . . .172 F4
Thame OX9 . . . . .147 F8
Cornmarket St OX1 . . . . . .261 B2
Corn St OX28 . . . . .118 A8
Cornwall Cl RG31 . . . . . . .257 B4
Cornwallis Cl OX4 . . . . . . .142 A5
Cornwallis Rd OX4 . . . . . . .142 A5
CORNWELL 41 C3
Cornwell OX7 . . . . .41 C3
Coromandel OX14. . . . . . . .179 D4
Coronation Cotts OX18 . . .152 E8
Coronation La OX17 . . . . . . .8 D7
Corpus Christi Coll OX1 . . .261 C2
Corunna Cres OX4 . . . . . . .142 E6
COSCOTE 218 D5
Cosford Gdns OX26 . . . . . .66 A4
Cosin Cl OX4 . . . . .142 A8
Costar Cl OX4. . . . . .142 D3
COTE 136 A2
Cote Rd OX18 . . . . .135 F3
COTHILL 158 E3
Cothill House Prep Sch
OX13. . . . . .158 E4
Cothill National Nature
Reserve★ OX13 . . . . .158 D3
Cothill Rd OX13 . . . . .158 F4
Cotman Cl OX14 . . . . .179 E5
Cotmore Cl OX9 . . . . .148 B7
Cotmore Field OX9. . . . . . .148 B7
Cotmore Gdns OX9. . . . . . .148 B7
Cot's Gn OX5 . . . . .92 D1
Cotshill Gdns OX7. . . . . . . .42 F3
Cotswold Cl
Minster Lovell OX29 . . . . . .102 E2
Sibford Ferris OX15 . . . . . . .19 B7
Cotswold Cnr OX7 . . . . . .29 A3
Cotswold Cres
Chipping Norton OX7 . . . . . .42 E1
Marston OX3 . . . . .123 F5
Cotswold Crescent Bglws
OX7 . . . . .42 E1
Cotswold Dene OX29 . . . . .137 A5
Cotswold Mdw OX28 . . . . .117 D7
Cotswold Pk OX11 . . . . . . .200 C2
Cotswold Rd OX2 . . . . .140 B6
Cotswold Terr OX7 . . . . . . .42 E1
Cotswold View OX7 . . . . . . .73 B4
Cotswold Way
Carterton OX18 . . . . .115 D4
Reading RG31 . . . . .257 C2
**Cotswold Wildlife Park &
Gardens★** OX18 . . . . . . .114 C5
Cottage Rd SN7 . . . . .194 D8
Cottages The
Burford OX18 . . . . .114 A5
Long Crendon HP18. . . . . . .129 C6
Cottesmore La OX10 . . . . .204 D5
Cottesmore Rd OX4 . . . . . .142 A3
COTTISFORD 37 F3
Cotton Grass Cl OX4 . . . . .142 E1
Cotwold Bsns Pk OX28 . . .103 B1
Couching St OX49. . . . . . . .186 B1
Coulings Cl OX12 . . . . . . .216 D7
Council Cotts RG4 . . . . . .252 B5
Council Hos
Binfield Heath RG9 . . . . . . .254 B2
Bloxham OX15 . . . . .21 D3
Great Tew OX7 . . . . .45 C7
Spelsbury OX7 . . . . .72 F4
Council Hos The
Barford St Michael OX15. . . .32 F5
Charlbury OX7 . . . . .73 B3
Hanwell OX17 . . . . .8 E3
Nettlebed RG9 . . . . .224 E2
Council Houses The OX17 10 F8
County Rd NN13 . . . . .24 A6
County Trad Est OX4 . . . . .142 F4
County View OX15 . . . . . . .34 A5
Coupland Rd OX13 . . . . . . .159 A6
Court Cl
Kidlington OX5. . . . . .108 D8
Shipton-under-Wychwood
OX7. . . . . .85 D7
Warmington OX17 . . . . .3 A4
Court Close Rd OX9 . . . . . .148 E7
Court Dr OX10 . . . . .203 B5
Courtenay Cl OX14 . . . . . . .200 A1
Courtenay Dr RG4. . . . . . . .259 B7
Courtenay Rd OX12 . . . . . .214 E5
Court Farm Barns OX5 . . . .77 B6
Court Farm Rd OX4 . . . . . .141 F3
Courtfield Rd OX33 . . . . . . .125 D7
Court Gdns RG8. . . . . .249 C7
Court Hill Rd
Letcombe Bassett OX12 . . .232 C7
Letcombe Regis OX12 . . . . .214 A1
Courtiers Gn OX14 . . . . . . .181 D4
Courtington La OX15 . . . . . .21 D5
Courtland Rd OX4 . . . . . . .142 A4
Courtlands Hill RG8 . . . . . .256 C4
Courtlands Rd OX7. . . . . . . .85 D8
Court Place Gdns OX4. . . . .141 F3
Court Pl OX12 . . . . .214 A2
Courts Gdns OX28 . . . . . . .118 D8
Court The OX14 . . . . .159 E1
Courtyard The
Aston OX18 . . . . .135 D3
Banbury OX17 . . . . .17 D5
Crawley OX29 . . . . .103 D5
Tadmarton OX15 . . . . .21 A6
Covent Cl OX14 . . . . .160 B3
Coverley Rd OX3 . . . . .142 D7
Covert The OX20 . . . . .91 C5
Cowdaroy Pl SN7 . . . . .194 E7

Cow La
Denchworth OX12, SN7 . . . .195 E4
Didcot OX11. . . . . .200 F2
Grove OX12 . . . . .196 E5
Harwell OX11. . . . . .217 F8
Kennington OX1. . . . . .141 E1
Longworth OX13 . . . . .156 C3
Marcham OX13 . . . . .178 D8
Moulsford OX10. . . . . .238 F3
Reading RG1 . . . . .258 E1
Steeple Aston OX25. . . . . . .62 B8
Sutton Courtenay OX11. . . .199 F2
Cowleaze OX39 . . . . .168 B6
Cowleaze Cl SN6. . . . . . . .209 B6
Cowleaze Cnr OX18 . . . . . .134 C2
COWLEY 142 E5
Cowley Bsns Ctr OX4. . . . . .142 F3
Cowley Junc OX4 . . . . .142 E4
Cowley Pl OX4 . . . . .141 E8
Cowley Rd
Oxford, Littlemore OX4 . . . .142 B2
Oxford OX4 . . . . .142 A7
Cowper Cl ◼ OX26 . . . . . . .65 C4
Coxfield Cl HP14 . . . . .188 F5
Cox La
Chipping Norton OX7 . . . . . .42 B2
Stanton St John OX33. . . . .125 D7
COXLEASE 226 A5
Coxmoor Cl OX7 . . . . .54 F4
Cox's Alley OX3 . . . . .124 E3
Cox's Ct SN7 . . . . .194 E7
Cox's Ground OX2 . . . . . . .123 A5
Cox's La
Crowmarsh Gifford
OX10. . . . . .222 A6
Enstone OX7 . . . . .58 F4
Stoke Row RG9 . . . . .242 A5
Cox's Rd SN6 . . . . .209 B6
Coxwell Gdns SN7 . . . . . . .172 F3
Coxwell Hall Mews SN7 . . .172 F1
Coxwell Lodge Dr SN7 . . . .172 E1
Coxwell Rd SN7 . . . . .172 E1
Coxwell St SN7 . . . . .172 F3
Cozens La OX7 . . . . .54 F4
Crab Tree Cl OX15 . . . . . . .21 E6
Crabtree Cnr OX10 . . . . . . .240 D7
Crabtree La OX14 . . . . .179 B2
Crabtree Pl OX14 . . . . .180 B7
Crabtree Rd
Haddenham HP17 . . . . . . .130 F5
Oxford OX2 . . . . .140 D8
Crafts End OX11 . . . . .235 E8
Cranberry Rd OX28. . . . . . .104 E1
Cranbourne Gdns RG30 . . .258 A2
Cranbrook Cl OX28. . . . . . .118 A6
Cranbrook Dr OX1 . . . . . . .160 E7
Crane Furlong SN6. . . . . . .190 A7
Cranesbill Dr OX26. . . . . . .65 D5
Cranesbill Way ◼ OX4 . . . .142 E1
Cranford House Sch
OX10. . . . . .238 F5
Cranham St OX2 . . . . .261 A4
Cranham Terr OX2 . . . . . . .261 A4
Cranleigh Cl OX16 . . . . . . .16 A4
Cranley Rd OX3. . . . . .124 F4
Cranmer Cl RG31 . . . . .257 B3
Cranmer Rd OX4 . . . . .142 E6
Cranston Ct ◼ OX4 . . . . . .142 B3
Cranwell Ave OX18. . . . . . .115 F2
Craster Ct OX16 . . . . .16 B3
Cratlands Cl OX44. . . . . . . .163 C2
Craufurd Rd OX4 . . . . .142 E6
Craven Comm SN7 . . . . . .211 D7
Craven Way OX11 . . . . . . .218 E7
Crawborough Rd OX7 . . . . .73 C4
Crawborough Terr OX7. . . . .73 C4
Crawborough Villas OX7 . . .73 C4
CRAWLEY 103 D4
Crawley Mill Ind Est
OX29 . . . . .103 D4
Crawley Rd OX28 . . . . .104 A2
Crawshay Dr RG4 . . . . . . .259 B7
Cray Ct OX11 . . . . .200 F4
Craysleaze RG4. . . . . .252 D3
CRAY'S POND 250 E6
Crays Pond Cl RG8 . . . . . .250 D6
CRAZIES HILL 255 F6
Crazies Hill CE Prim Sch
RG10. . . . . .255 F6
CR Bates Ind Est HP14. . . .188 E5
Creampot Cl OX17 . . . . .5 A2
Creampot Cres OX17. . . . . .4 F2
Creampot La OX17 . . . . .4 F2
Crecy Hill Nature Reserve★
OX5. . . . . .77 C7
Crecy Wlk OX30 . . . . .91 C5
Cremyll Rd RG1. . . . . .258 F1
Crendon Ct ◼ RG4. . . . . . .259 A2
Crescent Cl OX4. . . . . .142 D6
Crescent Ct OX4 . . . . .142 D6
Crescent Rd
Oxford OX4 . . . . .142 D6
Reading RG31 . . . . .257 D1
Crescent The
Adderbury OX17 . . . . .23 A5
Bicester OX26 . . . . .65 D3
Carterton OX18 . . . . .133 C8
East Hagbourne OX11. . . . .218 F6
Long Wittenham OX14 . . . . .201 D8
Lower Shiplake RG9 . . . . . .255 B4
Oxford OX2 . . . . .123 A3
Sandford-on-Thames OX4 . .161 C8
Steeple Aston OX25. . . . . . .62 B7
Witney OX29 . . . . .104 C2
Crescent Way OX10 . . . . . .220 F1
Cress Hill Pl OX3. . . . . . . .124 F4
Crest The
Bledlow Ridge HP14 . . . . . .189 F8

Crest The continued
Reading RG4 . . . . .259 C5
Cricket Ground HP14. . . . . .188 D5
Cricklade Rd SN6 . . . . .190 A5
Crick Rd OX2 . . . . .123 C4
Cripley Pl OX2. . . . . .123 A1
Cripley Rd OX2 . . . . .123 A1
Crispin Cl RG4 . . . . .258 D5
Crispin Pl OX10 . . . . .221 D7
Crisp Rd RG9 . . . . .244 C3
Croasdell Cl OX14 . . . . . . .179 E4
Crocker End RG9 . . . . .224 F2
Crockwell Cl OX26 . . . . . . .65 E2
Crockwell St CV36 . . . . . . .27 F7
Croft Ave OX5 . . . . .108 F8
Croft Cl
Marston OX3 . . . . .123 F4
Merton OX25 . . . . .95 D8
Thame OX9 . . . . .148 A7
Croft Cotts OX14 . . . . .181 E5
Croft Ct OX14 . . . . .148 A7
Croft Ctyd HP17 . . . . .130 F5
Croft End OX12 . . . . .214 A2
Croft Terr ◼ OX10 . . . . . . .221 D7
Croft The
Aston Tirrold OX11 . . . . . . .219 F1
Didcot OX11. . . . . .218 F8
East Hagbourne OX11 . . . . .218 F5
Haddenham HP17 . . . . . . .130 F5
Harwell OX11. . . . . .217 A2
Nuneham Courtenay OX44 . .162 A4
Oxford OX3 . . . . .124 C3
West Hanney OX12 . . . . . . .196 F7
Croft Villas ◼ OX10 . . . . . .221 C7
Croft Way RG8. . . . . .250 F8
Cromer Cl RG31. . . . . .257 C1
Cromwell Ave OX9 . . . . . . .130 A1
Cromwell Cl
Chalgrove OX44 . . . . .184 E6
Faringdon SN7 . . . . .173 A3
Henley-on-Thames RG9 . . . .254 E8
Marston OX3 . . . . .123 F4
Cromwell Ct OX16 . . . . . . .16 B7
Cromwell Dr OX11 . . . . . . .219 A7
Cromwell Pk OX7 . . . . .42 F4
Cromwell Rd
Banbury OX16 . . . . .16 A6
Henley-on-Thames RG9 . . . .254 E8
Reading RG31 . . . . .259 B2
Cromwell St OX1. . . . . . . .261 B1
Cromwell Way OX5 . . . . . . .109 A7
Cronshaw Cl OX11 . . . . . . .200 E2
Crookdale Beck OX11 . . . . .201 A3
Crook's Terr OX11. . . . . . . .214 D5
Croom Cotts OX11 . . . . . . .217 A7
CROPREDY 4 E2
Cropredy CE Prim Sch
OX17. . . . . .4 F1
Cross Ave OX10 . . . . .204 D2
Cross Cl OX10 . . . . .204 E2
Cross Hill Rd OX17 . . . . . . .22 F4
Cross Keys Rd RG8. . . . . . .239 C4
Crosslands OX27 . . . . .52 D6
Crosslands Dr OX14 . . . . . .159 E1
Cross Leys OX7 . . . . .42 E2
Cross Rd OX10 . . . . .220 F2
Cross's La OX7. . . . . .56 E1
Cross St OX4 . . . . .141 F8
Cross The OX29 . . . . .89 C7
Cross Tree La GL7 . . . . . . .132 B5
Crossville Cres OX11. . . . . .200 D2
Crossway OX7 . . . . .60 F8
Crossways The OX27 . . . . . .50 C4
Crotch Cres OX3 . . . . .124 A4
Crouch Hill Rd OX16 . . . . . .16 A4
Crouch St OX16 . . . . .16 C5
CROUGHTON 36 D7
Croughton All Saints CE Prim
Sch NN13 . . . . .36 D8
Croughton Elementary Sch
NN13. . . . . .36 E6
Croughton Mid Sch NN13 . .36 F7
Croughton Rd OX17 . . . . . .35 D7
Crowberry Rd OX4 . . . . . . .142 F2
Crowcastle La OX5 . . . . . . .77 F6
CROWELL 168 B4
CROWELL HILL 168 C5
Crowell Rd
Chinnor OX39 . . . . .168 B5
Oxford OX4 . . . . .142 C4
Crow La
Great Bourton OX17 . . . . . .9 D7
Wootton OX20 . . . . .75 C7
CROWMARSH GIFFORD . . .221 F7
Crowmarsh Gifford CE Prim
Sch OX10. . . . . .221 D7
Crowmarsh Hill OX10 . . . . .222 B6
Crowmarsh Rd OX27 . . . . . .64 F6
Crown La
Benson OX10 . . . . .203 F4
Dorchester OX10. . . . . . . .182 D1
South Moreton OX11. . . . . .220 A7
Crown Mdw OX12. . . . . . . .197 C7
Crown Mews ◼ OX14 . . . . .179 E7
Crown Rd
Kidlington OX5. . . . . .108 D8

Crown Rd continued
Wheatley OX33 . . . . .144 B8
Crown Sq
Benson OX10 . . . . .204 A4
Wheatley OX33 . . . . .144 B8
Crown St OX4. . . . . .141 F7
Crown Wlk OX26 . . . . .65 E1
CROWSLEY 253 C4
Crowsley Rd RG9 . . . . . . .255 A3
Crowsley Way RG4 . . . . . .252 E5
Croxford Gdns OX5 . . . . . .108 E6
Crozier Cl OX2 . . . . .140 D8
Crumps Butts OX26 . . . . . .65 E2
Crutch Furlong OX10. . . . . .182 C6
Cuckamus La OX29 . . . . . .105 B6
Cuckoo Cl OX27. . . . . .65 F6
Cuckoo La OX29 . . . . .106 A3
CUDDESDON 144 B3
Cuddesdon Cl RG8 . . . . . .250 F8
Cuddesdon Rd OX33 . . . . .143 E5
Cuddesdon Way OX4 . . . . .142 F2
Cuddeston Rd OX44 . . . . . .163 A6
Cues La SN6 . . . . .227 C4
CULHAM 180 B2
Culham Cl OX14 . . . . .160 A1
Culham No 1 Site OX14. . . .181 A3
Culham Parochial CE Prim
Sch OX14. . . . . .180 B3
Culham Science Ctr OX14 . .B4 0
Culham Sta OX14 . . . . . . .180 B3
Cullen Pl OX11. . . . . .218 E8
Cullerne Cl OX14. . . . . . . .160 A3
Cullerns The SN6 . . . . .190 A6
Cullum Ho OX33 . . . . .144 C8
Cullum Rd OX33 . . . . .144 C7
Culworth Rd OX17 . . . . . . .5 F6
Cumberford 21 D3
Cumberford Cl OX15 . . . . . .21 C4
Cumberford Hill OX15. . . . . .21 C4
Cumberland Rd OX4 . . . . . .142 B7
Cumberlege Cl OX3 . . . . . .123 E7
Cummings Cl OX3. . . . . . . .124 E2
CUMNOR 139 D5
Cumnor CE Prim Sch
OX2. . . . . .139 E5
CUMNOR HILL 140 C7
Cumnor Hill OX2. . . . . .140 B7
Cumnor Rd
Cumnor OX2 . . . . .139 C8
Wootton, Boars Hill OX1 . . .159 A8
Cumnor Rise Rd OX2. . . . . .140 C8
Cunliffe Cl OX2 . . . . .123 C4
Cup & Saucer OX17 . . . . . .4 F2
CURBRIDGE 117 C6
Curbridge Bsns Pk OX28 . .103 B1
Curbridge Rd
Ducklington OX29 . . . . . . .118 A4
Witney OX28 . . . . .117 E7
Curie Ave OX11 . . . . .217 B3
Cursus The GL7 . . . . .150 C5
Curtis Ave OX14 . . . . .180 B7
Curtis Rd
Kidlington OX5. . . . . .92 E1
Shrivenham SN6 . . . . .209 A6
Curtiss Cl OX26 . . . . .66 A5
Curtyn Cl OX14 . . . . .179 D8
Curzon Gate Ct HP14 . . . . .188 E7
Cuthwine Pl GL7. . . . . .150 C5
CUTTESLOWE 109 B2
Cutteslowe Prim Sch
OX2. . . . . .109 C1
Cuttle Brook Gdns OX9. . . .129 E1
Cuttle Brook Nature
Reserve★ OX9 . . . . .147 C8
CUXHAM 185 D3
Cuxham Rd OX49 . . . . .186 A2
Cwmcarn RG4 . . . . .258 F6
Cygnet Cl OX9 . . . . .166 B8
Cygnet Ct OX14 . . . . .179 E6
Cypress Gdns OX26 . . . . . .65 F5
Cyprus Terr OX2 . . . . .122 F8

D

Dacey Dr OX25. . . . . .63 B8
Dacre Ave RG4. . . . . .259 C4
Daedings The OX15 . . . . . .33 E4
Dagdale Dr OX11. . . . . .200 F3
Daimler Ave OX16. . . . . . . .15 F4
Dairyground The OX15 . . . .14 A5
Daisy Bank OX14. . . . . . . .180 B8
Daisy Hill OX25 . . . . .47 D5
Dale Cl
Brackley NN13 . . . . .24 A7
Oxford OX1 . . . . .261 A1
Dale Pl OX5 . . . . .92 E1
Dale The OX3. . . . . .125 A4
Dale Wlk OX29. . . . . .118 A5
Dalton Ave OX11. . . . . .217 A2
Damer Gdns RG9 . . . . .254 E8
Damson Trees SN6. . . . . . .209 A6
Dancers Hill OX7. . . . . .73 C3
Danesmoor OX16 . . . . .16 B8
Danes Rd OX26 . . . . .65 C2
Danvers Cl OX15 . . . . .15 C2
Danvers Rd
Broughton OX15 . . . . .15 C2
Oxford OX4 . . . . .142 A3
Darcey Lode OX11 . . . . . . .201 B2
Darell Rd RG4 . . . . .258 F3
Darent Pl OX11 . . . . .201 A2
Dark La
Great Coxwell SN7. . . . . . .192 C8
Reading RG31 . . . . .257 B2
Sunningwell OX13 . . . . . . .159 E5
Wargrave RG10 . . . . .255 D2

Dark La continued
Witney OX28 104 A1
Wroxton OX15 15 A8
Darnell Wlk OX26 65 E4
Darrell Way OX14 159 F1
Dart Dr OX11 200 E3
Dart Rd OX13 159 C3
Dashwood Ave OX5 108 B5
Dashwood Ct OX49 167 D3
Dashwood Mews OX5 77 F4
Dashwood Prim Sch 19 OX16 16 D5
Dashwood Rd
Banbury OX16 16 C5
Oxford OX4 142 A3
Dashwood Rise OX25 47 D6
Dashwood Terr 1 OX16 16 C5
Dasset Rd OX17 3 E8
Datchet Gn OX10 202 F2
Daubeny Rd OX4 141 F6
Daubigny Mead OX18 116 C4
Davenant Ct OX2 109 A1
Davenant Rd OX2 123 A8
Davenport Pl OX49 186 B1
Davenport Rd OX28 103 F1
Daventry Rd
Banbury OX16 9 F1
Banbury OX16 16 F7
David Nicholls Cl OX4 142 B2
David Walter Cl OX2 109 B1
Davis Cl OX18 115 E2
Davis Gdns OX27 65 F7
Dawls Cl OX7 71 B1
Dawson St 1 OX4 141 E8
DAYLESFORD 54 D8
Days Ground SN6 209 C7
Day's La OX10 204 F2
Deacon Field RG8 239 C3
Deacon Way
Banbury OX16 16 B5
Reading RG30 258 A2
Deadman's La RG8 251 C4
DEAN 57 E1
Dean Butler Cl OX12 214 C5
Dean Cl OX16 16 E8
DEAN COURT 140 B8
Dean Court Rd OX2 140 B7
Deanes Cl OX13 198 F4
Deanfield Ave RG9 244 D1
Deanfield Rd
Henley-on-Thames RG9 244 D1
Oxford OX2 122 B1
Deans Ct OX26 65 F1
Deans Farm RG4 259 D1
Dean Wood Cl RG8 240 E1
Dearlove Cl OX14 159 E2
Deaufort Cl OX5 92 E1
DEDDINGTON 33 E4
Deddington Castle Earthworks* OX15 34 A4
Deddington CE Prim Sch OX15 33 F4
Deddington Hill OX15 33 F6
Deene Cl OX17 23 B4
Deerhurst Cl GL56 26 F1
Deer Park Rd OX28 117 D7
Deers Cl OX15 22 E8
Deers Farm OX15 22 E7
Deer's Farm OX15 22 E7
Deer's La RG8 241 C2
Deer Wlk OX4 142 F1
Defence Academy Coll of Management & Tech SN6 209 E7
Defiant Cl OX26 66 A3
De Havilland Rd GL54 68 B5
De Havilland Way OX29 117 C8
Delafield Cl HP14 188 F4
Delamare Way OX2 140 B7
Delapre Dr OX16 16 F7
Delbush Ave OX3 125 B4
Dell Rd RG31 257 C2
Dell The HP14 188 F3
Dellwood Pk RG4 258 F4
Delly Cl OX29 104 A7
DELLY END 104 A8
Delly Hill OX29 104 A6
De Montfort Rd RG1 259 A1
Denbeigh Pl RG1 258 F1
Denbigh Cl OX16 15 F4
Denbigh Rd OX9 130 A1
Denby Way RG30 257 F1
Denchfield Rd OX16 16 D2
DENCHWORTH 196 A4
Denchworth Rd
Grove OX12 196 D2
Wantage OX12 214 C6
Denefield Gdns RG31 257 B2
Denefield Sch RG31 257 B3
Dene Hollow OX11 235 E8
Dene Rd OX3 142 D8
Dene Rise OX28 117 F8
Denman's La OX2 139 E5
Denmark St OX4 141 F7
DENTON 144 B1
Denton Cl
Abingdon OX14 180 B8
Oxford OX2 140 A8
Denton Hill OX44 144 B2
Denton La OX44 143 F1
Dents Cl OX3 124 A5
Derby Rd RG4 259 B3
Derwent Ave
Didcot OX11 201 A1
Oxford OX3 124 A4
Reading RG31 257 E2
Derwent Cl OX13 159 C2
Derwent Rd OX26 65 B3
Desborough Cres OX4 142 A3
Desmesne Furze OX3 124 C1
Des Roches Sq OX28 118 B7
Devereux Pl OX4 142 A3
Devil's Hill RG9 253 D6
De Vitre Pl OX12 214 D8
Devon Cl OX10 204 D3
Devon Dr RG4 259 E4
Devon Pl OX18 115 F2
Devonshire Gdns RG31 257 B3
Devon Way OX16 16 A8
Dexter Cl OX16 16 D4
Diamond Ct OX2 123 B6
Diamond Pl OX2 123 B6
Dibleys OX11 237 A8
Dickens Cl
Bicester OX26 65 C3
Reading RG4 259 D2
Dickenson Ct OX7 42 F3
Dickredge The OX25 62 B8
DIDCOT 200 D3
Didcot Girls' Sch OX11 200 D1
Didcot Hospl OX11 218 C8
Didcot L Ctr OX11 218 F7
Didcot Parkway Sta OX11 200 F2
Didcot Railway Ctr (Mus)* OX11 200 E2
Didcot Rd
Brightwell-cum-Sotwell OX10 202 D3
Didcot OX11 218 A8
Long Wittenham OX14 201 D8
Didcot Wave L Pool OX11 218 E7
Dido Rd OX11 217 A1
Digberry La RG9 224 C5
Digby Cl OX9 130 B1
Digging La OX13 157 C1
DIGGS 130 F5
Dillon Ct OX15 22 E8
Dirac Pl OX11 219 A8
Diston's La OX7 42 E3
Ditchend Cotts OX44 164 A5
Ditchley Rd OX7 73 E5
Dittander Cl OX26 65 D4
Divinity Rd OX4 142 A8
Dixon's Row OX12 214 E8
Dobson's La RG9 226 C1
Dobson's La RG9 244 C8
Dodgson Rd OX4 142 C4
Dodson Ct OX14 179 F8
Doe Lea OX11 200 F3
Dog Cl OX17 22 F3
Dogkennel La SN7 193 F7
Dog Kennel La OX7 85 C7
Dog La
Childrey OX12 213 C3
Rotherfield Peppard RG9 253 B8
DOGMORE END 241 D4
Doily Cl OX15 30 A7
Dollicott HP17 130 F6
Dolphin La OX18 100 F6
Don Boscoe Cl 3 OX4 142 D6
Don Cl OX11 201 A3
Donegal Cl RG4 259 C3
Donkin Hill RG4 259 C3
Donnington Bridge Rd OX4 141 F6
Donnington Cl OX28 117 D7
Donnington Lodge OX4 141 F6
Donnington Pl OX12 214 D6
Don Stuart Pl OX4 142 B7
Dora Carr Cl OX3 124 A5
Dorcas Rd OX16 17 A6
DORCHESTER 182 C1
Dorchester Abbey Mus* OX10 182 D1
Dorchester Cl OX3 124 F1
Dorchester Cres OX14 160 A1
Dorchester Ct
4 Kidlington OX5 108 F8
Oxford OX2 123 B6
Dorchester Gr OX16 15 F4
Dorchester Pl OX9 147 F8
Dorchester Rd OX10 182 F4
Dorchester St Birinus CE Prim Sch OX10 182 D1
Doris Field Cl OX3 124 A3
Dormer Rd OX9 148 B6
Dormers The SN6 190 B6
Dorn Cl OX7 60 F8
Dornford La OX20 76 D8
Dorn View OX20 76 A4
Dorothy Hodgkin Rd OX1 261 C3
DORTON 98 F1
Douglas Downes Cl OX3 124 E2
Douglas Rd RG4 259 D2
Dovecot Cl OX15 21 A2
Dovecote HP17 130 F6
Dovecote Cl
Haddenham HP17 130 F6
Milcombe OX15 21 A2
Dove Ct
3 Bicester OX26 65 E1
Carterton OX18 115 E4
Dovedale Cl RG4 258 F3
Dove Gn OX26 65 B3
Dovehouse Cl OX29 120 F8
Dove House Cl OX2 122 F8
Dove La RG9 252 D8
Doveleat OX39 168 D7
Dover Ave OX16 15 F6
D'Overbroeck's Coll OX2 123 B5
Dover Cl OX2 140 C7
Dovetrees OX18 115 E3
DOWN END 30 B7
Down End OX15 30 B7
Downhill La OX29 104 B4
DOWNINGTON 150 B3
Downlands SN7 192 D2
Downs Cl OX11 217 E6
Downside OX11 217 C1
Downside End OX3 125 A3
Downside Rd OX3 125 A3
Downsmead SN8 245 D1
Downs Rd
Aldworth RG20 247 A4
Curbridge OX29 117 B7
Didcot OX11 218 D7
Standlake OX29 137 B6
Witney OX29 103 B1
Downs The OX29 137 C5
Downs View
Aston Tirrold OX11 237 F8
Highworth SN6 190 A6
Downsview Rd OX12 214 B7
Downs Way
Chilton OX11 234 F8
Reading RG31 257 C2
Downsway Prim Sch RG31 257 C3
Dow St OX25 63 C8
Doyley Rd
Oxford OX2 141 A8
Wallingford OX10 203 C1
Dragonhill Rd SN7 211 B2
Dragon Sch OX2 123 C4
Drake Ave OX11 218 D8
Drake La OX28 104 D1
Drakes Dr HP18 129 E5
Drakes Farm HP18 129 E5
DRAYCOT 145 F8
Draycott Rd
Kingston Bagpuize OX13 156 D1
Longworth OX13 156 E2
Draymans Croft 10 OX26 65 E2
Drayman's Wlk 7 OX14 179 E6
Dray's La RG9 253 A8
DRAYTON
Abingdon 179 A1
Banbury 15 D8
Drayton East Way OX14 199 D8
Drayton Prim Sch OX14 179 B2
Drayton Rd
Abingdon OX14 179 D5
Berinsfield OX10 182 E3
Dorchester OX10 182 D2
Drayton OX14 179 D1
Sutton Courtenay OX14 199 F8
DRAYTON ST LEONARD 183 A5
Dresden Way RG30 257 F1
Drewett Ct OX2 122 E8
Drewitts Cnr OX11 217 E7
Drift Acre OX15 20 D7
Drift Ctr OX4 142 F6
Drinkwater Cl OX25 97 D7
Drivers La GL56 27 A1
Drive The OX7 58 F6
Drove Acre Rd OX4 142 A7
Drovers La RG9 226 C8
Droveside OX10 220 F1
Drove Way OX12 212 B4
Dr Radcliffes CE Prim Sch OX25 48 B1
Dr Souths CE Prim Sch OX5 93 E1
Druce Way OX4 142 F3
Druids Wlk
Chinnor OX39 168 C6
Didcot OX11 200 E2
Dryden Ave OX26 65 B3
Dry La OX29 103 D3
Drylands Rd OX29 102 E2
DRY SANDFORD 158 F5
Dry Sandford Prim Sch OX13 158 F6
Drysdale Cl OX14 160 E2
Duchess Cl RG8 256 D7
Duck End La OX29 120 C1
Duck La HP18 98 C8
DUCKLINGTON 118 A4
Ducklington CE Prim Sch OX29 118 B3
Ducklington La OX28 117 F7
Duck Sq OX39 168 C6
Dudgeon Dr OX4 142 B2
Dudley Cl RG31 257 E1
Dudley Ct OX2 123 B7
Dudley Gdns OX4 123 F1
Dudley La RG9 226 F7
Dudley Mews RG31 257 E1
Dudwell OX11 200 E3
Duffield Cl OX14 160 B2
Duffield Pl OX13 178 C7
Duffield Rd RG5 260 F1
Duke of York Ave OX14 199 D3
Dukes Cl HP18 128 C2
Dukes Meadow Dr OX16 9 B2
Dukes Rd OX5 108 F8
Duke St
Banbury OX16 16 E6
Henley-on-Thames RG9 244 E2
Oxford OX2 122 F1
Dulas Cl OX11 200 F2
Dumas Cl OX26 65 C2
Dumbarton Way RG4 259 E5
Dunbar Dr OX9 130 A1
Duncan Cl OX29 120 D8
Duncan Gdns RG8 257 C4
Dundas Cl OX14 180 B8
Dundas Ct SN7 172 E3
Dunkins Cl OX26 65 E2
Dunlin Ct
Banbury OX16 16 E3
Dunlin Ct continued
4 Bicester OX26 65 F1
Dunluce Gdns RG8 256 E5
Dunmore Prim Sch OX14 159 F1
Dunmore Rd OX14 159 E2
Dunnock Cl OX26 66 A1
Dunnock Way
Sandford-on-Thames OX4 142 F1
Wargrave RG10 255 E3
Dunsden Cl OX11 200 D1
DUNSDEN GREEN 259 F7
Dunsomer Hill OX11 220 A7
Dunstan Ave OX7 42 E2
Dunstan Rd OX3 124 C4
Dunstead La OX2 122 B6
Dunster Cl RG4 259 C6
DUNS TEW 47 D6
Duns Tew Rd OX7 47 C2
Dunthrop Rd OX7 44 A4
Durant Way RG31 257 D3
Durham La OX29 107 C1
Durham Mews 5 OX16 9 A1
DUXFORD 155 D4
Duxford Cl
Bicester OX26 66 B4
Carterton OX18 115 E3
Dyers Hill OX7 73 B4
Dyer Straits OX11 234 F8
Dynham Pl OX3 124 D1
Dysonswood La RG4 258 E8

E

Eady Rd OX25 63 B8
Eagle Ind Est OX28 118 A8
Eagle La SN6 191 C1
Eagles SN7 172 F3
Eagles Close Almshouses 7 OX12 214 D4
Eagle Sq SN7 192 E7
Earlsfield Cl RG4 259 E4
Earls La OX15 33 F4
Earl St OX2 122 F1
Earlstoke Cl OX16 16 E8
Early Rd OX28 104 D2
EASINGTON
Banbury 16 C3
Chalgrove 185 C7
Easington Gdns OX16 16 C4
Easington Rd OX16 16 C4
Eason Dr OX14 160 C1
EAST ADDERBURY 23 B3
East Allcourt GL7 150 C4
East Ave OX4 142 A8
Eastbrook Cl OX6 97 E7
Eastbury Ct 2 OX12 214 D5
EAST CHALLOW 214 A5
Eastchurch OX4 141 F3
East Cl OX16 16 F7
EASTEND 57 D1
EAST END
Adderbury 23 B4
Hook Norton 30 B7
Swerford 30 F3
East End
Combe OX29 90 D3
Hook Norton OX15 30 B7
Easterfield OX12 196 E1
Eastern Ave OX4 142 B3
Eastern By-Pass Rd OX3, OX4 142 E5
Eastern Ho OX4 142 B3
Eastern Terr OX15 22 E8
Eastfield OX11 237 A8
East Field Cl OX3 142 E7
Eastfield Ct 2 SN7 172 F4
Eastfield La
Whitchurch-on-Thames RG8 256 D7
Woodcote RG8 250 E6
Eastfield Pl OX4 142 F6
Eastfield Rd OX8, OX28 104 B3
Eastgate OX15 7 C7
EAST GINGE 216 B2
EAST HAGBOURNE 218 F6
EAST HANNEY 197 B6
East Hawthorn Rd OX25 81 D4
EAST HENDRED 216 E7
EASTLEACH MARTIN 131 B7
EASTLEACH TURVILLE 131 A8
EAST LOCKINGE 215 D3
Eastmanton La OX12 212 F3
East Oxford Prim Sch OX4 141 F8
East Paddocks OX14 199 D7
Eastrop SN6 190 B5
Eastrop Inf Sch SN6 190 A5
East St Helen St OX14 179 F6
East St
Banbury OX16 16 E7
Bicester OX26 65 D3
Bodicote OX15 22 E8
Didcot OX11 219 A8
Fritwell OX27 49 F7
Long Compton CV36 27 F6
Oxford OX2 123 A1
Thame OX9 148 A8
East View
Blackthorn OX25 82 A3
Kirtlington OX5 77 F3
East View Cl RG10 255 E2
East View Rd RG10 255 E2
Eastview Terr SN6 190 A6
East Way OX14 199 B8
Eastway Mobile Home Pk OX14 199 B8
Eastwood Rd
Stokenchurch HP14 188 F3
Witney OX29 103 C1
EATON 139 B3
Eaton Cl SN7 172 E2
Eaton Ct OX2 123 C8
EATON HASTINGS 171 E7
Eaton Rd OX13 139 B2
EATON WOOD 171 F5
Ebbes La OX12 197 B7
Eccles Cl RG4 259 C2
Eckersley Sch of English The OX1 261 A2
Edencroft SN6 190 B7
Eden Croft OX14 160 A2
Eden Ct OX11 201 A1
Eden Dr OX3 124 B4
Edenhall Cl RG31 257 D3
Eden Rd OX3 124 A4
Eden Way OX26 65 B2
Edgar Milward Cl RG30 258 A1
Edgecombe Rd OX3 124 F4
Edgehill OX9 129 F2
Edgehill Ctry Pk* OX17 2 D5
Edgeway Rd OX3 123 F3
Edgeworth Dr OX18 115 C2
Edinburgh Cl OX16 15 E7
Edinburgh Dr
Didcot OX11 200 F1
Kidlington OX5 109 A8
Edinburgh Way OX16 15 E6
Edington Pl OX12 196 D1
Edington Rd OX28 117 D8
Edington Sq OX28 117 D8
Edith Ct OX1 141 D1
Edith Moorhouse Prim Sch OX18 115 D2
Edith Rd OX1 141 C7
Edmonds Ct OX11 218 D8
Edmund Halley Rd OX4 142 B1
Edmund Rd OX4 142 C5
Edmunds Rd OX16 15 F5
Edon Bsns Pk OX33 145 A6
Edward Feild Prim Sch OX5 108 F7
Edward Rd OX1 141 E2
Edward St
Abingdon OX14 179 D7
Banbury OX16 16 F6
Edward Stone Rise OX7 42 D1
Edward Street Bsns Ctr OX16 16 F6
Edwin Ct OX2 122 F1
Edwin Rd OX11 218 D7
EF International Language Sch OX3 124 A2
Egerton Cl NN13 24 A7
Egerton Rd
Oxford OX4 142 A4
Wallingford OX10 221 C7
Eglin St OX25 63 A8
Egrove Cl OX1 141 E4
Eighth Ave OX3 142 F8
Eighth St OX11 217 B3
Elbourne OX11 218 C8
Elder Cl RG31 257 C1
Elderdene OX39 168 D8
Elderfield Cres OX11 235 D8
Elderfield Rd OX27 65 F7
Elder Way OX4 142 F1
Eldridge Cl OX14 159 F2
Eleanor Cl OX4 142 B4
Electric Ave OX2 141 A8
Eleventh St OX11 217 B2
Eliot Cl RG4 259 A4
Elizabeth Ave OX14 160 C2
Elizabeth Cl RG9 254 A8
Elizabeth Ct RG10 255 E2
Elizabeth Dr OX12 214 D6
Elizabeth Jennings Way OX2 123 A6
Elizabeth Rd
Henley-on-Thames RG9 254 B8
Stokenchurch HP14 188 F4
Elizabeth Rise OX16 16 B4
Ellesmere Cl RG4 259 B3
Ellesmere Rd OX4 142 A4
Elliots Way RG4 259 B2
Ellison Dr OX15 8 F1
Ell's La OX15 21 C7
Elm Bridge Rdbt OX10 203 D4
Elm Cl
Ambrosden OX25 81 C4
Bicester OX26 65 E4
Carterton OX18 115 F4
Chinnor OX39 168 C5
Tetsworth OX9 166 B8
Wheatley OX33 144 C7
Witney OX28 117 E8
Elm Cres OX7 73 C4
Elmcroft RG8 249 C5
Elm Ct
Henley-on-Thames RG9 254 D7
Sonning Common RG4 252 F4
Elm Dr
Chinnor OX39 168 C5
Garsington OX44 143 D2
Elm Farm Cl OX12 214 D7
Elm Gr
Brize Norton OX18 116 C5
Kidlington OX5 108 F6
Milton-under-Wychwood OX7 70 B1
Elmhurst Rd RG8 249 C7
Elmhurst Way OX18 115 E5

Elm La OX25 . . . . 81 C4
Elmleigh Ct RG4 . . . . 259 C3
Elm Pl OX29 . . . . 120 C8
Elm Rd
  Faringdon SN7 . . . . 172 E3
  North Moreton OX11 . . . . 220 A8
  Tokers Green RG4 . . . . . 258 D7
  Wantage OX12 . . . . 214 F6
Elmscote Rd OX16 . . . . . . 16 D2
Elms Dr OX3 . . . . 124 A5
Elmsfield Farm Ind Est
  OX7 . . . . 42 D3
Elmside SN7 . . . . 193 A5
Elms Par OX2 . . . . 122 D1
Elms Rd
  Cassington OX29 . . . . . . 107 C2
  Oxford OX2 . . . . 122 D1
  Thame OX9 . . . . 147 F8
Elms The
  Highworth SN6 . . . . 190 A5
  Langford GL7 . . . . 132 D1
Elmstone Dr RG31 . . . . . . 257 C1
Elms Way RG9 . . . . 224 D3
Elmthorpe Rd OX2 . . . . . . 122 E8
Elm Tree Cl
  Blackthorn OX25 . . . . . . 82 A4
  Oxford OX4 . . . . 142 B3
Elm Tree Farm OX25 . . . . 82 A4
Elm Trees HP18 . . . . 129 B7
Elm Tree Wlk OX13 . . . . . 159 C1
ELSFIELD 110 C1
Elsfield Rd OX3 . . . . 123 F6
Elsfield Way OX2 . . . . . . 109 B1
Elsley Rd RG31 . . . . 257 E3
Elstow Ave RG4 . . . . 259 C6
Elstree Rd RG31 . . . . 257 D2
Elswith Cl OX12 . . . . 214 D8
Eltham Ave RG4 . . . . 259 E5
Elton Cl OX3 . . . . 125 B4
Elton Cres OX33 . . . . 144 C7
Elton Rd OX16 . . . . 16 E2
Elvendon La RG8 . . . . 250 C7
Elvendon Rd RG8 . . . . . . 249 D7
Elwes Cl OX14 . . . . 180 B8
Elwes Rd OX13 . . . . 178 D6
Ely Cl
  Abingdon OX14 . . . . 179 C6
  Carterton OX18 . . . . 115 E3
Elyham RG8 . . . . 257 B5
Emden Ho OX3 . . . . 124 D4
Emma La RG10 . . . . 255 E2
Emmanuel Christian Sch
  OX4 . . . . 142 B2
Emmens Cl RG8 . . . . 241 D3
Emmens La RG8 . . . . 241 E2
EMMER GREEN 259 B6
Emmer Green Ct RG4 . . . . 259 C5
Emmer Green Prim Sch
  RG4 . . . . 259 B6
EMMINGTON 149 A1
Emperor Gdns OX4 . . . . . 142 E1
Empstead Ct RG9 . . . . . . 244 D2
Eney Cl OX14 . . . . 160 C2
English at Oxford OX1 . . . 261 A3
English La RG9 . . . . 223 E1
ENSLOW 77 C1
ENSTONE 58 F6
Enstone Airfield Complex
  (Ind Est) OX7 . . . . 59 D8
Enstone Prim Sch OX7 . . . 58 F5
Enstone Rd
  Charlbury OX7 . . . . 73 B4
  Little Tew OX7 . . . . 45 A5
  Middle Barton OX7 . . . . . 60 E8
EP Collier Prim Sch 🔟
  RG1 . . . . 259 A1
EPS Ind Est OX17 . . . . . . 5 E8
EPWELL 13 B6
Epwell Rd OX15 . . . . 13 E6
Erica Cl
  Banbury OX16 . . . . 9 A1
  Oxford OX4 . . . . 142 F3
Eric Ave RG4 . . . . 259 A6
Ermont Way OX16 . . . . . . 16 F4
Ernest Rd OX11 . . . . 218 E8
Ernicote Cl OX25 . . . . 81 E4
Essex Rd OX9 . . . . 148 B7
Essex St OX4 . . . . 142 A7
Essex Way RG4 . . . . 253 A3
Ester Carling La RG9 . . . . 252 D8
Estover Way OX39 . . . . . . 168 B6
Ethelhelm Cl OX14 . . . . . 160 C3
Ethelred Ct OX3 . . . . 124 C4
Eton Cl OX28 . . . . 118 D7
European Sch Culham The
  (Schola Europaea)
  OX14 . . . . 180 C4
Evans Cl OX29 . . . . 120 E8
Evans Ct OX5 . . . . 108 F8
Evans La OX5 . . . . 108 F8
Evans Rd OX29 . . . . 120 E8
Evans Yd 🔽 OX26 . . . . . . 65 E2
Evelin Rd OX14 . . . . 159 E1
Evelyn Cl OX2 . . . . 140 B8
Evenley Rd NN13 . . . . . . 24 D1
Evenlode Cl OX16 . . . . . . 16 B7
Evenlode Cl
  Bicester OX26 . . . . 65 D1
  Charlbury OX7 . . . . 73 B4
  Grove OX12 . . . . 196 D1
  North Leigh OX29 . . . . . 105 B6
Evenlode Cres OX5 . . . . . 92 A2
Evenlode Ct OX28 . . . . . . 118 B8
Evenlode Dr
  Berinsfield OX10 . . . . . . 182 C6

Evenlode Dr continued
  Didcot OX11 . . . . 200 F1
  Long Hanborough OX29 . . . 90 A1
Evenlode Pk OX26 . . . . . . 65 D2
Evenlode Pl OX26 . . . . . . 65 D2
Evenlode Twr OX4 . . . . . . 142 E1
Everard Cl 🔟 OX3 . . . . . . 124 D1
Eversley Cl OX7 . . . . 57 B1
Evesham Rd RG4 . . . . . . 259 B5
Ewart Cl OX26 . . . . 65 D2
EWELME 204 F4
Ewelme CE Prim Sch
  OX10 . . . . 204 F3
Ewelme Watercress Beds
  Nature Reserve★
  OX10 . . . . 204 D4
Ewert Pl OX2 . . . . 123 B6
Ewin Cl OX3 . . . . 123 F5
Ewin Ct OX3 . . . . 123 F5
Exbourne Rd OX14 . . . . . 179 D7
Exe Cl OX11 . . . . 200 F1
Exeter Coll OX1 . . . . 261 B2
Exeter Ct
  Didcot OX11 . . . . 219 B8
  🟧 Kidlington OX5 . . . . . 108 F8
Exeter Rd OX5 . . . . 92 E1
EXLADE STREET 251 B8
Eynsford Cl RG4 . . . . 259 E5
EYNSHAM 120 E7
Eynsham Ct OX29 . . . . . . 105 D5
Eynsham Prim Sch OX29 120 F8
Eynsham Rd
  Cassington OX29 . . . . . . 107 C2
  Farmoor OX2 . . . . 121 E1
  Oxford OX2 . . . . 140 B8
  Sutton OX29 . . . . 120 A2
Eyot Pl OX4 . . . . 141 E7
Eyres Cl OX10 . . . . 204 D4
Eyre's La OX10 . . . . 204 E5
Eyston Way OX14 . . . . . . 179 C7

F

Faber Cl OX4 . . . . 142 C2
Fairacres OX14 . . . . 179 C7
Fairacres Rd
  Didcot OX11 . . . . 218 E8
  Oxford OX4 . . . . 141 F6
Fairacres Shopping & Trad
  Est OX4 . . . . 179 C6
Fair Cl OX26 . . . . 65 F4
Fairfax Av OX3 . . . . 123 E4
Fairfax Cl
  Banbury OX16 . . . . 16 A5
  Reading RG4 . . . . 259 B3
  Thame OX9 . . . . 148 A8
Fairfax Ctr OX5 . . . . 108 F6
Fairfax Gate OX33 . . . . . . 144 C8
Fairfax Rd
  Chalgrove OX44 . . . . . . 184 D6
  Kidlington OX5 . . . . 108 F6
  Oxford OX4 . . . . 142 E6
Fairfield
  Cholsey OX10 . . . . 220 F1
  Standlake OX29 . . . . . . 136 F8
Fairfield Cl OX12 . . . . . . 214 D8
Fairfield Dr OX28 . . . . . . 117 F7
Fairfield Pl
  Abingdon OX14 . . . . 179 E8
  🟥 Carterton OX18 . . . . . 115 F5
Fairfield Rd RG8 . . . . 249 D7
Fairford Rd RG31 . . . . . . 257 C6
Fairford Way OX26 . . . . . 66 A4
Fairhaven Rd OX27 . . . . . 65 F7
Fairlawn End OX2 . . . . . . 122 F8
Fairlawn Flats OX2 . . . . . 122 F8
Fairlawn Wharf OX14 . . . . 179 F6
Fairlie Rd OX4 . . . . 142 B3
Fairmile Ct RG9 . . . . 244 D3
Fairspear Rd OX29 . . . . . 86 C3
Fairthorne Way SN6 . . . . 209 B6
Fair View OX3 . . . . 142 D7
Fairview Rd OX16 . . . . . . 16 D4
Fairview Trad Est RG9 . . . 254 F8
Fairways OX1 . . . . 160 E7
Fairway The OX16 . . . . . . 16 A6
Falcon Cl
  Banbury OX16 . . . . 16 A4
  Carterton OX18 . . . . 115 C3
  Oxford OX4 . . . . 142 D2
Falcon Mead OX26 . . . . . 81 A8
Falcon Villas OX7 . . . . . . 73 C5
Falkland Ho 🔟 OX18 . . . . 115 E2
Falkland Rd RG4 . . . . 259 B2
Falkner's Cl OX17 . . . . . . 23 A4
Fallowfield Cl RG4 . . . . . . 259 B4
Fallowfield Cres OX28 . . . 104 D1
Fallowfields OX26 . . . . . . 65 F2
Fallowfields Ct 🔳 OX26 . . 65 F2
Fallow Way OX16 . . . . . . 16 E2
Falstaff Cl OX29 . . . . 120 E8
Fane Cl OX26 . . . . 65 D4
Fane Dr OX10 . . . . 182 D6
Fane Ho 🔳 OX26 . . . . . . 65 E2
Fane Rd OX3 . . . . 123 E5
Fanshawe Pl OX4 . . . . . . 142 E5
Fanshawe Rd OX9 . . . . . . 148 B8
Faraday Ave OX11 . . . . . . 217 B2
Farbury End OX7 . . . . 29 B3
FARINGDON 172 E3
Faringdon Com Coll SN7 172 L1
Faringdon Inf Sch SN7 . . . 172 L4
Faringdon Jun Sch SN7 . . 172 F4
Faringdon L Ctr SN7 . . . . 172 F1

Faringdon Rd
  Abingdon, Gozzard's Ford
    OX13 . . . . 159 A2
  Abingdon OX14 . . . . 179 D8
  Cumnor OX2 . . . . 139 E2
  Gozzard's Ford OX13 . . . . 158 C2
  Kingston Bagpuize OX13 . . 156 E1
  Shrivenham SN6 . . . . . . 209 C2
  Stanford in the Vale SN7 . . 194 D7
  Watchfield SN6 . . . . 191 E1
  West Challow OX12 . . . . 213 E6
Farleigh Mews RG4 . . . . . 259 E5
Farleigh Rd SN6 . . . . 209 A6
Farley Cl OX29 . . . . 89 C8
Farley La OX29 . . . . 89 D8
Farlington Rd OX13 . . . . . 176 A8
Farman Cres GL54 . . . . . . 68 A4
Farm Cl
  Aston OX18 . . . . 135 E2
  Chalgrove OX44 . . . . . . 184 E6
  Ickford HP18 . . . . 127 F3
  Kidlington OX5 . . . . 92 F2
  Purley on Thames RG8 . . . 257 C5
  Sandford-on-Thames OX4 . 142 F1
  Sonning Common RG4 . . . 252 E5
Farm Close La OX33 . . . . . 144 B8
Farm Close Rd OX33 . . . . 144 B8
Farm Ct SN6 . . . . 227 D4
Farm End
  Grove OX12 . . . . 214 D8
  Woodstock OX20 . . . . . . 91 A7
Farmer Pl OX3 . . . . 123 F4
Farmers Cl OX28 . . . . 104 B2
Farmfield Rd
  Banbury OX16 . . . . 16 D3
  Calthorpe OX16 . . . . . . 16 D3
Farmhouse Cl OX29 . . . . . 138 A8
Farmhouse Mdw OX28 . . . 117 E7
Farmhouse Mews OX49 . . 186 B2
Farmiloe Cl RG8 . . . . 257 C4
Farmington Dr OX28 . . . . 117 E8
Farm La OX29 . . . . 103 D5
Farm Mill La OX28 . . . . . 118 B7
FARMOOR 121 C3
Farmoor Ct OX2 . . . . 121 C2
Farm Piece SN7 . . . . 194 D7
Farm Pl OX39 . . . . 149 E1
Farm Rd
  Abingdon OX14 . . . . 159 F2
  Brackley NN13 . . . . 24 A6
  Churchill OX7 . . . . 55 C8
  Goring RG8 . . . . 249 C6
  Henley-on-Thames RG9 . . . 254 F8
Farmstead Cl OX12 . . . . . 196 D1
Farm Way OX16 . . . . 16 F3
FARNBOROUGH 3 F8
Farnborough Hall★ OX17 . 3 E7
Farndon Rd OX2 . . . . 123 B4
Farnham Ct 🔟 OX5 . . . . . 108 F8
Farnham Dr RG4 . . . . 259 E4
Farriers Cl OX27 . . . . 52 C6
Farrier's Mead OX25 . . . . 80 A4
Farriers Mews OX14 . . . . 180 A7
Farriers Rd OX7 . . . . 60 E8
Farthings The OX13 . . . . . 178 C7
Faulder Ave OX18 . . . . . . 115 D3
Faulkner St OX1 . . . . 261 B1
Fawkner Way SN7 . . . . . . 194 D7
FAWLER
  Finstock 88 E7
  Uffington 211 F5
Fawler La OX7 . . . . 88 D7
Fawler Rd
  Charlbury OX7 . . . . 73 C2
  Uffington OX12, SN7 . . . . 211 E6
FAWLEY 226 D2
FAWLEY BOTTOM 226 B2
Fawley Bottom La RG9 . . . 226 B1
Fawley Cl OX12 . . . . 214 D6
Fawley Court Mus★ RG9 244 F5
FAWLEY GREEN 226 D2
Featherbed La
  Bishopstone SN6 . . . . . . 227 E6
  East Hendred OX12 . . . . 216 F8
  Milton Hill OX13 . . . . . . 199 A1
  Mixbury NN13 . . . . 38 D5
Feathers Yd 🔁 OX10 . . . . 221 D7
Feilden Cl OX29 . . . . 118 B4
Feilden Gr OX3 . . . . 124 A3
Fells Cl HP18 . . . . 129 D6
Feltwell Cl OX18 . . . . 115 E3
FENCOTT 95 D5
Fencott Rd OX5 . . . . 95 A4
Fenlock Ct OX29 . . . . 90 F1
Fenlock Rd OX29 . . . . 90 F1
Fennel Way OX14 . . . . . . 180 C8
Fenny Compton Rd OX17 . 1 D1
Fenway OX25 . . . . 48 A1
Ferguson Pl OX14 . . . . . . 180 C8
Ferguson Rd OX16 . . . . . . 16 E7
Fermi Ave OX11 . . . . 217 A1
Fernbrook Rd RG4 . . . . . . 258 E5
Ferndale Cl
  Reading RG31 . . . . 257 E3
  Stokenchurch HP14 . . . . 188 E4
Ferndale Ho OX16 . . . . . . 15 F7
Ferndale Sch 🔟 SN7 . . . . 172 F3
Ferndale St OX7 . . . . 173 A4
Ferne Cl RG8 . . . . 249 C2
Fern Glen RG31 . . . . 257 C1
Ferngrove 🟨 SN7 . . . . . . 172 F3
FERNHAM 193 A4
Fernham Gate SN7 . . . . . 172 E1
Fernham Rd
  Faringdon SN7 . . . . 172 E1
  Little Coxwell SN7 . . . . . 192 E8
  Longcot SN7 . . . . 192 D2
  Shellingford SN7 . . . . . . 193 D6

Fernhill Cl
  Kidlington OX5 . . . . 108 D8
  Milcombe OX15 . . . . 21 A2
  Tiddington OX9 . . . . 146 A6
Fernhill Rd OX5 . . . . 108 A8
Fern Hill Rd OX4 . . . . 142 E5
Fern La OX18 . . . . 115 F5
Ferny Cl OX14 . . . . 160 E3
Ferriston OX16 . . . . 9 A1
Ferry Ct OX14 . . . . 179 F6
Ferry Hinksey Rd OX2 . . . 123 A1
Ferry La
  Goring RG8 . . . . 249 B6
  Moulsford OX10 . . . . . . 239 A4
  South Stoke OX10, RG8 . . 239 B4
  Wargrave RG10 . . . . . . 255 C2
Ferry Mills OX2 . . . . 141 A8
Ferry Pool Rd OX2 . . . . . 123 C6
Ferry Rd
  Marston OX3 . . . . 123 F3
  South Stoke RG8 . . . . . . 239 B4
Ferry Sports Ctr RG6 . . . . 259 C6
Ferry Way OX10 . . . . 239 B8
Ferry Wlk OX14 . . . . 179 F6
Fetti Pl OX12 . . . . 214 F6
Fettiplace OX7 . . . . 70 B1
Fettiplace Cl OX13 . . . . . 158 A7
Fettiplace Rd
  Marcham OX13 . . . . 178 D6
  Oxford OX3 . . . . 124 C5
  Witney OX28 . . . . 117 E8
FEWCOTT 50 C5
Fewcott Gn OX27 . . . . . . 50 C4
Fewcott Rd OX27 . . . . . . 49 F7
FIDDLERS HILL 85 D6
Fiddlers Hill OX7 . . . . 85 E6
Fidlers Wlk RG10 . . . . . . 255 E2
FIELD ASSARTS 102 F8
Field Ave OX4 . . . . 142 F2
Field Cl
  Ickford HP18 . . . . 128 A3
  Kidlington OX5 . . . . 108 F8
  Kingston Bagpuize OX13 . . 156 D1
  Stonesfield OX29 . . . . . . 89 C8
  Yarnton OX5 . . . . 108 B6
Field Ct OX25 . . . . 47 C5
Fielden Cl OX10 . . . . 204 D2
Field End
  Long Crendon HP18 . . . . 129 F5
  Wargrave RG10 . . . . . . 255 F2
Fielden Rd OX10 . . . . 204 D2
Fieldfare Cl OX26 . . . . . . 65 F1
Fieldfare Rd OX4 . . . . 161 E8
Field Farm Bsns Ctr OX6 . 67 A5
Field Gdns
  East Challow OX12 . . . . 213 F5
  Steventon OX13 . . . . . . 199 A5
Field Ho OX2 . . . . 140 C8
Field House Dr OX2 . . . . . 123 A8
Field La OX44 . . . . 144 B3
Fieldmere Cl OX28 . . . . . 117 F8
Field Rd
  Kingham OX7 . . . . 54 F3
  Murcott OX5 . . . . 96 A5
Fieldside
  Abingdon OX14 . . . . 159 D1
  East Hagbourne OX11 . . . 219 A5
  Long Wittenham OX14 . . . 201 C8
  Upton OX11 . . . . 218 C2
Field St OX26 . . . . 65 E2
Field The OX13 . . . . 158 F6
Field View RG4 . . . . 259 B3
Fiennes Rd
  Banbury OX16 . . . . 16 A5
  Oxford OX4 . . . . 142 A3
FIFIELD 69 C2
Fifield Farm Barns OX10. 204 C5
Fifteenth St OX11 . . . . . . 217 A2
Fifth Ave NN13 . . . . 36 E7
Fifth St NN13 . . . . 36 E7
Fifth Street E NN13 . . . . . 36 E7
FILCHAMPSTEAD 139 C8
FILKINS 132 C5
Filkins Rd GL7 . . . . 132 C2
Finch Cl OX3 . . . . 124 C1
Finchdale Cl OX18 . . . . . . 115 D3
Finches La SN8 . . . . 245 E1
Finches The SN8 . . . . 245 C2
Finchley La OX25 . . . . . . 65 D1
Finham Brook OX11 . . . . . 200 F3
Finlay Dr RG9 . . . . 244 E2
Finlay Ho RG9 . . . . 244 E3
FINMERE 39 D6
Finmere CE Prim Sch
  MK18 . . . . 39 D6
Finmore Cl 🔳 OX14 . . . . . 179 E8
Finmore Rd OX2 . . . . 140 D8
Finsbury Pl OX7 . . . . 42 E3
FINSTOCK 88 C5
Finstock CE Prim Sch
  OX7 . . . . 88 C5
Finstock Sta OX7 . . . . . . 88 D7
Fir Cl OX10 . . . . 240 D7
Fircroft
  Banbury OX16 . . . . 16 D4
  Bicester OX26 . . . . 65 F5
Fircroft Cl RG31 . . . . 257 C1
Firebrass Hill OX10 . . . . . 204 F5
Fir La OX25 . . . . 48 B1
Firs Cl OX7 . . . . 54 D2
Firs Mdw OX4 . . . . 161 E8
First Ave
  Didcot OX11 . . . . 200 D2
  Oxford OX3 . . . . 142 F8
Firs The
  Oxford OX2 . . . . 123 B8
  Wroxton OX15 . . . . 15 A8

First St
  Croughton NN13 . . . . . . 36 F6
  Harwell OX11 . . . . 217 C2
First Turn OX2 . . . . 122 F8
Fir Tree Ave OX10 . . . . . . 221 B8
Firtree Cl OX16 . . . . 8 F1
Fir Tree Cl OX13 . . . . 156 E1
Fir Tree Cotts RG20 . . . . . 235 A2
Fir Tree Jun Sch OX10 . . . 221 B8
Fir Tree Paddock RG20. . . 235 A2
Fir Trees OX14 . . . . 160 E7
Fisher Cl
  Banbury OX16 . . . . 16 F8
  Drayton OX14 . . . . 179 A1
Fishermans Wharf OX14. . 179 F4
Fisher Row OX1 . . . . 261 A2
Fishers Cl OX29 . . . . 104 A6
Fishers Cotts RG4 . . . . . . 259 C6
Fishers Ct RG4 . . . . 259 C6
Fisher's La OX7 . . . . 73 B3
Fish Ponds OX9 . . . . 129 E1
Fitchett Yd OX14 . . . . . . 179 E7
Fitzcount Way OX10 . . . . 203 D1
Fitzharry's Rd OX14 . . . . 179 F8
Fitzharrys Sch OX14 . . . . 159 F1
Fitzherbert Cl OX4 . . . . . 141 F4
Fitzwaryn Sch OX12 . . . . 214 C6
Five Acre RG31 . . . . 257 B1
Fiveacres OX5 . . . . 95 E4
Five Acres Prim Sch
  OX25 . . . . 81 D4
Five Mile Dr OX2 . . . . . . 109 A1
Fiveways Cl SN6 . . . . 245 E1
Flambards 🔟 RG4 . . . . . . 259 C2
Flatford Pl OX5 . . . . 92 C2
Flavius Gate NN13 . . . . . 24 A7
Flaxfield Rd OX4 . . . . 142 F2
Fleet Way OX11 . . . . 219 A8
Fleetwood Way OX9 . . . . 129 F2
Fleming Cl
  Bicester OX26 . . . . 65 C4
  Middle Barton OX7 . . . . . 60 F8
Fleming Dr OX7 . . . . 60 F8
Flemings Rd OX20 . . . . . . 91 C6
Flemming Ave OX44 . . . . 184 C7
Fletcher Cl
  Faringdon SN7 . . . . 173 A3
  Yarnton OX5 . . . . 108 B5
Fletcher Rd OX4 . . . . 142 E6
Flexney Pl OX3 . . . . 124 D1
Flexneys Paddock OX29 . 138 A8
Flight Hill OX7 . . . . 46 B7
Flint Hollow OX39 . . . . . . 168 B6
Flint St HP17 . . . . 130 F5
Floral Cl OX12 . . . . 214 E8
Florence Cl OX5 . . . . 108 F8
FLORENCE PARK 142 B5
Florence Park Rd OX4. . . . 142 B5
Florey's Cl OX29 . . . . 104 C6
Flower's Hill RG8 . . . . . . 256 C5
Floyd's Row OX1 . . . . . . 261 B1
Fludger Cl OX10 . . . . 221 C7
Fluellen Pl OX26 . . . . 65 D5
Fogwell Rd OX2 . . . . 122 B1
Foliat Cl OX12 . . . . 214 E5
Foliat Dr OX12 . . . . 214 E5
Folland Cl OX7 . . . . 42 F4
Follets Cl OX5 . . . . 108 B5
Folly Bridge Ct OX1 . . . . 261 B1
Folly Cl SN6 . . . . 190 A7
Folly Cres
  Highworth SN6 . . . . 190 A7
  Watchfield SN6 . . . . 191 A1
Folly Ct OX15 . . . . 19 C7
Folly Dr SN6 . . . . 190 A7
Folly Gn RG8 . . . . 250 E8
Folly Orchard Rd RG8 . . . 240 E1
Folly View Cres SN7. . . . . 172 E2
Folly View Rd SN7 . . . . . 172 F2
Folly Way SN6 . . . . 190 A7
Ford La
  Drayton St Leonard
    OX10 . . . . 183 B6
  Frilford OX13 . . . . 178 A7
Fords Cl OX33 . . . . 143 C4
Ford's Cl HP14 . . . . 189 F8
FORDWELLS 102 D8
Fordy La OX12 . . . . 216 D6
Forest Cl
  Launton OX26 . . . . 66 D2
  Milton-under-Wychwood
    OX7 . . . . 70 B2
Foresters
  Beacon's Bottom HP14 . . . 189 C5
  Chinnor OX39 . . . . 168 B6
Foresters Tower OX3 . . . . 124 E1
Forest Farm Oxford
  Montessori Sch OX3 . . . 110 D2
FOREST HILL 125 F4
Forest Hill RG30 . . . . 257 F2
Forest Rd
  Charlbury OX7 . . . . 73 A4
  Oxford OX3 . . . . 124 F3
Forest Row OX10 . . . . . . 222 D3
Forestry Hos OX49 . . . . . 207 A7
Forest Side OX1 . . . . 141 D2
Forge Cl
  Benson OX10 . . . . 203 F4
  Horton-cum-Studley OX33. 112 B5
  Marsh Gibbon OX27 . . . . 67 F3
  Merton OX25 . . . . 95 D8
  Reading RG4 . . . . 259 C2
Forge La OX17 . . . . 3 E1
Forge Pl OX27 . . . . 49 F7
Forget-me-not Way 🔟
  OX4 . . . . 142 F1
Forgeway OX16 . . . . 9 A1
Forrest Cl SN6 . . . . 209 A6

Forster La OX2. . . . . 139 E4
Forsters La OX12. . . . . . 231 E6
Forsythia Cl OX26. . . . . . 65 E5
Forsythia Wlk OX16. . . . . .9 B1
Fortescue Dr OX26. . . . . 80 A7
Forties The OX44. . . . . . 145 A2
Fortnam Cl OX3. . . . . . . 124 B3
Forty Cross OX11. . . . . . 237 A8
Forty Gn HP27. . . . . . . 149 F3
FORTY GREEN 149 F3
Forty The
　Bishopstone SN6. . . . . .227 D5
　Cholsey OX10. . . . . 220 F2
FOSCOT 69 D8
Foscote Hospl The (Private)
　OX16. . . . . 16 D4
Foscote Rise OX16. . . . . 16 E4
Fosseway Cl GL7. . . . . . 150 C5
Fosseway The OX18. . . . 116 C3
Foster Rd OX14. . . . . . . 159 F3
Fothergill Pl OX9. . . . . . 147 F8
Foudry Cl OX11. . . . . . . 201 A2
Foundry St OX16. . . . . . . 16 C6
Fountain Ct OX14. . . . . . 179 F8
FOUR POINTS 247 E2
Fourteenth St OX11. . . . 217 B3
Fourth Ave
　Croughton NN13. . . . . . . 36 E6
　Oxford OX3. . . . . 142 F8
Fourth St
　Croughton NN13. . . . . . . 36 E6
　Harwell OX11. . . . . 217 B3
Fowler Rd OX16. . . . . 16 E7
Fowlers Ct OX7. . . . . 43 A3
Fowlers Farm Rd HP14. . . 188 E4
Fowler's Rd OX7. . . . . . . 55 A4
Foxborough Rd OX14. . . . 160 E2
Foxburrow Cl OX29. . . . . 120 A1
Foxburrow La OX29. . . . . 103 F4
Foxbury La 2 OX18. . . . . 115 E5
Fox Cl
　Bampton OX18. . . . . 134 F3
　Chipping Norton OX7. . . . . 42 F2
　Garsington OX44. . . . . . . 143 D2
　Hailey OX29. . . . . 104 A4
Foxcombe Ct OX14. . . . . 179 C8
FOXCOMBE HILL 159 F8
Foxcombe La OX1. . . . . . 141 A1
Foxcombe Rd
　Boars Hill OX1. . . . . 140 F1
　Sunningwell OX1. . . . . . . 141 A2
Fox Cover OX39. . . . . . . 168 C6
Fox Cres OX1. . . . . 141 E5
Foxcroft Dr OX18. . . . . . 115 D1
Foxden Way OX17. . . . . . . 9 D7
Foxdown Cl OX5. . . . . 92 E1
Foxfield OX7. . . . . 42 F2
Foxfield Ct OX7. . . . . 42 F2
Fox Furlong OX4. . . . . . . 142 A1
Foxglove Cl
　Bicester OX26 . . . . 65 E4
　7 Sandford-on-Thames
　　OX4. . . . . 142 E1
Foxglove La OX11. . . . . . 218 D4
Foxglove Rd OX5. . . . . . 108 B8
Foxhall Manor Pk OX11. 200 D2
Foxhall Rd OX11. . . . . . 200 D1
Fox Hill OX5. . . . . 77 A7
Foxhill Cl RG4. . . . . 260 A5
Foxhill La
　Reading RG4. . . . . 259 E6
　Souldern OX27. . . . . 35 E3
Foxholes Nature Reserve★
　OX7. . . . . 69 E5
Fox La
　Bicester OX26 . . . . 65 D1
　Middle Barton OX7. . . . . . 60 E8
　Souldern OX27. . . . . 35 E3
　Wootton OX1. . . . . 159 D7
Foxton Cl OX2. . . . . 108 F1
Foxtowns Gn OX5. . . . . . 78 A5
Foxwell Dr OX3. . . . . . . 124 C5
Foxwood OX18. . . . . 135 E3
Foxwood Cl
　Aston OX18. . . . . 135 E3
　Banbury OX16. . . . . 16 C2
Foxwood La OX18. . . . . . 114 C6
Framlands Cl OX12. . . . . 214 B5
Framlingham Dr RG4. . . . 259 C1
Frampton Cl RG5. . . . . . 260 E1
Frances Rd OX7. . . . . 60 F8
Francis Little Dr OX14. . . 179 D6
Frank Cook Ct OX5. . . . . 92 F1
Franklin Cl
　Chalgrove OX44. . . . . . . 184 D6
　Kidlington OX5. . . . . 92 F1
Franklin Rd OX3. . . . . . . 124 B3
Franklyn Cl OX14. . . . . . 159 F2
Frank's La OX13. . . . . . . 198 F4
Frank Wise Sch OX16. . . . 16 B5
Fraser Ave RG4. . . . . . . 259 C6
Fraser Cl OX16. . . . . 16 E6
Fraser Gdns OX10. . . . . . 221 C6
Frax Cl OX13. . . . . 156 F1
Frederick Rd OX4. . . . . . 142 D4
Freeborn Cl OX5. . . . . . . 92 F2
Freehold St OX25. . . . . . . 62 D6
FREELAND 106 A7
Freeland CE Prim Sch
　OX29. . . . . 106 A7
Freelands Cotts OX33. . . 125 D7
Freelands Rd OX4. . . . . . 141 F5
Freeman Rd OX11. . . . . . 200 C1
Freemans Cl SN7. . . . . . 211 C7
Freemans Rd OX15. . . . . 22 E8
Frenchay Rd OX2. . . . . . 123 A5
French Cl OX28. . . . . . . 117 F7

French Laurence Way
　OX44. . . . . 184 D6
Frensham Cl OX16. . . . . . 9 A1
Frethern Cl OX18. . . . . . 100 E4
Frewin Ct OX1. . . . . 261 B2
Friars Cl SN6. . . . . 209 A6
Friar's Ct OX18. . . . . . . 152 F6
Friars' Entry OX1. . . . . . 261 B2
Friars Furlong HP18. . . . 129 B7
Friars Wharf OX1. . . . . . 261 B1
Friday Ct OX9. . . . . 129 F1
Friday La OX33. . . . . . . 144 B8
Friday St RG9. . . . . 244 E2
Friends' Cl OX29. . . . . . . 89 C7
Frieze Way OX5. . . . . . . 108 F4
FRILFORD 178 A7
Frilford Rd OX13. . . . . . 178 C6
Frilsham St OX14. . . . . . 200 A7
FRINGFORD 52 D6
Fringford CE Prim Sch
　OX27. . . . . 52 C6
Frith The OX11. . . . . . . 201 B2
Fritillary Mews OX29. . . . 118 C3
FRITWELL 49 F7
Fritwell St OX2. . . . . 49 E7
Fritwell CE Prim Sch
　OX27. . . . . 49 F7
Fritwell Rd OX27. . . . . . . 50 B1
Frog La
　Bloxham OX15. . . . . 21 D4
　Milton-under-Wychwood
　　OX7. . . . . 70 B1
Frogmore La
　Long Crendon HP18. . . . . 129 C5
　Stanford in the Vale SN7. . 194 E8
FROGS' ISLAND 202 C2
Frome Rd OX11. . . . . . . 217 C1
Frouds Cl OX12. . . . . . . 213 C4
Fruitlands OX29. . . . . . . 120 D8
Fry Ct RG4. . . . . 259 B3
Frys Hill OX4. . . . . 142 E1
Fuchsia Wlk OX16. . . . . . .9 B1
FULBROOK 100 F7
Fullbrook Cres RG31. . . . 257 D3
Fullers Field OX44. . . . . 145 C2
Fullers Rd OX11. . . . . . . 219 E1
Fullwell Cl OX14. . . . . . 159 F1
Fulmar Ct OX26. . . . . . . 66 B4
Fulmar Pl OX12. . . . . . . 196 D1
FULWELL
　Enstone. 58 F3
　Westbury. 25 A2
Fulwell Rd
　Finmere MK18. . . . . 39 C7
　Westbury NN13. . . . . 25 A4
Furlong Cl OX4. . . . . 142 D3
Furlong Row OX18. . . . . 152 E8
Furlongs The OX9. . . . . . 147 C6
Furlong The OX29. . . . . . 137 B6
FYFIELD
　Kingston Bagpuize. 157 C2
　Lechlade-on-Thames. 131 B4
Fyfield Cl OX12. . . . . . . 214 F4
Fyfield Rd OX2. . . . . 123 C4

G

Gadge Cl OX9. . . . . 129 E1
GAGINGWELL 59 F7
GAINFIELD 174 F3
Gainsborough Cres RG9. . 254 C8
Gainsborough Gn OX14. . . 179 E5
Gainsborough Hill RG9. . 254 D8
Gainsborough Rd RG9. . . 254 C8
Gaisford Rd OX4. . . . . . . 142 C4
Gales Ct GL7. . . . . 150 C4
Galingale Dr OX26. . . . . . 65 E4
Gall Cl OX14. . . . . 180 C8
Galley Field OX14. . . . . . 180 B8
GALLOWSTREE
　COMMON. 252 C5
Gallowstree Rd RG9. . . . 252 E7
Galpin Cl OX14. . . . . 142 A7
Galsworthy Dr RG4. . . . . 259 E5
Gangsdown Hill RG9. . . . 223 E4
Gap The RG4. . . . . 259 A3
Gap Way RG8. . . . . 250 E8
Garage Yd OX7. . . . . 70 A5
GARDEN CITY. 108 E5
Garden City OX9. . . . . . 148 B7
Garden Cl
　Banbury OX16. . . . . 16 C7
　Didcot OX11. . . . . 218 C7
Gardens Cl HP14. . . . . . 188 F4
Gardens The
　Langford GL7. . . . . 132 D2
　South Stoke RG8. . . . . . 239 C3
Garde Rd RG4. . . . . 260 E3
Gardiner Cl
　Abingdon OX14. . . . . 180 C8
　Wheatley OX33. . . . . 144 B8
Gardiner St OX3. . . . . . . 124 D2
GARFORD 177 D5
Garford Cl OX14. . . . . . . 160 B2
Garford Rd OX2. . . . . . . 123 C5
Garner Cl OX18. . . . . . . 115 C5
Garne's La OX18. . . . . . . 100 F6
GARSINGTON 143 E1
Garsington CE Prim Sch
　OX44. . . . . 143 E2
Garsington Rd OX4. . . . . 142 E4
Garsons La OX10. . . . . . 240 E6
Garston Cl OX12. . . . . . . 214 E5
Garston Ct OX18. . . . . . . 116 B5
Garston La OX12. . . . . . 214 E5
Garth Rd OX11. . . . . . . 200 E1

Garth The
　Oxford OX2. . . . . 140 D8
　Yarnton OX5. . . . . 108 B6
Garton End
　Cray's Pond RG8. . . . . . 250 D6
　Whitchurch Hill RG8. . . . 250 E3
Gas Alley OX9. . . . . 148 A8
Gascoigne Way OX15. . . . 21 E2
Gaskells End RG4. . . . . . 258 D8
Gas La OX7. . . . . 85 D8
Gassons Mead OX18. . . . 133 C5
Gassons Rd GL7. . . . . . . 150 C5
Gassons The GL7. . . . . . 132 B5
Gassons Way GL7. . . . . . 150 C4
Gate Fernham SN7. . . . . 172 E1
Gatehampton Rd RG8. . . 249 C5
Gateley OX33. . . . . 143 D6
Gateridge St OX16. . . . . . 16 D5
Gauntlets Cl OX15. . . . . . 21 E5
Gaveston Gdns OX15. . . . 33 E4
Gaveston Rd OX11. . . . . 217 E7
Gavray Dr OX26. . . . . . . 66 B1
Gaydon Cl OX18. . . . . . . 115 E3
Gaydon Wlk 2 OX26. . . . 64 A4
Gayhurst Cl RG4. . . . . . . 259 D6
Gelt Burn OX11. . . . . . . 201 B2
Gentian Cl OX26. . . . . . . 65 D5
Gentian Rd OX4. . . . . . . 142 F2
Geoffrey Barbour Rd
　OX14. . . . . 179 F8
Geoffreyson Rd RG4. . . . 258 E5
Geoffrey Tuttle Dr OX10. 204 C2
George Moore Cl OX4. . . 142 A6
George Morland Ho 8
　OX14. . . . . 179 F6
George Rd HP14. . . . . . . 188 E5
George St
　Banbury OX16. . . . . 16 D5
　Bicester OX26 . . . . 65 D5
　Oxford OX1. . . . . 261 B2
　Reading RG1, RG4. . . . . 259 B1
George Street Mews
　OX1. . . . . 261 A2
Gerard Pl OX4. . . . . 142 C5
Germander Way OX26. . . . 65 D5
Gibbs Cres OX2. . . . . . . 261 A1
Gibbs Rd OX16. . . . . 16 E7
GIBRALTAR 77 B1
Gibson Cl OX14. . . . . . . 160 A3
Gibson Dr OX25. . . . . . . 63 C7
Gidley Way OX33. . . . . . 143 D6
Giernalls Rd OX39. . . . . 104 A6
Giffard Way HP18. . . . . . 129 C7
Gifford Cl RG4. . . . . 259 E5
Giles Cl OX4. . . . . 142 B2
Giles Ctr OX18. . . . . 115 E2
Giles Rd OX4. . . . . 142 C2
Gilkes Yd OX16. . . . . 16 B5
Gillett Cl OX16. . . . . 16 B5
Gillett Rd OX16. . . . . 16 B5
Gillians Way OX4. . . . . . 142 B5
Gillotts Cl RG9. . . . . . . 254 B8
Gillotts' Hill RG9. . . . . . 254 C7
Gillott's La RG9. . . . . . . 254 B7
Gillotts Sch RG9. . . . . . 254 B7
Ginge Brook OX14. . . . . 199 F8
Ginge Cl OX14. . . . . 160 B2
Ginge Rd OX12. . . . . . . 216 B5
Gipsy La
　Great Coxwell SN7. . . . . 192 C8
　Grove OX12. . . . . 214 F8
　Oxford OX3. . . . . 124 B1
　Reading RG30. . . . . 257 E1
Girdlestone Cl OX3. . . . . 124 D1
Girdlestone Rd OX3. . . . . 124 D1
Glades The OX26. . . . . . . 66 D2
Gladstone Ct OX3. . . . . . 124 E3
Gladstone Rd OX3. . . . . . 124 E3
Glamis Pl OX16. . . . . 15 F6
Glanville Cl OX16. . . . . . . 16 B6
Glanville Rd OX4. . . . . . 142 B7
Glean Cotts OX28. . . . . . 104 D1
Glebe Cl
　Ambrosden OX25. . . . . . . 81 D4
　Moulsford OX10. . . . . . . 238 F5
Glebe Cotts
　Postcombe OX9. . . . . . . 166 F4
　South Stoke RG8. . . . . . 239 C3
Glebe Ct OX25. . . . . 47 D5
Glebe Dr NN13. . . . . 24 A7
Glebe Gdns
　Grove OX12. . . . . 196 E1
　Sonning RG4. . . . . 260 E3
Glebe House Dr MK18. . . 25 E6
Glebe La RG4. . . . . 260 E3
Glebelands
　Bampton OX18. . . . . 134 E4
　Oxford OX3. . . . . 142 D7
Glebe Pl SN6. . . . . 190 A6
Glebe Rd
　Cumnor OX2. . . . . 139 E5
　Didcot OX11. . . . . 218 E4
　Purley on Thames RG8. . . 257 B5
　Stanford in the Vale SN7. . 194 D7
Glebe Ride RG8. . . . . . . 249 B6
Glebe St OX4. . . . . 123 F1
Glebe The
　Aldworth RG8 . . . . 247 F3
　Aynho OX17. . . . . 35 D7
　Culham OX14. . . . . 180 B3
　Cumnor OX2. . . . . 139 E5
　Highmoor Cross RG9. . . . 242 E5
　Hook Norton OX15. . . . . . 30 B8
　Lewknor OX49. . . . . 187 B8
　Standlake OX29. . . . . . . 137 C4

Glebe The continued
　West Challow OX12. . . . . 213 D5
　Wheatley OX33. . . . . 144 B8
Glen Cl OX27. . . . . 52 D1
Glenham Rd OX9. . . . . . . 148 B8
Glenmore Bsns Ctr OX29 103 C1
Glenmore Rd OX18. . . . . 115 D4
Glenrhondda RG4. . . . . . 258 F6
Gliffard Ho 5 RG4. . . . . . 259 C1
Glimbers Gr OX39. . . . . . 168 C5
Glissand Way OX18. . . . . 114 C6
Glory Farm Prim Sch
　OX26. . . . . 66 A4
Gloucester Court Mews
　OX28 . . . . 104 B1
Gloucester Gn OX1. . . . . 261 B2
Gloucester La OX1. . . . . 261 A2
Gloucester Mews 4
　SN7. . . . . 172 F4
Gloucester Pl OX28. . . . . 104 B1
Gloucester St
　Faringdon SN7. . . . . 172 F4
　Oxford OX1. . . . . 261 B2
Glover Mews OX20. . . . . . 91 B6
Glovers Cl
　Chipping Norton OX7. . . . . 42 E2
　Woodstock OX20. . . . . . . 91 C6
Glovers La OX17. . . . . . . 10 F1
Glyme Cl
　Abingdon OX14. . . . . 160 B1
　Woodstock OX20. . . . . . . 91 B7
Glyme Dr OX10. . . . . 182 D6
Glyme Way OX29. . . . . . 106 B8
GLYMPTON 75 D8
Glympton Rd OX20. . . . . . 75 E6
Glyn Ave OX11. . . . . 218 D8
Glyncastle RG4. . . . . 258 F5
Glyndebourne Gdns OX16 . 9 A1
Glyn Rd OX10. . . . . 203 D1
Glynswood OX39. . . . . . . 168 C6
Gobles Ct OX26. . . . . 65 F1
Goddards La OX7. . . . . . . 42 E3
Godfrey Cl
　6 Abingdon OX14. . . . . 179 E6
　Oxford OX3. . . . . 124 C1
Godfreys Cl
　Brill HP18. . . . . 98 B1
　Grove OX12. . . . . 196 F1
GODINGTON 53 E3
Godstow Cl RG5. . . . . . . 260 E1
Godstow Rd OX2. . . . . . . 122 D8
Godwyn Cl OX14. . . . . . . 179 E8
Goffe Cl OX9. . . . . 148 A8
Goggs The OX49. . . . . . . 186 A1
Golafre Rd OX14. . . . . . . 179 E5
Goldbury Cotts OX12. . . . 216 B4
Goldcrest Way OX26. . . . . 81 A8
GOLDEN BALLS 182 A8
Golden Cross OX1. . . . . . 261 B2
Golden Hills OX39. . . . . . 168 D6
Golden La OX7. . . . . 42 A5
Golden Rd OX4. . . . . 142 A7
Golden Villa Cl OX16. . . . . 16 A6
Golder's Cl HP18. . . . . . . 127 F3
Goldfinch Cl OX26. . . . . . 65 F1
Goldfinch La OX11. . . . . 221 A2
Goldsmith's Cl 3 OX26. . . 65 C4
Goldsmith's La OX10. . . . 221 D7
Goldsmith's Terr 7
　OX10. . . . . 221 D7
Gold St OX44. . . . . 163 F6
Gooch OX11. . . . . 200 E4
Goodall Cl RG9. . . . . 244 D1
Goodey Cl RG4. . . . . 142 C3
Goodlake Ave 2 SN7. . . . 172 F3
Goodliffe Gdns RG31. . . . 257 C4
Goodrich Cl RG4. . . . . . . 259 E5
Goodrington Cl OX16. . . . . 16 B6
Goodson Wlk OX3. . . . . . 123 F3
Goor La SN8. . . . . 245 C4
Gooseacre OX14. . . . . . . 160 E2
Goosecroft La RG8. . . . . 257 B5
Goose Gn OX15. . . . . 33 F5
Goose Green Cl OX2. . . . 122 E8
Goose La OX15. . . . . 22 D8
Goose Wlk OX15. . . . . . . 21 D4
GOOSEY 195 B4
GOOSEY GREEN 195 B4
Goosey La SN7. . . . . 195 A4
Gordon Cl OX3. . . . . 123 F5
Gordon Dr OX14. . . . . . . 160 C1
Gordon Pl RG30. . . . . . . 258 C1
Gordon Rd OX25. . . . . . . 63 C8
Gordon St OX1. . . . . 141 D6
Gordon Way OX28. . . . . . 118 A7
Gordon Woodward Way
　OX1. . . . . 141 D5
GORING 249 D6
Goring CE Prim Sch
　RG8. . . . . 249 C6
GORING HEATH 251 A3
Goring Lodge 7 OX1. . . . 141 C7
Goring Rd RG8. . . . . 250 E8
Goring & Streatley Sta
　RG8 . . . . 249 C6
Gorselands RG4. . . . . . . 259 A6
Gorse Leas OX3. . . . . . . 124 B5
Gorton Playne OX7. . . . . . 70 D1
Gorwell OX49. . . . . 186 B2
Gosbrook Ho 4 RG4. . . . . 259 C1
Gosbrook Rd RG4. . . . . . 259 B2
GOSFORD 108 F7
Gosford Cl OX5. . . . . 108 F6
Gosford Hill Ct OX5. . . . . 108 F7
Gosford Hill Sch OX5. . . . 108 F7
Goslyn Cl 3 OX3. . . . . . . 124 D1
Gossway Fields OX5. . . . . 78 A3

Gott Cl OX27. . . . . 66 A6
Goulders Cotts RG10. . . . 255 F7
Gouldland Gdns OX3. . . . 124 B5
Goulds Villas OX16. . . . . . 16 A5
GOZZARD'S FORD 158 E2
GRAFTON 152 C6
Grafton Ho OX39. . . . . . . 168 C7
Grafton Lodge 17 OX16. . . 16 D5
Grafton Orch OX11. . . . . 168 D7
Graham Cl OX11. . . . . . . 237 A8
Grahame Ave RG8. . . . . . 256 D5
Graham Rd OX26. . . . . . . 65 D3
Grainge Cl NN13. . . . . . . 25 A5
Grammar School Hill OX7 73 B3
Gramp's Hill OX12. . . . . . 231 E6
Grandison Ho RG9. . . . . . 244 E3
GRANDPONT 141 D7
Grandpont Pl OX1. . . . . . 261 B1
Grange Ave RG9. . . . . . . 253 A8
Grange Beck OX11. . . . . . 201 A3
Grange Cl
　Goring RG8. . . . . 249 B6
　Highworth SN6. . . . . 190 A5
Grange Ct OX2. . . . . 140 B8
Grange Farm Rd HP14. . . 189 B7
Grange La
　3 Carterton OX18. . . . . 115 E5
　Sibford Ferris OX15. . . . . 19 D7
Grange Mews OX26. . . . . 66 E2
Grange Mill Ct OX29. . . . 120 D7
Grange Pk OX25. . . . . . . 48 A1
Grange Prim Sch The
　OX16. . . . . 16 D3
Grange Rd
　Banbury OX16. . . . . 16 D2
　Henley-on-Thames RG9. . . 244 E3
　Oxford OX4. . . . . 142 B2
Grangers Pl OX28. . . . . . 104 B1
Grange The
　Kingham OX7. . . . . 55 A4
　Reading RG4. . . . . 258 D6
Grantham Ho OX2. . . . . . 261 A4
Grants Mews 2 OX4. . . . 141 F8
Granville Ct OX3. . . . . . . 124 A1
Granville Way OX26. . . . . 66 B2
Grasmere Ave RG30. . . . 257 F2
Grass Hill RG4. . . . . 258 E3
Grates The OX4. . . . . . . 142 C4
Gravel Cl OX10. . . . . 203 F4
Gravel Hill
　Henley-on-Thames RG9. . . 244 D2
　Reading RG4. . . . . 258 F6
　Sonning Common RG9. . . 252 F6
Gravel Hill Cres RG9. . . . 252 F6
Gravel La
　Drayton OX14. . . . . 179 B1
　Warborough OX10. . . . . . 203 B7
Gravel Pits La OX5. . . . . 108 B6
Gravel Rd RG4, RG9. . . . 253 F1
Gravel Wlk
　Drayton St Leonard
　　OX10. . . . . 183 B5
　Faringdon SN7. . . . . 172 F3
Graveney Dr RG4. . . . . . 258 E3
Gravenhill Road N OX26. . 81 A7
Gravett Cl RG9. . . . . 254 C8
Grayling Ct 9 RG1. . . . . . 259 A1
Grays Cl OX44. . . . . 184 C7
Grays Rd OX3. . . . . 124 B2
GREAT BARRINGTON. . . . 99 C3
GREAT BOURTON 9 D8
Great Clarendon St OX2. 261 A3
Great Close Rd OX5. . . . . 108 C5
GREAT COXWELL 192 C7
Great Coxwell Barn★
　SN7. . . . . 172 B1
GREAT HALCOMBE 183 E6
GREAT HASELEY 164 E8
Great Mead
　Didcot OX11. . . . . 219 A6
　Oxford OX1. . . . . 261 A3
GREAT MILTON 145 B2
Great Milton Prim Sch
　OX44. . . . . 145 C3
GREAT RISSINGTON 83 A7
Great Rissington Prim Sch
　GL54. . . . . 83 A7
GREAT ROLLRIGHT 29 B3
Great Rollright CE Prim Sch
　OX7. . . . . 29 B3
GREAT TEW. 45 D7
Great Tew Prim Sch OX7 . 45 D7
GREAT WESTERN 200 E2
Great Western Dr OX11. . 200 E2
Grebe Cl
　Abingdon OX14. . . . . 179 F5
　Sandford-on-Thames OX4 . 142 E1
Grebe Rd
　Banbury OX16. . . . . 16 E3
　Bicester OX26 . . . . 65 F1
Grebe Sq GL54. . . . . 68 B4
Greenacres OX14. . . . . . 179 B2
Greenacres Dr OX12. . . . 214 C4
Greenacres La OX18. . . . 135 D3
Green Cl
　Benson OX10. . . . . 204 A5
　Bicester OX26 . . . . 65 F2
　Didcot OX11. . . . . 218 F6
　Steventon OX13. . . . . . . 198 F5
　Wallingford OX10. . . . . . 221 C7
Green Cnr OX28. . . . . . . 104 C2
Green Dean Hill RG4. . . . 252 C1
GREENEND 72 A7
Green End Rd HP14. . . . . 189 E5
Greene's Tutorial Coll
　OX1. . . . . 261 B2

Green Farm OX17 . . . . 23 A4
GREENFIELD 207 A4
Greenfield Cres
  Stonesfield OX29 . . . . 89 D7
  Wallingford OX10 . . . . 221 B8
Greenfield Rd OX29 . . . . . . 89 D7
Greenfields OX25 . . . . 96 D7
Greenfinch Cl OX14 . . . . . . 142 F1
Green Furlong OX10 . . . . . 182 C5
Greengates 5 SN7 . . . . 172 F3
Green Ground OX33 . . . . . 127 A2
Greenheart Way OX13 . . . 156 E1
Green Hill OX4 . . . . 143 A2
Greenhill Ct OX16 . . . . 16 D4
Greenhills Pk OX15 . . . . . . 21 D4
Green Hitchings OX44 . . . 145 C2
Green La
  Banbury OX16 . . . . 16 D4
  Binfield Heath RG9 . . . . . 254 A1
  Bledlow Ridge HP14 . . . . 189 D5
  Chesterton OX26 . . . . 79 F7
  Ewelme OX10 . . . . 204 D4
  Henley-on-Thames RG9 . . 254 D8
  Little Tew OX7 . . . . 44 D5
  Longworth OX13 . . . . 156 C2
  Milton-under-Wychwood
   OX7 . . . . 70 B1
  North Leigh OX29 . . . . . . 105 A7
  Oxford OX2 . . . . 140 A8
  Pangbourne RG8 . . . . 256 C5
  Sonning Common RG4 . . . 252 F5
  South Newington OX15 . . . 31 F7
  Stokenchurch HP14 . . . . . 188 C5
  Sunningwell OX13 . . . . . . 160 A6
  Swalcliffe OX15 . . . . 14 A1
  Uffington SN7 . . . . 211 C7
  Upper Arncott OX25 . . . . . 96 E7
  Warborough OX10 . . . . . . 203 B7
  Woodcote RG8 . . . . 250 F7
  Woodstock OX20 . . . . 91 B7
  Wootton OX13 . . . . 159 A5
Greenlands OX7 . . . . 70 A1
Green Lane Flats OX10 . . 202 E3
Greenleas Ave RG4 . . . . . . 259 B7
Greenmere OX10 . . . . 202 E3
Greenmore RG8 . . . . 250 F8
Green N The OX10 . . . . . . 203 C8
Green Pl OX1 . . . . 141 D6
Green Rd
  Didcot OX11 . . . . 218 F7
  Kidlington OX5 . . . . 108 E8
  Oxford OX3 . . . . 124 F3
  Shillingford OX10 . . . . . . 203 B4
Green Ridges OX3 . . . . . . 125 A4
Greens Garth OX15 . . . . . . 21 F5
Greens Keep HP17 . . . . . . 130 E8
Green's Rd OX29 . . . . 120 E8
Green St OX4 . . . . 142 A7
Green S The OX10 . . . . . . 203 C8
Greensward The OX17 . . . . . 5 E1
Green Templeton Coll
  OX2 . . . . 261 A4
GREEN THE
  Ludgershall 98 C8
  North Aston 48 A6
Green The
  Adderbury OX17 . . . . 23 A4
  Alvescot OX18 . . . . 133 C5
  Ascott-under-Wychwood
   OX7 . . . . 71 C2
  Aston Rowant OX49 . . . . 167 D3
  Barford St Michael OX15 . . 32 E6
  Baydon SN8 . . . . 245 E1
  Bladon SN8 . . . . 91 B2
  Bledington OX7 . . . . 54 C2
  Cassington OX29 . . . . . . 107 C2
  Chalgrove OX44 . . . . 184 D6
  Charlbury OX7 . . . . 73 C4
  Charney Bassett OX12 . . 176 A2
  Chesterton OX26 . . . . 79 F7
  Chilton OX11 . . . . 235 E8
  Chipping Norton OX7 . . . . 42 E2
  Clanfield OX18 . . . . 152 E8
  Cuddesdon OX44 . . . . . . 144 B2
  Culham OX14 . . . . 180 A3
  Drayton OX14 . . . . 179 B1
  East Hanney OX12 . . . . . 197 B7
  Fawler OX7 . . . . 88 E6
  Fernham SN7 . . . . 193 A4
  Fifield OX7 . . . . 69 C2
  Freeland OX29 . . . . 106 B5
  Fringford OX27 . . . . 52 C6
  Garsington OX44 . . . . . . 143 E1
  Great Bourton OX17 . . . . . 9 D8
  Great Milton OX44 . . . . . 145 B2
  Great Rollright OX7 . . . . . 29 A3
  Great Tew OX7 . . . . 45 D7
  Highworth SN6 . . . . 190 A5
  Hook Norton OX15 . . . . . . 30 B7
  Hornton OX15 . . . . 7 C6
  Horspath OX33 . . . . 143 C5
  Horton-cum-Studley OX33 112 A5
  Kingham OX7 . . . . 55 A5
  Launton OX26 . . . . 66 E2
  Longcot SN7 . . . . 192 C2
  Lyford OX12 . . . . 176 C1
  Marcham OX13 . . . . 178 D6
  Middle Assendon RG9 . . 243 F8
  Milcombe OX15 . . . . 20 F2
  Nettlebed RG9 . . . . 224 E2
  North Aston OX25 . . . . . . 48 B7
  North Leigh OX29 . . . . . . 89 D2
  Salford OX7 . . . . 42 A5
  Shrivenham SN6 . . . . 209 A6
  Shutford OX15 . . . . 14 B5

Green The continued
  Stadhampton OX44 . . . . . 163 D2
  Standlake OX29 . . . . 137 D3
  Stanton Harcourt OX29 . . 138 A8
  Steventon OX13 . . . . 199 A5
  Stoke Lyne OX27 . . . . 51 B5
  Sutton Courtenay OX14 . . 180 A1
  Swalcliffe OX15 . . . . 19 F8
  Tackley OX5 . . . . 77 B5
  Turweston NN13 . . . . 24 C8
  Uffington SN7 . . . . 211 D7
  Upper Heyford OX25 . . . . 62 F8
  West Hanney OX12 . . . . . 196 E5
Green Trees RG9 . . . . 252 F7
Greenway
  Haddenham HP17 . . . . . 130 F5
  Lower Heyford OX25 . . . . 63 A4
  Thame OX9 . . . . 129 F1
Greenways RG8 . . . . 256 D5
Greenway The OX12 . . . . 216 B6
Greenwich La OX29 . . . . . . 87 B3
Greenwood Ave OX39 . . . 168 C5
Greenwood Dr OX26 . . . . . 65 B3
Greenwood Mdw OX39 . . 168 D6
Gregory Est OX49 . . . . . . 185 C3
Grenoble Rd
  Oxford OX4 . . . . 143 A1
  Sandford-on-Thames OX4 142 D1
Grenville Way OX9 . . . . . . 130 B1
Gresham Way RG30 . . . . . 258 A2
Gresham Way Ind Est
  RG30 . . . . 258 A2
Greycotes Oxford High Sch
  1 OX2 . . . . 123 C5
Greygoose La GL56 . . . . . . 41 B6
Greyhound La OX9 . . . . . . 129 F1
Greyhound Wlk OX9 . . . . . 147 F8
Grey La OX28 . . . . 104 D1
Greys Cl OX16 . . . . 15 F6
Greys Court ★ RG9 . . . . . 243 C3
GREYS GREEN 243 C2
Greys Hill RG9 . . . . 244 D1
Greys Rd RG9 . . . . 254 D8
Greystoke Rd RG4 . . . . . . 259 C4
Greystones Ct
  Alvescot OX18 . . . . 133 C5
  Kidlington OX5 . . . . 92 D1
Griffin Cl OX17 . . . . 23 A5
Griffin Rd OX9 . . . . 148 C8
Griffiths Cl OX29 . . . . 138 C3
Griffiths Gdns OX27 . . . . . 66 A4
Grimbly Pl OX2 . . . . 123 B8
Grimmer Way RG8 . . . . . . 250 F8
GRIMSBURY 16 F5
Grimsbury Dr OX16 . . . . . . 16 F7
Grimsbury Gn OX16 . . . . . . 16 E8
Grimsbury Green OX16 . . . 16 E8
Grimsbury Sq OX16 . . . . . . 16 F7
Grindon La OX11 . . . . 205 B1
Grosvenor Pl OX12 . . . . . 214 B5
Grosvenor Rd
  7 Banbury OX16 . . . . . . 16 D5
  Oxford OX2 . . . . 140 E6
  Reading RG4 . . . . 259 C4
GROVE 196 F1
Grove Cotts
  Brightwell-cum-Sotwell
   OX10 . . . . 202 D2
  Little Coxwell SN7 . . . . . 192 E7
  Reading RG4 . . . . 259 A5
Grove Ct
  Deddington OX15 . . . . . . 33 F4
  Oxford OX4 . . . . 142 A5
Grove Farm The OX14 . . . 199 C1
Grove Hill
  Highworth SN6 . . . . 190 A7
  Reading RG4 . . . . 259 A4
  Woodstock OX20 . . . . . . 91 A6
Grove La
  Ewelme OX10, OX49 . . . . 205 A6
  Spelsbury OX7 . . . . 72 E8
Grovelands OX5 . . . . 108 D8
Grovelands Ctr OX12 . . . . 196 D1
Grovelands Rd OX3 . . . . . 125 A2
Grove Mews RG4 . . . . 259 B5
Grove Park Dr
  Ardington OX12 . . . . 215 C7
  Grove OX12 . . . . 197 B1
Grove Rd
  Bladon OX20 . . . . 91 C3
  Grove OX12 . . . . 214 E7
  Harwell OX11 . . . . 217 D8
  Henley-on-Thames RG9 . . 244 E1
  Reading RG4 . . . . 259 B6
  Sonning Common RG4 . . 252 F5
  South Stoke RG8 . . . . . . 239 E2
Groves Ind Est OX7 . . . . . . 70 B1
Grove St
  Banbury OX16 . . . . 16 D5
  Oxford OX2 . . . . 123 B7
  Wantage OX12 . . . . 214 D5
Grove Terr OX11 . . . . 218 D4
Grove The
  Abingdon OX14 . . . . 160 B2
  Bourton SN6 . . . . 209 A3
  Deddington OX15 . . . . . . 33 F4
Grundy Cl OX14 . . . . 180 B8
Grundy Cres OX1 . . . . 141 E1
Grunsell Cl OX3 . . . . 124 C5
Guardian Ct 3 OX16 . . . . 16 E6
Guelder Rd OX4 . . . . 142 D1
Guernsey Way OX16 . . . . . 9 A1
Guildenford OX18 . . . . . . 100 E5
Guildford Ct 7 OX5 . . . . 108 F8
Guild Ho The 2 OX12 . . . 214 E4
Gulley Row OX25 . . . . 95 D8

Gullicote La OX17 . . . . 8 E3
Gulliver's Cl OX15 . . . . 8 B4
Gurden Pl OX3 . . . . 124 E4
Gurl Cl OX3 . . . . 124 E4
Gurney Cl RG4 . . . . 258 D5
Gurney Dr RG4 . . . . 258 D5
Gwilym Ct 5 OX10 . . . . . 221 C7
Gwyneth Rd OX4 . . . . 142 A2
Gwynne Cl RG31 . . . . 257 D3

H

Hackers La OX7 . . . . 55 E4
Hack La CV36 . . . . 27 E8
Haddenham Bsns Pk
  HP17 . . . . 130 E6
Haddenham & Thame
  Parkway Sta HP17 . . . . 130 E6
Hadden Hill OX11 . . . . 201 D1
Hadland Rd OX14 . . . . . . 180 C8
Hadleigh Rise RG4 . . . . . . 259 E5
Hadow Rd OX3 . . . . 124 A4
Hadrian's Gate NN13 . . . . 24 A7
Hafod RG4 . . . . 258 F6
Hagbourne CE Prim Sch
  OX11 . . . . 218 E5
Hagbourne Cl RG8 . . . . . . 250 F8
Hagbourne Rd
  Didcot OX11 . . . . 219 A8
  East Hagbourne OX11 . . 219 D2
HAILEY
  Wallingford 240 E8
  Witney 104 A6
Hailey Ave OX7 . . . . 42 E1
Hailey CE Prim Sch
  OX29 . . . . 104 A6
Hailey Cres OX7 . . . . 42 E1
Hailey Croft OX39 . . . . . . 168 B6
Hailey Rd
  Chipping Norton OX7 . . . . 42 D1
  Witney OX8, OX28 . . . . . 104 B3
Hailles Gdns 1 OX26 . . . . 65 E2
Haines Cl OX3 . . . . 178 D7
Haldane Rd
  Oxford OX4 . . . . 142 E2
  Reading RG4 . . . . 258 E5
Hale Rd OX10 . . . . 203 F5
Halfpenny La OX10 . . . . . 238 E5
Halifax Rd OX26 . . . . 66 A3
Hall Cl OX49 . . . . 186 B4
Hall Cl The OX25 . . . . 48 B6
Hallett Cl OX12 . . . . 214 E4
Halliday Hill OX3 . . . . 124 B5
Halls Cl
  Drayton OX14 . . . . 179 C1
  Oxford OX2 . . . . 140 B7
Halls La OX12 . . . . 197 B7
Hallsmead Ct 8 RG1 . . . . 259 A1
Halse Water OX11 . . . . . . 201 A2
Halton Rd OX18 . . . . 115 F2
Hambidge La OX7 . . . . . . 150 C5
Hamble Dr OX10 . . . . 221 B8
Hamble Dr OX1 . . . . 160 B1
Hamble Rd OX11 . . . . 201 A1
Hambleside OX26 . . . . 65 B2
Hamcroft OX12 . . . . 214 C5
Hamels La OX1 . . . . 140 F1
Hamel The OX1 . . . . 261 A2
Hamfield OX12 . . . . 214 C4
Hamilton Ave RG9 . . . . . . 244 E1
Hamilton Cl
  Banbury OX16 . . . . 16 E7
  Bicester OX26 . . . . 65 E3
Hamilton Rd
  Oxford OX2 . . . . 123 B7
  Thame OX9 . . . . 130 A1
  Wargrave RG10 . . . . 255 E2
Ham La OX18 . . . . 135 E1
Hamlet The RG4 . . . . 252 B5
Hamlyn Cl OX12 . . . . 214 A2
Hammer La OX10 . . . . 183 A1
Hammett Pl OX18 . . . . . . 115 D1
Hammond's End RG8 . . . . 241 B4
Hampden Ave OX9 . . . . . . 147 F7
Hampden Cl
  Banbury OX16 . . . . 15 F5
  Bicester OX26 . . . . 66 A3
  Chalgrove OX44 . . . . 184 D6
  Faringdon SN7 . . . . 173 A3
Hampden Dr OX5 . . . . 108 F6
Hampden Rd
  Oxford OX4 . . . . 142 C4
  Reading RG4 . . . . 259 B2
  Wantage OX12 . . . . 214 E5
Hampden Way OX10 . . . . 204 F4
Hampdon Villas OX27 . . . . 67 F7
Hampstead Hill RG9 . . . . . 260 C8
Hampton Dr OX17 . . . . . . 23 F6
HAMPTON GAY 92 D5
HAMPTON POYLE 93 B4
Ham Rd OX12 . . . . 214 C4
Hamstyles OX49 . . . . 205 E7
Hanborough Bsns Pk
  OX29 . . . . 90 C1
Hanborough Ct OX29 . . . . 120 E8
Hanborough Manor CE Sch
  OX29 . . . . 90 C1
Hanborough Rd OX29 . . . 120 E8
Hanborough Sta OX29 . . . 90 E1
Handlo Pl OX3 . . . . 124 F4
Hanney Rd
  Kingston Bagpuize OX13 . 176 D7
  Steventon OX13 . . . . 198 C6
Hannis Rd OX7 . . . . 42 D1
Hanover Cl OX7 . . . . 73 C3

Hanover Ct
  Didcot OX11 . . . . 218 E7
  Reading RG4 . . . . 259 C6
  9 Wallingford OX10 . . . 221 C7
Hanover Gdns
  Bicester OX26 . . . . 65 E1
  Wargrave RG10 . . . . 255 F3
Hans Ave OX12 . . . . 214 E5
Hanson Rd OX14 . . . . 159 F3
HANWELL 8 F4
Hanwell Ct OX17 . . . . 8 F4
HANWELL FIELDS 9 B1
Hanwell Fields Com Sch
  OX16 . . . . 9 B1
Hanwood Cl RG5 . . . . 260 C1
Harberton Mead
  Marston OX3 . . . . 123 F3
  Oxford OX3 . . . . 124 A3
Harbord Rd OX2 . . . . 109 B2
Harborne Rd OX5 . . . . 77 C5
Harcourt Arboretum ★
  OX44 . . . . 161 E1
Harcourt Cl RG9 . . . . 244 C1
Harcourt Gn OX12 . . . . . . 214 F6
HARCOURT HILL 140 E6
Harcourt Hill OX2 . . . . . . 140 E6
Harcourt Ho 5 OX26 . . . . 65 E2
Harcourt Rd OX12 . . . . . . 214 E5
Harcourt Terr OX3 . . . . . . 124 B2
Harcourt Way
  Abingdon OX14 . . . . 159 F1
  Wantage OX12 . . . . 214 E5
Harding Cl SN7 . . . . 173 A3
Harding Rd OX14 . . . . 179 D8
Hardings OX44 . . . . 184 D6
Hardings Cl OX4 . . . . 142 B3
Hardings Strings OX11 . . . 218 E7
Hardwell Ct OX12 . . . . . . 196 D1
HARDWICK
  Banbury 9 A1
  Stoke Lyne 51 D8
  Witney 118 F1
Hardwick Ave OX5 . . . . . . 108 E7
Hardwick Bsns Pk OX16 . . . 9 E2
Hardwick Hill OX16 . . . . . . 9 D3
Hardwick Pk OX16 . . . . . . 9 E2
Hardwick Prim Sch OX16 . 16 A8
Hardwick Rd
  Hethe OX27 . . . . 52 A7
  Mapledurham RG8 . . . . . 257 B8
  Whitchurch-on-Thames
   RG8 . . . . 256 D7
Hardy Cl RG4 . . . . 259 C2
Harebell Rd OX4 . . . . 142 F2
Harebell Way OX26 . . . . . . 65 D4
Harecourt OX12 . . . . 214 F4
Harefields OX2 . . . . 109 B1
HARESFIELD 190 B8
Hare Warren Ct RG4 . . . . 259 B4
Harewood Rd OX16 . . . . . 16 E2
Harlech Ave RG4 . . . . 259 D6
Harlech Cl OX16 . . . . 15 F5
Harlequin Way OX16 . . . . . 9 B1
Harley Rd
  Oxford OX2 . . . . 122 F1
  Reading RG4 . . . . 259 B2
Harlington Ave OX12 . . . . 196 E1
Harlow Way OX3 . . . . 123 F7
Harmon Cl OX27 . . . . 66 A6
Harolde Cl OX3 . . . . 124 D4
Harold Hicks Pl OX4 . . . . 141 F6
Harolds Cl OX29 . . . . 87 A3
Harold White Cl OX3 . . . . 124 F2
Harper Cl OX25 . . . . 96 D7
Harpes Rd OX2 . . . . 123 B8
HARPSDEN 254 D6
Harpsden Bsns Pk OX16 . . . 9 E2
Harpsden Rd RG9 . . . . . . 254 E8
Harpsden Way RG9 . . . . . 254 E7
Harpsichord Pl OX4 . . . . . 123 F1
Harrier Pk OX11 . . . . 200 D3
Harriers Ground Prim Sch
  OX16 . . . . 16 C4
Harriers View OX16 . . . . . 16 C4
Harrier Way OX26 . . . . 66 A4
Harris Gdns GL54 . . . . 68 B4
Harris Manchester Coll
  OX1 . . . . 261 C3
Harrison Pl OX9 . . . . 129 F1
Harrison's La OX20 . . . . . . 91 A6
Harris Rd OX25 . . . . 63 C7
Harris's La OX13 . . . . 156 C2
Harrisville OX25 . . . . 62 B8
Harroell
  Long Crendon HP18 . . . . 129 D5
  Long Crendon HP18 . . . . 129 D6
Harrogate Rd RG4 . . . . . . 258 E4
Harrowby Ct OX16 . . . . . . 16 D2
Harrowby Rd OX16 . . . . . . 16 D2
Harrow Rd OX4 . . . . 142 F3
Hart Ave SN7 . . . . 172 F3
Hart Cl
  Abingdon OX14 . . . . 180 C8
  Banbury OX16 . . . . 9 C1
Hartley Cl OX10 . . . . 203 B6
Hartleys Barns OX7 . . . . . . 85 D7
Hart Moor Cl HP14 . . . . . 188 E4
Hart Pl OX26 . . . . 66 A4
Harts Cl OX5 . . . . 108 D7
Hartslock Bridleway
  Whitchurch Hill RG8 . . . . 250 B1
  Whitchurch-on-Thames
   RG8 . . . . 256 B6
Hartslock Ct RG8 . . . . 256 B6
Hartslock View RG8 . . . . . 249 E2
Hartslock Way RG31 . . . . 257 C2
Hart St
  Henley-on-Thames RG9 . . 244 E2

Hart St continued
  Oxford OX2 . . . . 261 A3
  11 Wallingford OX10 . . . 221 D7
Hart-Synnot Ho OX2 . . . . 261 A4
Harvest Cres OX18 . . . . . 115 F5
Harvest Gr OX28 . . . . 104 E2
Harvest Pl RG10 . . . . 255 E1
Harvest Way OX28 . . . . . 104 E2
Harveys Nurseries Pk Cvn
  Site RG4 . . . . 259 C4
HARWELL 217 F7
Harwell Cl OX14 . . . . 160 A1
Harwell Int Bsns Ctr
  OX11 . . . . 217 A1
Harwell Prim Sch OX11 . 217 D7
Harwell Rd OX14 . . . . 199 F6
Harwell Science &
  Innovation Campus
  OX11 . . . . 217 C2
Harwood Rd OX11 . . . . . . 218 F5
Haseley Rd OX44 . . . . 163 F6
Haseley Trading Est
  OX44 . . . . 145 C1
Haslemere Gdns OX2 . . . . 109 A2
Haslemere Tramway Est
  OX16 . . . . 16 E5
Haslemere Way OX16 . . . . 16 E5
Hastings Cl OX16 . . . . 15 F6
Hastings Dr OX18 . . . . . . 115 F2
Hastings Hill OX7 . . . . 55 E5
Hastings Rd OX16 . . . . 15 F7
Hastoe Grange OX3 . . . . . 124 A4
Hatch Cl OX5 . . . . 77 F4
Hatch End OX5 . . . . 77 F4
Hatch End Ind Est OX25 . . 48 B2
Hatchet Hill SN4 . . . . 227 A4
Hatch Gate La RG10 . . . . 255 F7
Hatching La OX29 . . . . 87 A4
Hatch Way OX5 . . . . 77 F4
Hatfield Pits La OX29 . . . . 104 C7
HATFORD 174 D4
Hathaways OX33 . . . . 144 B8
Hatwell Row OX18 . . . . . . 115 E2
Havelock Rd OX4 . . . . 142 C5
Haven Cl OX10 . . . . 202 D8
Haven Vale OX12 . . . . 214 E5
Havers Ave OX14 . . . . 199 D2
Hawke La OX15 . . . . 21 D4
Hawker Sq GL54 . . . . 68 B4
Hawkins Ho 5 OX18 . . . . 115 E2
Hawkins St 1 OX4 . . . . . 141 F7
Hawkins Way OX13 . . . . . 159 B6
Hawk's La OX15 . . . . 19 C8
Hawksmead OX26 . . . . 81 A8
Hawksmoor Rd OX3 . . . . 109 B1
Hawkswell Gdns OX2 . . . . 123 C7
Hawkswell Ho OX2 . . . . . 123 C7
Hawksworth OX11 . . . . . . 200 D4
Hawksworth Cl OX12 . . . . 196 D1
HAWKWELL 68 D6
Haw La
  Aldworth RG8 . . . . 247 E1
  Bledlow Ridge HP14 . . . . 189 F8
Hawlings Row OX4 . . . . . 143 A1
Hawthorn Ave
  Oxford OX3 . . . . 124 D3
  Thame OX9 . . . . 147 E8
Hawthorn Cl
  Oxford OX2 . . . . 140 D8
  Wallingford OX10 . . . . . . 221 C7
Hawthorn Cres OX12 . . . . 214 E8
Hawthorn Dr
  Burford OX18 . . . . 114 C7
  Stoke Row RG9 . . . . 242 A1
Hawthorne Ave OX13 . . . . 159 C2
Hawthorne Rd RG4 . . . . . 259 E4
Hawthornes RG31 . . . . . . 257 B3
Hawthorn Gr OX18 . . . . . . 115 D1
Hawthorn Rd
  Eynsham OX29 . . . . 120 E8
  Faringdon SN7 . . . . 172 E3
Hawthorns The OX16 . . . . 16 D3
Hawthorn Way
  Kidlington OX5 . . . . 108 E7
  Sonning RG4 . . . . 260 D3
Hawthorn Wlk 2 OX26 . . . 65 F4
Hayden La RG9 . . . . 224 A3
Haydon Rd OX11 . . . . 200 E1
Hayes Ave OX13 . . . . 176 D8
Hayes Cl OX3 . . . . 123 F3
Hayes The OX1 . . . . 261 B2
Hayfield Rd OX2 . . . . 123 B5
Hayford Ho 5 OX18 . . . . 115 F5
Haynes Rd OX3 . . . . 123 C5
Hayward Dr OX18 . . . . . . 115 D1
Hayward Rd OX2 . . . . 109 B2
Haywards Cl
  Henley-on-Thames RG9 . . 244 C1
  Wantage OX12 . . . . 214 E5
Haywards Rd OX14 . . . . . 199 B7
Hayway La OX15 . . . . 29 F8
Hazel Ave OX9 . . . . 147 E8
Hazel Cl
  Abingdon OX14 . . . . 159 E1
  Witney OX28 . . . . 104 E2
Hazel Cres OX5 . . . . 108 F6
Hazeldene GL7 . . . . 150 D5
Hazeldene Cl OX29 . . . . . 105 B6
Hazeldene Gdns OX16 . . . 16 D3
Hazel End OX44 . . . . 143 C2
Hazel Gdns RG4 . . . . 252 F5
Hazel Gr
  Bicester OX26 . . . . 65 F4
  Stoke Row RG9 . . . . 242 B2
  Wallingford OX10 . . . . . . 221 C7
Hazells La SN6 . . . . 209 C6
Hazell's La SN6 . . . . 209 C6
Hazelmoor La RG4 . . . . . . 252 D4

Hazelnut Path OX14..... 160 E7
Hazel Rd
  Oxford OX2 ....122 C1
  Purley on Thames RG8...257 C4
Hazelrig Or OX9 ....148 A8
Hazelton Cl OX9 ....147 E8
Hazel Wlk OX5.........108 F6
Hazelwood Cl RG31 ....257 C1
HEADINGTON 124 C4
HEADINGTON HILL.....124 A2
Headington Prep Sch **1**
  OX3................124 C2
HEADINGTON QUARRY..124 E2
Headington Rd OX3 ....124 A2
Headington Rdbt OX3...124 F3
Headington Sch OX3....124 B2
Headley Ho OX3 ....124 A4
Headley Way OX3 ......124 B3
Healey Cl OX14 ....179 E6
Hean Cl OX14 ....160 B2
Hearns La RG4.........252 C5
Hearthway OX16........9 B1
Heath Cl
  Milcombe OX15.......20 F2
  Oxford OX3 ....142 D8
Heathcote Ave OX16....16 E2
Heathcote Pl OX14.....160 C1
Heath Ct OX15........30 B7
Heath Dr RG9.........254 A1
Heather Cl
  Carterton OX18........115 E4
  Sonning Common RG4...253 A5
Heather Pl OX3........123 F4
Heather Rd
  Bicester OX26........65 E5
  Milton OX14..........199 D6
Heath Farm La OX29...105 A6
Heathfield Ave RG9....254 A1
Heathfield Cl RG9.....254 B2
HEATHFIELD VILLAGE...93 E6
Heath La OX20........91 B1
Heath The OX7........70 A2
Hedge End OX20.......91 C6
Hedge Hill Rd OX12....213 F5
Hedgemead Ave OX14...160 C2
Hedgerley OX39.......168 B6
Hedges Cl OX3........124 E3
Hedges The OX15......14 B8
Heigham Ct SN7......194 D7
Helen Rd OX2.........122 F1
Hellebourine Cl OX4...142 F1
Helwys Pl OX5........92 D2
Hemdean Hill RG4.....259 A3
Hemdean House Sch
  RG4................259 A3
Hemdean Rd RG4......259 A3
Hemdean Rise RG4.....259 A3
Hemingway Dr OX26...65 C2
Hemplands
  Great Rollright OX7....29 A3
  Poffley End OX29......104 C6
HEMPTON 33 B4
Hempton Rd
  Barford St Michael OX15...32 F5
  Deddington OX15......33 E4
HEMPTON WAINHILL...168 F7
Henderson Ho OX10....221 B7
Hendon Pl OX26.......66 A4
Hendreds CE Prim Sch The
  OX12...............216 D6
Hendred St OX4........142 B6
Hendred Way OX14.....160 B1
Henfield View OX10....203 B8
Hengest Gate OX11....217 E7
Hengrove Cl OX3.......124 D5
Henley Ave OX4.......142 A5
Henley Coll The (Deanfield
  Bldgs) RG9..........244 D1
Henley Coll The (Rotherfield
  Bldgs) RG9..........244 C1
Henley Dr SN6........190 A7
Henley Gdns **9** OX26...65 E2
Henley L Ctr RG9......254 B7
HENLEY-ON-THAMES....244 B1
Henley-on-Thames Sta
  RG9................244 E1
Henley Rd
  Reading RG4.........259 D3
  Sandford-on-Thames OX4..161 B8
  Shillingford, Bridge End
    OX10..............202 F7
  Shillingford OX10.....203 A6
  Shiplake RG9.........260 C8
Henleys La OX14......179 B1
Henley St OX4........141 F7
Henley (Townlands) Com
  Hospl RG9...........244 D2
Hennef Way OX16......16 E8
Henor Mill Cl OX14....160 B2
Henrietta Rd OX9......130 A1
Henry Box Cl OX18.....118 A7
Henry Box Sch The
  OX28...............118 A7
Henry Gepp Cl OX17....23 B4
Henry Rd OX2.........122 F1
Henry Taunt Cl OX3....124 E5
HENSINGTON 91 D7
Hensington Cl OX20....91 C6
Hensington Rd OX20...91 B6
Hensington Wlk OX20...91 C6
HENTON 149 E2
HENWOOD 140 A1
Henwood Cotts OX1...139 F1
Henwood Dr OX1......140 A1
Herald Way **3** OX26...66 A4
Herbert Cl OX4........142 B7
Herb Farm The ★ RG4..253 A4

Hereford Way OX16.....9 A1
Heritage La OX7......71 B2
Herman Cl OX14......180 B8
Hermitage Rd OX14...179 E6
Hernes Cl OX2........123 B8
Hernes Cres OX2......123 B8
Hernes Oak OX39.....168 D8
Hernes Rd OX2.......123 B8
Heron Cl OX18........115 C3
Heron Ct
  Abingdon OX14.......179 F4
  Bicester OX26........66 B1
Heron Dr OX26........66 B1
Heron Island RG4......259 C1
Heron Rd OX10.......204 D3
Heron Shaw RG8......249 C7
Herons Pl OX2........123 B8
Heron's Wlk OX14.....159 F1
Heron Way OX16......16 A4
Herringcote OX10.....182 D2
Herschel Cres OX4.....142 C3
Herschel Ct OX4......142 C3
Hertford Cl
  Bicester OX26........65 F3
  Reading RG4.........259 D6
Hertford Coll OX1.....261 C2
Hertford Ct **8** OX5...108 F8
Hertford St OX4.......142 A7
HETHE 52 A8
Hethe Rd
  Cottisford NN13.......38 A3
  Hardwick OX27.......51 D8
Hewett Ave RG4......258 D4
Hewett Cl RG4........258 D4
Hewgate Ct RG9......244 E1
Hewitts Cl OX29......87 A3
Hey Croft OX29......120 E7
Heyford Cl OX29......137 C5
Heyford Hill La OX4...141 E2
Heyford Hill Rdbt OX4...141 F2
Heyford Ho **7** OX16...16 E6
Heyford Mead **2** OX5...92 D1
Heyford Pk OX25......63 C8
Heyford Rd
  Kirtlington OX5.......78 A5
  Middleton Stoney OX25...64 A4
  Steeple Aston OX25....62 B7
Heyford Sta OX25.....62 C6
HEYTHROP 44 A4
Hibiscus Way OX18...115 E5
Hicks Cl OX29........104 A6
Hid's Copse Rd OX2...140 B7
Higgs Cl OX11........219 A6
High Acres OX16......16 E4
Highbridge Cl RG4....259 E5
Highclere Gdns
  Banbury OX16........15 E6
  Wantage OX12........214 D6
Highcliffe Cl RG5.....260 F1
HIGH COGGES........118 F6
High Cogges OX29....118 F7
High Cross OX29....124 E5
Highdown Ave RG4...259 A6
Highdown Hill Rd RG4...259 A6
Highdown Sch RG4...259 A5
HIGHFIELD 65 C3
Highfield HP18.......129 C7
Highfield Ave OX3....124 C1
Highfield Cl OX7......147 C8
Highfield Pk RG10....255 F3
Highfield Rd RG31....257 C4
High Furlong OX16....16 B8
High House OX18.....152 E8
High Land Cl HP18...98 A1
Highlands
  Banbury OX16........9 A1
  Hardwick OX16........9 B1
  Lower Tadmarton OX15...21 A6
Highlands La RG9.....254 A8
Highlands Sch The RG31 257 D1
High Mdw
  Reading RG4.........258 D3
  Sibford Gower OX15...13 A1
HIGHMOOR 242 D7
HIGHMOOR CROSS.....242 E5
Highmoor Rd RG4.....258 F3
High Rd
  Brightwell-cum-Sotwell
    OX10..............202 E3
  Brightwell-cum-Sotwell, Slade
    End OX10..........203 A2
High Road Cotts OX10...202 D3
High St
  Abingdon OX14.......179 F7
  Adderbury OX17......23 A4
  Ardington OX12......215 E5
  Ascott-under-Wychwood
    OX7...............71 C2
  Ashbury SN6.........228 A7
  Aston OX18..........135 D3
  Bampton OX18........134 F3
  Barford St Michael OX15...32 F5
  Beckley OX3.........111 A3
  Benson OX10.........203 F4
  Bishopstone SN6.....227 D4
  Bloxham OX15........21 E5
  Bodicote OX15........22 B8
  Burford OX18.........100 E5
  Chalgrove OX44......184 C5
  Charlton-on-Otmoor OX5...95 A4
  Childrey OX12........213 C4
  Chinnor OX39........168 D7
  Chipping Norton OX7...42 E3
  Clifton Hampden OX14...181 D3
  Cropredy OX17........4 F2
  Croughton NN13......36 C8
  Cuddesdon OX44.....144 B2

High St continued
  Culham OX14........180 B3
  Cumnor OX2.........139 D5
  Deddington OX15.....33 F4
  Didcot OX11.........218 F8
  Dorchester OX10.....182 D1
  Drayton OX14........179 B1
  Drayton St Leonard OX10..183 B5
  East Hendred OX12...216 E6
  Ewelme OX10.........204 E4
  Eynsham OX29........120 E7
  Fernham SN7.........193 A4
  Fifield OX7..........69 B2
  Finstock OX7.........88 B5
  Goring RG8..........249 A6
  Great Rollright OX7....29 A3
  Haddenham HP17.....130 F6
  Harwell OX11........217 E7
  Highworth SN6.......190 A5
  Hinton Waldrist SN7...155 F2
  Hook Norton OX15....30 B7
  Islip OX5............93 F1
  Kidlington OX5.......92 E1
  Kingston Blount OX9...167 F3
  Lechlade-on-Thames GL7..150 A4
  Lewknor OX49........187 B8
  Little Milton OX44....163 F6
  Long Crendon HP18...129 D6
  Long Wittenham OX14...201 D8
  Longworth OX13......156 B3
  Ludgershall HP18.....98 B8
  Lyneham OX7.........70 D5
  Middleton Cheney OX17...17 F8
  Milton OX14..........199 D5
  Milton-under-Wychwood
    OX7...............70 A1
  Nettlebed RG9........224 D2
  North Moreton OX11...220 A7
  Oxford OX1..........261 C2
  Pangbourne RG8......256 C5
  Ramsden OX7........88 A3
  Ratley OX15..........2 A3
  Shipton-under-Wychwood
    OX7...............85 D8
  Shrivenham SN6......209 C6
  Shutford OX15........14 A5
  Sonning RG4.........260 D4
  Souldern OX27.......35 E3
  South Moreton OX11...219 F5
  South Newington OX15...31 F7
  Standlake OX29......137 D8
  Stanford in the Vale SN7..194 E7
  Steventon OX13......199 A4
  Stonesfield OX29......89 C7
  Streatley RG8........249 C6
  Sutton Courtenay OX14...200 A8
  Tetsworth OX9.......166 B8
  Thame OX9...........129 E1
  Uffington SN7........211 D7
  Upper Heyford OX25...48 F1
  Upton OX11..........218 C2
  Wallingford OX10.....221 D7
  Wargrave RG10.......255 D2
  Watchfield SN6.......191 D1
  Watlington OX49......186 B2
  Wheatley OX33.......144 B8
  Whitchurch-on-Thames
    RG8...............256 C7
  Witney OX28.........118 B8
  Woodstock OX20.....91 B6
Hightown Gdns OX16...16 D3
Hightown Leyes OX16...16 D3
Hightown Rd OX16....16 D4
High View OX12.......214 A4
HIGHWORTH 190 B6
Highworth Pl OX28....118 A7
Highworth Rd
  Faringdon SN7.......172 E2
  Shrivenham SN6......209 A7
Highworth Warneford Sch
  SN6................190 A4
Highworth Way RG31...257 B2
Hikers Way HP18......129 F4
Hillary Dr OX11.......218 E7
Hillary Way OX33.....144 C7
HILL BOTTOM.........250 E3
Hill Bottom Cl RG8....250 E3
Hill Cl
  Charlbury OX7.......73 C3
  Chipping Norton OX7...42 E1
  East Challow OX12....214 A4
Hillcraft Rd OX33.....125 D7
Hill Cres OX7.........88 C5
Hillcrest La RG9......252 F7
Hill Ct OX18.........115 D4
Hill Farm Ct OX39....168 D6
Hill Farm La OX25....47 D6
Hill Gdns RG8........249 A6
Hill Ho OX25.........62 A8
Hilliard Ho OX14.....179 E5
Hilliat Fields OX14....179 B1
Hilliers Cl OX14......200 A8
Hill Lands RG10......255 D2
Hill Lawn Ct OX7.....42 E3
Hill Piece OX11.......235 E7
Hill Prim Sch The RG4...259 C5
Hill Rd
  Chinnor OX39........168 D5
  Lewknor OX49.......187 C6
  Watchfield SN6.......191 D1
  Watlington OX49.....206 E8
Hill Rise
  Great Rollright OX7....29 A3
  Horspath OX33.......143 D6
Hillsborough Cl **3** OX4..142 B3
Hillsborough Rd OX4...142 B4

Hillside
  Harwell OX11........217 B3
  Oxford OX2..........140 B6
  Whitchurch-on-Thames
    RG8...............256 D8
Hillside Cl
  Banbury OX16........16 E3
  Upper Arncott OX25...96 E7
Hillside Cotts OX14...202 A6
Hillside Rd OX7.......46 E1
Hill The
  Aynho OX17.........35 C7
  Bourton SN6.........209 A3
  Burford OX18........100 E4
  Burford, Westwell OX18...99 F1
  Garsington OX44.....143 E1
  Shilton OX18.........115 B5
Hilltop HP18.........129 D5
Hilltop Ct OX4.......142 B8
Hilltop Gdns OX5.....93 F1
Hill Top La OX39.....168 F4
Hilltop Rd RG4.......258 D5
Hill Top Rd OX4......142 B8
Hill View
  Carterton OX18......115 D4
  Kingston Lisle OX12...212 B4
  Oxford OX3..........125 A4
Hill View Cl OX16....16 A7
Hill View Cres OX16...16 A7
Hill View La OX1.....159 A8
Hill View Prim Sch OX16..16 A7
Hillview Rd
  Abingdon OX14......159 F2
  Oxford OX3..........123 A1
Hillwerke OX39.......168 C6
Hillyard Barns OX14...200 A8
Hilton Rd OX16.......16 B6
Hinksey Bsns Ctr OX2...122 D1
Hinksey Hill OX1......141 B3
Hinksey Hill Interchange
  OX1...............141 C3
Hinksey Pool (Outdoor)
  OX26...............141 C6
Hinshelwood Rd OX1...261 C3
Hinton Hill SN4.......227 A3
HINTON PARVA.......227 A3
Hinton Rd OX13......156 D3
Hinton Springs SN4...227 B3
HINTON WALDRIST....155 F3
Hirstwood RG30......257 E1
Hiskins OX12.........214 B5
Hitching Ct OX14....179 C7
Hitchman Dr OX7.....42 E2
Hithercroft Ct OX10...221 B6
Hithercroft Ind Est OX10...221 B7
Hithercroft Rd
  Cholsey OX10, OX11...220 D5
  Wallingford OX10.....221 B7
  West End OX10.......220 E1
Hive Mews **3** OX14...179 F6
Hixet Wood OX7......73 B3
Hobbs Cl OX14.......180 B8
Hobbs End RG9.......254 B8
Hobby Ct OX4........142 F1
Hobbyhorse La OX14...200 B7
Hobson Rd OX2......123 B7
Hocker Bench SN6....227 D4
Hocketts Cl RG8......250 E3
Hockmore St OX4.....142 C4
Hodge Cl OX1........141 C7
Hodges Cl HP14......188 F4
Hodgson Cl OX27.....49 F7
Hogarth Pl OX14.....179 E5
Hogg End
  Bloxham OX15........21 E4
  Chipping Warden OX17...5 F6
Holborn Hill OX12....231 D7
Holcombe La OX10...183 D6
Holford Rd OX28......117 F7
Holkam Cl RG30......257 F1
Holland Cl OX39......168 D7
Holland Pl OX3.......142 E8
Holland Rd OX14.....160 A2
Hollandridge La OX49,
  RG9................207 D4
Holland Rise OX17....23 F4
Holley Cres OX3......124 C3
Holliers Cl
  Sydenham OX39......167 D8
  Thame OX9..........147 F8
Holliers Cres OX7.....60 F8
Hollies Ct The **9** OX16...16 D5
Hollington HP18......129 B7
Hollis Cl OX28.......118 D7
Holloway Hill OX15...12 A2
Holloway La
  Northend RG9........207 F5
  Winderton OX15......12 A1
Holloway Rd
  Wheatley OX33......144 A8
  Witney OX28.........118 A8
Holloway Rd The SN7...192 B4
Holloway The
  Harwell OX11........217 E6
  Mollington OX17......4 A3
Hollow Furlong OX29...107 C2
Hollow Rd The SN7....172 B1
HOLLOWS THE 28 A4
Hollow Way
  Aynho OX17.........35 C7
  Childrey OX12.......213 C3
  Oxford OX3, OX4.....142 D6
Hollybush Rd
  Carterton OX18......115 D2
  Hook Norton OX15....30 B8
Hollybush Row OX1...261 B2

Holly Cl
  Bicester OX26........65 F5
  Highmoor Cross RG9...242 E5
  Kidlington OX5.......108 E7
Holly Ct OX4.........142 E5
Hollyhocks OX11.....217 B7
Holmemoor Dr RG4...260 E2
Holme Park Farm La
  RG4................260 C2
Holmlea Rd RG8......249 C5
Holm Sq OX26........65 E5
Holm Way OX26......65 F5
HOLTON 126 C2
Holt The
  Abingdon OX14......179 F8
  Mollington OX17......3 E3
  Purley on Thames RG8...257 D4
Holt Weer Cl OX2.....109 B1
HOLWELL 114 A7
Holyoake Rd OX3.....124 D3
Holyrood Cl RG4......259 D6
Holy Trinity RC Prim Sch
  OX7...............42 F3
Holywell Bsns Ctr OX2..141 A8
Holywell Cl OX14.....160 C2
Holywell Music Room ★
  OX1...............261 C3
Holywell St OX1......261 C3
Home Cl
  Carterton OX18......115 D2
  Kidlington OX5.......92 E1
  Shabbington HP18....128 D3
  Wolvercote OX2......122 D8
  Wootton OX13........159 B7
Home Croft RG31.....257 B1
Home Farm
  Ardington OX12......215 D5
  Crowmarsh Gifford OX10..221 F7
Home Farm Barns OX18..133 B6
Home Farm Cl
  Ambrosden OX25.....81 C3
  East Hendred OX12...216 D7
  Shipton-under-Wychwood
    OX7...............85 D7
Home Farm Cotts
  Leafield OX29........102 F8
  Rousham OX25.......62 A4
Home Farm Ct OX17...23 B4
Home Farm Dr OX15...6 D8
Home Farm Mews OX12..196 A4
Homefield Cl HP14....188 E4
Homelands Way RG9...244 D1
Homeleaze Rd SN6....209 E8
Homestall OX2........122 B1
Homestead Cres OX25...63 A8
Homestead Rd OX16...16 E2
Homestead The
  Binfield Heath RG9...254 B1
  Bladon OX20.........91 C3
  Kidlington OX5.......108 D8
  Thame OX9..........129 E1
Hone Ct OX7.........73 B3
Honeybottom La OX13...159 B5
Honeyham OX18......116 C3
Honey La OX10.......220 F1
Honey Meadow Cl RG4..259 C6
Honeysuckle Cl OX26...65 F5
Honeysuckle Gr OX4...143 A2
Honor Cl OX5.........108 F8
HOOK END 251 E7
Hookend La RG8......251 D8
Hook End La RG8.....249 B1
HOOK NORTON.......30 A8
Hook Norton Brewery ★
  OX15...............29 F7
Hook Norton CE Prim Sch
  OX15...............30 B8
Hook Norton Rd
  Great Rollright OX7....29 B4
  Sibford Ferris OX15...19 B7
Hooks Cl GL7.........132 E1
Hopcraft Cl OX25.....96 E7
Hopcraft La OX15....33 F4
Hop Gdns RG9........244 E1
Hopkins Ct **4** OX4...142 D6
Hopton Rd OX3.......130 A1
Hordern Cl HP17......130 F6
HORLEY 8 B4
Horley Path Rd OX15...8 B1
Hornbeam Cl
  Banbury OX16........16 B5
  Purley on Thames RG8...257 C5
Hornbeam Dr OX4....143 A2
Hornbeam Rd OX26...65 F5
Horne OX27..........66 A7
Horn Hill OX15.......32 F6
Horn Hill Rd OX17....22 F3
Horn La
  Chastleton GL56......40 A6
  East Hendred OX12...216 D5
Hornsea Cl RG30......257 E1
Horns Way OX29......137 C3
HORNTON 7 C7
Hornton Hollow OX15...21 D4
Hornton Prim Sch OX15...7 C6
Horse Close Cotts OX44..164 D8
Horse Cl The RG4.....259 C4
Horsecroft SN7.......194 E7
Horsecroft Way RG31...257 B4
Horse Fair
  Banbury OX16........16 C6
  Chipping Norton OX7...42 E3
  Deddington OX15.....33 F4
Horseman Cl OX3.....124 A5
Horsemere La OX29...107 D2

Horsepath Park Cvn Site
　OX33. . . . . **143** D6
Horsepond Rd RG4. . . . . . **252** B5
Horseshoe La OX20. . . . . . **75** F4
Horse Shoe La OX7. . . . . . . **72** B8
Horseshoe Pk RG8. . . . . . **256** D5
Horseshoe Rd
　Bledlow Ridge HP14. . . . . **189** C8
　Pangbourne RG8. . . . . . . **256** D5
Horsham Cl OX16. . . . . **8** F1
HORSLEYS GREEN. **189** C3
HORSPATH. **143** D6
Horspath Athletics & Sports
　Gd OX4. . . . . **143** A6
Horspath CE Prim Sch
　OX33. . . . . **143** C7
Horspath Driftway OX3. . **142** E7
Horspath Rd OX4. . . . . **142** E6
Horspath Rd Ind Est OX4 **142** F6
Horton Ave OX9. . . . . **148** A7
Horton Cl OX9. . . . . **148** A7
HORTON-CUM-
　STUDLEY. **112** A6
Horton Hospl The OX16 . . **16** D4
Horton La OX15. . . . . **21** A2
Horton Rd OX33. . . . . **111** C1
Horton View OX16. . . . . **16** C3
Horwood Cl OX3. . . . . **124** C3
Hosker Cl OX3. . . . . **125** A3
Hound Cl OX14. . . . . **160** C2
Howard Ave OX12. . . . . **196** E1
Howard Cornish Rd
　OX13. . . . . **178** D7
Howard Rd OX16. . . . . **16** F6
Howard St OX4. . . . . **142** A6
Howbery Farm OX10. . . . . **221** F7
Howe Cl OX33. . . . . **144** A8
Howe Hill OX49. . . . . **206** D4
Howe Rd OX49. . . . . **206** C8
Howes La OX26. . . . . **65** B3
Howgate Dr RG8. . . . . **249** C7
Howland Rd OX9. . . . . **148** B7
Hoyle Cl OX28. . . . . **104** A3
Hubble Cl OX3. . . . . **124** E5
Huckleberry Cl RG8. . . . . **257** C4
Hudleston Ave OX10. . . . . **204** C2
Hudson Ct OX15. . . . . **33** F4
Hudson St
　Bicester OX26. . . . . **65** D3
　Deddington OX15. . . . . **33** F4
Hugh Allen Cres OX3. . . . **123** F3
Hughes Cl OX7. . . . . **73** C2
Hughes Cres SN7. . . . . **192** C3
Hughes Ho OX4. . . . . **141** F8
Hugh Price Ho OX4. . . . . . **142** B7
Humber Cl
　Didcot OX11. . . . . **201** A1
　Wantage OX12. . . . . **214** E5
Humber St OX15. . . . . **21** E4
Humber Wlk OX16. . . . . **15** F8
Humfrey Rd OX3. . . . . **124** F4
Humphries Cl OX18. . . . . . **115** E3
Hunder Ct OX1. . . . . **141** D2
Hundley Way OX7. . . . . **73** C4
Hundred Acres Cl OX3. . . **142** E7
HUNGERFORD GREEN. . . . **247** F4
Hungerford Rd OX13. . . . . **217** B8
Hunsdon Rd OX4. . . . . **142** A4
Hunt Cl OX26. . . . . **65** E2
Hunt Ct HP14. . . . . **188** F4
Hunter Cl
　Abingdon OX14. . . . . **160** B3
　Oxford OX4. . . . . **142** E6
HUNTERCOMBE END. **224** B4
Huntercombe End La
　RG9. . . . . **224** B4
Hunters Chase RG4. . . . . **258** F5
Hunters Cl OX12. . . . . **196** C1
Hunters Field SN7. . . . . . **194** E7
Hunters Piece SN6. . . . . . **209** A2
Hunters Point OX39. . . . . **168** C6
Hunt Rd OX9. . . . . **148** B7
Hunts Cl OX18. . . . . **100** E4
Hunt's Cl OX8. . . . . **89** C7
HUNT'S GREEN. **254** B6
Hurdeswell OX29. . . . . **90** A1
Hurdlers Gn OX49. . . . . . . **186** A2
Hurst Cl OX10. . . . . **221** C6
Hurst La
　Freeland OX29. . . . . **106** A7
　Oxford OX2. . . . . **140** B6
Hurst Rise Rd OX2. . . . . . **140** C8
Hurst St OX4. . . . . **141** F7
Huscarle Way RG31. . . . . **257** C4
Hutchcombe Farm Cl
　OX2. . . . . **140** C7
Hutchcomb Rd OX2. . . . . . **140** C8
Huxley Cl
　Bicester OX26. . . . . **65** C3
　Wootton OX13. . . . . **159** B6
Hyacinth Wlk OX4. . . . . . . **161** E8
Hyde Copse OX14. . . . . . . **178** D7
Hyde Gr OX15. . . . . **21** C3
Hyde Mdw View **3**
　OX28. . . . . **104** A1
Hyde Pl
　Abingdon OX14. . . . . **179** D5
　Oxford OX2. . . . . **123** A4
Hyde Rd OX12. . . . . **196** A5
Hydes The RG31. . . . . **257** C4
Hyde The OX14. . . . . **179** D5
Hydrangea Wlk OX16. . . . . . **9** B1

Hythe Bridge St OX1 . . . . **261** A2

I

Ian Mikardo Way RG4 . . . **259** D2
Ibstone Ave RG4. . . . . **259** E5
Ibstone Rd HP14. . . . . **188** C3
ICKFORD. **128** A3
Ickford Comb Sch HP18 . . **128** A3
Ickford Rd
　Shabbington HP18. . . . . . **128** D2
　Tiddington OX9. . . . . **145** F8
　Worminghall HP18. . . . . . **127** E6
Ickleton Rd OX12. . . . . . . **214** B4
Icknield Cl
　Chinnor OX39. . . . . **168** A4
　Didcot OX11. . . . . **200** C1
Icknield Com Coll OX49 . **186** B2
Icknield Cotts RG8. . . . . . **249** A6
Icknield La OX12. . . . . **214** E4
Icknield Line The (Chinnor &
　Princess Risborough Rly)★
　OX39. . . . . **168** E7
Icknield Pl OX18. . . . . **249** D8
Icknield Rd RG8. . . . . **249** D8
Icknield Way SN6. . . . . . . **227** C4
IDBURY. **69** B4
Idbury Cl OX28. . . . . **117** D7
Idbury Rd OX7. . . . . **69** A3
IDSTONE. **227** F5
Idstone Hill SN6. . . . . **228** A4
Idstone Rd SN6. . . . . **228** A6
IFFLEY. **141** F4
Iffley Mdw Nature Reserve★
　OX1. . . . . **141** E5
Iffley Mead Sch OX4 . . . . **141** F5
Iffley Rd OX4. . . . . **141** F7
Iffley Turn OX4. . . . . **142** A5
Ilchester Mews RG4. . . . . **259** E6
Ilex Cl RG4. . . . . **252** F4
Ilges La OX10. . . . . **221** A2
Ilkley Rd RG4. . . . . **258** E3
Illingworth Ave RG4. . . . . **259** E6
ILMER. **149** F8
Ilsley Cl RG4. . . . . **252** F5
Ilsley Rd OX3. . . . . **124** E4
Imperial Ct RG9. . . . . **244** E1
Independent Bsns Pk
　HP14. . . . . **188** C5
Ingham La OX49. . . . . **186** B1
Ingleby Paddocks OX5 . . . **77** D1
Ingle Cl OX3. . . . . **124** B4
INGLESHAM. **150** B1
Inglewood Cl RG4. . . . . . . **252** F6
Ingrebourne Way OX11. . **200** F3
Inkerman Cl OX14. . . . . . . **159** D1
Innsworth Rd OX18. . . . . . **115** E3
Inott Furze OX3. . . . . **142** D7
Insall Rd OX7. . . . . **42** E4
Inst of Virology &
　Experimental Microbiology
　OX1. . . . . **261** C3
IPSDEN. **240** C7
Iqra Sch OX4. . . . . **142** B2
Ireland Cl OX44. . . . . **184** D6
Ireton Ct OX9. . . . . **129** F1
Iron Down Hill OX15, OX7 . **32** C3
Ironside Dr SN6. . . . . **191** D1
Ironstone Hollow OX15. . . **30** C8
Ironstones OX16. . . . . **16** A8
Ishree Cotts RG9. . . . . . . **242** A5
Isis Ave OX26. . . . . **65** B2
Isis Bsns Ctr OX4. . . . . . . **142** F6
Isis Cl
　Abingdon OX14. . . . . **160** B1
　Long Hanborough OX29. . **106** B8
　South Hinksey OX1. . . . . **141** E5
Isis Ct RG1. . . . . **259** B1
ISLIP. **109** F8
Islip Rd
　Bletchingdon OX5. . . . . . . **93** A7
　Oxford OX2. . . . . **123** B8
Islip Sta OX5. . . . . **93** F1
Itchen Ct OX11. . . . . **201** A3
Ivatt Wlk OX16. . . . . **16** E8
Ivybank RG31. . . . . **257** C1
Ivy Cl OX4. . . . . **142** D5
Ivydene Rd RG30. . . . . . . **258** C1
Ivy La
　Mollington OX17. . . . . **4** A3
　Oxford OX3. . . . . **124** C4
　Shutford OX15. . . . . **14** B5

J

Jack Argent Cl **16** OX4 . . **142** F1
Jackdaw La OX4. . . . . **141** E7
Jackies La OX33. . . . . **144** C7
Jackman Cl OX14. . . . . . . **180** A7
Jackson Cl OX18. . . . . **115** D2
Jackson Cole Ho OX1. . . . **261** A2
Jackson Dr OX1. . . . . **141** D2
Jackson Rd
　Bledington OX7. . . . . **54** D2
　Cutteslowe OX2. . . . . **109** B1
Jacksons La RG4. . . . . **258** B5
Jack Straw's La OX3 . . . . **124** A3
Jacobs Cl OX28. . . . . **104** B1
Jacobs Yd OX7. . . . . **60** F8
James Ct OX18. . . . . **152** E8
James St OX4. . . . . **141** F8
James Wolfe Rd OX4. . . . **142** E7
Janaway OX4. . . . . **142** A1
Jane Morbey Rd OX9. . . . **148** A7
Jane Seaman Ct OX4 . . . . **143** A1
Japonica Cl OX26. . . . . **65** F5

Japonica Wlk OX16. . . . . . . **9** B1
Jarn Way OX1. . . . . **140** D1
Jarvis' La OX26. . . . . **66** B2
Jasmine Cl OX4. . . . . **142** F3
Jasmine Pl OX26. . . . . **65** F5
Jasmine Way **10** OX18. . . **115** E5
Jasmine Wlk OX16. . . . . . . **9** B1
Javelin Way OX10. . . . . . . **204** D3
Jay Cl OX26. . . . . **81** A8
Jaynes Cl OX16. . . . . **16** D2
Jefferson Cl RG4. . . . . **259** C7
Jeffersons Piece OX7. . . . **73** C4
Jefferson Way OX9. . . . . . **148** A7
Jeff's Terr OX7. . . . . **73** B4
Jemmetts Cl OX10. . . . . . **182** D1
Jennings La OX11. . . . . . . **217** E7
Jenyns Ct OX14. . . . . **179** C6
JERICHO. **261** A3
Jericho St OX2. . . . . **261** A4
Jerome Way OX5. . . . . **92** B6
Jersey Dr **1** OX16. . . . . **9** A1
Jersey Rd OX4. . . . . **142** A3
Jervis Cl OX7. . . . . **60** F8
Jespers Hill SN7. . . . . **173** A3
Jesse's La HP18. . . . . **129** C6
Jessops Cl
　Marston OX3. . . . . **123** C5
　Oxford OX3. . . . . **124** A5
Jesus Coll OX1. . . . . **261** B2
Jethro Tull Gdns OX10 . . **221** E7
Jetty The OX17. . . . . **5** E1
Jeune Hall **1** OX4 . . . . . . **141** F8
Jeune St OX4. . . . . **141** F8
Joan Lawrence Pl OX3 . . **124** E1
John Allen Ctr OX4. . . . . . **142** C5
John Blandy VC Prim Sch
　OX13. . . . . **156** E1
John Buchan Rd OX3. . . . **124** B5
John Garne Way OX3. . . . **124** A2
John Hampden Prim Sch
　OX9. . . . . **148** A7
John Henry Newman Prim
　Sch OX4. . . . . **142** B2
John Kallie Ho OX4. . . . . . **142** B6
John Lopes Rd OX29 . . . . **120** E7
John Mason Rd OX14. . . . **180** A8
John Mason Sch OX14 . . **179** E8
John Morris Rd OX14. . . . **179** E5
John Piers La OX1. . . . . . . **141** C5
John Radcliffe Hospl
　OX3. . . . . **124** B4
John Radcliffe Hospl Sch
　OX3. . . . . **124** C4
John Smith Dr OX4. . . . . . **142** D4
John Snow Pl OX3. . . . . . . **124** E3
Johnson Cl OX44. . . . . **143** D2
Johnstone Pl **12** OX10. . . **221** D7
Johnstones SN7. . . . . **195** A4
Johnston's Way OX7 . . . . . **42** E2
John Towle Cl OX1. . . . . . . **141** E5
John Watson Sch OX33. . **144** A8
Jordan Cl
　Didcot OX11. . . . . **201** A2
　Reading RG4. . . . . **259** E5
Jordan Hill OX2. . . . . **109** A2
Jordan Hill Rd OX2. . . . . . **109** A2
Jordans Ct OX7. . . . . **88** A3
Jordon Hill Bsns Pk OX2 **109** A2
Josey Cl RG4. . . . . **252** F6
Jourdain Rd OX4. . . . . **142** F3
Jowett Wlk OX1. . . . . **261** C3
Joyce's Rd SN7. . . . . **194** D8
Jubilee Cl OX25. . . . . **62** A8
Jubilee Cotts OX12. . . . . . **215** E5
Jubilee Ct OX16. . . . . **16** D5
Jubilee Gdns OX9. . . . . . . **147** D8
Jubilee La OX7. . . . . **85** A8
Jubilee Rd HP14. . . . . **188** F3
Jubilee Terr OX1. . . . . **261** B1
Jubilee Way
　Didcot OX11. . . . . **219** A8
　Witney OX28. . . . . **104** E1
Judds Cl OX28. . . . . **118** D8
Judges Cl OX5. . . . . **108** D8
Judges Rd RG9. . . . . **241** E4
Jugglers Cl OX16. . . . . **16** E8
Junction Rd
　Banbury OX16. . . . . **16** E6
　Churchill OX7. . . . . **55** E4
　Oxford OX4. . . . . **142** D6
Juniper Cl OX16. . . . . **9** B1
Juniper Ct
　4 Abingdon OX14. . . . . . **179** D7
　4 Banbury OX16. . . . . . . **16** D5
Juniper Dr OX4. . . . . **142** F2
Juniper Gdns OX26. . . . . . **65** E5
JUNIPER HILL. **37** D6
Juniper Way RG31. . . . . . **257** D2
Juxon St OX2. . . . . **261** A4

K

Kames Cl OX4. . . . . **142** B5
Karenza HP14. . . . . **188** A5
Kassam Stad (Oxford Utd FC)
　OX4. . . . . **142** D1
Katchside OX14. . . . . **199** F6
Katherine's Wlk GL7 . . . . **150** D4
Keats Cl **4** OX26. . . . . **65** C4
Keats Rd OX16. . . . . **16** A4
Keble Cl GL7. . . . . **150** D5
Keble Coll OX1. . . . . **261** B4
Keble Rd
　Bicester OX26. . . . . **65** F3
　Oxford OX1. . . . . **261** B4
Kedleston Rise OX16. . . . . **16** E2
Keene Cl OX4. . . . . **161** B8

Keens Cl OX7. . . . . **58** F5
Keens La OX39. . . . . **168** D6
Keeys Cl OX27. . . . . **50** C4
Kelburne Rd OX4. . . . . **142** B4
Kelham Hall Dr OX33. . . . **144** B7
Kellogg Coll (Norham
　Manor) OX2. . . . . **123** C4
Kellogg Coll (Rewley House)
　OX1. . . . . **261** B3
Kelly's Rd OX33. . . . . **143** F8
KELMSCOTT. **151** D3
Kelmscott Cl RG4. . . . . . . **258** F3
Kelmscott Manor★ GL7. . **151** E2
Kelso Mews RG4. . . . . **259** E6
Kelvedon Way RG4. . . . . . **258** E5
Kempson Cres OX4 . . . . . **142** A2
Kemps Rd OX17. . . . . **23** A5
Kempster Cl OX14. . . . . . . **180** B8
Kenchester OX14. . . . . **132** C5
Kendal Ave RG4. . . . . **259** E5
Kendall Cres OX2. . . . . . . **109** B1
Kendal Piece OX7. . . . . **73** C4
Kenhill Rd OX15. . . . . **6** E2
Kenilworth Ave OX4. . . . . **142** B7
Kenilworth Ct OX4. . . . . . **142** A7
Kenilworth Rd OX2. . . . . . **139** E4
Kenilworth Way OX16. . . . . **15** F5
Kenley Ave OX18. . . . . **115** E3
Kennedy Cl OX4. . . . . **142** E7
Kennedy Cres OX10 . . . . . **220** F1
Kennedy Dr RG8. . . . . **256** F5
Kennedy Ho OX16. . . . . **16** B6
Kennedy Rd OX26. . . . . . . **65** C1
Kennel La
　Chipping Norton OX7. . . . . **42** B2
　Steventon OX13. . . . . . . **199** A5
Kennet Cl
　Berinsfield OX10. . . . . . . **182** C4
　Bicester OX26. . . . . **65** D1
　Grove OX12. . . . . **196** D1
Kennet Rd
　Abingdon OX14. . . . . **160** B1
　Harwell OX11. . . . . **217** C1
Kennett Pl **3** OX11. . . . . **219** A8
Kennett Rd OX3. . . . . **124** D2
Kennetts Hos OX15. . . . . . **21** D4
KENNINGTON. **160** E7
Kennington Rd
　Kennington OX1. . . . . **141** E2
　Kennington OX1, OX14. . **160** E6
Kennington Rdbt OX1. . . . **141** D3
Kennylands Rd RG4. . . . . **253** A3
Kensington Cl
　Abingdon OX14. . . . . **179** E4
　Kings Sutton OX17. . . . . . **23** F6
Kent Cl
　Abingdon OX14. . . . . **180** B8
　Oxford OX4. . . . . **142** E3
Kenton's La RG10. . . . . . . **255** D7
Kentwood Cl
　Cholsey OX10. . . . . **220** F1
　Reading RG30. . . . . **257** E1
Kentwood Hill RG31. . . . . **257** E1
Kenville Rd OX1. . . . . **141** D2
Kernham Dr RG31. . . . . . . **257** C4
Kerry Cl **2** OX16. . . . . **9** A1
Kersington Cres OX4 . . . . **142** D3
Kerwood Cl OX20. . . . . **91** C7
Keston Cl RG4. . . . . **259** C2
Kestrel Cl OX18. . . . . **115** D3
Kestrel Cres OX4. . . . . **142** D2
Kestrels The OX12. . . . . . . **196** D2
Kestrel Way OX26. . . . . **81** A7
Ketchmere Cl HP18. . . . . **129** C6
Kew Win OX11. . . . . **201** A3
Keydale Rd OX33. . . . . **143** F8
Keyser Rd OX15. . . . . **22** E8
Keyte's Cl OX17. . . . . **23** B4
Kibble Cl OX11. . . . . **219** A8
KIDDINGTON. **60** B2
Kiddington Dr OX7. . . . . . . **74** D7
Kiddington Rd OX7. . . . . . . **60** E8
KIDLINGTON. **108** D7
Kidlington Ctr The **3**
　OX5. . . . . **92** E1
Kidlington & Gosford Sports
　Ctr OX5. . . . . **108** F7
Kidlington Rd OX5. . . . . . . **93** E1
KIDMORE END. **252** D3
Kidmore End CE Prim Sch
　RG4. . . . . **252** D3
Kidmore End Rd RG4. . . . **252** E4
Kidmore Rd RG4. . . . . **258** F5
Kilbale Cres OX16. . . . . **16** D4
Kildare Gdns RG4. . . . . . . **259** C3
Kilkenny La OX18. . . . . . . **115** C9
Kiln Cl
　Aston OX18. . . . . **135** D3
　Sandford-on-Thames OX4 **161** C8
Kiln La
　Garsington OX44. . . . . . . **143** C2
　Oxford OX3. . . . . **124** C4
　Shiplake Row RG9. . . . . . **254** C2
　Wheatley OX33. . . . . **144** B8
Kiln Rd RG4. . . . . **259** D8
Kiln Terr SN7. . . . . **173** B3
Kimbells Cl HP18. . . . . . . **128** D2
Kimber Cl OX33. . . . . **144** B8
Kimberley Villas **12** OX16 . **16** D5
Kimber Rd OX14. . . . . **179** C7
Kimbers Cl OX12. . . . . **196** A4
Kinecroft OX10. . . . . **221** D7
Kineton Rd OX1. . . . . **141** C7
King Alfred Dr OX11. . . . . **200** F1
King Alfred's Specialist
　Sports Coll (Centre Site)
　OX12. . . . . **214** D4

King Alfred's Specialist
　Sports Coll (East Site)
　OX12. . . . . **214** F4
King Alfred's Specialist
　Sports Coll (West Site)
　OX12. . . . . **214** B4
King Edward St OX1. . . . . **261** C2
Kingfisher Cl OX14. . . . . . **179** F5
Kingfisher Dr
　Banbury OX16. . . . . **16** E3
　Witney OX28. . . . . **118** A6
Kingfisher Gn OX4. . . . . . **142** F1
Kingfishers OX12. . . . . . . **214** E8
Kingfisher Sch OX14. . . . **180** B8
Kingfisher Way OX26. . . . . **81** A8
KINGHAM. **55** A4
Kingham Dr OX18. . . . . . . **115** D2
Kingham Hill Sch OX7. . . . **41** B1
Kingham Prim Sch OX7. . . **55** A5
Kingham Rd OX7. . . . . **55** E5
Kingham Sta OX7. . . . . **54** F2
King James Way RG9. . . . **254** C8
Kings Ave
　Bicester OX26. . . . . **65** D1
　Highworth SN6. . . . . **190** A5
　Marcham OX13. . . . . **178** D7
Kings Cl
　Ashbury SN6. . . . . **228** A7
　Henley-on-Thames RG9. . **244** D2
　Letcombe Regis OX12. . . **214** A2
　Worminghall HP18. . . . . . **127** D5
King's Cl OX9. . . . . **147** F8
Kingsclere Rd OX26. . . . . . **65** D2
Kings Common Cl RG9. . . **254** B1
King's Cross Rd OX2 . . . . **123** B7
Kings Ct OX18. . . . . **115** C9
KING'S END. **65** D1
King's End OX26. . . . . **65** E1
Kingsey Rd
　Thame OX9. . . . . **148** B8
　Towersey OX9. . . . . **130** D1
Kings Farm La RG9. . . . . . **253** E6
Kingsfield Cres OX28. . . . **104** C1
Kingsgate OX4. . . . . **142** D4
King's Head La OX5. . . . . . **93** F1
King's Head Mews OX7. . . **42** E3
Kingsholme Cl OX11. . . . . **218** F5
Kings La
　Filkins GL7. . . . . **132** D4
　Harwell OX11. . . . . **217** E7
King's La OX7. . . . . **192** C3
Kingsley Rd **5** OX26 . . . . . **65** C4
Kingsmead GL7. . . . . **150** C5
Kings Meadow Ind Est
　OX2. . . . . **140** F8
Kings Meadow Prim Sch
　OX26. . . . . **65** B3
King's Mill La OX3. . . . . . . **123** F2
King's Orch OX10. . . . . . . **202** E3
Kings Rd
　Bloxham OX15. . . . . **21** D4
　Henley-on-Thames RG9. . **244** E2
King's Rd
　Banbury OX16. . . . . **16** B6
　Henley-on-Thames RG9. . **244** D2
　Reading RG4. . . . . **259** C2
　Thame OX9. . . . . **148** A8
Kings Row HP14. . . . . **188** C5
King's School Oxford **5**
　OX4. . . . . **142** D6
King's Sch The (Primary)
　OX29. . . . . **104** D3
King's Sch The (Seniors)
　OX28. . . . . **118** B8
Kings Stile OX17. . . . . **10** F1
KINGS SUTTON. **23** F6
Kings Sutton Sta OX17 . . . **23** E5
King St OX2. . . . . **261** A4
KINGSTON BAGPUIZE. . . . **156** E2
Kingston Bagpuize House★
　OX13. . . . . **176** E8
KINGSTON BLOUNT. **167** F3
Kingston Bsns Pk OX13. . **176** F8
Kingston Cl OX14. . . . . . . **179** F8
Kingston Ct OX2. . . . . **261** A4
KINGSTONE WINSLOW. . . **228** B8
Kingston Hill OX39. . . . . . **188** B8
Kingston Hts OX29. . . . . . **105** B7
KINGSTON LISLE. **212** A4
Kingston Lisle Bsns Ctr
　OX12. . . . . **212** B4
Kingston Rd
　Frilford OX13. . . . . **177** D7
　Oxford OX2. . . . . **123** A4
KINGSTON STERT. **167** D7
Kingsway
　Banbury OX16. . . . . **16** B5
　Reading RG4. . . . . **259** E6
Kingsway Cotts OX18. . . . **135** D2
Kingsway Dr OX5. . . . . **109** A8
Kings Wlk RG9. . . . . **244** D5
Kingswood La HP18. . . . . . **98** F6
King Wlk OX11. . . . . **200** D2
Kinson Rd RG30. . . . . **258** A1
Kipling Cl OX26. . . . . **65** C4
Kirby Cl
　Middle Barton OX7. . . . . . **60** F8
　South Moreton OX11. . . . **219** D5
Kirby Pl OX4. . . . . **142** D5
Kirby Rd GL54. . . . . **68** B3
Kirk Cl
　Cutteslowe OX2. . . . . **109** A1
　Kennington OX1. . . . . **160** E8
Kirkfell Cl OX31. . . . . **257** C2
Kirkham Cl RG4. . . . . **259** E6
KIRTLINGTON. **77** F4
Kirtlington CE Prim Sch
　OX5. . . . . **78** A4

Kirtlington Quarry Nature Reserve★ OX5..........77 E4
Kirtlington Rd OX25..........63 A7
KITEBROOK..........26 D3
Kitebrook House Sch GL56..........26 C3
Kit La RG8..........241 D6
Knapp Cl OX14..........179 D8
Knappe OX9..........254 C8
Knapton's Croft OX25..........62 D6
KNIGHTON..........210 E3
Knighton Cl RG4..........259 A3
Knighton Hill SN6..........210 E1
Knightsbridge La OX49..........186 B5
Knights Ho OX3..........124 F2
Knights Rd OX4..........142 E2
Knights Way RG4..........259 B5
Knoll Cl OX12..........231 E7
Knolles Dr SN7..........194 D7
Knolles Rd OX4..........142 C5
Knoll The RG31..........257 B2
Knollys Cl OX14..........160 A3
Knott Oaks OX29..........89 F5
Knowlands SN6..........190 A4
Knowle Cl RG4..........258 D4
KNOWLE END..........2 A5
Knowle La OX25..........79 B1
Knowsley Rd RG31..........257 C3
Kybald St OX1..........261 C2
Kyetts Cnr OX17..........4 F2
Kynaston Rd OX11..........218 F8
Kysbie Cl OX14..........159 F3

L
Laburnum Ave OX13..........159 C1
Laburnum Cl
  Ambrosden OX25..........81 C3
  Carterton OX18..........115 F4
Laburnum Cres OX5..........108 E6
Laburnum Gr
  Banbury OX16..........16 D2
  Didcot OX11..........218 F8
Laburnum Rd OX2..........140 D7
Lacemakers
  Chinnor OX39..........168 C6
  Long Crendon HP18..........129 C7
Lacey Dr OX9..........148 B7
Lackmore Gdns RG8..........250 F8
Ladburn La OX18..........115 A6
Ladder Hill OX33..........144 A7
Ladenham Rd OX4..........142 E3
Ladman Villas SN7..........173 E7
Ladycroft Cvn Pk OX11..........219 A1
Lady Gr OX11, OX11..........201 B4
Ladygrove Paddock OX14..........179 D6
Ladygrove Park Prim Sch OX11..........200 F2
Ladygrove Rd OX14..........179 D6
Lady Jane Ct RG4..........259 B3
Lady Margaret Hall Coll OX2..........123 D4
Lady Pl OX14..........200 A8
Ladywell Cl OX29..........105 C6
Lady Wlk SN7..........211 C7
Laggots Cl SN7..........155 F2
Lains Ct OX12..........214 D7
Lakefield Rd OX4..........142 B1
Lake Rd
  East Hagbourne OX11..........218 E6
  Shrivenham SN6..........209 A8
Lake Sch of English The OX1..........261 A2
Lakeside
  Cutteslowe OX2..........108 F2
  Witney OX28..........118 A6
Lakeside Ind Est OX29..........137 F7
Lakesmere Cl OX5..........92 C3
Lake St OX1..........141 D6
Lake View NN13..........38 A3
Lake Wlk OX17..........23 B4
Lamarsh Rd OX2..........122 C1
Lambe Ave OX14..........199 C3
Lambert Wlk OX9..........129 F1
Lamb La OX20..........91 B2
Lamborough Hill OX13..........159 B6
Lambourne Cres OX26..........65 C1
Lambourne Rd RG4..........252 E5
Lambourne Way OX17..........23 B4
Lambourn Rd OX4..........142 A3
Lambrick Way OX14..........179 E4
Lambridge La RG9..........244 C3
Lambridge Wood Rd RG9..........244 B4
Lambs Cl OX5..........92 E2
Lamb's Cres OX16..........16 E4
Lamb's La OX20..........75 F4
Lambton Cl OX14..........159 A7
Lambwath Stream OX11..........200 F3
Lammas Ct OX14..........159 F1
Lamorna Cres RG31..........257 C1
Lampitts Gn OX15..........15 A8
Lancaster Ave OX10..........204 D3
Lancaster Cl OX26..........66 A4
Lancaster Dr GL54..........68 B4
Lancaster Pl OX18..........115 E1
Lanchester Dr OX16..........15 F8
Lancott La OX29..........137 B4
Lancut Rd OX28..........103 E1
Landells OX18..........134 E4
Landscape Cl OX25..........79 A5
Landseer Rd OX25..........79 A5
Landseer Wlk OX14..........179 E5
Lane Cl
  Horley OX15..........8 B4
  Kidlington OX5..........108 D8

Lane End OX10..........222 A7
Lanes End OX26..........66 E2
Lanes The OX18..........134 F3
Lane The
  Ashbury SN6..........228 A7
  Chastleton GL56..........40 D7
  Chilton OX11..........235 E8
  Cuddesdon OX44..........144 B2
  Fritwell OX27..........49 F7
  Great Tew OX7..........45 C7
  Hempton OX15..........33 B4
  Hinton Parva SN4..........227 A4
  Lower Heyford OX25..........62 D6
  Uffington SN7..........211 C7
  Woolstone SN7..........211 A5
Langdale Ct OX18..........118 B8
Langdale Gate OX28..........118 B8
Langdale Rd OX9..........148 A8
LANGFORD..........132 C2
Langford Bsns Pk The OX5..........92 B2
Langford Cl RG4..........259 C5
Langford Gdns OX26..........65 C2
Langford La
  Kidlington OX5..........92 A2
  Wendlebury OX25..........80 D5
Langford Locks OX5..........92 C2
Langford Village CP Sch OX26..........81 A8
Langhams Way RG10..........255 E2
LANGLEY..........86 C4
Langley Cl OX3..........124 D2
Langley La OX18..........152 E5
Langley Rd
  Abingdon OX14..........159 F2
  Chalgrove OX44..........184 C6
Langley's La OX29..........137 C1
Langston Cl OX7..........55 E5
Langston Priory Workshops OX7..........54 F2
Langton Ave OX25..........81 C4
Langtree Sch RG8..........250 F8
Lanham Way OX4..........142 B2
Lansdown OX25..........16 B3
Lansdowne Rd OX13..........159 A6
Lansdown Rd SN7..........173 A3
Lapsley Dr OX29..........9 C2
Lapwing Cl OX26..........81 A8
Lapwing La OX10..........221 A1
Larch Cl
  Bicester OX26..........65 E4
  Kingston Bagpuize OX13..........156 C1
  Oxford OX2..........140 D8
Larch Ct RG4..........259 B3
Larch End OX44..........143 D2
Larches The
  Carterton OX18..........115 D2
  Oxford OX3..........125 A3
Larch La OX28..........104 D1
Lardon Cotts RG8..........249 A6
Larissa Cl RG31..........257 C5
Larkdown OX12..........214 F4
Larkfield OX10..........221 A1
Larkfields OX3..........124 E2
Lark Hill
  Ardington OX12..........215 A2
  Oxford OX2..........123 A6
Larkhill Pl OX14..........159 D1
Larkhill Rd OX14..........179 E8
Larkins La OX3..........124 D4
Lark Rise
  Charlbury OX7..........73 C3
  Kidlington OX5..........92 D2
Larkmead Sch OX14..........179 C8
Larkrise First Sch OX4..........142 A6
Larksfield Cl OX18..........133 C8
Larksfield Rd OX16..........16 D2
Larkspur Gr OX28..........104 D1
Larkspur Sq OX26..........65 E4
Larkswood Cl RG31..........257 C5
Larsen Rd OX25..........63 D8
LASHBROOK..........255 B4
Lashbrook Mead RG9..........255 B4
Lashbrook Rd RG9..........255 B4
Lashford La OX13..........158 F7
Lashlake Rd OX9..........129 F1
Latcham Ct OX7..........43 A3
LATCHFORD..........165 B7
Latchford La OX44..........164 F7
Lathbury Rd OX2..........123 B5
Latimer Grange OX3..........124 C2
Latimer Rd
  Carterton OX18..........115 C2
  Oxford OX3..........124 C2
Latton Cl
  Chilton OX11..........235 E8
  Kingston Bagpuize OX13..........156 D1
Laud's Cl RG9..........244 C1
Laughton Hill OX8..........89 C7
Launceston Ave RG4..........259 E6
Laundry Cotts GL56..........40 C2
Laundry La OX18..........135 D3
LAUNTON..........66 D1
Launton Bsns Ctr OX26..........66 A2
Launton CE Prim Sch OX26..........66 D2
Launton Rd
  Bicester OX26..........66 A3
  Stratton Audley OX27..........66 D8
Launton Road Ret Pk OX26..........66 B3
Laurel Cl
  Banbury OX16..........16 D2
  Carterton OX18..........115 D3
  Chalgrove OX44..........184 D7
Laurel Cres OX12..........214 E8
Laurel Ct OX4..........142 A8
Laurel Dr
  Hornton OX15..........6 E8
  Kingston Bagpuize OX13..........156 E1
Laurel Farm Cl OX3..........124 C4

Laurels The
  Fringford OX27..........52 C6
  Great Coxwell SN7..........192 C8
  Pangbourne RG8..........256 D5
  Sonning RG5..........260 E1
  Stadhampton OX44..........163 C2
  Tetsworth OX9..........166 B8
Laurence Allison Mews RG4..........258 E2
Lavender Cl OX16..........9 B1
Lavender Pl
  Bampton OX18..........134 F3
  Carterton OX18..........115 C2
Lavender Sq OX18..........134 F3
Lavender View OX28..........104 D2
Lavender Way OX28..........104 E2
Lawns The HP18..........98 B1
Lawrence Cl OX12..........213 C4
Lawrence Fields OX25..........62 B8
Lawrence La OX18..........100 E5
Lawrence Rd OX4..........142 C5
Lawrence Way OX26..........65 C2
Lawson Dr RG4..........258 E5
Lawson La OX11..........235 E8
Lawson Rd RG9..........254 F7
Lawton Ave OX18..........115 D2
Laxton Way OX16..........8 F1
Lay Ave OX10..........182 C6
Laytom Rise RG31..........257 C3
Leabrook Cl OX16..........16 D2
Leach Rd
  Berinsfield OX10..........182 D5
  Bicester OX26..........65 C2
LEAFIELD..........86 E3
Leafield CE Prim Sch OX29..........86 F3
Leafield Rd
  Crawley OX29..........103 E5
  Oxford OX4..........142 C6
  Ramsden Heath OX7..........87 E4
  Shipton-under-Wychwood OX7, OX29..........86 B5
Leafield Tech Ctr OX29..........86 C3
Lea Gr OX11..........200 F3
Lea La HP18..........129 F4
Leamington Dr SN7..........172 E2
Leander Way OX1..........141 E4
Lea Rd RG4..........252 F4
Leaver Rd RG9..........244 C1
LECHLADE-ON-THAMES..........150 D3
Lechlade Rd
  Buscot SN7..........171 C7
  Faringdon SN7..........172 C5
  Highworth SN6..........190 A7
  Langford GL7..........132 D2
  Lechlade-on-Thames GL7..........151 A7
  Lechlade-on-Thames GL7, SN7..........150 E2
Leckford Pl OX2..........261 A4
Leckford Pl Sch OX2..........261 A4
Leckford Rd OX2..........261 A4
Ledbury Cl RG30..........258 C1
Ledgers Cl OX4..........142 C2
LEDWELL..........46 C5
Ledwell Rd OX7..........46 B2
Lee Ave OX14..........180 B8
Lee Cl
  Charlbury OX7..........73 C3
  Kidlington OX5..........92 D2
Lee Ct OX9..........147 F8
Lee Rd HP27..........169 F6
Lees Hts OX7..........73 C3
Lees The SN7..........172 F3
Le Hall Pl OX17..........22 F3
Leicester Cl RG9..........244 D3
Leiden Rd OX3..........142 E8
Leigh Cl OX29..........105 B5
Leigh Croft OX13..........159 A7
Leigh Rd OX16..........16 C5
Lely Ct OX14..........179 E5
Lennox Gdns OX16..........16 A4
Lenthal OX5..........93 A7
Lenthall Rd
  Abingdon OX14..........179 F8
  Oxford OX4..........141 F3
Lenton Rd OX16..........16 D2
Leoline Jenkins Ho OX4..........142 B7
Leon Cl OX4..........141 F8
Leopold St OX4..........142 A7
Lerwick Croft OX26..........66 A4
Lesparre Cl OX14..........179 B2
Lester Cl OX17..........23 A6
Lester Way OX10..........221 B7
Letcombe Ave OX14..........179 F8
LETCOMBE BASSETT..........231 F7
Letcombe Ct OX12..........214 E4
Letcombe Hill OX12..........214 A4
LETCOMBE REGIS..........214 B2
Letcombe Wlk OX12..........196 D1
Level The OX15..........6 E2
Levenot Cl OX16..........16 F6
Leverkus Ho OX39..........168 C6
Leverton Gdns OX12..........214 C5
Levery Cl OX14..........180 C8
LEW..........117 B1
Lewell Ave OX3..........123 F4
Lewin Cl [1] OX4..........142 C4
Lewington Cl OX44..........164 D8
Lewis Cl OX3..........125 A2
Lewis Rd OX7..........42 D2
LEWKNOR..........187 B8
Lewknor CE Prim Sch OX49..........187 B8
Leyburne Gdns OX39..........168 C7
Leyesland Ct OX16..........16 D3

Leyes The OX15..........33 F4
Leys App OX7..........42 E2
Leys Cl OX15..........15 A8
Leys Ho OX16..........16 C6
Leyshon Rd OX33..........144 C7
Leys Pl OX4..........142 A7
Leys Rd OX2..........139 C5
LEYS THE..........118 A7
Leys The
  Adderbury OX17..........22 F3
  Chipping Norton OX7..........42 D2
  Lyneham OX7..........70 E5
  Salford OX7..........41 F5
Leys View GL7..........132 C1
Leys Villas OX28..........118 A7
Ley The OX20..........91 C6
Library Ave OX11..........217 B2
Liddell Rd OX4..........142 C4
Lidderdale Rd GL54..........68 B3
Liddiard Cl
  Kennington OX1..........160 E8
  Wantage OX12..........214 D6
Liddiard's Row [7] SN7..........172 F3
Liddon Rd OX44..........184 D6
Lido Rd OX11..........234 F8
Lidsey Rd OX16..........16 A5
LIDSTONE..........58 B6
Lidstone Rd OX7..........58 D5
Lilac Cl RG8..........257 C5
Lilacs Pl OX49..........186 B1
Lily Cl OX26..........65 D5
Limborough Rd OX12..........214 D5
Lime Ave
  Banbury OX16..........16 E4
  Stoke Row RG9..........242 A1
Lime Cres OX26..........65 F5
Lime Gr
  Chinnor OX39..........168 D6
  Kingston Bagpuize OX13..........156 D1
Lime Kiln Rd OX5..........77 D1
Lime Rd OX2..........140 D7
Limes The
  Crowmarsh Gifford OX10..........221 F7
  Dorchester OX10..........182 D2
  Stratton Audley OX27..........52 D1
Limes Way HP18..........128 D2
Limetree Cl OX12..........196 F1
Lime Tree Ct OX18..........115 D3
Lime Tree Rd RG8..........249 B6
Limetrees OX11..........217 E1
Lime Wlk
  Oxford OX3..........124 C2
  Witney OX28..........104 E1
Limmings La OX9..........148 A6
Linacre Cl OX11..........219 B8
Linacre Coll OX1..........261 C3
Linacre Ct OX3..........124 F2
Lince La OX5..........77 E2
Linch Farm OX2..........122 B6
Linch Hill Fishery★ OX29..........138 B5
Lincoln Cl
  Banbury OX16..........16 B6
  Bicester OX26..........66 A4
  Standlake OX29..........137 D4
  Upper Rissington GL54..........68 B4
Lincoln Coll OX1..........261 B2
Lincoln Gdns OX11..........219 B8
Lincoln Pk NN13..........24 A5
Lincoln Pl OX9..........147 F8
Lincoln Rd OX1..........141 D5
Lincombe La OX1..........159 E2
Lincraft Cl OX5..........108 E2
Linden Cotts RG8..........250 E2
Linden Cres OX12..........196 F1
Linden Ct OX3..........124 D3
Linden Gate OX11..........217 E1
Linden Rd OX26..........65 F2
Lindsay Dr OX14..........160 B2
Linkside Ave OX2..........108 F2
Links Rd OX1..........160 E8
Link The
  Banbury OX16..........16 A6
  Marston OX3..........123 E4
  Oxford OX3..........124 F3
Linkwood Rd OX29..........103 C1
Linnet Cl
  Clifton Hampden OX14..........182 B4
  Oxford OX4..........142 C6
Linton Rd OX2..........123 C5
Lion Brewery The OX1..........261 A2
Lion Mdw RG9..........224 D2
Lipscombe Pl OX18..........115 D4
Lister Cl RG8..........257 C5
Litchfield Cl OX7..........58 F5
Lithgow Rd GL54..........68 B3
Little Acreage OX3..........123 F4
Little Baldon Farm Cotts OX44..........162 B1
LITTLE BARRINGTON..........99 B6
Little Blenheim OX5..........108 B5
LITTLE BOURTON..........9 D5
Little Bowden La RG8..........256 A4
Little Brewery St OX4..........123 F1
Little Bridge Rd OX15..........21 D4
Littlebrook Mdw OX7..........70 D1
Little Bury OX4..........143 A2
LITTLE CHESTERTON..........79 F5
LITTLE CLANFIELD..........152 B7
Little Clarendon St OX1..........261 B3
LITTLE COMPTON..........27 A1
LITTLE COXWELL..........192 C5
Little Croft Rd RG8..........249 C5
Little Cl OX12..........214 D7
LITTLE FARINGDON..........150 F8
Little Field OX4..........142 D5
Littlegate St OX1..........261 B1

Little Glebe RG4..........260 E3
Little Gn OX15..........21 D4
Little Ground OX15..........22 C3
LITTLE HASELEY..........164 D6
LITTLE HEATH..........250 C6
Little Howe Cl OX14..........160 E3
LITTLE ICKFORD..........128 B3
Littlejohn's La RG30..........258 C1
Little La
  Aynho OX17..........35 C7
  Bledington OX7..........54 D2
  Horley OX15..........8 B4
  Milton OX14..........199 C5
Little Langlands OX11..........218 F7
Little Lees OX7..........73 C3
LITTLE LONDON..........160 D8
LITTLE MILTON..........164 A6
Little Milton CE Prim Sch OX44..........163 F6
LITTLE MINSTER..........102 C3
LITTLEMORE..........142 C1
Littlemore Rd OX4..........142 C4
Littlemore Rdbt OX4..........142 B3
Little Paddock OX27..........52 C7
LITTLE ROLLRIGHT..........28 A1
Littlestead Cl RG4..........259 E5
LITTLESTEAD GREEN..........259 E5
LITTLE TEW..........45 A5
LITTLE TINGEWICK..........39 E6
LITTLE WITTENHAM..........202 B7
Little Wittenham Rd OX14..........201 F8
Little Wood HP14..........188 E5
LITTLEWORTH
  Benson..........203 E4
  Faringdon..........173 E4
  Wheatley..........143 F7
Littleworth Bsns Ctr OX33..........143 F7
Littleworth Ind Est OX11..........214 C5
Littleworth Pk OX33..........143 F7
Littleworth Rd
  Benson..........203 F4
  Wheatley OX33..........144 A8
Livingstone Cl OX5..........108 B7
Lobelia Rd OX4..........142 F2
Lock Cres OX5..........108 C6
Lockheart Cres OX4..........142 D4
Lockheed Cl OX16..........16 C8
Lockinge Cl OX11..........218 E7
Locks La OX12..........214 C4
Lockstile Mead RG8..........249 C6
Lockstile Way RG8..........249 C6
Lockway OX14..........199 A8
Locombe Hill OX12..........131 B8
Lodden Ave OX10..........182 C5
Loddon Cl
  Abingdon OX14..........160 B1
  Bicester OX26..........65 D1
Loddon Dr
  Didcot OX11..........201 B1
  Wargrave RG10..........255 B1
Loder Rd OX11..........217 C5
Lodersfield GL7..........150 C4
Lodge Cl
  Banbury OX16..........16 D4
  Bicester OX26..........65 E5
  Marston OX3..........123 D7
Lodge Hill OX14..........160 B4
Lodge Hill Intc OX14..........160 B5
Lodge Rd OX29..........90 F1
Lodge Terr OX7..........42 F3
Lombard St
  [5] Abingdon OX14..........179 F7
  Eynsham OX29..........120 E7
Lombard Way OX16..........17 A7
Lomond Ave RG4..........259 C5
London Ct OX3..........124 C2
London La OX7..........71 C2
London Pl OX4..........123 F1
London Rd
  Aston Rowant OX49..........167 C1
  Bicester OX26..........80 F8
  Blewbury OX11..........236 B3
  Chipping Norton OX7..........43 B3
  Milton Common OX9..........146 B3
  Oxford OX3..........124 D3
  Postcombe OX9..........166 F4
  Sonning RG6..........260 C1
  Tiddington OX9, OX44..........145 E5
  Wheatley OX33..........144 D7
London St SN7..........173 B4
London Wlk OX7..........43 A3
London Yd [1] OX16..........16 C6
Long Acre OX5..........6 D2
Long Alley Almshouses [10] OX14..........179 F6
Long Barn OX14..........200 A4
Long Barrow OX17..........5 F7
Long Cl
  Oxford, Dean Court OX2..........122 B1
  Oxford, New Headington OX3..........142 E8
LONG COMPTON..........27 F6
LONGCOT..........192 C2
Longcot & Fernham CE Prim Sch SN7..........192 C2
Longcot Rd
  Longcot SN7..........192 B1
  Shrivenham SN6..........209 D6
LONG CRENDON..........129 B6
Long Crendon Courthouse★ HP18..........129 D7

Long Crendon Ind Est HP18 . . 129 E5
Long Crendon Rd HP18 . . 128 D3
Long Crendon Sch HP18 129 C7
Longelandes Cl OX16. . . . 16 A8
Longelandes Way OX16 . . 16 B8
Longfellow Cl 1 OX26 . . 65 C3
Longfellow Dr OX14. . . . 179 C5
Longfellow Rd OX16 . . . . 16 B4
Longfields
  Bicester OX26 . . . . 65 F2
  Marcham OX13 . . . . . . 178 D7
Longfields Ct OX26. . . . . 65 F2
Longfields Prim Sch OX26 65 F2
Long Ford Cl OX1. . . . . 141 C7
Longford Way OX11. . . . 200 F2
Long Furlong HP17. . . . 130 F6
Long Furlong Prim Sch OX14. . 160 A3
Long Furlong Rd OX13 . 159 D4
LONG HANBOROUGH. . . . 90 B1
Longhurst Cl RG4 . . . . . 259 C3
Long La
  Oxford OX4 . . . . 142 C3
  Reading RG31. . . . . . . 257 B3
Longlands Rd OX4 . . . . 142 E3
RG31. . . . . 257 B3
Longleat Cl OX16 . . . . . 16 E2
Longleat Dr RG31 . . . . . 257 B3
Long Mdw RG8 . . . . . . 249 B5
Longmead OX14 . . . . . . 159 E1
Longmore Ave GL54. . . . 68 B3
Longore Ct OX29. . . . . . 89 C8
Longore OX29. . . . . 89 D8
Long Toll RG8 . . . . 251 A5
Long Tow OX13 . . . . . . 159 D2
Longwall OX4 . . . . 142 B3
Long Wall HP17. . . . . . 130 F5
Long Wall OX17 . . . . . . 23 B4
Longwall St OX1. . . . . . 261 C2
LONG WITTENHAM 201 D8
Long Wittenham CE Prim Sch OX14. . 201 D8
Long Wittenham Rd OX11. . 219 F8
LONGWORTH. 156 C3
Longworth Cl OX16 . . . . 16 E7
Longworth Prim Sch OX13. . 156 C3
Longworth Rd
  Charney Bassett OX12. . . 176 A3
  Longworth OX13 . . . . . 156 A3
  Oxford OX2 . . . . 261 A4
Lonsdale Ct OX7. . . . . . 29 A3
Lonsdale Rd OX2. . . . . . 123 B7
Lord Cl OX18 . . . . 115 D3
Lord Grandison Way OX16. 9 C2
Lords Piece Rd OX7. . . . 42 D1
Lord William's Lower Sch OX9. . 148 B8
Lord William's Sch OX9 . 147 D8
Lostock Pl OX11 . . . . . . 200 F2
Lovatt Cl OX18. . . . . . . 115 D5
Lovegrove's La RG8 . . . 241 C4
Love La OX49 . . . . 186 B2
Lovelace Cl OX14 . . . . . 160 A3
Lovelace Dr OX5 . . . . . 109 A8
Lovelace Rd OX2 . . . . . 109 A1
Lovelace Sq OX2. . . . . . 109 A1
Lovell Cl
  Ducklington OX29 . . . . 118 B4
  Henley-on-Thames RG9. . 254 C8
  Minster Lovell OX29 . . . 102 C2
Loverock Rd RG30 . . . . 258 D1
Lowell Pl OX28 . . . . . . 118 A8
Lower Armour Rd RG31 . 257 D1
LOWER ARNCOTT. 81 C1
LOWER ASSENDON. . . . 244 A6
LOWER BASILDON. 249 E2
LOWER BOURTON. 208 F3
LOWER CAVERSHAM. . . . 259 B5
Lower Cherwell St OX16. . 16 D5
Lower Church St HP14 . . 188 E5
Lower Cl OX15 . . . . 22 E8
Lower Comm SN7 . . . . . 211 D8
Lower Cres OX29 . . . . . 102 E3
Lower Elmstone Dr RG31. . 257 C1
LOWER END
  Alvescot. 133 C5
  Leafield 87 A4
  Long Crendon 129 B7
Lower End
  Great Milton OX44. . . . 145 B3
  Piddington OX25 . . . . . 97 E8
  Salford OX7. . . . . 41 F4
  Shutford OX15. . . . . . . 14 B5
Lower End Cotts CV47. . . 2 F8
Lower Farm Barns OX27. . 65 A8
Lower Farm Cl HP18 . . . 128 D3
Lower Farm La
  Mollington OX17. . . . . . 3 F3
  Sandford-on-Thames OX4. 161 B6
Lower Hades Rd OX5. . . 77 B6
Lower Henley Rd RG4 . . 259 C3
LOWER HEYFORD 62 D6
Lower Heyford Rd OX25. . 63 B5
LOWER HIGHMOOR. . . . 242 F6
Lower High St OX18. . . 100 E5
Lower Icknield Way OX39. . 168 D8
LOWER ODINGTON. . . . 54 A8
LOWER RADLEY. 161 A3

Lower Radley Cvn Pk OX14 . . 160 F2
Lower Rd
  Blackthorn OX25 . . . . . 82 A4
  Chilton OX11 . . . . 235 D8
  Chinnor OX39. . . . . . . 168 C7
  Long Hanborough OX29. . 90 F1
  Postcombe OX9 . . . . . . 166 F4
  Southend SN44 . . . . . . 162 F6
LOWER SHIPLAKE. 255 A3
Lower St
  Barford St Michael OX15. . 32 E6
  Islip OX5 . . . . 93 F1
LOWER TADMARTON. . . 20 F7
LOWER WAINHILL. 168 E7
Lower Wharf OX11. . . . . 221 D7
Lower Whitley Rd OX2. . 139 C8
LOWER WOLVERCOTE. . 122 D7
Lowes Cl
  Lower Shiplake RG9 . . . 255 B4
  Stokenchurch HP14. . . . 188 C5
Lowfield Ct RG4 . . . . . . 259 C5
Lowfield Gn RG4. . . . . . 259 E4
Lowfield Rd RG4. . . . . . 259 D5
Loyd Cl OX14 . . . . 160 A3
Loyd Rd OX11. . . . . . . 218 D6
Lucas Pl OX4 . . . . 141 F5
Lucca Dr OX14 . . . . . . 179 D4
Lucerne Ave OX26 . . . . 65 D4
Lucerne Dr OX44. . . . . 163 C2
Lucerne Rd OX2 . . . . . 123 C8
Lucey Cl RG31 . . . . 257 B3
Lucky La OX16 . . . . 16 C5
Ludford Gdns OX15 . . . . 21 D3
LUDGERSHALL. 98 D8
Ludgershall Rd OX25. . . 97 E7
Ludlow Dr
  Banbury OX16. . . . . . . 15 F8
  Thame OX9 . . . . 148 A8
Ludsden Gr OX9 . . . . . . 148 A8
Luker Ave RG9 . . . . . . 244 D3
Lumberd Rd OX14. . . . . 160 B2
Lune Cl OX11 . . . . 201 A1
Lupin La 4 OX18 . . . . . 115 E5
Lupton Rd
  Thame OX9 . . . . 148 A6
  Wallingford OX10 . . . . 221 B7
Luscombe Cl RG4 . . . . . 259 D2
Luther Cl OX1 . . . . 261 B1
Luther St OX1 . . . . 261 B1
Lych Gate La OX44 . . . . 145 B2
Lycroft Cl RG8 . . . . . . 249 C7
Lydalls Cl OX11 . . . . . . 200 D1
Lydalls Rd OX11. . . . . . 200 E1
Lydia Cl OX3 . . . . 124 F4
Lydsee Gate OX12. . . . . 214 B5
Lyefield Ct RG4 . . . . . . 259 B6
Lye Valley OX3 . . . . . . 142 D7
Lye Valley Nature Reserve★ OX3. . 142 D8
LYFORD. 176 C1
Lyford Cl OX14. . . . . . . 179 B2
Lyford Way OX14 . . . . . 160 B2
Lymbrook Cl OX29 . . . . 119 C5
Lyme Gr RG31 . . . . 257 D1
Lymington Gate RG4 . . . 258 E5
Lynams Sch OX2 . . . . . 123 A7
Lynch The OX12. . . . . . 216 D5
Lyndene Rd OX11 . . . . . 200 D3
Lyndhurst Rd
  Goring RG8 . . . . 249 C6
  Reading RG30 . . . . . . 258 A1
Lyndworth Cl OX3. . . . . 124 E4
Lyndworth Mews OX3 . . 124 E3
LYNEHAM. 70 E5
Lyneham Cl
  Carterton OX18 . . . . . 115 E3
  Witney OX28 . . . . 103 E1
Lyneham Ct OX12 . . . . 214 F4
Lyneham Rd
  Bicester OX26 . . . . . . 66 B3
  Milton-under-Wychwood OX7. . 70 B3
Lyne Rd OX5. . . . . 92 D1
Lynges Cl OX14 . . . . . . 160 B2
Lynmouth Ct RG1 . . . . . 259 B1
Lynmouth Rd
  Didcot OX11. . . . . 218 E8
  Reading RG1. . . . . 259 A1
Lynn Cl OX3. . . . . 123 F4
Lynt Farm Cotts SN6 . . . 170 B6
Lynton Ct 10 RG1 . . . . . 259 A1
Lynton La OX29 . . . . . . 107 D2
Lynt Rd SN6 . . . . 170 A5
Lyon Cl OX14 . . . . 160 A1
Lysander Cl 5 OX26 . . . 66 A4
Lytham End RG31. . . . . 257 B3
Lytton Rd OX4 . . . . . . 142 B5

M

Mabel Prichard Sch OX4 142 E2
Maberley Cl OX14. . . . . 179 C6
Mably Gr OX12. . . . . . . 214 D6
Mably Way OX12. . . . . . 214 D7
MacAulay Cl 6 OX26. . . 65 C3
McCabe Pl OX3 . . . . . . 124 A3
McCrae's Wlk RG10 . . . 255 D2
MacDonald Cl OX11. . . . 200 D1
McKay Trad Est OX26 . . 80 F8
McKee Sq OX10. . . . . . 204 D2
McKeever Pl 5 OX16 . . . 16 E6
Mackenzie Ave OX14 . . . 199 D3
Mackenzie Cl 5 OX26. . . 65 C3
Mackley Cl OX15. . . . . . 33 E4
MACKNEY. 220 D8
Mackney La OX10. . . . . 202 E1

McMullan Cl OX10 . . . . 221 C8
Macray Rd OX29 . . . . . 118 B4
Maddle Rd RG17. . . . . . 229 C1
Madley Brook La OX28 . 104 E2
Madley Brook Prim Sch OX28. . 104 D2
Madley Way OX28. . . . . 104 E2
Mafeking Row OX49. . . . 186 E4
Magdalen Cl OX26 . . . . 65 F3
Magdalen Coll OX1 . . . . 123 C1
Magdalen Coll Sch OX4. 141 E8
Magdalen Pl OX18 . . . . 115 D2
Magdalen Rd OX4. . . . . 141 F7
Magdalen St OX1 . . . . . 261 B2
Magnette Cl OX14 . . . . 179 F7
Magnolia Cl OX5. . . . . . 108 E7
Magnolias The
  Banbury OX16. . . . . . . 9 B1
  2 Bicester OX26. . . . . . 65 F5
Magnolia Way OX18. . . . 115 E4
Magpie Alley OX7. . . . . 85 D8
Magpie La OX1 . . . . . . 261 C2
Maharajah's Well★ RG9. 241 F5
Maidcroft Rd OX4. . . . . 142 C5
Maiden's Cl SN6 . . . . . 191 D1
MAIDENSGROVE 225 C5
Maidley Cl OX28 . . . . . 104 C2
Main Ave OX4 . . . . 161 C8
Main Pk OX18. . . . . . . 133 D8
Main Rd
  Alvescot OX18 . . . . . . 133 B6
  Appleford OX14 . . . . . 200 F7
  Broughton OX15 . . . . . 15 C1
  Curbridge OX29. . . . . . 117 C6
  East Hagbourne OX11. . 218 E5
  Fyfield OX13 . . . . 157 C2
  Long Hanborough OX29. . 90 D1
  Middleton Cheney OX17. . 17 F8
  Stanton Harcourt OX29. . 138 B8
  Tadmarton OX15 . . . . . 20 C8
Main St
  Adlestrop GL56 . . . . . . 40 C3
  Bledington OX7 . . . . . . 54 D2
  Charney Bassett OX12. . 175 F2
  Chilton OX11 . . . . 235 D8
  Clanfield OX18. . . . . . 152 E7
  Claydon OX17 . . . . 1 D1
  Duns Tew OX25 . . . . . 47 D5
  East Hanney OX12 . . . . 197 B6
  Fawler OX7. . . . . 88 E7
  Forest Hill OX33 . . . . . 125 E4
  Fringford OX27 . . . . . . 52 C6
  Grove OX12 . . . . 214 E8
  Hanwell OX17 . . . . . . 8 F4
  Hethe OX26. . . . . 52 A8
  Letcombe Regis OX12. . . 214 A2
  Long Compton CV36 . . . 27 F6
  Mollington OX17. . . . . . 4 A3
  North Newington OX15. . 15 B4
  Over Norton OX7. . . . . 42 F5
  Poundon OX27. . . . . . . 67 F7
  Shalstone MK18. . . . . . 25 E6
  Sibford Ferris OX15. . . . 19 B7
  Sibford Gower OX15 . . . 19 A8
  Tadmarton OX15 . . . . . 20 B8
  Turweston NN13 . . . . . 24 C8
  Westbury NN13. . . . . . 25 A4
  West Hagbourne OX11. . 218 C4
  West Hanney OX12 . . . . 196 E6
  West Ilsley RG20. . . . . 235 A4
  Wroxton OX15. . . . . . . 15 A8
Maisonettes The RG8 . . 249 D8
Majors Rd SN6. . . . . . . 191 D2
Makins Rd RG9 . . . . . . 254 B8
Malet Cl HP14 . . . . 188 F5
Malford Rd OX3. . . . . . 124 F4
Mallard Cl OX4 . . . . . . 142 D2
Mallard Dr OX28 . . . . . 118 A6
Mallards Way
  Bicester OX26 . . . . . . 66 A1
  Bicester OX26 . . . . . . 80 F8
Mallard Way OX12 . . . . 196 D1
Mallins La SN7. . . . . . . 192 D3
Mallinson Cl OX2 . . . . . 123 A1
Mallory Ave RG4 . . . . . 259 D6
Mall The SN6 . . . . 209 E7
Maltfield Rd OX3. . . . . . 124 B5
Malthouse SN6. . . . . . . 228 A7
Malthouse Cl SN6 . . . . 228 B7
Malthouse La
  Bodicote OX15 . . . . . . 22 D8
  Dorchester OX10. . . . . 182 D1
  Long Compton CV36 . . . 27 F6
  Shutford OX15 . . . . . . 14 B5
Malthouse Paddock SN7 174 E8
Malthouses The SN6 . . . 228 B7
Malthouse Wlk 4 OX16 . 16 D6
Maltings Ct OX15 . . . . . 21 D4
Maltings The
  2 Carterton OX18 . . . . 115 F5
  West Ilsley RG20. . . . . 235 B1
Maltsters OX29 . . . . . . 89 C7
Malvern Cl
  Banbury OX16. . . . . . . 16 D2
  Didcot OX11. . . . . 200 C2
Malyns Cl OX39 . . . . . . 168 C7
Malyns Way RG31. . . . . 257 B4
Managua Cl RG4 . . . . . 259 E2
Manchester Terr 2 OX26. 65 F2
Mandarin Pl OX12. . . . . 196 D1
Mandeville Cl OX14 . . . 160 A2
Mandhill Cl OX12 . . . . . 214 E8
Mandlebrote Dr OX4. . . 142 B1
Manning Cl OX15 . . . . . 21 E2
Mannings Cl OX15 . . . . 19 B7

Manor Ave GL7 . . . . . . 150 E3
Manor Barns Bsns Pk OX7. . 88 C6
Manor Cl
  Appleford OX14 . . . . . 200 F8
  Aston OX18 . . . . 135 E2
  Cassington OX29 . . . . . 107 C2
  Chilton OX11 . . . . 217 E1
  Drayton OX14 . . . . . . 179 B1
  Enstone OX7 . . . . 58 F5
  Great Bourton OX17 . . . 9 D8
  Shrivenham SN6 . . . . . 209 B7
  West Hagbourne OX11. . 218 C4
Manor Cotts OX29. . . . . 138 B7
Manor Court Yd OX33 . . 127 B2
Manor Cres
  Didcot OX11. . . . . 200 D1
  Standlake OX29 . . . . . 137 D3
  Stanford in the Vale SN7. 194 E7
Manor Ct
  Abingdon OX14 . . . . . 179 E6
  Banbury OX16. . . . . . . 16 E7
  Carterton OX18 . . . . . 115 D2
  Chadlington OX7 . . . . . 57 C1
  Wootton OX20 . . . . . . 75 F4
Manor Dr OX33 . . . . . . 143 C6
Manor Farm OX14. . . . . 180 A2
Manor Farm Barns OX5. . 95 A4
Manor Farm Cl
  Fernham SN7. . . . . . . 193 A4
  Kingham OX7 . . . . 54 F5
  Merton OX25 . . . . 95 D8
Manor Farm Cotts
  Garford OX13 . . . . 177 D5
  Wendlebury OX25 . . . . 80 A3
Manor Farm La RG8. . . 256 C2
Manor Farm Rd
  Chesterton OX26 . . . . . 80 A7
  Dorchester OX10. . . . . 182 D1
  Horspath OX33 . . . . . . 143 C6
Manor Field OX12. . . . . 214 A2
Manor Gdns GL7 . . . . . 150 C4
Manor Gn
  Harwell OX11 . . . . 217 E7
  Stanford in the Vale SN7. 194 E7
Manor Gr OX1. . . . . . . 160 E7
Manor Ho★ OX5. . . . . . 108 B4
Manor Hospl The OX3. . 124 C3
Manor La
  Clanfield OX18. . . . . . 152 E8
  Shrivenham SN6 . . . . . 209 B6
  West Hendred OX12 . . . 216 B5
Manor Orch OX15 . . . . . 8 B4
Manor Pk
  Claydon OX17 . . . . 1 D1
  Oxford OX3 . . . . 124 C3
Manor Pl OX1. . . . . . . 123 E2
Manor Prep Sch OX13. . 159 C1
Manor Prim Sch OX11. . 200 D1
Manor Rd
  Adderbury OX17 . . . . . 22 E3
  Banbury OX16. . . . . . . 16 F8
  Bladon OX20 . . . . 91 B2
  Brize Norton OX18. . . . 116 B4
  Carterton OX18 . . . . . 115 D5
  Chinnor OX9. . . . . 149 A6
  Didcot OX11. . . . . 200 D1
  Ducklington OX29 . . . . 118 A4
  Fringford OX27 . . . . . . 52 D7
  Goring RG8 . . . . 249 B5
  Great Bourton OX17 . . . 9 D8
  Henley-on-Thames RG9. . 254 D8
  Oxford OX1 . . . . 123 E2
  Sandford St Martin OX7. . 46 C1
  South Hinksey OX1 . . . 141 B5
  Towersey OX9 . . . . . . 148 F7
  Wantage OX12. . . . . . 232 C5
  Whitchurch-on-Thames RG8. . 256 C7
  Witney OX28 . . . . 118 C7
  Woodstock OX20 . . . . . 91 A7
  Wootton OX13 . . . . . . 159 A7
Manor View
  Bampton OX18. . . . . . . 134 E4
  Bucknell OX27 . . . . . . 64 F8
Manor Way OX5 . . . . . . 92 F2
Manor Wood Gate RG9. . 255 A4
Manor Yd OX27 . . . . . . 52 D7
Mansell Cl OX29 . . . . . 106 D6
Mansell Pl OX18 . . . . . 115 D1
Mansfield Coll OX1 . . . . 261 C3
Mansfield Gdns OX11 . . 219 B8
Mansfield Rd OX1. . . . . 261 C3
Mansion Hill OX17 . . . . 17 F8
Mansmoor Rd OX5 . . . . 94 F7
Manston Cl OX26 . . . . . 66 B3
Manzel Rd OX27 . . . . . 66 A6
Manzil Way OX4 . . . . . 142 A8
Maple Ave OX5 . . . . . . 108 E7
Maple Cl
  Bodicote OX15 . . . . . . 16 E1
  Oxford OX2 . . . . 140 D8
  Sonning Common RG4. . 253 A4
Maple Cotts SN7 . . . . . 172 E3
Maple Gr RG5. . . . . . . 260 E1
Maple Ho RG4 . . . . . . 259 C3

Maple Rd
  Bicester OX26 . . . . . . 65 F2
  Faringdon SN7 . . . . . . 172 E3
  Thame OX9 . . . . 147 D8
Maples The
  Carterton OX18 . . . . . 115 D1
  Grove OX12. . . . . 196 D2
Maple Way OX7. . . . . . 71 B2
Maplewell OX29 . . . . . . 89 C7
Maplewell Ho OX29. . . . 89 D7
MARCHAM. 178 D6
Marcham CE Prim Sch OX13. . 178 D6
Marcham Rd
  Abingdon OX14 . . . . . 179 C6
  Drayton OX14 . . . . . . 179 A6
  Marcham OX13 . . . . . . 178 D6
March Rd OX17 . . . . . . 3 D3
Marchwood Ave RG4. . . 259 C8
Marcourt Rd HP14 . . . . 188 F3
Mardy RG4 . . . . 258 E5
Margaret Cl
  Banbury OX16. . . . . . . 16 A5
  Bicester OX26 . . . . . . 65 D4
Margaret Rd
  Adderbury OX17 . . . . . 23 B5
  Oxford OX3 . . . . 124 E2
Maria Cres OX12. . . . . . 214 E5
Marie Cl OX27 . . . . 67 F7
Marigold Cl 12 OX14 . . 142 F1
Marigold Wlk 1 OX26. . 65 E5
Marina Way OX14 . . . . 179 F4
Marines Dr SN7. . . . . . 172 F2
Mariot Ct 8 OX10. . . . 221 D7
Marjoram Cl OX4 . . . . . 143 A2
Market End Ct OX26. . . 65 D3
Market End Way OX26. . 65 D3
Market Pl
  4 Abingdon OX14. . . . 179 F7
  Banbury OX16. . . . . . . 16 D6
  Chipping Norton OX7. . . 42 E3
  Deddington OX15. . . . . 33 F4
  Didcot OX11. . . . . 200 F1
  Faringdon SN7 . . . . . . 172 F4
  Henley-on-Thames RG9. . 244 D2
  Highworth SN6 . . . . . . 190 A5
  Lechlade-on-Thames GL7. 150 C4
  3 Wallingford OX10. . . 221 D7
  Wantage OX12. . . . . . 214 D4
  Woodstock OX20 . . . . . 91 A6
Market Place Mews RG9 244 D2
Market Sq
  Bampton OX18. . . . . . . 134 E3
  Bicester OX26 . . . . . . 65 F1
  Lower Heyford OX25. . . 62 D6
  Witney OX28 . . . . 118 B8
Market St
  Charlbury OX7 . . . . . . 73 B4
  Chipping Norton OX7. . . 42 E3
  Oxford OX1 . . . . 261 B2
  Woodstock OX20 . . . . . 91 B6
Mark Rd OX3. . . . . 124 C4
Marlborough Ave OX5. . 92 D2
Marlborough Cl
  Carterton OX18 . . . . . 115 E1
  Eynsham OX29. . . . . . 120 E8
  Faringdon SN7 . . . . . . 172 F3
  Kidlington OX5. . . . . . 92 D2
  Oxford OX4 . . . . 142 B2
Marlborough Cres
  Long Hanborough OX29. . 106 B8
  Woodstock OX20 . . . . . 91 A7
Marlborough Ct OX2 . . . 122 F1
Marlborough Dr OX29. . 107 C5
Marlborough Gdns SN7. 172 F2
Marlborough Ho 18 OX16. 16 D5
Marlborough La
  Stanford in the Vale SN7. 194 E7
  Witney OX28 . . . . 118 A8
Marlborough Pl
  2 Banbury OX16 . . . . . 16 D5
  Charlbury OX7 . . . . . . 73 B3
  Eynsham OX29. . . . . . 120 E8
  Faringdon SN7 . . . . . . 172 E2
Marlborough Rd
  Banbury OX16. . . . . . . 16 D5
  Chipping Norton OX7. . . 42 F4
  Oxford OX1 . . . . 141 C7
Marlborough Sch OX20. . 91 D6
Marlborough St SN7 . . . 172 F3
Marlborough Terr OX29. 90 A4
Marley Ind Est OX16. . . 16 D8
Marley La OX44 . . . . . . 184 C7
Marley Way OX16. . . . . 16 D7
Marling Cl RG31 . . . . . 257 C2
Marlow Cl OX10. . . . . . 221 B8
Marlow Cres RG4 . . . . . 259 D3
Marlowe Cl OX16 . . . . . 15 F6
Marlow Rd
  Henley-on-Thames RG9. . 244 E3
  Stokenchurch HP14 . . . 188 F3
Marmyon Ho RG9 . . . . 244 E3
Marns Hey OX12 . . . . . 214 C5
Marriott Cl
  Cutteslowe OX2. . . . . . 109 B1
  Wootton OX20 . . . . . . 76 A4
Marriotts Cl OX28. . . . . 118 B8
Marriott's Cl HP17 . . . . 130 F6
Marriott's La HP17. . . . 130 F6
Marriott's Way HP17. . . 130 F6
Marsack St RG4. . . . . . 259 C2
Marshall Cl
  Chipping Norton OX7. . . 42 E1
  Purley on Thames RG8. . 257 C4
Marshall Cres OX7 . . . . 46 E1
Marshall Rd
  9 Banbury OX16 . . . . . 16 E6

Mar–Mor 277

Marshall Rd *continued*
Oxford OX4 142 D6
Marshalls Cl OX15 6 E2
MARSH BALDON 162 B3
Marsh Baldon CE Prim Sch
OX44 162 A4
Marsh Cl OX5 108 C5
Marsh Ct OX14 179 F8
Marsh End OX9 147 B1
MARSH GIBBON 67 F3
Marsh Gibbon CE Sch
OX27 67 F3
Marsh La
Clanfield OX18 152 F8
Clanfield OX18, SN7 153 B7
Crowmarsh Gifford OX10 222 A8
East Challow OX12 213 F7
Fyfield OX13 157 B4
Marston OX3 124 A5
Witney OX28 104 B1
Marshland Sq RG4 259 B5
Marsh Pl RG8 256 D5
Marsh Rd
Oxford OX4 142 C6
Shabbington HP18 128 D3
Marsh Way SN7 211 A5
MARSTON 123 E6
Marston Ferry Ct OX2 123 C6
Marston Ferry Rd OX2 123 D6
Marston Rd
Marston OX3, OX4 123 F3
Thame OX9 130 A1
Marston St OX4 141 F8
Marten Gate OX16 16 E3
Marten Pl RG31 257 C3
Martens Cl SN6 209 A6
Martens Lake OX13 156 C2
Martens Rd SN6 209 B6
Martin Cl OX26 80 F8
Martin Ct OX2 123 B7
Martins La OX29 137 C4
Martin's La OX10 182 D2
Martyn's Way OX10 204 F4
Maryfield OX12 214 E4
Marygreen OX12 214 D8
Marylands Gn OX44 162 D2
Marymead OX10 220 F2
Mary Price Cl OX3 124 A3
Mary Towerton First Sch
HP14 189 D3
Mary Whipple Cl OX12 214 C4
Mascall Ave OX3 142 E7
Mascord Cl OX16 16 A5
Mascord Rd OX16 16 A5
Masefield Cl 3 OX26 65 C3
Masefield Cres OX14 179 C5
Masefield Rd OX16 16 A4
Masey Cl 4 OX3 124 D1
Masons Ct OX12 215 E6
Masons Rd OX3 124 E1
Mathematical Inst Univ of Oxford OX1 261 B3
Mather Rd OX3 124 F4
Mathews Way OX13 159 B6
Matlock Rd RG4 258 E4
Matson Dr RG9 244 F2
Matthew Arnold Sch
OX2 140 C7
Mattock Cl OX3 124 D2
Mattock Way OX14 160 B3
Maud Cl OX26 65 C4
Maud Hale Cotts 11
OX14 179 F6
Maud Ho OX12 214 F5
Maule Cl OX15 21 E2
Maunds The OX15 33 F4
Mavor Cl OX20 91 A7
Mawkes Cl SN7 194 D7
Mawle Ct 1 OX16 16 D5
Mawles La OX7 85 D8
Maxwell Ave OX11 217 B3
Maycroft 4 OX26 65 F4
Mayfair Rd OX4 142 B4
Mayfield Ave OX12 196 F1
Mayfield Cl
Carterton OX18 115 D1
Chalgrove OX44 184 D6
Mayfield Dr RG4 259 D3
Mayfield Rd
Banbury OX16 16 D2
Farmoor OX2 121 B2
Oxford OX2 123 B7
Mayott's Rd 1 OX14 179 E7
May's Cl OX27 49 F7
MAYS GREEN 254 B5
May Tree Cl OX26 65 E3
Maytree Wlk RG4 259 E4
Mead Cl RG4 259 D2
Meaden Hill OX3 124 B5
Mead La
Longcot SN7 192 D2
Lower Basildon RG8 249 F1
Witney OX28 104 B1
Meadow Bank SN7 172 F3
Meadowbank Cl
Ascott-under-Wychwood OX7 71 B2
Long Crendon HP18 129 C7
Meadow Cl
Farmoor OX2 121 B3
Goring RG8 249 C6
Grove OX12 196 E1
Moulsford OX10 238 F4
Shipton-under-Wychwood OX7 70 D1
Meadow End OX18 100 E6
Meadow La
Crowmarsh Gifford OX10 222 A6
Fulbrook OX18 100 F6
Long Crendon HP18 129 E4
Oxford OX4 141 E7
Oxford OX4 141 F5
Pangbourne RG8 256 D5
Shipton-under-Wychwood OX7 70 D1
6 Witney OX28 104 A1
Meadow Pl OX7 55 D5
Meadow Prospect OX2 122 D8
Meadow Rd
Chinnor OX39 168 D6
Henley-on-Thames RG9 244 E1
Reading RG1 258 F1
Watchfield SN6 191 E2
Meadowside
Abingdon OX14 179 E6
Reading RG31 257 B1
Meadowside Ct 1 OX14 179 E6
Meadowside Rd RG8 256 D5
Meadows The OX49 186 B2
Meadowsweet Way OX16 9 A2
Meadow View
Adderbury OX17 23 A4
Banbury OX16 16 E4
Kidlington OX5 92 E2
Long Crendon HP18 129 E4
Oxford OX2 123 C8
Wendlebury OX25 79 F3
Witney OX28 118 C8
Meadow View Rd OX1 160 F8
Meadow Way
Carterton OX18 115 F5
Didcot OX11 218 C7
Faringdon SN7 172 F2
Kingham OX7 54 F3
Lower Caversham RG4 259 D2
Thame OX9 129 F1
Yarnton OX5 108 C5
Meadow Wlk OX20 91 C6
Mead Platt HP14 188 D5
Mead Rd
Barford St Michael OX15 32 F7
Yarnton OX5 108 C4
Meads Cl OX14 179 B2
Meadside OX10 202 E8
Meads The OX12 196 E7
Mead The OX17 3 F3
Mead Way OX5 92 E2
Mead Wlk OX11 200 E2
Meashill Way OX11 234 F8
Medcroft Rd OX5 77 B6
Medhurst Way OX4 142 B2
Medill Cl RG8 250 E8
Medina Cl OX11 201 B1
Medina Gdns OX26 65 B2
Medlar Rd SN6 209 C7
Medlicott Dr OX14 179 C6
Medlock Gr OX11 200 F3
Medway OX12 197 B6
Medway Cl OX13 159 C3
Medway Gr 5 OX11 219 A8
Medway Rd OX13 159 C3
Meer The OX10 204 A5
Melbourne Cl OX16 16 E3
Melford Gn RG4 259 E6
Melrose Ct OX16 8 F1
Melton Dr OX11 200 E1
Melville Cl OX26 65 B2
Membury Way OX12 214 D8
Memorial Ave RG9 254 E2
Mendip Hts OX11 200 C2
Menmarsh Rd HP18 127 E6
Menpes Rd RG31 257 C4
Mercury Cl OX18 134 F3
Mercury Ct OX18 134 F3
Mercury Rd OX4 143 A2
Meredith Cl OX26 65 C3
Mere Dyke Rd OX13 198 F5
Mere La MK18 39 E6
Mereland Rd OX11 218 E7
Mere Rd
Finmere MK18 39 D6
Wolvercote OX2 122 F8
Merewood Ave OX3 125 A4
Merganser Dr OX26 81 B8
Meriden Ct OX10 221 C7
Merlin Cl
Benson OX10 204 D2
Carterton OX18 115 D3
Merlin Rd
Abingdon OX13 159 B2
Oxford OX4 142 E2
Merlin Way OX26 81 B8
Merritt Rd OX11 200 C1
Merrivale's La OX15 21 E4
Merrivale Sq OX2 123 A4
Merrymouth Rd OX7 69 A2
Mersey Way OX11 201 A3
Merthyr Vale RG4 259 A6
MERTON 95 D8
Merton Cl
Didcot OX11 219 B8
Eynsham OX29 120 D7
Merton Coll OX1 261 C2
Merton Ct OX2 123 A4
Merton Rd OX25 81 C3
Merton St
Banbury OX16 16 E6
Oxford OX1 261 C2
Merton Way OX5 108 B5
Merton Wlk OX26 65 F3
Metcalfe Cl
Abingdon OX14 179 E4
Drayton OX15 15 D8
Meteor Cl OX26 66 A3
Mewburn Rd OX16 16 B5
Mews The
Baydon SN8 245 B5
Highworth SN6 190 A6
Sonning RG4 260 D4
Warborough OX10 203 B5
Watchfield SN6 191 D1
Meyseys Cl OX3 142 E7
Michaelmas Cl OX17 10 F1
Michaels Chase RG4 259 C3
Micklands Prim Sch
RG4 259 D4
Micklands Rd RG4 259 E4
Mickle Way OX33 125 E4
Middi Haines Ct SN6 190 A6
MIDDLE ASSENDON 243 F7
MIDDLE ASTON 48 B3
Middle Aston La OX25 48 A4
Middle Aston Rd OX25 48 A6
MIDDLE BARTON 60 F7
Middle Barton Rd OX25 47 D5
Middle Barton Sch OX7 61 A8
Middle Furlong OX11 201 B2
Middle Hill OX15 30 B7
Middle La
Balscote OX15 14 C8
Shotteswell OX17 8 D8
Middle Orch OX7 54 D2
Middle Rd
Burford OX18 99 B6
Stanton St John OX33 125 D7
Middle Row
Chipping Norton OX7 42 E3
Great Rollright OX7 29 A3
Middle Springs RG8 249 C8
Middle St OX5 93 F1
MIDDLETON CHENEY 11 A1
Middleton Cheney Prim Sch
OX17 17 F8
Middleton Cl OX16 17 A7
Middleton Pk OX25 63 E3
Middleton Rd
Banbury OX16 16 F7
Bucknell OX27 64 F8
Chacombe OX17 10 E4
MIDDLETON STONEY 64 B3
Middleton Stoney Rd
OX26 65 C1
MIDDLETOWN 104 A6
Middle Way
Chinnor OX39 168 B6
Islip OX5 93 F1
Oxford OX2 123 B7
Middleway Bottom OX12 213 C2
Midget Cl OX14 179 D5
Midsummer Mdw RG4 258 F6
Midway OX17 11 A1
Midwinter Ave OX14 199 C3
MILCOMBE 21 B2
Miles Dr OX12 214 E8
Milestone Ave RG10 260 F6
Milestone Cl HP14 188 E5
Milestone Rd OX18 115 D1
Milestone View Ct RG4 259 E4
Mileway Gdns OX3 124 C1
Milford Pl OX20 76 A4
Milking La OX28, OX29 104 A3
Millar Cl OX10 203 F5
Mill Arts Ctr★ OX16 16 D6
Millaway La SN7 195 C5
Millbank OX2 141 A8
Millbrook Cl
Blewbury OX11 219 A1
Wallingford OX10 221 C7
Millbrook Prim Sch
OX12 196 D1
Millbrook Sq OX12 196 E1
Millbuck Ind Est OX28 118 B6
Mill Cl
Chadlington OX7 57 A1
Charlton-on-Otmoor OX5 95 A5
Deddington OX15 33 E4
Middle Assendon RG9 243 F8
Milldown Ave RG8 249 C7
Milldown Rd RG8 249 C7
MILLEND 57 A2
Mill End OX5 93 A1
Miller Ho OX16 16 A6
Miller Rd
Banbury OX16 16 A6
Wheatley OX33 144 C7
Miller's Acre 1 OX2 109 B1
Millers Cl
Chalgrove OX44 184 C7
Goring RG8 249 B7
Millers Ct RG4 259 D1
Millers La OX15 7 C7
Millers Mews OX28 104 B1
Millers Turn OX39 168 B6
Millets Farm Cotts OX13 177 D5
Millfield Ave OX27 67 F3
Millfield Cl OX27 67 F3
Millford Rd RG1 258 F1
Mill Gn
Bampton OX18 134 E2
Reading RG4 259 C1
Mill Green Cl OX18 134 E2
Millham The OX12 216 B6
Millington Rd OX10 221 C8
Mill La
Adderbury OX17 23 A3
Alvescot OX18 133 C6
Ascott-under-Wychwood OX7 71 D2
Benson OX10 203 F4
Black Bourton OX18 133 F5
Brackley NN13 24 A6
Mill La *continued*
Cassington OX29 106 F2
Chalgrove OX44 184 C6
Charlton-on-Otmoor OX5 95 A5
Chinnor OX39 168 B7
Chipping Warden OX17 5 F6
Clanfield OX18 152 D8
Croughton NN13 36 C7
Drayton OX15 15 D8
East Challow OX12 213 E7
East Hendred OX12 216 D6
Great Bourton OX17 9 F7
Great Haseley OX44 164 D8
Grove OX12 214 E7
Haddenham OX9 130 B3
Henley-on-Thames RG9 254 F8
Horton-cum-Studley OX33 112 A6
Islip OX5 109 E8
Kidmore End RG4 252 C1
Kings Sutton OX17 23 F4
Kirtlington OX5 77 F4
Lechlade-on-Thames GL7 150 F4
Lower Heyford OX6 62 D6
Lower Shiplake RG9 255 A2
Marston OX3 123 E8
Marston OX3 123 F7
Middle Barton OX7 60 F8
Milton OX14 199 C6
Oxford OX4 141 F4
Sandford St Martin OX7 46 B1
Shenington OX15 6 E2
South Moreton OX11 220 A5
Stokenchurch HP14 188 C5
Sutton Courtenay OX14 199 F7
Upper Arncott OX25 96 E7
Upper Heyford OX25 48 F1
Wallingford OX10 221 D7
Westbury NN13 25 A4
West Hendred OX12 216 C6
Weston-on-the-Green OX25 79 A2
Wootton OX20 75 F4
Mill Lane Prim Sch
OX39 168 B7
Millmoor Cres OX29 120 E8
Mill Orch OX12 197 A6
Mill Paddock
7 Abingdon OX14 179 F6
Letcombe Regis OX12 214 A2
Mill Rd
Abingdon OX14 179 C5
Goring RG8 249 C7
Lower Shiplake RG9 255 B3
Marcham OX13 178 D5
Nettlebed RG9 224 E3
Reading RG4 259 C1
Shabbington HP18 128 E1
Stokenchurch HP14 188 C5
Stratton Audley OX6 52 E1
Wolvercote OX2 122 D8
Mill St Mews OX29 120 E7
Mills La OX15 15 A8
Mill St
Eynsham OX29 120 E8
Islip OX5 109 E8
Kidlington OX5 92 F1
Oxford OX2 123 A1
Stanton St John OX33 125 E8
Steventon OX13 198 F3
Wantage OX12 214 D5
Witney OX28 104 A1
Millstream Ct OX2 122 D8
Mill The OX7 42 C2
Millview OX7 42 E2
Mill View OX49 185 D3
Millway Cl OX2 122 F8
Millway La OX13 157 E6
Millwood End OX29 90 A1
Millwood Farm Barns
OX29 90 A1
Millwood Vale OX29 90 A1
Millwright Cl 3 OX16 16 B6
Milne Pl OX3 124 B5
MILTON
Banbury 22 C3
Didcot 199 C5
Milton Bsns & Tech Ctr
OX13 199 A2
Milton CE Prim Sch
OX14 199 C2
Milton Cl
4 Bicester OX26 65 C3
Henley-on-Thames RG9 244 D2
MILTON COMMON 146 B3
Milton Cres OX33 125 F4
MILTON HEIGHTS 199 C2
MILTON HILL 199 B2
Milton Hill OX13 199 B2
Milton Intc OX14 199 C3
Milton La OX13 199 A5
Milton Manor Dr OX44 163 F6
Milton Manor House★
OX14 199 C5
Milton Park Est OX14 199 E4
Milton Rd
Bloxham OX15 21 E3
Didcot OX11 200 B3
Milton OX17 22 C2
Oxford OX4 142 B6
Shipton-under-Wychwood OX7 70 C1
Stadhampton OX44 163 C2
Sutton Courtenay OX14 199 F6
Milton St OX16 16 C5
MILTON-UNDER-WYCHWOOD 70 C1
Milvery Way OX4 142 B3
Minchery Farm Cotts
OX4 142 C1
Minchery Rd OX4 142 C1
Minchins Cl OX14 180 C8
Minnow La OX18 99 B6
Minns Rd OX12 196 F1
Minster Ind Pk OX29 103 B1
MINSTER LOVELL 102 F2
Minster Lovell Hall & Dovecote★ OX29 103 A3
Minster Rd
Brize Norton OX18 116 B5
Oxford OX4 142 A8
Minster Riding OX29 102 F4
Minton Cl RG30 257 F1
Mint The 1 OX10 221 D7
Minty Cl OX18 115 C1
Mirfield Rd OX28 117 E8
Mistletoe Gn OX4 142 E1
Mitchell Cl
Thame OX9 147 E8
Wootton OX13 159 A7
Mitford Cotts OX18 99 E1
MIXBURY 24 D1
Moat Cl OX18 116 B3
Moat La OX27 67 F2
Moat's Cres OX9 148 A8
Moat The OX7 54 F5
Mobbs La OX15 30 B7
Moberly Cl OX4 141 F8
Model Cotts OX18 133 F4
Modern Art Oxford★
OX1 261 B2
Moir Ct OX12 214 D5
Mold Cres OX16 16 A6
Mole Pl
Oxford OX4 143 A1
17 Sandford-on-Thames OX4 142 F1
MOLLINGTON 4 A3
Mollington La OX17 3 B4
Mollington Rd
Claydon OX17 4 D8
Shotteswell OX17 8 D8
Molyneux Dr OX15 22 E8
Molyns Ho RG9 244 E3
Monarchs Ct OX10 203 F4
Monard Terr 2 OX4 141 F7
MONGEWELL 221 E4
Monique Ct 6 OX16 9 A1
Monkley Ct 2 RG4 259 C1
Monks Cl
Carterton OX18 115 D5
Dorchester OX10 182 E1
Oxford OX4 142 D2
West Hanney OX12 196 E6
Monks Dene Bsns Ctr
OX7 42 E3
Monks Lode OX11 200 F3
Monks Mead OX10 202 E2
Monks Wlk GL7 150 E3
Monmouth Ct 5 RG1 259 A1
Monmouth Rd OX1 141 D5
Monnhan Way OX18 115 F4
Mons Way OX14 159 D1
Montabaur Rd NN13 24 A7
Montague St RG4 259 C2
Montagu Rd OX2 140 D8
Montfort Gate RG4 259 E4
Montgomery Rd OX27 66 A7
Montpelier Dr RG4 259 D5
Montrose Way OX9 148 A8
Monument Ind Pk OX44 184 F7
Monument Rd OX44 184 E6
Monument St OX16 16 C5
Moody Rd OX3 123 F3
Moonraker La OX18 134 F3
Moor Ave OX28 104 A1
Moorbank OX4 142 E2
Moorbrook OX11 200 D4
Moorend La
Thame OX9 129 F1
Thame OX9 130 A2
Moorfield Ct OX16 16 E6
Moorgate GL7 150 B4
Moorhen Wlk OX4 142 E1
Moor La OX15 31 F7
Moorland Cl OX28 103 F1
Moorland Rd OX28 117 F8
Moorlands The
Benson OX10 204 A4
Kidlington OX5 92 E2
Moor Pond Cl OX26 65 F2
Moors Cl OX29 118 A5
Moors Dr The OX17 17 F8
MOORS THE 118 A5
Moors The
Kidlington OX5 92 D2
Pangbourne RG8 256 D5
Morecambe Ave RG4 258 E5
MORETON
Appleton 157 A7
Thame 147 D5
Moreton Ave OX10 221 B7
Moreton La
Newbridge OX29 156 F7
Thame OX9 147 E8
Moreton Rd
Aston Tirrold OX11 219 F2
Moreton OX9 147 C6
Oxford OX2 123 B6
Morgan Cl OX16 15 F8
Morlais RG4 259 A5
Morland Cl OX33 144 B8
Morland Rd OX13 178 D6
Morlands OX12 197 B7
Morrell Ave OX4 142 A8

Morrell Cl OX5. . . . . . . .108 D8
Morrell Cres OX4 . . . . . .142 A2
Morrells Cl OX11. . . . . . .200 D1
Morris Cres OX4 . . . . . . .142 B6
Morris Dr OX16 . . . . .15 F8
Morris Ho OX4. . . . . .142 C4
Morse Rd OX11 . . . . .218 D6
Mortimer Dr OX3 . . . . . .123 F4
Mortimer Rd OX4 . . . . . .141 F3
Morton Ave OX5 . . . . . . .108 E7
Morton Cl
  Abingdon OX14 . . . . . . .180 C8
  Kidlington OX5. . . . . . . .108 E8
Morton King Cl HP18. . . .128 D3
Mortree Ct SN6 . . . . .209 B6
Mosquito La OX10. . . . . .204 D2
Moss Cl RG4. . . . . .259 C3
Motte The OX14. . . . . . . .179 F7
MOULSFORD. 238 F4
Moulsford Prep Sch
  OX10. . . . . .239 A6
Mountfield RG8. . . . . . . .249 C7
Mountfield Rd OX28. . . . .117 F7
Mount Owen Rd OX18. . . .135 A3
Mount Pl OX2. . . . . .261 A3
Mount Pleasant
  Bishopstone SN6. . . . . . .227 D4
  Lechlade-on-Thames GL7 . .150 C4
  Shipton-under-Wychwood
    OX7. . . . . .85 E7
  Wardington OX17 . . . . . . .5 E1
Mount Pleasant Cotts
  OX12 . . . . .216 D6
MOUNT SKIPPETT 88 A4
Mount St OX1. . . . . .123 A2
Mount The
  Reading RG4. . . . . .258 F3
  Tetsworth OX9. . . . . . . .166 B8
Mount View OX10 . . . . . .244 D2
Mount View Ct RG9 . . . . .244 D2
Mousey La OX10 . . . . . . .221 D7
Mowbray Dr RG30. . . . . .258 A1
Mowbray Fields Nature
  Reserve★ OX11. . . . . . .218 E6
Mowbray Rd OX11 . . . . . .218 E6
Mowforth Cl RG8 . . . . . .240 E1
Mulberries The OX12. . . .197 A6
Mulberry Bush Sch
  OX29. . . . . .137 C2
Mulberry Ct OX2. . . . . . .123 A8
Mulberry Dr
  Bicester OX26 . . . . .65 E5
  Wheatley OX33 . . . . . . .144 B8
Mulcaster Ave OX5. . . . . .108 F8
Mullard Way OX14 . . . . . .179 E7
Mullein Rd OX26. . . . . . . .65 E5
Mullens Terr RG4. . . . . . .258 D8
Mumbery Hill RG10 . . . . .255 E1
MURCOTT. 95 F4
Murcott Rd OX25. . . . . . . .96 D6
Murdock Cl OX15. . . . . . . .33 E4
Murdock Rd OX26. . . . . . . .66 A2
Murray Ct OX2. . . . . .123 C4
Murren Croft OX10. . . . . .221 E7
Murren The OX10. . . . . . .221 D6
Museum of the History of
  Science★ OX12. . . . . . .261 B2
Museum Rd OX1. . . . . . . .261 B3
Musgrave Rd OX39. . . . . .168 D7
Musgrave Wlk HP14. . . . .188 F5
Mus of Oxford★ OX1. . . .261 B2
Musson Cl 🔳 OX4. . . . . .179 E6
Mustard La RG4. . . . . . . .260 E2
Myrtle Cl
  Long Hanborough OX29. . . .90 B1
  Reading RG31 . . . . .257 C3

N

Nalderton OX12 . . . . . . .214 C5
Napier Ct OX14 . . . . .180 B7
Napier Rd OX4. . . . . .142 D5
Nappins Cl HP18. . . . . . .129 D5
Narrow Hill OX28 . . . . . .104 B2
Naseby Cl OX9 . . . . .130 B1
Nash Ct OX4. . . . . .142 D4
Nash Dr OX4. . . . . .179 C6
Nash La OX29. . . . . .106 A7
National Herb Ctr The★
  OX17. . . . . .3 A3
Navigation Way OX2 . . . .123 A5
Neal's La RG9. . . . . .242 A4
NEAT ENSTONE 58 F5
Neave Mews 🔳 OX14. . . .179 F6
NEITHROP. 16 A6
Neithrop Ave OX16 . . . . . .16 B7
Neithrop Cl OX16 . . . . . . .16 B7
Nell Hill SN6. . . . . .227 D4
Nelson Cl OX10 . . . . .221 C8
Nelson Rd RG4. . . . . .259 C2
Nelson St
  Oxford OX2 . . . . .261 A3
  Thame OX9 . . . . .147 F8
Nene Gr OX11 . . . . .201 B2
Nene Rd OX13 . . . . .159 C2
Netheravon Cl OX18. . . . .115 E2
Nether Cl NN13 . . . . .24 A7
NETHERCOTE. 17 B7
Nethercote La OX49. . . . .167 A1
Nethercote Mdw CV36 . . .27 F7
NETHERCOTT. 77 D6
Nether Durnford Cl OX3 . .142 F7
NETHERTON. 157 B3

Netherton La OX13 . . . . .157 C3
Netherton Rd OX13 . . . . .157 E6
NETHER WESTCOTE 68 F5
NETHER WORTON. 32 C1
Netherworton Rd OX15. . . .32 E5
Netley Rd RG4. . . . . .259 E6
Netting St OX15. . . . . .30 A7
NETTLEBED. 224 D2
Nettlebed Com Sch RG9 .224 D2
Nettlebed Mead OX4. . . .142 E1
Nettleton Dr OX25 . . . . . .63 A7
Neunkirchen Way OX26 . . .81 A7
Neville Way SN7. . . . . . . .194 E7
Nevis Rd RG31 . . . . .257 D3
Newalls Rise RG10. . . . . .255 E2
Newbarn Cl OX9 . . . . . . .148 A7
Newbery Cl RG31 . . . . . .257 D1
New Bldgs
  Uffington SN7 . . . . .211 D8
  Whitchurch Hill RG8 . . . .250 D2
Newbold Cl OX16 . . . . . . .16 E4
NEW BOTLEY. 122 E1
NEWBRIDGE. 156 E8
New Bridge St OX28. . . . .104 B1
Newbury Rd
  East Hendred OX12 . . . . .216 E5
  Rowstock OX11 . . . . . . .217 B6
Newbury St OX12 . . . . . .214 D4
New Close Farm Rd
  OX39. . . . . .149 C3
New Close La OX28 . . . . .117 F5
New Coll OX1. . . . . .261 C2
New College La OX1. . . . .261 C2
New College Sch OX1. . . .261 C3
New College Sq OX25 . . . .48 F1
Newcombe Cl OX15 . . . . . .21 A1
Newcombe Ct OX4. . . . . .123 A7
New Cross Rd OX3. . . . . .124 E3
Newells Cl OX44 . . . . . . .163 C1
Newell's La RG4. . . . . . . .258 B7
Newfield Rd RG4. . . . . . .252 F6
Newgate Rd OX5. . . . . . . .95 E5
NEW HEADINGTON. 124 C1
New High St OX3. . . . . . .124 C2
New Hill RG8 . . . . .257 C5
NEW HINKSEY 141 D6
New Hinksey CE Prim Sch
  OX1. . . . . .141 C6
New Hope Terr 🔳 RG1. . . .259 A1
New House Yd OX7 . . . . . .42 A5
NEWINGTON. 183 E6
Newington Rd OX44. . . . .163 C1
New Inn Hall St OX1. . . . .261 B2
New Inn Rd OX3. . . . . . . .111 A2
NEWLAND. 118 D8
Newland OX28. . . . . .104 C1
Newland Cl OX29 . . . . . .120 E7
Newland Mill OX28. . . . . .104 C1
Newland Pl OX16 . . . . . . .16 D5
Newland Rd OX16. . . . . . .16 D5
Newlands Ave
  Didcot OX11. . . . . .218 E7
  Reading RG4. . . . . .259 B3
Newlands Dr OX12 . . . . . .196 C1
Newlands La RG9 . . . . . . .242 B5
Newland St OX29 . . . . . . .120 E8
Newlin Cl OX4 . . . . .141 F3
New Look Mobile Home Pk
  OX18 . . . . .115 E1
Newman Ct
  Oxford OX4 . . . . .123 F1
  Witney OX29 . . . . .103 C1
Newman La OX14 . . . . . . .179 B2
Newman Rd OX4. . . . . . . .142 B3
Newmans Cl OX11 . . . . . .218 C3
NEW MARSTON. 123 F4
New Marston Prim Sch
  OX3. . . . . .124 A5
Newmill La OX28. . . . . . .103 F2
New Mill Mews 🔳 OX28 .104 A1
Newnham Gn OX10. . . . . .221 F7
Newnhamhill Bottom
  RG9. . . . . .242 B5
NEWNHAM MURREN. 221 E6
NEW OSNEY 261 A2
New Pl OX17. . . . . .4 F2
New Pond La OX5. . . . . . . .95 A5
Newport Cl OX5. . . . . . . .108 D7
Newport Rd RG1. . . . . . . .259 A1
Newport Terr 🔳 OX26. . . .65 F2
New Rd
  Adderbury OX17 . . . . .22 F3
  Bampton OX18. . . . . . . .134 F4
  Banbury OX16 . . . . .16 C5
  Beckley OX3. . . . . .111 B2
  Bledington OX7 . . . . .54 D2
  Bletchingdon OX5 . . . . . . .93 B8
  Charney Bassett OX12. . .175 F2
  Childrey OX12 . . . . .213 B6
  East Hagbourne OX11. . . .219 A6
  Glympton OX20 . . . . .75 D8
  Great Tew OX7. . . . . .45 D7
  Hailey OX29. . . . . .104 A6
  Kingham OX7. . . . . .54 F4
  Long Hanborough OX29. . . .90 B1
  Lower Shiplake RG9 . . . . .255 A3
  Marcham OX13 . . . . .178 C6
  Milcombe OX15 . . . . .21 A1
  Oxford OX1. . . . . .261 B2
  Radley OX14 . . . . .160 E2
  Ratley OX15. . . . . .2 A4
  Shiplake Row RG9. . . . . .254 B2
  Shotteswell OX17 . . . . . . .8 C8
  Shrivenham SN6 . . . . . . .209 E3
  Stokenchurch HP14. . . . .188 F4
  Sutton OX29. . . . . .120 A1
  Wallingford OX10 . . . . . .221 D7

New Rd continued
  Warborough OX10. . . . . .203 B6
  Watlington OX49. . . . . . .186 B2
  Woodstock OX20. . . . . . . .91 B6
New Row
  Ambrosden OX25. . . . . . . .81 C3
  Bucknell OX27. . . . . .64 F8
Newscut La OX17. . . . . .4 F2
New St
  Abingdon OX14 . . . . . . .179 F7
  Bicester OX26 . . . . .65 E3
  Chipping Norton OX7. . . . .42 E3
  Deddington OX15. . . . . . .33 F3
  Henley-on-Thames RG9 . . .244 E2
Newtec Pl OX4. . . . . .141 F7
New Theatre★ OX1. . . . . .261 B2
Newton Ave RG4. . . . . . . .259 D5
NEWTON PURCELL 39 B2
Newton Rd OX1. . . . . . . .141 C7
Newton Way OX10 . . . . . .204 A5
NEWTOWN
  Henley-on-Thames. 254 F8
  Wallingford 221 E1
Newtown OX10 . . . . .240 C7
New Town GL56. . . . . .40 F8
New Town Cotts SN6. . . .227 D4
Newtown Gdns RG9. . . . .254 E8
New Town La SN6. . . . . . .227 D4
Newtown Rd RG9 . . . . . . .254 F8
NEW YATT. 104 E7
New Yatt Bsns Ctr OX29. .104 E7
New Yatt La OX29. . . . . . .104 D7
New Yatt Rd OX28, OX29 .104 E4
Niagara Rd RG9. . . . . . . .254 E8
Nicholas Ave OX3. . . . . . .123 F4
Nicholas Rd RG9. . . . . . . .254 B8
Nichol Ct 🔳 SN7. . . . . . . .172 F3
Nicholson Rd OX3. . . . . . .123 F3
Nigel Ct NN13 . . . . .24 A5
Nightingale Ave OX4 . . . .142 F1
Nightingale La SN3 . . . . .208 A5
Nightingale Pl OX26. . . . . .81 A8
Nine Acres Cl OX7 . . . . . . .73 B4
Nine Acres La OX7 . . . . . . .73 B4
Nineteenth St OX11 . . . . .217 A1
Ninety Cut Hill OX18 . . . .102 A4
Ninth Ave OX3, OX4. . . . .142 F7
Ninth St OX11. . . . . .217 B2
Nixon Rd OX4. . . . . .141 F5
Nizewell Head OX25. . . . . .62 B8
Noble Rd RG9. . . . . .254 F8
Nobles Cl
  Grove OX12 . . . . .196 D1
  Oxford OX2 . . . . .140 A8
Nobles La OX2. . . . . .140 A8
NOKE. 110 C7
Noral Way OX16 . . . . .9 D2
Nor Brook Cl OX14 . . . . . .160 C2
Norcot Rd RG30. . . . . . . .258 A1
Norfolk Cl OX14. . . . . . . .160 E2
Norfolk St OX1. . . . . .261 B1
Norham End OX2. . . . . . . .123 C4
Norham Gdns OX2 . . . . . .261 B4
NORHAM MANOR. 261 C4
Norham Rd OX2. . . . . . . .123 C4
Norman Ave
  Abingdon OX14 . . . . . . .160 A1
  Henley-on-Thames RG9 . . .244 E1
Normandy Cres OX4 . . . . .142 E5
Norman Pl RG1. . . . . .259 B1
Norman Rd RG4. . . . . . . .259 C4
Norman Smith Rd 🔳
  OX4. . . . . .142 F1
Normanstead RG9. . . . . . .244 D1
Norman Way OX10 . . . . . .221 C7
Norreys Ave OX1. . . . . . . .141 D6
Norreys Cl OX11 . . . . . . .218 D7
Norreys Rd
  Cumnor OX2. . . . . .139 F5
  Didcot OX11. . . . . .218 D8
Norries Dr OX10 . . . . . . .203 D1
Norris Cl
  Abingdon OX14 . . . . . . .160 B2
  Adderbury OX17 . . . . . . .22 F2
Norris Rd OX25. . . . . .96 E8
Northampton Rd
  Oxford OX1 . . . . .141 D5
  Weston-on-the-Green OX25 .79 A4
NORTH ASTON. 48 B6
North Aston Rd OX25. . . . .47 D6
North Ave OX14. . . . . . . .160 A2
North Bar Pl OX16 . . . . . . .16 C6
North Bar St OX16 . . . . . . .16 C6
Northbourne CE Prim Sch
  OX11. . . . . .218 E2
Northbourne Ct OX11 . . . .218 F8
Northbourne Prim Sch
  OX11. . . . . .218 D7
NORTHBROOK. 62 E1
Northbrook Ho 🔳 OX4. . .142 E2
Northbrook Rd RG4. . . . . .259 D6
North Bush Furlong
  OX11. . . . . .201 B1
North Cl OX9. . . . . .145 F7
Northcot La OX16. . . . . . . .16 B7
NORTHCOURT. 160 A1
Northcourt La OX14. . . . .160 A1
Northcourt Mews OX14. . .159 F1
Northcourt Rd OX14. . . . .159 F1
Northcourt Wlk OX14 . . . .180 A8
North Croft OX11 . . . . . . .218 F7
North Culham Est OX14 . .181 A5
North Dr
  Grove OX12 . . . . .196 E2
  Harwell OX11. . . . . .217 C4
  Swerford Heath OX7 . . . . .31 E2
NORTHEND. 207 E6

Northern By-Pass Rd
  Cutteslowe OX2. . . . . . . .108 E1
  Oxford OX2 . . . . .124 C5
Northern House Sch
  OX2. . . . . .123 B7
Northfld Ave RG9 . . . . . . .255 A4
Northfield Cl OX4. . . . . . .142 C2
Northfield Cotts OX2. . . . .122 A8
Northfield Ct RG9. . . . . . .244 D3
Northfield End RG9 . . . . . .244 D3
Northfield Rd
  Abingdon OX14 . . . . . . .160 A3
  Lower Shiplake RG9 . . . . .255 B4
  Oxford OX3 . . . . .124 E4
  Reading RG1 . . . . .259 A1
  Woodgreen OX28 . . . . . . .104 D1
Northfield Row 🔳 OX28. .104 C1
Northfield Sch OX4 . . . . . .142 D1
Northfield Sq OX28 . . . . .104 D1
Northford Cl SN6 . . . . . . .209 C8
Northford Ind Est SN6. . .209 C8
North Gn
  Kirtlington OX5 . . . . .77 F4
  West Hanney OX12 . . . . .196 F7
North Hill HP18 . . . . .98 A1
North Hinksey CE Prim Sch
  OX2. . . . . .140 E8
North Hinksey La OX2. . . .140 E8
NORTH HINKSEY
  VILLAGE. 140 E8
North Hinksey Village
  OX2. . . . . .140 F7
North Kidlington Prim Sch 🔳
  OX5. . . . . .92 D1
North La OX25 . . . . .79 A2
NORTH LEIGH 105 B7
North Leigh Bsns Pk
  OX29 . . . . .105 C7
North Leigh CE Prim Sch
  OX29. . . . . .105 B6
North Leigh Roman Villa★
  OX29. . . . . .89 D3
North Lodge OX2 . . . . . . .122 D1
North Manor OX44 . . . . . .143 E2
North Manor Estate The
  OX44. . . . . .143 E2
Northmead La OX12. . . . .196 A7
North Mill Rd HP27. . . . . .149 F5
NORTHMOOR. 138 C2
Northmoor Pk OX29. . . . .138 C2
Northmoor Pl OX2 . . . . . .123 C5
Northmoor Rd OX2. . . . . .123 C5
NORTH MORETON 220 A7
NORTH NEWINGTON 15 B4
Northolt Rd OX18 . . . . . . .115 E3
North Oxfordshire Acad
  OX16. . . . . .15 E8
North Parade Ave OX2 . . .123 C4
North Pl OX3. . . . . .124 D3
North Quay OX14 . . . . . . .179 F4
North Rd
  Didcot OX11. . . . . .200 D2
  Moulsford OX10. . . . . . . .238 F4
North Side OX25 . . . . .48 A1
North St
  Aston OX18 . . . . .135 E3
  Banbury OX16 . . . . .16 E7
  Bicester OX26 . . . . .65 E2
  Fritwell OX27. . . . . .49 E7
  Islip OX5 . . . . .93 F1
  Marcham OX13 . . . . .178 C6
  Middle Barton OX7 . . . . . .60 F8
  Oxford OX2 . . . . .123 A1
  Reading RG4. . . . . .259 B2
  Thame OX9 . . . . .129 F1
  Watchfield SN6 . . . . .191 D1
NORTH STOKE. 221 D1
Northumberland Ct 🔳
  OX16. . . . . .16 E6
Northview Prim Sch
  SN6. . . . . .190 A7
North Way
  Cutteslowe OX2. . . . . . . .109 A1
  Oxford OX3 . . . . .124 E4
  Steventon OX13. . . . . . . .198 F4
NORTH WESTON. 146 F8
Northwood Cres OX18. . . .115 E4
Northwood Rd OX29 . . . . .103 C1
Norton Cl OX3. . . . . .124 D2
Norton Green Ct OX7. . . . .42 E2
Norton Pk OX7. . . . . .42 F4
Norton Terr OX29 . . . . . . .102 D8
Norton Way OX18 . . . . . . .115 F3
Norwood Ave OX13 . . . . .156 E1
Nosworthy Way OX10 . . . .221 E5
Notley Pl RG4. . . . . .259 B4
Nottingham Fee OX11. . . .236 E8
Nottwood La RG9. . . . . . .242 A5
Nourse Cl OX3. . . . . .110 B5
Nowell Rd OX4. . . . . .142 A3
NUFFIELD. 223 D3
Nuffield Cl
  Bicester OX26 . . . . .65 F3
  🔳 Didcot OX11. . . . . . . .219 A8
Nuffield Coll OX1 . . . . . . .261 A2
Nuffield Dr OX16. . . . . . . .16 A8
Nuffield Hill RG9. . . . . . . .223 C4
Nuffield Ind Est OX4 . . . .142 C2
Nuffield La OX10. . . . . . . .222 C5
Nuffield Orthopaedic Ctr
  OX3. . . . . .124 D1
Nuffield Rd OX3. . . . . . . .124 F1
Nuffield Way OX14. . . . . .179 C7
NUNEHAM COURTENAY . . .161 E3
Nuneham Sq OX14 . . . . . .179 F8
NUNEY GREEN 251 E3
Nunhide La RG8. . . . . . . .256 F1
Nunnery Cl OX4. . . . . . . .142 D2

Nunney Brook OX11. . . . .200 F3
Nun's Acre RG8. . . . . . . .249 B7
Nurseries Rd OX5. . . . . . .108 D8
Nursery Cl
  Lower Shiplake RG9 . . . . .255 A4
  Oxford OX3 . . . . .124 C1
Nursery Dr OX16 . . . . .16 C7
Nursery Gdns RG8 . . . . . .257 B5
Nursery La OX16 . . . . .16 C7
Nursery Rd OX29. . . . . . .105 C7
Nursery The OX14. . . . . . .200 A8
Nursery View SN7. . . . . . .173 B3
Nuthatch Cl 🔳 OX4 . . . . .142 E1
Nut Hatch Cotts RG8. . . .241 D3
Nuthatch Way OX26. . . . . .65 F1
Nyatt Rd OX14. . . . . .180 C8
Nye Bevan Cl OX4. . . . . . .142 A8

O

Oak Ave OX14. . . . . .160 E6
Oak Cl OX26. . . . . .65 F4
Oak Cotts OX10 . . . . .239 D6
Oakdale Ct 🔳 OX10 . . . . .221 C7
Oakdale La OX28. . . . . . .104 E3
Oakdale Rd OX28 . . . . . . .104 D3
Oakdene RG8. . . . . .250 F7
Oakdown Cl RG8. . . . . . . .250 E3
Oak Dr OX5. . . . . .92 F1
Oak End Way OX39. . . . . .168 D6
Oakes La OX2. . . . . .121 C2
Oakey Cl OX18. . . . . .133 C5
Oak Farm Cl OX9. . . . . . .166 B7
Oakfield Ind Est OX29 . . .120 D6
Oakfield Pl OX28. . . . . . . .118 B7
Oakfield Rd OX18 . . . . . . .115 D1
Oakham Cl RG31 . . . . . . .257 D2
Oakham Rd GL56. . . . . . . .27 B1
Oak La
  Ambrosden OX25. . . . . . . .81 D4
  Stanford in the Vale SN7. .194 F6
Oakland Cl OX29 . . . . . . .105 F7
Oakland Rd OX16 . . . . .16 D2
Oaklands OX2 . . . . .121 B3
Oaklands Rd OX2. . . . . . . .122 F1
OAKLEY. 168 B5
Oakley Cl OX10 . . . . .222 F5
Oakley Ho OX13. . . . . . . .158 C2
Oakley La OX39 . . . . .168 B6
Oakley Rd
  Chinnor OX39. . . . . .168 C6
  Horton-cum-Studley OX33 .112 C5
  Reading RG4. . . . . .258 F4
Oakmead OX28 . . . . .104 D2
Oak Rd SN6. . . . . .191 C1
Oaks Meade OX18. . . . . . .115 F4
Oaksmere OX13. . . . . . . .158 A6
Oaks Rd RG9. . . . . .255 A4
Oak St GL7. . . . . .150 C4
Oaks The OX18 . . . . .115 E4
Oakthorpe Pl OX2. . . . . . .123 B6
Oakthorpe Rd OX2. . . . . .123 B6
Oak Tree Copse RG31 . . .257 E3
Oak Tree Rd RG31. . . . . .257 E2
Oak Tree Wlk RG8 . . . . . .257 D5
Oak View OX14. . . . . . . .114 C7
Oasis Pk OX29 . . . . .120 D6
Oathurst Est OX18 . . . . . .134 F3
Oatland Rd OX11. . . . . . .218 E8
Oatlands Cl OX10 . . . . . . .203 B7
Oatlands Rd OX2. . . . . . . .122 F1
Observatory Cl OX10 . . . .204 A4
Observatory St OX2 . . . . .261 A4
Ock Dr OX10. . . . . .182 D5
Ockham Ct OX2. . . . . . . .123 C4
Ockley Brook OX11. . . . . .201 A3
Ock Meadow Nature
  Reserve★ OX14. . . . . . .179 B5
Ock Mews 🔳 OX14. . . . . .179 E7
Ock Mill Cl OX14 . . . . . . .179 D6
Ock St OX14. . . . . .179 D6
O'Connors Rd OX29 . . . . .102 E2
Octavian Way NN13 . . . . .24 A7
ODDINGTON 94 E2
Oddley La HP27. . . . . . . .169 D8
Odiham Ave RG4. . . . . . . .259 E5
Odiham Cl OX18 . . . . . . .115 F3
Offas Cl OX10. . . . . .204 A5
Offlands Ct OX10. . . . . . .238 F6
Ogbourne Cl OX12 . . . . . .214 B5
OISE Oxford OX1. . . . . . .261 B2
Old Arncott Rd OX26. . . . . .81 C3
Old Bakery The OX1. . . . .261 A2
Old Barn Cl
  Benson OX10. . . . . .204 A4
  Reading RG4. . . . . .259 A6
Old Barn Ground OX3. . . .142 F7
Old Bath Rd
  Sonning RG4. . . . . .260 D1
  Sonning RG4. . . . . .260 E2
Old Bix Rd RG9 . . . . .243 F5
Old Blackalls Dr OX10. . . .221 A3
Old Bldgs 🔳 OX10 . . . . . .221 D7
Old Boars Hill
  Boars Hill OX1. . . . . .140 D1
  Wootton OX1. . . . . .159 C8
Old Bourne OX11. . . . . . .200 F3
Old Brewery La RG9. . . . .244 E2
Old Bridge Rd OX15. . . . . .21 E4
Old Bryers Cl HP18. . . . . .128 C3
Old Burford Rd OX7. . . . . .54 D1
Old Chapel Cl OX5. . . . . . .92 E1
Old Coach Rd OX13 . . . . .157 F2
Old Coachyard The 🔳
  OX28. . . . . .104 B1
Old Copse Gdns RG4. . . . .252 F6

Old Council Hos The
Horley OX15 . . . . **8** B4
South Newington OX15 . . . . **31** F7
Old Croft Cl OX39 . . . . **167** F4
Old Dashwood Hill HP14 . **189** F2
Oldean Cl RG31 . . . . **257** D1
Old Farm Cl
Abingdon OX14 . . . . **180** C8
Worminghall HP18 . . . . . . **127** D5
Old Farm Cres RG31 . . . . . **257** C2
Old Field OX44 . . . . **164** A7
Old Forge Cl OX7 . . . . **54** D2
Old Forge Rd OX7 . . . . **29** A3
Old Forge The RG8 . . . . . . **249** A6
Old George Yd OX18 . . . . . **100** E5
Old Glebe OX15 . . . . **20** C8
Old Gn The OX33 . . . . **112** A5
Old Greyfriars St OX1 . . . **261** B1
Old Grimsbury Rd OX16 . . **16** E7
Old High St OX3 . . . . **124** D3
Old Johns Cl OX7 . . . . **60** F8
Old Kiln★ RG9 . . . . **224** E2
Old Kiln The RG9 . . . . **224** E2
Old London Rd
Benson OX10 . . . . **204** A4
Chipping Norton OX7 . . . . . **56** C7
Nuffield OX10 . . . . **223** A7
Tiddington OX9 . . . . **145** F4
Wheatley OX33 . . . . **144** D8
Old Luxters Farm Brewery★
RG9 . . . . **226** F7
Old Maltings The OX9 . . . **129** E1
Old Manor Ct OX14 . . . . . . **214** A2
Old Man's La OX12 . . . . . . **197** B4
Old Marston Rd OX3 . . . . . **123** F4
Old Mill Cl OX12 . . . . **196** E1
Old Mill The
Pangbourne RG8 . . . . **256** D6
6 Wantage OX12 . . . . . . **214** D4
Old Moor OX14 . . . . **199** D5
Old Moor Cl OX10 . . . . **221** C7
Old Nursery View OX1 . . **141** D3
Old Orchard OX39 . . . . **149** E2
Old Parr Cl OX16 . . . . **16** D5
Old Parr Rd OX16 . . . . **16** D4
Old Place Yd OX26 . . . . **65** E1
Old Plough Wlk OX15 . . . . . **33** A4
Old Pound The OX13 . . . . . **159** B6
Old Rd
East Hendred OX12 . . . . . . **216** E6
Great Tew OX7 . . . . **45** D7
Littleworth OX33 . . . . **143** E8
Oxford OX3 . . . . **124** E1
Ratley OX15 . . . . **2** A4
Old Rd The RG9 . . . . **225** C8
Old Reading Rd OX10 . . . . **221** F5
Old Rectory OX25 . . . . **48** F1
Old Rectory Ct OX25 . . . . . **80** A4
Old Rectory Mews OX28 . **118** A7
Old Sawmills Rd SN7 . . . . **172** F2
Old Sch La OX27 . . . . **49** F7
Old School Cl OX27 . . . . **65** F7
Old School End OX15 . . . . . **30** A7
Old School Ho The OX7 . . . **70** B2
Old School La OX12 . . . . . **213** F5
Old School Pl
Banbury OX16 . . . . **16** E6
Watlington OX49 . . . . **186** B1
Old School The OX4 . . . . . **142** C6
Old Stables The OX3 . . . . . **124** C4
Old Stables Yd OX12 . . . . . **214** A1
Old Station Yd **6** OX14 . . **179** F7
OLD TOWN **24** A7
Old Town NN13 . . . . **24** A7
Old Vicarage La SN3 . . . . . **208** A3
Old Wallingford Way
OX14 . . . . **200** B8
Old Warehouse Flats The
OX28 . . . . **104** C1
OLD WARREN **246** E6
Old Well Ct RG4 . . . . **260** D4
Old Wharf Rd SN7 . . . . **210** C8
Old Windmill Way HP18 . **129** C7
Old Witney Rd OX29 . . . . . **120** D8
OLD WOODSTOCK **91** A7
Oliver Rd OX4 . . . . **142** E5
Olson Cotts HP14 . . . . **188** F4
Omega Pk OX11 . . . . **200** E3
One End La OX10 . . . . **203** F4
Onley Ct **8** OX1 . . . . **141** C7
Onslow Dr OX9 . . . . **130** B1
Onslow Gdns RG4 . . . . **259** C3
Oracle Parkway RG5 . . . . . **260** A1
Orange Cl SN6 . . . . **190** A6
Oratory Prep Sch The
RG8 . . . . **250** D4
Oratory Sch The RG8 . . . . **251** A8
Orchard Ave RG4 . . . . **252** E5
Orchard Cl
Abingdon OX14 . . . . **160** A1
Banbury OX16 . . . . **16** B6
Buckland SN7 . . . . **174** E8
Cassington OX29 . . . . **107** C2
Chalgrove OX44 . . . . **184** D7
Charney Bassett OX12 . . . **175** F2
Combe OX29 . . . . **90** A4
Didcot OX11 . . . . **200** E1
East Hanney OX12 . . . . . . **197** B6
East Hendred OX12 . . . . . . **216** D7
Eynsham OX29 . . . . **120** F7
Henley-on-Thames RG9 . . **244** E1
Lechlade-on-Thames GL7 . **150** C4
Reading RG31 . . . . **257** C3
Salford OX7 . . . . **41** F3
Shiplake RG9 . . . . **254** C4
Thame OX9 . . . . **148** A8
Upton OX11 . . . . **218** C2
Wallingford OX10 . . . . . . **221** D6

Orchard Cl continued
Warborough OX10 . . . . . . **203** B7
Wheatley OX33 . . . . **144** B7
Orchard Coombe RG8 . . . **250** D3
Orchard Cotts OX7 . . . . **57** B1
Orchard Ct OX4 . . . . **142** B4
Orchard Ctr The OX11 . . . **200** F1
Orchard Field RG4 . . . . . . **252** C5
Orchard Field La OX12 . . . **91** D3
Orchard Fields Com Sch
OX16 . . . . **16** A6
Orchard Furlong OX12 . . . **213** C4
Orchard Gdns OX12 . . . . . **213** D5
Orchard Gr
Bloxham OX15 . . . . **21** D3
Reading RG4 . . . . **259** E4
Orchard Ground OX7 . . . . . **69** C2
Orchard Haven OX10 . . . . **202** D8
Orchard Hill SN7 . . . . **172** E3
Orchard La
Boars Hill OX1 . . . . **140** C1
East Hendred OX12 . . . . . . **216** D6
Upper Heyford OX25 . . . . . **62** F8
Orchard Meadow Prim Sch
OX4 . . . . **142** E2
Orchard Piece OX17 . . . . . . **4** A3
Orchard Pl
Upper Heyford OX25 . . . . . **62** F8
Westbury NN13 . . . . **25** A4
Orchard Rd
Ardley OX27 . . . . **50** B4
Buckland SN7 . . . . **174** E8
Hook Norton OX15 . . . . **30** B8
Oxford OX2 . . . . **140** A8
Orchard Rise
Burford OX18 . . . . **100** E4
Chesterton OX26 . . . . **79** F8
Orchard Row OX18 . . . . . . **100** F6
Orchard The
Appleton OX13 . . . . **158** A8
Ascott-under-Wychwood
OX7 . . . . **71** B1
Brighthampton OX29 . . . . **137** A4
East Challow OX12 . . . . . . **214** A5
Horton-cum-Studley OX33 . **112** C6
Merton OX25 . . . . **95** D8
Orchard View OX17 . . . . **4** F2
Orchard Way
Banbury OX16 . . . . **16** B6
Bicester OX26 . . . . **65** C3
Chinnor OX39 . . . . **168** C6
Harwell OX11 . . . . **217** D7
Kidlington OX5 . . . . **108** F8
Kingham OX7 . . . . **54** F4
Marcham OX13 . . . . **178** D6
Middle Barton OX7 . . . . **46** E1
Wantage OX12 . . . . **214** E4
Witney OX28 . . . . **118** A8
Orchard Wlk OX49 . . . . . . **186** C2
Orchid Cl OX26 . . . . **65** E5
Orchids The OX11 . . . . **235** D7
Orchid Way OX18 . . . . **115** E4
Ordnance Rd OX11 . . . . . . **200** D2
Oregon Ave RG31 . . . . **257** D3
Oriel Coll OX1 . . . . **261** C2
Oriel Ct OX11 . . . . **219** B8
Oriel Sq OX1 . . . . **261** C2
Oriel St OX1 . . . . **261** C2
Oriel Way OX26 . . . . **65** F3
Orkney Pl OX28 . . . . **117** F8
Ormond Rd
Thame OX9 . . . . **130** A1
Wantage OX12 . . . . **214** A4
Orpine Cl OX26 . . . . **65** D5
Orpwood Way OX14 . . . . . **179** C6
Orwell Cl RG4 . . . . **258** F4
Orwell Dr OX11 . . . . **201** A1
Osberton Rd OX2 . . . . **123** A7
Osborne Cl
Bicester OX26 . . . . **65** C3
Kidlington OX5 . . . . **108** D7
Wolvercote OX2 . . . . **122** F8
Osiers The OX10 . . . . **183** B5
Osler Rd OX3 . . . . **124** C3
OSNEY **123** A1
Osney Cl OX15 . . . . **30** B7
Osney La
Oxford OX1 . . . . **123** A1
Oxford OX1 . . . . **261** A2
Osney Mead OX2 . . . . **141** A8
Osney Mead Ind Est OX2 **141** A8
Osney Mews OX2 . . . . **123** A1
Osprey Cl OX26 . . . . **81** B8
Osterley Dr RG4 . . . . **259** E6
Osterley Gr OX16 . . . . **16** B4
Oswestry Rd OX1 . . . . **141** D5
Otmoor La
Beckley OX3 . . . . **111** B4
Charlton-on-Otmoor OX5 . . **95** A4
Otmoor View OX25 . . . . **95** C8
Otters Reach OX1 . . . . **141** E1
Ottery Way OX11 . . . . **201** A2
Otwell Cl OX14 . . . . **160** B2
Our Lady of Lourdes RC Prim
Sch **1** OX28 . . . . **117** E7
Our Ladys Convent Jun &
Senior Sch OX4 . . . . . . **180** A8
Our Ladys RC Prim Sch
OX4 . . . . **142** D5
Ouse Cl OX11 . . . . **200** F3
Ouseley Cl OX3 . . . . **123** F4
Outram Rd OX4 . . . . **142** B5
Oval The
Bicester OX26 . . . . **65** D3
Didcot OX11 . . . . **200** C2
Oxford OX4 . . . . **142** A3
Overbrooke Gdns OX4 . . . **143** A2

Overbury **1** OX18 . . . . . . **115** E5
Overdale Cl OX4 . . . . **124** E4
Overdown Rd RG31 . . . . . . **257** D3
OVER KIDDINGTON **60** A1
Overlanders End RG31 . . **257** E3
Overmead OX14 . . . . **179** E4
Overmead Gn OX4 . . . . . . **142** E2
OVER NORTON **42** E5
Over Norton Rd OX7 . . . . . **42** F4
Overstrand Cl OX26 . . . . . . **66** A4
OVERTHORPE **17** D6
Overthorpe Prep Sch
OX17 . . . . **17** C8
Overthorpe Rd OX16 . . . . . **17** A6
OVER WORTON **46** D7
Owens Way OX4 . . . . **142** E4
Owlington Cl OX2 . . . . **122** C1
Ox Cl OX14 . . . . **180** A8
Oxen Piece OX44 . . . . **145** C2
Oxeye Ct OX4 . . . . **161** E8
OXFORD **261** C1
Oxford Acad OX4 . . . . **142** C2
Oxford Airport OX5 . . . . . . **92** A4
Oxford Brookes Univ
(Harcourt Hill Campus)
OX2 . . . . **140** D6
Oxford Brookes Univ
(Headington Campus:Gipsy
La) OX3 . . . . **124** B2
Oxford Brookes Univ
(Headington
Campus:Headington Hill)
OX3 . . . . **124** A2
Oxford Brookes Univ
(Marston Road Site)
OX3 . . . . **124** A3
Oxford Brookes Univ
(Wheatley Campus)
OX33 . . . . **144** C3
Oxford Bsns Ctr The
OX1 . . . . **261** A1
Oxford Bsns Park N OX4 **142** D5
Oxford Bsns Park S OX4 **142** D4
Oxford Bsns Pk QX2 . . . . **109** A2
Oxford Bus Mus★ OX29 . . **90** C1
Oxford Castle Unlocked★
OX1 . . . . **261** A2
Oxford & Cherwell Valley
Coll (Banbury Campus)
OX16 . . . . **16** B5
Oxford & Cherwell Valley
Coll (Bicester Campus)
OX26 . . . . **66** B3
Oxford & Cherwell Valley
Coll (Blackbird Leys
Campus) OX4 . . . . **142** A2
Oxford & Cherwell Valley
Coll (Oxford Campus)
OX1 . . . . **261** A1
Oxford Cl
Kingston Bagpuize OX13 . . **156** F1
Kirtlington OX5 . . . . **77** F4
Oxford Cres OX11 . . . . **218** C8
Oxford Ct OX25 . . . . **79** A2
Oxford English Ctr The **4**
OX2 . . . . **123** C5
Oxford High Sch OX2 . . . . **123** C6
Oxford Hill OX28, OX29 . . . **118** D8
Oxford House Sch of English
OX33 . . . . **144** B8
Oxford Ice Rink★ OX1 . . . **261** A1
Oxford Int Coll of Beauty **2**
OX28 . . . . **104** B1
Oxford La OX12 . . . . **196** E2
Oxford Media & Bsns Sch
OX1 . . . . **261** B1
Oxford Motor Pk OX5 . . . . . **92** B2
Oxford Playhouse★ OX1 . **261** B3
Oxford Rd
Abingdon OX1, OX13,
OX14 . . . . **160** B5
Adderbury OX17 . . . . **23** A3
Benson OX10 . . . . **203** E4
Bicester OX25, OX26 . . . . . **80** D8
Bletchingdon OX5 . . . . **93** A7
Bodicote OX15 . . . . **16** D3
Burford OX18 . . . . **100** E4
Clifton Hampden OX14,
OX44 . . . . **181** E6
Cumnor OX2 . . . . **139** F5
Cutteslowe OX2 . . . . **109** A3
Dorchester OX10 . . . . **182** D2
Dorchester OX10 . . . . **182** E2
Duns Tew OX25 . . . . **47** F5
Enstone OX7 . . . . **58** F5
Eynsham OX29 . . . . **120** F7
Farmoor 2, OX29 . . . . **121** A4
Frilford OX13 . . . . **178** A7
Garsington OX44 . . . . **143** C2
Hampton Poyle OX5 . . . . . . **93** B3
Horspath OX33 . . . . **143** B6
Kidlington OX5 . . . . **108** F7
Kingston Bagpuize OX13 . . **156** D1
Kirtlington OX5 . . . . **77** F3
Marston OX3 . . . . **123** F5
Middleton Stoney OX25 . . . **64** A3
Oxford, Littlemore OX4 . . . **142** B3
Oxford, Temple Cowley
OX4 . . . . **142** C5
Reading RG8, RG30, RG31 **257** D4
South Newington OX15 . . . **31** A2
Stokenchurch HP14 . . . . . **188** C5
Thame OX9 . . . . **147** D8
Tiddington OX9 . . . . **145** E6
Woodcote RG8 . . . . **240** E1
Woodstock OX20 . . . . **91** C5
Oxford Retail Pk OX4 . . . . **142** E4

Oxford Said Bsns Sch
OX1 . . . . **261** A2
Oxford Sch OX4 . . . . **142** B7
Oxford Sch of English
OX1 . . . . **261** B2
Oxford Science Pk The
OX4 . . . . **142** C1
Oxfordshire Hospital Sch **6**
OX3 . . . . **124** D1
Oxfordshire Mus The★
OX20 . . . . **91** A6
Oxford Spires Bsns Pk
OX5 . . . . **92** B3
Oxford Sq SN6 . . . . **191** C1
Oxford St
Reading RG4 . . . . **259** A2
Woodstock OX20 . . . . **91** B6
Oxford Sta OX2 . . . . **123** A1
Oxford Study Ctr OX2 . . . . **109** A1
Oxford Tutorial Coll
OX1 . . . . **261** C2
Oxford Union The★ OX1 . **261** B2
Oxford Univ OX1 . . . . **261** B4
Oxford University Press
OX2 . . . . **261** A3
Oxford Univ Inst Of
Experimental Psychology
OX1 . . . . **261** C1
Oxford Univ Mus of Natural
History The★ OX1 . . . . **261** B3
Oxhey Hill OX17 . . . . **4** D3
Oxhey Rise OX15 . . . . **31** B7
Oxlease OX28 . . . . **118** C8
Oxlip Leyes OX26 . . . . **65** D4
Oxon Pl SN6 . . . . **227** D4
Oxpens Rd OX1 . . . . **261** A1
Ozone L Pk OX4 . . . . **142** D1

P

Packhorse La OX13 . . . . . . **178** D6
Pack La OX7 . . . . **61** B7
Pack & Prime La RG9 . . . . **244** C2
Paddick Cl RG4 . . . . **260** E3
Paddock Cl
Benson OX10 . . . . **204** A4
Chalgrove OX44 . . . . **184** D7
Wantage OX12 . . . . **214** F6
Paddock Farm La OX15 . . . **22** D8
Paddock Mews OX13 . . . . **156** D1
Paddock Rd
Ardley OX27 . . . . **50** B4
Reading RG4 . . . . **259** D1
Wallingford OX10 . . . . . . **221** D7
Paddocks The
Aston OX18 . . . . **135** E2
Bampton OX18 . . . . **134** E1
Deddington OX15 . . . . **33** E4
East Hanney OX12 . . . . . . **197** B6
Mollington OX17 . . . . **3** F3
Souldern OX27 . . . . **35** E3
Yarnton OX5 . . . . **108** B5
Paddock The
Chilton OX11 . . . . **235** D8
Highworth SN6 . . . . **190** A5
Kennington OX1 . . . . **160** E7
Kingston Bagpuize OX13 . . **156** D1
Somerton OX25 . . . . **48** F5
Paddox The OX2 . . . . **123** A8
Page Furlong OX10 . . . . . . **182** D2
Pages Cl OX15 . . . . **7** C6
Pages Orch RG4 . . . . **252** E5
Paget Rd OX4 . . . . **142** E6
Pagisters Rd OX14 . . . . . . **160** C2
Paines Hill OX25 . . . . **62** B8
Painswick Cl OX28 . . . . . . **103** E1
Painters Cl OX15 . . . . **21** D4
Pain Way OX10 . . . . **183** B3
Palladian Ct OX14 . . . . . . **142** B6
Palmer Ave OX25 . . . . **96** F8
Palmer Pl OX14 . . . . **179** E5
Palmer Rd OX3 . . . . **124** E1
Palmers OX12 . . . . **214** F5
Pampas Cl OX18 . . . . **115** E1
PANGBOURNE **256** C6
Pangbourne Coll RG8 . . . . **256** A4
Pangbourne Hill RG8 . . . . **256** C5
Pangbourne Mews RG8 . . **256** D6
Pangbourne Pl RG8 . . . . . **256** D6
Pangbourne Prim Sch
RG8 . . . . **256** E5
Pangbourne St RG30 . . . . **258** B1
Pangbourne Sta RG8 . . . . **256** D6
Panters Rd OX10 . . . . **221** N4
Paper Mill Cotts OX18 . . . . **99** D6
Paper Mill La OX11 . . . . . . **220** A5
Papist Way
Cholsey OX10 . . . . **239** B8
West End OX10 . . . . **220** F1
Parade The
Kidlington OX5 . . . . **108** F6
Oxford OX3 . . . . **124** D3
Paradise Cl OX15 . . . . **21** A2
Paradise Mews RG9 . . . . . **244** D2
Paradise Rd RG9 . . . . **244** C1
Paradise Sq OX1 . . . . **261** A1
Paradise St OX1 . . . . **261** A2
Paradise Terr OX7 . . . . **42** D1
Park 34 OX11 . . . . **200** E3
Park Ave
Highworth SN6 . . . . **190** A5
Kidlington OX5 . . . . **92** D2
Shrivenham SN6 . . . . **209** D7
Park Cl
Avon Dassett CV47 . . . . **2** F8
Banbury OX16 . . . . **16** C6

Park Cl continued
Bladon OX20 . . . . **91** B3
Cutteslowe OX2 . . . . **109** B2
Didcot OX11 . . . . **218** D8
Hanwell OX17 . . . . **8** F4
Hook Norton OX15 . . . . **30** B6
Kirtlington OX5 . . . . **77** F5
Middleton Stoney OX25 . . . **64** A4
North Leigh OX29 . . . . **105** C6
Sonning Common RG4 . . . **253** A6
Yarnton OX5 . . . . **108** B4
PARK CORNER **224** C6
Park Cres OX14 . . . . **179** E7
Park Ct OX9 . . . . **148** A8
Park End
Bodicote OX15 . . . . **16** E1
Croughton NN13 . . . . **36** D8
Park End Cl OX15 . . . . **16** E1
Park End Ct OX15 . . . . **16** E1
Park End Pl OX1 . . . . **261** A2
Park End St OX1 . . . . **261** A2
Park End Works NN13 . . . . **36** D7
Parkers Cir OX7 . . . . **43** A3
Parkers Cl SN7 . . . . **173** A3
Parkers Hill OX9 . . . . **166** B8
Parkers Rd OX7 . . . . **43** A3
Parker St OX4 . . . . **141** F6
Park Farm Cl OX25 . . . . **81** C3
Park Farm Cotts OX25 . . . . **63** E5
Park Hill
Hook Norton OX15 . . . . **30** B7
Wheatley OX33 . . . . **126** B1
Parkhill Dr RG31 . . . . **257** D2
Park Hospl for Children
OX3 . . . . **124** C1
Park La
Appleton OX13 . . . . **158** A7
Ardington OX12 . . . . **215** D3
Bladon OX20 . . . . **91** B2
Checkendon RG4 . . . . **251** E6
Kingston Blount OX39 . . . **167** F3
Long Hanborough OX29 . . . **90** D1
North Newington OX15 . . . **15** C4
Stanford in the Vale SN7 . . **195** B6
Stokenchurch HP14 . . . . . **188** E6
Stonor RG9 . . . . **225** D6
Swalcliffe OX15 . . . . **19** E7
Woodstock OX20 . . . . **91** B6
Parkland Pl OX26 . . . . **80** F8
Parklands
Banbury OX16 . . . . **16** B7
Farmoor OX2 . . . . **121** E2
Freeland OX29 . . . . **105** F7
Oxford OX3 . . . . **124** E1
Park Rd
Abingdon OX14 . . . . **179** E7
Banbury OX16 . . . . **16** B6
Chipping Norton OX7 . . . . . **42** F4
Combe OX29 . . . . **90** B5
Didcot OX11 . . . . **218** B4
Ducklington OX29 . . . . . . **118** A4
Faringdon SN7 . . . . **172** F2
Henley-on-Thames RG9 . . **244** E1
Hook Norton OX15 . . . . **30** B7
Kiddington OX20 . . . . **60** A2
North Leigh OX29 . . . . **105** B6
Witney OX28 . . . . **103** F1
Park Rise OX25 . . . . **81** C3
Parkside
Checkendon RG8 . . . . **241** D3
Cuddesdon OX44 . . . . **144** C3
Henley-on-Thames RG9 . . **244** C2
North Leigh OX29 . . . . **105** C6
Witney OX28 . . . . **118** B6
Park Side
Marcham OX13 . . . . **178** C6
Woodstock OX20 . . . . **91** C6
Park Sports Ctr The
OX33 . . . . **126** B1
Parks Rd OX1 . . . . **261** B3
Park St
Bladon OX20 . . . . **91** B2
Charlbury OX7 . . . . **73** B3
Thame OX9 . . . . **148** A7
Woodstock OX20 . . . . **91** A6
Park Terr
East Challow OX12 . . . . . . **214** A5
Thame OX9 . . . . **148** A7
Park The
Cumnor OX2 . . . . **139** E4
East Challow OX12 . . . . . . **214** A5
Harwell OX11 . . . . **217** E6
PARK TOWN **123** D4
Park Town OX2 . . . . **123** C4
Park View
Crowmarsh Gifford
OX10 . . . . **222** A6
Sydenham OX39 . . . . **148** F1
Wantage OX12 . . . . **214** E5
Park View La OX18 . . . . . . **115** E5
Park View Rd OX28 . . . . . . **104** D1
Park Wall La RG8 . . . . **249** D1
Park Way OX3 . . . . **123** F7
Parkway Cl OX4 . . . . **142** D4
Parkway Dr RG4 . . . . **260** E3
Park Wlk RG8 . . . . **257** D5
Parliament Rd OX9 . . . . . . **129** F1
Parma Ho OX2 . . . . **123** B7
Parrs Rd HP14 . . . . **188** E4
Parry Cl OX3 . . . . **123** F3
Parsley Pl OX16 . . . . **9** A2
Parslow Ho OX49 . . . . **186** C1
Parsonage Cl OX12 . . . . . **215** A6
Parsonage Ct SN6 . . . . . . **190** A6
PARSONAGE GREEN **247** E4

Parson's La OX10 . . . . 204 F3
Parsons Mead OX14 . . . . . 159 E2
Parsons Pl OX4 . . . . 142 A8
Parsons St OX17 . . . . 23 A4
Parson's St OX16 . . . . 16 D6
Partridge Chase OX26 . . . . 81 A8
Partridge Cl **4** OX12 . . . . 214 E4
Partridge Ct OX17 . . . . 22 F3
Partridge Pl OX5 . . . . 92 C1
Partridge Wlk OX4 . . . . . 143 A1
Pascali Pl OX16 . . . . 9 A1
Passey Cres OX10 . . . . . . 204 A4
Patemore La OX49, RG9 . . 206 E2
Paternoster La OX10 . . . . 220 F1
PATH HILL 251 A1
Patrick Haugh Rd OX25 . . 96 F7
Patrick Rd RG4 . . . . 259 B2
Patricks Orch SN7 . . . . . . 211 D7
Pattison Pl OX4 . . . . 142 A3
Pauling Rd OX3 . . . . 124 E1
Pauls Way OX49 . . . . 186 B2
Paxmans Pl OX16 . . . . 16 C4
Paynes End OX27 . . . . 65 F6
PEACHCROFT 160 C2
Peachcroft Rd OX14 . . . . . 160 B2
Peacock Ho **8** OX12 . . . . 214 D4
Peacock Rd OX3 . . . . 123 F3
Peaks La OX29 . . . . 89 C7
Pearce Cl OX9 . . . . 147 F8
Pearce Dr OX7 . . . . 42 E2
Pearces Mdw RG9 . . . . . 224 D3
Pearce's Orch RG9 . . . . . 244 D3
Pearce Way OX5 . . . . 148 B7
Pearson Rd RG4 . . . . 260 D3
Peartree Cl **2** OX4 . . . . . 142 F1
Pear Tree Cl OX7 . . . . 70 B1
Pear Tree Cotts RG9 . . . . 243 D1
Pear Tree Farm Ind Units
  OX27 . . . . 67 E2
Peartree Interchange
  OX2 . . . . 108 E2
Pear Tree Wlk OX18 . . . . 115 E5
Peascroft HP18 . . . . 129 D6
Pease Pl OX11 . . . . 218 F8
Peat Moors OX3 . . . . 142 D8
Pebble Cl OX18 . . . . 101 D5
Pebble Hill OX44 . . . . 162 B4
Pebble La NN13 . . . . 24 A7
Peeble Dr OX11 . . . . 219 A8
Peeble Hill Mobile Home Pk
  OX14 . . . . 160 E6
Peel Cl
  Ducklington OX29 . . . . 118 B4
  Reading RG4 . . . . 259 D2
Peel Pl
  Carterton OX18 . . . . . . 115 E2
  Oxford OX1 . . . . 141 D5
Peep-O-Day La OX14 . . . . 179 F3
Pegasus Ct **5** OX1 . . . . . 141 C7
Pegasus First Sch OX4 . . 142 F2
Pegasus Rd OX4 . . . . 142 F2
Pegswell La OX44 . . . . . . 145 B2
Pelham Rd OX9 . . . . 130 B1
Pelican Pl OX29 . . . . 120 E8
Pembroke Coll OX1 . . . . . 261 B1
Pembroke Ct **3** OX4 . . . . 141 F8
Pembroke Ho **6** RG4 . . . 259 C1
Pembroke La OX14 . . . . . 199 D5
Pembroke Pl
  Bampton OX18 . . . . 134 F4
  Reading RG4 . . . . 259 C3
Pembroke Sq OX1 . . . . . . 261 B1
Pembroke St OX1 . . . . . . 261 B2
Pembroke Way OX26 . . . . 65 F3
Pemscott Cl OX18 . . . . . . 133 C5
Pendennis Ave RG4 . . . . . 259 E6
Pendles Paddock HP14 . . 188 F2
Pendon Mus★ OX14 . . . . 201 C8
Penfield Ct OX3 . . . . 124 B5
Penfold Ct OX3 . . . . 124 B5
Penhill Ind Pk OX16 . . . . . 9 B1
Penhurst Sch OX7 . . . . . . 42 E3
Pen La OX13, OX14 . . . . . 159 F5
Penley Cl OX39 . . . . 168 B6
Penlon Pl OX14 . . . . 180 A7
Penn Cl
  Abingdon OX14 . . . . . . 160 C2
  Reading RG4 . . . . 259 A6
Pennington Pl OX9 . . . . . 130 B1
Penn The OX7 . . . . 42 E5
Pennycress Rd OX4 . . . . . 143 A2
Pennyfarthing Pl OX1 . . . 261 B2
Pennyhooks La SN6 . . . . 209 B8
Penny Piece RG8 . . . . . . 249 C7
Pennyroyal RG8 . . . . 250 F5
Pennywell Dr OX2 . . . . . . 109 B1
Penpont Water OX11 . . . . 201 A2
Penrhyn Cl OX16 . . . . 15 E7
Penrose Cl OX16 . . . . 16 A5
Penrose Dr OX16 . . . . 16 A6
Pensclose OX28 . . . . 104 C1
Pensfield OX10 . . . . 203 E4
Penson's Gdns OX4 . . . . 123 E1
Penstones Ct SN7 . . . . . . 194 E7
Pentagon The OX14 . . . . . 180 B7
Pen Way OX16 . . . . .9 B1
Peppard CE Prim Sch
  RG9 . . . . 253 A8
PEPPARD COMMON 252 F8
Peppard Hill RG9 . . . . . . 252 F8
Peppard La RG9 . . . . 254 E7
Peppard Rd RG4 . . . . 253 B3
Pepper Alley
  2 Banbury OX16 . . . . 16 D6
  Deddington OX15 . . . . . 34 E4

Peppercorn Ave OX3 . . . . 142 E8
Percy St OX4 . . . . 141 F6
Peregrine Rd OX4 . . . . . . 142 D2
Peregrine Way
  Bicester OX26 . . . . 81 A8
  Grove OX12 . . . . 196 D1
Periam Cl RG9 . . . . 254 C8
Perimeter Rd OX11 . . . . . 217 C1
Periwinkle Pl **3** OX4 . . . 142 F2
Perkins OX1 . . . . 141 D2
Perkins Cl OX15 . . . . 7 C7
Perpetual Park Dr RG9 . . 254 F8
Perrinsfield GL7 . . . . 150 D6
Perrin St OX3 . . . . 124 C2
Perrott Cl OX29 . . . . 105 A7
Perry's Rd SN7 . . . . 194 D8
Perseverance Hill RG9 . . 254 A5
Peterley Rd OX4 . . . . 142 F6
Peter's Way OX4 . . . . 142 C3
Pether Rd OX3 . . . . 124 E1
Pethers Piece OX18 . . . . 100 D5
Petre Pl OX5 . . . . 92 F1
Pettiwell OX44 . . . . 162 D8
Pevensey Ave RG4 . . . . . 259 E5
Pheasant Wlk OX4 . . . . . 142 A1
Phelps Pl OX4 . . . . 123 F1
Phelps The OX5 . . . . 108 D8
Philcote St OX15 . . . . 33 F4
Phillimore Rd RG4 . . . . . 259 C8
Phipps Rd OX4 . . . . 142 D4
Phoebe Ct OX2 . . . . 123 A5
Phyllis Court Dr RG9 . . . 244 E3
Pickenfield OX9 . . . . 148 B7
Pickering Row OX12 . . . . 214 D6
Pickett Ave OX3 . . . . 142 E7
Picklers Hill OX14 . . . . . . 160 A2
Picton Way RG4 . . . . 259 B4
PIDDINGTON 97 E7
PIDDINGTON COW LEYS . 82 D3
Piddington Rd HP18 . . . . . 98 A8
Pieces The OX18 . . . . 134 F3
Pierce's Hill RG31 . . . . . . 257 C1
Piers Row OX15 . . . . 33 E4
Pigeon Farm Rd HP14 . . . 188 E5
Pigeonhouse La OX5 . . . . 95 F3
Pigeon House La OX29 . . 106 C6
Piggott's Rd **1** RG4 . . . . 259 C1
Pikeshaw Way RG31 . . . . 257 C2
Pike Terr OX1 . . . . 261 B1
Pilcher Ct OX4 . . . . 123 F1
Pilgrims Cl SN6 . . . . 191 F2
Pill La GL56 . . . . 26 F1
Pimpernel Cl OX4 . . . . . . 143 A2
Pinchester Cl GL56 . . . . . 27 A1
Pinchgate La OX5 . . . . . . 93 D7
Pine Cl
  Bicester OX26 . . . . 65 F5
  Garsington OX44 . . . . . 143 C2
  Oxford OX4 . . . . 142 F3
Pinecroft OX18 . . . . 115 D2
Pine Rise OX28 . . . . 104 D2
Pines The SN7 . . . . 172 E3
Pinetree Ct RG4 . . . . 259 A5
Pinewood Cl **1** OX18 . . . 115 E2
Pinewood Dr RG4 . . . . . . 258 E5
Pinewood Sch OX4 . . . . . 209 A2
Pine Woods Rd OX13 . . . 156 B1
Pingle Dr OX26 . . . . 80 E8
Pinhill Rd OX16 . . . . 16 B7
Pinkhill La OX29 . . . . 120 E6
Pinnocks Way OX2 . . . . . 140 B8
Pinsley Rd OX29 . . . . 106 B8
Pioneer Rd
  Bicester OX26 . . . . 81 B6
  Faringdon SN7 . . . . . . 172 F2
Pipe Line La OX16 . . . . . . 16 D7
Pipers Croft OX16 . . . . . . 16 A4
Piper St OX3 . . . . 124 D2
Pipit Cl OX4 . . . . 142 E1
Pipits Croft OX26 . . . . . . 81 A8
Pipkin Way OX4 . . . . 142 A6
Pipley Furlong OX4 . . . . . 142 B2
Pitch The HP14 . . . . 189 D3
Pitmaston Cl OX16 . . . . . . 8 F1
Pitreavie Ave OX18 . . . . . 115 E4
Pitters Piece HP18 . . . . . 129 B7
Pitts La OX7 . . . . 46 B3
Pitts Rd OX3 . . . . 124 E3
Pixey Pl OX2 . . . . 122 F8
Pixton Cl OX11 . . . . 218 D8
Plain Rd The OX15 . . . . . . 14 B5
Plain The OX4 . . . . 141 E8
Plane Tree Way OX20 . . . 91 C6
Plantation Rd
  Chilton OX11 . . . . 234 F8
  Oxford OX2 . . . . 261 A4
Plantation The OX17 . . . . . 4 F1
Plater Dr OX2 . . . . 123 A4
PLATT THE 163 A7
Playfield Rd OX1 . . . . 160 E7
Playford OX9 . . . . 147 F8
PLAY HATCH 259 F5
Playhatch Rd RG4 . . . . . . 260 B5
Playing Cl The OX7 . . . . . 73 B4
Playing Field Rd NN13 . . . 25 A4
Pleck La OX39 . . . . 167 F4
Plot Rd OX15 . . . . 14 B6
Plough Cl
  Warborough OX10 . . . . 203 B6
  Wolvercote OX2 . . . . . 122 F8

Plough Cnr OX39 . . . . . . 148 F1
Plough La RG9 . . . . 254 E1
Ploughley Cl
  Ardley OX27 . . . . 50 C4
  Kidlington OX5 . . . . . . 108 D8
Ploughley Rd
  Ambrosden OX25 . . . . . 81 D3
  Upper Arncott OX25 . . . 96 E8
Plover Dr OX4 . . . . 142 E1
Plowden Pk OX49 . . . . . . 167 E3
Plowden Way RG9 . . . . . 254 E1
Plumbe Ct OX12 . . . . 214 D6
Plum Cl OX7 . . . . 85 D7
Pluto Rd OX11 . . . . 234 F8
Plym Dr OX11 . . . . 201 A2
Pochard Pl **8** OX4 . . . . . 142 F1
Pococks Cl OX14 . . . . . . 134 F3
POFFLEY END 104 C6
Poffley End La OX29 . . . . 104 B5
Polecat End La OX33 . . . 125 F4
Pollard Pl OX18 . . . . 134 F4
Pollocks La OX10 . . . . . . 221 C1
Polstead Rd OX2 . . . . . . 123 B4
Polsted Rd RG31 . . . . . . 257 D1
Pond Cl
  Oxford OX3 . . . . 125 A3
  West Ilsley OX12 . . . . . 233 E1
Pond End Rd RG4 . . . . . . 253 A6
Pond Hill OX8 . . . . 89 C7
Pond La RG4 . . . . 258 A6
Ponds La OX3 . . . . 123 F6
Pony Rd OX4 . . . . 142 F6
Pool Cl GL56 . . . . 26 F1
Pool Close Cotts GL56 . . 26 F1
Pooles La OX7 . . . . 73 B3
Poolside Cl OX16 . . . . . . 16 B5
Popes Acre HP17 . . . . . . 130 F5
Pope's Piece OX28 . . . . . 103 F1
Poplar Cl
  Banbury OX16 . . . . 16 E2
  Garsington OX44 . . . . . 143 C2
  Kidlington OX5 . . . . . . 108 F7
Poplar Farm Cl OX7 . . . . 70 A1
Poplar Farm Rd OX44 . . . 184 D7
Poplar Gr OX2 . . . . 160 E8
Poplar Rd OX2 . . . . 122 C1
Poplars Rd OX17 . . . . 10 F4
Poplars The OX26 . . . . . . 66 D1
Poppy Cl OX5 . . . . 108 B7
Poppylands OX26 . . . . . . 65 D4
Poppy Terr OX18 . . . . . . 115 F5
Portal Cl OX25 . . . . 63 C8
Portal Drive N OX25 . . . . 63 C8
Portal Drive S OX25 . . . . 63 C7
Port Hill RG9 . . . . 224 B2
Port Hill Rd OX10 . . . . . . 203 F5
Portland Pl OX7 . . . . 42 F3
Portland Rd
  Milcombe OX15 . . . . . . 21 A2
  Oxford OX2 . . . . 123 B7
Portman Rd RG30 . . . . . . 258 C1
Portmeirion Gdns RG30 . 257 F1
Portway
  Aynho OX17 . . . . 35 D7
  Banbury OX16 . . . . 16 A8
  Croughton NN13 . . . . . . 36 E7
  Didcot OX11 . . . . 218 C7
  Faringdon SN7 . . . . . . 172 F3
  Wantage OX12 . . . . . . 214 D4
Portway Cres NN13 . . . . . 36 E7
Portway Dr NN13 . . . . 36 D7
Portway Gdns OX17 . . . . . 35 D7
Portway Mews OX12 . . . . 214 D4
PORTWAYS 207 B8
POSTCOMBE 166 F5
Post Office La
  Letcombe Regis OX12 . . 214 A1
  5 Wantage OX12 . . . . 214 D4
Potash Cl OX14 . . . . 160 C2
Potenger Way OX14 . . . . 179 D6
Potkiln La RG8 . . . . 250 E7
POTTER'S HILL 86 C2
Potters La OX10 . . . . 205 A1
Pottery Fields RG9 . . . . . 224 E2
Pottery Piece OX4 . . . . . 142 E1
Pottery Rd RG30 . . . . . . 257 F1
Pottle Cl OX2 . . . . 122 B1
Pott's Cl OX44 . . . . 145 B3
Poultney Rd OX18 . . . . . . 115 D3
Poulton Pl OX4 . . . . 142 F3
Pound Bank OX7 . . . . 46 B3
Pound Cl
  Ducklington OX29 . . . . 118 B4
  Kirtlington OX5 . . . . . . 77 F4
  Yarnton OX5 . . . . 108 B5
Pound Cotts RG8 . . . . . . 249 A6
Pound Croft OX12 . . . . . . 214 D8
Pound Ct OX15 . . . . 33 F4
Pound Field Cl OX3 . . . . . 124 E5
Pound Hill OX7 . . . . 73 A4
Pound La
  Cassington OX29 . . . . . 107 C2
  Cholsey OX10 . . . . 220 F2
  Clanfield OX18 . . . . . . 133 E1
  Sibford Gower OX15 . . . 13 A2
  Sonning RG4 . . . . 260 E2
  Stanton St John OX33 . 125 D8
  Upton OX11 . . . . 218 C2
POUNDON 67 E7
Pound Piece SN6 . . . . . . 228 A7
Pound The
  Bloxham OX15 . . . . 21 E5

Pound The continued
  Cholsey OX10 . . . . 220 F2
  North Newington OX15 . . 15 B4
  Wantage OX12 . . . . . . 215 A5
Pound Way **7** OX4 . . . . . 142 C4
Poveys Pl SN6 . . . . 227 D4
Powell Cl OX33 . . . . 125 F4
Powys Gr OX16 . . . . 15 F7
Preachers La OX1 . . . . . . 261 B1
Preece Ct OX18 . . . . 115 E1
Prescott Ave OX16 . . . . . 15 F6
Prescott Cl OX16 . . . . 16 A6
Prestidge Pl OX5 . . . . . . 108 F8
PRESTON CROWMARSH . 203 F2
Preston Rd OX14 . . . . . . 179 E4
Prestwich Pl OX2 . . . . . . 122 F1
Prestwick Burn OX11 . . . 200 F3
Prew Cotts OX7 . . . . 29 A3
Price Cl OX26 . . . . 65 F3
Prichard Rd OX3 . . . . 124 A3
Priest Cl RG9 . . . . 224 D3
Priest End OX9 . . . . 129 E1
Priest Hill RG4 . . . . 259 A3
Priest Hill La OX29 . . . . . 103 F5
Primrose
  Purley on Thames RG8 . 257 C5
  Witney OX28 . . . . 104 E1
Primrose Dr OX26 . . . . . . 65 E4
Primrose La OX18 . . . . . . 134 E2
Primrose Pl **20** OX4 . . . . 142 F1
Primsdown Ind Est OX7 . 42 C3
Prince Christian Victor
Berkshire Memorial Homes
  OX12 . . . . 214 D2
Prince Gr OX14 . . . . 160 A3
Princes Ride OX20 . . . . . . 91 C6
Princess Gdns OX12 . . . . 214 C6
Princess St OX4 . . . . 141 F8
Princethorpe Dr OX16 . . . 16 F7
Prince William Dr RG31 . 257 C1
Prior's Forge OX2 . . . . . . 109 B1
Prior's La SN7 . . . . 155 F3
Priors Wlk GL7 . . . . 150 E3
Priory Ave RG4 . . . . 259 A2
Priory Bank Cotts OX44 . 145 C2
Priory Cl
  Bicester OX26 . . . . 65 F1
  Horton-cum-Studley OX33 . 112 B5
  Reading RG4 . . . . 259 A2
Priory Copse RG9 . . . . . . 252 F6
Priory Cotts★ OX13 . . . . 198 F3
Priory Ct
  4 Bicester OX26 . . . . . 65 E1
  Cutteslowe OX2 . . . . . . 109 B1
  Reading RG4 . . . . 259 A2
Priory Farm Cotts OX27 . 67 E2
Priory Gn
  Highworth SN6 . . . . . . 190 A6
  Highworth SN6 . . . . . . 190 B6
Priory La
  Bicester OX26 . . . . 65 E1
  Burford OX18 . . . . 100 E5
  Lyneham OX7 . . . . 70 D5
  Marcham OX13 . . . . . . 178 D6
Priory Mead SN7 . . . . . . 192 D2
Priory Mews **14** OX10 . . . 221 D7
Priory Orch OX12 . . . . . . 214 C5
Priory Rd
  Bicester OX26 . . . . 65 F1
  Chipping Norton OX7 . . 43 A3
  Lyneham OX7 . . . . 70 D5
  Oxford OX4 . . . . 142 C2
  Wantage OX12 . . . . . . 214 D4
Priory Vale Rd OX16 . . . . 16 F7
Pritchard Cl OX10 . . . . . . 182 C6
Project Timescape★
  OX14 . . . . 202 A6
Promenade Rd RG4 . . . . 259 A4
Prospect Cl OX29 . . . . . . 89 C7
Prospect Pk OX33 . . . . . 143 C7
Prospect Pl OX49 . . . . . . 186 B2
Prospect Rd
  Banbury OX16 . . . . 16 D5
  Upton OX11 . . . . 218 C2
Prospect St RG4 . . . . 259 B2
Prunus Cl OX4 . . . . 142 F3
Pryor Cl RG31 . . . . 257 B4
Puck La OX28 . . . . 104 B1
Puddleduck La SN7 . . . . . 192 B8
Pudlicote La OX7 . . . . 71 E6
Pudsey Cl OX4 . . . . 179 E4
Pugsden La OX13 . . . . . . 199 A4
Pulker Cl OX4 . . . . 142 C4
Pullens Field OX3 . . . . . . 124 A2
Pullens La OX3 . . . . 124 A2
Pulling Cl SN7 . . . . 172 F3
Pulpit Hill OX12 . . . . 213 A4
Puma Cl OX10 . . . . 204 D2
Pumbro OX29 . . . . 89 C7
Purcell Rd OX3 . . . . 123 F3
Purchas Rd OX11 . . . . . . 200 C4
Purfield Dr RG10 . . . . . . 255 F2
Purland Cl OX4 . . . . 142 C6
Purley CE Inf Sch RG8 . . 257 C5
Purley La RG8 . . . . 257 C5
PURLEY ON THAMES . . . 257 B6
Purley Rise RG8 . . . . 257 A5
Purley Village RG8 . . . . . 257 C5
Purley Way RG8 . . . . 256 E5
Purrants La OX29 . . . . . . 86 E1
Purslane OX14 . . . . 180 B8
Purslane Dr OX26 . . . . . . 65 D4
Purslane Rd OX26 . . . . . . 65 D5
PUSEY 175 B6
Pusey La OX1 . . . . 261 B3
Pusey St OX1 . . . . 261 B3
Putman Cl OX9 . . . . 148 B8
Putman Pl RG9 . . . . 244 E1

Pye St SN7 . . . . 173 A3
Pykes Cl OX14 . . . . 160 B2
Pym Wlk OX9 . . . . 129 F1
PYRTON 186 B4
Pyrton La OX49 . . . . 186 A2
Pytenry Cl OX14 . . . . 160 B3
Pytt's La OX18 . . . . 100 E5

Q

Quadrangle The
  Bicester OX26 . . . . 65 E1
  Wolvercote OX2 . . . . . . 122 F8
  Woodstock OX20 . . . . . 91 C7
Quadrant The OX14 . . . . . 180 B7
Quaker La OX10 . . . . 203 B8
Quakers Ct **10** OX14 . . . . 179 F7
Quantock Ave RG4 . . . . . 259 D5
Quantock View OX11 . . . 200 C2
Quarhill Cl OX7 . . . . 42 E5
Quarrington Pl OX49 . . . . 186 B1
Quarry Cl
  Bloxham OX15 . . . . 21 C4
  Enstone OX7 . . . . 59 A5
  Long Crendon HP18 . . . 129 C7
Quarry End OX5 . . . . 108 B8
Quarry Ground
  Fifield OX7 . . . . 69 B2
  Idbury OX7 . . . . 69 A5
Quarry High St OX3 . . . . 124 E1
Quarry Hollow OX3 . . . . . 124 E2
Quarry La
  Charlbury OX7 . . . . 73 C4
  Lower Shiplake RG9 . . . 255 A4
Quarry Rd
  Chadlington OX7 . . . . . 57 B2
  Hornton OX15 . . . . 7 A8
  Oxford OX3 . . . . 124 E1
  Sunningwell OX13 . . . . 159 F7
  Witney OX28 . . . . 104 A2
Quarry School Pl OX3 . . . 124 E2
Quarry The OX13 . . . . . . 159 F7
Quartermain Cl OX4 . . . . 142 A6
Quartermain Rd OX44 . . . 184 C7
Quebec Rd RG9 . . . . 254 C3
Queen Annes Gate RG4 . 259 C3
Queen Annes Sch RG4 . . 259 B3
Queen Cl RG9 . . . . 244 E1
Queen Eleanor Ct OX29 . 106 B8
Queen Elizabeth Cl **8**
  OX11 . . . . 219 A8
Queen Elizabeth Ho OX1 261 B1
Queen Emma's Dyke
  OX28 . . . . 117 F8
Queenford Farm OX10 . . 182 E2
Queen St Mews RG9 . . . 244 E1
Queens Ave
  Bicester OX26 . . . . 65 E2
  Highworth SN6 . . . . . . 190 A6
  Kidlington OX5 . . . . . . 109 A8
Queen's Ave OX10 . . . . . 203 B1
Queensborough Dr RG4 . 258 E5
Queens Cl
  Dorchester OX10 . . . . . 182 D1
  Oxford OX2 . . . . 140 B8
  Thame OX9 . . . . 129 F2
Queen's Cl OX29 . . . . . . 120 E7
Queens Coll The OX1 . . . 261 C2
Queen's Cres
  Clanfield OX18 . . . . . . 152 E8
  Drayton OX15 . . . . 15 D8
Queens Ct OX26 . . . . 65 E2
Queens Dyke Prim Sch
  OX28 . . . . 117 F7
Queens La OX29 . . . . . . 120 E7
Queen's La OX1 . . . . 261 C2
Queens Rd OX10 . . . . . . 220 F1
Queen's Rd
  Banbury OX16 . . . . 16 B6
  Carterton OX18 . . . . . . 115 E1
  Reading RG4 . . . . 259 C1
  Thame OX9 . . . . 148 B7
Queens St OX15 . . . . 21 D4
Queen St
  Abingdon OX14 . . . . . . 179 F7
  Bampton OX18 . . . . 134 F3
  Dorchester OX10 . . . . . 182 D1
  Eynsham OX29 . . . . . . 120 E7
  Henley-on-Thames RG9 . 244 E1
  Hook Norton OX15 . . . . 30 B7
  Middleton Cheney OX17 . 17 F8
  Oxford OX1 . . . . 261 B2
  Reading RG4 . . . . 259 A3
Queensway
  Banbury OX16 . . . . 16 B4
  Didcot OX11 . . . . 218 E7
  Reading RG4 . . . . 259 D6
Queens Way OX11 . . . . . 219 F8
Queensway Prim Sch
  OX16 . . . . 16 A4
Quercus Ct OX2 . . . . 123 B6
Quickset Cl OX7 . . . . 72 F8
Quintan Ave OX25 . . . . . . 81 D4

R

Race Farm Cotts OX13 . . 176 E8
Race Farm La OX13 . . . . 176 F8
RACK END 137 E3
Rack End OX29 . . . . 137 E3
Rackham Pl OX2 . . . . 123 A6
Radbone Hill OX7 . . . . . . 42 F6
Radcliffe Camera Liby
  OX1 . . . . 261 C2
Radcliffe Rd OX4 . . . . . . 141 F5

Radcliffe Science Liby
OX1 . . . . 261 B3
Radcliffe Sq OX1 . . . . . . 261 C2
RADCOT 152 F4
Radcot Cl RG5 . . . . 260 E1
Radcot Rd SN7 . . . . 172 F6
RADFORD 59 F5
Radford Cl OX4 . . . . 141 F3
RADLEY 160 E3
Radley CE Prim Sch
OX14 . . . . 160 E3
Radley Coll OX14 . . . . . 160 D4
Radley Ct OX14 . . . . 160 B1
Radley Ho OX2 . . . . 123 C6
Radley Rd OX14 . . . . 160 C1
Radley Road Ind Est
OX14 . . . . 160 B1
Radley Sta OX14 . . . . . . 160 F2
RADNAGE 189 D8
Radnage CE Inf Sch
HP14 . . . . 189 D6
Radnage Common Rd
HP14 . . . . 189 D5
Radnage La HP14 . . . . . 169 D2
Radnor Cl RG9 . . . . 244 E2
Radnor Rd OX10 . . . . . . 221 B8
RAF Benson Prim Sch
OX10 . . . . 204 D2
Raghouse La OX27 . . . . . . 49 F5
Raglan Gdns RG4 . . . . . 259 C4
Ragley Mews RG4 . . . . . 259 D6
Ragnall's La OX33 . . . . . 111 F7
Rahere Rd OX4 . . . . 142 C4
Railway Cotts SN7 . . . . 195 A4
Railway La OX4 . . . . 142 B2
Railways Cotts RG8 . . . 249 C6
Railway Terr GL7 . . . . . . 150 D5
Railway View RG8 . . . . . 256 D6
Rainbow Way OX14 . . . . 160 B3
Raincliffe Cl OX17 . . . . . . 35 C7
Raleigh Cres OX28 . . . . 117 D7
Raleigh Park Rd OX2 . . 140 E2
Ramilles Ho 3 OX18 . . . 115 E2
Rampion Cl OX4 . . . . 143 A2
RAMSDEN 88 A3
RAMSDEN HEATH 87 F4
Ramsey Rd OX3 . . . . 124 E3
Ramsons Way OX14 . . . . 180 C8
Randall Rd GL54 . . . . 68 B3
Randolph Rd RG1 . . . . . 259 A1
Randolph St 7 OX4 . . . . 141 F8
Range Rd OX28, OX29 . . 117 C8
Rannal Dr OX39 . . . . 168 C6
Rastel Ho 2 OX16 . . . . . . 16 E6
RATLEY 2 A4
Rattlecombe Rd OX15 . . . 6 D2
Rau Ct OX27 . . . . 66 A7
Ravencroft OX26 . . . . . . 81 A7
Raven Rd HP14 . . . . 188 F4
Ravensbourne Dr RG5 . . 260 E1
Ravenscroft Rd RG9 . . . 244 D2
Ravensmead
Banbury OX16 . . . . 16 A4
Chinnor OX39 . . . . 168 D6
Rawdon Way SN7 . . . . . 173 A2
Rawlings Gr OX14 . . . . . 179 D8
Rawlins Cl OX17 . . . . 23 A5
Rawlinson Cl OX7 . . . . . . 57 B1
Rawlinson Rd OX2 . . . . 123 B5
Rawson Cl OX2 . . . . 108 F1
Rawthey Ave OX11 . . . . 200 F4
Ray Ct OX11 . . . . 201 A2
Raymond Rd OX26 . . . . . 65 C4
Raymund Rd OX3 . . . . . 123 F5
Raynham Ct OX18 . . . . . 115 E4
Rayson Ho OX3 . . . . 124 B4
Ray View OX5 . . . . 94 F4
Reade Ave OX14 . . . . . . 180 B8
Reade Cl OX7 . . . . 70 B1
Reades La RG4 . . . . 252 A6
Reade's La RG4 . . . . 252 D4
READING 259 A4
Reading Blue Coat Sch
RG4 . . . . 260 C3
Reading Ct 2 OX26 . . . . . 65 E3
Reading Rd
Aldworth RG8 . . . . 248 A2
Cholsey OX10 . . . . 239 A7
Goring RG8 . . . . 249 E6
Harwell OX11 . . . . 217 D6
Henley-on-Thames RG9 . . 254 F8
Pangbourne RG8 . . . . . . 256 D5
Streatley RG8 . . . . 249 A6
Wallingford OX10 . . . . . . 221 D6
Wallingford, Winterbrook
OX10 . . . . 221 C4
West Hendred OX12 . . . . 216 B7
Woodcote RG8 . . . . 240 F1
Reading Ret Pk RG30 . . 258 B1
Recreation Rd
Wargrave RG10 . . . . 255 E2
Woodstock OX20 . . . . 91 C6
Rectory Cl
Marsh Gibbon OX27 . . . . 67 F3
Upper Hayford OX25 . . . . 48 F1
Warmington OX17 . . . . . . 3 A4
Wendlebury OX25 . . . . . . 80 A4
Rectory Cres OX7 . . . . . . 60 E8
Rectory Ct OX49 . . . . . . 187 B8
Rectory Farm Cl OX12 . . 196 F7
Rectory Gdns OX15 . . . . 15 D8
Rectory Hill RG9 . . . . . . 206 A1
Rectory La
Aston Tirrold OX11 . . . . 237 F8
Bix RG9 . . . . 243 D7
Fringford OX27 . . . . 52 C6
Kingston Bagpuize OX13 . . 176 F8

Rectory La continued
Letcombe Bassett OX12 . . 231 E7
Longworth OX13 . . . . . . 156 B3
Middleton Cheney OX17 . . 10 F1
South Weston OX9 . . . . 166 E1
Woodstock OX20 . . . . 91 A6
Rectory Lane Trad Est
OX13 . . . . 176 F7
Rectory Mdw OX39 . . . . 168 D7
Rectory Rd
Great Haseley OX44 . . . 164 E8
Hook Norton OX15 . . . . . 30 B8
Oxford OX4 . . . . 141 F8
Reading RG4 . . . . 259 A2
Streatley RG8 . . . . 248 C7
Redberry Cl RG4 . . . . . . 259 D5
Red Bridge Hollow OX1 . 141 C4
Red Copse La
Boars Hill OX1 . . . . 140 F2
Sunningwell OX1 . . . . . . 141 A2
Red Cross Rd RG8 . . . . . 249 C6
Rede Ct OX3 . . . . 124 E1
Red Hill RG9 . . . . 253 F5
Red House Dr RG4 . . . . 253 A5
Red House Rd OX15 . . . . 22 E8
Red La
Chinnor OX39 . . . . 168 F3
Ewelme OX49, RG9 . . . . 206 D2
Woodcote RG8 . . . . 240 C5
Redland Rd OX3 . . . . . . 124 B5
Redlands Cl SN6 . . . . . . 190 A4
Redlands Row GL56 . . . . 27 A1
Red Lion Dr HP14 . . . . . 188 D5
Red Lion Mews SN6 . . . 190 A6
Red Lion Sq OX1 . . . . . . 261 B2
Red Lion St
Cropredy OX17 . . . . 4 F2
Kings Sutton OX17 . . . . . 23 F5
Redmayes OX18 . . . . . . 135 E2
Redmoor Cl OX4 . . . . . . 142 C2
Redmoor Cl OX26 . . . . . . 65 C3
Red Poll Cl OX16 . . . . . . 16 A8
Redwing Cl OX26 . . . . . . 66 A1
Redwood Cl
Kingston Bagpuize OX13 . 156 E1
Oxford OX4 . . . . 143 A2
Redwood Way RG31 . . . 257 D3
Reed Cl OX28 . . . . 104 E2
Reedmace Cl OX4 . . . . . 143 A2
Reedmace Rd OX26 . . . . 65 E4
Reeds Cl OX12 . . . . 214 C5
Reema Hos The SN6 . . . 190 B1
Regal Cl 11 OX14 . . . . . 179 F7
Regal Ct 2 OX26 . . . . . . 65 F1
Regal Way SN7 . . . . 172 F3
Regency Hts RG4 . . . . . 258 E4
Regent Gdns OX11 . . . . 219 B8
Regent Mews SN7 . . . . . 172 F4
Regent Sch OX2 . . . . . . 123 C5
Regents Park Coll OX1 . . 261 B3
Regents Riverside 7
RG1 . . . . 259 A1
Regent St OX4 . . . . 141 F8
Regis Pl OX12 . . . . 214 A2
Reid Cl OX16 . . . . 16 B6
Reid Pl OX25 . . . . 63 B7
Reliance Way OX4 . . . . . 142 B7
REMENHAM 244 F3
Remenham La RG9 . . . . 244 F3
Remenham Row RG9 . . . 244 F2
Remus Gate NN13 . . . . . 24 A4
Remy Pl OX4 . . . . 141 F5
Renault Ho OX4 . . . . . . 141 F6
Rest Harrow 2 OX4 . . . 142 F2
Restharrow Mead OX26 . . 65 C4
Retford Cl RG5 . . . . 260 F1
Retreat Gdns OX10 . . . . 221 E7
Retreat La HP14 . . . . . . 169 D2
Revell Cl OX10 . . . . 221 C7
Rewley Abbey Ct OX1 . . 261 A2
Rewley Rd OX1 . . . . 261 A2
Reynard Ct 3 OX26 . . . . 65 E2
Reynolds Cl OX7 . . . . 70 D1
Reynolds Way
Abingdon OX14 . . . . 179 E5
East Challow OX12 . . . . 213 F5
Rhigos RG4 . . . . 258 F6
Rhine Cl RG4 . . . . 259 D2
Rhodes Ho OX1 . . . . 261 C3
Ribstone Pl OX16 . . . . 8 F1
Richard Gray Ct OX1 . . 261 A3
Richard Nevill Ct 2 RG4 259 C2
Richards La OX2 . . . . . . 123 A7
Richardson Ct OX4 . . . . 123 F1
Richards Way OX3 . . . . 124 F2
Richens Dr OX18 . . . . . . 115 C2
Richfield Ave RG1 . . . . . 258 F1
Richman Gdns OX16 . . . . 15 F8
Richmere Rd OX18 . . . . 115 F7
Richmond Rd
Oxford OX1 . . . . 261 A3
Reading RG4 . . . . 258 E4
Richmond St OX17 . . . . . 23 F5
Rickyard Cl OX1 . . . . . . 261 A3
Rickyard The
Ardington OX12 . . . . 215 D5
Chalgrove OX44 . . . . . . 184 C6
Fulbrook OX18 . . . . 100 F6
Shutford OX15 . . . . 14 A5
Riddell Pl OX2 . . . . 109 A1
Riders Way OX39 . . . . . 168 C6
Ride The OX13 . . . . 158 B5
Ridge Cl OX16 . . . . 16 D4
Ridgefield Rd OX4 . . . . 142 A7
Ridge Hall Cl RG4 . . . . 258 E3
Ridgemont Cl OX2 . . . . 123 A7
Ridgemount Cl RG31 . . 257 B2

Ridge The
Lower Basildon RG8 . . . 249 F1
Tackley RG8 . . . . 77 C6
Ridgeway
Boars Hill OX1 . . . . 140 D1
Wargrave RG10 . . . . 255 F6
Ridge Way HP18 . . . . . . 129 F5
Ridgeway CE Prim Sch The
OX12 . . . . 213 B3
Ridgeway Ct RG9 . . . . . 223 D3
Ridgeway Ct OX12 . . . . 214 D7
Ridgeway Rd
Didcot OX11 . . . . 218 F7
Oxford OX3 . . . . 124 F3
Ridgeway The
Bloxham OX15 . . . . 21 E4
Chilton OX12 . . . . 234 D3
Nettlebed RG9 . . . . 224 D2
Reading RG4 . . . . 259 B3
Wantage OX12 . . . . 232 D5
Riding La OX29 . . . . 103 C7
Ridings Bglws OX29 . . . . 86 E3
Ridings The
Banbury OX16 . . . . 16 F7
Kidlington OX5 . . . . 92 C1
Leafield OX29 . . . . 86 E2
Oxford OX3 . . . . 142 F8
Reading RG4 . . . . 259 C8
Stonesfield OX29 . . . . . . 89 C8
Ridley Rd OX4 . . . . 142 E6
Riely Cl OX29 . . . . 90 C1
Riley Cl OX14 . . . . 179 D6
Riley Dr OX16 . . . . 15 F8
Riley Ho OX4 . . . . 142 C4
Rimes Cl OX13 . . . . 156 F1
Rimmer Cl OX3 . . . . 123 F5
Ring The OX17 . . . . 10 E4
Ringwood Rd
Oxford OX3 . . . . 125 A3
Reading RG30 . . . . 258 A1
Ripley Ave OX29 . . . . . . 102 E2
Ripley Rd OX29 . . . . . . 258 A1
Ripon Coll OX44 . . . . . . 144 B3
Rippington Ct OX14 . . . 179 B2
Rippington Dr OX3 . . . . 123 F4
Rise The
Adderbury OX17 . . . . 23 A4
Islip OX5 . . . . 93 F1
Kingston Blount OX39 . . 167 F4
Reading RG4 . . . . 259 B4
Rising Hill OX25 . . . . 48 E1
RISINGHURST 125 A3
Rissington Bsns Pk GL54 . . 68 B3
Rissington Cl RG31 . . . . 257 E3
Rissington Dr OX28 . . . 117 E8
Rivacres RG8 . . . . 250 E3
River Cl OX14 . . . . 179 E5
River Gdns RG8 . . . . . . 257 D5
Rivermead L Complex
RG1 . . . . 258 F2
Rivermead Rd OX4 . . . . 141 F3
River Rd RG4 . . . . 258 D3
River & Rowing Mus★
RG9 . . . . 244 F1
Riverside OX16 . . . . 16 E5
Riverside Ct
Oxford OX1 . . . . 141 C7
2 Reading RG4 . . . . . . 259 A2
Riverside Gdns OX28 . . 104 B1
Riverside Pk & Pools
OX10 . . . . 221 E8
Riverside Rd OX2 . . . . . 122 F1
River View
Kennington OX1 . . . . 141 E1
Sandford-on-Thames OX4 . 161 A7
Shillingford OX10 . . . . . 203 B4
Riverview Rd RG8 . . . . . 256 C5
River View Terr OX14 . . 179 E6
Rivington Glebe GL56 . . . 27 A1
Rivy Cl OX14 . . . . 180 C8
Road Eight OX11 . . . . . 217 B1
Road Eighteen OX11 . . . 217 B1
Road Eleven OX11 . . . . 217 A1
Road Fifteen OX11 . . . . 217 A1
Road Five OX11 . . . . . . 217 B1
Road Four OX11 . . . . . . 217 B1
Road Nine OX11 . . . . . . 217 B1
Road One OX11 . . . . . . 217 A1
Roadside Cotts SN7 . . . 171 E6
Road Six OX11 . . . . 217 B1
Road Thirteen OX11 . . . 217 B1
Road Twelve OX11 . . . . 217 A1
Road Two OX11 . . . . . . 217 A1
Robert Palmer Cotts The
RG4 . . . . 260 D3
Robert Piggott CE Inf Sch
The RG10 . . . . 255 E1
Robert Piggott CE Jun Sch
The RG10 . . . . 255 F1
Robert Robinson Ave
OX4 . . . . 142 C1
Roberts Cl OX3 . . . . 125 A4
Robert Sparrow Gdns
OX10 . . . . 222 A6
Robin Cl OX14 . . . . 179 D8
Robin Hill OX29 . . . . 90 A4
Robin Pl OX4 . . . . 142 E1
Robins Cl
Barford St Michael OX15 . . 32 F6
Great Rollright OX7 . . . . . 29 B3
Robinson Cl
Blewbury OX11 . . . . 237 A8
Carterton OX18 . . . . . . 115 D3
Robinson Rd OX1 . . . . . 159 A7
Robins Platt OX39 . . . . 168 B6
Robins Way OX26 . . . . . . 81 A7
Robinswood OX16 . . . . . 16 A4
Robsart Pl OX2 . . . . 139 E4

Rochester Ave RG5 . . . . 260 E1
Rochester Pl OX7 . . . . . . 73 C3
Rochester Way OX7 . . . . 23 B5
Rochford Gdns OX26 . . . 66 A4
Rockbourne Gdns RG30 258 A1
Rock Cl OX18 . . . . 115 D3
Rock Edge OX3 . . . . 124 D2
Rock Edge Nature Reserve★
OX3 . . . . 124 D1
Rock Farm La OX4 . . . . 161 B8
Rockfort Ind Est OX10 . . 221 B7
Rock Hill OX7 . . . . 42 F3
Rockhill Farm Ct OX7 . . . 42 F3
Rockley Cotts OX2 . . . . 139 E1
Rock Rd OX18 . . . . 115 D3
Rock The OX15 . . . . 32 F6
Rocky Banks OX18 . . . . 115 F6
Rocky La RG9 . . . . 243 B4
Roding Way OX11 . . . . . 201 A2
Rodney Pl OX13 . . . . . . 156 C3
Rodway Rd RG30 . . . . . 257 F1
Roebuck Ct OX11 . . . . . 219 A8
Roebuck Rise OX3 . . . . 257 D3
Roentgen Ave OX11 . . . 217 A2
Rofford La OX44 . . . . . . 164 B3
Roger Bacon La OX1 . . 261 B1
Roger Dudman Way OX1,
OX2 . . . . 123 A2
Rogers St OX2 . . . . 123 B7
ROKE 204 B7
Rokeby Dr RG4 . . . . 258 D8
ROKEMARSH 204 A6
Rolfe Pl OX3 . . . . 124 A3
Rollright Stones★ OX7 . . 28 B2
Rolls Ct OX12 . . . . 214 D5
Roman Pl OX11 . . . . 200 D3
Roman Rd OX33 . . . . . . 144 C3
Roman Way
Beckley OX3 . . . . 111 B3
Bicester OX26 . . . . 65 E2
Brackley NN13 . . . . 24 A7
Lechlade-on-Thames GL7 . 150 D5
Oxford OX4 . . . . 142 F5
Wantage OX12 . . . . 214 C6
Roman Wlk SN6 . . . . . . 191 E2
Romany Cl RG30 . . . . . . 258 A1
Romany La RG30 . . . . . 258 A1
Romney Rd OX16 . . . . 8 F1
Romsey Rd RG30 . . . . . 258 A1
Romulus Way NN13 . . . . 24 A6
Rookery Cl
Abingdon OX13 . . . . 159 B1
Bodicote OX15 . . . . 22 E8
Rookery Ho OX44 . . . . . 143 E1
Rookery The 11 OX5 . . . . 92 D1
Rookery Way OX26 . . . . . 65 D3
Rooks La OX9 . . . . 147 F8
Roosevelt Dr OX3 . . . . . 124 C1
Roosevelt Rd OX29 . . . . 106 B8
Roper Rd OX25 . . . . 63 C8
Rope Way OX15 . . . . 30 B6
Rope Wlk 5 OX16 . . . . . . 16 D6
Rosamund Dr OX20 . . . . 91 A7
Rosamund Rd OX2 . . . . 122 E8
Rose Ave OX14 . . . . 159 F3
Rosebank OX15 . . . . 21 E5
Rosebay Cres OX12 . . . 214 D8
Rosebery Rd RG4 . . . . . 258 D7
Rose Cl
Bucknell OX27 . . . . 64 F7
Carterton OX18 . . . . . . 115 D2
Rose Cnr HP14 . . . . 188 E5
Rose Cott OX17 . . . . 8 F4
Rose & Crown OX29 . . . . 89 C7
Rose Ct 2 OX4 . . . . 142 B3
Rosedale Ave OX16 . . . . . 9 A1
Rose Gdns OX2 . . . . 140 C8
ROSE HILL 142 B4
Rose Hill OX4 . . . . 142 B4
Rosehill Ho RG4 . . . . . . 259 B4
Rosehill Pk RG4 . . . . . . 259 C7
Rose Hill Prim Sch OX4 . 142 A3
Rose La OX1 . . . . 261 C2
Rosemary Ct OX4 . . . . . 141 F7
Rosemary La OX18 . . . . 134 E3
Rosemead Ave RG31 . . 257 B3
Rose Pl OX1 . . . . 261 B1
Roses La OX7 . . . . 41 F5
Rose Terr OX12 . . . . 196 A4
Rosina Wlk OX16 . . . . 9 A1
Rosmary Dr OX16 . . . . . . 9 A1
Ross Ct OX1 . . . . 141 C1
Rossendale Rd RG4 . . . 259 D3
Ross Rd 3 RG1 . . . . 259 A1
Rotary Way OX16 . . . . . . 9 B2
Rotha Field Rd OX2 . . . 109 A1
ROTHERFIELD GREYS . . 243 D1
ROTHERFIELD
PEPPARD 253 A8
Rotherfield Rd RG9 . . . 254 E7
Rotherfield Way RG4 . . 259 B4
Rother Garth OX11 . . . . 201 A3
Rother Rd OX16 . . . . 8 F1
Rothwell Gdns RG5 . . . 260 F1
Rothwells Cl OX10 . . . . 221 A2
Rothwell Wlk RG4 . . . . 259 D2
Rotten Row OX10 . . . . . 182 C6
Round Close Rd
Adderbury OX17 . . . . 22 F3
Hook Norton OX15 . . . . . 30 A7
Roundham Cl OX5 . . . . . 92 D1
Roundhead Dr OX9 . . . . 129 F2
Roundhill Ct HP17 . . . . 130 E8
Roundhills Mead SN6 . . 190 B7
Roundtown OX17 . . . . . . 35 C7
Roundway The OX3 . . . . 124 F3
Rouses La GL7 . . . . 132 B5
ROUSHAM 62 B4

Rousham Park House &
Gdn★ OX25 . . . . 62 B5
Rousham Rd OX5 . . . . . . 77 C7
Routh Rd OX3 . . . . 124 F4
Routs Gn HP14 . . . . 169 D2
ROUT'S GREEN 169 D2
Roves Farm★ SN6 . . . . 208 B6
Roves La SN6 . . . . 208 B7
Rowallan Cl RG4 . . . . . . 259 D6
Rowan Cl
Ambrosden OX25 . . . . . . 81 C3
Carterton OX18 . . . . . . 115 C3
Kidlington OX5 . . . . 108 E7
Sonning Common RG4 . . 252 F4
Rowan Dr OX28 . . . . . . 104 E2
Rowan Gr OX4 . . . . 143 A1
Rowan Rd OX26 . . . . 65 E3
Rowans The OX10 . . . . . 220 E1
Rowborough La SN3 . . . 208 A4
Rowel Dr OX5 . . . . 92 B1
Rowell Way OX7 . . . . 42 F3
Row La RG4 . . . . 259 E7
Rowland Cl
Benson OX10 . . . . 204 D3
Wallingford OX10 . . . . . . 203 C1
Wolvercote OX2 . . . . . . 122 D8
Rowland Hill Ct OX1 . . 261 A2
Rowland Rd OX10 . . . . . 221 A1
Rowlands Ho OX3 . . . . . 125 A3
Rowles Cl OX1 . . . . 141 E1
Rowles Paddock RG20 . . 235 A2
Rowney Pl OX4 . . . . 142 A4
ROWSTOCK 217 B7
Row The
Bletchingdon OX5 . . . . . . 93 A8
Glympton OX20 . . . . 75 D8
Hinton Waldrist SN7 . . . 155 F2
Lechlade-on-Thames GL7 . 150 F7
Lyneham OX7 . . . . 70 D5
Mollington OX17 . . . . 3 F3
Stanton Harcourt OX29 . . 138 A8
Roxburgh Dr OX11 . . . . 200 D3
Royal Berkshire Ct OX11 218 F7
Royal Mans RG9 . . . . . . 244 E1
Ruck Keene Cl OX26 . . . 65 C2
Rufus Isaacs Rd RG4 . . 259 B2
Rugge Furlong OX11 . . . 201 B1
Rumbolds Cl OX10 . . . . 203 F5
Rumsey's La OX11 . . . . 237 A8
Rupert Cl
Chalgrove OX44 . . . . . . 184 D6
Henley-on-Thames RG9 . . 244 E3
Rupert Rd
Chalgrove OX44 . . . . . . 184 E6
Oxford OX4 . . . . 142 E6
Rupert's La RG9 . . . . . . 244 E3
Rupert Way OX9 . . . . . . 130 A1
RUSCOTE 16 A7
Ruscote Arc OX16 . . . . . 16 B8
Ruscote Ave OX16 . . . . . 16 B8
Ruscote Sq OX16 . . . . . . 16 B7
Rushall Rd OX9 . . . . 130 A1
Rushbeds Wood Nature
Reserve★ HP18 . . . . 98 D4
Rush Common Prim Sch
OX14 . . . . 160 B1
Rushmead Copse OX14 . 160 C2
Ruskin RG4 . . . . 259 D3
Ruskin Ave OX14 . . . . . 179 E5
Ruskin Cl OX11 . . . . 219 A8
Ruskin Coll
Oxford, Headington OX3 . 124 C4
Oxford OX1 . . . . 261 A3
Ruskin Rd OX16 . . . . 16 C3
Ruskin Wlk OX26 . . . . . . 65 F3
Russell Ct OX2 . . . . 123 B4
Russell Jackson Cl OX10 182 C6
Russell Rd RG4 . . . . 258 D7
Russell St OX2 . . . . 123 A1
RUSSELL'S WATER 224 F8
Russet Ave GL7 . . . . . . 150 E3
Russet Cl RG4 . . . . 252 E5
Russet Glade RG4 . . . . 259 C7
Russet Rd OX27 . . . . 50 C4
Russett Ave OX18 . . . . 115 F5
Russley Gn SN8 . . . . . . 245 D1
Rutherford Ave OX11 . . 217 B3
Rutherford Cl OX14 . . . 160 A1
Rutherford Pl OX11 . . . 218 D7
Rutherway OX2 . . . . 123 A3
Rutten La OX5 . . . . 108 A6
Rutters Cl OX5 . . . . 108 D8
Rycote La OX9 . . . . 146 C5
Rydal Ave RG30 . . . . . . 257 F2
Ryder Cl
Summertown OX2 . . . . . 123 A6
Yarnton OX5 . . . . 108 B6
Rydes Cl OX15 . . . . 22 E8
Rydes The OX15 . . . . 22 E8
Rye Cl OX16 . . . . 8 F1
Ryecote Chapel★ OX9 . . 146 D6
Ryecroft Cl
Sonning RG5 . . . . 260 E1
Wargrave RG10 . . . . 255 E2
Rye Grass OX20 . . . . 91 C6
Rye St Antony Sch OX3 . 124 B3
Rylands OX3 . . . . 123 F5
Rymans Cres OX11 . . . . 219 A6
Rymers La OX4 . . . . 142 B5

S

Sackler Liby OX1 . . . . . 261 B3
Sackville Ct OX17 . . . . . . 8 E4
Sacred Heart RC Prim Sch
  RG9 . . . . 244 D1
Sadlers Cl SN7 . . . . . . 172 E2
Sadlers Croft OX44 . . . . 143 E1
Sadlers Ct OX14 . . . . . 160 B3
Sadlers The RG31 . . . . 257 B1
Sadler Wlk OX1 . . . . . . 261 A1
Saffron Cl OX26 . . . . . . 65 D5
Saffron Cres OX18 . . . . 115 E4
Saffron Ct OX14 . . . . . 180 B8
Sage Cl OX16 . . . . 8 F1
Sage Rd RG31 . . . . . . 257 C3
Sage Wlk **7** OX4 . . . . . 142 F1
St Alban's Ct **5** OX10 . . 221 D7
St Aldate's OX1 . . . . . . 261 B1
St Aloysius RC Prim Sch
  OX2 . . . . 123 B4
St Amand Dr OX14 . . . . 179 E6
St Amands RC Prim Sch
  OX12 . . . . 216 E5
St Andrews CE Prim Sch
  Chinnor OX39 . . . . . 168 C7
  Oxford OX3 . . . . . . 124 D3
St Andrews Cl OX14 . . . 160 C2
St Andrews Ct OX9 . . . . 147 F8
St Andrews Ho OX3 . . . 168 C6
St Andrew's La OX3 . . . 124 D4
St Andrew's Rd
  Chinnor OX39 . . . . . 168 C5
  Didcot OX11 . . . . . . 218 F8
  Henley-on-Thames RG9 . 254 D8
  Oxford OX3 . . . . . . 124 C4
  Reading RG4 . . . . . . 258 F4
St Andrews Sch **5** OX12 214 E4
St Andrews Sq OX20 . . . 91 A7
St Anne's Cl
  Bicester OX26 . . . . . . 65 F4
  Henley-on-Thames RG9 . 244 D1
St Anne's Coll OX2 . . . . 261 B4
St Annes Ct OX11 . . . . 219 B7
St Annes RC Prim Sch
  RG4 . . . . 259 B2
St Anne's Rd
  Banbury OX16 . . . . . . 16 D3
  Oxford OX3 . . . . . . 124 D2
  Reading RG4 . . . . . . 259 A2
St Anthony's Wlk OX26 . . 66 A3
St Antony's Coll OX2 . . . 261 A4
St Barnabas CE First Sch
  . . . . 261 A3
St Barnabas Rd RG4 . . . 259 A6
St Barnabas St OX2 . . . 261 A3
St Benets Way RG4 . . . 259 C6
St Bernard's Rd OX2 . . . 261 A4
St Birinus Ct GL7 . . . . . 150 C5
St Birinus Sch OX11 . . . 218 F7
St Catherines Coll OX1 . . 123 E2
St Catherines Ho OX4 . . 123 E1
St Christophers CE First Sch
  OX4 . . . . 142 C6
St Christophers CE Prim Sch
  GL7 . . . . 132 C1
St Christopher's Pl OX4 . 142 C6
St Clares Bardwell Rd Ctr **2**
  OX2 . . . . 123 C5
St Clares Oxford OX2 . . . 123 B6
St Clement's St OX4 . . . 123 F1
St Cristopher Cotts **4**
  SN7 . . . . 172 F3
St Cross Bldg OX1 . . . . 261 C3
St Cross Coll OX1 . . . . 261 B3
St Cross Coll (Annexe)
  OX1 . . . . 261 B3
St Cross Rd OX1 . . . . . 261 C3
St David's Ct RG4 . . . . 258 F5
St David's Ct NN13 . . . . 24 A8
St Denys Ct SN7 . . . . . 194 E7
St Ebbe's CE Prim Sch
  OX1 . . . . 141 C7
St Ebbes St OX1 . . . . . 261 B2
St Edburg's Cl OX26 . . . 65 C2
St Edburg's Prim Sch
  OX26 . . . . 65 E1
St Edith's Way OX26 . . . 65 C2
St Edmund Hall OX1 . . . 261 C2
St Edmund's La **4** OX14 . 179 F6
St Edmunds RC Prim Sch
  OX14 . . . . 180 A8
St Edward's Ave
  Oxford OX2 . . . . . . 123 A7
  Summertown OX2 . . . 123 A6
St Edwards Ct OX2 . . . . 123 B6
St Edwards Sch
  Oxford OX2 . . . . . . 123 A7
  Oxford OX2 . . . . . . 123 B6
SS Mary & John CE Prim Sch
  1 OX4 . . . . 142 A4
SS Philip & James CE Prim
  Sch OX2 . . . . 123 A4
St Francis CE Prim Sch
  OX4 . . . . 142 E6
St Francis Ct OX3 . . . . 142 E7
St Francis Rd HP14 . . . 189 D3
St Fridewides Ct OX11 . . 218 E8
St George's Cl OX10 . . . 220 F1
St Georges Cres OX16 . . 16 C4
St Georges Gate OX1 . . . 261 A2
St Georges Gn OX10 . . . 203 C1
St George's Pl OX1 . . . . 261 B2

St Georges Rd OX10 . . . 221 C8
St George's Rd SN7 . . . 154 D1
St Giles OX5 . . . . 93 A8
St Giles' OX1 . . . . 261 B3
St Giles Cl OX25 . . . . . 80 A4
St Gregory the Great RC Sec
  Sch OX4 . . . . 142 A6
St Helen's Ave OX10 . . . 203 F3
St Helen's Cres OX10 . . 204 A3
St Helen's Ct OX14 . . . 179 F6
St Helen's Mews **5**
  OX14 . . . . 179 F6
St Helen's Mill **12** OX14 . 179 F6
St Helen's Pas OX1 . . . 261 C2
St Helens Way OX10 . . . 203 F4
St Helen's Wharf OX14 . . 179 F6
St Hildas Cl OX11 . . . . 219 B7
St Hilda's Cl OX26 . . . . . 65 F4
St Hildas Coll OX4 . . . . 141 E8
St Hughs Cl OX16 . . . . . 16 C3
St Hugh's Cl
  Bicester OX26 . . . . . . 65 F4
  Stokenchurch HP14 . . 188 F4
St Hugh's Coll OX2 . . . . 123 B4
St Hugh's Pl HP14 . . . . 188 F4
St Hughs Rise OX11 . . . 219 B7
St Hughs Sch SN7 . . . . 174 B8
St Ives La OX12 . . . . . 214 E8
St Ives Rd OX12 . . . . . 214 E8
St James OX12 . . . . . . 214 D6
St James CE Prim Sch
  OX12 . . . . 197 A6
St James Cl RG8 . . . . . 256 C6
St James Ct OX29 . . . . . 89 C7
St James Rd OX14 . . . . 160 E3
St James Terr OX14 . . . 160 E2
St James View OX12 . . . 197 B6
St John Fisher Prim Sch
  OX4 . . . . 142 D3
St Johns OX12 . . . . . . 212 F4
St John's Cl
  Didcot OX11 . . . . . . 219 A8
  Fyfield OX13 . . . . . . 157 C2
St John's Coll OX1 . . . . 261 B3
St John's Cl
  3 Banbury OX16 . . . 16 D5
  Grove OX12 . . . . . . 196 E1
St Johns Dr
  Carterton OX18 . . . . 115 E3
  Kidlington OX5 . . . . . 92 F1
St John's Gn **18** OX10 . . 221 D7
St John's Ho **2** OX16 . . 16 C5
St Johns Prim Sch OX10 221 C7
St Johns Priory Sch **3**
  OX16 . . . . 16 C5
St Johns RC Prim Sch
  OX16 . . . . 16 E3
St Johns Rd OX5 . . . . . 77 C6
St John's Rd
  Abingdon OX14 . . . . 180 A8
  Banbury OX16 . . . . . . 16 C5
  Grove OX12 . . . . . . 196 E1
  Reading RG4 . . . . . . 259 C2
  Wallingford OX10 . . . 221 C7
St John's Row OX14 . . . 201 C8
St John's St
  Bicester OX26 . . . . . . 65 E2
  Lechlade-on-Thames GL7 . 150 D4
St John St OX1 . . . . . . 261 B3
St John's Terr **7** OX10 . . 221 C7
St John's Way OX15 . . . 33 B4
St John the Evangelist Prim
  Sch OX18 . . . . 115 F4
St Josephs RC Prim Sch
  Banbury OX16 . . . . . . 15 F6
  Carterton OX18 . . . . 115 D7
  Oxford OX3 . . . . . . 124 A4
St Joseph's RC Prim Sch
  OX9 . . . . 147 D8
St Katherine's Rd RG9 . . 254 D7
St Kenelm's CE Sch
  OX29 . . . . 102 E2
St Kenelms Cl OX29 . . . 102 E2
St Laurence CE Prim Sch
  OX10 . . . . 203 B7
St Lawrence CE Prim Sch
  GL7 . . . . 150 D3
St Lawrence Cl OX10 . . 203 B8
St Lawrence Ho OX10 . . 203 B8
St Lawrence Rd
  Lechlade-on-Thames
  GL7 . . . . 150 D4
  South Hinksey OX1 . . 141 B5
St Leonards CE Prim Sch
  OX16 . . . . 16 F6
St Leonards Cl OX49 . . 186 B2
St Leonard's Cl OX16 . . . 16 E6
St Leonards Ct OX7 . . . 54 D2
St Leonard's Ct OX11 . . 221 D6
St Leonard's La OX10 . . 221 D7
St Leonard's Rd OX3 . . . 124 D3
St Leonard's Sq **10** OX10 221 D7
St Lucian's La OX10 . . . 221 D6
St Lukes Ct RG4 . . . . . 259 B4
St Luke's Rd OX4 . . . . 142 D5
St Lukes Way RG4 . . . . 259 B5
St Margaret's Rd OX2 . . 123 B4
St Mark's Rd RG9 . . . . 254 D8
St Martins RC Prim Sch
  RG4 . . . . 259 E6
St Martin's Rd OX4 . . . 142 A3
St Mary & John CE First Sch
  1 OX4 . . . . 142 A4
St Mary's Ave RG8 . . . . 257 D5
St Marys CE Inf Sch
  OX28 . . . . 118 B7

St Marys CE Prim Sch
  Banbury OX16 . . . . . . 16 C6
  Chipping Norton OX7 . . 42 E2
St Mary's Cl
  2 Banbury OX16 . . . 16 C6
  Bicester OX26 . . . . . . 65 D1
  Chalgrove OX44 . . . . 184 D6
  Henley-on-Thames RG9 . 254 A8
  Kidlington OX5 . . . . . 92 E2
  Oxford OX4 . . . . . . 142 B2
  Wheatley OX33 . . . . 144 B8
St Mary's Ct OX18 . . . . 134 E2
St Mary's Ct OX28 . . . . 118 A7
St Mary's Gn OX14 . . . 159 F1
St Mary's Ho OX33 . . . 144 B8
St Mary's La OX7 . . . . . 30 E3
St Marys Mead OX28 . . . 118 B7
St Marys RC Prim Sch
  OX26 . . . . 65 E2
St Mary's Rd
  Adderbury OX17 . . . . . 22 F2
  East Hendred OX12 . . 216 E6
  Oxford OX4 . . . . . . 141 F7
St Marys Sch OX12 . . . 214 D4
St Mary's St OX10 . . . . 221 D7
St Mary's Way OX12 . . . 214 C5
St Mary's Wlk OX27 . . . 50 C3
St Michaels OX12 . . . . 214 D4
St Michael's Ave
  Abingdon OX14 . . . . 179 E7
  Highworth SN6 . . . . 190 A5
St Michaels CE First Sch
  . . . . 123 F2
St Michaels CE Prim Sch
  OX13 . . . . 198 F4
St Michaels Cl OX7 . . . . 85 D8
St Michael's Ct OX27 . . . 52 D6
St Michael's La OX5 . . . 107 F8
St Michael's St OX1 . . . 261 B2
St Michael's Way OX13 . . 198 F4
St Nicholas CE Inf Sch
  OX10 . . . . 221 C8
St Nicholas CE Prim Sch
  OX12 . . . . 213 F4
St Nicholas' Gn OX14 . . 159 F1
St Nicholas Pk (Cvn Pk)
  OX3 . . . . 123 F7
St Nicholas Prim Sch
  OX3 . . . . 123 F5
St Nicholas Rd
  Oxford OX4 . . . . . . 142 C2
  Tackley OX5 . . . . . . 77 C6
  Wallingford OX10 . . . 221 C8
St Nicolas CE Prim Sch
  OX14 . . . . 179 F8
St Omer Rd OX14 . . . . 142 C5
St Paul's Cres OX2 . . . . 140 D8
St Peter's Ave RG4 . . . 258 E3
St Peters CE Inf Sch
  OX18 . . . . 133 C5
St Peters CE Prim Sch
  OX29 . . . . 107 C2
St Peters Cl OX15 . . . . . 31 F7
St Peter's Cl
  Cassington OX29 . . . 107 D2
  Stoke Lyne OX27 . . . . 51 B5
  Wootton OX13 . . . . . 159 B6
St Peter's Coll OX1 . . . 261 B2
St Peter's Cres OX26 . . . 65 F4
St Peter's Gate NN13 . . . 24 A7
St Peter's Hill RG4 . . . 258 F3
St Peter's Pl **4** OX10 . . 221 D7
St Peter's Rd
  Abingdon OX14 . . . . 160 C1
  Brackley NN13 . . . . . 24 A8
  Didcot OX11 . . . . . . 218 E8
  Wolvercote OX2 . . . . 122 F8
St Peter's St OX10 . . . . 221 D7
St Ruald's Cl **15** OX10 . . 221 D7
St Rumbold's Rd OX10 . . 221 D7
St Stephens Cl **5** RG4 . . 259 A2
St Swithuns CE Prim Sch
  OX1 . . . . 160 E8
St Swithun's Rd OX1 . . 160 E8
St Thomas More RC Prim
  Sch **1** OX5 . . . . . . 108 E7
St Thomas' Cl SN7 . . . . 155 F2
St Thomas St OX15 . . . 33 F3
St Thomas' St OX1 . . . . 261 A2
Salegate La OX4 . . . . . 142 D5
Salesian Gdns OX4 . . . 142 D6
Salesian Ho **1** OX4 . . 142 D6
SALFORD 41 F5
Salford Rd OX3 . . . . . . 123 E4
Salisbury Cres OX2 . . . 123 B8
Sallow Cl OX26 . . . . . . 65 F5
Salmon Cl OX15 . . . . . . 21 F6
Salop Cl SN6 . . . . 209 B6
Salter Cl OX1 . . . . 141 C7
Salters Cl HP18 . . . . . . 98 C8
Salters La HP18 . . . . . . 98 C8
Salt La OX9 . . . . 166 E2
Saltway Nature Reserve*
  OX7 . . . . 74 B3
Salvia Cl OX16 . . . . 9 B1
Samian Way OX10 . . . 202 D8
Samor Way OX11 . . . . 218 D8
Samphire Rd OX4 . . . . 142 F2
Samuelson Ct **16** OX16 . . 16 D5
Sandcroft Rd RG4 . . . . 258 B6
Sandell Cl OX16 . . . . . 16 B5
Sanderling Cl OX26 . . . 81 A8
Sanderling Wlk OX16 . . . 16 B3
Sandfield Rd OX3 . . . . 124 B3
Sandfine Rd OX15 . . . . 15 B2
Sandford Cl
  Abingdon OX14 . . . . 160 B2
  Woodcote RG8 . . . . 250 F8

Sandford Dr RG5 . . . . 260 F1
Sandford Gn OX16 . . . . 15 F7
Sandford La OX1 . . . . 160 F7
Sandford Mount OX7 . . . 73 C3
SANDFORD-ON-
  THAMES 161 B7
Sandford Park OX7 . . . 73 C3
Sandford Rd OX4 . . . . 142 A1
Sandford Rise OX7 . . . 73 C3
SANDFORD ST MARTIN . . 46 C2
Sandford St Martin Rd
  OX7 . . . . 46 C1
Sandgate Ave RG30 . . . 257 F2
Sand Hill SN6 . . . . . . 209 A7
Sandhill Rd OX5 . . . . . 108 A8
SANDHILLS 125 B4
Sandhills Prim Sch OX3 . 125 B4
Sand La OX3 . . . . 111 A2
Sandleigh Rd OX13 . . . 159 A2
Sandpiper Cl OX26 . . . . 81 A8
Sandpit Hill MK18 . . . . . 39 F6
Sandpit La RG4 . . . . . 259 F8
Sandringham Rd
  Didcot OX11 . . . . . . 219 B8
  Kings Sutton OX17 . . . 23 F5
Sands Cl
  Bletchingdon OX5 . . . . 93 A8
  Cumnor OX2 . . . . . . 139 E5
Sands La OX15 . . . . . . 31 F7
Sands Rd OX11 . . . . . 219 F6
Sands The
  Benson OX10 . . . . . 204 C6
  Milton-under-Wychwood
  OX7 . . . . 70 B1
Sands Way OX10 . . . . 203 F5
Sand View SN7 . . . . . 172 F2
Sandy La
  Boars Hill OX1 . . . . . 140 C2
  Cholsey OX10 . . . . . 220 F1
  Hatford OX7 . . . . . . 174 C4
  Kingston Bagpuize OX13 . 156 E1
  Long Crendon HP18 . . 129 B6
  Oxford OX4 . . . . . . 142 E3
  Shrivenham SN6 . . . . 209 B6
  Tiddington OX9 . . . . 145 F5
  Upper Rissington GL54 . 68 A4
  Yarnton OX5 . . . . . . 108 C7
Sandy Lane Ct GL54 . . . 68 A4
Sandy Lane Est OX9 . . . 145 F7
Sandy Lane W OX4 . . . 142 D3
Sarajac Ave OX12 . . . . 213 F4
SARSDEN 55 F3
Sarsden Cl OX7 . . . . . . 57 B1
SARSDEN HALT 55 D6
Sarsden Rd OX7 . . . . . 55 F4
Sarum Cl OX18 . . . . . . 115 F3
Satin La OX15 . . . . 33 F3
SATWELL 242 E4
Satwell Cl RG9 . . . . . . 243 A3
Saunders Cl OX49 . . . . 186 B2
Saunders Ct RG8 . . . . . 257 B5
Saunders Rd OX4 . . . . 142 B6
Saunders Wood Copse
  HP14 . . . . 188 F4
Savile Rd OX1 . . . . . . 261 C3
Savile Way OX12 . . . . 196 D1
Saw Cl OX44 . . . . 184 C7
Sawpit Rd OX4 . . . . . . 142 E3
Sawpits La GL56 . . . . . . 40 A1
Saxel Cl OX18 . . . . . . 135 E3
Saxifrage Sq **5** OX4 . . 142 E1
Saxon Cl OX10 . . . . . . 221 C7
Saxon Ct
  Benson OX10 . . . . . 203 F4
  Bicester OX26 . . . . . . 65 F1
  Oxford OX3 . . . . . . 124 C3
Saxon Orch SN6 . . . . . 191 D2
Saxon Pl
  Pangbourne RG8 . . . 256 D6
  Wantage OX12 . . . . 214 B5
Saxons Cl GL7 . . . . . . 132 B5
Saxons Heath OX14 . . . 201 D7
Saxons Way OX11 . . . . 219 A7
Saxon Way
  Oxford OX3 . . . . . . 124 B4
  Witney OX28 . . . . . . 118 A7
Saxton Rd OX14 . . . . . 179 E5
Sayer Milward Terr **20**
  OX10 . . . . 221 D7
Sayers Orch OX11 . . . . 200 D1
Scafell Cl OX11 . . . . . 218 E8
Scampton Cl OX26 . . . . 66 E3
Schilling St OX25 . . . . . 63 A8
Sch of Geography OX1 . . 261 C3
Schofield Ave OX28 . . . 104 A3
Schofield Gdns OX28 . . 104 A3
Schofields Way OX15 . . . 21 E5
Scholar Cl SN6 . . . . . . 191 F2
Scholar Pl OX2 . . . . . . 140 C7
Scholars Acre OX18 . . . 115 D4
Scholars Cl RG4 . . . . . 258 F2
Scholar's Mews OX2 . . . 123 B6
Schongau Cl OX14 . . . 179 D4
School Cl
  Ickford HP18 . . . . . . 128 A3
  Long Compton CV36 . . . 27 F5
  Longworth OX13 . . . . 156 C3
  Steventon OX13 . . . . 198 F4
School Cotts RG9 . . . . 243 D3
School Ct OX2 . . . . . . 261 A3
School End
  Aynho OX17 . . . . 35 C7
  Chetwode MK18 . . . . . 53 D8
Schooler's La GL56 . . . . 40 C3
School Hill
  Minster Lovell OX29 . . 102 F3
  Mollington OX17 . . . . . 3 F3
  Wargrave RG10 . . . . 255 D1

School La
  Appleford OX14 . . . . 200 F8
  Aston Rowant OX9 . . . 167 E3
  Black Bourton OX18 . . 133 F5
  Chilson OX7 . . . . 71 F3
  Coleshill SN6 . . . . . . 191 B8
  Great Bourton OX17 . . . 9 D7
  Grove OX12 . . . . . . 196 E1
  Harwell OX11 . . . . . 217 E7
  Kingston Bagpuize OX13 . 156 F1
  Middleton Stoney OX25 . 64 A4
  Milton Heights OX14 . . 199 C3
  Milton OX14 . . . . . . 199 D5
  Minster Lovell OX29 . . 102 E3
  North Newington OX15 . 15 C4
  Reading, Emmer Green
  RG4 . . . . 259 B6
  Reading RG4 . . . . . . 259 A2
  Shabbington HP18 . . . 128 D3
  Stadhampton OX44 . . 163 C2
  Stoke Lyne OX27 . . . . 51 B5
  Stoke Row RG9 . . . . 241 F4
  Upper Heyford OX6 . . . 62 F8
  Wargrave RG10 . . . . 255 D2
  Warmington OX17 . . . . 3 A4
School of St Helen & St
  Katherine OX14 . . . . 179 D8
School Paddock OX27 . . 64 F8
School Pl OX1 . . . . . . 141 D6
School Rd
  Ardington OX12 . . . . 215 D5
  Finstock OX7 . . . . . . 88 C5
  Kidlington OX5 . . . . . 92 E1
  West Hanney OX12 . . 196 F6
School Row OX16 . . . . . 16 F6
School View OX16 . . . . . 16 F6
School Yd OX44 . . . . . 163 C2
Science Oxford★ OX4 . . 123 F1
SCOTLAND END 30 A7
Scotland End OX15 . . . . 30 A7
Scotsgrove Cotts OX9 . . 130 A4
Scotsgrove Hill OX9 . . . 130 A3
Scott Cl
  Bicester OX26 . . . . . . 65 C3
  Kidlington OX5 . . . . . 108 D8
  Reading RG4 . . . . . . 259 A5
Scott Rd OX2 . . . . . . 123 B8
Scotts Cnr NN13 . . . . . 25 A4
Scotts House Sch OX29 105 D5
Scotts La OX27 . . . . . . 67 E2
Scours La RG30 . . . . . 258 B1
Scrutton Cl OX3 . . . . . 124 E3
Seacourt Rd OX2 . . . . 122 C1
Sealham Rd OX29 . . . . 118 B4
Second Ave OX11 . . . . 200 D2
Second St
  Croughton NN13 . . . . . 36 E6
  Harwell OX11 . . . . . 217 C3
Sedgefield Cl RG4 . . . . 252 F6
Sedgemoor Dr OX9 . . . 130 A1
Sedgewell Rd RG4 . . . 252 F6
Seelscheid Way OX26 . . 81 A7
Seesen Way OX12 . . . . 214 E4
Sefton Pl OX15 . . . . . . 22 E7
Sefton Rd OX3 . . . . . . 124 E3
Segrave Cl RG10 . . . . 260 E2
Segsbury Ct OX12 . . . 214 B5
Segsbury Rd OX12 . . . 214 B5
Selborne Gdns RG30 . . 258 A4
Sellwood Dr OX18 . . . . 115 E3
Sellwood Rd OX14 . . . 159 F1
Selwyn Cres OX14 . . . 160 E2
Send Rd RG4 . . . . . . 259 C1
Sermon Cl OX3 . . . . . 124 F2
Setler Ho **1** OX16 . . . . 16 E6
Setts The SN7 . . . . . . 172 E2
Seven Acres
  Long Crendon HP18 . . 129 B7
  Thame OX9 . . . . . . 148 A8
Sevenfields SN6 . . . . . 190 A7
SEVENHAMPTON 190 B2
Seventeenth St OX11 . . 217 A2
Seventh Ave OX3 . . . . 142 E6
Severalls Cl OX10 . . . . 203 D1
Severalls Cotts OX10 . . 203 B3
Severn Cl OX26 . . . . . . 65 B3
Severn Cres **2** OX11 . . 219 A8
Severn Rd
  Abingdon OX13 . . . . 159 D2
  Harwell OX11 . . . . . 217 B1
Sewell Cl OX14 . . . . . 160 C1
Sewell's La OX39 . . . . 167 C9
SHABBINGTON 128 D3
Shackleton Cl **4** OX26 . . 66 A4
Shades The OX16 . . . . . 16 C5
Shadwell Rd OX10 . . . 182 C5
Shaftesbury Rd OX3 . . . 124 E5
Shakenoak OX29 . . . . 105 C6
Shakespeare Cl RG4 . . 259 D5
Shakespeare Dr OX26 . . 65 C3
Shakespeare Rd OX29 . . 120 D8
SHALSTONE 25 E6
Shannon Cl OX12 . . . . 196 F1
Shannon Rd
  Bicester OX26 . . . . . . 65 B2
  1 Didcot OX11 . . . . 219 A8
Sharland Cl OX12 . . . . 214 E8
Sharman Beer Ct OX7 . . 147 E8
Sharpes Cotts OX26 . . . 66 E2
Shaw Cl OX26 . . . . 65 C3
Shaw's Copse OX14 . . . 160 F2
Sheards La SN7 . . . . . 194 E7
Shearings The OX15 . . . 30 A7
Shearwater Dr OX26 . . . 81 B8
Sheen Cl OX27 . . . . . . 65 F6
Sheep St
  Bicester OX26 . . . . . . 65 E2
  Burford OX18 . . . . . 100 E5

Sheep St continued
Charlbury OX7 . . . .**73** B3
Highworth SN6 . . . .**190** A5
Sheepstead Rd OX13 . . . .**178** C8
Sheepwash La OX13. . . . .**199** A4
Sheepway Ct OX4 . . . .**142** A4
Sheepways La RG4. . . . . .**258** B8
Sheep Wlk RG4 . . . .**259** B4
Sheerstock HP17. . . . . . .**130** E5
Sheldonian Theatre★
OX1. . . . .**261** C2
Sheldon Rd HP18 . . . . . .**128** A3
Sheldons Piece OX49. . . .**186** A2
Sheldon Way OX4. . . . . .**142** C3
Shelford Pl OX3. . . . .**124** D1
Shelley Cl
Abingdon OX14 . . . .**160** A1
Banbury OX16 . . . .**16** A3
2 Bicester OX26 . . . . . .**65** C3
Oxford OX3 . . . .**124** C1
Shelley Rd OX4 . . . .**142** B6
SHELLINGFORD **193** F7
Shellingford CE Prim Sch
SN7. . . . .**193** F7
SHENINGTON **6** E2
Shenington CE Prim Sch
OX15. . . . .**6** F2
Shenington Kart Club★
OX15. . . . .**6** C2
Shepard Way OX7. . . . . . .**42** F3
Shepherd Gdns OX14. . . .**179** C6
Shepherds Cl
Grove OX12 . . . .**196** D2
Sibford Gower OX15 . . . . .**19** B8
Weston-on-the-Green OX25 **79** A2
Shepherds Gn RG9. . . . . .**243** A3
SHEPHERD'S GREEN **243** A3
Shepherds Hill
Sandford-on-Thames
OX4. . . . .**142** F1
Sonning RG6 . . . .**260** C1
Steeple Aston OX25. . . . . .**48** A1
Shepherds La RG4 . . . . . .**258** D6
Sheraton Dr RG31. . . . . .**257** B1
Sherborne Rd GL7. . . . . .**150** C4
Sherbourne Rd OX28. . . .**117** D8
Sheridan Ave RG4. . . . . .**258** F4
Sheriff's Dr OX2 . . . .**122** F8
Sherwood Ave OX14. . . . .**180** A7
Sherwood Cl OX26 . . . . . .**66** D2
Sherwood Gdns RG9 . . . .**254** C8
Sherwood Pl
Barton OX3. . . . .**124** E4
Purley on Thames RG8. . .**257** B4
Sherwood Rd OX11 . . . . .**218** D8
Sherwood Rise RG8. . . . .**257** B5
SHIFFORD **136** E1
Shifford La OX29. . . . . . .**137** C2
Shilbrook Manor OX18 . .**133** F4
Shilbrook Ave OX18 . . . .**115** D5
Shilldeane Dr OX18 . . . .**115** D4
SHILLINGFORD **203** B6
Shillingford Rd OX10. . .**203** C3
Shilson La OX7. . . . .**73** B3
SHILTON **115** B5
Shilton Rd
Burford OX18. . . . .**100** F3
Carterton OX18 . . . .**115** D4
SHINMOOR **254** F2
Shinmoor Cl OX11 . . . . . .**201** B2
SHIPLAKE **254** F2
Shiplake Bottom RG9 . . .**252** F6
Shiplake CE Prim Sch
RG9. . . . .**254** E2
Shiplake Coll RG9. . . . . . .**254** F1
SHIPLAKE ROW **254** C2
Shiplake Sta RG9 . . . . . .**255** B4
SHIPPON **159** C1
Ship St OX1 . . . .**261** B2
Shipston Cl CV36 . . . .**27** E7
Shipton Cl RG31 . . . .**257** C2
**SHIPTON-ON-
CHERWELL** **92** B6
Shipton Rd
Ascott-under-Wychwood
OX7. . . . .**71** B1
Shipton-under-Wychwood
OX7. . . . .**70** B1
Woodstock OX20 . . . .**91** D6
Shipton Sta OX7 . . . .**70** E2
**SHIPTON UNDER
WYCHWOOD** **85** E8
SHIRBURN **186** D4
Shirburn Rd OX49. . . . . .**186** C2
Shirburn St OX49. . . . . .**186** C2
Shire Lake Cl OX1. . . . . .**261** B1
Shires Bsns Pk The NN13 .**24** A6
Shires Rd NN13. . . . .**24** A6
Shirley Pl OX2. . . . .**261** A4
Shirville Hill RG8 . . . . . .**250** E7
Shoe La
East Hagbourne OX11 . . .**218** F5
Oxford OX1 . . . .**261** B2
Shooter's Hill RG8 . . . . .**256** C6
SHORES GREEN **118** F8
Shorte Cl OX3 . . . .**142** E7
Short Furlong OX11 . . . .**201** B2
SHORTHAMPTON **72** B5
Shortlands Hill OX10 . . .**238** D4
Short St
Pangbourne RG8 . . . . . .**256** D5
1 Reading RG4. . . . .**259** B4
Watchfield SN6. . . . .**191** D1
Short The RG8. . . . .**257** D5
Shotover SN7. . . . .**211** C6
Shotover Ctry Pk★ OX3 .**143** B8
Shotover Kilns OX3 . . . .**124** F1
Shotover Trad Est OX3 . .**124** F1
SHOTTESWELL **8** D7

Shrewsbury Pl OX18 . . . .**134** E3
Shrieves Cl OX14. . . . . . .**160** B2
SHRIVENHAM **209** B7
Shrivenham CE Prim Sch
SN6. . . . .**209** B7
Shrivenham Hundred
SN6. . . . .**191** D2
**Shrivenham Hundred Bsns
Pk** SN6 . . . .**191** D2
Shrivenham Rd
Highworth SN6 . . . .**190** B3
Longcot SN7 . . . .**192** C2
Shrubbery The GL7 . . . . .**150** C4
Shute Ave SN6. . . . .**209** D8
SHUTFORD **14** B6
Shutford Rd
North Newington OX15 . . .**15** B4
Tadmarton OX15 . . . .**20** E8
Siareys Cl OX39. . . . .**168** C6
SIBFORD FERRIS **19** A7
SIBFORD GOWER. **19** A8
Sibford Gower Prim Sch
OX15. . . . .**19** A8
Sibford Rd
Hook Norton OX15. . . . . .**30** B8
Shutford OX15 . . . .**13** E3
Sibford Sch OX15 . . . .**19** B7
Sibthorp Rd OX1 . . . . . .**261** C3
Sideleigh Rd OX15 . . . . . .**22** E8
Sidings Ind Est The NN13 .**24** A8
Sidings Rd OX7 . . . .**55** E5
Sidings The OX10. . . . . .**221** C7
Sidney St OX4 . . . .**141** F7
SIGNET **100** C1
Signet End OX18 . . . .**100** E3
Silkdale Cl OX4 . . . .**142** D5
Silver Birches OX33. . . . .**125** E7
Silverdale Rd RG10. . . . .**255** E1
Silver La OX12 . . . .**213** D6
Silvermead HP18 . . . . . .**127** D5
Silver Rd OX4 . . . .**142** A7
Silver St
Bourton SN6. . . . .**209** A2
Chacombe OX17 . . . .**10** E4
Fernham SN7. . . . .**193** A4
Tetsworth OX9. . . . .**166** B8
Wroxton OX15 . . . .**15** B8
Silver Street N OX17 . . . . .**10** E4
Silverthorne Dr RG4. . . .**258** E6
Simmns Cl OX33 . . . .**125** D7
Simmonds Wlk OX12 . . . .**214** D6
Simmons Rd RG9. . . . . . .**244** D3
Simmons Way OX9. . . . . .**129** F1
Simon Ho OX3. . . . .**124** D3
Simons Cl RG31. . . . .**257** C4
Simon's Cl OX33 . . . .**144** A8
Simons La OX7. . . . .**85** D7
Simon's Way MK18. . . . . .**25** E7
Simpsons Way OX1. . . . . .**160** E8
Sinclair Ave OX16. . . . . . .**16** A7
Sinclair Dr OX16. . . . .**16** A7
Singers Cl RG9 . . . .**254** E8
Singers La RG9 . . . .**244** E1
Singletree OX4 . . . .**142** B4
Sinnels Field OX7 . . . .**85** E8
Sinnet Ct OX4 . . . .**142** A8
Sinodum Cl OX14 . . . . . .**201** D7
Sinodun Rd
Didcot OX11. . . . .**218** F7
Wallingford OX10 . . . . .**203** C1
Sinodun Row OX14. . . . .**200** F7
Sinodun View OX10. . . . .**203** B8
Sint Niklaas Cl OX14 . . . .**179** D4
Sires Hill
Long Wittenham OX11,
OX14. . . . .**201** E5
North Moreton OX11. . . .**202** C4
Sir Georges La OX17 . . . . .**23** A4
Sir Henry Jake Cl OX16. . . .**9** C4
Sir Mortimer's Terr
OX14. . . . .**199** D6
**Sir William Dunn Sch of
Pathology** OX1 . . . .**261** C4
Siskin Rd
Bicester OX26. . . . .**66** A1
Upper Rissington GL54 . . .**68** A5
Sixpenny La OX44. . . . . .**184** E6
Sixteenth St OX11. . . . . .**217** B3
Sixth St
Croughton NN13 . . . .**36** E7
Harwell OX11. . . . .**217** B3
Skarries View RG4. . . . . .**258** D8
Skelton Ct OX4 . . . .**123** F1
Skene Cl OX3 . . . .**124** C1
Skerritt Way RG8 . . . . . .**257** C4
Skilton Rd RG31 . . . .**257** C3
Skimmingdish La
Bicester, Caversfield
OX27. . . . .**65** F6
Bicester OX26. . . . .**66** B5
Skinner Rd OX26. . . . .**66** D2
Skippett La OX7. . . . .**88** A4
Skippon Way OX9. . . . . .**129** F2
Skittle Alley OX17. . . . . . .**35** C7
Skylark Pl OX4 . . . .**142** D2
Slade Cl OX3 . . . .**124** D1
SLADE END **202** F1
Slade End OX10. . . . .**202** F2
Slade End Rdbt OX10. . . .**203** A2
Slade Farm Cotts OX5 . . . .**63** B1
Slade Hill OX14 . . . .**24** D1
Slade Rd
Cholsey OX10. . . . .**221** A2
Didcot OX11. . . . .**200** C1
Stokenchurch HP14. . . . .**188** E4
Slade The
Charlbury OX7 . . . .**73** C4
Oxford OX3 . . . .**142** E8

Slatters Ct OX29 . . . .**90** A1
Slave Hill HP17. . . . .**130** F5
Slaymaker Cl OX3. . . . . .**124** F2
Sloane Cl RG8 . . . .**249** C6
Slopes The RG4. . . . .**259** D2
Small Ho OX15. . . . .**19** C7
Smith Barry Cir GL54. . . . .**68** A4
Smith Barry Cres GL54 . . .**68** B4
Smith Barry Rd GL54 . . . .**68** A4
Smith Cl RG4 . . . .**252** F5
Smith's Cl OX18. . . . .**135** E2
Smiths Cvn Site OX15 . . . .**21** F3
Smiths Farm La OX11 . . . .**200** D1
Smith's Hill OX12 . . . . . .**231** F5
Smiths Rickyard OX12 . . .**216** D7
Smiths Wharf **3** OX12. . .**214** D5
Snakehill La OX15. . . . . . .**33** B4
Snipe Rd GL54 . . . .**68** A4
Snowdon Mede OX3 . . . . .**124** A4
Snowshill Dr OX28 . . . . .**117** D8
Snows La OX33 . . . .**125** D8
Snowswick La SN7. . . . . .**170** E5
Snuff La OX17 . . . .**8** C8
Snuggs La OX12 . . . .**197** B7
Soane End RG4 . . . .**259** A7
Soden Pl OX13. . . . .**156** D1
Soden Rd OX25 . . . .**63** D8
Sollershott OX2. . . . .**108** F2
SOMERTON **48** F6
Somerton Rd
Ardley OX27. . . . .**50** B4
North Aston OX25 . . . . . .**48** B3
Upper Heyford OX25 . . . .**48** F1
Somerville OX11 . . . .**219** B8
Somerville Coll OX2. . . . .**261** A3
Somerville Rd OX11. . . . .**219** B8
Somerville Dr OX26 . . . . .**65** F4
Songers Cl OX2 . . . .**140** B8
SONNING **260** E4
Sonning CE Prim Sch
RG4. . . . .**260** D3
SONNING COMMON. **252** E5
Sonning Common Prim Sch
RG4. . . . .**252** F5
SONNING EYE. **260** C5
Sonning Gate RG10 . . . . .**260** E2
Sonning La RG4. . . . .**260** C2
Sonning Mdws RG4 . . . . .**260** C1
Soot La OX17 . . . .**3** A4
Sopwith Rd GL54. . . . .**68** A5
Sorrel Mead OX26 . . . .**65** D4
Sorrel Rd OX4 . . . .**143** A2
Sorrel Way OX18. . . . . . .**115** E4
Sotwell St OX10. . . . .**202** F2
SOULDERN **35** E4
Southampton St
Faringdon SN7. . . . .**172** F3
3 Faringdon SN7. . . . . .**172** F4
Southam Rd
Banbury, Little Bourton
OX17. . . . .**9** D4
Banbury OX16 . . . .**16** C7
Mollington OX17 . . . .**4** A3
South Ave
Abingdon OX14 . . . .**159** F2
Henley-on-Thames RG9 . .**254** E8
Kidlington OX5. . . . .**108** F6
South Bank
South Stoke RG8 . . . . . .**239** C3
Turweston NN13 . . . .**24** C7
South Bar St OX16 . . . . . .**16** C5
South Bridge Row OX1 . .**261** B1
Southby OX18 . . . .**134** F4
Southby Cl OX13. . . . . . .**158** A8
South Cl OX5 . . . .**108** F5
SOUTHCOOMBE **43** D3
Southcroft OX3. . . . .**123** F6
Southdale Rd OX2. . . . . .**123** B8
Southdown Ct SN7. . . . . .**194** E7
Southdown Rd RG4. . . . .**259** B5
South Dr
Harwell OX11. . . . .**217** C3
Sonning RG4 . . . .**260** C1
SOUTHEND
Garsington. **162** E8
Henley-on-Thames **226** C8
Southend OX44. . . . .**162** E8
South End
Great Rollright OX7 . . . . .**29** A3
Haddenham HP17. . . . . .**130** F5
Southend Cotts OX5 . . . . .**78** A3
Southern By-Pass Rd
Kennington OX1. . . . . . .**141** D4
Oxford, Botley OX2. . . . .**140** E8
Southerndene Cl RG31 . . .**257** C2
Southern Rd OX9. . . . . . .**147** E8
Southfield Dr OX14 . . . . .**199** F7
Southfield Jun Sch SN6 .**190** A5
Southfield La OX27. . . . . . .**49** F7
Southfield Pk OX4 . . . . . .**142** B8
Southfield Rd OX4 . . . . . .**142** A8
South Gate Ct GL54. . . . . .**68** A3
South Gn OX5 . . . .**78** A1
South Hills HP18 . . . .**98** A1
SOUTH HINKSEY **141** C5
Southlands OX18. . . . . . .**135** E2
SOUTH LAWN **85** F2
Southlawn OX28 . . . .**117** F7
SOUTH LEIGH **119** C6
South Leigh Rd OX29. . . .**119** A7
South Lodge The **2** OX26 **65** E1
South Mdw OX25 . . . .**81** C3
South Mere OX18 . . . .**116** C3
SOUTHMOOR **156** D1
Southmoor Pl OX2. . . . . .**123** B4
Southmoor Rd OX2 . . . . .**123** A4
Southmoor Way OX14. . . .**179** E8

SOUTH MORETON **219** F5
South Moreton Prim Sch
OX11. . . . .**219** F5
SOUTH NEWINGTON **31** E7
South Newington Rd
Barford St Michael OX15. . .**32** D6
Bloxham OX15 . . . .**21** B1
South Par OX2. . . . .**123** A4
South Park Ave OX11. . . .**218** D7
South Park Ct **5** OX4 . . .**141** F8
South Parks Rd OX1. . . . .**261** C3
South Quay OX14 . . . . . .**179** F4
SOUTHROP
Hook Norton **30** B6
Lechlade-on-Thames **131** A3
Southrop CE Prim Sch
GL7. . . . .**131** A4
Southrop Rd OX15 . . . . . .**30** B6
South Row OX11 . . . .**235** D7
South Side OX25. . . . .**62** A8
South St
Banbury OX16 . . . .**16** E7
Blewbury OX11 . . . .**237** A8
Caulcott OX25 . . . .**63** B5
Letcombe Regis OX12 . . .**214** A1
Middle Barton OX7 . . . . .**60** F8
Oxford OX2 . . . .**141** A8
Reading RG4 . . . .**259** B2
Watchfield SN6. . . . .**191** D1
SOUTH STOKE **239** C4
South Stoke Prim Sch
RG8. . . . .**239** B4
South Stoke Rd RG8. . . . .**240** B2
South View
Great Bourton OX17 . . . . .**9** D7
Tiddington OX9 . . . .**145** F7
4 Wallingford OX10 . . . .**221** C7
South View Ave RG4 . . . .**259** C2
South View Pk RG4 . . . . .**259** C2
SOUTH WESTON **166** E1
Southwold **3** OX26 . . . . . .**65** F4
Southwold Cty Prim Sch **7**
OX26. . . . .**65** E5
Southwood Rd OX29 . . . .**103** C1
Sovereign Cl OX11 . . . . . .**219** A8
Sovereign Pl OX10 . . . . . .**221** C7
Spa Cl SN6 . . . .**190** B7
Span Hill RG4. . . . .**260** B7
Spareacre La OX29 . . . . . .**120** E8
Sparrow Way OX4. . . . . .**142** F1
Sparsey Pl OX2 . . . .**109** B1
SPARSHOLT **212** F4
Sparsholt St OX12. . . . . .**212** F4
Spears The OX5. . . . .**108** B6
Speedwell Croft **2** OX26 .**65** E5
Speedwell St OX1. . . . . . .**261** B1
SPELSBURY **72** F8
Spencer Ave OX5. . . . . . .**108** B5
Spencer Cres OX4 . . . . . .**142** B4
Spencer Ct **14** OX16 . . . . . .**16** D5
Spencers Cl SN7. . . . .**194** D7
Spendlove Ctr The OX7. . .**73** B4
Spenlove Cl OX14 . . . . . .**159** F2
Spenser Cl OX26 . . . .**65** C3
Spey Rd OX13. . . . .**159** C3
Speyside OX18 . . . .**115** D5
Spiceball Country Pk★
OX16. . . . .**16** D7
Spiceball Park Rd OX16 . .**16** D6
Spiceball Park Sp Ctr
OX16. . . . .**16** D6
Spier's La OX27 . . . .**67** F2
Spinage Cl SN7 . . . .**173** A3
Spindleberry Cl OX4 . . . .**142** E2
Spindlers OX5 . . . .**92** F2
Spindleside **1** OX26 . . . . . .**65** F4
Spinney Bank OX17 . . . . .**23** F5
Spinney Cl RG4 . . . .**259** B7
Spinney Dr OX26 . . . .**16** E3
Spinney Field OX4 . . . . . .**142** E1
Spinneys Cl OX14 . . . . . .**160** F3
Spinneys The OX7. . . . . . .**58** F5
Spinney The
Abingdon OX14 . . . .**159** D1
East Hendred OX12. . . . .**216** D6
Launton OX26 . . . .**66** D2
Lechlade-on-Thames GL7 .**150** C4
Spitfire Cl
Benson OX10. . . . .**204** B2
Bicester OX26. . . . .**66** A3
Spooner Cl OX3. . . . .**124** E3
SPRIG'S ALLEY **168** F1
Sprigs Holly La HP14 . . . .**189** B8
Spring Cl OX28 . . . .**118** A7
Spring Copse OX1. . . . . .**141** C3
Springdale **6** OX10 . . . . .**221** C7
Spring Farm Mews RG8 . .**239** C1
Springfield OX17. . . . .**8** F4
Springfield Ave OX16. . . .**16** C3
Springfield Dr
Shrivenham SN6 . . . . . .**209** B6
Watlington OX49 . . . . . .**186** C1
Springfield Dr OX4 . . . . .**179** E8
Springfield End RG8 . . . .**249** C8
Springfield Gdns OX39 . .**168** C7
Springfield Hollow HP14 .**188** E5
Springfield Mews RG9 . . .**259** B4
Springfield Oval OX28 . . .**103** C3
Springfield Pk OX28. . . . .**103** F1
Springfield Rd
Bicester OX27. . . . .**65** F7
Kidlington OX5. . . . .**108** F8
Oxford OX2 . . . .**140** C8
Stokenchurch HP14. . . . .**188** F4
Wantage OX12. . . . .**214** A4
Springfield Sch OX28 . . .**104** D2
Spring Gdns
Abingdon OX14 . . . .**179** D7

Spring Gdns continued
Lechlade-on-Thames GL7 .**150** C4
Spring Hill OX13 . . . .**176** C8
Springhill Rd RG8. . . . . .**249** C8
Spring Hill Rd OX5 . . . . .**107** F8
Spring La
Aston Tirrold OX11 . . . . .**237** E8
Great Bourton OX17 . . . . .**9** D5
Horspath OX33 . . . .**143** C7
Idbury OX7 . . . .**69** B4
Oxford, Headington Quarry
OX3. . . . .**124** F2
Oxford OX4 . . . .**142** D2
Playhatch RG4 . . . .**260** B5
Watlington OX49 . . . . . .**186** C1
Spring Meadows Bsns Ctr
RG10 . . . .**255** F5
Spring Path OX9 . . . .**147** E8
Spring Pl OX14 . . . .**42** E2
Spring Rd OX14. . . . .**179** D7
Spring St OX7 . . . .**42** E3
Springs The OX28 . . . . . .**118** A7
Spring Terr **2** OX14. . . . .**179** D7
Springwell Cl OX5 . . . .**93** A8
Springwell Hill OX5 . . . . .**78** A1
Springwell Ho **6** OX16 . . .**16** D5
Spring Wlk OX10. . . . . . .**255** D1
Springwood La RG9 . . . . .**253** A7
Spruce Dr OX26 . . . .**65** F5
Spruce Gdns OX4 . . . . . .**161** E8
Spruce Rd OX5 . . . .**108** E7
Spur The RG10. . . . .**255** E3
Square Firs OX29 . . . .**90** A5
SQUARE THE **59** A6
Square The
3 Abingdon OX14. . . . . .**179** F7
Aston OX18 . . . .**135** E3
Aynho OX17 . . . .**35** C7
Brightwell-cum-Sotwell
OX10. . . . .**202** D2
Churchill OX7. . . . .**55** E5
Ducklington OX29 . . . . .**118** B4
Eynsham OX29 . . . .**120** E7
Great Tew OX7 . . . .**45** D7
Kings Sutton OX17. . . . . .**23** F5
Long Crendon HP18. . . . .**129** C6
Longworth OX13 . . . . . .**156** B3
Milton-under-Wychwood
OX7. . . . .**70** B1
Oxford, Botley OX2. . . . .**122** D1
2 Oxford OX4. . . . .**142** C4
Pangbourne RG8 . . . . . .**256** D6
Swalcliffe OX15 . . . .**19** F8
Squires OX18 . . . .**116** C3
Squires Ho **5** OX12 . . . . .**214** D5
Squires Rd SN6. . . . .**191** D1
Squire's Wlk QX10 . . . . .**221** C7
Squitchey La OX2 . . . . . .**123** A8
Stable Cl
Finmere MK18 . . . .**39** C7
Oxford OX1 . . . .**261** A2
Stable Cotts GL56. . . . . . .**40** C2
Stable Rd OX26 . . . .**65** E3
Stables The GL7 . . . .**150** D5
Staddlestone Cl RG31 . . .**257** C2
STADHAMPTON **163** D2
Stadhampton Prim Sch
OX44. . . . .**163** D2
Stadhampton Rd
Drayton St Leonard
OX10. . . . .**183** B6
Little Milton OX44 . . . . .**163** F5
Stadium Ind Est RG30 . . .**258** B1
Stadium Way RG30 . . . . .**258** B1
Staffordshire Cl RG30. . . .**257** F1
Stainer Pl OX3. . . . .**123** F4
Stainfield Rd OX3. . . . . . .**124** B5
Stainswick La SN6. . . . . .**209** C4
Stallpits Rd SN6. . . . .**209** A7
Stanbridge Cl OX16 . . . . .**16** A5
STANDLAKE **137** D4
Standlake CE Prim Sch
OX29. . . . .**137** D3
Standlake Rd
Ducklington OX29 . . . . .**118** C3
Hardwick OX29 . . . .**118** E2
Northmoor OX29 . . . . . .**138** A2
Standon Ct OX3. . . . .**124** C2
Stanford Dr OX14 . . . . . .**179** F8
**STANFORD IN THE
VALE** **194** F7
Stanford in the Vale CE Prim
Sch SN7 . . . .**194** E7
Stanford Rd SN7. . . . . . .**173** B3
Stanier Pl OX16. . . . .**16** E7
Staniland Ct OX14. . . . . .**179** F8
Stanley Cl
Oxford OX4 . . . .**140** D8
Yarnton OX5 . . . .**108** B7
Stanley Rd OX4 . . . .**141** F7
Stanmore Cres OX18 . . . .**115** E3
Stansfeld Pl OX3. . . . .**124** E1
Stansfield Cl OX3. . . . . . .**124** F1
Stanton Cl OX28 . . . .**117** E8
Stanton Cotts OX33 . . . . .**125** D7
STANTON HARCOURT. **138** A8
Stanton Harcourt CE Prim
Sch OX29 . . . .**138** B8
Stanton Harcourt Ind Est
OX29. . . . .**138** A7
Stanton Harcourt Rd
Eynsham OX29. . . . .**120** D5
South Leigh OX29 . . . . .**119** D5
Witney, Cogges OX28 . . .**118** C8
Witney OX28 . . . .**118** D7

Stanton Rd
Forest Hill OX33 . . . . 125 E4
Oxford OX2 . . . . 140 E6
STANTON ST JOHN 125 E7
Stanville Rd OX2 . . . . 140 B7
Stanway OX28 . . . . 103 D1
Stanway Cl OX3 . . . . 125 A3
Stanwell Cl OX17 . . . . 11 A1
Stanwell Dr OX17 . . . . 11 A1
Stanwell La OX17 . . . . 9 D8
Stanwell Lea OX17 . . . . 11 A2
Stapleton Rd OX3 . . . . 124 C2
Starina Croft OX16 . . . . 9 A1
Star La SN6 . . . . 191 C1
Starnham Rd OX29 . . . . . . 118 A4
Star Rd RG4 . . . . 259 C2
Starveall Rd RG8 . . . . 247 D6
Starwort Path 4 OX4 . . . . 142 F2
Station App
Bicester OX26 . . . . 65 F1
Kidlington OX5 . . . . 92 C2
Station Field Ind Est OX5. 92 C2
Station La OX28 . . . . 118 B6
Station Rd
Alvescot OX18 . . . . 133 E5
Ardley OX27 . . . . 50 C3
Ashbury SN6 . . . . 228 A4
Aynho OX17 . . . . 35 B6
Bampton OX18 . . . . 134 E6
Blackthorn OX25 . . . . 82 A4
Bletchingdon OX5 . . . . . . 93 A8
Brize Norton OX18 . . . . . . 116 C3
Chinnor OX39 . . . . 168 C6
Chipping Norton OX7 . . . 42 D2
Cholsey OX10 . . . . 220 F1
Cropredy OX17 . . . . 4 F1
Culham OX14 . . . . 180 F3
Didcot OX11 . . . . 200 F1
Enslow OX5 . . . . 77 B1
Eynsham OX29 . . . . 120 E7
Faringdon SN7 . . . . 172 F3
Goring RG8 . . . . 249 C6
Grove OX12 . . . . 214 E8
Haddenham HP17 . . . . . . 130 E5
Henley-on-Thames RG9 . . 244 E1
Highworth SN6 . . . . 190 A6
Hook Norton OX15 . . . . . . 30 C8
Kingham OX7 . . . . 54 F3
Langford GL7 . . . . 132 D2
Launton OX26 . . . . 66 E3
Lechlade-on-Thames GL7 . 150 D5
Lower Heyford OX25 . . . . . 62 D6
Lower Shiplake RG9 . . . . . 255 A4
Marsh Gibbon OX27 . . . . . 67 F3
Pangbourne RG8 . . . . 256 C6
Shipton-under-Wychwood
OX7 . . . . 70 C1
Shrivenham SN6 . . . . 209 B5
South Leigh OX29 . . . . . . 119 C5
Uffington SN7 . . . . 211 E8
Upton OX11 . . . . 218 C2
Wallingford OX10 . . . . . . 221 C8
Wargrave RG10 . . . . 255 C1
Wheatley OX33 . . . . 144 B8
Station Road Ind Est
OX11 . . . . 200 F1
Station Yard Ind Est
Adderbury OX17 . . . . 23 B2
Chipping Norton OX7 . . . . 42 D2
Station Yd
Steventon OX13 . . . . 199 A4
Thame OX9 . . . . 148 A7
Staunton Rd OX3 . . . . 124 B3
Staverton Rd OX2 . . . . 123 B5
Steady's La OX29 . . . . 138 B7
STEEPLE ASTON 62 A7
STEEPLE BARTON 61 D7
Steeple Cl OX15 . . . . 21 E4
Steepness Hill OX15 . . . . . 32 F4
Steep Rise OX3 . . . . 124 C5
Stenter La OX28 . . . . 104 A1
Stenter Mews 5 OX28 . . . 104 A1
Stenter Rise 4 OX28 . . . . 104 A1
Stenter Sq OX14 . . . . 104 A2
Stenton Cl OX3 . . . . 179 E5
Stephen Ct OX3 . . . . 124 C3
Stephen Freeman Prim Sch
OX11 . . . . 200 C2
Stephen Rd OX3 . . . . 124 C3
Stephenson Ho OX1 . . . . . 261 B1
Steppingstone La SN6 . . . 209 A4
Steptoe Cl OX12 . . . . 196 D2
Sterling Cl
Bicester OX26 . . . . 66 A3
Kidlington OX5 . . . . 108 E8
Sterling Rd OX5 . . . . 108 E8
Sterling Road App OX5 . . 92 E1
Sterling Way RG30 . . . . . . 258 B1
Stert Rd OX39 . . . . 167 E4
Stert St OX14 . . . . 179 F7
Stevens Cl OX2 . . . . 123 B4
Stevens La RG9 . . . . 252 D8
Stevenson Cl OX26 . . . . . . 65 C3
Stevenson Dr OX14 . . . . . 179 D8
STEVENTON 198 E4
Steventon Rd
Drayton OX14 . . . . 199 B7
East Hanney OX12, OX13 . 197 E7
Stewart St OX1 . . . . 141 C6
Stile Rd OX3 . . . . 124 D3
Stileway Rd
Chilton OX11 . . . . 234 F8
East Hendred OX12 . . . . . 216 F3
Stimpsons Cl OX2 . . . . . . 122 B1

Stirling Cl
Carterton OX18 . . . . 115 C3
Reading RG4 . . . . 259 D6
Wantage OX12 . . . . 214 E5
Stirling Ct OX16 . . . . 15 F6
Stirlings Rd 4 OX12 . . . . 214 D4
STITCHENS GREEN 248 F3
Stockey End OX14 . . . . . . 160 C2
Stockfields Pl HP14 . . . . . 188 D5
Stockham Pk OX12 . . . . . 214 C5
Stockham Prim Sch
OX12 . . . . 214 C5
Stockham Way OX12 . . . . 214 C5
Stocking La OX15 . . . . 6 D2
Stockleys Rd OX3 . . . . . . 124 A5
Stockmore St OX4 . . . . . 141 F8
Stocks Gn OX18 . . . . 115 E4
Stocks La
Carterton OX18 . . . . 115 E4
Steventon OX13 . . . . 198 F4
Stocks The OX7 . . . . 57 B1
Stocks Tree Cl OX5 . . . . . 108 B5
Stocks Wlk OX18 . . . . 115 E4
Stockwell HP17 . . . . 130 F5
STOKE LYNE 51 B5
Stoke Lyne Rd OX27 . . . . 52 D1
STOKENCHURCH 188 E5
Stokenchurch Prim Sch
HP14 . . . . 188 B5
Stoke Pl OX3 . . . . 124 C4
STOKE ROW 241 F4
Stoke Row CE Prim Sch
RG9 . . . . 241 F4
Stoke Row Rd
Rotherfield Peppard RG9 . 252 E8
Stoke Row RG9 . . . . 242 A4
Stokes View RG8 . . . . 256 C5
STOKE TALMAGE 165 F3
Stonebridge Rd OX13 . . . 198 F5
Stoneburge Cres OX26 . . . 65 E3
Stonebury Cl OX12 . . . . . 214 E5
Stone Cl OX2 . . . . 122 B1
Stonecrop Leyes 3 OX26. 65 E5
Stone Ct
11 Banbury OX16 . . . . . . 16 D5
Great Rollright OX7 . . . . . 29 A3
Stonefield Cl SN6 . . . . . . 209 C6
Stonefield Dr SN6 . . . . . . 190 A4
Stonegables OX28 . . . . . . 118 A6
Stone Hill OX15 . . . . 21 D4
Stonehill La
Abingdon OX14 . . . . 179 D3
Kingston Bagpuize OX13 . 176 D8
Stonehill Wlk OX14 . . . . . 179 D4
Stonehouse RG8 . . . . 249 E2
Stone House Cl OX13 . . . 156 E1
Stoneleigh Cl OX7 . . . . . . 57 B1
Stoneleigh Dr OX18 . . . . 115 D5
Stone Mdw OX2 . . . . 123 A5
Stone Quarry La OX4 . . . 142 A4
STONESFIELD 89 D7
Stonesfield OX11 . . . . 219 A7
Stonesfield La OX7 . . . . . . 73 C2
Stonesfield Prim Sch
OX29 . . . . 89 C7
Stonesfield Rd OX29 . . . . 90 A5
Stonesfield Riding OX29 . 74 D2
Stone St
Oxford OX4 . . . . 142 A8
Reading RG30 . . . . 258 B1
Stoney La OX9, OX49 . . . . 185 E8
Stonhouse Cres OX14 . . . 160 E2
STONOR 225 D2
Stonor Cl OX11 . . . . 200 E1
Stonor Gn OX49 . . . . 186 B1
Stonor Ho ★ RG9 . . . . . . 226 A7
Stonor Pl OX3 . . . . 124 B2
Stort Cl OX11 . . . . 200 F3
Stour Cl OX11 . . . . 201 A1
Stoutsfield Cl OX5 . . . . . 108 A5
Stow Ave OX28 . . . . 117 D8
Stowford Ct OX3 . . . . . . 124 F5
Stowford Rd OX3 . . . . . . 124 F4
Stowhill OX12 . . . . 213 C3
Stowood Cl OX14 . . . . . . 124 E4
Stow Rd
Bledington OX7 . . . . 54 C2
Fifield OX7 . . . . 69 B2
Strachay Cl RG8 . . . . 256 C2
Strafford Way OX9 . . . . . 148 A8
Straight Mile Rd OX33 . . 111 F3
Strainges Cl OX29 . . . . . 118 B4
Stranks Cl SN6 . . . . 190 A4
Stratfield Rd
Kidlington OX5 . . . . 108 E6
Oxford OX2 . . . . 123 B6
Stratford Dr OX29 . . . . . 120 D8
Stratford La OX20 . . . . . . 76 B2
Stratford Rd
Drayton OX15 . . . . 15 E8
Shenington OX15 . . . . 6 F7
Stratford St OX4 . . . . 141 F7
Strathmore Cl OX18 . . . . 115 D5
STRATTON AUDLEY 52 D1
Stratton Audley Manor
OX27 . . . . 52 D1
Stratton Audley Rd
Fringford OX27 . . . . 52 D5
Stoke Lyne OX27 . . . . 51 B5
Stratton Way OX14 . . . . . 179 F7
Strawberry Hill OX15 . . . 21 E5
Strawberry Path OX4 . . . 142 F2
Strawberry Terr OX15 . . . 21 E5
Stream Rd OX11 . . . . 218 C2
STREATLEY 249 A7
Streatley CE Prim Sch
RG8 . . . . 248 F5
Streatley Hill RG8 . . . . . . 248 F6

Streatley Lodge 6 OX1 . 141 C7
Street The
Crowmarsh Gifford OX10 . 221 F7
Ipsden OX10 . . . . 240 C7
Moulsford OX10 . . . . 239 A6
North Stoke OX10 . . . . . 221 E1
South Stoke RG8 . . . . . . 239 B3
Stoke Lyne OX27 . . . . 51 B5
Tidmarsh RG8 . . . . 256 D2
Stroud Cl OX16 . . . . 16 E8
Stuart Cl RG4 . . . . 259 B5
Stuart Way OX9 . . . . 130 A1
Stubble Cl OX2 . . . . 140 A8
Stubbs Ave OX3 . . . . 142 E7
Stuchfield Cl OX25 . . . . . 79 F4
Studdridge Ct HP14 . . . . 188 C4
Stud Farm Cl OX17 . . . . . . 5 E1
STUDLEY GREEN 189 E3
Sturges Cl OX3 . . . . 124 D5
Sturt Cl OX7 . . . . 73 C2
Sturt Rd OX7 . . . . 73 C3
Styles Cl OX27 . . . . 67 E2
Styles The OX11 . . . . 217 D7
Sudbury Ct SN7 . . . . 173 A4
Sudbury La OX13 . . . . . . 156 C3
Suffolk Ct OX17 . . . . 67 F3
Suffolk Ho OX10 . . . . 204 E4
Suffolk Way OX14 . . . . . 179 D6
Sugarswell La OX15 . . . . . 6 B6
Sugworth Cres OX14 . . . 160 E6
Sugworth La OX14 . . . . . 160 D6
SULHAM 256 E2
Sulham La RG8 . . . . 256 E3
Summerfield OX1 . . . . . . 141 D6
Summerfield Rd OX2 . . . 123 B7
Summerfield Rise RG8 . . 249 D7
Summer Fields OX14 . . . 160 B3
Summer Fields Sch OX2 . 123 B7
Summerhill Rd OX2 . . . . 123 B7
Summer Ley OX15 . . . . . . 32 F6
Summers Cl OX17 . . . . . . 23 A5
Summerside SN7 . . . . . . 174 F8
Summerside Rd SN7 . . . 174 E8
Summerton Pl OX7 . . . . . 42 F3
SUMMERTOWN 123 C7
Summertown OX12 . . . . 197 B6
Summertown Ct OX2 . . . 123 A7
Summertown Ho OX2 . . . 123 A8
Summit House OX18 . . . 250 F7
Sunderland Ave OX2 . . . 109 A1
Sunderland Dr OX26 . . . . 66 A4
Sundew Cl OX4 . . . . 143 A2
SUNNINGWELL 159 E6
Sunningwell CE Prim Sch
OX13 . . . . 159 E6
Sunningwell Rd
Oxford OX1 . . . . 141 D6
Sunningwell OX13 . . . . . 159 E4
Sunny Bank OX7 . . . . 29 A3
SUNNYMEAD 123 B8
Sunnymeade Ct 2 OX2 . 109 B1
Sunny Rise OX33 . . . . . . 143 D6
Sunnyside
Benson OX10 . . . . 203 F5
Oxford OX4 . . . . 142 D6
Wheatley OX33 . . . . 144 C8
Sun Rising Hill OX15 . . . . . 6 C8
Supergas Ind Est OX28 . 103 B1
Surley Row RG4 . . . . 259 A5
Sussex Dr OX16 . . . . 15 F8
Sutherland Beck OX11 . . 200 E3
SUTTON 120 B1
Sutton Cl OX14 . . . . 179 F7
SUTTON COURTENAY . . . 200 B8
Sutton Courtenay La
OX14 . . . . 199 F5
SUTTON GREEN 120 B2
Sutton La OX29 . . . . 120 B1
Sutton Rd
Milton OX14 . . . . 199 E6
Oxford OX3 . . . . 124 B5
SUTTON WICK 179 C2
Sutton Wick La OX14 . . . 179 C2
Suzan Cres OX12 . . . . . . 214 E5
Swain Ct OX28 . . . . 118 A6
SWALCLIFFE 19 E7
Swalcliffe Barn ★ OX15 . 19 F8
Swalcliffe Lea OX15 . . . . . 14 B1
Swalcliffe Park Sch OX15 . 19 F8
Swalcliffe Rd OX15 . . . . . 20 B8
Swale Dr OX11 . . . . 201 A2
Swallow Cl
Bicester OX26 . . . . 81 A8
15 Sandford-on-Thames
OX4 . . . . 142 F1
Swan Cl
Blackthorn OX25 . . . . 82 A3
Grove OX12 . . . . 196 D1
Lechlade-on-Thames GL7 . 150 C4
Middleton Cheney OX17 . . 17 F8
Swan Close Rd OX16 . . . . 16 D5
Swan Ct
Oxford OX1 . . . . 261 A2
7 Witney OX28 . . . . 118 A8
Swan Gdns OX9 . . . . 166 B8
Swanhall La OX29 . . . . . 104 B5
Swan La
Burford OX18 . . . . 100 E5
Faringdon SN7 . . . . 172 F4
Great Bourton OX17 . . . . . 9 D8
Long Hanborough OX29 . . 90 B1
Swanlands Ho OX29 . . . . 120 E7
Swan Lane Cl OX18 . . . . 100 E5
Swan Wlk OX17 . . . . 147 F8
Swan Sch of English
OX2 . . . . 123 B5
Swansea Rd RG1 . . . . . . 259 A1
Swansea Terr RG31 . . . . . 257 D1

Swansfield
Bicester OX26 . . . . 81 A7
Lechlade-on-Thames GL7 . 150 D6
Swan St
Eynsham OX29 . . . . 120 E7
Oxford OX2 . . . . 123 A1
Swanston Field RG8 . . . . 256 D7
Swarbourne Cl OX11 . . . 200 F2
Sweeps La OX18 . . . . 100 E5
Sweet Briar OX13 . . . . . . 178 C6
Sweet Green Cl OX3 . . . . 125 B4
Sweetmans Rd OX2 . . . . 140 E7
SWERFORD 30 E3
SWERFORD HEATH 31 C4
Swerford Rd OX15 . . . . . . 30 B5
Swift Cl
Bicester OX26 . . . . 65 C3
Oxford OX4 . . . . 143 A1
19 Sandford-on-Thames
OX4 . . . . 142 F1
Swift Way OX10 . . . . 204 D3
Swinbourne Rd OX4 . . . 142 B6
SWINBROOK 101 E5
Swinbrook Cl RG31 . . . . 257 D3
Swinbrook Ct OX28 . . . . 118 B7
Swinbrook Rd
Carterton OX18 . . . . 115 D2
Carterton OX18 . . . . 115 D5
Shipton-under-Wychwood
OX7 . . . . 85 E6
Swinburne Rd
Abingdon OX14 . . . . 180 A8
Oxford OX4 . . . . 141 F6
Swindon Rd SN6 . . . . 190 A5
Swindon St SN6 . . . . 190 A5
SWINFORD 121 B5
Swinford Mus ★ GL7 . . . . 132 B5
Swingburn Pl OX28 . . . . 118 A8
Swin La OX18 . . . . 101 E5
Swinnerton Ho RG9 . . . . 244 E3
Swinstead Ct OX44 . . . . 184 D6
Sworford La OX33 . . . . . 144 F5
Sycamore Cl
Abingdon OX13 . . . . 159 C1
Long Crendon HP18 . . . . 129 C6
Sibford Gower OX15 . . . . . 19 A8
Watlington OX49 . . . . . . 186 A2
Witney OX28 . . . . 104 C2
Sycamore Cres OX14 . . . 160 E7
Sycamore Ct RG8 . . . . . . 256 C6
Sycamore Dr
Banbury OX16 . . . . 16 D2
Carterton OX18 . . . . 115 D3
Thame OX9 . . . . 147 D8
Sycamore Gdns OX26 . . . 65 F4
Sycamore Pl OX18 . . . . . 114 D7
Sycamore Rd
Ambrosden OX25 . . . . . . 81 C4
Launton OX26 . . . . 66 D2
Oxford OX2 . . . . 140 D7
Sycamores The OX3 . . . . 124 E4
Sycamore Terr OX15 . . . . 21 D4
Sycamore Wlk OX12 . . . 196 D1
SYDENHAM 167 E8
Sydenham Cl OX17 . . . . . 23 B4
Sydenham Gr
Sydenham OX39 . . . . 167 E8
Sydenham OX39 . . . . 167 E8
Sylvester Cl OX18 . . . . . . 100 E5
Symeon Pl RG4 . . . . 258 F3
Sympson Cl 5 OX14 . . . . 179 E6
Synderford Cl OX11 . . . . 201 A2
Syringa Wlk OX16 . . . . 9 B1

T

TACKLEY 77 C5
Tackley CE Prim Sch OX5 . 77 C6
Tackley Pl OX2 . . . . 123 A7
Tackley Rd OX25 . . . . 62 B2
Tackley Sta OX5 . . . . 77 C6
Tacks La HP17 . . . . 130 F6
TADMARTON 20 C8
Tadmarton Park OX15 . . . 21 A6
Tadmarton Rd OX15 . . . . 21 B5
TADPOLE 154 C5
Taggs Gate OX3 . . . . 124 F5
Tait Dr OX25 . . . . 63 B7
Talbot Cl
Banbury OX16 . . . . 15 F8
Reading RG4 . . . . 259 D2
Talbot Fields OX18 . . . . . 135 A3
Talbot Rd OX2 . . . . 109 A2
Talbot Way RG31 . . . . . . 257 C3
Talisman Bsns Ctr The
OX26 . . . . 80 F8
Talisman Rd OX26 . . . . . . 80 F8
Tamar Cres OX26 . . . . . . 65 B3
Tamarisk Cres OX18 . . . . 115 E4
Tamarisk Gdns 7 OX26 . . 65 E5
Tamar Way OX11 . . . . . . 201 A2
Tamesis Pl RG4 . . . . 259 B1
Tangmere Ave OX18 . . . 115 E4
Tangmere Ct OX26 . . . . . 66 B4
Tanners Cl OX7 . . . . 73 B3
Tanners La
Adderbury OX17 . . . . 22 F3
Burford OX18 . . . . 100 D4
Eynsham OX29 . . . . 120 F7
Tokers Green RG4 . . . . . 258 E8
Tannery Cl OX18 . . . . . . 100 E5
Tannery Yd OX18 . . . . . . 100 F5
Tansy Way OX18 . . . . . . 115 E5
Taphouse Ave OX28 . . . . 104 B2
Tarragon Dr OX4 . . . . . . 142 F1
Tarrant Ave OX28 . . . . . 104 D2
Tar Rd OX29 . . . . 118 F4

Tarret Burn OX11 . . . . . . 200 F2
TASTON 58 B1
Taston Rd OX7 . . . . 73 A8
Tatham Rd OX14 . . . . . . 159 F1
Tatlings Rd OX13 . . . . . . 198 F5
Taverner Pl OX3 . . . . 123 F4
Tavistock Ave OX11 . . . . 218 D7
Tavy Cl OX11 . . . . 200 F3
Tawney St OX4 . . . . 142 A8
Tay Gdns OX26 . . . . 65 C3
Taylor Cl OX26 . . . . 65 E4
Taylor Inst Main Liby
OX1 . . . . 261 B3
TAYNTON 100 A8
Tays Gateway OX15 . . . . . 33 F4
Tchure The OX15 . . . . 33 F4
Teal Cl
Banbury OX16 . . . . 16 E3
Grove OX12 . . . . 196 D1
Sandford-on-Thames OX4 . 142 F1
Teale Cl OX25 . . . . 96 E7
Teasel Way OX18 . . . . . . 115 F5
Teescroft OX11 . . . . 201 A3
Telford Cres RG5 . . . . . . 260 F1
Telford Rd OX26 . . . . 66 B3
Telford Road Ind Est
OX26 . . . . 66 B3
Templar Ho OX4 . . . . . . 142 C5
Templar Rd OX2 . . . . 109 B1
Templars Cl OX33 . . . . . 144 A8
Templars Square Sh Ctr 5
OX4 . . . . 142 C4
Temple Cloisters 2
OX4 . . . . 142 D5
TEMPLE COWLEY 142 C5
Temple Cowley Pool &
Fitness Ctr OX4 . . . . . . 142 C6
Temple Ho RG9 . . . . 244 E3
Temple Mill Rd OX15 . . . . 19 A8
Temple Rd OX4 . . . . 142 C6
Temple St
Brill HP18 . . . . 98 B1
Oxford OX4 . . . . 141 E8
Templeton Ho RG9 . . . . 254 F7
Tenby Ave RG4 . . . . 259 D5
Tenlands OX17 . . . . 17 F8
Tennis The OX7 . . . . 107 D2
Tennyson Cl OX16 . . . . . . 16 A3
Tennyson Dr OX14 . . . . . 179 C5
Tenpenny OX10 . . . . 202 D8
Tenth St OX11 . . . . 217 B3
Tern Wlk OX4 . . . . 142 E1
Terrace The OX7 . . . . 70 A1
Terrett Ave OX3 . . . . 125 B4
Terrington Cl OX14 . . . . 160 A2
Tessa Rd RG1 . . . . 258 F1
Tetbury Dr OX28 . . . . . . 103 D1
TETSWORTH 166 A8
Tetsworth Prim Sch OX9 . 166 B8
Tewer The OX8 . . . . 89 C7
Tew La OX20 . . . . 75 F6
Tew Rd OX7 . . . . 59 A5
TF Smith Bldgs OX28 . . . 118 C8
Thackley End OX2 . . . . . 123 B5
THAME 148 C7
Thame Com Hospl OX9 . . 148 A8
Thame La
Clifton Hampden OX14 . . 181 B5
Culham OX14 . . . . 180 D4
Thame L Ctr OX9 . . . . . . 147 D8
Thame Park Rd OX9 . . . . 147 F6
Thame Pk Bsns Ctr OX9 . 148 A7
Thame Rd
Blackthorn OX25 . . . . 82 A3
Chinnor OX39 . . . . 168 B8
Great Haseley OX44 . . . . 164 E8
Great Milton OX44 . . . . . 145 C2
Haddenham HP17 . . . . . 130 D5
Little Milton OX44 . . . . . 163 F7
Long Crendon HP18, OX9 . 129 C4
Piddington OX25, HP18 . . 97 D6
Stadhampton OX44 . . . . 163 C1
Sydenham OX39 . . . . . . 148 F1
Towersey OX9 . . . . 148 E7
Warborough OX10 . . . . . 203 B4
Thames Ave
Bicester OX26 . . . . 65 B3
Pangbourne RG8 . . . . . . 256 D6
Reading RG1 . . . . 259 A1
Thames Bank RG8 . . . . . 249 B7
Thames Ct
Abingdon OX14 . . . . 180 A7
4 Didcot OX11 . . . . 219 A8
Eynsham OX29 . . . . 120 E7
Goring RG8 . . . . 249 B6
Oxford OX1 . . . . 261 B1
Thames Dr RG10 . . . . . . 260 F7
Thames Gdns OX7 . . . . . . 73 B4
Thames Ho RG9 . . . . 244 E3
Thameside RG9 . . . . 244 E2
Thameside Court Residential
Pk OX29 . . . . 138 E5
Thameside Ct OX29 . . . . 138 E5
Thameside Mansion
OX10 . . . . 221 E8
Thameside Prim Sch
Abingdon OX14 . . . . 179 D5
Reading RG4 . . . . 259 B1
Thameside Reach OX10 . 239 A4
Thames International 8
OX28 . . . . 118 A8
Thames Mead OX10 . . . . 221 E7
Thames Pk OX10 . . . . . . 221 B8
Thames Rd
Goring RG8 . . . . 249 B6
Harwell OX11 . . . . 217 A3
Thames Reach RG8 . . . . 257 D5
Thames Side 6 RG1 . . . . 259 A1

Thames Side Prom RG4 . 259 A2
Thames St
 Abingdon OX14 . . . . 179 F6
 Charlbury OX7 . . . . 73 B4
 Eynsham OX29 . . . . 120 E7
 Lechlade-on-Thames GL7 150 C3
 Oxford OX1 . . . . 261 B1
 Sonning RG4 . . . . 260 D4
 Wallingford OX10 . . . . . 221 D7
Thames Valley Bsns Pk
 RG6 . . . . 260 A1
Thames Valley Park Dr
 RG6 . . . . 260 B1
Thames View OX14 . . . . 180 A7
Thames View Bsns Ctr
 OX14 . . . . 180 A7
Thames View Ind Pk
 OX14 . . . . 180 A7
Thames View Rd OX4 . . 141 F3
Thatchers Cl OX15 . . . . 13 A5
Thelwall Ho OX4 . . . . . 142 B7
Thenford Rd OX17 . . . . 11 D1
Theobald Dr RG31 . . . . 257 D4
Thesiger Rd OX14 . . . . 179 F8
Third Acre Rise OX2 . . 140 B8
Third St NN13 . . . . 36 E6
Thirlmere Ave OX11 . . 257 F1
Thirteenth St OX11 . . . 217 A2
Thistlecroft Cl OX14 . . 160 B2
Thistledown RG31 . . . . 257 C1
Thistle Down Cl OX4 . . 161 E8
Thistle Dr OX4 . . . . . . 143 A2
Thomas Mews OX4 . . . 123 F1
Thomas Reade Prim Sch
 OX14 . . . . 180 B8
Thompson Dr OX27 . . . 65 F2
Thomson Ave OX11 . . . 217 B3
Thomson Terr OX4 . . . 142 A2
Thornbury Rd OX29 . . . 120 D7
Thornbury Rise OX16 . . 15 F5
Thorncliffe Rd OX2 . . . 123 B6
Thorne Cl
 Henley-on-Thames RG9 . 254 B7
 Kidlington OX5 . . . . 92 C1
Thorney Leys OX28 . . . 117 E6
Thorney Leys Ind Pk
 OX28 . . . . 117 F6
Thornhill OX11 . . . . . . 10 F4
 Sutton Courtenay OX14 . 200 A1
Thornhill Cl OX12 . . . . 214 D5
Thornhill Wlk OX14 . . . 159 E1
Thorningdown OX11 . . . 235 D8
Thorpe Cl OX16 . . . . . . 16 F6
Thorpe Dr OX16 . . . . . 16 F6
Thorpe La OX16 . . . . . . 16 F6
Thorpe Mead OX16 . . . 16 F5
Thorpe Pl OX16 . . . . . . 16 F6
Thorpe Rd
 Chacombe OX17 . . . . . . 10 E4
 Wardington OX17 . . . . . 10 F8
Thorpes Field OX18 . . . 133 C5
Thorpe St OX11 . . . . . 219 E1
Thorpe Way OX16 . . . . 16 F6
Three Corners Rd OX4 . 143 A2
Three Fields Rd OX3 . . 142 E8
Three Gables La RG8 . . 249 A7
Three Pigeons Cl 3
 OX12 . . . . 214 E4
Three Poplar Mobile Home
 Pk OX14 . . . . 201 C7
Threshers Ct 3 OX18 . 115 F5
Thrift Pl OX4 . . . . 142 F2
THRUPP
 Faringdon 153 A2
 Kidlington 92 C4
Thrupp La OX14 . . . . . 160 D1
Thrupp Turn SN7 . . . . 172 F8
Thurne View OX11 . . . . 201 A1
Thurston Cl 4 OX4 . . . 179 E6
Thyme Cl 11 OX16 . . . . 9 A1
Tichborne OX9 . . . . . . 148 A8
Ticknell Piece Rd OX7 . 73 C4
TIDDINGTON 145 F7
Tidford Cotts GL7 . . . . 150 C3
TIDMARSH 256 C2
Tidmarsh La
 Oxford OX1 . . . . 261 A2
 Tidmarsh RG8 . . . . 256 B2
Tidmarsh Rd RG8 . . . . 256 C4
Tidmarsh St RG30 . . . . 258 B1
Tidmore La RG8 . . . . . 240 F1
Tidworth Row OX18 . . . 152 E8
Tigel Mews RG30 . . . . 257 E1
Tilbury Cl RG4 . . . . . . 259 C3
Tilbury La OX2 . . . . . . 122 C1
Tilebarn Cl RG9 . . . . . 244 C1
Tilebarn La RG9 . . . . . 254 B8
Tilehouse Cl OX3 . . . . 124 E3
TILEHURST 257 E1
Tilehurst Sta RG31 . . . 257 E3
Tilgarsley Rd OX29 . . . 120 D8
Tilling Cl RG31 . . . . . . 257 B2
Tilsley Pk OX14 . . . . . 159 E3
Tilsley Rd OX7 . . . . . . 42 D1
Timbers La RG4 . . . . . 223 D2
Timber Way OX39 . . . . 168 C6
Timber Yard Cotts OX7 . 74 C8
Timms Rd OX16 . . . . . 16 D2
Timothy Way 5 OX4 . . 142 F2
Timsbury Ct OX13 . . . . 199 A4
Tinkerbush La OX12 . . . 214 D6
Tinkers La
 Bicester OX26 . . . . 65 E2
 Mollington OX17 . . . . . . 3 F3
Tirrold Way OX12 . . . . 214 F5
Titchener Cl OX26 . . . . 65 D4
Tite La OX15 . . . . 30 B7
Tithe Ct OX16 . . . . 16 A5

Tithe La OX15 . . . . 34 D5
Tithings The OX15 . . . . 19 F8
Titup Hall Dr OX3 . . . . 124 E1
Tiverton Cl RG5 . . . . . 260 E1
TOKERS GREEN 258 D8
Tokers Green La RG4 . . 258 D7
Tolgate Seat 11 OX26 . 65 E2
Tollbrook Cnr OX5 . . . . 78 D1
Tollgate Ho 4 OX26 . . 65 E2
Tollgate Rd OX14 . . . . 180 B3
Tollington Ct SN7 . . . . 172 E1
Tolsey Mus* 5 OX18 . . 100 E5
Tom Brown's School Mus*
 SN7 . . . . 211 C7
Tomkin's Almshouses 4
 OX14 . . . . 179 E7
Tompkins La OX27 . . . . 67 E2
TOOT BALDON 162 B6
Toot Hill Butts OX3 . . . 124 F3
Top La OX20 . . . . 75 F3
Top Station Rd NN13 . . 24 A8
Top Station Road Ind Est
 NN13 . . . . 24 A8
Torridge Dr OX11 . . . . 201 A2
Tothill OX7 . . . . 70 D1
TOUCHBRIDGE 97 E1
Tower Cl
 Abingdon OX14 . . . . . . 179 D6
 Marcham OX13 . . . . . . 178 D6
 Reading RG4 . . . . 259 C8
Tower Cres OX1 . . . . . 261 B2
Tower Ct
 Carterton OX18 . . . . . . 115 C2
 Witney OX28 . . . . 103 F1
Tower Est OX44 . . . . . 185 A7
Tower Gdns OX11 . . . . 200 C2
Tower Hill OX28 . . . . . 117 F8
Tower Hill Bsns Pk OX27 . 67 D7
Tower Hill Prim Sch
 OX28 . . . . 104 A1
Tower Rd OX10 . . . . . . 182 D6
TOWERSEY 148 E2
Towersey Dr OX9 . . . . 148 B7
Towersey Rd OX9 . . . . 148 B8
Tower View SN7 . . . . . 172 F2
Town Cl
 Finmere MK18 . . . . 39 D6
 Sutton Courtenay OX14 . 200 A1
TOWNEND 215 F5
TOWN END 189 C8
Town End Rd
 Bledlow Ridge HP14 . . . 189 C8
 Faringdon SN7 . . . . 172 F2
Town Farm Cl
 Lewknor OX49 . . . . 187 B8
 Thame OX9 . . . . 147 D4
Town Furlong
 Appleton OX13 . . . . . . 158 A8
 Bodicote OX15 . . . . 22 D8
Town Furze OX4 . . . . . 142 D7
Town Hill OX15 . . . . . . 2 A3
Town Pond La OX13 . . . 176 D8
TOWNSEND
 Grove 196 D2
 Wantage 214 A4
 Wheatley 127 B2
Town's End OX7 . . . . . 67 D2
Townsend
 Abingdon OX14 . . . . . . 179 F5
 Banbury OX16 . . . . 16 B6
 Barford St Michael OX15 . 32 F5
 Harwell, Chilton OX11 . . 217 D1
 Harwell OX11 . . . . 217 E8
 Marsh Gibbon OX27 . . . 67 E2
Towns End OX29 . . . . . 104 A6
Townsend La
 Marsh Gibbon OX27 . . . 67 E2
 Middleton Cheney OX17 . 11 F6
Townsend Rd
 Aldworth RG8 . . . . 247 E3
 Shrivenham SN6 . . . . . 209 A6
 Streatley RG8 . . . . 249 A7
Townside HP17 . . . . . . 130 F5
Town The OX15 . . . . . . 31 F7
Town Well End OX27 . . 49 E7
Toy La OX7 . . . . 42 C2
Toynbee Cl OX2 . . . . . 140 D8
Trafford Rd
 Oxford OX3 . . . . 124 E3
 Reading RG1 . . . . 258 E1
Traitor's Ford La OX15 . 18 D4
Tramhill HP18 . . . . 98 B2
Tramway Ind Est The
 OX16 . . . . 16 E5
Tramway Rd OX16 . . . . 16 E5
Treadwells SN7 . . . . . 194 E7
Treble House Terr OX11 . 237 A8
Tredegar Rd RG4 . . . . 259 A6
Tree Close Bay OX4 . . . 142 A4
Treeground Pl OX5 . . . . 108 E8
Tree La OX4 . . . . 142 A4
Trefoil Dr OX26 . . . . . . 65 C4
Trefoil Pl OX4 . . . . 143 A2
Trefoil Way OX18 . . . . 115 F5
Treforgan RG4 . . . . . . 258 F5
Trelawney Dr RG31 . . . 257 B1
Trenchard Ave OX14 . . 199 C3
Trenchard Circ OX25 . . 49 D1
Trenchard Ct OX10 . . . 221 C7
TRENCH GREEN 258 A6
Trendell Pl OX14 . . . . . 159 E1
Trent Cres OX26 . . . . . 65 B3
Trenthams Cl RG8 . . . . 257 B5
Trent Rd OX11 . . . . . . 201 A2
Trevor Pl OX4 . . . . 142 B5

Trill Mill Ct OX1 . . . . . 261 B1
Trinder Rd OX12 . . . . . 214 E4
Tring Rd RG31 . . . . . . 257 C2
Trinity CE Prim Sch RG9 244 D1
Trinity Cl
 Abingdon OX14 . . . . . . 160 B2
 Banbury OX16 . . . . 15 E7
 Bicester OX26 . . . . 65 F3
Trinity Coll OX1 . . . . . 261 B3
Trinity Ct OX7 . . . . . . 43 A3
Trinity Rd
 Chipping Norton OX7 . . . 43 A3
 Oxford OX3 . . . . 124 F2
Trinity Sq OX1 . . . . . . 43 A3
Trinity St OX1 . . . . . . 261 B1
Trinity Way OX17 . . . . 23 D3
Tristram Rd OX29 . . . . 118 B4
Troika Cl 4 OX16 . . . . 9 A1
Trot's La OX7 . . . . 85 D7
Trout Hollow HP27 . . . 169 E8
Truelocks Way OX12 . . 214 F6
Truemper Gr OX27 . . . 65 F7
Trust Cnr RG9 . . . . . . 254 E8
Tubb Cl OX14 . . . . 160 B2
Tubbs Cl OX12 . . . . . . 214 D8
Tubbs La OX26 . . . . . . 80 A7
Tubbs Yd OX26 . . . . . . 80 A7
TUBNEY 157 F2
Tucker Rd OX4 . . . . . . 142 E5
Tuckers La SN4 . . . . . 227 A3
Tuckers Rd SN7 . . . . . 173 A3
Tuckmill Mdws Nature
 Reserve* SN6 . . . . 209 B8
Tuck's La OX13 . . . . . 156 B4
Tudor Cl
 Banbury OX16 . . . . 16 D2
 Oxford OX4 . . . . 141 F4
 8 Wallingford OX10 . . . 221 C7
Tudor Ct OX2 . . . . 140 A8
Tudor Hall Sch OX16 . . 22 A8
Tudor Wlk OX11 . . . . . 217 B7
Tuer The
 Chadlington OX7 . . . . . 57 A2
 Eynsham OX29 . . . . . . 120 E7
Tullis Cl OX14 . . . . . . 199 F7
Tulwick Ct OX12 . . . . . 214 D7
Tulwick La OX12 . . . . . 197 A2
Tumbledown Hill OX2 . . 139 D6
Tumbling Bay Ct OX2 . . 123 A1
Tuns La RG9 . . . . 244 E2
Turberville Cl OX14 . . . 179 E6
Turley La OX29 . . . . . . 104 A8
Turl St OX1 . . . . 261 B2
Turnagain La OX14 . . . 179 F6
Turn Again La OX1 . . . 261 B1
Turnberry Cl OX26 . . . . 66 B4
Turner Cl OX4 . . . . 142 D6
Turner Ct OX5 . . . . . . 108 F7
Turner Rd OX14 . . . . . 179 D5
Turners Cl OX14 . . . . . 160 F2
Turner's Gn OX49 . . . . 205 D7
Turner's Green La
 Britwell Salome OX49 . . 205 D8
 Cuxham OX49 . . . . 185 C2
Turnfields HP18 . . . . . 128 A3
Turnpike Rd
 Bicester OX27 . . . . 66 A6
 Highworth SN6 . . . . . . 190 A6
 Oxford OX2 . . . . 140 B6
Turnstone Cl OX26 . . . 81 A8
Turret Ho OX3 . . . . . . 124 C3
TURVILLE PARK 207 F3
TURWESTON 24 C8
Turweston Manor NN13 . 24 C8
Tuscan Cl RG30 . . . . . 257 E1
Tweed Cres OX26 . . . . 65 B3
Tweed Dr OX11 . . . . . . 200 F4
Twelve Acre Dr OX14 . . 160 C3
Twentieth St OX12 . . . 216 F2
Twin Oaks RG4 . . . . . . 259 B6
Two Rivers Ind Est OX28 . 118 B4
Two Tree Hill RG9 . . . . 254 B8
TWYFORD 23 B5
Twyford Ave OX17 . . . 23 A6
Twyford Gdns OX17 . . . 23 A6
Twyford Gr OX17 . . . . 23 A6
Twyford Mill Ind Est
 OX17 . . . . 23 A2
Twyford Rd OX17 . . . . 23 C7
Twynhams Rd OX5 . . . 77 C6
Tyburn Glen OX11 . . . . 200 F2
Ty-Craig OX26 . . . . . . 65 F2
Tyler Cl RG4 . . . . 258 E5
Tylorstown RG4 . . . . . 258 F5
Tymawr RG4 . . . . 258 F5
Tyndale Cl 6 OX18 . . . 115 E2
Tyndale Pl OX33 . . . . . 144 C8
Tyndale Rd OX4 . . . . . 141 E8
Tyne Ave OX11 . . . . . . 200 F2
Tyne Cl OX11 . . . . 159 C2
Tyne Sq 6 OX11 . . . . . 219 A8
Tyrell Cl SN7 . . . . 194 D7
Tyrrells Cl OX11 . . . . . 217 D6
Tyrrell's Way OX11 . . . 199 E6
Tyte End OX7 . . . . 29 B3
Tythings The OX17 . . . 10 F2

Uffington White Horse*
 SN7 . . . . 211 C2
Ulfgar Rd OX2 . . . . . . 122 F8
Ullswater Dr RG31 . . . 257 D3
Ulster Cl RG4 . . . . 259 D5
Underhill OX10 . . . . . . 239 A4
Underhill Cir OX3 . . . . 124 F4
Unicorn Sch The 5
 OX14 . . . . 179 D7
Unicorn St OX15 . . . . . 21 D4
Union Sq OX20 . . . . . . 75 F4
Union St
 Banbury OX16 . . . . 16 B6
 Oxford OX4 . . . . 141 F8
 Woodstock OX20 . . . . . 91 B6
Union Way OX28 . . . . . 117 F8
Unity Cl RG4 . . . . 259 B6
Unity Ct RG4 . . . . 259 B5
University Coll OX1 . . . 261 C2
University Coll (Annexe)
 OX2 . . . . 123 B5
Untons Pl SN7 . . . . . . 173 A3
Upavon Way OX18 . . . 115 C3
Upland Park Rd OX2 . . 123 A8
Upland Rise OX17 . . . . 9 D5
Uplands Rd RG4 . . . . . 258 E5
UPPER ARNCOTT 96 E7
Upper Barr 3 OX4 . . . 142 C4
Upper Brook Hill OX20 . 91 B6
Upper Campsfield Rd
 OX20 . . . . 91 E5
Upper Common La SN7 . 211 D7
Upper Crale SN7 . . . . . 194 D8
Upper Cres OX29 . . . . 102 E2
Upper Cross La OX11 . . 218 F5
Upper End
 Fulbrook OX18 . . . . . . 100 F7
 Shipton-under-Wychwood
 OX7 . . . . 85 D6
Upper Fisher Row 1 OX1 . 261 A2
Upper Gn SN7 . . . . . . 194 E8
UPPER HEYFORD 62 E8
Upper High St OX9 . . . 147 F8
Upper Icknield Way
 HP27 . . . . 169 E7
UPPER INGLESHAM . . . 170 B6
UPPER
 MAIDENSGROVE 225 A7
UPPER MILTON 84 F7
Upper Rd OX1 . . . . . . 141 E2
Upper Red Cross Rd
 RG8 . . . . 249 C6
UPPER RISSINGTON . . 68 B4
UPPERTON 185 A1
UPPER WARDINGTON . . 10 F8
UPPER WARGRAVE . . . 255 F2
Upper Warren Ave RG4 . 258 D3
Upperway Furlong OX11 . 201 B2
Upper Windsor St OX16 . 16 D4
UPPER WOLVERCOTE . 122 F8
Upper Woodcote Rd
 RG4 . . . . 258 D5
Uppingham Dr RG5 . . . 260 F1
Uppingham Gdns RG4 . 259 D6
Upthorpe Dr OX12 . . . 214 E6
UPTON
 Burford 100 C5
 Didcot 218 C2
Upton Cl
 Abingdon OX14 . . . . . . 160 A1
 Henley-on-Thames RG9 . 244 E1
 Oxford OX4 . . . . 142 C2
Upton Ct OX16 . . . . . . 16 C5
Upton House* OX15 . . . 6 D8
Upway Rd OX3 . . . . . . 124 B5
Upwood Dr OX18 . . . . 115 E4
Urquhart La OX10 . . . . 241 A7
Ushercombe View OX15 . 20 B8
Usher Dr OX5 . . . . 8 F1
Usk Way OX11 . . . . . . 201 B3
Uxmore Rd RG8 . . . . . 241 E4

V

Vale Ave OX12 . . . . . . 196 C2
Vale Cres RG30 . . . . . 257 E1
Vale & Downland Mus*
 OX12 . . . . 214 D4
Valence Cres OX28 . . . 103 E1
Valentia Cl OX5 . . . . . 92 F8
Valentia Rd OX3 . . . . . 124 C2
Valentine Cres RG4 . . . 259 C4
Vale Rd
 Harwell OX11 . . . . 217 B3
 Witney OX28 . . . . 117 E8
Valetta Way OX10 . . . . 204 D3
Valley Cl
 Brackley NN13 . . . . 24 A8
 Goring RG8 . . . . 249 C6
 Reading RG4 . . . . 259 A4
Valley Cotts RG9 . . . . 243 F8
Valley Cres NN13 . . . . 24 A8
Valley Rd
 Banbury OX16 . . . . 16 D4
 Brackley NN13 . . . . 24 A8
 Finmere MK18 . . . . 39 D6
 Henley-on-Thames RG9 . 254 B8
 Horspath OX33 . . . . . . 143 E6
Valley Rise NN13 . . . . 24 A8
Valley View
 Great Bourton OX17 . . . 9 D8
 Lower Heyford OX25 . . . 62 E6
Van Alloys Bsns Pk RG9 242 A4
Vanbrugh Cl OX20 . . . . 91 A7
Van Dieman's SN7 . . . 194 D8

Van-Dieman's La OX4 . 142 C3
Van Dieman's Rd OX9 . 147 F7
Van Diemens Cl OX39 . 168 C7
Vane Rd OX9 . . . . 148 B8
Vanner Rd OX28 . . . . . 104 C2
Vastern Rd RG1 . . . . . 259 A1
Vauxhall Way OX11 . . . 200 D3
Venables Cl OX2 . . . . . 261 A4
Venetia Cl RG4 . . . . . . 259 C7
Venneit Cl OX1 . . . . . . 123 A2
Venners Water OX11 . . 201 A3
Ventfield Cl OX33 . . . . 112 A5
Ventnor Rd RG31 . . . . 257 D1
Venvell Cl OX7 . . . . . . 58 F5
Verbena Way 2 OX4 . . 142 E1
Verinia Cl OX20 . . . . . 91 C6
Verlam Gr OX11 . . . . . 201 B2
Vermont Dr OX20 . . . . 91 A7
Vernon Ave OX2 . . . . . 140 E6
Vernon Ho OX7 . . . . . 42 C2
Vervain Cl 4 OX26 . . . 65 E5
Vestry Cl OX12 . . . . . . 196 D2
Vetch Pl OX4 . . . . 142 F2
Vicarage Cl
 Aston OX18 . . . . 135 D2
 Chalgrove OX44 . . . . . 184 D7
 Grove OX12 . . . . 196 E1
 Oxford OX4 . . . . 142 B2
Vicarage Ct
 5 Banbury OX16 . . . . . 16 D5
 Oxford OX1 . . . . 141 D6
Vicarage Flats OX17 . . . 4 F2
Vicarage Gdns OX17 . . . 4 F2
Vicarage Hill OX12 . . . 214 A4
Vicarage La
 Highworth SN6 . . . . . . 190 A6
 Long Compton CV36 . . . 27 F6
 Oxford OX1 . . . . 141 C6
 Piddington OX25 . . . . . 97 E6
 Shrivenham SN6 . . . . . 209 C6
Vicarage Rd
 Didcot OX11 . . . . 218 F8
 Henley-on-Thames RG9 . 254 E8
 Kidlington OX5 . . . . . . 92 F1
 Oxford OX1 . . . . 141 D6
 Steventon OX13 . . . . . 198 E4
Vicarage Wood Way
 RG31 . . . . 257 B1
Vicars Row 2 OX12 . . . 214 A4
Vickers Rd GL54 . . . . . 68 B5
Vicks Cl OX18 . . . . . . 100 E5
Victoria Cotts OX18 . . . 134 E3
Victoria Ct
 Bicester OX26 . . . . 65 F1
 Henley-on-Thames RG9 . 244 E1
 Oxford, Headington OX3 . 124 B2
 Oxford OX1 . . . . 261 B1
Victoria Gate OX2 . . . . 123 B8
Victoria Mead OX9 . . . 148 A7
Victoria Pl
 12 Banbury OX16 . . . . 16 E6
 Banbury OX16 . . . . 16 E6
 Chipping Norton OX7 . . . 42 E3
Victoria Rd
 Abingdon OX14 . . . . . . 179 D7
 Bicester OX26 . . . . 65 F2
 Oxford OX2 . . . . 123 B8
 Reading RG4 . . . . 259 A3
 Reading, Tilehurst RG31 . 257 D1
 Wargrave RG10 . . . . . . 255 E2
Victoria Terr OX15 . . . 33 F4
Victor St OX2 . . . . 261 A3
Viking Dr OX11 . . . . . . 219 A7
Viking Terr OX10 . . . . 204 D3
Village Farm Ct OX25 . . 79 A2
Village Rd OX17 . . . . . 3 A4
Villeboys Cl OX14 . . . . 180 C8
Villiers Cl OX4 . . . . . . 142 B4
Villiers La OX4 . . . . . . 142 B4
Villiers Rd OX26 . . . . . 65 D2
Vine Cotts
 5 Bicester OX26 . . . . . 65 E1
 Cuddesdon OX44 . . . . . 144 B2
Viner Cl OX28 . . . . . . 104 C2
Vinery Pl RG10 . . . . . . 255 D2
Vines The 2 OX4 . . . . 179 F7
Vine The HP18 . . . . . . 128 D3
Vineyard OX14 . . . . . . 179 F7
Vineyard Cl OX16 . . . . 16 C7
Vinters Ho RG31 . . . . . 257 D1
Vintner Rd 9 OX14 . . . 179 F7
Violet Way OX4 . . . . . 161 E8
Virginia Gdns HP14 . . . 189 F8
Virginia Way OX14 . . . 179 D4
Viscount Ind Est
 Bampton OX18 . . . . . . 134 D8
 Brize Norton OX18 . . . . 116 D1
Vivienne Ct OX3 . . . . . 124 C1
Volunteer Way SN7 . . . 173 A2
Vorda Rd SN6 . . . . . . 190 A7

W

Wadard's Mdw OX28 . . 118 D8
Wadham Cl OX26 . . . . 65 F3
Wadham Coll OX1 . . . . 261 B3
Waggon Pl OX13 . . . . . 156 D1
Waine Rush View OX28 . 118 B8
Wainwrights HP18 . . . 129 D6
Waites Cl OX18 . . . . . . 135 E2
WALCOT 72 F4
WALES 23 F5
Wales St OX17 . . . . . . 23 F5
Waleys Pl 3 RG4 . . . . 259 C2

Walford Rd OX15 .... 19 B7
Walker Cl RG8 .... 240 E1
Walkers Cl OX29 .... 106 B6
Walker's Cl OX18 .... 101 F3
Walkers Dr OX9 .... 148 B7
Walker's Ht OX7 .... 88 C5
Walk The OX5 .... 93 F1
Wallace Cl OX14 .... 179 E5
Wallbrook Ct OX2 .... 122 D1
Walled Gdns OX14 .... 160 E3
Walled Gdns The OX26 ... 65 E2
Walled Gdn The RG10 ... 255 D2
Waller Ct RG4 .... 259 B2
Waller Dr OX16 .... 16 A3
WALLINGFORD 221 C6
Wallingford Com Hospl
OX10 .... 221 C6
Wallingford Mus★ OX10 221 D8
Wallingford Rd
Cholsey OX10 .... 221 B3
Crowmarsh Gifford OX10 . 221 F2
Goring RG8 .... 249 C8
North Moreton OX11 .... 202 A1
South Stoke OX10, RG8 ... 239 C5
Streatley RG8 .... 249 A7
Warborough OX10 .... 203 B5
Wallingford Sch OX10 ... 221 D8
Wallingford St OX12 .... 214 E4
Wallingford Sta★ OX10 .. 221 B7
Walls The SN7 .... 194 E7
Wally Cnr OX10 .... 182 E4
Walmer Rd RG5 .... 260 F1
Walnut Cl
Bicester OX26 .... 65 F5
Deddington OX15 .... 34 E4
Long Crendon HP18 ..... 129 C7
Sonning Common RG4 .... 252 E5
Witney OX28 .... 117 F8
Wootton OX20 .... 75 F4
Walnut Ct SN7 .... 172 F3
Walnut Gdns OX17 .... 1 D1
Walnut Rise OX25 .... 48 F6
Walnut Row OX18 .... 100 E6
Walnut Tree Ct RG8 ..... 249 C6
Walnut Trees Hill SN6 ... 228 B7
Walpole Cl 7 OX26 ...... 65 C4
Walsingham Cl OX15 ..... 21 C4
Walter Bigg Way OX10 .. 221 C8
Walterbush Rd OX7 .... 42 E1
Walter's Row OX4 .... 123 F1
Waltham Ct RG8 .... 249 C8
Waltham Gdns OX16 ...... 17 A6
Walton Ave
Adderbury OX17 .... 23 B5
Henley-on-Thames RG9 ... 254 E8
Walton Cl OX15 .... 22 E8
Walton Cres OX1 .... 261 A3
Walton La OX1 .... 261 A3
WALTON MANOR 261 A4
Walton Manor Ct OX2 ... 261 A4
Walton St OX1, OX2 ..... 261 A3
Walton Well Rd OX2 .... 123 A3
Wanbourne La RG9 ...... 224 D2
Wandhope Way RG31 ... 257 C2
Wandle Beck OX11 ...... 200 F3
Wansbeck Dr OX26 .... 65 B3
Wansbeck Wood OX11 .. 201 A3
WANTAGE 214 E3
Wantage Com Hospl
OX12 .... 214 E5
Wantage L Ctr OX12 .... 214 D4
Wantage Prim Sch OX12 214 D3
Wantage Rd
Didcot OX11 .... 218 C8
Frilford OX13 .... 177 F5
Harwell OX11 .... 217 D6
Rowstock OX11 .... 217 A7
Streatley RG8 .... 248 F8
Wallingford OX10 .... 203 B1
Wapping HP18 .... 129 D6
Warbler Wlk OX4 .... 142 E1
WARBOROUGH 203 B8
Warborough Rd
Letcombe Bassett OX12 .. 232 A7
Warborough OX10 .... 203 B6
Warbreck Dr RG31 ...... 257 B3
Warburg Cres OX4 ...... 142 F3
Warburg Nature Reserve★
RG9 .... 225 B5
WARDINGTON 5 E2
Wardington Rd OX17 ..... 10 D6
Wardle Ave RG31 .... 257 D1
Ward Rd NN13 .... 24 A5
Wards Cres OX15 .... 22 E7
Ward's La OX7 .... 88 C5
Wards Rd OX7 .... 42 F3
Ware Leys Cl OX27 .... 67 E3
Ware Rd SN7 .... 194 C7
WARGRAVE 255 D1
Wargrave Hill RG10 .... 255 D2
Wargrave Rd
Henley-on-Thames, Newton
RG9 .... 255 B8
Henley-on-Thames, Remenham
RG9 .... 244 F1
Wargrave Sta RG10 .... 255 C1
WARKWORTH 17 D5
Warkworth Cl OX16 ...... 15 F8
Warkworth Rd OX17 ...... 17 E7
Warley Rise RG31 ...... 257 C3
Warmans Cl OX12 ...... 214 B5
War Memorial Pl RG9 ... 254 E7
WARMINGTON 3 A4
Warnborough Rd OX2 ... 123 B4
Warneford Hospl OX3,
OX4 .... 124 B1
Warneford La OX3, OX4 .. 124 B1
Warneford Rd OX4 ...... 142 A8
Warner Cres OX11 ...... 218 D7
Warping House Cotts
OX7 .... 42 C2
WARPSGROVE 164 F1
Warren Barn Farm OX44. 163 E7
Warren Ct RG4 .... 258 F2
Warren Hill OX44 .... 163 C1
Warren Ho RG4 .... 258 F2
Warren House Ct RG4 ... 258 F2
Warren Rd RG5 .... 260 D1
Warren Row Rd RG10 ... 255 F7
Warren The
Abingdon OX14 .... 180 B8
Hinton Waldrist SN7 .... 156 A2
Reading RG4 .... 258 D3
Warren View OX44 ...... 163 F7
Warriner Sch The OX15 ... 21 F6
Warwick Cl
Abingdon OX14 .... 180 A8
Carterton OX18 .... 115 C3
Stanford in the Vale SN7 .. 194 E7
Warwick Ct 1 OX26 ...... 66 A4
Warwick Rd
Banbury OX16 .... 16 C6
Banbury, Ruscote OX16 .... 16 A7
Hanwell OX16 .... 8 E3
Warwick St OX4 .... 141 F7
Wasbrough Ave OX12 ... 214 C6
Washford Glen OX11 .... 201 A2
Washington Rd RG4 ..... 259 B2
Washington Terr OX7 .... 60 F8
Wastie's Orch OX29 ...... 90 B1
WATCHFIELD 191 F1
Watchfield Prim Sch
SN6 .... 191 D1
Watcombe Manor Ind Est
OX49 .... 186 B1
Watcombe Rd OX49 ..... 186 B1
Watercress Cl OX15 ...... 22 E8
WATER EATON 109 D5
Water Eaton La OX5 .... 109 A7
Water Eaton Rd OX2 .... 123 C8
WATEREND 189 C5
Water End Rd
Beacon's Bottom HP14 ... 189 D3
Bledlow Ridge HP14 ..... 189 C5
Waterford La OX28 ..... 104 D1
Waterford Rd OX28 ..... 104 D1
Waterfowl Sanctuary &
Children's Farm The★
OX15 .... 20 A1
Water La
Adderbury OX17 .... 23 A3
Ardley OX27 .... 50 C4
Bloxham OX15 .... 21 E5
Brackley NN13 .... 24 A7
Drayton St Leonard OX10 . 183 B5
Little Tew OX7 .... 45 A6
Steeple Aston OX25 ...... 62 A8
Witney OX28 .... 104 E2
Waterloo Cl OX10 .... 239 A7
Waterloo Dr OX16 .... 16 E6
Waterloo Way OX28 ..... 118 B8
Waterman Pl RG1 .... 259 A1
Waterman's Rd RG9 ..... 254 F8
Watermans Reach 2
OX1 .... 141 C7
Waterman's Way RG10 .. 255 C1
Watermead OX5 .... 109 A8
Watermill Way OX3 ..... 125 A4
WATERPERRY 127 B1
Waterperry OX33 .... 127 B1
Waterperry Ct 8 OX16 ... 16 E6
Waterperry Gdns & Mus of
Rural Life★ OX33 ...... 127 B1
Waterperry Rd HP18 .... 127 D5
Waterside Cotts RG4 .... 260 B4
Waterside Dr RG8 ...... 257 D5
Waterside Villas OX14 ... 181 F4
Waters La OX17 .... 11 B1
Waterslade Pens HP17 .. 130 E6
Water St OX25 .... 48 F6
WATERSTOCK 145 D8
Watery La
Brackley NN13 .... 24 A7
Clifton Hampden OX14 ... 181 D4
Hook Norton OX15 .... 30 A7
Sparsholt OX12 .... 212 F4
Wates Way OX16 .... 16 E8
Watling La OX10 .... 182 D1
WATLINGTON 186 C2
Watlington Chalk Pit Nature
Reserve★ OX49 .... 186 D1
Watlington Hill★ OX49 .. 206 E8
Watlington Ind Est OX49. 186 A2
Watlington Prim Sch
OX49 .... 186 B2
Watlington Rd
Benson OX10 .... 203 F4
Garsington OX44 .... 162 D7
Lewknor OX49 .... 187 A7
Oxford OX4, OX44 .... 143 B2
Shirburn OX49 .... 186 E6
Watlington St RG9 ..... 224 E2
Watson Cres OX13 ...... 159 A7
Watsons Cl OX18 .... 115 E1
Watt's La OX11 .... 237 A8
Watts Way 1 OX5 .... 92 E1
Waveney Cl
Bicester OX26 .... 65 B2
Didcot OX11 .... 201 A1
Waverley Ave OX5 ...... 109 A8
Waverley Cl OX17 .... 23 F5
Wavers Ground OX18 .... 115 F3
Waxes Cl OX14 .... 160 C2
Wayfaring Cl OX4 .... 161 E8
Wayfarings OX26 .... 65 E5
Wayland Cres OX11 ..... 217 C1
Wayland Rd OX12 ...... 196 D1
Wayland's Smithy (Long
Barrow)★ SN6 .... 228 E7
Waynflete Rd OX3 ...... 125 A4
Wayside Gn RG8 .... 240 E1
Wayside Ho 4 OX26 ..... 65 E3
WEALD 134 D1
Wealden Way RG30 ..... 257 E1
Weald Rise RG30 .... 257 F2
Weald St OX18 .... 134 E2
Wear Rd OX26 .... 65 B2
Weaver Croft OX11 ..... 201 A3
Weavers Cl OX28 .... 118 A7
Weavers Cotts CV36 ...... 27 F5
Weavers Cl 4 OX18 ..... 115 F5
Webb Cl OX16 .... 16 E7
Webb Cres OX7 .... 42 D2
Webbs Cl OX7 .... 57 B1
Webb's Cl OX2 .... 122 D8
Webb's Way OX5 .... 92 F1
Webster Cl OX9 .... 129 F1
Websters Cl OX29 ...... 106 A6
Wedgewood Way RG30 .. 257 F1
Wedgwood Rd OX26 ..... 66 A3
Weedon Cl OX10 .... 239 A8
Weedon Ct OX10 .... 221 C8
Weeping Cross OX15 ..... 22 E8
Weighbridge Row RG1 .. 258 F1
Weir La OX25 .... 82 A5
Weirs La OX1 .... 141 D5
Welch Way 2 OX28 ..... 118 A8
Weldon Rd OX3 .... 123 F3
Weldon Way OX9 .... 148 A8
Welford Gdns OX14 ..... 160 A2
Welland Ave OX11 ...... 201 B2
Welland Cl
Abingdon OX13 .... 159 C2
Reading RG31 .... 257 C1
Welland Croft OX26 ...... 65 B3
Well Bank OX15 .... 30 B7
Weller Cl OX10 .... 204 A8
Wellesbourne Cl OX14 .. 180 B8
Wellesley Cl OX16 .... 16 E6
Well Hill OX7 .... 88 C5
Wellington Ave OX16 ..... 16 E6
Wellington Cl OX26 ...... 66 A3
Wellington Cotts OX7 .... 73 B2
Wellington Pl OX1 ...... 261 B3
Wellington Rd GL54 ...... 68 B4
Wellington Sq
Oxford OX1 .... 261 B3
Watchfield SN6 .... 191 D1
Wellington St
Oxford OX2 .... 261 A3
Thame OX9 .... 148 A8
Well La
Curbridge OX29 .... 117 C6
Shenington OX15 .... 6 F2
Stonesfield OX29 .... 89 C7
WELL PLACE 240 F7
Wellshead La OX11 ..... 217 E6
Wellsprings OX10 ...... 202 E2
Well St OX12 .... 215 E5
Well View RG9 .... 241 F5
WENDLEBURY 80 A4
Wendlebury Rd OX25,
OX26 .... 80 B5
Wenlock Cl OX11 ...... 200 C2
Wenman Rd
Thame OX9 .... 148 A6
Witney OX28 .... 117 E8
Wenrisc Dr OX29 ...... 102 E2
Wensum Cres OX26 ...... 65 B3
Wensum Dr OX11 ...... 201 A2
Wentworth Rd
Oxford OX2 .... 123 B8
Thame OX9 .... 148 A8
Werrell Dr OX1 .... 159 A7
Wesley Cl
Bicester OX26 .... 65 C4
Oxford OX4 .... 142 E3
Wesley Dr OX16 .... 16 B4
Wesley La 6 OX26 .... 65 E2
Wesley Pl OX17 .... 10 E4
Wesley Wlk OX28 ...... 118 B8
Wessex Cl SN7 .... 173 A3
Wessex Ind Est OX28 ... 118 B6
Wessex Rd
Benson OX10 .... 204 D2
Didcot OX11 .... 218 F8
Wessex Way
Bicester OX26 .... 65 F1
Grove OX12 .... 214 D8
Highworth SN6 .... 190 B7
Westacott Rd OX26 ...... 81 A6
WEST ADDERBURY 22 E3
West Allcourt GL7 ..... 150 C4
West Ave OX14 .... 160 A2
West Bar St OX16 .... 16 C5
Westbeech Ct OX16 ..... 16 C5
Westbourne Ct OX15 ..... 21 E3
Westbrook
Faringdon SN7 .... 172 F3
Grove OX12 .... 196 E2
Westbrook Gn OX11 .... 236 F8
Westbrook Rd RG30 .... 258 C1
Westbrook St OX11 .... 236 F8
WESTBURY 25 B4
Westbury Court Bsns Ctr
OX27 .... 67 E3
Westbury Cres OX4 ..... 142 B4
Westbury Ct Bsns Pk
OX27 .... 67 E3
Westbury La RG8 ...... 257 A6
Westbury Terr OX27 ..... 67 E2
WEST CHALLOW 213 C6
West Chiltern RG8 ...... 250 E8
WESTCOT 212 D3
Westcote Cl OX28 ...... 117 D7
Westcote Pl OX7 .... 42 F3
Westcot La OX12 .... 212 E5
WESTCOTT BARTON 60 D8
West Cotts OX27 .... 52 D1
West Croft OX10 .... 182 C5
West Ct
Banbury OX16 .... 16 E6
Sonning RG4 .... 260 E2
Westdene Cres RG4 .... 258 E4
West Dr
Harwell OX11 .... 217 A3
Sonning RG4 .... 260 D1
West Edge OX27 .... 67 E2
WESTEND 57 B1
WEST END
Cholsey 220 F1
Stanton Harcourt 138 C5
West End
Brightwell-cum-Sotwell
OX10 .... 202 D2
Chipping Norton OX7 ..... 42 E2
Cholsey OX10 .... 220 E1
Combe OX29 .... 90 A4
Hornton OX15 .... 7 C6
Kingham OX7 .... 54 F4
Launton OX26 .... 66 D1
Shilton OX18 .... 115 A5
Witney OX28 .... 104 B2
Wootton OX20 .... 75 F4
West End Cl OX26 .... 66 D1
West End Ind Est OX28 .. 104 B1
West End La
Bishopstone SN6 .... 227 C4
Merton OX25 .... 95 D8
Western Ave
7 Didcot OX11 .... 219 A8
Henley-on-Thames RG9 .. 254 E8
Sonning RG5 .... 260 E1
Western By-Pass Rd
Cutteslowe OX2 .... 108 E1
Wytham OX2 .... 122 C5
Western Cl RG9 .... 254 E8
Western Cres OX16 ...... 16 E4
Western Oaks RG31 ..... 257 E2
Western Rd
Henley-on-Thames RG9 .. 254 E8
Oxford OX1 .... 141 C7
Westfield OX11 .... 217 D7
Westfield Cl
Benson OX10 .... 204 A4
Grove OX12 .... 214 D7
Oxford OX4 .... 142 B6
Westfield Cres RG9 ..... 255 B3
Westfield Rd
Benson OX10 .... 204 A4
Cholsey OX10 .... 238 D6
Long Wittenham OX14 ... 201 D8
Reading RG4 .... 259 B2
Wheatley OX33 .... 126 A1
Witney OX28 .... 104 B2
Westfields OX14 .... 179 D7
Westfield Way OX12 ..... 215 A6
Westgate OX7 .... 85 D8
Westgate Sh Ctr OX1 .... 261 B2
WEST GINGE 216 A2
West Gr OX2 .... 123 B8
WEST HAGBOURNE 218 D4
WESTHALL HILL 100 D6
WEST HANNEY 196 F6
West Hawthorn Rd OX25 . 81 D4
WEST HENDRED 216 C6
West Hill OX12 .... 214 C4
Westholme Ct OX26 ...... 65 F1
WEST ILSLEY 235 B1
West Ilsley Ho RG20 .... 235 B1
West Kidlington Prim Sch 2
OX5 .... 108 E7
West La RG9 .... 244 D2
Westland Rd SN7 .... 172 E2
Westlands Ave OX25 ..... 79 A2
Westlands Dr OX3 ...... 124 B5
Westland Way OX20 ...... 91 A7
Westleigh Dr RG4 ...... 252 F4
WEST LOCKINGE 215 C4
Westminster Cl NN13 .... 24 A7
Westminster Cres NN13 .. 24 A7
Westminster Way
Banbury OX16 .... 16 F6
Oxford OX2 .... 140 E8
Westonbirt Dr RG4 ..... 258 E3
Weston Bldgs OX1 ...... 261 B2
Weston Bsns Pk OX5 ..... 78 F5
Weston Cotts SN7 ...... 170 D8
Weston Ct CV36 .... 28 A6
Weston La OX9 .... 146 F8
Weston Old Bsns Pk OX25 79 A5
WESTON-ON-THE-
GREEN 79 B2
Weston Rd
Bletchingdon OX5 .... 93 A8
Lewknor OX49 .... 187 A8
West Oxford Prim Sch
OX2 .... 123 A1
West Oxon Ind Pk OX18 . 115 F3
West Quay OX14 .... 179 F4
Westridge Ave RG8 ..... 257 C5
WESTRIDGE GREEN 248 B4
Westrop SN6 .... 190 A6
Westrup Cl OX3 .... 123 F3
West St Helen St OX14 .. 179 F6
West St
Banbury OX16 .... 16 E7
Bicester OX26 .... 65 D3
West St *continued*
Childrey OX12 .... 213 B3
Chipping Norton OX7 ..... 42 E2
Henley-on-Thames RG9 .. 244 D2
Kingham OX7 .... 54 F5
Oxford OX2 .... 123 A1
Shutford OX15 .... 14 A5
Sparsholt OX12 .... 212 F4
West View
Oxford OX4 .... 142 A4
Somerton OX25 .... 49 A6
Westwater Way OX11 ... 201 B2
Westway RG8 .... 249 C8
West Way
Lechlade-on-Thames
GL7 .... 150 C5
Oxford OX2 .... 122 D1
WESTWELL 99 E1
West Witney Cty Prim Sch
OX28 .... 117 E8
Westwood Farm Inf Sch
RG31 .... 257 C3
Westwood Farm Jun Sch
RG31 .... 257 C3
Westwood Glen RG31 ... 257 C1
Westwood Rd
Reading RG31 .... 257 D1
Witney OX29 .... 103 C1
Westwood Row RG31 ... 257 C2
Wetherby Cl RG4 ...... 259 C6
Weycroft OX11 .... 201 A3
Weyland Rd OX3 .... 124 E2
Wey Rd OX10 .... 182 D5
W & G Ind Est OX12 .... 213 E6
Whales La OX27 .... 67 E2
Wharf Cl OX14 .... 179 F6
Wharfe La RG9 .... 244 E2
Wharf La
Lechlade-on-Thames
GL7 .... 150 D4
Somerton OX25 .... 48 F6
Souldern OX27 .... 35 B4
Wharf Rd OX10 .... 203 A6
Wharf The
Pangbourne RG8 .... 256 C6
7 Wantage OX12 ...... 214 D5
Wharton Rd OX3 .... 124 D3
Whatleys Orch SN6 ..... 227 C4
Wheatcroft Cl OX14 .... 160 A2
WHEATFIELD 166 B3
Wheatfields OX11 ...... 218 C7
WHEATLEY 144 A8
Wheatley Bsns Ctr OX33. 144 C8
Wheatley CE Prim Sch
OX33 .... 144 A8
Wheatley Cl OX16 .... 16 E2
Wheatley Park Sch OX33 126 B2
Wheatley Rd
Cuddesdon OX44 .... 144 B4
Forest Hill OX33 .... 125 F4
Garsington OX44 .... 143 E3
Islip OX5 .... 109 F8
Wheeler Ct RG31 ...... 257 E1
Wheelers End OX39 .... 168 C6
Wheeler's Rise NN13 .... 36 C8
Wheel Wright Ct SN7 ... 174 F8
Whimbrel Cl OX26 .... 66 A1
Whimbrel Way OX16 ..... 16 E3
Whirlwind Way OX10 ... 204 D3
Whitamore Row RG9 .... 254 E8
Whitby Ct RG4 .... 259 D6
Whitby Gn RG4 .... 259 D6
WHITCHURCH HILL 250 E2
WHITCHURCH-ON-
THAMES 256 C7
Whitchurch Prim Sch
RG8 .... 256 E7
Whitchurch Rd RG8 .... 256 D6
White Barn OX1 .... 140 C2
Whitecross OX13 ...... 159 D4
Whitecross Rd HP17 .... 130 F5
WHITEHALL 241 D3
Whitehall Cl OX29 ..... 102 D2
Whitehall La RG8 ...... 241 D3
White Hart OX3 .... 123 F6
White Hart Cl
Benson OX10 .... 203 F4
Ludgershall HP18 .... 98 B7
White Hart Wlk 1 SN7 .. 172 F3
White Hill
Burford OX18 .... 101 B3
Henley-on-Thames RG9 .. 244 F2
Hinton Parva SN4 ...... 227 A2
Hunt's Green RG9 ...... 254 A5
White Hill La OX1 ..... 140 A1
Whitehills Gn RG8 ..... 249 C6
Whitehorns Farm Rd
OX12 .... 215 A5
Whitehorns Way OX14 .. 179 A1
White Horse SN7 ...... 211 D7
White Horse Bsns Pk
SN7 .... 194 C7
White Horse Cres OX12 .. 214 C8
White Horse Ho OX12 .. 214 D7
White Horse Leisure &
Tennis Ctr OX14 .... 180 C8
White Horse Mews OX18 100 E4
White Horses Cl OX15 .... 22 F8
White Hos MK18 .... 39 D6
Whitehouse Cl OX13 ... 159 C1
Whitehouse La OX7 ...... 42 E3
Whitehouse Rd
North Stoke OX10 ...... 239 F8
Oxford OX1 .... 141 C7
Woodcote RG8 .... 250 E8
White La RG9 .... 243 E8
White Leys Cl OX11 .... 200 F1
White Lion Wlk 1 OX16 .. 16 D6

Whitelock Rd OX14 159 F1
White Lodge Cl RG31 257 B3
WHITEOAK GREEN 87 F1
White Post Rd OX15 16 E1
White Rd
Chilton OX11 217 D1
East Hendred OX12 216 E7
Oxford OX4 142 E6
Whites Forge OX13 158 A7
White Shoot OX11 237 A5
White's La OX14 160 D3
Whites Orch OX11 219 A1
Whitethorn Way 3 OX4 142 E2
Whiteway OX17 3 F3
White Way OX5 108 E8
Whitings La OX29 104 B7
Whitley Cres OX26 66 A3
Whitley Dr OX25 63 C8
Whitley Rd OX10 221 B7
Whitney Rd OX13 156 F1
Whitson Pl OX4 142 A7
Whittall St OX17 23 F5
Whittington Pl OX18 115 D1
Whittle Rd OX9 148 B8
Whittons Cl OX15 30 B8
Whitworth Pl OX2 123 A2
Wick Cl
Abingdon OX14 160 C2
Oxford OX3 124 E4
Wick Farm Pk OX3 124 E5
Wick Gn OX12 196 D2
WICK GREEN 196 E2
Wick Hall OX14 180 D8
Wicks Cl OX18 152 E8
WIDFORD 101 B4
Widmore La RG4 253 A6
Widnell La OX25 97 C7
Wigan's La HP14 169 C5
WIGGINTON 31 B7
WIGGINTON HEATH 20 B3
Wigginton Rd OX15 31 D7
Wigmore La RG30 258 C1
Wigod Way OX10 203 C1
Wilberforce St OX3 124 D2
Wilcher Cl OX11 218 F6
WILCOTE 88 E3
Wilcote La OX7 88 B3
Wilcote Rd OX3 124 F4
Wilcote Riding OX7 88 D5
Wilcote View OX29 105 C6
Wilcox Rd OX7 42 E4
Wilder Ave RG8 256 E5
Wilding Rd OX10 203 C1
Wildmere Ind Est OX16 16 F8
Wildmere Rd OX16 9 F1
WILDMOOR 159 F1
Wildmoor Gate OX14 159 E1
Wilkins Ho OX7 42 E1
Wilkinson Pl OX28 103 F1
Wilkins Rd OX4 142 E6
Willes Cl SN7 172 F3
William Bliss Ave OX7 42 E2
William Cl OX16 15 F7
William Fletcher Prim Sch OX5 108 A5
William Kimber Cres OX3 124 E3
William Lucy Way OX2 123 A3
William Morris Prim Sch OX16 15 F7
William Orchard Cl OX3 124 C4
WILLIAMSCOT 10 C8
Williamscot Hill OX17 10 A5
Williams Hill OX20 75 F3
Williams Mews OX28 118 A7
William Smith Cl OX7 55 E4
Williamson Way OX4 142 A3
William St OX3 123 F3
Willis Ct OX7 70 D1
Willoughby Rd OX16 16 D2
Willow Bank Jun & Inf Sch RG5 260 F1
Willowbrook
Lower Arncott OX25 81 E1
Stanton Harcourt OX29 137 F8
Willow Brook OX14 179 D7
Willow Cl
Garsington OX44 143 D2
Watlington OX49 186 A2
Yarnton OX5 108 B6
Willow Court La OX10 238 F5
Willowcroft Com Sch OX11 218 F8
Willow Dr
Bicester OX26 65 E4
Carterton OX18 115 F4
Willow End
Ambrosden OX25 81 C4
Little Compton GL56 27 A1
Willow Gdns RG31 257 B2
Willow La
Milton OX14 199 D5
Wantage OX12 214 D3
Wargrave RG10 255 C4
Willow Mead OX44 184 D6
Willow Rd
Ambrosden OX25 81 C4
Banbury OX16 16 D2
Brackley NN13 24 A6
Chinnor OX39 168 C6
Thame OX9 129 F1
Willows Ct RG8 256 C6
Willows Edge OX29 120 D8
Willows Gate OX27 52 D1
Willowside RG5 260 F1
Willows Lodge OX27 52 D1
Willows The
Grove OX12 214 D7
Willows The *continued*
Highworth SN6 190 B5
Reading RG4 259 A2
Witney OX28 104 C1
Wootton OX1 159 A7
Willow Tree Cl OX13 159 C1
Willow Way
Begbroke OX5 92 A1
Kennington OX14 160 E7
Oxford OX4 142 E2
Willow Wlk OX12 214 D6
Wills Rd OX11 200 C1
Wilmot Cl OX28 117 F6
Wilmots OX44 162 A6
Wilmot Way OX12 214 F6
Wilsdon Way OX5 92 D1
Wilsham Rd OX14 179 F5
Wilson Ave RG9 254 E8
Wilsons Cl OX14 201 C8
Wilson Way OX27 65 F7
Wilwyne Cl RG4 259 C4
Wimblestraw Rd OX10 182 C5
Wimborn Cl OX15 33 E4
Wimborne Ave OX16 16 B6
Wimbourne Gdns RG30 258 A1
Winaway OX11 217 D6
Winchelsea Cl OX16 8 F1
Winchester Cl OX16 16 F7
Winchester Rd OX2 123 B4
Winchester Way OX12 214 C5
Wincroft Rd RG4 258 E5
Windale Ave OX4 142 E1
Windale Ho 3 OX4 142 E2
Windale Prim Sch OX4 142 E1
WINDERTON 12 B6
Windle Gdns OX26 65 C2
Windmill Ave OX26 65 E4
Windmill Cl Banbury OX16 16 D4
Deddington OX15 33 E4
North Leigh OX29 105 B6
Towersey OX9 148 E7
Windmill Hts OX29 105 B6
Windmill La OX33 143 F7
Windmill Piece OX49 186 A1
Windmill Pl OX12 213 F4
Windmill Prim Sch OX3 124 D2
Windmill Rd
Haddenham HP17 130 F6
North Leigh OX29 105 B6
Oxford OX3 124 D2
Thame OX9 147 F7
Towersey OX9 148 E8
Windmill St Brill HP18 98 A1
Deddington OX15 33 E4
Windows Ct OX33 144 C7
Windrush OX16 16 B8
Windrush Cl
Bicester OX26 65 D1
Burford OX18 100 E4
Grove OX12 196 D1
Witney OX28 117 E8
Windrush Ct
Abingdon OX14 179 C7
Burford OX18 100 E4
Windrush Ind Pk OX29 103 C1
Windrush L Ctr OX28 118 B8
Windrush Mews OX11 201 A3
Windrush Park Rd OX29 103 C1
Windrush Pl OX29 138 B2
Windrush Rd OX10 182 C4
Windrush Twr OX4 142 E2
Windrush Valley Prep Sch OX7 71 C2
Windrush Valley Rd OX28 103 E1
Windrush Way
Abingdon OX14 160 B1
Standlake OX29 137 C5
Windsor Cl
Carterton OX18 115 C2
Didcot OX11 219 A8
Kings Sutton OX17 23 F6
Windsor Cotts OX18 134 E3
Windsor Cres
East Hagbourne OX11 218 F6
Marston OX3 123 E5
Windsor Dr OX10 221 C7
Windsor Ho RG9 254 E8
Windsor St Banbury OX16 16 D5
Oxford OX3 124 D2
Windsor Terr 15 OX16 16 D5
Windy Ridge SN7 173 A3
Wingate Cl OX4 142 E3
Wingfield Cl OX10 204 E3
Wingfield Ct OX4 123 F1
Winnyards The OX2 139 E4
Winslet Pl RG30 258 B1
Winsmore La 2 OX14 179 F6
Winston Cl OX5 108 E7
Winston Dr OX17 8 F1
Winston Way RG8 257 B5
Winterberry Way RG4 258 E6
Winterborne Rd OX14 179 D7
Winterbourne Cl OX26 65 D2
WINTERBROOK 221 C5
Winterbrook OX10 221 D5
Winterbrook La OX10 221 C5
Winter Gdns Way OX16 9 A2
Wintergreen La OX10 221 C5
Winter La OX12 196 F7
Wintersfield OX10 221 F7
Winter's Field OX10 221 F7
Winters Way OX15 21 D4
Wintringham Way RG8 257 D5
Wise Ave OX5 92 D1
Wise Cl OX15 22 F8
Wise Cres OX27 52 C6
Wise Ct 3 OX26 65 E3
Wisterias The OX16 9 B1
Witan Pk OX28 118 B6
Witan Way
Wantage OX12 214 D6
Witney OX28 118 B8
Witheridge Cross OX29 104 B5
Withers Ct OX7 42 E3
Withers Way OX7 42 E2
Withington Ct OX14 179 F7
Withington Rd OX26 65 F2
Withycombe Dr OX16 15 F6
WITNEY 118 C7
Witney Com Hospl OX28 118 A8
Witney Com Prim Sch OX28 104 A3
Witney & District Mus★ OX28 104 B1
Witney Hill OX29 103 E4
Witney La OX29 86 F3
Witney Prim Sch OX28 104 B3
Witney Rd
Brize Norton OX18 116 D5
Crawley OX29 103 F3
Ducklington OX29 118 A5
Eynsham OX29 120 D8
Finstock OX7 88 B5
Leafield OX29 87 A1
Long Hanborough OX29 90 A1
Standlake OX29 137 A4
Whiteoak Green OX7, OX29 87 E2
Witney St OX18 100 E5
Wittenham Cl
Wallingford OX10 203 D1
Woodcote RG8 250 F8
Wittenham La OX10 202 D8
Woburn Cl Banbury OX16 16 F7
Reading RG4 258 E4
Wolage Dr OX12 214 D7
Wolfson Coll OX2 123 C5
Wolseley Cl OX16 16 A8
Wolsely Ho OX4 142 C4
Wolsey Ct OX20 91 F3
Wolsey Rd
Cutteslowe OX2 109 B1
Reading RG4 259 A2
WOLVERCOTE 122 E8
Wolvercote Gn OX2 122 F8
Wolvercote Prim Sch OX2 122 F8
Wolvercote Rdbt OX2 108 F1
Woodberry Cl RG4 259 A5
Woodbine Pl OX1 261 A2
Woodbridge Cl OX18 135 E2
WOODCOTE 250 E7
Woodcote Prim Sch RG8 240 F1
Woodcote Rd
Bicester OX27 66 A7
Reading RG4 258 E4
South Stoke RG8 239 E4
Woodcote Way
Abingdon OX14 179 E4
Reading RG4 258 D5
Woodcroft OX1 141 E1
WOODEATON 110 B4
Woodeaton Manor Sch OX3 110 A5
Wood End OX16 16 E3
Wood Farm Prim Sch OX3 124 E1
Wood Farm Rd OX3 124 E1
Woodfield OX16 16 B8
Woodfield Cotts RG8 249 A6
Woodfield Dr OX7 73 C3
Woodfield Rd OX26 65 E3
WOODFIELDS 65 D4
Woodford Cl Enstone OX7 58 F5
Reading RG4 258 E4
Woodford Mill OX28 104 A1
Woodford Way 3 OX28 118 A8
Woodgate Cl OX12 196 D1
Wood Gn RG8 250 E8
WOODGREEN 104 D2
Woodgreen OX28 104 C1
Woodgreen Ave OX16 16 A5
Woodgreen Hill 5 OX28 104 B1
Wood Green Sch OX28 104 D1
Woodhall Dr OX16 16 E3
Woodhill Dr OX12 214 D8
Woodhill La
East Challow OX12 214 A7
Grove OX12 196 A1
Woodhill Lane Cvn Pk OX12 213 F6
Woodhouse Way OX4 142 A4
Woodins Way OX1 261 A2
Wood La Hailey OX29 104 A7
Kidmore End RG4 252 C4
Leafield OX29 87 E1
Sonning Common RG4 252 F5
Whiteoak Green OX29 103 F8
Woodcote RG8 250 D8
Woodland Park Cvn Site The OX14 160 E7
Woodland Rise OX29 89 C7
Woodlands
Banbury OX16 16 B5
Carterton OX18 115 F4
Freeland OX29 106 A7
Kidlington OX5 109 A8
Standlake OX29 137 D3
Woodlands Cl
Milton-under-Wychwood OX7 70 B1
Oxford OX3 124 B3
Woodlands Ct OX28 104 C2
Woodlands Gr RG4 259 E4
Woodlands Rd
Didcot OX11 218 C8
Oxford OX3 124 B3
Shiplake RG9 254 E4
Sonning Common RG4 252 F6
Witney OX28 104 C1
Woodlands The OX26 79 F7
Woodland Wlk OX1 140 F1
Wood Lane Cl RG4 252 F5
Woodley Cl OX14 159 F3
Woodley Gn OX28 104 E2
Woodman Ct OX4 123 F1
Woodman Villas OX3 124 C2
Woodpecker Cl OX26 66 A1
Woodpecker Gn 13 OX4 142 F1
Woodperry Rd OX3 111 B2
Woodpery Hill OX33 111 D2
Woodpiece Rd OX25 96 E7
Woodrow 5 OX18 115 E5
Woodrow Ct RG4 258 F2
Woodruff Cl
Bicester OX26 65 D5
Oxford OX4 142 F2
Woodrush Gdns OX18 115 F4
Wood's Farm Rd OX12 216 D8
Woodside OX29 105 C6
Woodside Dr OX18 114 C6
Woodside La RG4 252 C5
Woods Rd RG4 259 E4
Wood St OX10 221 D7
WOODSTOCK 91 B5
Woodstock CE Prim Sch OX20 91 C6
Woodstock Cl OX2 123 A8
Woodstock Close Flats OX2 123 A8
Woodstock Ct OX2 123 A7
Woodstock Open Air Pool OX20 91 D6
Woodstock Rd
Charlbury OX7 73 C2
Kidlington OX20 91 F3
Oxford OX2 123 B5
Stonesfield OX8 89 D7
Witney OX28 104 D2
Wolvercote OX2 108 D4
Woodstock Road E OX5 91 F1
Woodstock Road W OX20 91 F1
Woodthorne Cl RG31 257 B4
Woodview SN7 172 E4
Woodview Rd RG8 256 D5
Woodville OX39 168 C5
Woodway Farm Ind Est HP18 128 F8
Woodway Rd
Blewbury OX11 237 A7
Middle Barton OX7 60 E8
Sibford Ferris OX15 19 A7
Woolgate Sh Ctr OX28 118 B8
WOOLSTONE 211 B4
Woolstone Rd
Uffington SN7 211 C7
Woolstone SN7 211 B5
Wootten Dr OX4 142 A4
WOOTTON
Abingdon 159 A6
Woodstock 75 F5
Wootton Bsns Pk OX1 158 F7
Wootton-by-Woodstock CE Prim Sch OX20 75 F4
Wootton CE Prim Sch OX1 159 B8
Wootton End OX29 89 D8
Wootton Rd
Abingdon OX13, OX14 159 E2
Abingdon OX14 179 E8
Henley-on-Thames RG9 254 C8
Wootton Road Ind Est OX14 159 E1
WOOTTON VILLAGE 159 B8
Worcester Coll OX1 261 A3
Worcester Dr OX11 219 B8
Worcester Pl
Kingston Bagpuize OX13 156 D1
Oxford OX1 261 A3
Worcester Rd OX7 42 B2
Worcester Road Ind Est OX7 42 C3
Worcester St OX1 261 A2
Wordsworth Cl
6 Bicester OX26 65 C4
Stanford in the Vale SN7 194 D8
Wordsworth Ct RG4 259 C7
Wordsworth Rd OX14 179 D5
Workhouse La OX15 21 D5
Work House Yd OX20 75 F4
Wormald Rd OX10 221 C6
WORMINGHALL 127 E6
Worminghall Rd HP18 127 F4
WORMLEIGHTON 1 B8
Wormsley Cres HP14 188 C4
Wornal Pk HP18 127 C8
WORSHAM 102 B2
Worsham Turn OX29 102 B5
Wortham Rd OX11 200 D2
Worthington Way OX12 214 D6
WORTON 107 E3
Worton Rd OX7 46 E1
Wotton End HP18 98 C7
Wren Cl OX33 144 B8
Wrenfield Dr RG4 258 F5
Wren Rd OX2 109 C1
Wren Way OX26 80 F8
Wretchwick Way OX26 81 B8
Wright Cl GL54 68 A5
Wright Rd GL54 68 A5
Wrightson Cl OX33 143 C6
Wroslyn Rd OX29 106 A7
Wroslyn Road Ind Est OX29 105 F8
WROXTON 15 A8
Wroxton CE Prim Sch OX15 15 A8
Wroxton Coll OX15 15 B8
Wroxton Ct OX15 15 A8
Wroxton Ho OX15 15 B8
Wyatt Rd 7 OX2 109 B1
Wychcotes RG4 258 F3
Wychwood Brewery★ 10 OX28 118 A8
Wychwood CE Prim Sch OX7 70 C1
Wychwood Cl
Benson OX10 204 A4
Carterton OX18 115 D5
Charlbury OX7 73 C4
Milton-under-Wychwood OX7 70 A1
Sonning Common RG4 252 F5
Witney OX28 117 E8
Wychwood Dr OX7 70 A1
Wychwood Gdns OX16 16 A4
Wychwood La
Oxford OX3 125 A2
Rissinghurst OX3 125 A2
Wychwood National Nature Reserve★ OX7 87 D6
Wychwood Paddocks OX7 73 B4
Wychwood Sch 3 OX2 123 C4
Wychwood View OX29 102 E2
Wycliffe Hall OX2 261 B4
Wycombe Rd HP14 189 D3
Wycombe Way OX18 115 E2
Wye Cl OX26 65 B3
Wyfold Ct RG9 242 A1
Wyfold La RG4, RG9 252 C8
Wykeham Cres OX4 142 B4
Wykeham Gate HP17 130 F5
Wykeham Pk OX9 148 A8
Wykeham Rise OX39 168 D6
Wykeham Way HP17 130 F6
Wykham Gdns OX16 16 B3
Wykham La
Banbury OX16 16 B1
Broughton OX15 15 E1
Wykham Pl OX16 16 B3
Wylie Cl OX3 124 D1
Wynbush Rd OX4 142 A3
Wynchway Ho OX15 33 F4
Wyncies The SN6 227 D4
Wyndale Cl RG9 244 E1
Wyndham Cres RG5 260 D1
Wyndham Gdns OX10 221 D6
Wyndham Way OX2 123 A8
Wyndyke Furlong OX14 179 C8
Wyre Ct RG31 257 C3
Wysdom Way OX18 100 F4
WYTHAM 122 B6
Wytham Cl OX29 120 E8
Wytham St OX1 141 D5
Wytham View OX29 120 E8

Y

Yare Cl OX11 201 B2
Yarnell's Hill OX2 140 D7
Yarnell's Rd OX2 140 E8
YARNTON 108 A6
Yarnton Cl RG4 259 C6
Yarnton Ct OX5 108 E8
Yarnton La OX5 108 D6
Yarnton Rd
Cassington OX29 107 D3
Kidlington OX5 108 E8
Yarrow Cl OX4 142 E1
Yatesbury Rd OX18 115 E4
Yealm Cl OX11 200 F4
Yeates Cl OX9 129 F1
Yeats Cl OX4 142 E6
Yeftly Dr OX4 142 A1
Yeld Hall Rd OX14 160 B2
YELFORD 136 B6
Yeomans Cl NN13 24 A8
Yew Cl
Bicester OX26 65 E5
Oxford OX4 143 A2
Yew Tree Cl OX9 166 B8
Yew Tree Ct RG8 249 C6
Yewtree Mews OX14 179 F7
Yew Tree Mews OX29 118 B4
Yew Tree Rise NN13 36 D8
Yew Wlk OX12 215 D3
Yolsum Cl HP17 130 E6
York Ave OX3 124 E1
York Cl OX26 66 A3
York Pl OX4 123 E1
York Rd
Carterton OX18 115 E4
Henley-on-Thames RG9 244 D2
Oxford OX3 124 E2
Reading RG1 259 A1
West Hagbourne OX11 218 C4
Youens Dr OX9 148 A7
Youghal Cl SN6 209 B6
Ypres Way OX14 159 D1
Yule Ct 1 OX16 16 B6

Z

Zedcor Bsns Pk 3 OX28 104 B1

PHILIP'S MAPS

the Gold Standard for drivers

◆ **Philip's street atlases cover all of England, Wales, Northern Ireland and much of Scotland**

◆ Every named street is shown, including alleys, lanes and walkways

◆ Thousands of additional features marked: stations, public buildings, car parks, places of interest

◆ Route-planning maps to get you close to your destination

◆ Postcodes on the maps and in the index

◆ Widely used by the emergency services, transport companies and local authorities

BEST BUY • BEST BUY
Auto EXPRESS
BEST BUY • BEST BUY

PHILIP'S
STREET ATLAS
London
More streets
More lanes and alleys
More named build...
More house numbers
More clear routes
'Absolutely fabulou...'
'Must buy' Evening Standa...

PHILIP'S
STREET ATLAS
Greater Manchester
Bolton, Bury, Manchester, Oldham, Rochdale,
Salford, Stockport, Tameside, Trafford, Wigan
Altrincham, Ashton-under-Lyne, Cleckheaton, Eccles, Glossop,
Hyde, Leigh, Middleton, Prestwich, Radcliffe, Sale, Stretford,
Tyldesley, Urmston, Wilmslow, Wythenshawe

PHILIP'S
STREET ATLAS
Dorset
Bournemouth and Poole
Christchurch, Dorchester, Weymouth

PHILIP'S
STREET ATLAS
Co Armagh Co Down
Armagh, Bangor, Craigavon,
Downpatrick, Newry, Newtownards
Includes route-planning map

PHILIP'S
NEW EDITION
NAVIGATOR
Britain
'The reigning champion of road atlases'
The Sunday Times
With speed cameras
from PocketGPSWorld.com
Britain's most detailed road mapping
Spot the best breakfast competition
in our survey of motorway services

For national mapping, choose
Philip's Navigator Britain
the most detailed road atlas available of England, Wales and Scotland. Hailed by Auto Express as 'the ultimate road atlas', Navigator shows every road and lane in Britain.

Street atlases currently available

England

Bedfordshire and Luton	Surrey
Berkshire	East Sussex
Birmingham and West Midlands	West Sussex
Bristol and Bath	Tyne and Wear
Buckinghamshire and Milton Keynes	Warwickshire and Coventry
Cambridgeshire and Peterborough	Wiltshire and Swindon
Cheshire	Worcestershire
Cornwall	East Yorkshire Northern Lincolnshire
Cumbria	North Yorkshire
Derbyshire	South Yorkshire
Devon	West Yorkshire
Dorset	
County Durham and Teesside	**Wales**
Essex	Anglesey, Conwy and Gwynedd
North Essex	Cardiff, Swansea and The Valleys
South Essex	Carmarthenshire, Pembrokeshire and Swansea
Gloucestershire and Bristol	Ceredigion and South Gwynedd
Hampshire	
North Hampshire	Denbighshire, Flintshire, Wrexham
South Hampshire	Herefordshire Monmouthshire
Herefordshire Monmouthshire	Powys
Hertfordshire	
Isle of Wight	**Scotland**
Kent	Aberdeenshire
East Kent	Ayrshire
West Kent	Dumfries and Galloway
Lancashire	Edinburgh and East Central Scotland
Leicestershire and Rutland	Fife and Tayside
Lincolnshire	Glasgow and West Central Scotland
Liverpool and Merseyside	Inverness and Moray
London	Lanarkshire
Greater Manchester	Scottish Borders
Norfolk	
Northamptonshire	**Northern Ireland**
Northumberland	County Antrim and County Londonderry
Nottinghamshire	County Armagh and County Down
Oxfordshire	
Shropshire	Belfast
Somerset	County Tyrone and County Fermanagh
Staffordshire	
Suffolk	

Philip's maps and atlases are available from bookshops, motorway services and petrol stations

For further details visit
www.philips-maps.co.uk